INVITATION
to the
NEW
TESTAMENT

INVITATION
to the
NEW
TESTAMENT

First Things
Second Edition

BEN WITHERINGTON III

Oxford   New York
Oxford University Press

Oxford University Press is a department of the University of Oxford.
It furthers the University's objective of excellence in research, scholarship,
and education by publishing worldwide. Oxford is a registered trade
mark of Oxford University Press in the UK and certain other countries.

Published in the United States of America by Oxford University Press
198 Madison Avenue, New York, NY 10016, United States of America.

For titles covered by Section 112 of the US Higher Education Opportunity Act,
please visit www.oup.com/us/he for the latest information about
pricing and alternate formats.

Library of Congress Cataloging-in-Publication Data

Names: Witherington, Ben, III, 1951– author.
Title: Invitation to the New Testament: first things / Ben Witherington III.
Description: Second edition. | New York, NY: Oxford University Press, 2017.
  | Includes bibliographical references and index.
Identifiers: LCCN 2016021919 | ISBN 9780190491949 (pbk.)
Subjects: LCSH: Bible. New Testament—Introductions.
Classification: LCC BS2330.3 .W575 2017 | DDC 225.6/1—dc23 LC record available
at https://lccn.loc.gov/2016021919

9 8 7 6 5 4 3 2 1

Printed by Sheridan Books, Inc., United States of America

ENTRY INTO THE CITY
Copyright 2012 by John August Swanson
Giclee, 36" by 48"
www.JohnAugustSwanson.com
Los Angeles artist John August Swanson is noted for his finely detailed, brilliantly colored paintings and
original prints. His works are found in the Smithsonian Institution's National Museum of American
History, London's Tate Gallery, the Vatican Museum's Collection of Modern Religious Art, and the
Bibliothèque Nationale, Paris.

This book is dedicated in loving memory and honor of our daughter Christy Ann (1979–2012), who was born in Durham, England, and studied Shakespeare at Oxford. Christy loved books of all kinds, especially British ones. I think she would have really enjoyed this one, produced by Oxford University Press.

BRIEF CONTENTS

Foreword   *xv*
Acknowledgments   *xvi*
The Plan of This Book   *xviii*

PART I   BACKGROUND and FOREGROUND 1

CHAPTER 1
The TEXTURE of the TEXT of the NEW TESTAMENT 3

CHAPTER 2
The LITERATURE of the NEW TESTAMENT 11

CHAPTER 3
JESUS of NAZARETH in HIS EARLY JEWISH SETTING 23

CHAPTER 4
FIRST CENTURY FAMILY VALUES 41

PART II   The GOSPELS and ACTS 55

CHAPTER 5
The EARLIEST GOOD NEWS—MARK'S GOSPEL 57

CHAPTER 6
The MOST POPULAR GOSPEL— MATTHEW 83

CHAPTER 7
LUKE the HISTORIAN'S TWO-VOLUME
          WORK—LUKE–ACTS 103

CHAPTER 8
The LAST WORD on JESUS—The BELOVED DISCIPLE'S
          TESTIMONY in the GOSPEL of JOHN 133

PART III PAUL and HIS RHETORICAL LETTERS 157

CHAPTER 9
PAUL—OUTLINES of the LIFE and LETTERS
          of the APOSTLE 159

CHAPTER 10
PAUL the LETTER WRITER PART ONE:
          The EARLIER LETTERS 193

CHAPTER 11
PAUL the LETTER WRITER PART TWO: The CAPITAL
    PAULINE EPISTLES 209

CHAPTER 12
PAUL the LETTER WRITER PART THREE:
    The CAPTIVITY EPISTLES 231

CHAPTER 13
PAUL the LETTER WRITER PART FOUR: The PASTORAL EPISTLES
    and the PROBLEM of PSEUDONYMOUS LETTERS 251

PART IV LETTERS and HOMILIES for
    JEWISH CHRISTIANS 269

CHAPTER 14
The SERMON of JAMES the JUST—JESUS' BROTHER 271

CHAPTER 15
The OTHER BROTHER and HIS ESCHATOLOGICAL
    THINKING—JUDE 293

CHAPTER 16
The SUFFERING SERVANT—1 PETER 307

CHAPTER 17
The SERMON of the FAMOUS ANONYMOUS
    PREACHER—HEBREWS 331

CHAPTER 18
A BELOVED SERMON and TWO ELDERLY LETTERS—1–3 JOHN 351

PART V In the END—APOCALYPSE—and
    THEREAFTER 375

CHAPTER 19
PICKING UP the PIECES, FORMING UP the CANON—2 PETER 377

CHAPTER 20
APOCALYPSE LATER—The BOOK of REVELATION 399

CHAPTER 21
The MAKING of the NEW TESTAMENT—DID the
    CANON MISFIRE? 433

Appendix A 453
Appendix B 462
Glossary 472
Index 484

CONTENTS

Foreword   xv
Acknowledgments   xvi
The Plan of This Book   xviii

PART I   BACKGROUND and FOREGROUND 1

CHAPTER 1
The TEXTURE of the TEXT of the
NEW TESTAMENT 3
    The Material Used 4
    Why a Continuous Flow of Letters? 5
    The Oral and Rhetorical World of the New
        Testament 7
    Implications of What We Have Learned 8

CHAPTER 2
The LITERATURE of the NEW TESTAMENT 11
    What Are the Gospels (and Acts)? 12
    What about the "Letters" of the New Testament? 14
    In the End, Apocalypse 15
    What Is the Story the New Testament Seeks to Tell? 16
    What Sort of History Is This? 18
    Implications 20

CHAPTER 3
JESUS of NAZARETH in HIS EARLY JEWISH
SETTING 23
    Did Jesus Even Exist? 25
    What Manner of Man Was He? 26
    What Is a Miracle? 31
    Were There "Lost Christianities"? 33

CHAPTER 4
FIRST CENTURY FAMILY VALUES 41
    Greece and Rome Will Not Leave Us Alone 42
    Social History and Ordinary Life 47
    Implications 51

PART II   The GOSPELS and ACTS 55

CHAPTER 5
The EARLIEST GOOD NEWS—MARK'S GOSPEL 57
    Who Was Mark, and When Did He Write? 60
    How Is Mark's Gospel Arranged? 62
    Brief Contents of Mark's Gospel 64
    The Presentation of and Reflection on Christ in Mark 68
    Marking Time 72
    The Kingdom Comes with Teaching and Healing 73
    A CLOSER LOOK Jesus' Wisdom Teachings—Parables,
            Aphorisms, Riddles 74
    The Dramatic, Surprise Ending of Mark's Gospel 76
    Implications 80

CHAPTER 6
The MOST POPULAR GOSPEL— MATTHEW 83
    Describing a Scribe 84
    The Audience, Date, and Character of Matthew's Gospel 87
    Matthew's Special Contributions to the Story of Jesus 90
    The Sermon on the Mount 91
    The Peter Principle 95
    The Grand Finale 97
    Implications 100

CHAPTER 7
LUKE the HISTORIAN'S TWO-VOLUME
WORK—LUKE–ACTS 103
    Luke's Hellenistic, Yet Jewish,
         Historical Approach to Jesus and "The Way" 104
    Who Was Theophilus? 106
    Who Was Luke? 107
    The Logical and Theological Structuring of Luke–Acts 109
    The Gospel of the Holy Spirit 115
    Luke's Views of Jesus 119
    Synopsis of the Content of Luke–Acts 124
    Implications 128

CHAPTER **8**
The LAST WORD on JESUS—The BELOVED DISCIPLE'S
TESTIMONY in the GOSPEL of JOHN 133
    First Things 134
    The Theological Structure of the Fourth Gospel 140
    A CLOSER LOOK The I Am Sayings 142
    In Passing—Meaningful Asides in the Gospel of John 146
    A Glimpse of Glory—Special Moments in the Gospel
         of John with Nicodemus, The Samaritan
            Woman, Mary Magdalene, and Peter 147
    Synopsis of Contents 153
    Implications 154

PART III PAUL and HIS RHETORICAL LETTERS 157

CHAPTER **9**
PAUL—OUTLINES of the LIFE and LETTERS of the APOSTLE 159
    The Trinity of Paul's Identity 173
    Paul the Multilingual, Multicultural Apostle 176
    Rhetoric in the Greco-Roman World 177
    Paul's Rhetorical Letters 182
    Paul's Narrative Thought World 185
    Five Stories That Shook and Shaped Paul's
         World and Worldview 187
    Implications 187

CHAPTER **10**
PAUL the LETTER WRITER PART ONE: The EARLIER LETTERS 193
    Paul's First Salvo—Galatians 194
    Synopsis of Contents 196
    1 and 2 Thessalonians 200
    Synopsis of Contents 200
    Implications 205

CHAPTER **11**
PAUL the LETTER WRITER PART TWO: The CAPITAL
PAULINE EPISTLES 209
    1 and 2 Corinthians 209

Synopsis of Contents 210
A CLOSER LOOK 212
Synopsis of Contents 216
Romans—The Righteousness of God and
            the Setting Right of Human Beings 219
Synopsis of Contents 221
Implications 229

CHAPTER 12
PAUL the LETTER WRITER PART THREE: The CAPTIVITY EPISTLES 231
Synopsis of Colossians and Ephesians 234
Colossians 3.18–4.1/Ephesians 5.21–6.9—The
            Household Codes 236
Synopsis of Contents 238
Philemon 239
Philippians 240
Implications 247

CHAPTER 13
PAUL the LETTER WRITER PART FOUR: The PASTORAL
EPISTLES and the PROBLEM of PSEUDONYMOUS LETTERS 251
Why the Authorship Issue Matters 252
The Pastoral Epistles—What Sort of Rhetoric Is This? 255
Outlines and Synopses of Contents of the Pastorals 258
Implications 266

PART IV LETTERS and HOMILIES for JEWISH
            CHRISTIANS 269

CHAPTER 14
The SERMON of JAMES the JUST—JESUS' BROTHER 271
General Epistles? 271
James—a Wisdom Sermon in Encyclical Form 273
The Language, Wisdom, and Rhetorical Style of James 275
The Authorship and Provenance Question 280
What Kind of Document Is James? 282
Synopsis of Contents 284
Implications 288

CHAPTER **15**
The OTHER BROTHER and HIS ESCHATOLOGICAL
THINKING—JUDE 293
    Jude—The Man 294
    Jude the Book 298
    Jude's Audience 300
    Synopsis of Contents 302
    Implications 303

CHAPTER **16**
The SUFFERING SERVANT—1 PETER 307
    The Social World of Early Christianity 308
    The Authorship, Audience, and Social Milieu of 1 Peter 309
    The Rhetorical Outline of 1 Peter 316
    Synopsis of Contents 318
    Implications 326

CHAPTER **17**
The SERMON of the FAMOUS ANONYMOUS
PREACHER—HEBREWS 331
    The Authorship, Audience, and Provenance of Hebrews 331
    The Rhetoric of Hebrews 339
    Core Samplings 343
    Implications 346

CHAPTER **18**
A BELOVED SERMON and TWO ELDERLY LETTERS—1–3 JOHN 351
    The Authorship Issues 352
    The Social Context of the Johannine Epistles 356
    The Date and Provenance of the Johannine Epistles 359
    The Rhetoric of the Johannine Epistles 363
    The Rhetorical Structure of 1 John 365
    The Rhetorical Structure of 2 John 366
    The Rhetorical Structure of 3 John 366
    Core Samplings—1 John 4 367
    Implications 371

PART V In the END—APOCALYPSE—and THEREAFTER 375

CHAPTER 19
PICKING UP the PIECES, FORMING UP the CANON—2 PETER 377
  Preliminary Considerations 377
  The Mystery That Is 2 Peter 378
  Putting Together the Pieces 384
  The Rhetoric of 2 Peter 385
  Core Samplings—2 Peter 1.12–21 388
  Implications 395

CHAPTER 20
APOCALYPSE LATER—The BOOK of REVELATION 399
  Who, What, When, Where, and Why? 400
  The Particularity of Revelation 402
  The Rhetoric and Resources of Revelation 404
  Revelation in Its Social Setting in Western Asia Minor 412
  The Christology of Revelation 415
  The Genre of Revelation 419
  Core Samplings: Revelation 11 424
  Implications 427

CHAPTER 21
The MAKING of the NEW TESTAMENT—DID the CANON
MISFIRE? 433
  Canon Consciousness and Scripture Consciousness 434
  The Rise of New Testament Scripture and
        Canon Consciousness 437
  The Organizing of Orthodoxy and Orthopraxy 447
  In the End 447
  Implications 448

Appendix A 453
Appendix B 462
Glossary 473
Index 484

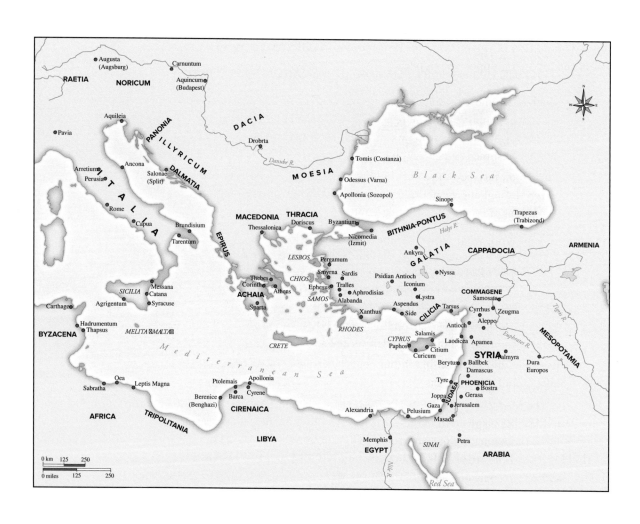

FOREWORD

The second edition of *Invitation to the New Testament* differs from the first edition in the following important respects:

- Much of the more complex historical and contextual coverage has been reduced or simplified and more essential discussion of the content of the New Testament itself has been added, making the book more accessible for freshmen students taking the survey course.
- The greater focus on the content of the New Testament itself is now woven throughout the narrative in section-by-section content outlines; summaries of events and teachings; and reflections on theological interpretation.
- A revised and expanded Part Three (now including five rather than four chapters) provides more comprehensive coverage of Paul's letters. The chapters on Paul's letters are now divided in a more accessible way (earlier letters, capital epistles, pastoral epistles, and captivity epistles) allowing for more thorough coverage of each letter.
- A glossary at the end of the text defines key terms.
- Revisions and streamlining throughout the text make for a more accessible overall presentation.

Many thanks should be given to the seven reviewers who have helped make this second edition a more accessible and useful college textbook.

Thanks are also in order to Joy Vaughan, my teaching assistant at Asbury, who has labored tirelessly on the second edition of this manuscript, simplifying things and adding proper definitions. I owe her a considerable debt for her attention to the details of this manuscript.

Last, I want to also thank Robert Miller my editor (and fellow lover of the Tar Heels!) who has been patient with me and the whole process of getting this book into its most useful shape for the audience he knew this book would serve well.

EASTER 2016

ACKNOWLEDGMENTS

This book could not have been completed without the considerable help of many people. Here, I wish to give special thanks to those who granted me permission to use either pictures or edited forms of some of my previous publications.

First and foremost, I must thank my colleague and friend Mark Fairchild for permission to use a large number of his excellent pictures of the Biblical World. These are sprinkled throughout the text and each one is credited to Mark Fairchild.

Second, I must thank my longtime illustrator Rev. Rick Danielson for the reuse of various of his pen-and-ink sketches.

Third, any unidentified pictures or images in the text are my own.

Fourth, a special thanks to the creators of the *St. John's Bible* for permission to use a variety of their wonderful illustrations from the latest and one of the finest illuminated manuscripts to ever have been created. These too appear throughout the manuscript and are identified at each juncture.

Fifth, a profound thanks to InterVarsity Press for permission to reuse small and edited portions of several of my previous commentaries and theology volumes, namely, from *Letters and Homilies for Hellenized Christians, Volumes One and Two*, and *Letters and Homilies for Jewish Christians* (2006–2008), and from *The Indelible Image, Volumes One and Two* (2008–2009). A further thanks to my various other publishers including Baylor U. Press, Eerdmans, Smyth and Helwys, Westminster/John Knox, and Cambridge University Press for allowing me to write commentaries for you and allowing me to continue to use this material in other forms in other books. Some of the material in this book you will find is a simplified version of some of the things I wrote for your fine publishing houses.

Sixth, I wish to thank Rev. Laverna Patterson and Teachhearts.org for permission to use the colorful map of Biblical Sites.

Also, many thanks to all of the reviewers:

Gary E. Blackwell, William Carey University

Craig L. Blomberg, Denver Seminary

Darrell L. Bock, Dallas Theological Seminary

Andy Chambers, Missouri Baptist University

Gladys Childs, Texas Wesleyan University

Robert C. Crosby, Southern University, College of Christian Ministries and Religion

David A. Croteau, Liberty University

Donald Denton, Southwest Baptist University

Travis Derico, Huntington University

David A. deSilva, Ashland Theological Seminary

Craig A. Evans, Acadia University— Acadia Divinity College

Mark R. Fairchild, Huntington University

Matthew E. Gordley, Regent University School of Divinity

Matthew James Hamilton, Carson-
Newman University
Steven A. Hunt, Gordon College
Karl Kuhn, Lakeland College
Joseph M. Martin, Belhaven University
David L. Mathewson, Denver Seminary
Kevin W. McFadden, Louisiana Col-
lege and Caskey School of Divinity
Josh McNall, Oklahoma Wesleyan
University
W.E. Nunnally, Evangel University
Viktor Roudkovski, LeTourneau
University
James B. Shelton, Oral Roberts
University, College of Theology and
Ministry

Rob Starner, Southwestern Assemblies
of God University, College of Bible
and Church Ministries
Todd D. Still, George W. Truett, Theo-
logical Seminary of Baylor University
Grady T. Tew, Charleston Southern
University
E. Jerome Van Kuiken, Oklahoma
Wesleyan University
Andrew H. Wakefield, Campbell Uni-
versity Divinity School
Edward W. Watson, Oral Roberts
University, College of Theology and
Ministry
Jonathan M. Watt, Geneva College

The PLAN of THIS BOOK

This *Introduction to the New Testament* has 21 chapters (and two appendixes), some shorter and some longer, depending on the needs of the subject matter. In these chapters, you will find an explanation of the origins and character of each of the 27 books of the New Testament insofar as we can discern them, discussing the usual subjects of author, audience, date, and structure of these documents in addition to other issues. You will also find throughout a reconstruction of earliest Christian history based on the clues we find in these same books. One of the distinctive features of this book is that you will also find an analysis of the social and rhetorical dimensions of the New Testament books. To get the most benefit out of this book, it is best to read the New Testament book with its corresponding chapter here. In the case of the Pauline letters, which are covered in four chapters, I would suggest reading all of the Pauline letters with the first two Pauline chapters, except the pastoral epistles, which one should read in tandem with the third Pauline chapter.

In the right-hand margin, you will find a box at the beginning of each chapter (after the four Introductory chapters) called "At a Glance," which summarizes some of the basic conclusions and points of the chapter. This will let you know where the chapter is going and what its focus will be. You will also find some sections called "Core Samplings," which give a detailed look into a particular sample passage from the New Testament book in question. There are also a few "A Closer Look" sections, for example, about the crucifixion of Jesus, for those who want to explore the material in more detail.

The text of this book is geared to entry-level college courses in the New Testament, but some of the supplemental materials will help more advanced students to go beyond what they already know, students who may nonetheless be required to take the entry-level course.

In the margins, you will find key definitions of terms, and you will also find a variety of quotations from Greco-Roman writers of the period under the heading "Clues from the Culture" to give you a flavor of what the cultures the Christians lived in were like as they tried to bring the Good News of Jesus Christ to a very diverse, and very non-Christian world.

At the end of most chapters, you will find the following sections: (1) "Implications" of the material discussed in the chapter, (2) "For Further Reading" containing suggestions for additional study, and (3) "Study Questions" that arise from the chapter itself.

Throughout, you will benefit from various maps and charts, the many pictures by Mark Fairchild and others, the beautiful paintings done for the St. John's Bible, and the wonderful line drawings of Rick Danielson (who has done drawings for several of my books). It is my hope that through the collective impact of all this material you will not merely learn a lot about the New Testament but that you will get excited about studying one of the most important and influential documents ever produced in human history.

INVITATION
to the
NEW
TESTAMENT

PART I

BACKGROUND and FOREGROUND

The temple mount looking through the window at Dominus Flevit Chapel.
(© Mark R. Fairchild, Ph.D.)

1

The TEXTURE of the TEXT of the NEW TESTAMENT

LOOK CAREFULLY AT the picture of the ancient manuscript in Figure 1.1. What do you see? Notice both what we would call the paper and also the writing on the paper.

What you are looking at is one page of the Greek New Testament, written in all capital letters with little or no spacing between words, sentences, or paragraphs; little or no guides to punctuation; and definitely no headings or chapter and verse markers. If a modern person copying a New Testament document did it like this, we would think he or she was crazy. We might complain, "It's impossible to read the document like that! Who knows where the words start and stop, much less the sentences!"

Figure 1.1 All ancient manuscripts were written on either papyrus, from the papyrus reeds in the Nile, or on animal skin, parchment.

Perhaps you know the famous example in English of what a continuous flow of letters looks like—JESUSISNOWHERE. What do those words say or mean? They could mean "Jesus is nowhere," but they could also mean "Jesus is now here." The first act of interpreting an ancient document with a continuous flow of Greek letters is to figure out where the words start and stop.

You may be surprised to learn that what you are looking at is a *typical* ancient manuscript page of the New Testament, and it reminds us of something critically important—the past is indeed like a foreign country, and they did things differently then and there. If we want to understand the New Testament and its world, we have to enter into that world and begin to think as they thought. So let's explore why that manuscript looks like it does.

THE MATERIAL USED

By far, in the world of the earliest Christians, the most common material used to write on was papyrus. What is papyrus? It is a reed with a long, triangularly shaped stem found in the marshes in the Nile River in Egypt. The stem is harvested, then cut into long thin strips. These strips are laid horizontally and then vertically at right angles, and then they are rolled and hammered together, with the natural sap of the stem gluing the strips together. The resulting individual pages or portions are hung up and allowed to dry. After drying, the papyrus is polished with a smooth stone or sometimes with a bone. Although the manuscript in Figure 1.1 is yellowish in color, originally it would have been very white and quite flexible, so it could be rolled up. While commonly only one side of the papyrus was written on (as it was quite thin, and the writing would bleed through and be visible on the other side), sometimes both sides would be used because papyrus was very expensive, as was ink, and the labor of the scribes or secretaries who composed the documents was expensive as well.

It was expensive not merely because the materials were expensive but also because the historical evidence suggests that only 10 to 20 percent of the ancient world could read or write, and actually those were two different skills. More people could read than could write with accurately formed letters in straight lines. The document in Figure 1.1 was copied by a professional scribe in a "fair hand." In other words, it took skill in writing, skill obtained by training and education, which only a minority of people had access to, and that minority was usually from the socially more elite and wealthy members of society. The copier of the document in Figure 1.1 was not merely literate, he was skilled. While it is true that graffiti found at Pompeii and elsewhere in the ancient Roman world reminds us that many people could read or even write a few brief phrases in Greek, that is very different from having the ability to compose any of the documents we find in the New Testament, especially the longer and more complex ones.

The average papyrus sheet was about 11 inches high by 8 inches wide, although this could vary. What would normally happen is that pages would be glued together side by side, making rolls. Sometimes those papyrus rolls could be enormous, stretching some 20 feet long or more at times. Imagine carrying around a New Testament in a roll that was 30 feet long or more! It makes you appreciate Kindle technology. In fact, more than 20 sheets glued together was usually about the maximum because any more than that became much too bulky and cumbersome.

Our longest Gospel (by word count), Luke's Gospel, contains about the maximum number of letters and words that one could get on 20 papyrus sheets glued together. Because the papyrus was so thin, even 20 sheets glued together could be rolled up into something that looked like a large baton or stick several inches thick. When a document was produced for a library, whether a personal or a public library like the famous one in Alexandria, Egypt, it would often have a tag sewn to one end bearing the title of the work. Ancients were like us in this regard—they did not tend to rewind the scroll they read, so sometimes the tags would be at the end, not the beginning, of the document!

There were pluses and minuses to using papyrus for composing documents. Compared to parchment, which is the scraped skins of animals, papyrus was much more lightweight and flexible, and thus easier to carry around. It was not, however, as durable, particularly in a wet climate. Papyrus is vegetable matter, and so in a wet locale, it will rot. If you are wondering why so many ancient Jewish and Christian papyrus scrolls have been found in Egypt or the desert region of Judea at the Dead Sea, it is because of the arid, or very dry, climate. By contrast, Galilee, in the northern part of the Holy Land, and Mediterranean countries like Turkey, Greece, and Italy, have a considerable rainy season from November into the late spring. One main reason so few papyrus documents have been found in those places is not because no one was literate but due to the climate.

Another virtue of papyrus is that you could wash it, wash off the ink, and reuse the scroll. Usually, however, after washing, the scribe would wisely use the other side of the scroll. It was much more difficult to scrape the words off an animal skin because the ink would penetrate the skin's surface. And as expensive as a papyrus roll might have been, it was always cheaper than a parchment roll composed of several different animals' hides.

WHY A CONTINUOUS FLOW OF LETTERS?

On one hand, there was a very good reason why ancient documents almost always had a continuous flow of letters—economics. The less papyrus used, the cheaper the document was to produce. There was another reason as well. Ancient documents were not normally produced for the general public but for patrons, or clients, or libraries of and for the wealthy. The general public (1) could not afford to buy such documents, as most could not read them anyway (they had enough trouble just reading short inscriptions on tombstones and public proclamations of the Emperor); and (2) reading and writing had been the provenance of the wealthy, in particular of royal courts and temples since time immemorial. There was no concept in antiquity of "the general public's right to know"—or to be educated, for that matter. The very use of a continuous flow of letters suggests an insider talking to another literate insider, and this brings up an interesting point.

The earliest Christians were evangelistic to a fault. They believed it was their job to share the Good News of Jesus Christ with all and sundry, from the least, last, and lost to the foremost, first, and found. Their message was not just for the cultured or wealthy or literate. Yet, in the production of their documents, they also used the continuous flow of letters, presumably for practical economic reasons. And many of their documents were written to whole groups of people—the church in Corinth or Philippi, for example. They were *public* communications in ways that many ancient documents were not, and they were public communications for the whole spectrum of society from the elites right down to the slaves and children. These were ethnic and gender inclusive documents as well, not just written for literate males. But how did Christians with their evangelistic zeal make these documents accessible to the widest possible audience, including the illiterate?

The answer is they used literate readers, who already knew the document and would read it out to a whole congregation. Today we might call such a person a **lector**. Two examples from the New Testament make my point.

In the last document in the New Testament, the Revelation of John of Patmos, we find the following at Rev. 1.3: "Blessed is the one who reads aloud the words of this prophecy, and blessed are those who hear it and take to heart what is written in it." John of Patmos was the author of the document, but he was in exile on the island of Patmos off the west coast of modern Turkey. He would not be the person who read these words out loud to the churches in Ephesus, Smyrna, and elsewhere. No, that would be the job of the lector, who, with scroll in hand, and with an advance knowledge of its contents, would be able to read the continuous flow of letters and perhaps explain some things along the way. The *hearers* in Rev. 1.3 are clearly distinguished from the reader of the document. And notice that the word *reader* is in the singular here.

We find the very same Greek phrase and phenomenon in Mark 13.14. In the midst of a discussion about the defiling of the temple in Jerusalem by what is called "an abomination which makes desolate" (using a phrase from an Old Testament prophetic book called Daniel), the author inserted the parenthetical remark "let the reader understand." Notice that the word *reader* is again in the singular. This is because while Mark's audience was a group of people, they were

LECTOR

A literate person trained to read an important manuscript (a sacred text, a public proclamation) to an audience with appropriate feeling, pauses, and insight.

merely the hearers of the document. The singular reader of the document was the lector sent to undertake the job of reading it out loud, and perhaps explaining it, to the many hearers who could not read it themselves. This brings us to a further crucial observation.

THE ORAL AND RHETORICAL WORLD OF THE NEW TESTAMENT

All of the ancient cultures of the Biblical world were oral cultures, not cultures based on texts! Whereas in our culture, we tend to think of texts as primary sources of information, and oral conversations or proclamation as secondary, it was just the opposite in the world of the Bible. The oral word was primary, and documents were entirely secondary. There is a reason that Jesus said to his disciples "let those with two good ears hear." The oral word was given pride of place, not least because of the low literacy rate. Not only was the oral word the dominant form of ancient communication, the oral nature of the culture shaped the way people wrote and read documents—they were oral documents, meant to be read out loud.

By this I mean the New Testament documents, like so many other ancient documents, reflect oral speech—they have rhythm, rhyme, alliteration, assonance, and various aural devices. Especially when a person wanted to persuade someone else about something, they would seek to make what was said pleasing, interesting, intriguing to the ear, and not merely memorable but even memorizable.

Early Christianity was an evangelistic religion, so the early Christians produced documents that could be proclaimed or used for the persuasion of nonbelievers, documents that were meant to be heard in the original Greek, not primarily read silently in private. There is a renowned anecdote about two very famous early Christian thinkers named Ambrose and Augustine. Augustine once said that he found Ambrose to be the most remarkable man he had ever met because *he could read a document without moving his lips or making a sound.* This was highly unusual in Augustine's view. Almost all ancient reading was done out loud, even if you were only reading to yourself! Libraries in antiquity must have been very noisy places.

Precisely because the earliest Christians were part of such an **oral culture**, and precisely because they so deeply wanted others to believe in Jesus, they took care to compose their documents in ways that would be aurally effective, and indeed persuasive. Later in our study of the New Testament, we will have occasion to discuss ancient rhetoric (the art of persuasion and speaking well in public) and its use in the New Testament; but here it is enough to say that the earliest Christians used all the oral and rhetorical tools available to them to try

ORAL CULTURE

A culture in which a large part of the communication takes place by the spoken word rather than by written text.

CLUES FROM THE CULTURE

For what man among you would pardon me one **solecism** or condone the barbarous pronunciation of so much as one syllable? But you subject every word I utter to the closest examination.

—*Apuleius* Florida 9

SOLECISM

A grammatical mistake or error.

to convince, convict, and convert people to the following of Jesus Christ. Some of the implications of what we have been discussing in this chapter are enormous as we try to understand the New Testament, and we must explore some of them here as we draw this first chapter to a close.

IMPLICATIONS OF WHAT WE HAVE LEARNED

We are all familiar with the phrase "some things get lost in translation." This is definitely true. If you have ever studied any foreign language at all, you know that some words in one language have no one-to-one corresponding term in another language; and some phrases in one language would not have the same meaning if simply literally translated into another language—some things do get lost in translation. This is why, ideally, if you really want to understand the New Testament, you need to read and study it in the original Greek, not in English. For most of you, this is not possible, so rest assured that this textbook was written only after I studied the New Testament in its original language for many decades. What you will hear in the following chapters is not based merely on one or another interpretation of one or another popular English translation of the New Testament. It is based on the original Greek text of the New Testament.

Obviously, one of the things that absolutely gets lost in translation is all the poetic devices—rhyme, rhythm, and alliteration, for example, cannot be simply produced—and so to a large degree, we lose the oral and aural effect of the words of the New Testament by hearing or reading it in translated languages. We will do our best to compensate for that as we go along, but it would be wise for you, the reader, to use a good modern translation of the New Testament. Several can be recommended: the New Revised Standard Version (NRSV), Today's New International Version (TNIV), the New Living Translation (NLT), or the Common English Bible (CEB) are all excellent choices. The New (or Old) King James Translation is acceptable for most passages, but not always, so it would be better if you used one of the four recommended translations.

There is another good reason why this Introduction is based on the Greek New Testament rather than on some particular English translation. *Every English translation is already an interpretation of the original Greek text.* In other words, translators cannot avoid making decisions about the meanings of various Greek words that have no direct equivalent in English, or have multiple meanings in Greek, or are frankly ambiguous Greek terms. Once a decision is made about the choice of an English term, this already slants the meaning of the English text in a particular direction. What you will get in this Introduction is an interaction with the Greek text as it is, not on the basis of later English translations. One illustration must suffice.

Let us take a particularly popular verse, Hebrews 12.2, which reads literally "fixing our eyes on Jesus the pioneer and perfecter of faith." Unfortunately, there are many English translations that render the verse "fixing our eyes on Jesus the pioneer and perfecter of *our faith.*" Yet the original Greek text of this verse does not have the word "our." It is nowhere to be found, and the context of Hebrews 12.2 does not favor this translation either because Jesus was being presented as the climax of a long list in Hebrews 11 of people who exhibited exemplary faith in God. The whole context suggests that Jesus is portrayed as the paradigm and paragon who exhibited great trust in God, modeling it for his followers. There are many more such examples, but this one is sufficient to show the importance of dealing with the original language, not merely a translation, however helpful and accurate. In chapter 2, we must begin to discuss the various types of literature found in the New Testament—ancient biographies, historical monographs, letters, sermons, and a book of prophecies.

KEY TERMS

Lector   Solecism
Oral Culture

FOR FURTHER READING

Gamble, H. Y. *Books and Readers in the Early Church.* New Haven, CT: Yale University Press, 1995.

Houston, G. W., *Inside Roman Libraries. Book Collection and Their Management in Antiquity.* Chapel Hill: University of North Carolina Press, 2014.

Millard, A. *Reading and Writing in the Time of Jesus.* Sheffield, UK: Sheffield Academic Press, 2000.

STUDY QUESTIONS

Take a few minutes to look over the first chapter about the nature of ancient texts. What is an oral culture? How do texts function in an oral culture? How does this differ from how texts function in our modern culture? Why is this important for the study of the New Testament?

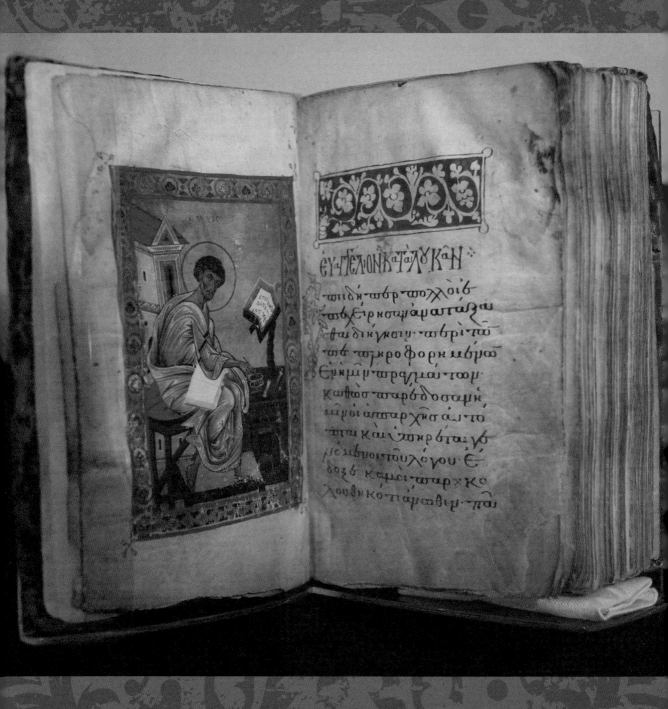

Ancient papyrus was often subject to mold and rot, hence holes and tears. See the picture above.

2

The LITERATURE of the NEW TESTAMENT

THE NEW TESTAMENT IS A COMPENDIUM—not a single book but rather a collection of 27 books. These 27 books are not all of one sort either. Four are Gospels, one is some sort of history (called the Acts of the Apostles), 21 are either letters or sermons or discourses, and the last book of the New Testament is a book of some sort of prophecy. In other words, we have at least five different kinds of literature in the New Testament, if we are talking about whole documents. Within these documents, there are various other kinds of literature—for example, the parables of Jesus. This is important because different kinds of literature are written according to different kinds of literary conventions, and what you can expect out of them is in part determined by what sort of literature it is. C. S. Lewis once stated it this way:

> The first qualification for judging any piece of workmanship from a cork-screw to a cathedral is to know *what* it is—what it was intended to do, and how it is meant to be used![1]

GENRE

From French: *genre*, "kind" or "sort"; from Latin: *genus* (stem gener-); from Greek: *genos,* the term for any category of literature or other forms of art or culture, and in general, any type of discourse, whether written or spoken, auditory or visual, based on some set of stylistic criteria. Genres are formed by conventions that change over time as new genres are invented and old ones are discontinued.

BIOGRAPHY

A written account of a person's life history.

Figure 2.1 A Gospel lectionary.

This assertion is especially true when it comes to dealing with literature. Different types of literature have different **genres**, a French word meaning a literary type. Different genre of literature convey different kinds of information in varying ways. For example, you would not go to a dictionary to look up someone's phone number. That is a category, or genre, mistake. Similarly, if you come to the reading of the New Testament without understanding what sorts of information these documents are trying to give you, you are bound to misread the text.

It is important at the outset to discuss briefly each of the differing types of literature in the New Testament and figure out exactly what they are, so we can understand how to properly read them. Let's start with the Gospels.

WHAT ARE THE GOSPELS (AND ACTS)?

On the surface of things, the Gospels may simply appear to be stories about Jesus. That is true so far as it goes, but if we look more closely, we will notice that the four Gospels differ from one another in noticeable ways. One Gospel begins with a genealogy (Matthew); one Gospel begins with a sort of thesis statement ("This is the beginning of the Good News about Jesus"—Mark); one Gospel begins with a historical preface ("Inasmuch as many have undertaken to give an account of the things which have happened among us"—Luke); and one Gospel begins with a theological prologue ("In the beginning was the Word and the Word was with God, and the Word was God"—John).

Beginnings of documents are especially important in the case of ancient documents because, as we saw in chapter 1, documents were written without headers or paragraphing or even separation of words usually. The only way to figure out what sort of document you were looking at was by reading the first few lines of it. Normally, the genre signals would be given at the outset of the scroll.

Scholars and laypeople have long debated what sort of literature the Gospels are. Some have even seen the Gospels as modern history or modern **biography**. Modern biographies, however, tend to be womb-to-tomb chronicles of someone's life, usually in chronological order, like Carl Sandburg's massive book on the life of Abraham Lincoln.

Even a brief scrutiny of Matthew, Mark, Luke, and John reveal that they are not like that. For one thing, the Gospels are very selective in their presentation. Only two Gospels really tell of Jesus' birth and infancy (Matthew and Luke), and only one Gospel says anything at all about Jesus as a youth (Luke—in only one story—Luke 2.41–52). All four

Gospels focus on the last one to three years of Jesus' life. *In fact, a third or more of each of these Gospels is devoted to only the last week of Jesus' life.* This is hardly the way people write biographies today. Imagine a modern biography of President John Fitzgerald Kennedy that spent a full third of its verbiage on the last week of his life. It would be accused of being grossly out of balance in its coverage, even though the week he was assassinated deserves detailed attention. In fact, this is what happens in our Gospels, as they are really **passion narratives** (33% spent on the last week of Jesus' life) with long introductions.

And for those who are keen on chronology, even a brief study of the four Gospels in the New Testament reveals that the Gospel writers must have felt some freedom to arrange their material in ways other than strict chronology—for example, while in all four Gospels Jesus cleanses the temple in Jerusalem only once, in John, this is recounted near the beginning of the story (in John 2); whereas in the other three Gospels, the temple account is part of the more detailed chronicling of the last week of Jesus' life. Some principle of arrangement of material other than strict chronology must apply at least for John's account.

Or consider works of modern history—for instance, some of the accounts of the American Civil War. Bruce Catton's famous chronicle is incredibly detailed and comprehensive, as is the more literate approach of Shelby Foote. Both authors seek to show how the particular events of the American Civil War relate to larger historical events before, during, and after it. When we look at the four Gospels, only Luke shows any interest at all in linking the macro-history of Judaism or the Greco-Roman world with the micro-history of Jesus and his followers. The other three Gospel writers show little or no interest in this at all. *A fair-minded person should conclude on the basis of such facts and comparisons that the Gospel writers were not writing according to modern conventions for biographies or* **historical monographs**.

This does not mean, however, that the Gospels are not like some sort of biographies or historical monographs. In fact, as we will see when we examine each of these Gospels individually, three of them are written according to the conventions of ancient biography writing (Matthew, Mark, and John); and one author decided to write a two-volume ancient historical monograph, which today is called Luke's Gospel and the Acts of the Apostles. Occasionally, however, some scholars have suggested that the Gospels have very little historical substance or interest at all because they are written more like ancient legends or myths. Let's consider those suggestions for a moment.

The problems with these sorts of suggestions are many. First, the Gospels were written within the lifetime of some of the **eyewitnesses** of the ministry of Jesus, or at least the lifetime of some of those who knew and consulted the eyewitnesses. Notice, for example, that Luke 1.2 says that the author is passing on information that he received *from the original eyewitnesses and servants of the Word* (presumably the original preachers of the story of Jesus).

PASSION NARRATIVE

A term that is commonly used to refer to the narrative of Jesus' suffering and death.

HISTORICAL MONOGRAPH

A written account of a certain period within history. For example, Luke's Gospel and the Acts of the Apostles are a two-volume ancient historical monograph which document the life and death of Jesus and the growth of the New Testament church.

EYEWITNESS

A person who is present to witness an event personally and is able to present an account of the event from his/her own perspective.

CLUES FROM THE
CULTURE

As for necessary reading, Homer comes first and in the middle, and last, in that he gives to every boy and adult and old man just as much as each of them can take.

—Dio Chrysostom (Or. 18.8)

Legends, such as we find, for example, in Homer's *Odyssey* or *Iliad*, although they have some small amount of grounding in historical fact, were in fact written centuries later, after the stories had outlived the people they chronicled. They were written at a time when there were no historical constraints, such as eyewitnesses who could object to the account where it went wrong, for expanding the stories in legendary ways. In fact, the Gospels do not have anywhere near that long a gestation period. The vast majority of scholars believe that Matthew, Mark, Luke, and John were all written in the first century A.D. *The Gospels then are not like ancient legends.*

Nor are the Gospels like ancient mythological stories, for example, about the Greek gods Zeus, Athena, or Apollo, and the like. Such stories focus on the activities of the gods themselves, including their various squabbles on Mount Olympus and elsewhere. The Gospels, however, are telling a tale about a historical person, Jesus of Nazareth, and about other historical persons who met and interacted with him. While the person called God the Father certainly plays a role in the Gospel stories, the story in the main is not his story, but rather the Gospels tell the tale of the redemption of human beings, focusing particularly on Jews and Israel.

No ancient person picking up the Gospels would have mistaken these works for Greek or Roman mythological tales. This is especially true because the hero Jesus, in all four forms of the Gospel story, dies the most shameful form of death known in antiquity—crucifixion. You will look in vain for ancient legends or myths about a human and yet divine figure who suffers the ultimate humiliation of crucifixion. If you wanted people in the ancient Greco-Roman world to believe in a figure called Jesus, you would not make up a story about his dying on a cross. This is not the stuff of which legends or myths or heroes are made in antiquity.

In the coming chapters, we will have occasion to examine Mark, Matthew, Luke–Acts, and John (in that order), but here we stress that *the Gospel writers were following the ancient biographical and historical conventions and genre of their day in writing about Jesus.*

CLUES FROM THE
CULTURE

O Queen of heaven, whether you be bountiful Ceres, or heavenly Venus, or Phoebus, or dreaded Proserpina—by whatever name, with whatever rite, in whatever image it is right to invoke you, defend me now!

—Apuleius (Met. 11.2)

WHAT ABOUT THE "LETTERS" OF THE NEW TESTAMENT?

It is in some ways very surprising that we have 27 New Testament texts of some sort from the earliest followers of Jesus, much less that some 21 of them have been called letters. When it comes to ancient letters, they were mainly viewed as poor substitutes or surrogates for face-to-face conversations with a person or group of persons who could not be present to have such a conversation. In fact, ancient letters are often nothing more than transcripts of what a person would have said orally if he or she had been there in person. Letters are to a large extent "oral texts"—texts meant to be read out loud and heard, as an expression of the living voice. They are not meant to be read silently, thus missing all the cadences, rhythm, assonance, and alliteration of oral speech.

What did an ancient letter actually look like? Most of them are very ordinary and brief. For example, consider the following document written at about the same time as one of the earliest New Testament documents (1 Thessalonians) was being composed.

> Mystarion to his own Stoetis: Greetings. I have sent Blastus to get the forked sticks for my olive groves. See that he does not loiter, for you know I need him every hour. Farewell.
> *(written September 13,* A.D. *50)*

Most ancient letters were about this length or only a little longer. The only two New Testament documents that are as succinct and short as this letter are 2–3 John. All the rest of the New Testament "letters" are much longer, and once you get past the initial or closing greetings and addressor/addressee parts, they hardly look like ancient letters at all. In fact, they are far more like **rhetorical discourses** than like ancient letters when it comes to the vast majority of the content of these documents.

It was only from the time of Cicero (in the first century B.C.) forward that letter writing took on something more like a literary function and at times had more literary pretensions. And it was only from the time of Cicero on that there began to be educational training in the skill of writing letters well. In other words, the conventions of letter writing were not well developed before the time of Cicero. But the art of speaking well, or rhetoric, had been a staple of education for centuries before the time of the writing of the New Testament.

My point in mentioning this is that the so-called letters of the New Testament owe far more to oral speech conventions than to letter-writing conventions, as we shall see. Some of them, such as 1 John, can hardly be called letters at all, as they have no letter features. Some of them, such as Hebrews, appear to be long sermons, but sermons sent from some distance, so they have letter features only at the close of the documents (the end of Hebrews 13). What 19 of the 21 so-called letters are NOT is like ordinary ancient letters. They are not like the perfunctory note we quoted earlier from Mystarion.

IN THE END, APOCALYPSE

Perhaps no book in the New Testament has been more debated when it comes to both form and content than the book of the Revelation of John, the last book in the whole Bible. Is it a book of real prophecy, about both the present

RHETORICAL DISCOURSE

A discourse that employs rhetoric in order to persuade an audience.

CLUES FROM THE **CULTURE**

You have so many delightful spectacles to behold: Orators, writers, poets, and like gorgeous peacocks, sophists in great numbers, men who are lifted aloft as on wings by their fame and their disciples.

—*Dio Chrysostom (Or. 12.5)*

PSEUDONYMOUS

A book falsely, and usually deliberately, attributed to a famous person as if he or she authored it.

TESTAMENT OF ABRAHAM

A Jewish work written sometime during the 1st or 2nd century A.D. about events surrounding Abraham's death.

APOCALYPTIC LITERATURE

A genre of revelatory literature with a narrative framework, in which a revelation is mediated by an otherworldly being to a human recipient, disclosing a transcendent reality that is both temporal, insofar as it envisages eschatological salvation, and spatial insofar as it involves another, supernatural world.

CLUES FROM THE CULTURE

The manner of her prophesying was not that of many other men and women said to be inspired: She did not gasp for breath, whirl her head about or try to terrify with her glances.

—*Dio Chrysostom (Or. 1.56)*

and future, or is it like other early Jewish *apocalyptic* documents?[2] Early Jewish apocalyptic documents tended to be **pseudonymous**, which means a document with a person's name appended to it that was not actually the name of the author of the document.

For example, the **Testament of Abraham** was written long after the death of Abraham, and the parables of Enoch were written long after the time of Enoch. What is actually going on in such **apocalyptic literature** is that history is being written up as if it were prophecy by putting it in the mouth of an ancient luminary of the faith. Thus, it is not really prophecy at all but rather historical commentary disguised as prophecy. This, however, is precisely *not* what is going on in Revelation. We know the actual author's name, John, because he identifies himself at the outset of the first chapter of his book (Revelation 1), and he is literally speaking about his and his audience's own present, and their eventual future, including the final future when Christ returns.

For this reason, scholars have usually concluded that Revelation should be called apocalyptic prophecy or prophecy with apocalyptic images, set within an epistolary framework (see Rev. 2–3 and Rev. 22 on the letter elements in the document). In other words, the last book of the Bible is of mixed genre, that is, it reflects the conventions of several different kinds of literature. In fact, one could make the case that this final book of the New Testament sums up all the different kinds of literature that came earlier in the New Testament: It is one part story, one part history, one part visionary prophecy, one part letter, and one part exhortation or sermon—all of which are presented with the use of amazing apocalyptic images and symbolic numbers.

WHAT IS THE STORY THE NEW TESTAMENT SEEKS TO TELL?

It is one thing to describe what kind of literature we find in the New Testament. It is another matter entirely to ask what is the foundational story that not only the Gospel writers, but also all the writers, of the New Testament are seeking to tell or assume to be true?

In one sense, the New Testament story is part of an ongoing and much larger story, the story of the whole Bible from Adam to Abraham to Moses to David and so on. The New Testament joins the storytelling a long way into the story. Jesus appears in this larger Biblical story some thousands of years after it began. And we are constantly having quotations, allusions to, or echoes of these earlier stories in the New Testament itself. The very first New Testament book, the Gospel of Matthew, begins with a genealogy that runs from Abraham all the way to Jesus, connecting him directly with the royal line of King David, the most famous of all Jewish kings. None of this would have obvious meaning to someone who knew nothing of the contents of the Old Testament. The New

Testament was largely written by Jews who became followers of Jesus, and so it is not a surprise that they do their best to connect the story of Jesus with the larger story of Israel and its major figures, and thus with the Hebrew Scriptures that Christians call the Old Testament.

It is not just that they tried to connect these stories to the Jesus story, it is that the writers of the New Testament all agreed that the stories found in the Old Testament are inspired stories, sacred stories; and so "they are Scriptures" suitable for learning the truth about God and for training in righteousness as well. The Old Testament then is seen as foundational for the beliefs and practices of the earliest Christians, and they told their stories about Jesus in ways that show he is the culmination, the climax, and the fulfillment of all these previous stories. Indeed, they insisted that Jesus is the person to whom all these earlier texts were pointing. It may surprise you to realize that the only Bible the earliest Christians had was the Old Testament; so, for example, when we read in 2 Timothy 3.16 that all Scripture is God-breathed and profitable for a host of educational purposes, the term "Scripture" refers to what we call the Old Testament.

Figure 2.2 The glorified Christ in a ceiling mosaic at the Chora Church, Istanbul. (© Mark R. Fairchild, Ph.D.)

All of the writers of the New Testament documents were committed followers of Jesus, and thus the New Testament documents were not attempts at objective newspaper-like reporting of the story of Jesus. Nevertheless, these writers insisted that their interpretations of the Jesus story were correct ones, correct drawings out of the true implications of who Jesus was, and what the historical and religious significance was of what he said and did. They are all in agreement that "his story" is true "history"—indeed, the most important history of all, a history that changed and is changing the world. It is the story of how God came in person, the person of his Son, to redeem his lost creatures—all of humanity.

Sometimes, the story of Christ is on the surface of a New Testament document, such as in the Gospels, or in the sermon summaries in Acts (see, e.g., Peter's sermon in Acts 2). Sometimes, the story is briefly quoted, as we find in 1 Corinthians 11, where Paul quotes a portion of the Last Supper story from the life of Jesus; or in Revelation 12, where we hear of the birth of Jesus and his ascension. Sometimes, the story is retold in hymnic fashion, as in Philippians 2.5–11. Sometimes, we merely hear echoes of the Jesus story or of his teachings or deeds. For example, in James, we have some 20 or more partial uses of Jesus' teachings found in Matthew 5–7: the so-called Sermon on the Mount.

The point is, all the New Testament writers assumed that the story of Jesus is foundational for Christian belief and for all that they were trying to say and do. There is a unity to the story of and stories in the New Testament, as they all are grounded or grow out of the story of Jesus. Indeed, people like Paul keep stressing that it is the believer's job to imitate Christ (1 Cor. 11.1), but you have to first know the ways and story of Christ in order to do that. This is why, after this short introduction, we start by examining the Gospels to see if we can get Jesus' story straight first. Before we do so, we need to make some final comments about the sort of history writing in the New Testament and talk some about the social context of the New Testament and about Jesus himself.

WHAT SORT OF HISTORY IS THIS?

When a modern person picks up and reads the Gospels and Acts, and indeed, the rest of the New Testament, almost immediately the question arises—is this a historical story, and if so, what sort of historical story is it? Modern history seldom spends time recounting miracles or stories of divine interventions. In this respect, modern history writing is very different from ancient history writing. For example, Herodotus, the father of all history writing, was perfectly comfortable with talking about the role of the divine—this god or that—in human affairs, including history. The New Testament writers all agreed with this broader and more open-minded approach to history writing. They don't exclude the divine part of the story from the outset like most modern historians do. For this reason, I would argue that we should call New Testament history *theological history telling.* Not theology without history, or history without theology, but rather the two together. Indeed, it can be said that the whole Bible is the story of God's dealings with and relationship with human beings.

There is, however, an even more important reason to say we have theological history writing in the New Testament. All the writers of the New Testament believe and assume the truth of what we find in John 1—namely, that God the Son took on flesh and became a human being, and he walked among us for a span of time. If, as the writers of the New Testament believe, Jesus was both divine and human, then even just telling the story of Jesus requires that we take into account both divine and human history, both God's dealings with humanity and human beings' attempts to relate to God. It is not in one or the other, but in both, that we find undergirding and overarching the whole New Testament, hence the term theological history writing. The great English cleric, John Donne, contemplating the grandeur of the story of humanity in its relationship with God, put it eloquently:

> 'Twas much that man was made like God before,
> But, that God should be made like man, much more.

The poignancy of these lines expresses well the view of the New Testament writers—they not only believed that human beings are made in the image of God, they also believed that the Son of God came down and took on the image of humanity in order to redeem humanity from its sins and sorrows, from disease, decay, and death. With this sort of worldview, the only kind of history that made sense to the earliest Christians was theological history.

Lest we think, however, that the New Testament writers were just historians who liked dwelling on the past, we need to remind ourselves that they also believed that Christ's history is the believer's destiny. By this we mean that the story of Jesus is being recapitulated in his followers' lives, such that one day they too will experience resurrection as Jesus did. Whatever else you say about this belief, it led to the writing of documents that are not only about the past, and the writers' present, but about the future of humanity as well, and they scarcely suffered from being dull.

The writers of the New Testament were saints standing on tiptoe eagerly waiting for the author of the human drama to come on the stage once more and conclude the story, for they believed that the future was as bright as the promises of God. Whether this is part of your faith or not, in order to understand the New Testament, you need to enter into the world of these writers sympathetically and give their writings a fair hearing. Above all, if we want to understand the most influential person in all of human history, Jesus, we need to undertake such a task. To that end, we will turn first to Jesus, then to the Gospels and Acts, and then to the rest of the New Testament.

IMPLICATIONS

Sometimes, it is necessary to divest oneself of certain ideas, presuppositions, and feelings before reading an important document. Think for a moment of a time when you received an e-mail from a person who had deeply wounded you. You were predisposed to expect this to be another nasty and unpleasant exchange, and all your negative feelings were aroused just from seeing the return address on the e-mail. You might not have even wanted to open the e-mail and read it. For many people, they already have strong feelings about the Bible, either negative or positive, and sometimes this gets in the way of reading the text fairly and with an open mind. It is my hope that you will be fair and open-minded as you read this textbook.

For those for whom the Bible is already familiar territory, I promise you will learn some things you never knew before. For those for whom the Bible is like an unknown land, there will be many more surprises. It is the necessary presupposition of any good or fair reading of a text that one approach the text without prejudice. Indeed, it is better to approach the text with curiosity, sympathy, and willingness to learn, and then be surprised, giving the writers the benefit of the doubt as you read.

There is a famous saying of Johannes Bengel—"Apply yourself wholly to the text [i.e., give it your full attention], and apply the text wholly to yourself." Even if you must wrestle and struggle with some of the content and concepts in the New Testament, if like Jacob wrestling with the angel, you stay at it long enough, you will come away not just with more knowledge, but with a blessing, and not just with information, but with inspiration.

KEY TERMS

Apocalyptic Literature	Passion Narrative
Biography	Pseudonymous
Eyewitnesses	Rhetorical Discourse
Genre	Testament of Abraham
Historical Monograph	

FOR FURTHER READING

Hubbard, Moyer V. *Christianity in the Greco-Roman World.* Peabody, MA: Hendrickson, 2010.

Witherington, B. *New Testament History: A Narrative Account.* Grand Rapids, MI: Baker, 2003.

Witherington, B. *The New Testament Story.* Grand Rapids, MI: Eerdmans, 2004.

STUDY QUESTIONS

The literature found in the New Testament comprises various genres. What does the term *genre* mean, and why is it important to know the genre of literature when you examine it? How does this help us understand the New Testament better?

NOTES

1. C. S. Lewis, *A Preface to Paradise Lost* (Oxford, England: Oxford University Press, 1942), 1.
2. See the full definition of apocalyptic on p. 16.

The Porch of the Maidens on the Acropolis opposite
the Parthenon. (© Mark R. Fairchild, Ph.D.)

3

JESUS of NAZARETH in his EARLY JEWISH SETTING

Whoever he was or was not, whoever he thought he was, whoever
he has become in the memories since and will go on becoming for as long
as men remember him—exalted, sentimentalized, debunked, made and
remade to the measure of each generation's desire, dread, indifference—
he was a man once, whatever else he may have been.
And he had a man's face, a human face.
—FREDERICK BUECHNER, *THE FACES OF JESUS*[1]

HAVE YOU EVER READ THE GOSPELS, looking for a description of what Jesus looked like? Have you wondered if he perhaps looked like the picture of the **Pharisee** in Figure 3.1? You will look in vain, for unlike our image- and appearance-obsessed culture, outward appearance did not matter nearly as much as reality in Jesus' world. It was your character, not the color of your eyes, that

PHARISEE

This term seems to derive from the Hebrew root *prs*, which means either "separate" or "interpret"—probably the former. The Pharisees were the "separate ones," probably because of their attempt to distinguish themselves in the careful observance of the law from less-observant Jews and from Gentiles. It is possible to say that Pharisees were a holiness movement that believed that the way to purify the land was not by violence but through a more detailed attention to the Levitical laws. The Pharisees, unlike the Sadducees, believed that oral traditions were passed on by Moses since Mt. Sinai and were as binding on a Jew as the written traditions in the Old Testament. They used these oral traditions to meet new dilemmas and situations. The Sadducees, by contrast, were for strict adherence to the letter of the Old Testament, particularly the Pentateuch.

JOSEPHUS

A Jewish historian who lived during the first century A.D. and referred to Jesus in his writing. Key writings include *The Jewish War, Antiquities of the Jews* and *Against Apion*.

Figure 3.1 A Pharisee was identifiable by his religious attire, including the prayer shawl. (© *Rick Danielson*)

mattered. What we have in the four Gospels is four portraits of the character of Jesus, not descriptions of his physical appearance.

I emphasize the word *portrait*, for the Gospels are not like modern digital photographs. Rather, they are like beautiful portraits, inherently interpretive and presenting Jesus from various angles of incidence, various vantage points. The basic difference between an ordinary photograph and a portrait is that the latter is indeed an interpretation of the subject, not merely a physical representation of the subject. We have no real idea what Jesus looked like, but we do know who he was, what kind of person he was.

In a sense, the ancient Gospel writers already knew and affirmed the dream of Martin Luther King Jr., a dream of a day when a person would be judged not on the basis of the color of their skin (or any aspect of their outward appearance) but rather on the basis of the content of their character. The Gospels are character sketches, portraits, and they are not merely "true to life": they are true, too true for mere surface descriptions or outward impressions to be allowed to get in the way.

Like other ancient biographers and historians, the Evangelists decided to take an indirect approach to revealing the character of Jesus, what manner of person he actually was. It is the words and deeds of Jesus that are used to reveal his person and character. Substance is preferred over form, and reality over a physical account of his image. Using this indirect method of portraiture, the Gospel writers reveal what they want us to know about Jesus. Interestingly, they do so without a lot of side commentary or explanation. Yes, there are a few parenthetical comments in the Gospels (see, e.g., Mark 7.11, 19; John 4.2, 9), but surprisingly few; and most of those comments by the Gospel writers simply explain foreign terms or customs, they do not usually attempt to explain the meaning of Jesus' teaching, much less the meaning of Jesus himself. The Gospel story is allowed to carry the weight all by itself.

DID JESUS EVEN EXIST?

In our own cynical and skeptical age, there are even some persons who have doubted the very existence of Jesus. No responsible historian of antiquity takes this view for the very good reason that we have more evidence for the existence of Jesus of Nazareth than for almost any other comparable figure from that era. We have Jewish, Roman, and Christian evidence that he was a real person. The Jewish historian **Josephus**, even if we eliminate possible later additions to his text by Christians, certainly refers to Jesus, just as he does to John the Baptist (see "Clues from the Culture: Josephus on Jesus"); and the Roman historian **Tacitus**, who like Josephus also lived in the first century A.D., refers to Jesus who was crucified on a cross by Pontius Pilate. Then there are myriad of early Christian testimonies to the life and death of Jesus from the first century, much of which we find in the New Testament itself. Peter, James the brother of Jesus, and perhaps even Paul all knew or had seen Jesus and knew directly about his crucifixion.

This is but a passing reference, and something Josephus certainly could have said. Portions of the other passage may well have some Christian insertions in them, which I have highlighted in bold.

> Now there was about this time Jesus, a wise man, **if it be lawful to call him a man,** for he was a doer of wonderful works, a teacher of such men as receive the truth with pleasure. He drew over to him both many of the Jews, and many of the Gentiles. **He was the Christ,** and when Pilate, at the suggestion of the principal men among us, had condemned him to the cross, those that loved him at the first did not forsake him; **for he appeared to them alive again the third day; as the divine prophets had foretold these and ten thousand other wonderful things concerning him.** And the tribe of Christians so named from him are not extinct at this day.
> —Antiquities 20.9.1 (bold added)

Josephus lived in the Holy Land during and after the time of Jesus and was in a position to know something of Jesus' story, although Josephus was not a follower of Jesus. If he inclined to any one Jewish group, it was the Pharisees. The majority of scholars of whatever stripe accept some edited version of the preceding paragraph as being penned by Josephus himself. I agree with that judgment.

This report (see "Clues from the Culture, Tacitus on Jesus") comes from an important Roman senator and historian who had access to official documents from provinces like Judaea, which is presumably where he got the information about Jesus' death. He likely wrote this late in the first century A.D. as he was compiling and drawing on his own memoirs.

TACITUS

A Roman historian who lived in the first century A.D. and referred in his writing to Jesus who was crucified on a cross by Pontius Pilate. Key writings include his *Annals* and his *Histories* which report historical events contemporaneous with his lifetime.

CLUES FROM THE CULTURE
JOSEPHUS ON JESUS

There are two passages in Josephus's Antiquities of the Jews *that refer to Jesus. The first is affirmed as authentic by historians of all sorts and is not really under debate. It reads as follows:*

But the younger Ananus who, as we said, received the high priesthood, was of a bold disposition and exceptionally daring; he followed the party of the Sadducees, who are severe in judgment above all the Jews, as we have already shown. As therefore Ananus was of such a disposition, he thought he had now a good opportunity, as Festus was now dead, and Albinus was still on the road; so he assembled a council of judges, and brought before it the brother of Jesus the so-called Christ, whose name was James, together with some others, and having accused them as lawbreakers, he delivered them over to be stoned.

—Antiquities 20.9.1

We may then put aside extreme skepticism about the existence of Jesus. The evidence is stronger for his existence than even for a figure like Julius Caesar; and in terms of ancient manuscripts, we have more copies of very ancient Christian manuscripts referring to Jesus than manuscripts referring to any other comparable historical figure.

WHAT MANNER OF MAN WAS HE?

Perhaps the first thing to say about Jesus is that he was a Jew, and as a Jew he lived in a highly Jewish environment in Jewish ways. You may not need this reminder, but it would be **anachronistic** to say Jesus was a Christian, although he certainly is the source and focus of the early Christian movement, and I would stress that Jesus had an exalted and messianic view of himself. We will say much more about that later in this textbook.

Jesus was born somewhere between 2 and 6 B.C. This should strike you as odd, and it is all because a monk called Dionysius the Short reckoned that Jesus was born at or just before 1 A.D. He was off by a few years, but the modern calendar that makes this year 2017 is based on Dionysius's errant calculations.

What we know with some certainty is that Jesus was born while Herod the Great was king over all of the Holy Land (see Matthew 2). Herod the Great, however, died somewhere between 1 and 4 B.C. Ergo, Jesus has to have been born before then. Luke 3.23 tells us that Jesus was about 30 years old when he began his ministry. If we count backward from the date of his death, which was probably A.D. 30, this means his ministry probably began about A.D. 27 (lasting about 3 years), which in turn means he was likely born somewhere around 2–3 B.C.

As a Jew, Jesus had many discussions about the Law of Moses found in the first five books of the Old Testament, and we find him debating things like laws of clean and unclean, appropriate behavior on the Sabbath, what the greatest commandment of that Mosaic Law was, and so on. The contrast between Jesus' discussions and arguments with other Jewish leaders, such as the Pharisees, and Paul's discussion at the **Areopagus** (see Acts 17.16–34) with Greeks, in which he quotes Greek poets and philosophers, could hardly be more

Figure 3.2 The Gezer Calendar, shown in the Istanbul Archaeological Museum, may be one of the earliest examples of Hebrew writing.

Figure 3.3 The Court called Areopagus is thought to have stood on Mars Hill by some, but more likely it was in the agora below the hill. (© *Mark R. Fairchild, Ph.D.*)

ANACHRONISTIC

The description of a term, concept, idea or event that does not fit accurately into the time in which it is being discussed. In other words, the usage is chronologically incorrect. For example, it would be anachronistic (or an anachronism) to refer to the use of cell phones in the first century A.D.

AREOPAGUS

This word literally means Mars Hill and refers to a locale in Athens. It is debated whether the reference is to a little knoll in the shadow of the acropolis and the Parthenon, or if in fact Acts 17 is referring to the court in the stoa or marketplace below which Paul was tried for preaching new deities.

dramatic. Jesus lived and died in a very different world from the world of some of the earliest Christians, especially the Gentile ones who had never set foot in the Holy Land. As different as our 21st century world is from all of the ancient world, even within the ancient Jewish and Greco-Roman worlds of the New Testament, one culture often differed from another as much as, say, modern American culture differs from Afghanistan's culture today. In order to understand Jesus and the earliest Christians and their writings, a person needs to begin to understand the character of the world, the cultures, and the ethos of the first century A.D.

The second major thing to say about Jesus is that we don't know nearly as much about his life as we would like to know. For example, we know next to nothing about what he was doing between the ages of infancy and when he began his public ministry at about the age of 30. We can assume he had a normal early Jewish life—his family was composed of devout Jews. He attended synagogue. Joseph and Jesus himself practiced a trade, namely, they were artisans (the Greek word *tekton* refers to those skilled in working in wood and stone).[2] The family went on religious pilgrimages to Jerusalem like many other Galilean Jews (see Luke 2.41–52). We can assume he had a normal early Jewish diet—eating fruits, nuts, grains, bread, and not much meat except during a feast or festival occasion.

Figure 3.4 Grain was the most precious of commodities for survival in the Ancient Near East, as there were often famines. (© Rick Danielson)

PEASANT

A class of people who lived in an agrarian society. Peasants were part of the lower class, often illiterate and were not landowners.

What we *cannot* assume, despite the assertions of some scholars is that (1) Jesus was a **peasant**. First of all, the New Testament depicts him as an artisan, working in wood and stone, and it depicts his family as having a home in Nazareth. His family is neither without property, nor are they tenant farmers. (2) The evidence as we have it indicates that Jesus could read (see Luke 4). Persons who could not read the Torah were not allowed to teach the Torah in early Jewish synagogues. Jesus was not illiterate. (3) Southern Galilee was not a monolingual region. Greek, Hebrew, and Aramaic were all used in this region, with Aramaic being the dominant language spoken. Greek was necessary because of the cities of the Decapolis, which were either actually in this part of the Holy Land (i.e., Scythopolis) or very nearby and visited regularly by Jews like Jesus (i.e., Caesarea Philippi—see Mark 8.27–30, or Gadara). We will say a good deal more about how much Greek culture had influenced this region long before the time of Jesus later in this study. See chapter 15 on Jude (p. 293), the brother of Jesus, and Galilee in their day.

What set Jesus apart from the ordinary was controversy, and the controversy does not seem to have begun until Jesus actually began his ministry somewhere around A.D. 27 or 28. What seems to have prompted Jesus' ministry as much as anything else was the earlier ministry of his cousin, the man we know as John the Baptizer. We will say much more about that as we examine the Gospels themselves.

Here it is enough to say that Jesus was born, lived, and died a Jew within his Jewish environment; so far as we know, he almost never left the land of Israel at all, except for small excursions across the borders near to the Sea of Galilee and points north. Nor do any of the earliest followers of Jesus suggest that he ever wrote anything down, such as his own teachings. But some of Jesus' disciples certainly began writing down things he said and likely did so at an early juncture. Jesus was well known by friend, foe, and the indifferent as a remarkable teacher and healer who drew considerable crowds clamoring to hear and be healed.

The all too brief life of Jesus came to an abrupt halt in about A.D. 30, when the Roman authorities, chiefly Pontius Pilate, had him crucified on a wooden cross outside the city walls of Jerusalem. He was no more than about 33 years old when this happened. It is fair to say that we would have probably never heard of Jesus at all if crucifixion was in fact the historical end of his story. One of the great problems for modern historians in dealing with Jesus is explaining *why* a movement of Jesus followers, and even Jesus worshippers, arose after the crucifixion of Jesus, if in fact crucifixion was the dead end to which his life and story came.

Crucifixion was considered the most horrible and shameful way to die in antiquity. Ancient people tended to believe that a person's origins and birth and how a person died revealed their character. This is one reason why various writers of the Gospel spent so much time on Jesus' origins and death, especially his death. In Jesus' world, a death by crucifixion would be taken as proof that Jesus was a wicked person, even that Jesus was a person cursed by God, because few early Jews could imagine that God would allow a special prophet or king, much less God's son, to die a hideous, shameful death like that. If Jesus was crucified, so went the logic, then at a minimum he couldn't be anyone good, anyone im-

Figure 3.5 The modern Via Dolorosa, or way of the cross, which Christian pilgrims take from the Antonio Fortress to the Church of the Holy Sepulcher, seeking to follow the path Jesus took to the cross. (© Rick Danielson)

portant, anyone that God had anointed. To the contrary, crucifixion proved that he was a false prophet and someone God never endorsed, or at least that God in the end abandoned him. Some have even pointed to the last words of Jesus on the cross—"My God, my God, why have you forsaken me" as proof that he was no one special (see Mark 15.34).

Indeed, even Jesus' sympathizers and various of his followers had given up hope he was anyone special once he was crucified, and they were prepared to abandon their belief in Jesus. Look at the story in Luke 24 of the two followers of Jesus who are leaving Jerusalem with their heads down once Jesus was crucified. Notice what they say to the "stranger" they meet on the road as they leave town—"But we had *hoped* (past tense) that he was the one to redeem Israel" (Luke 24.21). Clearly, the hope was gone now that Jesus had died on a cross. Even knowing that the tomb was found empty and that some women claimed to have had a vision of angels who told them he was alive again did not prevent these disciples from abandoning hope in Jesus.

Figure 3.6 An image of a garden tomb that is empty with the stone rolled back. (© Rick Danielson)

It is for this reason that something dramatic and historic had to have happened to Jesus after his crucifixion and death to change the crushed hopes of the earliest disciples into joy, devotion, and a lifelong commitment to following Jesus, proclaiming Jesus, worshipping Jesus, and even dying for Jesus. They would not do all that for a lie, for a person they believed was cursed by God and simply died on a cross, ending an otherwise interesting, helpful, and healing three years of ministry.

There were plenty of famous early Jewish, and for that matter Greco-Roman, teachers who lived normal lives and died normal deaths, not on a cross, and none of them spawned evangelistic movements that have endured for 2,000 years and continue even now to grow. Even the secular historian has to explain how we get from a crucified Jesus to the early Christian movement; and as Martin Dibelius once said, the X that one puts in the equation between those two historical facts has to be large enough to explain why the latter events happened after the former event of crucifixion.

I would suggest that the earliest followers of Jesus were telling the truth when they claimed they saw Jesus alive again after his death, and they walked with him, talked with him, supped with him, and even touched him after he had died. In other words, a miracle happened to the miracle worker himself after his crucifixion. The story of Jesus cannot be adequately told or explained without the miracle. Indeed, the story of Jesus is full of miracles—miracles that he performed and miracles that happened to and for him at the beginning and end of his human story.

WHAT IS A MIRACLE?

If you look up the dictionary definition of a miracle, you will find something like this:

> 1. A surprising and welcome event that is not explicable by natural or scientific laws and is considered to be divine. 2. A highly improbable or extraordinary event, development, or accomplishment.

In the old days, you sometimes even heard a definition that suggested a miracle was something that "violated" the laws of nature, but this was shown to make little sense because if there is a God who set up the laws of nature in the first place, what sense would it make to say he then violated them? Hence, we have definitions such as the ones just given. What these definitions rightly suggest is that miracles in the proper sense are out of the ordinary happenings, and often they are not explicable on the basis of our current knowledge, scientific or otherwise.

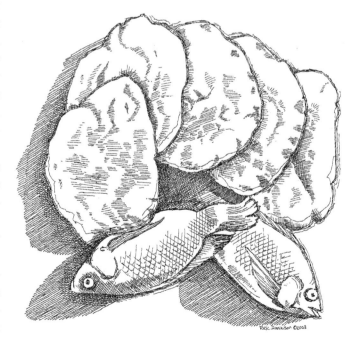

A fair-minded person will admit there are many things that happen in this world that are currently inexplicable. Even the most committed scientist, if not given over to hubris, has to admit that we do not actually know the limits of what is possible in this world, and we do not even fully know the parameters of the laws of nature. Whatever those parameters are, however, it was the conviction of the writers of the New Testament that *God can and does on occasion go beyond the known laws of nature, without going against*

Figure 3.7 Loaves and fishes were the most basic food stuffs in Galilee. (© Rick Danielson)

them. This is miracle with a capital *M,* something that will probably never be fully explicable on the basis of normal processes of causation or natural law.

For a modern person who has grown up in the scientific era, it is important, of course, to evaluate claims about miracles critically, but at the same time with an open mind. Open-mindedness does not mean that one has to be gullible or easily duped about things. Some claims about miracles are false, but some, I would suggest, are true. I like the dictum of my grandmother—"Don't be so open-minded that your brains fall out." At the same time, you should not be so close-minded that you assert dogmatically that "miracles don't happen because they can't happen." In fact, no one knows enough to be able to make that dogmatic statement—no one.

I am stressing this at the beginning of our exploration into the New Testament because as you read the New Testament, you will find one report about a miracle after another after another. You will not be able to fairly evaluate these stories and these documents unless you approach them with not only an open mind but also some good, careful, critical thinking. Faith is not the opposite of knowledge. No students of the New Testament should ever be asked to check their brains at the door in order to believe what the New Testament says about Jesus or various other topics. Indeed, the mind is a gift from God, just as faith is. This introduction seeks to do justice to both reason and faith when it comes to Jesus and the New Testament, not just one or the other.

When it comes to miracles then, while it is possibly true that some of the miracle stories in the New Testament (such as the healing of a person who seems to be having an epileptic fit) may reflect primitive ideas about disease and unclean spirits that today we would describe in more scientific and natural terms, it is not the case that we can explain *all* the miracles in the New Testament, or even all the miracles performed by Jesus, in purely naturalistic terms. Dead men tell no tales, and they do not rise from actual death without a miracle. To an important extent, you need to be open to the possibility of miracles if you are going to try to understand Jesus and the writings of the New Testament, never mind if you want to embrace Jesus and these documents as important to your own faith journey. Ironically, you can only fully know and understand the historical Jesus and his words and deeds and life if you allow that he just might be more than an ordinary historical person. And you can only fully appreciate the writings of the New Testament if you approach them with an open mind. Once you admit the possibility of divine activity in the human sphere, then you have opened yourself up to the question of the relationship of the historical Jesus to the exalted Christ of faith.

Mark Allan Powell frames the issue this way:

> There is one passage in the Gospel of Matthew in which Jesus says to his disciples, "You always have the poor with you, but you will not always have me" (26.11). Then [only a little] later in Matthew's

Gospel, Jesus says to these same disciples "I will always be with you" (28.20). The first passage refers to what scholars call the earthly historical figure of Jesus. . . . But then, in the second passage, when Jesus says "I will be with you always," he must be referring to something else. Christian theologians would say that the eternal exalted Jesus . . . remains present in a way that the earthly, historical figure does not.[3]

It is not just that there is more to Jesus than quite literally meets the eye, but that the person we call Jesus is more than just a historical figure. The name "Jesus" applies especially to his earthly ministry and career. It is the name his parents gave to him at his birth. Sometimes, because of an antisupernatural bias, some scholars assume that the Jesus of history was a real person, but that the Christ of faith is just a figment of human hope and faith. What the writers of the New Testament insist, however, is that the divine Christ is just as real as the historical Jesus; indeed, it is the same person, although the exalted Christ is present too and with his disciples now in a different and nonmaterial way. Thus, the New Testament writers suggested that while we can distinguish the Jesus of history from the Christ of faith, we cannot divide the two. In fact, they would say Jesus' earthly ministry is just one phase of the career of the Son of God.

WERE THERE "LOST CHRISTIANITIES"?

It is fair to say that there are two main competing visions of early Christianity in play in the scholarly world today. On one hand, there is the more traditional view (which is still the majority view among scholars worldwide) that although certainly there was some diversity in early Christianity, one could not speak of multiple Christianities in the first century A.D. vying with one another for converts to their brand of a new religion (with some of them later suppressed in a fourth-century crackdown on heresy—the so-called lost Christianities). Instead, a rather unified small group of Jewish Christians and a growing number of Gentile Christians had a strong sense of what theological and ethical **orthodoxy** was and embraced it, and the New Testament documents reflect this fact. The movement was largely unified and had a shared core of convictions about belief and behavior.

On the other hand, there is the perspective that early Christianity took myriad forms and involved a wide diversity of beliefs almost right from the beginning. In this view, there was no such thing as orthodoxy or **orthopraxy** in the first century A.D. when it comes to the beliefs and behaviors of these early followers of Jesus. To the contrary, it is argued, orthodoxy was something later imposed on Christianity through a ruler like Constantine and through meetings like the Council of Nicea in A.D. 325.

ORTHODOXY

A term used to describe correct or approved theological and ethical beliefs. Heresy occurs when a belief does not agree with orthodox beliefs.

ORTHOPRAXY

A term used to describe correct practices based upon proper theological and ethical beliefs.

Figure 3.8 Drawing of a Galilean fishing boat based on the one found in the mud by the sea of Galilee. (© Rick Danielson)

You may have encountered a version of this approach to the origins of Christianity in the form of a novel from a decade ago, *The Da Vinci Code,*[4] but you could also have come across it in New Testament introductory textbooks.[5] Despite the claim that this is a more historical approach to this subject than one finds in more traditional introductions to the New Testament, unfortunately this view involves a "myth of origins" and is largely an argument from silence. The historical evidence as we have it, which is largely limited to the New Testament documents themselves, is against this view. Why do I say this?

First, all of the earliest followers of Jesus, both during his ministry and immediately thereafter, were Jews—monotheistic Jews. There was already a sense of both orthodoxy and orthopraxy that the earliest followers of Jesus had, before they ever believed Jesus was the risen Lord. They did not suddenly abandon a belief, for example, in monotheism, that "God is One," after the death and resurrection of Jesus. They *did* come to understand that belief in fresh ways, but the point is that their template was what they had been taught first in the Old Testament and second by Jesus himself, a monotheistic Jew. The Old Testament continued to be the sacred Scriptures of the new "Christian" movement throughout the first century A.D. and beyond, and the teachings of Jesus continued to be important throughout the first century A.D. The proof of this is that no fewer than four Gospels containing the story of the life and teachings of Jesus *were likely all produced in the last third of the first century* A.D., *when the parting of the ways of Christians with early Judaism had already largely happened.*

Second, so far as we can tell, the majority of Christians well into the first century, and after the New Testament documents began to be written about mid-century, were still Jews or Gentiles who had had connections with the synagogue before becoming followers of Jesus. There is not a shred of historical evidence that there were, for example, "Gnostic Christians" producing **Gnostic** documents in the first century A.D.

Despite sensationalistic claims made in the last two decades, the historical evidence is clear that documents like the Gospel of Judas, the Gospel of

Philip, the Gospel of Mary, or even the Gospel of Thomas were all created in the second through fourth centuries A.D., as the Gnostic movement arose during that period and *in reaction to and dependence on the earlier Christian documents.* The Gnostic movement was a largely Gentile movement deeply indebted to Greco-Roman dualistic ideas about matter being evil and spirit being good, reacting against the earlier Jewish Christian movement in various ways, and in some cases rejecting the Old Testament and the God of the Old Testament altogether.

As soon as this movement began to gain steam in the second and third centuries A.D., it was immediately condemned by those who stood in the stream of the original Jewish Christian version of the Jesus movement. There was a sense of orthodoxy and orthopraxy from the beginnings of early Christianity, which is precisely why we read critiques of false prophets and teachers in a variety of different documents now in the New Testament.

We can see this early orthodoxy already being a crucial part of original Christian worship at the beginning of the second century if we consider two important texts—one by a Christian from Smyrna named Justin Martyr (A.D. 110–165), the other by Pliny, a Roman governor of a province called Bithynia in the same general region (modern-day Turkey). Here is what they say:

> On the day called Sunday, all who live in the cities or in the country gather together, to one place, and the *memoirs of the apostles* or the writings of the prophets are read, as long as time permits, then when the reader has ceased, the President verbally instructs and exhorts to the imitation of these good things. Then we all rise together and pray, . . . and when our prayer is ended, bread and wine and water are brought, and the President in like manner offers prayers and thanksgivings, according to his ability, and the people assent, saying Amen, and there is the distribution to each . . . and to those absent a portion is sent by the deacons. . . . But Sunday is the day on which we hold our common assembly, because it is the first day on which God . . . made the world, and Jesus Christ our Savior on the same day rose from the dead.
> (Justin Martyr, First Apology, 65–67)

Pliny, writing from Bithynia, also in the middle of the second century, said the Christians themselves that he interrogated confessed that

> They were accustomed to meet on a fixed day before dawn and sing responsively a hymn to Christ as to a god, and to bind themselves by oath, not to do some crime, but not to commit fraud, theft, or adultery, not falsify their trust, nor to refuse to return a trust when

GNOSTICISM

The English term "Gnosticism" derives from the use of the Greek adjective *gnostikos* ("learned," "intellectual") by Irenaeus (ca. A.D. 185) to describe the school of Valentinus as "the heresy called Learned (gnostic)." This occurs in the context of Irenaeus's work, *On the Detection and Overthrow of Knowledge Falsely So Called.* There is no clear historical evidence of a Gnostic movement before sometime in the second century A.D. The movement was mainly called Gnostic because of its claims to have special, even secret, knowledge about reality.

called upon to do so. When this was over, it was their custom to depart and to assemble again to partake of food—but ordinary and innocent food.

(Letter to Trajan 10.96)

There are several components to these testimonies, but the essential things to note are as follows: (1) singing to Christ as a God; (2) praying and sharing a meal together; (3) exhortations about ethical matters and commitments to follow the exhortations; and (4) worship on a fixed day, namely, Sunday. To this, Justin added that there were readings from sacred texts, both Christian and Jewish. The reference to the "memoirs of the apostles" probably includes both Gospels and some readings from Paul, at a minimum, as well as readings from Old Testament prophets. In addition, Justin referred to leaders of the worship meetings, presidents, deacons, and readers of the sacred texts. Notice as well the reference to creation theology in connection with the first day of the week. There are several aspects of this that Gnostics in the second century and later would have found unacceptable. First, they would not have liked the use of the Old Testament, nor the theology of creation affirmed. Second, they would not have wanted the Christian readings to be limited to first-century Christian apostles because *none of them were Gnostics.* Rather, they were Jewish Christians.[6]

When we examine closely the 27 books that did make it into the New Testament, *they can be traced back to a handful of persons, all of whom were either eyewitnesses to the original events or in contact with those who were eyewitnesses of Jesus himself, or, in some cases, with the earliest post-Easter followers of Jesus.* Think about it for a minute. About a third of the New Testament, including all its very earliest documents, is attributed to one person—Paul, a Jew who lived in Jerusalem during the time of the ministry of Jesus. Second, another quarter or so of the New Testament, namely, the Gospel of Luke and the Acts of the Apostles, is attributed to and probably written by another individual person, Luke, who was in contact with the original eyewitnesses and preachers of the Good News and was a sometime companion of Paul (see Luke 1.1–4). Still another 15 percent of the New Testament came from the mind and the heart of someone called "the Beloved Disciple," who was responsible for the Fourth Gospel and perhaps 1 John as well. Thus, three persons probably produced some 70 percent of the New Testament, and they were either Jewish Christians or, in the case of Luke, persons deeply steeped in the Old Testament and its beliefs and ethics. *We would not expect persons with this background and orientation who still deeply appreciated and were indebted to early Judaism and its Scriptures and monotheistic beliefs to spawn a movement that had a wild variety of contradictory beliefs and behaviors in play, and they did not do so. Indeed, the latest studies confirm that even the Gospels reflect the eyewitness testimonies of those most involved in the events.*

Consider for a moment the conclusion of Robert K. McIver after a detailed study of how memory, and more particularly eyewitness memory and testimony, works:

> The strong social cohesion known to exist in first century Mediterranean groups, and visible in the book of Acts, undoubtedly led to a strong collective memory of the teachings and deeds of the one central to the existence of the groups: Jesus. That eyewitness accounts both contributed to this process and ensured that the traditions did not stray too far from the reality of the memories of Jesus can be taken for granted. So it is hard to gainsay the observation that there was considerable eyewitness input in the early formation of traditions about Jesus. Indeed, it is possible to name some of those who are likely to have contributed to the tradition [e.g., Peter].[7]

The social networks of earliest Christianity were small and close-knit, and the spectrum of beliefs of this minority religious group was not broad at the outset or, for that matter, during the New Testament period itself. This began to change when the Jewish Christian presence in the movement began to dwindle and became a small minority, and there arose non-Jewish ideas, voices, and prejudices against things Jewish in the second century A.D. and later.

What about the disputes that we do hear about in the New Testament itself—disputes recorded in Galatians 1 between Paul and Barnabas and between Peter and the *Judaizers* (Jewish Christians who insisted that Gentiles had to become Jews, keeping the whole Mosaic covenant, in order to be followers of Jesus)? The dispute recorded there, as well as the disputes that led to the Jerusalem Council mentioned in Acts 15, had to do largely with **praxis**, that is, with whether Gentiles would be required to be circumcised, observe food laws, and observe the Sabbath in order to be part of the fellowship of Christians. *It did not have to do with debates about (1) is Jesus both human and divine or not; (2) is the Old Testament God's Word; or (3) should the monotheism and basic ethical codes of the Old Testament be continually practiced by Christians or not. In fact, the debates between Paul and the Judaizers were not about their beliefs about Jesus at all (which both sides shared in common), nor were they about what constituted proper behavior when it came to things such as murder, adultery, theft, and the like.*

In short, there was diversity in early Christianity when it came to approaches to praxis as Christians tried to unite Jews and Gentiles into one coherent fellowship of believers; but the notion that there was a wide variety of theological and ethical viewpoints in early Christianity about the essentials is historically false, and the New Testament itself is the proof of this. Even when one looks at

PRAXIS

The application or practice of a concept or idea.

very early non-canonical Christian texts like the Didache or 1 Clement, these documents as well do not reflect the later non-Jewish and even anti-Jewish beliefs of Gnostics and others during the period when Christianity was losing its Jewish moorings and re-envisioning its Jewish heritage, including the Old Testament.

As suggested at the outset of this portion of the book, the alternative vision of the origin of Christianity is that it was a natural development of the Jesus movement, well grounded in the teachings of the Old Testament and of Jesus himself, differing from early Judaism chiefly because of its belief in Jesus as the messiah, Son of God, and savior of the world, a belief most Jews did not come to share in the first century A.D. There were a handful of key persons, mostly Jews or God-fearing Gentiles (such as Luke), who led the Christian movement throughout the first two-thirds of the first century A.D. These included persons like James, the brother of Jesus; Peter, the leader of the 12 apostles; and Paul, a very early convert who was in touch with the Jerusalem church leaders of the movement who sought and got approval for the Gentile mission and continued to touch base with the Jerusalem leadership from time to time.

The idea that earliest Christianity was like dueling banjos when it came to basic theology and ethics is largely a myth. The arguments within the Christian movement had to do mainly with "how then shall we all live together as Jew and Gentile united in Christ"? We will have much more to say about this as we work our way through the New Testament itself.[8]

KEY TERMS

Anachronistic	Orthopraxy
Areopagus	Peasant
Gnostic	Pharisee
Josephus	Praxis
Orthodoxy	Tacitus

FOR FURTHER READING

Burridge, Richard A., *What Are the Gospels?: A Comparison with Graeco-Roman Biography*. Grand Rapids, MI: Eerdmans, 2004.

Wright, N. T. *Simply Jesus: A New Vision of Who He Was, What He Did, and Why He Matters*. San Francisco: Harper, 2011.

STUDY QUESTIONS

Obviously, Jesus is the most important figure in the New Testament. Why is it important to understand him in light of his early Jewish setting? In what ways was he like other first-century Jews, and in what ways was he different from them?

NOTES

1. F. Buechner, *The Faces of Jesus* (Brewster, MA: Paraclete Press, 2005), viii–xi.

2. What we know about the terrain of Nazareth in Jesus' day is that an artisan was more likely to work with stone than wood, for wood was more scarce and precious. The famous cedars used to build the Temple in Jerusalem had to be imported from Lebanon.

3. M. A. Powell, *Introducing the New Testament* (Grand Rapids, MI: Baker, 2009), 65.

4. Dan Brown, *The Da Vinci Code* (New York: Doubleday, 2003).

5. See, for example, the very popular B. Ehrman, *The New Testament: A Historical Introduction to the Early Christian Writings* (New York: Oxford University Press, 2008).

6. To this could also be added the Didache, another early, non-canonical document perhaps from the first century, which also indicates there was a sense of orthodoxy and orthopraxy that needed to be followed; and if false prophets showed up and offered false teaching or false behavior, they were to be shown the door.

7. R. K. McIver, *Memory, Jesus, and the Synoptic Gospels* (Atlanta, GA: Society of Biblical Literature, 2011), 128.

8. The student interested in the origins of Christianity should consult my books, *The Gospel Code: Novel Claims about Jesus, Mary Magdalene, and Da Vinci* (Downers Grove, IL: InterVarsity, 2004); and *What Have They Done with Jesus?: Beyond Strange Theories and Bad History—Why We Can Trust the Bible* (San Francisco: HarperSanFrancisco, 2006).

An aqueduct for the transportation of water.
(© Rick Danielson)

4

FIRST CENTURY FAMILY VALUES

The past is like a foreign country, they do things differently there.
—L. P. HARTLEY[1]

WHEN YOU TURN THE PAGE FROM THE END OF MALACHI to the first page of Matthew in your Bibles, you may not realize that centuries have passed, and the situation and even some of the beliefs of God's people in the Holy Land have changed drastically. In many New Testament introductions, you will get a long section on the historical events that led up to the New Testament. This sort of background is certainly important in various ways, and we will say some things about that history as we discuss the various books of the New Testament. But in most ways, the more important history is the social or cultural story of day-to-day life as the persons we encounter in the New Testament would have experienced it, and we will focus on this in this chapter. First, however, a brief mention of some highlights about the history between the Old and New Testaments is in order. It is important to say something about this

GYMNASIUM

The term itself refers to a place where youths train their bodies in the nude (the very meaning of the Greek word *gymnos* is "naked"). Gymnasium complexes, however, were more than just places for physical training or places with adjoining baths near gyms, although these were included. There were also educational facilities involved in a gymnasium complex, as the Greek ideal was the complete training and discipline of both mind and body.

ARAMAIC

Aramaic is a Semitic language (not to be confused with Arabic) like Hebrew, which Jews acquired while they were in exile in Persia. The name itself comes from the region called Aram in central Syria. It is thus a northwest Semitic language like Hebrew and Phoenician. During its 3,000-year written history, Aramaic has served as a language of administration of empires and a language of worship. It was the day-to-day language of Israel in the Second Temple period (539 B.C.–A.D. 70.), was the language spoken by Jesus, is the language of sections of the biblical books of Daniel and Ezra, and is the main language of the later collection of Jewish teachings called the Talmud.

for the very good reasons that (1) it is not the history mentioned in the New Testament, which almost exclusively refers to the history recorded in the Old Testament itself; and (2) this history from between the eras explains a variety of things about the New Testament—for example, why it is all written in Greek.

GREECE AND ROME WILL NOT LEAVE US ALONE

Despite a brief period between about 167 and 63 B.C. when Jews had independence and self-rule, called the Maccabean period, during most of the time between the end of the Old Testament and the beginning of the New Testament, the Holy Land was once again a political football being tossed back and forth as the prize between one Empire and another. The Jews who returned from the Babylonian and Persian exile in about 525 B.C. had not really been masters of their own fate. Alexander the Great had soon swept through the land and conquered the whole region, and his successors ruled in the region up until the Maccabean revolt.

The major legacy left behind when Alexander's forces occupied the land was the Greek language and various aspects of Greek culture, including a devotion to Olympic-style games and a combination of games and education available through the **gymnasium**. That legacy was still in evidence when Jesus was born. Herod the Great fancied himself a great world ruler and had built Greek-style buildings and held Greek-style games and theater productions, which made the skin of devout conservative Jews crawl. Greek was a known and spoken language, as well as a written language, in the world of Jesus. He lived in a world where **Aramaic** (a cousin of Hebrew) was the main spoken tongue, Hebrew and Greek were both written and read (and in certain contexts Greek was spoken),

Figure 4.1 Roman coins had images of living emperors and often proclaimed them as sons of the divine Augustus. (© *Rick Danielson*)

and Latin was the official language of jurisprudence in the province of Judea. Many Jews were not comfortable with these ongoing foreign influences, though some had less of an allergic reaction to things Greek and Roman than others.

The Roman Empire already existed by the time the story begins in the Gospels, and by the time Jesus' ministry began, Judea was a province of the Roman Empire run directly by a Roman governor; whereas in Galilee, there was still a descendant of Herod the Great, named Herod Antipas, ruling as a puppet king with the permission of Rome. God's people were not free at the time, even if they lived within their own land of Israel. Herod Antipas was only partially Jewish (he was mainly an Idumean, which is to say he was a descendant of the Edomites with some Jewish ancestry), and of course Pontius Pilate was a Roman, pure and simple. In other words, Jews were by and large under foreign rule during the time of Jesus.

Figure 4.2 Notice how close the gymnasium (the large building beyond the synagogue wall on the right of the picture) in Sardis is to the synagogue, which is in the foreground of this picture. The synagogue itself is remarkably Hellenized, showing the influence of Greek culture on Jews outside the Holy Land. (© *Mark R. Fairchild, Ph.D.*)

WISDOM OF SOLOMON

A pseudonymous work (attributed to but not actually written by King Solomon) written by a Hellenized Jew. The sapiential work discusses matters of righteousness and wisdom in the Jewish context.

1 ENOCH

An apocalyptic Jewish writing that describes the fall of the angels and the story of the joining of the angels with the daughters of men (referred to in Genesis 6.2). Further, it tells of Enoch's trip to heaven as well as his dreams and visions.

QUMRAN

The home of a Jewish community, possibly the Essenes. The Dead Sea Scrolls were discovered in caves at Qumran starting in 1947.

SIRACH

A Jewish writing from the 2nd century B.C. that discusses Jewish wisdom and promotes the study and observance of the Mosaic Law.

ESSENES

The Essenes felt that they were the true Jewish people, and they separated themselves from the Jews in Jerusalem. The community consisted of mostly males (Philo and Josephus record their number at about 4,000). Discipline

continued

It should not be surprising that in these circumstances many devout Jews felt (1) that their land was unclean, so they constantly needed to purify themselves; (2) that their way of life was under threat; (3) that Zealots and revolutionary bands rose up from time to time to protest the census because the census would lead to more taxes; and (4) that Jews were so concerned about the corruption in the halls of power in Jerusalem that they had anathematized Herod's temple in Jerusalem as unclean and gone out to the Dead Sea and set up a base camp, awaiting for God's judgment to fall upon the land. John the Baptizer apparently shared that sort of apocalyptic worldview as well. In John's view, Israel had better repent because judgment was going to begin with the household of God soon. Into this volatile and sometimes violent and culturally mixed milieu, Jesus came.[2]

But it is not just that the land was not free, the political system not entirely Jewish, and the Holy Land was more of a mixed-language milieu, but also that the thought world had changed between the Old Testament times and the New Testament era. Now early Jewish documents talked a great deal about demons, and heavens, and the afterlife, whether we are thinking of Jewish writings such as the **Wisdom of Solomon** or the Testaments of the Twelve Patriarchs or **1 Enoch**. Now, suddenly, the apocalyptic style that was found in only a few places in the Old Testament (Zechariah, Ezekiel, and Daniel) is found all over the place. And where exactly are prophetic books like that of Amos or Jeremiah? We do not really find them in the intertestamental period, unless one counts some of the material from **Qumran**.

What one mostly finds is wisdom literature like **Sirach**. The religious and cultural landscape of early Judaism had changed and was continuing to change when Jesus came on the scene. You will look in vain in the Old Testament for Pharisees or Sadducees or Zealots or **Essenes**, but they were definitely alive and well and affecting all of life in the Holy Land in Jesus' day. Some of those different kinds of religious Jews were to become conversation partners with Jesus, and even antagonists in some cases, when he debated issues important to all Jews, such as the Sabbath laws. But what is most revealing about the times in which Jesus lived is the social history rather than the political or even specifically the more specific religious history, and we turn to that in a moment. A few more words about the importance of the impact of the era just prior to the time of Jesus on Jesus and his fellow early Jews are in order.

Jesus did not appear on the early Jewish scene out of thin air. There was a long history of God's people before his day, and indeed there is a history not told in the Old Testament that happened between the time when the last events recorded in the Old Testament are mentioned and the time when Jesus was born. It is a mistake to underestimate the considerable impact of Greek language and culture on Jews, even in Israel. By the time we get to Jesus' day, Greek was the established common language of business and trade in the whole eastern part of the Mediterranean, including in Israel. The point of stressing this is threefold. First, the world in which Jesus and his first disciples lived was a multiple language milieu. While Jesus and his disciples mainly spoke Aramaic, it would be very surprising if they did not also have an oral and aural familiarity with some Greek. For example, if Jesus had a conversation with Pontius Pilate directly, who as a Roman would not know Aramaic, it would have to have been in Greek! Or again, when Peter spoke to Cornelius (Acts 10), he would likely have spoken at least some in Greek. Second, it is therefore no surprise that *the whole New Testament is written* in the common language of the eastern Roman Empire—Greek. Third, Jews by Jesus' day had adapted and adopted various Greek customs, such as reclining on couches for a formal meal; and educated Jews, such as Saul of Tarsus, even studied Greek philosophy and rhetoric in schools in Jerusalem. The impact of Hellenistic or Greek culture was considerable by the time of Jesus' era.

Thus, it is not enough to simply read the Old Testament and turn from the last page of Malachi to the first page of Matthew and think you know the background to the New Testament era. In the some 500 years between the Testaments, a lot of things had transpired, and not just at the political level of who ruled and how.

For example, during this interim period, the whole Old Testament was translated into Greek, the so-called Septuagint or LXX (called this because it was supposed to have been the work of 70 translators); and what we discover is that numerous New Testament writers use the LXX instead of the Hebrew Bible when they are quoting the Old Testament. Indeed, Luke does so almost exclusively, and so does the author of Hebrews. It was the Greek Old Testament that became the Bible for Jews outside the Holy Land who spoke Greek and read little Hebrew. There was in addition to the Bible a large corpus of Jewish writings of importance composed in the intertestamental period, *mainly in Greek,* that are not included in most Bibles—works like Sirach, Wisdom of Solomon, 1–3 Maccabees, the **Testament of Twelve Patriarchs**, **Tobit**, or **Judith**. These are all fascinating books, and they help to reveal the evolution of Jewish thinking on all kinds of subjects such as God and the afterlife (including resurrection). Some of the intertestamental books mention the rise of Jewish sects like the Pharisees, the Sadducees, and the Essenes, who were all active during the time of Jesus and afterward.

John the Baptizer did not come out of nowhere. He was not the first early Jew seeking reform of his people and the land since Old Testament times. Indeed, there were various prophetic and messianic figures before John, none of whom made the impact John did, but they were important enough to be mentioned by the Jewish historian Josephus (and see Acts 5.36–38; Josephus's *Antiquities* 20.97–98).[3] It is likely that John had spent time at the Dead Sea with the Essenes or Qumran community for his message of coming judgment, his concern

and study of the Scriptures characterized the activity of the community. Ceremonial baptisms were also performed. In addition, the group believed that they lived in the end times. As a result, they expected the coming of two messiahs: a priestly messiah and a kingly messiah.

TESTAMENT OF TWELVE PATRIARCHS

A Jewish writing which reports stories about the final words and the nearing of death of each of the twelve patriarchs. The stories tell of the character of the patriarchs and their thoughts of what would occur among their descendants after their deaths.

TOBIT

A Jewish story written in the 3rd – 2nd century B.C. about a righteous Jew named Tobit. The story centralizes around Tobias, Tobit's son, who while traveling with Raphael (an angel disguised as a man) meets a Jew named Sarah during his travels to collect money from his father's friend. Sarah's previous engagements had ended as just before the consummation of the marriages her seven fiancés were murdered by a demon named Asmodeus who loved Sarah. Tobias learns a prophylaxis from Raphael and is able to marry Sarah.

Figure 4.3 One of the famous Dead Sea Scrolls. (© Mark R. Fairchild, Ph.D.)

JUDITH

A Jewish story written in the second century B. C. about a heroine named Judith who devised a plan to save the people of Israel from the Assyrian king by using her beauty. When the King was found drunk Judith decapitated him and took his head as a trophy back to her people.

for ritual purity, and his ascetic diet; and even the theme verse used to describe him ("the voice of one crying in the wilderness, make straight a highway for our God") had already characterized the Qumran or Essene community at the Dead Sea from which the famous Dead Sea Scrolls come.

The point of briefly mentioning this intertestamental history is to make clear that when we get to the Gospel story itself, a lot of water had gone under the bridge since the days of Ezra and Nehemiah, and more to the point, that water had fertilized the land and changed its religious, linguistic, social, and historical topography in various ways. Jesus arose at a dangerous time, when the Holy Land was under foreign rule either directly, as in Judaea, or indirectly, as in the rest of the land.

Prophetic figures like John and Jesus would have been seen as dangerous to the fragile balance of power in the region and were closely watched, challenged, and debated: and finally, both were executed by the powers that be. Into this volatile and sometimes violent world came the message and the messenger of the Good News—Jesus of Nazareth.

Figure 4.4 Cave 4, which held the famous Dead Sea Scrolls. (© Rick Danielson)

SOCIAL HISTORY AND ORDINARY LIFE

The New Testament is telling the story of a micro-history, the history of Jesus and his followers, not world history and not war's history either. What is most helpful for understanding Jesus and the early Christians is what daily life was like and what cultural values guided that life. Let us consider the basic building blocks of the social situation that undergirds and is presupposed in the stories in the New Testament.

We must start with the fact that all of the cultures of the Ancient Near East (Egypt, Babylon, Syria, Persia, and Israel), as well as the cultures of the Greek and Roman world, were honor and shame cultures. By this is meant that the dominant or top value in the hierarchy of ethical values was not truth versus lies, or life and death, but rather honor and shame. Most people would rather lie or die than be publicly shamed in that world. Oriental culture, even today, or Mafia culture today, operates the same way to some degree. The most important thing is the honor of one's name and one's family's name. Life is further down the hierarchy of values, and truth is as well. The default in such a culture is to do what it takes to avoid shame and to achieve honor. This is why you see honorific columns all over the Greco-Roman and Ancient Near East world. It is probably the case that the reason the story of Judas Iscariot ends as it does, with Judas hanging himself, is because he became deeply ashamed of what he had done to Jesus, and he could not live with that shame, so he took his life. Feeling ashamed, however, is not the same thing as repentance or remorse.

Contrast this with modern American culture, where we have clichés such as "well, it's not a matter of life and death." This is a telltale sign that our own top value most of the time, for most people, is preserving life and avoiding death. By contrast, in Jesus' world, life was not worth living if you had to live in guilt and shame all the time. Social historians talk about paired values like honor and shame, and in a real sense, these values are a reflex of one another. When a culture loses its sense of honor, it also loses its sense of shame, and vice versa. The two ideas are linked together as opposites.

The second major cultural value of the world of Jesus and his followers was patriarchy. It was indeed a man's world, even in the more enlightened parts of the Roman Empire. Women in various subcultures of the empire did not have the privilege of choosing whom they would marry. Marriages were arranged, and when it came to divorce, this was also largely a male privilege. The same applied to property. In the more eastern part of the empire, women often could not inherit property, although they were entitled to be supported by their family property.

Women were occasionally rulers in antiquity—for instance, Cleopatra of Egypt—but the halls of political power were mostly controlled by men, and the military of whatever country was overwhelmingly controlled by and involved men. In religious life as well, men dominated the scene, especially in early Judaism. Although there were women priestesses in Greco-Roman religious groups, such as in the cult of Artemis in Ephesus, there were no Jewish priestesses in the temple in Jerusalem. In fact, so far as we can tell, no Jewish teachers before Jesus ever had female disciples—so Jesus was setting a precedent when he took Mary Magdalene and other women on the road with him.

In these patriarchal cultures, the basic "place" of women was in the home, having children, raising children, cooking and cleaning—and especially in an agricultural family, helping with the farm work. Their job was to focus on the inner life of the family and in large measure to run the household (see the wife described in Proverbs 31). The husband's job was to represent the public face of the family and to establish the family's honor in the city gate or town square and with the other male members of the community. The husband, of course, also worked, but it was his job to arrange the marriages for his daughters and make the property transactions (the marriage contract was seen as one form of such a transaction—hence the dowry). If he was a part of a priestly family, it was his task to perform the religious ceremonies in the temple or synagogue. The husband promoted the public honor of the family, whereas the wife kept the home fires burning, literally, and protected the inner life of the family from shame.

This led in many situations to a sexual double standard. Women were expected to be chaste and avoid even the hint of adultery, whereas men, especially in Greek and Roman settings, were allowed to be sexually active outside the home without loss of honor if no one else's wife was involved. Jews were more strict about extramarital intercourse even by men, but notice the stigma that falls solely on the woman caught in adultery in John 7.53–8.11. What we should have asked about that story is "Where is the man caught in adultery, because it takes two to tango?"

The third major building block of the social values of that world may come as the biggest shock. Sociologists call it **dyadic** or **collectivist personality**, by which is meant an identity chiefly formed by the group and

Figure 4.5 First-century Jewish home in Israel.
(© Mark R. Fairchild, Ph.D.)

the effect of the group on the individual. Basically, the culture in which Jesus and Paul and others lived was a collectivist culture, not an individualist culture. Of course, there were individual persons in antiquity, but their identities were chiefly formed not by the ways they stood out from the crowd but by what crowd they were part of. Did you ever notice that people in Jesus' culture don't really have last names? Last names are the designations that most individuate all of us from others.

In Jesus' world, geography, gender, and generation were thought to make people who they were. By this I mean *where they were born, what gender they were, and who their father was most determined their identity.* This can be seen in their names: Jesus is Jesus of Nazareth; Saul is Saul of Tarsus; and Mary Magdalene's name is actually Miriam of Migdal, a little fishing village by the sea of Galilee. I am trusting that you know that Jesus' last name was not Christ! Consider other names in the New Testament—Simon bar Jonah means Simon, son of John; James and John bar Zebedee are the sons of Zebedee. Or sometimes people were distinguished by their religious or political affiliation—Simon the Pharisee or Simon the Zealot. Sometimes, they were even distinguished by age or height— James the Less or Little or Pliny the Elder. The point is they did not have last names, so their identity was formed by whom they were related to or what kin or social group they were a part of. Jesus was acting like a normal ancient person when he asked his disciples, "Who do people say that I am?" (Mark 8.27–30). He was not asking because he had an identity crisis; he asked this way because people got a sense of their identity from what their group said about them.

Normal in that world was fitting into the crowd, not standing out from the crowd. Ancient peoples were often like self-conscious modern teenagers who do not want to be singled out but rather prefer to blend in and be part of the in-crowd. Standing out from the crowd made you abnormal: and yes, Jesus was seen as abnormal. Indeed, some even thought he was so abnormal that they thought he was possessed by demons.[4]

The thing about geography, gender, and generation was that you were born in that place, with that gender, and to that family. You did not have a choice about it. So ancient peoples quite naturally believed that one's identity was largely determined from birth. Not surprisingly, this led to the correlate belief that people don't change by in large, and if they do, it is not a good thing. It's aberrant behavior, not normal behavior. Conversion in that world was a tough sell in many contexts. The ancients had clichés like "can a leopard change its spots?" That Jesus went around changing people's lives, and calling them away from their livelihoods, was something radical and would have been seen by many as suspect.

Yet another of the building blocks of the ancient world was the political and religious situation. Let me first say that politics and religion were inherently and always intertwined in antiquity. For example, the high priest in the temple in Jerusalem only got to be that way with the permission of the Roman governor, in this case Pontius Pilate. The essence of all ancient religion comprised priests,

DYADIC OR COLLECTIVIST PERSONALITY

An identity chiefly formed by the group and the effect of the group on the individual. In other words, the identity of an individual was not defined by the ways one stood out from the crowd. Rather, individual identity was defined by what crowd one was associated with. As a result, individuals did not seek to form their own personal identity as identity was derived from group association.

CLUES FROM THE CULTURE

I meant to congratulate you on the way you preserve the distinctions in class and rank. Once these are thrown into confusion and destroyed, nothing is more unequal than so-called equality.

—*Pliny*, Letters 9.5.3

temples, and sacrifices, and the Romans were wise enough to know just how profoundly religious ancient people were. Religious activity was always political activity—often potentially politically dangerous activity, so it was regulated. Judaism was a recognized and sanctioned religion during the Roman Empire. Jews were allowed to make their own sacrifices and did not have to sacrifice to the emperor. Instead, they made prayers for the emperor.

The Romans' basic policy was to leave indigenous religion alone, so long as it did not disturb the social order. But when a new religion came along that had no long pedigree or established track record, it was considered a *superstitio,* a superstition and an illegal religion. One could be persecuted, prosecuted, and executed for practicing an illegal religion. The problem for early Christianity was that when it emerged from the womb of Judaism in the first century A.D., and it was realized by officials that it was not just another form of Judaism, a sanctioned religion, then it could be open season on Christians. Christians could be persecuted and their property seized. They could be brought to trial for making a public nuisance or for offending the Greco-Roman gods, and so on. The basic premise in that world was very different from our assumptions—when it came to religion, they did not assume that "the new is the true" and "the latest is the greatest." To the contrary, for a religion to be deemed valid and true, it had to be ancient and time-tested.

Another of the basic social building blocks of the New Testament world was the fact that (1) there were no democracies, and (2) the economy was not a free-market economy or, for that matter, a money economy, although money was increasingly being used in that world.[5] The world of the Roman Empire consisted basically of a bunch of barter economies where persons traded things and haggled to get a particular price.

Because of the patriarchal and hierarchal nature of all those cultures, in order to get ahead in life, it was truly a matter of reciprocity and patronage. One needed a patron, and so one sought to become a client of a more well-to-do person. All economic exchanges were reciprocity exchanges, and patron–client relationships were reciprocity relationships. It was a "you scratch my back, and I'll scratch yours" world. It was a "it's not what you know, it's who you know" world, if you wanted to prosper or get ahead in life. The client's role was to praise the patron, and in certain situations to help the patron get elected to important offices; and the patron's role was to bankroll the client, so he could survive and perhaps even thrive economically.

One of the interesting things about Jesus' immediate culture was that as a barter culture, money had a limited and very specific function—it was used to pay taxes, tolls, tithes, and tribute money. It thus had *strong negative associations for subjugated peoples like Jews. No wonder Jesus called money "unrighteous mammon"—it promoted pagan emperors and their values.* When Jesus was asked about whether it was OK to pay taxes to Caesar, notice he did not have a coin on his person. Coins were viewed not just as a means of exchange, they were propaganda pieces. So Jesus asked whose picture was on the coin, that is, the picture of the person who minted the coin (rulers controlled the making and dissemination of coins). Ancient coins did not feature dead presidents, they featured living emperors, some of whom even claimed divinity!

This brings us to the final social building block, which may seem counter-intuitive to us. The concept is "limited good." Ancient peoples by and large did not live in a world full of abundance. Famines caused crop shortages, and there was no agribusiness. Food, except for Egyptian grain, had to be generated and consumed locally, so everything depended on the local crops. Many people lived in poverty or at a subsistence level. They lived, as my grandparents used to say, "from hand to mouth." Praying for daily bread was a normal prayer for most ancients. In a world without refrigeration, the only time meat would be consumed was when there was a sacrifice at a temple or at a rare local celebration (see the parable of the prodigal son in Luke 15). Otherwise, the diet of the ancients consisted of bread, wine, fruits, nuts, and vegetables, and that was about it.

It is not surprising then that ancient peoples thought in terms of "limited good." By this is meant that there was only a limited number of goods and property to go around. If one man had a vineyard and another did not, in a world of limited arable land, the only way the second person could have a vineyard was if he bought or stole the vineyard (see the parable of the vineyard in Mark 12 and notice the comments of the tenants—if they kill the heir, they have squatters rights to the land). Where there was not abundance, the only way some people could survive was to "beg, borrow, or steal" something that belonged to others. We moderns live with a mythology of unlimited goods. We have clichés like "eat all you want—we'll make more." We have children so disconnected from the land and the facts about food that they think food comes from grocery stores, and it will always be on the shelves. But this is not true, as the nightly images of famine in Somalia or elsewhere in the world remind us. We do live in a world of limited goods. The ancients knew this better than we do.

IMPLICATIONS

If you think through the topics discussed in this chapter, you will see the truth in the phrase "the past is like a foreign country, they do things differently there." As was discussed, the social history of the period is as important, or more important, than the political history in understanding the people and their customs and cultures we encounter in the New Testament.

The good news is that the more you study the New Testament in its original contexts, the clearer it becomes and the better you understand it. What you also learn in the process is that just an English translation of the Bible and your modern brain is not enough to fully understand the Bible because it came from a very different time and set of cultures. All modern persons need help to understand the context of the Bible. In some ways you may say, "I am so glad I didn't live in that world," but in other ways you may well say, "if only I lived in that world, then I could have met and better understood people like Jesus and Paul." Because time travel is not possible, we must settle for diligent study of these ancient texts to properly interpret them. Knowing the various facets of culture and context mentioned in the last few chapters can help us to bridge the gap between then and now.

One of the things I regularly tell my students is that a text without a context is just a pretext for whatever you want it to mean. To read the New Testament with understanding, we have to enter into the world of the New Testament writers, not ask them to speak to us in our own modern ways. Accordingly, we will be examining the New Testament in light of its linguistic, textual, historical, literary, rhetorical, archaeological, and social contexts. Our goal is to hear the text as first-century people would have heard it in their world. This requires careful study of the New Testament in its various contexts.

Because this is an introductory textbook, it is not assumed that you have a great deal of advance knowledge of the content and the context of the New Testament. Maps, pictures, and charts are used in this book to aid your understanding. The goal, when you have completed studying this text, is that you will have a good entry-level understanding of the New Testament and how to read it with insight and without distorting the meaning of the text. We are ready now to begin the adventure of exploring these fascinating and most influential of all ancient texts.

KEY TERMS

1 Enoch	Qumran
Aramaic	Sirach
Dyadic/Collectivist Personality	Testament of Twelve Patriarchs
Essenes	Tobit
Gymnasium	Wisdom of Solomon
Judith	

FOR FURTHER READING

Bell, A. A., Jr. *Exploring the New Testament World.* Nashville, TN: Nelson, 1998.

Collins, John J. *The Scepter and the Star.* Grand Rapids, MI: Eerdmans, 2010.

Collins, John J., and G. Sterling, eds. *Hellenism in the Land of Israel.* Notre Dame, IN: University of Notre Dame Press, 2001.

deSilva, David A. *Honor, Patronage, Kinship & Purity: Unlocking New Testament Culture.* Downers Grove, IL: IVP Academic, 2000.

———. *Introducing the Apocrypha: Message, Context, and Significance.* Grand Rapids, MI: Baker, 2004.

Malina, Bruce. *The New Testament World: Insights from Cultural Anthropology.* 3rd ed. Louisville, KY: Westminster John Knox Press, 2001.

Witherington, Ben. *Jesus and Money: A Guide for Times of Financial Crisis.* Grand Rapids, MI: Brazos Press, 2010.

———. *Women and the Genesis of Christianity.* Edited by Ann Witherington. Cambridge, England: Cambridge University Press, 1990.

STUDY QUESTIONS

Did Jews stop writing books during the period between the end of the Old Testament era and the beginning of the New Testament era?

Why is the New Testament entirely in Greek?

This chapter was largely devoted to first-century cultural values. How different was the world of Jesus and Paul from our world in terms of money, food, politics, the role of women, and the like? What does the phrase *honor and shame* mean, and why was this a crucial value in antiquity?

What is the importance of studying Alexander and his empire for the study of the New Testament?

Did John the Baptizer have any similarities with the separatist group called the Essenes who had a base camp at the Dead Sea?

Who was Herod the Great, and why would Jews not have been happy with his ruling of the Holy Land?

In these first four chapters, you have been introduced to the world in which the New Testament was written. What seemed most strange to you about this world? What seemed most familiar to you?

NOTES

1. L. P. Hartley, *The Go Between* (New York: NYRB Classics, 2002), 1.

2. For a thorough overview of the history leading up to the New Testament period, see B. Witherington, *New Testament History: A Narrative Account* (Grand Rapids, MI: Baker, 2003).

3. For a discussion, see B. Witherington, *The Christology of Jesus* (Minneapolis, MN: Fortress Press, 1990).

4. For all of this section, see Bruce Malina's *The New Testament World: Insights from Cultural Anthropology*, 3rd ed. (Louisville, KY: Westminster John Knox Press, 2001); and especially David de Silva's *Honor, Patronage, Kinship, & Purity: Unlocking New Testament Culture* (Downers Grove, IL: IVP Academic, 2000).

5. See B. Witherington, *Jesus and Money: A Guide for Times of Financial Crisis* (Grand Rapids, MI: Brazos Press, 2010).

PART II

The GOSPELS and ACTS

A typical pair of rolling stone tombs near Jerusalem.
(© Mark R. Fairchild, Ph.D.)

5

The EARLIEST GOOD NEWS— MARK'S GOSPEL

> *Given the Gospels' continuing force on the lives of those around me, in the years to come I began to sense that any subsequent secular writer—even Shakespeare or Tolstoy—was hardly likely to equal the pull those brief works exert on the human minds with no resources but words and an invisible architecture as severe as the desert their hero frequents.*
> —REYNOLDS PRICE[1]

THE GOSPELS ARE NOT WRITTEN LIKE various sorts of modern literature, whether we are thinking of histories, or dramas, or novels, or modern biographies. In fact, at least three of the Gospels (Matthew, Mark, and John) are written like ancient biographies, whereas Luke–Acts is a two-volume ancient historical monograph. But what are ancient biographies like, and how do they differ from modern ones? We have already dealt with this briefly in our earlier discussion of the genre of the New Testament literature, and here we will simply offer a table of the characteristics of ancient biographies as written by Plutarch, Tacitus, Josephus, and Christians like Mark.

FEATURES OF ANCIENT BIOGRAPHIES

1. They are always tendentious, by which is meant that they always take a definite point of view about the person they are about, either strongly positive or strongly negative. There is no pretense at pure objectivity.
2. Ancient biographies do not attempt to psychologize or psychologically analyze their subject, so there is little said about motives, upbringing, and the like.
3. The real *focus* of an ancient biography is on the character of the person in question, and this is revealed through a portrayal of the person's words and deeds, with little or no overt commentary by the biographer.
4. Chronology is much less of a concern in ancient biographies than in ancient historical monographs; and even when there is some chronological interest, it is usually only in broad strokes, not in minutiae.
5. There are no footnotes, and very rarely does the author indicate sources, unless it is a Scriptural text. Parenthetical comments do occur, but they tend to be minimal and purely explanatory.
6. The style of narrative is very basic and straightforward, without a lot of description. Sometimes, it can even be called anecdotal in that the author picks a story about the author not because it is of great historical significance but because it aptly reveals the person's character.
7. The ethical character of biography is clear—it is meant to get the audience to emulate the good character of the subject or to avoid the subject's bad character.
8. Because of the competitive nature of ancient culture, the author would tend to stress how the biographical person was superior to others, including both friends and rivals (think of the portrayal of Jesus' relationship to John the Baptizer).
9. Because it was widely believed that how a person died most revealed his or her character, there would be a strong focus on the death of the biographical person, especially if he or she died tragically. There would also be a focus on explaining how his or her death was consistent with his or her life philosophy (think of Socrates).

10. There would be a concern with the legacy of the person and the ongoing impact he or she continued to have. All these factors explain why an ancient biography might seem imbalanced to a modern reader—spending too much time, say, on the last week of the person's life, as in the Gospels, and skipping over large portions of the rest of the person's life.[2]

The term **euangelion** is a Greek word that literally means "good news." It is the origin of the English word **Gospel** (based on the word's meaning) and also *evangelist* (based on the form of the word). The headings of the Gospels tell us we have the Good News (about Jesus) according to four different persons or sources. There are not very many things that almost all New Testament scholars agree on, but one of those things is that Mark's Gospel is probably the earliest one of these written Gospels. Shortly, we will see why that view is probably correct.

Whereas the four Gospels do begin the New Testament, they are not chronologically the earliest documents in the New Testament. That distinction belongs to Paul's letters, which began to be written about A.D. 49, and Paul wrote his last letter likely in the mid-60s of the first century. This means that *all of Paul's letters were probably written before any of our Gospels were written.* One reason the Gospels were put first in the New Testament is because they chronicle the story that set in motion the whole Christian movement, and so the contents of the four Gospels are the earliest part of the story the New Testament is telling.

Before Mark's Gospel was written, there was the oral preaching of the Good News, samples of which we find in Paul's letters and summaries of which we find in some of the speeches in Acts. In a largely oral world, it is not surprising that "Gospel" meant, in the first instance, the oral proclamation of Good News about Jesus, before it ever referred to a document, much less a document that came to be called "a Gospel." It is interesting that the main meaning of the phrase "word of God" in Acts and Paul is "the oral preaching of the Good News about Jesus." It did not, in the first instance, refer to a book. For example, consider 1 Thessalonians 2.13: "We constantly give thanks to God for this, that when you received the word of God which you *heard* from us, you accepted it not as a mere human word, but as what it really is—God's word, which is also at work in you believers." The phrase "word of God" here refers to an oral proclamation of the Good News about Jesus that the Thessalonians received and believed; and notice that Paul says it was not merely a religious opinion that he was conveying, not merely human words, but God's word, God's truth about Jesus. The Gospel was never seen as merely a message in which a human being was sharing his personal opinions about Jesus. It was seen as God's revelation of the truth about Jesus, and this is how it was proclaimed and why it was later written down in four different accounts. But who was this Mark?

EUANGELION

A Greek word that literally means "good news" and is the origin of the English words *Gospel* and *evangelist.*

GOSPEL

A term that originally meant the oral proclamation of the Good News about Jesus. Later it became common to use the term to refer to a document. In the New Testament the term refers to Matthew, Mark, Luke, and John.

WHO WAS MARK, AND WHEN DID HE WRITE?

at a Glance:
MARK

The Gospel of Mark was probably written A.D. 68 or a little after in Rome by John Mark, a sometime companion of Paul and Peter. The earliest and shortest Gospel, it is based on the memories of Peter and arranged like an ancient biography, but with an apocalyptic flavor to it. It makes clear that you need to know who Jesus is before you can understand his death on the cross.

PAPIAS

A church father who lived at the end of the first century A.D. and the beginning of the second century A.D. Papias was the Bishop of Hierapolis. His important writings include some fragments that discuss oral tradition and how the canonical gospels originated.

CHREIA

A short story or anecdote told about a person in order to reveal his or her character, usually concluding with a famous saying or deed of the person. Forming such tightly packed pithy narratives was part of elementary rhetorical training in antiquity, and Mark uses this form regularly.

According to Christian tradition, the author of the earliest Gospel was the John Mark referred to in the book of Acts as a sometime companion of his cousin Barnabas, and of Paul, and later of Peter. He apparently lived with his mother in Jerusalem (whose house became an early Christian meeting place—Acts 12.12). The earliest testimony that this man wrote a Gospel is that of the church father **Papias** who lived at the end of the first century A.D. and the beginning of the second century A.D. Here is what Papias said about Mark:

> . . . concerning Mark, who wrote the gospel. He [Papias] expounds with these [words]: "And the presbyter [i.e., John] also said this: 'Mark, being the interpreter of Peter, wrote accurately all that he remembered (but not, however, in order) [of] the things which were spoken or done by our Lord,' for he neither heard the Lord nor followed him, but later, as I said, [he followed] Peter (who provided instruction according to the *chreiae*, but not as to make an arrangement [orderly account] of the Lord's discourses); so that Mark did not err in anything in thus writing some things as he remembered them; for he was attentive to one thing, not to leave out anything that he heard or to make any false statements in them." So then these things were recounted by Papias concerning Mark.[3]

Sadly, we only have fragments of Papias's important original work, and this passage is found as a quotation of Papias in Eusebius's *Church History*, which was written two centuries later. Notice, however, that Papias was quoting a first-century Christian whom he called either John the elder (which could mean the older John), or the Elder John (referring to his church function). In either case, this John had known and talked with various original eyewitnesses during the first century and is a crucial source of information for Papias. For now, notice that Mark is said to be (1) the companion, (2) the interpreter of the great apostle Peter, and (3) that he wrote down what amounts to Peter's memoirs about Jesus. That the teaching of Peter is about Jesus is clear from the phrase "the Lord's discourses" in the quote.

Notice as well the disclaimer about Mark. He was not one of the original followers of Jesus, not one of the twelve or even the larger circle of disciples. All in all, this testimony has the earmarks of authenticity. It does not claim too much about Mark, but it does make clear that he wrote down the Lord's discourses based on the preaching or teaching of Peter. Notice as well that it denies that Mark arranged his Gospel material in some sort of strict chronological order. Mark was concerned (1) not to leave out anything he heard and remembered that Peter said and (2) not to say anything false about Jesus. Here, we have a believable account of the origins of the earliest Gospel. It is not surprising then that Peter played an important role in this earliest Gospel. And there is no good reason why the early church would make up the notion that a non-apostle, non-eyewitness was responsible for writing down the earliest Gospel because a premium was later placed on apostolic authorship of early Christian documents. This is why most scholars who have written commentaries on this interesting Gospel are disposed to accept this testimony of Papias about Mark's Gospel.

If Mark was indeed a sometime companion of Peter before Peter was martyred in Rome—sometime around A.D. 65–66 during the persecutions and executions of Christians in Rome by Nero—and Papias was suggesting that Mark wrote things down later on the basis of his memory of what Peter had said, then this means that the Gospel may have been written as early as A.D. 68 or a little later.

There may be an internal clue in Mark 13 that lets us know it was perhaps before A.D. 70. In Mark 13.14, in commenting on the coming destruction of

Figure 5.1 The famous Arch of Titus from a distance. (© Mark R. Fairchild, Ph.D.)

Figure 5.2 The Arch of Titus depicts the Romans carting off menorahs and temple apparatus after the sacking of Jerusalem in A.D. 70. (© *Mark R. Fairchild, Ph.D.*)

the temple in Jerusalem (A.D. 70), as Jesus predicted, Mark offered a parenthetical comment about the desolating sacrilege in that temple. Why would he say "attention reader, take note" unless he saw the demise of the temple on the near horizon? In fact, it took a rather long time for the city of Jerusalem to be captured and to fall to the hands of Emperor Vespasian's son Titus. Mark may have had news from Jerusalem about the siege and was suggesting to the oral proclaimer of his Gospel that he should let his hearers know it was happening in his own day. This date makes understandable why Mark spent so much time (in Mark 13) on the teaching of Jesus about the coming demise of the temple and the events that led up to it, whereas elsewhere in this Gospel there is only one other similar long block of teaching—the chapter about the parables in Mark 4.

HOW IS MARK'S GOSPEL ARRANGED?

Papias suggested that Mark did not arrange his Gospel in strict chronological order, but that, nonetheless, it had a definite order to it. I would say that we have, broadly speaking, a chronological order (baptism of Jesus by John, beginning of ministry, Passion week, then death and resurrection of Jesus); but when we look more closely, in fact, this Gospel has a theological order to it as follows:

QUESTIONS FROM MARK (1.1–8.26)

1.27	What is this?	Crowds
2.7	Who can forgive sins but God?	Scribes
2.16	Why does he eat with tax collectors and sinners?	Scribes
2.24	Why are they doing what is not lawful?	Pharisees
4.41	Who then is this that even wind and sea obey him?	Disciples
6.2	Where did this man get this Wisdom?	Hometown folks
7.5	Why do your disciples not live by tradition?	Pharisees
7.37	He has done all things well, he even makes the deaf hear and the dumb speak.	Crowd

The first half of Mark raises questions about who Jesus is. Then we have a dramatic turning point in the narrative at Mark 8.27–30. We have Peter's confession that Jesus is the Christ (i.e., the Jewish Messiah), the son of the living God. *The who question about Jesus has been finally answered, and the answer matches up with what Mark told us at Mark 1.1—"this is the beginning of the Good News about Jesus the Christ."* It is only *after* the *who* question is answered that we begin almost immediately to hear Jesus discuss his coming suffering, demise, and resurrection. Four times in three straight chapters Jesus tells his disciples that he must suffer many things, be killed, and on the third day rise—Mark 8.31, 9.31, 10.32–34, and 10.45.

What this indicates, from Mark's vantage point, is that until you know who Jesus is, you cannot know why he had to die and be raised again. Once the *who* question was answered, then the subject of his mission (the fact that Jesus was a man born to die) could be broached, and an explanation of the significance of his death was given in Mark 10.45—"the Son of Man did not come to be served, but to serve and to give his life as a ransom for the many."

Finally, once the *who* question was answered, and the mission stated, then the Passion and Easter narratives could be told in the remainder of this Gospel, in Mark 11–16. This leaves us with the following theological outline:

THEOLOGICAL OUTLINE OF MARK

Who and Why?	The Questions	1–8.27
Peter's confession of faith, Jesus is the Christ	The *who* question answered	8.27–30
A mission of suffering	What is the mission?	8.31, 9.31, 10.32, 10.45
The Passion narrative	Mission accomplished	11–16

Having looked at the big picture of the outline of the earliest Gospel writing, we can now look a little more closely.

BRIEF CONTENTS OF MARK'S GOSPEL

PART ONE: PRECEDENTS AND PREPARATIONS FOR JESUS' MINISTRY

1. The Heading—Mk. 1.1: The Beginning of the Good News
2. The Forerunner—Mk. 1.2–8: John the Baptizer's Preaching
3. The Baptism—Mk. 1.9–11: Jesus Is Baptized and Anointed with the Spirit
4. The Temptations—Mk. 1.12–13: Jesus in the Wilderness
5. The Summary Message—Mk. 1.14–15: "Repent for the Dominion Is at Hand"

PART TWO: THE MINISTRY OF THE MESSIAH—HIS WORDS AND DEEDS

BEGINNINGS BY THE SEA:

1. Calling the First Disciples—Mk. 1.16–20
2. Exorcism in the Synagogue in Capernaum—Mk. 1.21–27
3. Healing Simon's Mother-in-Law—Mk. 1.29–34
4. Withdrawal for Prayer—Mk. 1.35–39

TRAVELING, TEACHING, AND HEALING THROUGHOUT GALILEE AND NEARBY:

1. Healing the Man with Leprosy—Mk. 1.40–45
2. Healing and Forgiving the Paralytic—MK. 2.1–12
3. Calling the Tax Collector and Eating with Sinners—Mk. 2.13–17
4. Of Fasting and Food on the Sabbath—Mk. 2.18–28
5. Healing a Deformed Man on the Sabbath—Mk. 3.1–6
6. Jesus Draws a Crowd and Appoints Twelve—Mk. 3.7–19
7. Accusations by the Torah Teachers, Fears of the Family—Mk. 3.20–35
8. Parables by the Sea—Mk. 4.1–34
9. Stilling the Storm—Mk. 4.35–41
10. Exorcism on the Other Side of the Sea—Mk. 5.1–20

11. Jairus and the Jewess—MK. 5.21–43

12. Rejected in Nazareth—MK. 6.1–6

13. The Sending Out of the Twelve—Mk. 6.7–12

14. The Beheading of the Baptizer—Mk. 6.14–29

15. Feeding the Five Thousand—Mk. 6.30–44

16. Jesus Walks on Water—Mk. 6.45–58

17. The Debate About What Really Defiles—Mk. 7.1–23

18. A Healing in Tyre—Mk. 7.24–30

19. A Healing in the Decapolis—Mk. 7.31–37

20. Feeding of the Four Thousand—Mk. 8.1–13

21. The Warning About the Leaven of Leaders—Mk. 8.14–21

22. Healing a Blind Man in Bethsaida—Mk. 8.22–26

23. Peter's Confession in Caesarea Philippi—Mk. 8.27–30

24. Jesus First Prediction of His Death—Mk. 8.34–9.1

25. A Summit Meeting with Elijah and Moses—Mk. 9.2–13

26. Exorcising A Demon From a Young Boy—Mk. 9.14–29

27. Jesus' Second Prediction of His Death—Mk. 9.30–32

28. Recap in Capernaum: Principles of Leadership and Discipleship—Mk. 9.33–50

29. Jesus on Divorce, Little Children, and the Rich—Mk. 10.1–31

30. Jesus' Third Prediction of His Death—Mk. 10.32–34

31. The Request of James and John and the Quest of Jesus—Mk. 10.35–45

32. The Healing of Blind Bartimaeus in Jericho—Mk. 10.46–52

PART THREE: WORDS AND DEEDS IN JERUSALEM

1. The King Comes to Town—Mk. 11.1–11

2. The Cursing and the Cleansing—Mk. 11.12–25

3. The Authorities Challenge Jesus' Authority—Mk. 11.27–33

4. The Parable of the Tenants—Mk. 12.1–12

5. Render unto Caesar—Mk. 12.13–17

6. Marriage in the Afterlife?—Mk. 12.18–27

7. The Greatest Commandment—Mk. 12.28–34

8. Messiah: Son of David or David's Lord?—Mk. 12.35–37

9.   Warnings Against the Teachers—Mk. 12.38–40

10.   The Widow's Offering—Mk. 12.41–44

11.   The Temple of Doom and the Return of the Son of Man—Mk. 13.1–47

PART FOUR: THE PASSION AND RESURRECTION OF THE SON

1.   Anointing in Bethany—Mk. 14.1–11

2.   The Last Supper—Mk. 14.12–26

3.   The Prediction of Peter's Denials—Mk. 14.27–31

4.   Prayer in Gethsemane—Mk. 14.32–41

5.   The Betrayal and Arrest of Jesus—Mk. 14.43–52

6.   Jesus Before the Sanhedrin—Mk. 14.53–65

7.   The Threefold Denial by Peter—Mk. 14.66–72

8.   Jesus Before Pilate—Mk. 15.1–15

9.   The Mockery of the Messiah—Mk. 15.16–20

10.   The Crucifixion and Death of Jesus—Mk. 15.21–41

11.   The Burial of Jesus—Mk. 15.42–47

12.   Women at the Tomb and the Easter Message—Mk. 16.1–8

MESSIANIC SECRET

A theory proposed by William Wrede. Wrede purported that Mark imposed a "messianic secret motif" on his source material (material used as sources in the writing process) to cover up the historical fact that Jesus did not really present himself as a messianic figure during his lifetime. The theory does not hold up well in light of other evidence in Mark itself, the other Gospels, Pauline material, and elsewhere in the New Testament.

APOCALYPSIS

A Greek word, from which the English word *apocalyptic* is derived, which refers to the revelation of divine secrets.

[Our earliest and best manuscripts of Mark likely do not include verses 9–20, which appear to have been added in the second century after the original ending of Mark was lost. See the discussion at the end of this chapter.]

One of the things scholars have regularly commented on about the Gospel of Mark is what is called the "**Messianic secret.**" By this is meant the idea that in Mark's telling of the Good News about Jesus, there are regular commands to silence. Even the disciples at various junctures are told not to reveal what Jesus has said or done to the crowds or the general public. This stands in stark contrast with the Gospel of John where Jesus seems to be prepared to "tell all" to the general public.

German scholar William Wrede suggested that Mark imposed a "messianic secret motif" on his source material to cover up the historical fact that Jesus did not really present himself as a messianic figure during his lifetime. The problem with this theory is that there is too much evidence against it, not only in the other Gospels, but also in Mark itself and in Paul and elsewhere in the New Testament.[4] What then accounts for the atmosphere of secrecy and silence that broods over the text of the Gospel of Mark?

The answer to this question is that Mark was presenting the story of Jesus from an apocalyptic point of view. The Greek word ***apocalypsis***, from which the English word *apocalyptic* comes, refers to the revelation of divine secrets. (See the full discussion on apocalyptic thinking on p. 68.) The idea is that unless God reveals the truth about this or that, often in a vision or a dream, then no one will know it. Even Jesus is depicted at his baptism as needing a revelation from God to confirm his identity and begin his ministry.

Mark is telling us that what happened in the case of Jesus and his ministry is that God began to part the clouds of unknowing and reveal his character and will and plan in the person of his son, Jesus. Ched Myers should be credited for first fully seeing this as a key to understanding the Gospel of Mark.[5] He noticed that there are periodic apocalyptic or revelatory moments in Mark where Jesus' true or full identity is made known. Myers points to the following three:

BAPTISM	TRANSFIGURATION	CRUCIFIXION
Heavens torn	Garments turn to white	Sanctuary curtain torn
Dove descends	Cloud descends	Darkness descends
Voice from heaven	Voice from the cloud	Jesus' great voice
"You are my beloved son."	"This is my beloved son."	"Truly this man was God's son."
John the Baptizer as Elijah	Jesus appears with Elijah	"Is he calling Elijah?"

To this list of three we could add the story of the women at the tomb on Easter and their encounter with the angels, and perhaps the Caesarea Philippi episode in Mark 8 as well, where Peter confessed who Jesus is. The important point is that the whole story of Mark, from the beginning of the ministry to the end of Jesus' life, is punctuated by a few revelatory moments, and in between there is silence, silencing of the witnesses, and misunderstanding. Put another way, the commands to silence at particular junctures are balanced with commands to publication or proclamation *after one gains understanding.* The silence commands reveal that Jesus wanted to let people know who he was on his own timetable and on his own terms. He did not wish to be pigeonholed into preconceived messianic categories.

Even Jesus' public teaching is deliberately couched in the obscure form of parables, riddles, and **aphorisms**. When Jesus explained the purpose of the use of this metaphorical way of speaking, he quoted Isaiah 6 in Mark 4.12, saying that public teaching is in parables so that the people will look but not perceive, listen but not understand, unless they turn around, repent, and be forgiven.

The point of dark speech is to let God's people know that they are in the spiritual dark, and without repentance and revelations from God, they will not understand who they are, whose they are, and what is happening to them—and they certainly will not understand God's son, even if he is standing right in front of them! When a people dwell in darkness, unless they turn and see a great light, they will not be able to find their way along the path of life. The

APHORISM

A short saying that reveals a general truth.

basic premise of apocalyptic thinking is that there is a great gulf between God and the understanding of God by his people, and it takes a miracle, a revelation, from God to make things clear. This is why Mark's Gospel is punctuated with moments of revelation between which is dullness and lack of understanding, even on the part of the disciples.

Sometimes, scholars have complained that Mark is too hard on the disciples. From time to time, Jesus berates them, asking "Have you no faith?" (see, e.g., Mark 4.40 and contrast the same story in Matthew 8.26, where Jesus says, "O you of *little* faith"), but in fact all God's people are in spiritual darkness. Both advocates and adversaries require illumination to understand Jesus, both who he is and what the nature of his ministry is. Mark clearly believed that without revelation, repentance, and change in a person's life, the person could not understand, much less embrace, Jesus. The Good News is that Jesus is both the light and the light bringer, and when he comes, it can be said that "there is nothing hidden except to be disclosed, nor is anything secret except to come to light" (Mark 4.22). This leads us to discuss the Christology of Mark's Gospel, that is, Mark's reflections on the messianic character of Jesus.

Figure 5.3 Jesus emerges from the Jordan after having received a revelation. *"Baptism of Christ,"* Donald Jackson, Copyright 2002, The Saint John's Bible, *Order of Saint Benedict,* Collegeville, Minnesota, USA. Used by permission. All rights reserved.

THE PRESENTATION OF AND REFLECTION ON CHRIST IN MARK

As was said in the introduction to this book, what is in the Gospels and Acts is theological history writing—not theology added to history, like icing on a cake, but rather the two combined. Nowhere is this more evident than in the presentation of Jesus in the Gospel of Mark. Mark himself wants to emphasize that Jesus is God's son, the Messiah. This is clear from the first verse, Mark 1.1, but also from the revelatory passages listed earlier in this chapter. It is all the more revealing, then, that when we actually study the stories in Mark, the one phrase that keeps cropping up to identify Jesus on almost every page is "**Son of Man.**" This is the phrase Jesus regularly used to identify himself and to speak of his mission in life. To understand Mark's presentation of Jesus, we need to examine the use of this key phrase.

Although some scholars have tried to suggest that the phrase "Son of Man" is simply a circumlocution for "I" or for "a man in my position," this explanation of the phrase clearly would not have satisfied Mark, and I doubt it would have satisfied Jesus either. Mark is reading the story of Jesus in light of apocalyptic concepts and earlier Jewish apocalyptic literature. In particular, he was reading the story of Jesus in light of Daniel 7.13–14. This is especially clear in a text like Mark 14.62, where the reference to the Son of Man coming on the clouds is a dead giveaway that Daniel 7 stands in the background. To ignore the allusion to Daniel in the phrase "Son of Man" is to ignore a key that unlocks the understanding of Jesus in Mark.[6] So let us examine Daniel 7.13–14 a bit more closely.

> I saw in the night visions,
> and behold, with the clouds of heaven
> there came one like a Son of Man,
> and he came to the Ancient of Days
> and was presented before him.
> And to him was given dominion
> and glory and a kingdom,
> that all peoples, nations, and languages
> should worship him;
> his dominion is an everlasting dominion,
> which shall not pass away,
> and his kingdom one
> that shall not be destroyed.

The astute student of the Old Testament will immediately notice two striking things about this apocalyptic and visionary passage. First, it is the only place in the Old Testament where we find the Aramaic phrase *bar enash*, "son of man"; and second, it is absolutely the only place in the Old Testament where the two concepts most constantly found on the lips of Jesus—*Son of Man* and *kingdom of God*—are found. *Nowhere else in the Old Testament do you find these two concepts juxtaposed.* It surely cannot be an accident that these are the two phrases Jesus constantly used to refer to himself, and to refer to what his preaching, teaching, and healing inaugurated for God's people—namely, God's saving reign in their lives, God's rule, and God's kingdom. But there is more.

If you read Daniel 7 in light of Daniel 6 and the first part of the seventh chapter, you discover a climax in the visions of Daniel. He had previously seen a series of beastly empires with beastly rulers ruling the earth, and more particularly ruling God's people. These are superseded once and for all by a humane and truly human ruler of God's people, "one like a Son of Man."

The phrase "**ancient of days**" in Daniel 7 is a colorful way of speaking of God; and what happens in this vision is that God authorizes and empowers the Son of Man figure to rule the earth *forever,* and indeed to be worshipped and

SON OF MAN

The phrase regularly used by Jesus to identify himself and his mission in life. While some scholars suggest that the use is a circumlocution (a roundabout way of saying) for "I" or "a man in my position" this explanation does not do justice to the use of the phrase in Mark or by Jesus himself. Rather, the term refers both to a ruler who is human and yet so much more than human. The term also refers to Jesus' divinity as one who has God's authority to forgive sins, to change the way Sabbath is viewed and observed, to sit at the right hand of God, and to judge both the living and the dead.

ANCIENT OF DAYS

A phrase used to refer to God.

served by all nations (not just Israel) *forever.* One has to ask—what sort of figure can personally rule forever and deserves eternal service and worship by every tribe and tongue and people and nation? From a Jewish point of view, only an eternal figure, only a divine one, should receive that kind of devotion. In other words, here is a text that portrays a ruler who is both truly human and yet so much more than human, for he is worthy of everlasting service, worship, and rule.

If we contrast Daniel 7 with the promise given to David in 2 Samuel 7.12–17, the text becomes even more striking. There, David is promised to have descendants who will rule on his throne after he dies and maintain his kingdom. He is not said to rule forever as an individual; rather, he has a series of dynastic successors—a son, a grandson, and so on. The king in 2 Samuel 7 is mortal, and so requires successors, but the Son of Man figure in Daniel 7 is the end of the line—he personally will rule forever.

Ironically then, we might be tempted to see the phrase "Son of Man" as simply referring to Jesus' humanity and not his divinity. In fact, in the context of Daniel 7, Jesus picked the one phrase, the one concept in the Old Testament, that conjured up both the idea of a divine figure and the idea of a human figure combined in one person. I would suggest that this is indeed how Jesus viewed himself, and this is why Mark, taking down the testimony of Peter about Jesus, presented Jesus as the Son of Man referred to in Daniel.[7]

Let us consider a few examples of the use of Son of Man in Mark's Gospel. Interestingly, the phrase "Son of Man" is not used of Jesus in the first chapter of Mark's Gospel, but beginning in Mark 2, we find things such as the following:

1. "But that you may know that the Son of Man has authority to forgive sins" (2.10).

2. "The Sabbath was made for humankind, not humankind for the Sabbath, so the Son of Man is lord even over the Sabbath" (2.27—compare the image of Jesus as the strongest man who can bind Satan, called the "strong man," and release people from demonic possession in Mark 3.26–27).

3. Sometimes, we find the phrase *Son of Man* on Jesus' lips, and sometimes, it is Mark who calls him that. For instance, in Mark 8.31, "then he began to teach them that the Son of Man must undergo great suffering, and be rejected by the elders, chief priests, and scribes, and be killed, and after three days rise again." But later in the same chapter, we have the following saying of Jesus:

4. "Those who are ashamed of me and my words in this adulterous sinful generation, of them the Son of Man will be ashamed when he comes in the glory of his Father with the holy angels" (8.38).

5. "How then is it written that the Son of Man must suffer many things and be treated with contempt?" (9.12).

6. "The Son of Man is to be betrayed into human hands, and they will kill him, and three days after being killed, he will rise again" (9.31).

7. "See, we are going up to Jerusalem, and the Son of Man will be handed over to the chief priests and the scribes, and they will condemn him to death; then they will hand him over to the Gentiles; they will mock him, and spit upon him, and flog him, and kill him, and after three days he will rise again" (10.33–34).

8. "For the Son of Man came not to be served, but to serve and give his life as a ransom for the many" (10.45).

9. "Then they will see the Son of Man coming in the clouds with great power and glory" (13.26).

10. "For the Son of Man goes as it is written of him, but woe to that one by whom the Son of Man is betrayed!" (14.21).

11. "Enough! The hour has come; the Son of Man is betrayed into the hands of sinners" (14.41).

12. "I am. And you will see the Son of Man seated at the right hand of power and coming with the clouds of heaven" (14.62).

A careful examination of each of these 12 Son of Man sayings in Mark makes clear the two things we had already deduced from looking at the Son of Man saying in Daniel—this is a human figure, he is mortal, and he can suffer and die. In Daniel, the Son of Man is the representative of God's suffering people in exile. In Mark, the fourfold Passion predictions in Mark 8–10 always use the phrase Son of Man (see preceding list). Yet this Son of Man is clearly more than mortal—he has the authority of God to forgive sins; the authority of God to change the way the Sabbath is viewed and observed; and he sits at the right hand of God in heaven and will come to judge the living and the dead. In the climactic Son of Man saying in Mark 14.62, Jesus says he will be back to judge those who are judging him. It needs to be understood that the high priest does not see Jesus' claim to be Messiah, son of the blessed, as blasphemy. No, it is Jesus' claim to be the divine Son of Man coming to judge the world, something only God can and should do, that is seen as blasphemy and causes Caiaphas to tear his robes. It is this proclamation that seals Jesus' fate and leads to his being handed over to Pilate.

If Mark's Gospel is characterized by occasional revelations that Jesus is the Son of God, it is even more characterized by the twelvefold insistence that Jesus is the mortal yet divine Son of Man as well—not just Son of God, but also Son of Man. Notice as well that in the Passion predictions, resurrection is also predicted for the Son of Man, and *Son of Man* is the title Jesus was most comfortable using for himself with regularity. What of Jesus' teachings about something other than his personal identity and fate? To understand his teaching better, we need to understand a bit about how ancient Jews viewed time and timing, and how Mark presents these things.

MARKING TIME

EUTHUS

A Greek word loosely translated as "immediately." In Mark the term is not to be taken literally. Rather, it ought to be translated as "next," "after that," or "after awhile."

One of Mark's favorite adverbs is the Greek word **euthus**, loosely translated as "immediately." This word occurs about 40 times in Mark prior to the Passion narrative, and were we to take the term literally, we would get the impression of Jesus running around Galilee at a breakneck pace ("and immediately he got out of the boat . . . and immediately he went up into the hills to pray . . . and immediately he went to another village"). In fact, the term cannot be taken literally; it means something more like "next," or "after that," or in some cases what my grandfather meant by the word "directly" (as in "we will go to the ice cream parlor directly"). By *euthus,* Mark meant "after a while."

Many of the time references in the Bible are general time references, not specific ones. Ancient peoples did not run around with little sundials on their wrists worrying about hours and seconds, unlike modern persons. So for instance, in the Passion predictions in Mark 8–10, when Jesus says that he must be killed and "after three days rise," the phrase should not be pressed to mean three 24-hour days. This is because in reference to the same event in this same Gospel, there is the phrase "on the third day," which indicates that Jesus was in the grave for parts of three days— Friday evening, all day Saturday, and early Sunday morning. Many of the supposed chronological or time contradictions in the New Testament disappear when we take into account the general and generic ways ancients talked about time.

While we are discussing this matter, it is good to note that Jews reckoned time from sundown to sundown, not from midnight to midnight or sunrise to sunrise. The Romans began counting the hours of the day at dawn; so, for example, noon would be the sixth hour and 3 p.m. the ninth hour. This is relevant because Mark himself, probably writing in Rome for a largely Gentile audience, uses Roman ways of counting hours. Thus, in Mark 15.25, 33, and 34, we hear about the third, sixth, and ninth hours when Jesus was on the cross—beginning at 9 a.m. It is the Romans who gave us the abbreviations *ante meridiem* and *post meridiem,* or a.m. and p.m. *Meridiem* means middle of the day.

For a Jew, then, the new day began at sundown, and so the Sabbath for Jews runs from sundown Friday night to sundown Saturday night. I have been in the modern city of Jerusalem before and after sundown on Saturday and what a contrast. Suddenly, the coffee shop and shopping district on Ben Yehuda Street come alive after sundown Saturday, with shops opening, young people roaming the streets, and musicians playing on the corners. The new day, from the Jewish point of view, has begun, and the Sabbath is over.

THE KINGDOM COMES WITH TEACHING AND HEALING

The two things that characterize Jesus' ministry in all four Gospels found in the New Testament are healing and teaching, and both are connected to the coming of the kingdom of God on earth. Mark has lots of miracle stories in the first 11 chapters of his narrative. They are generally called **dynamis**, a Greek word meaning "mighty works" when applied to deeds. Thus, Mark is emphasizing the powerful, even stupendous, nature of Jesus' miracles.

There are a variety of miracles: (1) exorcisms (especially prevalent in Mark's account, by contrast with the fourth Gospel, which has no such tales), (2) healings of various sorts, (3) so-called nature miracles (showing control over nature—walking on water or cursing a fig tree), and (4) raising the dead. We might well think that raising the dead would cause the most surprise; but in fact, in that setting, it is exorcisms, such as the tale of the exorcism of the Gadarene demoniac on the Golan Heights in Mark 5 or giving sight to the blind, that cause the most amazement. After all, there were stories in the Old Testament of prophets raising the dead and healing people (see the stories about Elijah and Elisha in 1 Kings 17–19 and 2 Kings 1–9), but there are no recorded instances of sight being given to the blind or of exorcisms in the Old Testament.

These were new sorts of "mighty works" in Jesus' day, and the exorcisms especially frightened people. Jesus in Mark 3, because of his exorcisms, was accused of being in league with Satan and being Satan's agent. Jesus refutes this claim by pointing out that Satan wants demons in people, not demons exorcised from those who were bewitched, bothered, and bewildered by what Mark called "unclean spirits." In any case, Jesus painted the picture in Mark 3 of a ministry involving setting people free from what plagued them, both spiritual and physical maladies. These acts are seen as signs of God's saving activity, his divine reign on earth, his "kingdom"—or better said, his "dominion" or saving reign breaking into that world.

There is also a decided emphasis in Mark's Gospel on Jesus as a teacher. Jesus is even addressed as a famous teacher both by insiders, namely, his disciples, and outsiders (compare Mark 9.38 and 10.17). While various famous riddles and aphorisms of Jesus are sprinkled throughout Mark (e.g., Mark 10.25: "it is easier for a camel to go through the eye of a needle than for a rich person to enter the kingdom of God"), there are in fact only two major blocks of teachings in this Gospel—one in Mark 4, which is a collection of Jesus' "parables of the kingdom," and one in Mark 13, which is Jesus' prophetic teachings about the future. We will focus briefly on the former collection of teachings.

One of the reasons scholars are almost unanimous in agreeing that Mark is the earliest Gospel is that despite the emphasis on Jesus' preaching and teaching, we find *none of the Sermon on the Mount in Mark's Gospel!* (See Chapter 6 on Matthew 5–7.) Making this all the more surprising is that in Mark 1.38, Jesus

DYNAMIS

A Greek word meaning "mighty works" when applied to deeds.

CLUES FROM THE **CULTURE**

And I a sage, declare the splendor of His radiance in order to frighten and terrify all the spirits of the ravaging angels and the bastard spirits, demons . . . owls, and jackals.

—4Q510 Frag 1.4 from Qumran

said that his mission was not primarily to provide a healing service, but rather to proclaim the message of the breaking in of the kingdom of God. Jesus went out to teach, but when he performed acts of compassion, he stayed to heal the needy.

Notice that Jesus never said to his disciples, "Let us go to the next village so I can find some more people to heal," but he did say that about the teaching! Perhaps this emphasis is because healing of any kind is temporary. People will still go on and die eventually. But if Jesus gives them the Good News about salvation and the breaking in of the reign of God that could change their life and, indeed, give them everlasting life, the latter is more important.

Not only is the Sermon on the Mount missing in the earliest Gospel, so are most of our favorite parables—for instance, the parable of the prodigal son or the parable of the Good Samaritan (both of which are only in Luke's Gospel). This is significant because *each* of the four Gospels originally had particular, individual audiences in mind, and they were *not* written with the understanding that their audience could fill in the picture by reading the other Gospels. *Each Gospel stood on its own as a fully adequate, fully developed portrait of Jesus that was supposed to be sufficient for that audience.*

Mark's audience was likely Christians in Rome, particularly Gentile Christians who needed to know the basic story about Jesus. Had Mark had the Sermon on the Mount to use as a source for his Gospel, it is hard to imagine him *leaving it out* just so he could tell longer versions of some miracle tales than we find in the parallel accounts in Matthew or Luke. No, Mark gives us what he has from Peter's preaching and teaching, and in this case, he gives us a collection of agricultural parables (Mark 4).

Mark 4 begins with the famous parable of the sower, which is one of the few parables that has a full explanation by Jesus after the fact. Then at Mark 4.21 is the brief parable about the lamp. This is followed in 4.26 with the parable of the seed growing secretly, and then the famous parable of the mustard seed in 4.30–32. Mark 4.33–34 reminds us that Jesus mainly taught in parables when he spoke to outsiders. But what is a parable? It is a metaphorical form of speaking meant to tease the mind into active thought.

A CLOSER LOOK JESUS' WISDOM TEACHINGS—PARABLES, APHORISMS, RIDDLES

The Greek word *parabole,* from which we get the word *parable,* has a broader range of meaning than the English word *parable.* For example, in Luke 4.23, the metaphorical saying "physician heal yourself" is called a *parable.* So, what does this word mean in the Greek? Basically, it refers to metaphorical speech that involves an analogy ("the kingdom of God is like a sower who . . ."). The analogy can be short or long. It can involve a simple sentence, a proverb, or a riddle; or it can be as complex as a short story—such as the parable of the Good Samaritan. Note that metaphors or extended metaphors compare two things that are basically unalike, *except in some particular respect where they are similar.* So when the psalmist wrote that when God came down to judge the earth, and "the hills skipped like rams," there is only one way in which hills and rams are alike—they bounce or bound from time to time when danger or disaster is afoot. C. H. Dodd added that parables are meant to "tease the mind into active thought." They are not intended to be simple, obvious stories; they are meant to prompt deep reflection and musing.

Jesus was by no means the first person to tell parables. We certainly find them elsewhere in early Jewish literature, and occasionally in the Old Testament (e.g., the prophet Nathan's parable of the ewe lamb in 2 Samuel 12.1–7). What distinguishes Jesus' parable telling is (1) the sheer volume of parables, at least 43 of them in Mark, Matthew, and Luke alone; and (2) the fact that he related these parables to the subject of God's final salvation work, that is, God's final rule breaking into human history in and through his own ministry. In terms of numbers, we have 17 parables found only in Luke, 10 parables found only in Matthew, 6 parables found only in the sayings source called Q, and of the 9 parables in Mark, only 1 is not found in either Matthew or Luke, or both.

In terms of their literary form, parables are a form of wisdom literature, and it is important to realize that that involves a specific genre, a specific literary type of material. In other words, much of Jesus' public discourse stands in the tradition of the book of Proverbs or Ecclesiastes, offering wisdom for life of a metaphorical sort. The difference between Jesus' wisdom speech and earlier wisdom speech is that Jesus offered wisdom in light of the eschatological situation of God's final saving reign breaking into human history. By contrast, Proverbs, Ecclesiastes, and the wisdom Psalms give more generic life advice, sometimes based on the observation of nature ("go to the anthill, and learn the lesson") and sometimes based on acute observation of human nature ("a fool says in his heart, there is no God").

In Mark's Gospel, analogies are drawn mostly from nature—in the case of Mark 4, from the planting of seeds to garner a crop, or from the way certain kinds of seeds grow, quite apart from the action of the farmer. There is in fact a sliding scale between parable and allegory in early Jewish parables. Some have more symbolic elements that refer directly to things or persons outside the fictional parable. Some have less. So for example, in the parable of the sower, the sower in the first instance is Jesus, and then his disciples, and he commented on what sort of return he and they can reasonably expect from "sowing the word." Not every element in the parable is allegorical or symbolic, but some elements clearly are.

Similarly, in the parable of the tenants in Mark 12, Jesus presented himself as God's beloved son, the heir to the ownership of the vineyard, who is killed by the current tenants of the vineyard. This parable is based on the song of the vineyard in Isaiah 5, where the vineyard is clearly identified as Israel; so in Mark 12, the tenants have to be seen as some of the leadership in Judea whose job is to look after God's people, but in fact they make the mistake of doing away with God's son. Sometimes, the parables are stories Jesus told about himself, and sometimes they are more generally about the coming of the kingdom of God. But in all cases, these wisdom sayings are not stories told as moralizing tales about general human ethics; they are parables of and about the Kingdom, and the King who is bringing it in.

We need to say a bit more about what is meant by the word we translate most often as Kingdom. The Greek word in question *basileia,* and the Aramaic word behind it *malkuta,* can have either a more verbal or a noun sense. By this I mean it can refer to a reign or a realm, an activity or a place. If we simply translate the word as "kingdom" in English, then that always conveys the idea of a place, a domain that a king rules. However, a better translation would be "dominion" because in English, dominion can be a place, but it can also be an activity—"to have dominion over." In the Gospels, and in Paul as well, when we hear about inheriting, obtaining, or entering the "kingdom," Jesus or Paul is indeed referring to a future realm or place. But when *basileia* is used of something happening in the present, what it refers to is the dynamic saving activity of God that heals or helps or redeems someone. So, for example, when Jesus says "if I by the Spirit of God cast out demons, you will know the *basileia* has broken into your midst," he is referring to the final divine saving activity happening through his ministry—he is not referring to some invisible place. Because there is so much overlap between the Passion Narrative in Mark and the Passion Narrative in Matthew, we will reserve our more detailed survey of the content of the Passion Narrative for Chapter 6 in this textbook.

THE DRAMATIC, SURPRISE ENDING OF MARK'S GOSPEL

The Passion narrative in Mark's Gospel is both stark and dark. Jesus is condemned by the Jewish authorities, judged and sentenced by the Roman governor Pilate, and crucified between two Jewish revolutionaries or Zealots, with the ironic and mocking sign over his head—"King of the Jews." Jesus dies on a Roman cross with the sky turned ugly and black, crying out, "My God, my God, why have you forsaken me" (quoting the beginning of Psalm 22 in Aramaic). There are no other words of Jesus from the cross in Mark's Gospel. Jesus is abandoned by all the male disciples, having been betrayed by Judas, and denied three times by the leader of the 12, Peter himself. Jesus is alone, starkly alone, at death. Even God seems not to be present.

If that were not bad enough, the sequel is equally shocking. Jesus is hastily buried before the Sabbath and Passover begins. And after Sabbath and Passover are over, the women who come to change the linens wrapping the corpse of Jesus and re-anoint his body find the body missing, the tomb empty. There is the proclamation by angels to the women reassuring them: "Fear not. You are looking for Jesus of Nazareth, who was crucified. He has been raised, he is not here. Look there is the place they laid him. But go tell his disciples and Peter that he is going before you into Galilee; there you will see him, just as he told you." What is the response of the women to this exhortation? According to Mark 16.8, the response is fright and flight. They flee in terror from the tomb and say nothing to anyone because of their fears.

Although this ending might make for a good conclusion to a horror movie today, it is not how ancient biographies concluded in antiquity. They concluded with the hero of the biography vindicated and his legacy praised. This is not what is in Mark 16.8. It will come as a surprise to some readers that there are actually a good number of scholars who think Mark 16.8 is the original ending of the Gospel of Mark. Why?

Some scholars say that Mark begins abruptly, and so it is appropriate that it ends abruptly. This is not an adequate rationale because, although this Gospel begins abruptly with "The beginning of the Good News of Jesus, the Christ, the Son of God," it begins with Good News, not the downer of an empty tomb and women terrified and fleeing.

Some scholars have thought that because Mark's Gospel is apocalyptic in tone and color, Mark 16.8 might be an appropriately mysterious ending. The problem with this suggestion is that the apocalyptic prophecies of Jesus in Mark's Gospel point forward to not only the resurrection of Jesus but also the return of Jesus. In other words, they point forward to a personal appearance of Jesus. Mark 16.8 does not give us this.

Figure 5.4 Christ on the cross, the juxtaposing of the ghastly and the glorious. *"Crucifixion,"* Donald Jackson, *Copyright 2002,* The Saint John's Bible, *Order of Saint Benedict, Collegeville, Minnesota, USA. All rights reserved.*

Still other scholars who advocate Mark 16.8 as an ending suggest that it is deliberately open-ended so that the readers themselves would feel included in the story. The big problem with all these suggestions is that they ignore the way ancient biographies of hero figures ended, and they owe far too much to modern literary tastes and preferences.

Ancient peoples believed that how a person died most revealed their character. If this Gospel did not dramatically reverse the horrific tale of Jesus on the cross, and indeed provided a positive explanation for that death, showing that God vindicated and had not abandoned Jesus, this Gospel would not have been

Figure 5.5 A first-century rolling-stone tomb just outside Jerusalem. (© *Mark R. Fairchild, Ph.D.*)

seen as ending with Good News about Jesus. It would have suggested that Jesus was a criminal, and certainly not the Son of God, as the centurion says beneath the cross. But there is, as well, a textual reason why some scholars argue that Mark 16.8 was the original ending.

For one thing, our earliest and best Greek manuscripts of Mark do not appear to have had anything beyond Mark 16.8. The longer and shorter endings we find in Mark 16.9–20, or in the so-called shorter ending found in at least one major manuscript (which reads "And all that had been commanded them they told briefly to those around Peter. And afterward, Jesus himself sent out through them from east to west, the sacred and imperishable proclamation of eternal salvation.") are both likely later additions to the text because Mark 16.8 was deemed not an appropriate ending. In fact, Mark 16.9–20 appears to be a later composite of Gospel traditions from the other Gospels as from elsewhere, for they do not reflect Mark's style of Greek. The vast majority of scholars of Christian faith (or no Christian faith or somewhere in between) are convinced that these conclusions are not original to Mark's Gospel, yet there are still some conservative scholars who have argued for verses 9–20 being original—in part because they were included in early translations of Mark such as the 1611 version of the King James Bible, but those translators did not have the earlier Greek manuscripts of Mark that we now possess.

The very fact that there were these later additions should tell us something important—the early church did not think that Mark's Gospel could possibly have ended at Mark 16.8. Would there really be a Gospel that told of no appearances of the risen Jesus to his disciples, especially when the angel in Mark 16.7 tells the women that as Jesus promised, he would see them all, women and men, in Galilee?

Fright and flight are not a "Good News" conclusion to a story recounting the Good News of Jesus' life, death, and resurrection. Furthermore, there is no evidence at all of any whole ancient document, or even a chapter within an ancient document ending with a dangling connective word like "for" (the Greek text of Mark 16.8 ends with "they were afraid for. . . ."). In my own view, it is probable that the original ending of Mark's Gospel is lost, and the second-century church tried to fix the problem by creating at least two, or possibly three, proper conclusions to this ancient biography.

How could the original ending of Mark have gotten lost? It is easy enough to explain, based on what has already been discussed in this book about ancient scrolls. Ancient people, like modern people, tended not to follow the dictum "please be kind and rewind," which we used to hear a lot back in the days of videotapes, cassettes, and reel-to-reel recorders. When an ancient person finished unrolling and reading a scroll, the reader tended not to rewind the scroll. In fact, so prevalent was this practice of not rewinding that often the identifier tag on a scroll was attached to the end of the scroll! This means that the outermost edge and the end of the scroll were most subject to wear and tear. It is likely then that Mark's ending was lost through such a process of deterioration or even tearing. Papyrus was by no means as durable as parchment.[8]

Can we reconstruct the original ending of Mark? Probably we can, as over 95% of Mark's Gospel recurs in Matthew, as we shall see in Chapter 6. For now, I would suggest that we find the original ending of Mark in Matthew 28.9–10 and 28.16–20, with small editorial subtractions of Matthean verbiage. Mark's Gospel ended just as Mark 14 suggested, with Jesus appearing to women in Jerusalem and to the 12 apostles in Galilee. Now *that* ending qualifies as "the Good News about Jesus the Christ, the Son of God." Whichever of the three possibilities one favors (the Gospel originally ended at 16.8; the original ending is lost, but can be recovered from Matthew's use of it; the Gospel continued with verses 9–20), the angels do proclaim the Good News at the end of the Gospel that the tomb is empty and Jesus is risen, and it was time for the disciples to go spread this Good News to one and all.

IMPLICATIONS

The earliest Gospel, Mark, may seem simple on the surface, but as we have seen in this chapter, it is rich, varied, and full of interesting theological and historical substance. It is often a surprising Gospel, and repeatedly one can say, "These aren't the sort of stories one would make up, if one was creating a fictional narrative in the first century A.D. about the savior of both Jews and Gentiles." No indeed. First-century Jews, and even more so first-century Gentiles, were not looking for a crucified savior figure. That was an oxymoron. Just how much of an oxymoron it was can be seen in the *tufa* rock carving found in the pagan catacombs in Rome.

Figure 5.6 A drawing of the graffiti found in the Roman pagan catacombs, ridiculing the notion of worshipping a God who died on a cross. (© *Rick Danielson*)

Figure 5.6 shows a *graffito*, a cartoon drawing found in the pagan tombs beneath Rome. It depicts a person worshipping a crucified donkey who is said to be the worshipper's "god" in the inscription. In the mind of the graffiti artist, the whole notion of worshipping someone who was crucified was totally asinine—it made no sense. Had Jesus not been vindicated after he was crucified, it is doubtful anyone would have tried to tell the difficult tale of the Good News about a crucified man. Mark, however, did tell such a tale, and remarkably, he told it in the wake of the brutal deaths of two of his early Christian heroes—Peter and Paul in Rome. This took both courage and faith. It also took knowledge of the fact that Jesus appeared to his disciples after his death.

KEY TERMS

Ancient of Days	*Euthus*
Aphorism	Gospel
Apocalypsis	Messianic Secret
Chreia	Papias
Dynamis	Son of Man
Euangelion	

FOR FURTHER READING

Bryan, C. *A Preface to Mark*. Oxford: Oxford University Press, 1997.

Hooker, M. D. *The Gospel According to Saint Mark*. Black's New Testament Commentary. Baker Academic, Ada, MI: Hendrickson, 2009.

Witherington, B. *The Gospel of Mark: A Socio-Rhetorical Commentary*. Grand Rapids, MI: Eerdmans, 2001.

STUDY QUESTIONS

Why is it that the majority of scholars think that a non-apostle, non-eyewitness like John Mark wrote this Gospel?

What is the Messianic secret theory, and who came up with the idea? How does this relate to the notion of Mark's Gospel having an apocalyptic character?

Why is Mark 8.27–30 such a turning point in this Gospel, and what is predicted thereafter?

Why does Mark 16.8 make a bad ending for an ancient biography, particularly the biography of Jesus?

NOTES

1. Reynolds Price, *Three Gospels* (New York: Scribner, 1997), 14–15.
2. This list was partly inspired by my friend and colleague Mark Allan Powell, in *Introducing the New Testament: A Historical, Literary, and Theological Survey* (Grand Rapids, MI: Baker Academic, 2009), 84.
3. Here I am following Dr. Rod Decker's rendering of this passage in Eusebius's *Ecclesiastical History* (EH 3.39.14b–15) as posted on his blog on August 31, 2007, at http://ntresources.com/blog/?p=20. I am following his rather literal translation because I think it is more nearly right than the Loeb standard translation. I have, however, altered his translation of chreia.
4. And in fact, Wrede himself later had serious doubts about this theory as a late letter to Adolph van Harnack shows. See Michael Wilkins, "Peter's Declaration Concerning Jesus' Identity in Caesarea Philippi," in *Key Events in the Life of the Historical Jesus: A Collaborative Exploration of Context and Coherence,* ed. Darrell Bock and Robert Webb (Grand Rapids, MI: Eerdmans, 2010), 332–34, especially n. 143.
5. Ched Myers, *Binding the Strong Man: A Political Reading of Mark's Story of Jesus* (London: Orbis, 1988), 390–92.
6. Ignoring the allusion to Daniel 7 makes no sense of the Greek text because the phrase "Son of Man" in the New Testament is almost always preceded by the definite article—"the Son of Man," which surely means "the familiar, or well-known, or previously mentioned" Son of Man. The definite article makes it clear that the phrase was not used in some generic sense to mean "a human being."
7. On Jesus' self-understanding and self-presentation, see B. Witherington, *The Christology of Jesus* (Minneapolis, MN: Fortress Press, 1990).
8. On this whole matter, see the detailed study of N. Clayton Croy, *The Mutilation of Mark's Gospel* (Nashville, TN: Abingdon Press, 2003).

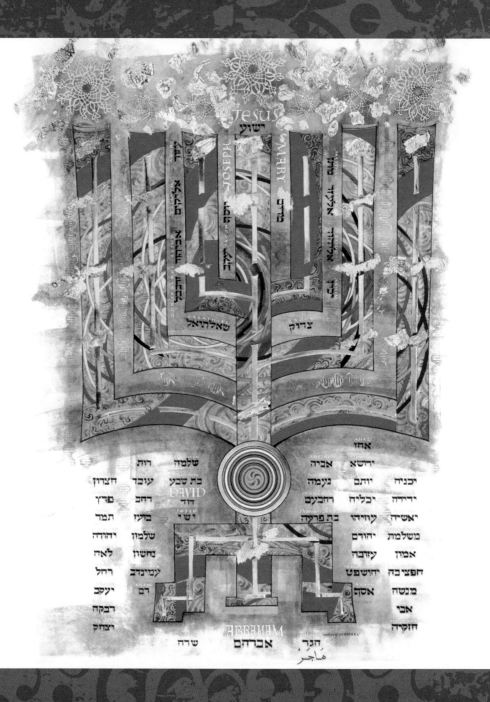

A painting of a menorah with its seven branches, like the sevenfold genealogy in Matthew 1. (*"Genealogy of Jesus,"* Donald Jackson, Copyright 2002, The Saint John's Bible, *Order of Saint Benedict, Collegeville, Minnesota USA.*)

6

The MOST POPULAR GOSPEL— MATTHEW

> *To us it would seem wrong to credit an editor with the work of an author. The author in our mind, is the intellectual source of the text, whereas an editor merely polishes; the former is the creative genius, the latter merely the technician. This distinction was obviously less important to the ancients. They did not place the same value on originality. To them, an author does not invent his text but merely arranges it; the content of the text exists first, before being laid down in writing.*
>
> —KAREL VAN DER TOORN[1]

IT IS AN IRONY that the more early Christianity grew, spread, and became a movement dominated by Gentiles, the more popular and widely used of the four Gospels was the most Jewish one—Matthew's Gospel! In the canon of the New Testament, Matthew's Gospel was placed first, perhaps because of its widespread popularity.

at a Glance

The Gospel of Matthew is a compilation of several sources, one or more of which likely came from Matthew, one of the original disciples. Matthew was literate, and may have been responsible for compiling Jesus' sayings in Aramaic. He may also have been responsible for the uniquely Matthean material in this Gospel. It was likely written in the A.D. 70s or 80s to Jewish Christians, either in Capernaum or Antioch.

EKKLESIA

A Greek word usually translated as "church" in modern translations.

There were a whole host of reasons why this Gospel became so popular. In the Western Church, certainly one reason was the prominence of Peter in this Gospel and his leadership role in relationship to Jesus' disciples in this Gospel. Matthew's Gospel was also popular because it offers some instructions on church order, being the only Gospel to actually use the word **ekklesia**, usually translated as "church." It was popular as well because it began with a genealogy for Jesus, and it ended with a full telling of the appearances of Jesus in both Jerusalem and Galilee. Indeed, this Gospel is much larger than Mark's, having 18,305 words compared to Mark's 11,242. Especially notable are both the birth narratives in Mt. 1–2 and all the additional teaching material in Mt. 5–7 (the Sermon on the Mount) and elsewhere in this Gospel. This is a Gospel ready made for teaching and discipling. In terms of the influence of this Gospel in the English-speaking world, phrases like "casting pearls before swine," "salt of the earth," "burning the midnight oil," "waiting until the 11th hour," "beware of wolves in sheep's clothing," "the blind leading the blind," and "the left hand not knowing what the right hand is doing" we owe to the early English translations of this Gospel (particularly the Tyndale and the King James translations).

Already in the second century A.D., this Gospel was put in codex or page and book form, making it easier to use than a Gospel on a scroll. It was already copied in a "fair" or elegant hand and treated as a special, even sacred text. The care lavished on the seven earliest papyri we have of this book reflects its status and teaching authority for worship and Christian life in the early church. Already in an early second-century document called 2 Clement, Mt. 9.13 is called *Scripture* along with the Old Testament. In that same century, we find amulets made for Christians with the Matthean form of the Lord's Prayer written on them meant to protect the wearer from disease or harm.

It is probably not too much to say that despite the ordinary Greek style of this Gospel, words from Matthew have been pronounced, prayed, preached, taught, and read more often than from any other author in human history. When we hear a Christian say "Jesus says" or even "the Bible says," it is this Gospel that is cited most often.[2] It is thus important to look more closely at this "feature-length, value-added" Gospel. The first question to be raised about it is, Why is it called Matthew's Gospel? We must examine in some detail ancient practices about ascribing authorship to a document that does not tell us directly within the document (as this Gospel does not) who wrote it.

DESCRIBING A SCRIBE

If we ask why exactly this most popular of all Gospels was ascribed to a relatively minor and more obscure disciple named Matthew, it is likely because someone named Matthew had something to do with this Gospel, either as a prominent source of the material in this Gospel or as its composer. Here again, we may gain some help by examining what the second-century church father Papias tells us about Matthew.

Consider this comment of Papias directly quoted by Eusebius, the father of church history (EH 3.39.4):

> But whenever someone who had followed the presbyters came along, I would carefully ask about the words of the presbyters, what Andrew or what Peter had said or what Philip or what Thomas or James or what John or Matthew or any other of the disciples of the Lord, and which Aristion and the presbyter John, disciples of the Lord say too. For I did not assume that whatever comes from books is as helpful to me as what comes from a living and lasting voice.

Here, we have early confirmation from outside the New Testament that there was an original disciple of Jesus named Matthew, and in Papias's day there were still some persons alive such as presbyter John (or John the Elder), who had been in contact with these persons and knew what they said. *Notice that Papias showed no interest in anonymous community traditions. He wanted to know what the important early eyewitnesses saw and said about it.*[3] Then Papias went on to say (H.E. 3.39.16): "Now Matthew compiled the words in a Hebrew dialect [i.e., Aramaic], but each interpreted them as he could."

It has often been debated what this last tantalizing sentence means. The first thing to notice about it is that Matthew can write. Indeed, as we shall see, he may have been a scribe, but even if he was only a head tax collector, he would have had to be able to read and write. "Compiled the words" (or perhaps "reports") sounds definitely like that kind of person. Furthermore, it is not clear whether Papias was talking about a full Gospel here or a collection of Jesus' sayings in Aramaic. It could be the latter, but the parallelism in construction with Papias's comment on Mark suggests that he was talking about a full Gospel—in Aramaic. Our Gospel of Matthew, however, is in Greek. You will also notice that Papias knew of several interpreters of this Aramaic text of Matthew.

Figure 6.1 Statue of an Egyptian scribe. (*Ben Witherington*)

Notice that over 90 percent of a Gospel written by a non-eyewitness, namely, Mark, shows up in Matthew's Gospel.[4] Doesn't this count against the notion that this Gospel might have been compiled by an original apostle? Why would he need a secondary source and adhere to it so religiously if he himself was an eyewitness of the things reported in this Gospel? This is a very good and fair question.

Although you could argue that Mark was giving Peter's testimony, and we can see why Matthew might use most of it almost verbatim in many places, I would suggest it makes better sense to conclude as follows: (1) Matthew the tax collector had writing and scribal skills; (2) he compiled some important stories about Jesus and some of Jesus' sayings—in the mother tongue of Jesus himself and his own mother tongue, Aramaic; (3) someone else, probably a non-apostle, non-eyewitness scribe came along and combined the Matthean material with Mark's Gospel, and perhaps **Q**. On this showing, Matthew may have contributed all the unique material in this Gospel—for instance, the birth narratives in Mt. 1–2 and some of the special Peter traditions. The scribe who compiled this Gospel did not have any desire, or authority, to claim the Gospel was by him when he was in fact drawing on earlier apostolic material directly from Matthew and indirectly from Mark. He was just the compiler and editor, not the author. But he was also the translator of Matthew's original material.

Q

An abbreviation for *Quelle* which means "source." Q is a hypothetical document that contains the non-Markan collection of Jesus' sayings. The contents of Q are typically drawn from Matthew and Luke.

Figure 6.2
House of Peter in Capernaum underneath the current chapel. It is perhaps the oldest place of Christian worship, with graffiti on the walls dating to the second century.
(© Mark R. Fairchild, Ph.D.)

There is a further possibility as well: Matthew himself originally compiled in Aramaic what scholars call Q. He could also have been responsible for both the M (or special Matthew) material in this Gospel as well as the Q (non-Markan sayings source) material. That is, he contributed a large portion of the material in this Gospel that the scribe translated, edited, and arranged. The finished document then was attributed to its apostolic contributor—Matthew, being the only eyewitness source used. Concepts of authorship were not as strictly individualistic as we moderns would view it (see the quote at the beginning of this chapter). In either case, we are clearly not dealing with an attempt at forgery or deception here.

Are there internal clues about Matthew or about the final composer of this Greek document, or both? Yes, there are both. There is a saying in Matthew that is not found in other Gospels. Matthew 13.52 reads, "Therefore every scribe who has been trained for the kingdom of heaven is like the master of a household who brings out of his treasure what is new and what is old." It is hard to doubt that this saying of Jesus had special relevance to both Matthew, as a compiler of some of the stories and sayings about Jesus, and the Christian scribe (notice that this scribe is trained for the kingdom of heaven Jesus was preaching) who put this document in its final form in Greek.

Notice especially that the role of a scribe who has been trained is to bring together something old (perhaps in this case the testimony of Peter as mediated through Mark in Greek) and something new (the collections of Jesus material from Matthew) into a coherent whole. Scribes were compilers, compendium makers, translators, and editors; but they did not view themselves as authors, and they did not append their names to documents unless they were the originators of the material in the document. Only rarely did a scribe make a statement about himself in the first person using his own name, when he was compiling documents by other persons (see Rom. 16.22 where Tertius sends greetings). We will say much more about the role of scribes in the composition of the New Testament later, when we come to the discussion of Paul's letters (see p. 159).

THE AUDIENCE, DATE, AND CHARACTER OF MATTHEW'S GOSPEL

Scholars who are experts in the Gospel of Matthew have often noted the more specifically Jewish flavor of this Gospel. Jesus is shown debating specifically Jewish ideas and practices in this Gospel more than in any other, and we have a whole chapter of denunciations of other early Jewish teachers—namely, the scribes and Pharisees, in Matthew 23. Instead of the word "God" in the phrase "Kingdom of God," Matthew frequently substitutes the most familiar roundabout way of saying the same thing—"kingdom of heaven." Most Matthew experts have concluded that this Gospel must have been written in an environment or locale

Figure 6.3 The black basalt bottom layer of this wall represents the original first-century synagogue foundation on which the synagogues of the second and third centuries were built. Jesus spoke in that original synagogue, having adopted Capernaum as his base camp for his traveling ministry in Galilee. (© *Mark R. Fairchild, Ph.D.*)

where there was still a great deal of contact, discussion, and debate between the followers of Jesus and other Jews.

There are two places that have been suggested as the possible locale where the audience of this Gospel resided—Antioch in ancient Syria (which is in modern-day southeastern Turkey) and Galilee itself, with Capernaum being a likely choice, the adopted hometown of Jesus, where there is evidence of the earliest house church in the "house of Peter" (see Figure 6.2). Wherever the audience is, it needs teaching material from Jesus to continue the often heated debate with non-Christian Jews, and this Gospel provides it with some five or six blocks of teaching and discipling materials (see the next section, "Matthew's Special Contributions to the Story of Jesus").

We may date this Gospel to the later A.D. 70s or so, after the Gospel of Mark had circulated beyond its original audience, also after collections of Jesus' sayings had begun to be amassed, and perhaps after the death of Matthew as well. As we shall now see, the Gospel of Matthew has a theological structuring, as does Mark, with the scribe compiling collections of thematically related sayings and traditions together.

THEOLOGICAL OUTLINE OF MATTHEW

1.1–2.23	Narrative	Birth stories
3.1–4.24	Narrative	Galilean ministry begins
5.1–7.29	Teaching	Sermon on the Mount
8.1–9.34	Narrative	On Christian discipleship
9.35–10.42	Teaching	Teaching on discipleship
11.1–12.50	Narrative	On the kingdom
13.1–52	Teaching	Teaching on kingdom parables
13.53–17.27	Narrative	On community order, discipline, worship
18.1–35	Teaching	Teaching on the same subjects
19.1–22.46	Narrative	Controversies in Jerusalem
23	Teaching	Judgment on Pharisees and scribes
24–25	Teaching	Apocalyptic discourse
26–28	Narrative	Passion and resurrection narratives

What one notices immediately is that this Gospel alternates between narrative and teaching sections. Although there are more narrative sections than blocks of teaching, nevertheless, there are five or six large blocks of teaching material. Scholars debate whether there are five or six blocks of teaching material based on whether they think Matthew 23 goes with Matthew 24–25 or should be seen as a separate block of teaching. The break in the teaching at Matthew 24.1 and the different setting for what follows in Matthew 24–25 likely indicates that we are meant to see two different blocks of teaching. The reason many scholars insist on five blocks of teaching is because they see Jesus being cast in the mold of a latter-day Moses in this Gospel. This idea may be present in this Gospel (see, e.g., the story in the birth narrative of the flight into Egypt and the return from there in Matthew 2), but the Evangelist clearly wants to indicate that Jesus is greater than Moses, not merely his equal. Hence in this view, there are six blocks of teaching, in contrast with the five books of Moses, which are the first five books of the Old Testament.

Furthermore, the Evangelist wants to present Jesus as a great sage, as one greater even than Solomon. The phrase "son of David" applied by outsiders to Jesus in this Gospel refers to his being like Solomon, even having the wisdom to cure people.[5] In this Gospel, Jesus is presented as greater than Moses, greater than Solomon. But who could be greater than them as a teacher of Israel? The answer is Wisdom come in the flesh, or as Matthew puts it, "God with us" (Immanuel). The Immanuel theme is distinctive to this Gospel, being found in the first and last chapters ("lo, I will be with you always"). This Gospel presents us with a very exalted view of Jesus as both human and more than human, as did Mark's Gospel. We need now to consider some of the special features of this Gospel.

MATTHEW'S SPECIAL CONTRIBUTIONS TO THE STORY OF JESUS

Clearly, this is a teacher's, and so a disciple's, Gospel, meant probably to be used to disciple Jewish Christians. But as the preceding outline suggests, it is a Gospel that wants to talk about order, discipline, and leadership in the community of Jesus, so it talks more about the first leader of the apostles, Peter, than did Mark. This Gospel has at its heart a concern about Christology (who Jesus was and what was his significance), discipleship (what it takes to follow him), and community (how the group of followers should relate to one another and to outsiders like other Jews). With its Jewish Christian character and audience, it is no surprise that we hear in this Gospel things like "I was sent only to the lost sheep of Israel," or "go nowhere among the Gentiles" (a command to the twelve at one point). Nor is it a surprise that there is such a strong critique of Pharisees, scribes, and Sadducees, which is to say the Jewish religious leadership of the day. This should be contrasted with the stress on the leadership of Jesus' disciples by Peter. But this Gospel from the very outset sounds like an early Jewish debate— in this case over a genealogy.

It is safe to say that no one before this Gospel was written had ever seen a genealogy quite like the one we find in Mt. 1.1–17. For one thing, it seems clearly to be Joseph's genealogy, but the author does not believe that Joseph is the biological father of Jesus! He believes that Jesus was conceived by means of miracle in Mary's womb, which Christians now call the virginal conception, a gift from God to Mary. For another thing, this genealogy includes some surprising persons, in particular some surprising women— Tamar, Rahab, Ruth, "the wife of Uriah" (i.e., Bathsheba), and then there is Mary—in Joseph's genealogy! In fact, there was no reason for there to be *any women* in this genealogy. It is about men who begat sons! There was no need for the women in the genealogy at all, so they must be there by design.

For a third thing, this is a schematized genealogy, by which I mean it deliberately leaves out names and whole groups of names so that it ends up with a perfect three sets of 14 generations—or put another way, Jesus is the seventh son of a seventh son of a seventh son of King David, whose very Hebrew name adds up to the number 14 according to the Jewish way of turning Hebrew letters into numbers. In early Jewish numerology, seven is the number of perfection—for example, the complete and perfect week that is "very good." And seven times seven is the number of the Jubilee year (see Lev. 25.10–23). Jesus is the one who comes to release people from their debts, their sins, like the Jubilee year. Lest we worry that Matthew needed some lessons in basic math, in fact it was common in royal genealogies to leave out whole generations and leave some skeletons in the closet. But in this genealogy, we have a few female skeletons out of the closet and walking around. What in the world is Matthew trying to say by this genealogy?

As we have suggested, Matthew wants us to know that Jesus is in the royal line of David, even if by a peculiar, roundabout means. In early Judaism, if a man adopted a son, then the son had a right to the father's full heritage, including his genealogy apparently. For a second thing, this genealogy is an exercise in apologetics. What it shows is that there were some irregularities, specifically, irregular unions, in the royal genealogy. Solomon, for example, came from such an irregular union, as did the father of King David, for that matter. These irregularities are meant to prepare us for the shock of the virginal conception story that follows this genealogy, which in fact makes a cameo appearance in the genealogy at Mt. 1.16. The genealogy takes a big left turn to Mary the wife of Joseph, at its end, because she alone was the actual biological human parent of Jesus according to this story. But it is not just the story of the conception of Jesus by a woman not impregnated by a man (and connected to Isaiah 7.14) that is surprising in this Gospel. The very teaching of Jesus is surprising, if one has only read Mark before reading Matthew.

THE SERMON ON THE MOUNT

Even though the Sermon on the Mount comes from the Q material (the non-Mark collection of Jesus' sayings), it is the Matthean presentation of some of this material, in Mt. 5–7, that has most come to be characterized in all of Christian history as the quintessential teaching of Jesus. It is certainly the most influential collection of theological ethics anywhere in the New Testament, and so we must spend a little time examining it. As C. Baumann once said, Mt. 5–7 has been dramatized, secularized, universalized, criticized, psychologized, politicized, and radicalized.[6] It will repay close scrutiny.

The First Evangelist has a very different strategy when it comes to arranging his source material than did Mark. After giving only a very brief summary of Jesus' Galilean ministry in Mt. 4.17–25, we turn very rapidly to this signature block of Jesus' teachings in Mt. 5–7. But teachings for whom? When Jesus sees the crowd (Mt. 5.1), he goes up the mount to teach the disciples. Whereas it contains a few parables, and many other sorts of wisdom teaching like beatitudes, the Sermon on the Mount is teaching for insiders, although the crowds are depicted as overhearing it. This is not an ethic for those who are not followers of Jesus, even though some have attempted to impose such an ethic on communities and cultures and countries ill-suited to obey it.

Those unfamiliar with Proverbs, Ecclesiastes, or early Jewish books like the Wisdom of Solomon or Sirach may not realize that the Sermon on the Mount is a virtual compendium of familiar and standing topics discussed by Jewish sages for ages—subjects like the dangers of wealth; self-control in regard to anger and sexual expression; the appeal to nature as an example of how to avoid anxiety; and instructions on prayer, fasting, and oath taking. What is different is that Jesus takes an eschatological or kingdom perspective on these topics, and in some cases he intensifies the demands (e.g., prohibiting adultery in the heart). What is also different is the counter-order wisdom Jesus sometimes offers—for example, he prohibits oath, whereas Moses allowed it. He also prohibits divorce (except on grounds of incest), whereas Moses allowed it; and most strikingly, he prohibits killing and even urges that his followers must love their enemies. There is also an ethic of nonresistance and non-retaliation to abuse in this sermon ("turn the other cheek"). We can also point to the exhortation to avoid the dangers of money and of accumulating wealth. This is something Solomon would never have said.

The overall impression one gets is that Jesus, like the aforementioned scribe, is offering something old and something new in this ethical compendium. More importantly, Jesus is exercising sovereign freedom over the Mosaic law—saying some of it is already fulfilled and therefore obsolete, some of it is intensified, and some of it is re-affirmed, sometimes with a new wrinkle—namely, that because God's final saving activity is in motion, new occasions and new situations require some new teaching and a new approach to ethics.

It needs to be stressed that Jesus is not trying to offer a utopian ethic. He believes that God's fresh outpouring of salvation and grace enables his followers to embrace and to walk through a narrow gate and follow a straighter path in life. In other words, Jesus expects obedience to his exhortations, but he knows that only God can enable obedience to an ethic like this.

The Sermon on the Mount begins with what we call the beatitudes. Basically, we can talk about the whole sermon as involving blessings, admonitions, and warnings. Jesus begins with the blessings, but what odd blessings these are. These are not general truisms, a sort of chicken soup for the soul, if you will. These are statements that those who are now in danger, having difficulties or sorrow, or doing the hard work of the kingdom will experience reversal or blessings later when the kingdom comes in full on earth. In other words, the blessings come later.

It is not true, here and now, that those who mourn are always comforted or that those who are merciful receive mercy. What is presupposed is that there is a sovereign God who one day will set things right, see that justice and salvation are done, and God's people are vindicated. Being satisfied, or obtaining mercy, or being called sons and daughters of God, or most clearly seeing God all refer to a destiny set aside for the faithful, not just anyone. There are, in fact, 28 beatitudes in Matthew alone, and all of these in Mt. 5 speak of vindication, victory, comfort, and blessing later when the kingdom comes fully on earth. Jesus is confident that the future is as bright as the promises of God. The alert student may have noticed a certain familiarity in these eight beatitudes given that they echo a Scripture Jesus seems to have believed he was called to fulfill—Isaiah 61.1–4, which proclaims the year of God's favor when all wrongs are righted, and all promises are fulfilled. This same text comes up in Jesus' inaugural sermon in Luke 4.

Matthew 5.17–20 are in some ways the most important verses in this "sermon," as they seem to indicate something of the purpose of this Gospel—to show that Jesus did not come to abolish the law or the prophets but to fulfill them. Whatever these verses mean, they cannot be seen to contradict what follows where we have antitheses ("you have heard it said . . . but I say to you"), where in some cases Jesus offers a new teaching that replaces some of the admonitions of the Mosaic law. Jesus seems to feel free to add to, subtract from, and substitute for, not to mention intensify the Mosaic law. The reason is that the new eschatological situation calls for a new covenant with a new law. This is confusing because the new law contains some of the old law, while replacing other parts of the old law with new teaching.

The word *fulfill* here is important, as it applies to both the law and the prophets. Jesus came to fulfill them both. What the word means in regard to the law is also what it means in regard to the prophets. But when a prophecy is completely fulfilled (in this case in and by the person and ministry of Jesus), then it is complete and done. The same applies to the law, for example, the law about atoning for sins. When Jesus accomplishes this on the cross, those laws are no longer binding on Jesus' followers.

The goal or purpose of such laws has been accomplished by and in Jesus. What is also important here is that Jesus is making clear that the law is *not* being replaced by grace alone. Indeed it is not. For one thing, grace and mercy were already in the

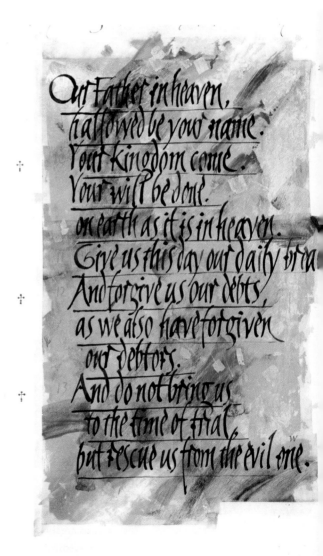

Figure 6.4 This painting of the Lord's prayer is from the *St. John's Bible*. "Lord's Prayer," Donald Jackson, Copyright 2002, The Saint John's Bible, *Order of Saint Benedict, Collegeville, Minnesota, USA. Used by permission. All rights reserved.*

Mosaic covenant. For another thing, Jesus expects a high standard of obedience from his disciples, obedience to the commands he gives. There is still law or demand in the new covenant just as there was in the old covenant.

The difference is that under the *new covenant, Jesus himself is the game changer* who has fulfilled the role Israel was to play of being the obedient son and the light to one and all, so now obedience to the new covenant has to do with pleasing Christ and emulating his character and behavior. Jesus clearly believes that God graciously enables his followers to do what he commands them to do. *By God's grace, even anger can be controlled, oaths and divorce can be avoided, enemies can be loved, retaliation can be avoided, and so on.*

We conclude this brief consideration of the Sermon on the Mount by examining the so-called Lord's Prayer in Mt. 6.9–13. This model prayer is not meant to list all the things that we can or ought to pray about and for but to give us a sense of the sorts or *types* of things to pray about. It is more naturally called the Disciple's Prayer, in which Jesus instructs us about the manner of proper praying. One thing Jesus clearly does not like is ostentatious public praying to impress others. He also recommends private prayer by oneself, but he certainly does not rule out some forms of public and corporate prayers. The Lord's Prayer is meant to be prayed with others—hence "give *us* this day . . . forgive *us*. . . ." This is a prayer disciples should pray together and help each other to live out. The prayer, which would originally have been given in Aramaic, begins with the word **Abba**, which means "father dearest" (it is not slang, and does not mean "daddy"). The term indicates an intimate relationship with God, but it is also a term of respect. God by definition dwells in his own dwelling place—heaven.

The next clause in the prayer is probably intended to be an invocation, not a statement—God's name is hallowed by the disciples and praying this prayer is part of doing so. Praying for God's kingdom to come fully on earth indicates that even during the ministry of Jesus, it had not yet fully done so. "Kingdom" here refers to God's final saving reign, which already exists in heaven and one day will fully come to fruition on earth. What this implies as well, in light of the next clause, is that God's will is not now fully being done on earth, or otherwise there would not be any purpose in praying for the kingdom to come and God's will to be done. It should be noticed that the first personal petition comes with the request for daily bread. This is a prayer about God providing the basic necessities of life like daily bread and regular forgiveness. We need food, but we also need a clean slate with God and with others to live a healthy and spiritually blessed life.

The petition about temptation has caused a lot of queries. Does God tempt people or lead them into temptation, and if not, why are we praying that God not do so? Here is where we note that the Greek term **peirasmos** can be translated either as "test" or "temptation." Probably the best translation here is "do not put us to the test, but rather deliver us from the evil one" (i.e., Satan). God will test us, and such a test is intended to strengthen one's character; by contrast,

ABBA

An Aramaic term which means "father dearest." The term is not slang for "daddy". The term denotes intimate relationship with deep respect.

CLUES FROM THE CULTURE

When we say that pleasure is a chief good, we are not speaking of the pleasures of the debauched person, or those which lie in sensual enjoyment, as some think . . . but we mean the freedom of the body from pain, and the soul from confusion. . . . It is impossible to live a life of true pleasure which is not a life of prudence, honor and justice.

—*Epicurus (cited in Diogenes Laertius*, Lives of Eminent Philosophers *10.131, 141).*

PEIRASMOS

A Greek word that can be translated as either "test" or "temptation."

Satan tempts the disciple, and the intent of the temptation is to destroy one's character. It is also possible that the original Aramaic form of the prayer meant "cause us not to yield to temptation" (see Mt. 26.41, "pray that you do not enter into temptation, the time of trial").

At the very end of the Sermon on the Mount, there is a little parable that suggests that if the instructions and commands are followed and obeyed, then one will be building one's life on solid rock rather than sand. As it turns out, Jesus' definition of the good life is one that involves rigor and vigor, challenges and obedience. Taking the path less traveled makes all the difference, however narrow the path may sometimes seem. At the end of the day, Mt. 5–7 contains the blueprint for imitating Christ and his own life pattern.

THE PETER PRINCIPLE

Probably no one tried harder to imitate Jesus and follow his instructions than Simon bar Jonah. His story is told more fully in this Gospel than elsewhere, and it will be well to review the things we learn from Matthew about him. Let's talk about his name first. Simon was a popular name in that era because of the Maccabees, whose great leader bore that name. Simon is named after a Jewish

Figure 6.5 Insula homes in Capernaum.

war hero who helped liberate Israel and Jerusalem for an all-too-brief century. Bar Jonah is a patronymic meaning son of Jonah or son of John. Simon was a fisherman, and if the excavations at Bethsaida are any clue, it was possible to make a good living fishing in the Sea of Galilee. The archaeological excavation of the House of the Fisherman in Peter's hometown of Bethsaida shows a large house with a courtyard, an outside kitchen, a large residence, and several other structures.

Our Evangelist is not satisfied with just reiterating Mark's Peter material, although Peter is certainly prominent in that earliest of Gospels. To the Markan material, we can add Mt. 10.2, 14.28–31, 15.15, 17.24–27, and 18.21 (cf. 16.15–20). To the Markan portrait of Peter as part of the inner circle of three among the twelve, with James and John and as always named first among the twelve, we find a fresh emphasis on the nickname Jesus gave Simon—Cephas, which in Greek is *Petros* (from which we get the English name Peter). But Cephas is not a proper name; it means "rock."

So Simon is called "Rocky" by Jesus—which in itself has a delicious ambiguity. One can be as solid as rock, or one can be rocky, and Simon Peter was both. There is also the non-Markan tale of Peter asking Jesus to allow him to walk on the water (Jesus having already set the precedent). And as Mt. 14.28–34 tells the tale, he does OK until he sees the strong wind and becomes frightened and starts sinking. Jesus reaches out and grabs him and says, "You of little faith, why did you start doubting?" You will notice, however, that no other disciple in the boat even attempts to walk on water. Peter deserves some credit for trying.

At Mt. 15.15, it is Peter who asks for clarification about the metaphorical teaching of Jesus about the blind leading the blind. Mt. 16.17–18 is perhaps the most famous of the special Matthean texts about Peter not found in Mark. Peter has called Jesus the Messiah, and Jesus returns the favor by calling Peter Cephas—the Rock. He proceeds to tell Simon that his true insight into Jesus' identity was a matter of him receiving a news flash, or revelation, from God.

Punning on Simon's new nickname, Jesus goes on to say that "on this rock I will build my community, and the gates of Hades will not prevail against it." This is one of the most debated verses in all of this Gospel. Does Jesus mean he will build his community on Peter himself, or does he mean he will build it on the true confession Peter made, or both? Perhaps he means his community will be built on Peter and those like him who make the good confession of Jesus, for the Greek word for rock here actually means a shelf of rocks, and so "rocks" plural. The comment about the gates of Hades in its original context probably refers to the gates into the land of the dead, and so Jesus would be saying that his community will never die out.

Matthew 17.24–27 gives us a uniquely Matthean fish tale. Peter asks if Jesus' disciples should pay the temple tax, and Jesus says that it should not be required because Jews are God's free children and should not be obligated to do this.

Nevertheless, Jesus says do it anyway, so as not to offend the collectors of the temple tax. But where does the money come from? Jesus tells Peter to go fishing and suggests the first fish he catches will have a coin in its mouth! It is not clear whether this is a joke (yes, Jesus had a sense of humor) or if Jesus is serious, as we are not told how Peter's fishing expedition turned out on this occasion.

Finally, in Mt. 18.21, it is Peter who asks Jesus if it is sufficient to forgive someone seven times who keeps sinning against him. Jesus replies seven times 70, which is probably an echo of the story of Lamech in Gen. 4.23–24, who says he will take revenge 70 times seven. Jesus then would be saying that his disciples should reverse the whole tendency of fallen persons to take revenge. They should just keep forgiving until the offense stops. The disciples are to be like the master in offering ongoing unconditional forgiveness. The net effect of all this material is that Peter is given more prominence in this Gospel than in Mark, and he is shown as the disciple taking the lead in various ways and at various times.

If, as we have hinted, this Gospel was written in Capernaum for an audience of Jewish Christians, it is completely understandable why it gives us more of the story of Peter because that was his second home and where his mother-in-law lived. In that village, if anywhere, there would have been access to oral traditions about Peter that would have been unavailable to Mark in Rome after Peter's death. On the whole, it appears that the special Matthean material found in the birth narratives and in the special Peter stories would ultimately have gone back to the Holy family and to Peter himself if, as is likely, they are historical reminiscences.

THE GRAND FINALE

The Passion narrative as recorded in Matthew is dramatic to say the least. Jesus rides into town on a donkey like a Solomon, the only time in the whole Gospel he elevates himself above the crowd, and the crowd responds with Hosannas to the Son of David, remembering once again that *the paradigmatic son of David was Solomon*, so quite naturally we expect Jesus to offer some wisdom in Jerusalem, which he does in Mt. 23 and in Mt. 24–25. The grand entrance is followed by an equally dramatic and authoritative prophetic sign act, namely, the cleansing of the temple. But he doesn't just cleanse the temple, he heals the blind and the lame there, and even the children cry out Hosanna when he does such mighty miracles (bearing in mind that nowhere in the Old Testament does a prophet or even Moses give sight to the blind). There is then a night spent in Bethany followed by the cursing of the fig tree and Jesus' authority being challenged by authority figures, to which he responds with parables about coming judgment and reversal of fortune—the tax collectors and prostitutes will enter the kingdom before those challenging him do so. Matthew expands the teaching material and ratchets up the tension with even more challenges to Jesus than we find in the Markan account. When the authorities try to play the game of stump the sage, they fail miserably. The chief priests, the elders, and the Pharisees all realize that Jesus is telling stories about them, and against them, and they have no adequate response to his powerful parables of judgment. Toward the end of Mt. 22, the Sadducees have a go at the game of stump the sage, and they too fail miserably, understanding neither the nature nor the power of a God who raises the dead. If all this were not sufficient to alienate all these authorities, then Jesus pronounces a whole set of woes on hypocritical leaders in Mt. 23, which we do not find in the parallel account in Mark. Jesus is clearly not following ancient or modern advice on how to be judicious in one's comments. He does not mince words in his pronouncements of condemnation, and this leads to the climactic teaching in Mt. 24–25, the so-called Olivet discourse, where Jesus lays out the prophetic scenario of coming judgment on the Temple after many trials, tribulations, false leaders, and fighting; and then as a further statement about the eschatological situation, Jesus explains that the Son of Man, by which he means himself, will be coming back at an unknown time thereafter to judge the quick and dead, the righteous and the wicked, even the high priest as we hear in the Jewish trial scene in Mt. 26.

Sandwiched between the apocalyptic discourse in Mt. 24–25 and the trial in Mt. 26 is the last supper, a Passover meal with a few disciples, the desertion of Judas, and then the betrayal in the Garden of Gethsemane, after Jesus has prayed for the cup of God's wrath to pass from him—but in the end, he submits to God's will in the matter. Prophetic sign acts lead to prophecies, lead to a prophetic revamping of the Passover meal so that the interpretation of the elements has to do with Jesus' coming death, not the ancient acts in Egypt leading to the Exodus from slavery and bondage. What is most telling about this account in Matthew is that Jesus is portrayed as symbolically distributing the benefits of his death—before he dies! It was to be a death that inaugurated the new covenant "in his blood." Thus Jesus sees his death as an atoning sacrifice for sin, whose benefits will be given to his disciples and those who will become his disciples later.

The disciples fail Jesus miserably—one betrays him, one denies him three times, the rest of the male disciples desert Jesus and leave him to his fate in the hands of Caiaphas the high priest and Pilate. Judas, realizing the magnitude of what he has done—betrayed an innocent man—goes out and hangs himself. Before Jesus is crucified between two revolutionaries (they are not thieves, but rather zealots), Pilate even offers to release either Jesus or a notorious revolutionary named Barabbas. The irony is thick because Jesus is the genuine son of the Father, but the name Barabbas means son of the father. Irony is piled upon irony because the genuine King of the Jews is mockingly crucified under the title "King of the Jews"; and as in Mark's account, Jesus' only word from the cross is a quoting of the beginning of Ps. 22—"My God, my God, why have you forsaken me." As he breathes his last, the earth quakes, the curtain in the Temple is torn asunder from top to bottom, as though the divine presence is leaving the building, and uniquely in Matthew a preview of coming events happens as some tombs are opened and some dead saints emerge alive (Mt. 27.52–53). The only disciples to witness the crucifixion and Jesus' burial, and the empty tomb, and in turn receive the first appearance of the risen Jesus, are the female disciples led by Mary Magdalene (Mt. 27.55–56).

A unique feature of the Matthean account is the guards at the tomb of Joseph of Arimathea where Jesus is laid to rest, and the sealing of the tomb itself. But no such provisions to prevent the body of Jesus leaving the tomb avail because an angel descends and an earthquake again transpires (Mt. 28.1–3); and while the guards shake and become as dead men, the angel shares the Easter message with the female disciples and they are commissioned to go and tell the male disciples Jesus is risen and is going before them into Galilee. No sooner do they leave to do so than Jesus appears to them and they grab him and bow down before him and worship him. When the report reaches the chief priests that the tomb is now empty, the guards are bribed to say nothing to Pilate at all about their failure.

The Gospel comes to an equally dramatic conclusion with Jesus appearing to the Eleven and numerous others in Galilee. Astoundingly it says many worshipped him, but still some doubted. As Jesus once said in his parable of the rich man and Lazarus, if someone will not believe God's word about Jesus, they will not believe even if someone rises from the dead. Jesus offers the great commission to the disciples to go and make disciples of all nations by baptizing and teaching them, and the baptism is to be in the name of the Trinity—Father, Son, and Holy Spirit. Finally, Jesus promises to be with his disciples spiritually forever. The Gospel, which began by telling us Jesus was Immanuel, God with us, concludes with the very same unique motif.

The story is dark and dramatic, and the tone often somber and full of pathos, yet still, throughout it all, Jesus is portrayed as being in charge every step of the way. The authorities cannot refute him, the chief priests and Pilate cannot accurately judge him, and even death cannot hold him. The male disciples desert him, and the female disciples are last at the cross, first at the tomb, first to see and proclaim the risen Jesus.

This story of tragedy and triumph has so many improbable elements in it that most have recognized that it can hardly be a made-up tale. You don't make up a story about a crucified messiah whom God vindicates by resurrection. Crucified messiah was an oxymoron to early Jews, and crucifixion was a sign that a person was cursed and had been publicly shamed. If you want to start a world religion, you especially don't make up a story about women being your chief witnesses of the crucial concluding and salvific events in Jesus' life! This is why many have said "this story is too improbable NOT to be true." You just can't make this stuff up if you're a Jew of the first century in an honor and shame culture that is male dominated and did not trust the witness of women. Thus, Matthew's Gospel ends with a bang, not a whimper, eclipsing whatever was the original ending of Mark's Gospel. It is no surprise that this Gospel quickly became the most popular and most used Gospel in early Christianity. One could call it a full-service Gospel that has everything one could want, and more, in such a narrative.

IMPLICATIONS

Studying the Gospel of Matthew is like sitting down at a great banquet and not knowing what to consume first. It is rich, it is varied, and one cannot take it all in at one, or even many, sittings. It repays close study over and over again. It is not a surprise that this Gospel was the early church's Gospel of first preference, as it is a complete telling of the story of the life of Jesus on earth, from womb to tomb and beyond. Indeed, the Gospel ends with the transition of power from Jesus to his disciples—commissioning them to go and make disciples of all nations. The church has been scrambling ever since to fulfill these famous last words of the risen Jesus.

Alfred Loisy was once credited with saying that Jesus preached the kingdom, but it was the church that showed up thereafter. If this Gospel is to be believed, Jesus also preached the continuation of his community of disciples, and both the divine saving reign of God and that community showed up after Easter. It is not an accident that this "disciples" Gospel has been the one that has most often been taken as the blueprint for wholeheartedly following Jesus whether by monastics like Francis of Assisi, separatists like the Amish, or ardent Protestants like John Wesley who made 11 sermons on the Sermon on the Mount part of his *Standard Sermons* for his Methodists, serving as an ethical touchstone. If you want to understand both the theological vigor and ethical rigor of Jesus, this Gospel is a good place to start.

KEY TERMS

Abba	*Peirasmos*
Ekklesia	Q

FOR FURTHER READING

Clarke, H. *The Gospel of Matthew and Its Readers: A Historical Introduction to the First Gospel.* Bloomington: Indiana University Press, 2003.

Keener, C. *The Gospel of Matthew: A Socio-Rhetorical Commentary.* Grand Rapids, MI: Eerdmans, 2009.

Witherington, B. *Matthew.* Macon, GA: Smyth and Helwys, 2006.

STUDY QUESTIONS

Why does it matter if the virginal conception happened to Jesus' mother Mary?

What should we make of the alternating structure in the middle of this Gospel, presenting in turn a block of narrative and then a block of teaching, and so on?

Why does this Gospel writer give so much attention to Peter?

Do you think Jesus really intended his disciples to live by the Sermon on the Mount? What would it look like if Christians really did follow this teaching in detail?

In what sense was Jesus a sage, or even God's wisdom come in the flesh? Why does the Evangelist portray Jesus this way?

What were the roles of scribes in antiquity, and how does understanding them help us better understand this Gospel and its composition?

NOTES

1. K. van der Toorn, *Scribal Culture and the Making of the Hebrew Bible* (Cambridge, MA: Harvard University Press, 2007), 47–48.
2. See the helpful discussion in H. Clarke, *The Gospel of Matthew and Its Readers: A Historical Introduction to the First Gospel* (Indianapolis: Indiana University Press, 2003), xxi.
3. See the detailed study by Richard Bauckham, *Jesus and the Eyewitnesses: The Gospels as Eyewitness Testimony* (Grand Rapids, MI: Eerdmans, 2006), 294.
4. On the use of Mark and other sources in the Gospels written later than Mark, please see Appendix A where the Synoptic Problem and Q, the sayings source, are both discussed.
5. Solomon was believed in early Judaism to have the wisdom of cures, indeed even the wisdom to perform exorcisms.
6. C. Bauman, *Sermon on the Mount: The Modern Quest for Its Meaning* (Macon, GA: Mercer University Press, 1985), 62.

The Lukan Nativity scene as depicted in the *St. John's Bible.* "Birth of Christ," Donald Jackson, Copyright 2002, The Saint John's Bible, *Order of Saint Benedict, Collegeville, Minnesota USA. Used by permission. All rights reserved.*

7 LUKE the HISTORIAN'S TWO-VOLUME WORK— LUKE-ACTS

On a spring morning in about the year 30 CE, *three men were executed by the Roman authorities in Judea. Two were "brigands" . . . the third was executed as another type of political criminal. He had not robbed, pillaged, murdered, or even stored arms. He was convicted, however, of having claimed to be "the King of the Jews"—a political title. Those who looked on doubtless thought that the world would little note what happened that spring morning. But it turned out that this third man, Jesus of Nazareth, would become the most important figure in human history.*
—E. P. SANDERS[1]

LUKE'S GOSPEL HAS SEVERAL NOTABLE DISTINCTIONS. First, it is the longest of the canonical Gospels by word count (although Matthew has 28 chapters, and Luke only 24, there are more words in Luke). In fact, papyrus experts say that Luke squeezed just about as many Greek letters as was humanly possible on one scroll when he wrote a Gospel. He had a lot to say. In fact, one could say that he wrote a Gospel that is so good, it has a sequel—the Acts of the Apostles.

at a Glance

Luke, the sometime companion of Paul, a second-generation Christian, and likely a Gentile synagogue adherent, is probably the author of Luke–Acts, a two-volume work composed in the A.D. 80s for Luke's patron, Theophilus, to help him understand his new faith and the Christian movement he joined and how it related to all things Roman.

Scholars have long debated whether we should see Luke–Acts as a two-volume effort at one project or two separate books by the same author. Most scholars these days say the former, and the hyphenated phrase Luke–Acts has become commonplace. When you count all the words in both these volumes, which are very long by ancient standards, you have about one-third of the New Testament.

As discussed earlier in this book, Luke's Gospel reads more like a work of ancient history than a work of ancient biography, and because Luke himself links the two volumes in Acts 1 ("In my first volume Theophilus . . ."), and the second volume is definitely not a biography but rather a historical monograph, there is no reason not to view both volumes that way. We need to consider in a bit more detail what an ancient historical monograph was like.

LUKE'S HELLENISTIC, YET JEWISH, HISTORICAL APPROACH TO JESUS AND "THE WAY"

We must be careful when we use the terminology *Luke–Acts* to make clear what sort of *unity* we have in mind by this term. The view that Luke and Acts were written by two different persons is not much discussed today by scholars because of the considerable linguistic, grammatical, thematic, and theological evidence that these volumes both come from the same hand. Most scholars in fact would argue for the theological and thematic similarity and unity of the two volumes. R. Tannehill has argued at length for the narrative unity of these two volumes in the sense that they are bound together by a consistent and continuous story pursuing a particular trajectory and sharing common themes and ideas.[2] More recently, P. Borgman has shown at some length that there are patterns, echoes, and interlocking themes that unite these two volumes.[3]

There are a variety of similar literary patterns in the two volumes—for example, in the parallel way the trials of Jesus and Paul are presented. These similarities have created a presumption in the mind of many that there is also some sort of generic unity shared by Luke and Acts. In regard to the possibility of the compositional unity of Luke–Acts, it must be remembered that writing in antiquity had certain constraints we do not face today.

For one thing, literary texts did not circulate in the same fashion as they do today. They tended first to be sent to patrons or friends who might have copies made for others. In other words, unless a manuscript was deliberately placed in one of the few great city libraries in antiquity, it normally had private circulation only. Occasionally, an author would take a manuscript to a bookshop in a large city like Rome, which would make and sell copies, but we must not think in terms of modern publication methods. The connection between Luke and Theophilus may be important in this regard, especially if Theophilus was Luke's patron.

Another constraint faced by ancient writers like Luke was the length of composition one could get on a papyrus roll. The content of Luke's Gospel represents about the maximum one could include on one normal papyrus roll, writing in a medium-sized Greek script, following the normal procedure of leaving no gaps between words or sentences. Luke's Gospel (19,404 words) would have fit on a 35-foot roll, and Acts (18,374 words) on a 32-foot roll if he wrote in a normal hand and with normal spacing. The sheer length of his Gospel required Luke to round off the narrative *close to* the point where he did, although he could have included a few brief additional narratives of about the same length as the material in Luke 24. What is clear enough is that Luke would never have included all of Luke and Acts on *one* papyrus roll, nor is it likely that Luke–Acts was ever included in one codex, apart from other early Christian literature. Luke and Acts are, respectively, the longest and second longest compositions in the New Testament, making up not quite one-third of the whole New Testament (27.85 percent to be precise).

It is worth noting that the very dimensions of the two volumes suggest that Luke is following ancient Greek historiographical conventions. "Greco-Roman authors often tried to keep the size of books roughly symmetrical (Diodorus *Bibliotheca Historica* 1.29.6, 1.41.10; Josephus *Against Apion* 1.320)."[4] Furthermore, it is surely no accident that the first volume covers roughly the same amount of time (from about 4 B.C. to A.D. 30) as the second volume does (from about A.D. 30 to 60, or to 62 if one counts the reference to "two whole years" in Acts 28). There is also a certain symmetry in the fact that the last 23 percent of Luke's Gospel (19.28–24.53) presents the events leading to and including Jesus' trial(s), death, resurrection, and ascension; while the last 24 percent of Acts (21.27–28.31) deals with Paul's arrest, trials, and arrival in Rome. The question then becomes this: Are there intimations in the third Gospel, *apart* from the preface itself, that suggest Luke intended a sequel?

C. K. Barrett has assembled the evidence, and the overall impression it leaves suggests a positive answer to the question.[5] In particular, the promise of light for the Gentiles, indeed "all flesh," in Luke 2.32 and 3.6, and of help for various non-Jewish peoples implied in the paradigmatic speech of Jesus in Luke 4.24–27, is not truly brought to fulfillment before the book of Acts. Nor, for that matter, is the fulfillment of the promise in Luke 24 of "power from on high" for the disciples recorded in the Gospel; in view of how important the empowerment of the Holy Spirit is in the Lukan schema of things, it is hard to doubt he intended at some point to record this promise's fulfillment.

There was space enough at the end of the roll to include at least some of the material in Acts 1–2 in his Gospel had Luke chosen to do so.[6] Another key foreshadowing comes at Luke 22.33, where Peter says he is prepared to go with Christ *to prison* and to death. The parallels in Matthew and Mark do not include the reference to prison, and "it is hard to resist the impression that this rendering of his words has been formulated with the incidents in Acts 4, 5, and especially

12 in mind."[7] Furthermore, the Lukan form of the telling of the parable of the great dinner in Luke 14.15–24 likely alludes to the gathering of Gentiles to the eschatological banquet. The Lukan form of the prophecy in Luke 21.12–13, which speaks about the witness the disciples would bear, should be compared to 24.48, where the disciples are informed they will be witnesses, a key theme that is then picked up in Acts 1.8. The fulfillment of Luke 21.12–13 is then portrayed in places like Acts 4.3; 5.18–25; 8.3; 12.1, 3–6; and 16.23.

Equally telling is the *omission* of the material in Mark 7 about clean and unclean in the parallel passage in Luke's Gospel, only to see the issue come to light in Acts 10 with Peter. One could also point to the omission in the Lukan Passion narrative of the charge about Jesus attacking the temple found in Mark 14.58, a charge that nevertheless surfaces in Acts 6.14 in the accusations against Stephen. Luke is a good and careful editor of his sources and does not wish to tread the same path twice if it can be avoided, unless there is some special point he is pressing, as with the three tellings of Saul's conversion in Acts 9, 22, and 26.

There are other telltale points in the Gospel that are picked up and further developed in Acts, such as the favorable attitude toward the Samaritans (cf. Luke 9.52–56, 17:11–19 to Acts 8), the idea that Judaism deserves a second chance (cf. Luke 13.6–9 to Paul's repeated returns to the synagogue in Acts), the role of women in the Jesus movement (cf. Luke 8.1–3 to Acts 16, 18 passim), and the clarification that John the Baptist was not the Messiah (cf. Luke 3.15 to Acts 13.25, 19.5).

A great deal more could be said along these lines, but this is sufficient to show that Luke planted some seeds in his Gospel that he did not intend to fully cultivate and bring to harvest before his second volume. The first volume was likely written with at least one eye already on the sequel. In short, there is indeed a compositional unity to Luke–Acts, so we may take the preface in Luke 1.1–4 as meant to talk about Luke's whole project.

Luke 1.1–4 indicates that Luke would do the Greek historian's job and consult eyewitnesses and the original servants of the word, and he would write an orderly account thereafter, so Theophilus could know the truth about "the things that have happened among us." This focus on significant events is characteristic of ancient historical chronicles. Luke would not be writing biographies of Jesus and Paul. He would be talking about what he took to be historic events. He would chronicle Jesus and the rise of a movement called "the Way" in its earliest days.

CLUES FROM THE CULTURE

The people of Claudiconium honored Lucius Pupius Praesens . . . Prefect of the Picentine Cavalary Squadron . . . their benefactor and founder.

—Inscription, Phrygia (cited in B. Levick[8])

WHO WAS THEOPHILUS?

It is possible that the two longest books in the New Testament may have been written to exactly one person, and that they may indeed be the only two books in the New Testament written for only one person. But who is this person? The phrase "most noble Theophilus" indicates that he was a high-status person, and there is good reason to think he was Luke's patron, who sponsored the writing of these long documents. In fact, we can say more than that.

The Greek word *Theophilus* is not likely a cipher for "lovers of God" in general (although that is the meaning of the name), especially not with the additional phrase "o noble . . . ," which was a standard way of impressing one's patron. What I am inclined to suggest is as follows: (1) Luke was not writing to a community writ large, but to Theophilus and his reading circle. (2) Some in the reading circle were literate Jewish Christians, some were Gentile Christians, and perhaps some God-fearers were now followers of Jesus. Theophilus himself was a Gentile, and a new Christian, but also the patron of Luke. (3) As the patron of Luke, he was the one responsible for having Luke's volumes copied and, in a limited sense of the term, "published" and distributed to certain ones among the literati. (4) Luke was well aware of this and writes not just for the reading circle of Christians, but with one eye on a possibly larger audience, say in Rome, that needed some convincing (and some apologetics) if they were to take seriously the claims about Jesus. Among other things, they needed some assurances about the relationship between being a Christian and being a Roman citizen, and about the Christian faith's approach to the state. Luke wrote as an ancient, rhetorically skilled historian in the tradition not just of **Polybius**, but also in the tradition of some of the writers in the LXX, the Greek translation of the Old Testament. He is somewhat concerned with chronological synchronisms between the micro-culture of growing Christianity and the macro-culture of the Roman Empire. We see a synching up of the micro- and macro-history in both volumes (see Luke 2.1–2, Luke 3.1–6, Acts 18.2).

WHO WAS LUKE?

The earliest extant manuscript, **p75**, of the first volume of Luke–Acts has at its end the ancient title *Euaggelion kata Loukan,* "the Gospel according to Luke." This papyrus codex is dated sometime between A.D. 175 and 225. Possibly even a little earlier (A.D. 170–80?) than that inscription is the old canon list known as the **Muratorian canon**, which refers to "Luke the physician and companion of Paul" as the author of a Gospel and Acts. At the end of the second century, there is the testimony of **Irenaeus** in his *Against Heresies* 3.1.1 and 3.14.1, which stresses that Luke was an inseparable companion of Paul, a conclusion also supported by various other patristic witnesses, at least in regard to Luke being a companion of Paul.[9] In fact, the testimony about Luke–Acts from both the manuscript evidence and the church fathers is basically unanimous, but which Luke of those mentioned in the New Testament are we discussing?

The name *Loukan* is a shortened Greek form of a Latin name—either Lucanus, Lucianus, Lucius, or Lucillus. This name does not give us any further clear

POLYBIUS

A Greek historian whose historical account entitled *The Histories* spanned the period between 264 to 146 B.C.

P75

An abbreviation for Papyrus 75 which is called Papyrus Bodmer. This early papyrus codex contains the first volume of Luke–Acts. At the end is the ancient title *Euangelion kata Loukan*, Greek for "the Gospel according to Luke." P75 dates to sometime between A.D. 175 and 225 (or a bit earlier).

MURATORIAN CANON

This ancient fragment is one of the first documents to contain a list of the books that were accepted as part of the New Testament. The canon dates to the second century A.D.

IRENAEUS

A church father who lived in the second century. Irenaeus was Bishop of Lugdunum in the Gaul region. One of Irenaeus' popular writings is titled *Against Heresies*. This work is an apologetic against Gnosticism.

clues about the author's identity, as it could have been used by a Diaspora Jew as well as by a Gentile.

In the New Testament, there are three candidates to be considered. There is first the Lucius mentioned in Rom. 16.21 as a kinsman of Paul, and thus a Jewish Christian. Origen (*Commentary on the Epistle to the Romans* 10.39) knew of various persons who thought this identification was correct. The problem with this conclusion is that elsewhere in Paul the person in question is identified as *Loukan* (Col. 4.14; 2 Tim. 4.11), not as *Loukion* as in Romans. Less plausible is the identification of our author with Lucius (*Loukion*) of Cyrene mentioned in Acts 13.1. This leaves us with the three references in Paul not yet discussed. The only reference in the undisputed Paulines is found at Philem. 24, where *Loukan* is said to be one of Paul's co-workers along with Mark, Aristarchus, and Demas. Although the matter is disputed, most scholars, including myself, still believe that Philemon, like Philippians, was written from a Roman setting while Paul was under some sort of house arrest.[10] This comports with the ending of Acts, which finds the author in Rome with Paul. In regard to the important term *sunergon,* in the Pauline Epistles, it refers to someone who has some sort of Christian leadership role, perhaps as an assistant to Paul in his missionary tasks.[11]

The second text is found in Col. 4.14 and is in some ways even more important. Most scholars still believe that Paul wrote Colossians, but even if he did not, there is no reason why Col. 4.14 could not reflect authentic Pauline tradition about Luke as a companion of Paul. There is no apparent reason why this passing reference would have been concocted by someone after the time of Paul, as it adds nothing to the substance or message of the letter, for it is simply a greeting. Luke is again grouped here with Demas. More important is that here is the only reference to Luke as "the beloved physician."[12] While it has been often noted that Luke's "scientific" preface in Luke 1.1–4 and the use of medical language in both Luke and Acts does not prove the author was a physician, it does comport with such a view.

Even more important than some of these reflections, we have the "we passages" in Acts, which taken on face value do suggest Luke was a sometime companion of Paul on his later missionary journeys. The important point is that these passages comport with other "we passages" in ancient works of history where it is clear that the author was present at the occasion. Acts 16.10–17, 20.5–15, 21.1–18, and 27–28 are the "we passages." If the author was trying to vouch for the eyewitness nature of much of his narrative by inserting a fictitious "we" into the story, we would have expected it to come much earlier and more often in Acts, and we would especially not have expected it to primarily occur in minor spots of no great historic significance—for instance, the brief sea journey between Troas and the port of Philippi.

We can also say that because Luke–Acts was written after "many" had undertaken to give an account of the things that happened in the life of Jesus, and perhaps in the earliest days of the early Christian movement, then we should probably not put Luke's chronicles any earlier than the A.D. 80s, after Mark and the sayings source called Q by scholars, as well as Matthew, had been written.

THE LOGICAL AND THEOLOGICAL STRUCTURING OF LUKE–ACTS

Luke, operating like an ancient historian, drew up his Gospel and arranged his materials according to his sources. The following table should help us see this fact. Notice that whereas in Matthew we alternate between narrative and teaching, in Luke we alternate between one source and another.

SOURCE	LOCATION IN LUKE	MARKAN PORTION USED
MARK	Luke 4.31–6.11	Mark 1.21–3.6
NON-MARK	Luke 6.12–8.3 (except 6.17–19)	Mark 3.7–11a
MARK	Luke 8.4–9.50	Mark 4.1–25, 3.31–35, 4.35–6.44, 8.27–9.40
NON-MARK	Lukan Travel Narrative Luke 9.51–18.11	
MARK	Luke 18.15–43	Mark 10.13–52
NON-MARK	Luke 19.1–28	
MARK	Luke 19.29–22.13	Mark 11.1–14.16

Figure 7.1 The Southern steps leading into the Temple Mount. Jesus surely must have used these on various occasions. (© Mark R. Fairchild, Ph.D.)

The overall structure then of Luke–Acts can be seen as follows:

1. Preface (Luke [Lk.] 1.1–4) followed by the Birth narratives of Jesus and John (Lk. 1–2)

2. The Ministry of John and His Baptizing of Jesus (Lk. 3)

3. The Temptations of Jesus and the Inaugural Sermon (Lk. 4.1–30)

4. The Ministry—the Early Days in Galilee (Lk. 4.31–9.50); Calling of the Twelve, Sermon on the Plain, healings and raising of the widow's son at Nain (Lk. 7.11–17); Queries from John the Baptizer; dinner at the house of Simon the Pharisee (7.36–50); traveling women disciples (Mary Magdalene, Joanna, others); parables; healings and exorcisms; raising of Jairus's daughter; Authorizing; Empowering and sending out of the Twelve; Return of the Twelve; the Transfiguration

5. The Turning Point—Lk. 9.51—Jesus sets his face to go to Jerusalem

6. The Journey up to Jerusalem—Lk. 9.52–19.28—(Sending out and Return of the Seventy, numerous parables found only in Luke—Good Samaritan, Prodigal Son, Rich Man and Lazarus, The Persistent Widow and the Pernicious Judge, The Pharisee and the Tax Collector, numerous healings, exorcisms, conversion of Zacchaeus the tax collector)

7. The Passion Week Events—Lk. 19.29–23.56—from Triumphal Entry to Execution on Friday

8. The Resurrection and the Appearances (all in Jerusalem, climaxing with the Emmaus Road narrative with the final command "stay in Jerusalem until you receive power from on High," and the Ascension)—Lk. 24

9. Preface to Acts—Acts 1.1–11—Recapitulation of Ascension story with command to stay in Jerusalem until the Holy Spirit is sent

10. Disciples Waiting in Jerusalem, choosing a new member of the Twelve, explaining the demise of Judas—Acts 1.12–26

11. The Pentecost Account—The reception of the Spirit, the miraculous speaking in foreign languages, the first proclamation of the Gospel by Peter, the first conversion—Acts 2

12. The Growth of the Church in Jerusalem and the Mounting Opposition, Climaxing with the Martyrdom of Stephen—Acts 3–7

13. First Forays beyond Jerusalem—to Samaria and elsewhere—Acts 8

14. The Conversion of Saul—Acts 9 (retold in Acts 22, 26)

15. The Conversion of Cornelius—Acts 10 (also retold twice more)

16. The First Missionary Journey of Saul and Barnabas—Acts 13–14

17. The Jerusalem Council and its Aftermath—Acts 15

18. The Second Missionary Journey—Acts 15.36–18.21 (Paul and Barnabas split over John Mark, and Paul acquires new co-workers—Silas, Timothy, Apollos, Priscilla, Aquila)

19. The Third Missionary Journey—Acts 18.22–22.30 (Paul returns to Jerusalem and is taken captive after an incident in the Temple)

20. Paul appears before the Sanhedrin, under House Arrest in Caesarea Maritima for two years awaiting trial and release, appearances before Felix and Festus the governors of Judaea ending in the appeal to Caesar (Acts 23–26)

21. The Journey to Rome, including Shipwreck on Malta—Acts 27.1–28.15

22. Paul in Rome under House Arrest awaiting trial for two years (Acts 28.15–31)

What you notice when you consider the outlines of the two volumes is how much they have in common—lots of speeches, some miracles, some major journeys, some trials—but eventually, the Gospel successfully reaches first Jerusalem; and then the Roman Empire between Jerusalem and Rome; and then Rome, the capital itself. The journeying motifs propel the story along as the Good News spreads further and further. Luke deliberately highlights the parallels between what happens to Jesus and what happens to his chief apostles—Peter and Paul— in various ways.

When Luke took up his two-volume work, he knew that, at least in regard to the Gospel volume, various others had tried their hand at writing such an account. Although there will continue to be some debate as to whether we should read Luke 1.1–4 to suggest that Luke proposed to set the record straight, which in turn would imply a somewhat negative evaluation of one or more of

Luke's predecessors, it seems clear enough from Luke 1.4 that Theophilus, not just Luke, had heard various things about the "things that have been fulfilled among us," and that Luke was seeking to offer the proper interpretation of these things. As J. B. Green has stressed, the issue would seem to be not validation but *signification*—How has the past been represented, what is its significance?[13]

In other words, Luke does not primarily intend to *defend* the record of the "things which have been fulfilled among us," but rather to present the story so as to explain it in an orderly fashion that will help Theophilus understand its sense and meaning. "Luke's purpose is hermeneutical. He is not hoping to prove *that* something happened, but rather to communicate *what these events signify.*"[14] By referring to "fulfillment," Luke was suggesting that one can only understand and properly interpret these things in the larger historical and biblical framework he intends to provide. To understand Luke's purposes, one needs to understand something about the way he structured his materials.

There is an overall structure to Luke–Acts that may be stated as follows: Using a broadly chronological framework, Luke recounts the spread of the Good News up and down the social scale from the least to the greatest in Israelite society; and in the course of doing that, a "from Galilee through Samaria to

Figure 7.2 The Pinnacle of the Temple Mount in Jerusalem from which Satan told Jesus to throw himself down. (© *Mark R. Fairchild, Ph.D.*)

Jerusalem" orientation in his Gospel was maintained. Jesus must, in the end, go up *to* Jerusalem; and in the end, the disciples must wait in Jerusalem until they receive power from on high. This stands in contrast to the "*from* Jerusalem to Rome" (and to other places in the Diaspora) orientation of the book of Acts.

Luke, in short, is interested in the universal spread of the Good News not only up and down the social scale but also geographically outward to the world. This theme of the universal scope of this Gospel is announced in Luke 2.30–32: "For my eyes have seen your salvation, which you have prepared in the presence of all peoples, a light for revelation to the Gentiles and for glory to your people Israel." The spread of this Good News even to the least, last, and lost is made clear in the paradigmatic speech in Luke 4.18–21 where Jesus quotes Isaiah 61.

Luke's Gospel focuses more on the vertical (up and down the social scale) universalization of the Gospel, whereas Acts focuses more on its horizontal universalization (to all peoples throughout the Empire). This means that one must take the material in Acts 2.1–21 as setting the agenda in Acts in the same way Luke 4.18–21 does in the Gospel. In Acts 2, various Jews from many nations hear the Good News in their own tongue, which suggests this news is for peoples of all tongues and nations, but to the Jew first. What lies behind this agenda is

Figure 7.3 Jerusalem Golden Gate. (© *Mark R. Fairchild, Ph.D.*)

that Luke believed that Jesus is the *one* savior for *all* peoples, and this is why he must be proclaimed *to* all peoples. There is stress on both continuity of the Jesus movement with Israel and its Scriptures in some ways and discontinuity with Israel in others throughout the two volumes. It is hard to doubt that what determines the discontinuity is the universalistic agenda—those facets of Judaism that make difficult or impossible the welcoming of other ethnic groups into the people of God purely on the basis of faith—and more particularly, faith in the Jewish Messiah Jesus—must be critiqued or be seen as obsolescent.

Even the geographical orientation of the Gospel of Luke is in part caused by the concern about salvation. Jesus *must* go up to Jerusalem, for it is the center from which Jews looked for salvation (Luke 9.51; 13.22, 33, 35; 17.11; 18.31; 19.11, 28). Jesus *must* accomplish or finish his earthly work there so that salvation and its message may go forth from Jerusalem to the world, as the Hebrew Scriptures had always suggested. The belief that salvation comes from the Jews engenders the "to Jerusalem" orientation of Luke's Gospel, which in turn explains why Luke relates the story of Jesus going up to the temple as a boy (Luke 2.22ff.), why the prophecies of Simeon and Anna about Jesus as the world's savior come from the temple (2.25–38), why Luke wishes to show that Jesus is in the line of the Old Testament prophets (Luke 13.33), and finally why Jesus' life and teaching are all presented as a fulfillment of the prophecies of the Old

Figure 7.4 Jerusalem garden tomb. (© *Mark R. Fairchild, Ph.D.*)

Testament (Luke 4.18–21; 16.31; 18.31; 24.27, 45). The disciples must remain in Jerusalem until they receive power from on high, for not only is Jerusalem the place from which salvation comes, but it is also the place from which empowerment to preach it comes (Luke 24.47, 53; Acts 1.4). Thus, Luke 24.47, rounding out the Gospel, foreshadows the fact that Acts will deal with the horizontal spread of the Gospel "beginning from Jerusalem" unto all the nations.

THE GOSPEL OF THE HOLY SPIRIT

The medium by which the Good News message is conveyed is the Holy Spirit, and Luke more than all other Gospel writers stresses the role of the Spirit in both his books. Thus, for instance, in the Gospel, it is by the Spirit that Mary is impregnated (Luke 1.35); the Spirit fills the mouths of the prophets (Luke 1.41, 67; 2.25); Jesus will baptize with that Spirit (Luke 3.16; 11.13; 24.49); but the Spirit had already empowered Jesus (Luke 3.22) and leads him (Luke 4.1) and teaches the disciples what they are to say when they go out and witness (Luke 12.12). The Holy Spirit, then, is the means that empowers the disciples as well as Jesus for preaching, teaching, and healing. The Spirit leads and guides the disciples in Acts as he did Jesus in the Gospel (cf. Acts 1.2, 16; 2.4, 13; 4.13; 10.44; 16.6 passim).

We cannot pause here to demonstrate the lengths Luke went to in his Gospel to show Jesus' concern for the least, last, and lost, including women and the poor.[15] Suffice it to say that when we turn to Acts, we find relatively the same agenda. For instance, Luke reveals the same interest in Acts regarding how the Good News comes to the poor, the oppressed, possessed, and imprisoned, with the Holy Spirit empowering those within the community as the church tries to minister to their needs. We also see reiterated in Acts another Lukan emphasis found in the Gospel—the intensification of demands ("take up [your] cross *daily,*" Luke 9.23; never look back, Luke 9.62; give up everything, Luke 14.26, 18.18–30). These themes are interlocking, and the Holy Spirit is the key that makes proclamation, salvation, liberation, and strenuous discipleship possible. At this point, we would like to give brief examples of how Luke's major theme of universalization of the Gospel to both the up-and-in and down-and-out, but with special concern for the poor, diseased, imprisoned, oppressed, and possessed, is evidenced. In addition, we note the evidence of intensification of demands.

On the poor	cf. Acts 6; 9.36ff.
On the diseased	cf. Acts 5.12–16; 9.32ff.
On women	cf. Acts 9.36–42; 12.12–17; 16.12–15, 40; 18.24ff.; 21.8–9
On the possessed	cf. Acts 8.4–8; 16.16ff.
On intensification of demands	cf. Acts 4.32–5.11

FIGURE 7.5 Call to repent and be baptized at Pentecost. *"Pentecost,"* Donald Jackson, Copyright 2002, The Saint John's Bible, *Order of Saint Benedict, Collegeville, Minnesota USA. Used by permission. All rights reserved.*

The references to the Holy Spirit in Acts are too numerous to list. It is interesting that Luke was not content to show that the universalization of the Gospel involved the oppressed (Luke 4.18). Rather, in truly universalistic fashion, he showed how Christ's Gospel was likewise for the oppressor, usually the upper echelon of the social ladder. They, too, were captives who needed to be set free, whether from money, power, or pious religiosity. Thus, we see Jesus eating with Levi and many other tax collectors (Luke 5.29) or with Simon the Pharisee (Luke 7.36). Jesus redeems Zacchaeus, a tax collector and a rich man who begins immediately to right his wrongs of overtaxing (Luke 19.1ff.). Luke pointed out that it is a Roman centurion, a representative of the Emperor Caesar, in whom Jesus finds more faith than in all of God's chosen people Israel (Luke 7.1–10). Luke even recorded Jesus calling a *rich* young ruler to give up all his money and follow him (cf. Luke 18.22).

These agendas in the Gospel are simply preparation for similar treatments in Acts of people like the Ethiopian eunuch, Cornelius, and others of some social status. One suspects that Theophilus would have seen himself in the telling of the story at various points and would have understood the degree to which the story was for him as well as for others. The universalization of the Gospel will embrace not only all ethnic diversity in the Empire but also people up and down the social scale, including both the oppressed and the oppressor. Furthermore, a concern will be shown in both Luke and Acts for the physical as well as the spiritual welfare of humankind, showing that the Gospel's liberation is meant not merely to come to all people but to affect every aspect of their lives.

Such a total salvation requires a total response of discipleship. One must be prepared to leave *everything* and follow (Luke 5.11), renounce all (Luke 14.33), take up one's cross *daily* (Luke 9.23), and put one's hand to the plow and not look back (Luke 9.62)—agendas reiterated in Acts 3–6 and elsewhere. The whole Gospel must be proclaimed to the whole person in the whole world, for there is one, all-sufficient savior for all, and therefore all must be for this one. You can see from this how Luke's historical and theological urgencies intersect and intertwine in this two-volume attempt at what can be called theological and historical and rhetorical narrative. At this point, we need to examine Luke's theology in a bit more detail.

Several dimensions of Luke's theologizing call for comment. We especially see Luke's hand in the way he structures his so-called travel narrative.

The middle of Luke's Gospel has been called the Lukan travel narrative (Jesus' journeying to Jerusalem between Luke 9.51 and 18.14, in which there is next to no Markan material, only Q and special L material alternating).[16] Luke 9.51 announces that Jesus has set his face like a flint to go up to Jerusalem, recognizing that the time was soon for him to go to heaven.

When we finally get to the triumphal entry in Luke 19, we feel like we have been on pilgrimage for a very long time. But then one gets that feeling with Paul as well as he seeks to journey to Rome via Jerusalem, and this journey has some amazing twists and turns as well (see Acts 21–28). Many scholars have rightly noted that there is a method to Luke's way of presenting materials, and it involves both volumes, with the second volume extending some of the structural elements that were vertical in the Gospels (up and down the social scale and in Judea, Galilee, Samaria) in a horizontal direction as the Word spreads from Jerusalem to Rome. This suggests that the book of Acts was not an afterthought but a continuation that Luke had in mind from the outset, hence all the parallel patterning. I would call this, to some extent, a theological and ethical structuring of materials. An example or two will have to suffice. There are two paradigmatic sermons that set up the narratives that follow them—Jesus' sermon in Luke 4 and Peter's in Acts 2. Luke had carefully structured this material such that his narrative that follows this sermon would demonstrate how the Scripture he cited here (Is. 61.1–2) was fulfilled. We can see this from the following table:

Figure 7.6 Luke's parable of the Good Samaritan. *"Luke Anthology,"* Donald Jackson *with contributions from Aidan Hart, Copyright 2002, The Saint John's Bible, Order of Saint Benedict, Collegeville, Minnesota, USA. All rights reserved.*

Luke 4.18–19	*Luke 4.38–44*	*Luke 8.1–3*
v. 18, Preach Good News and recovery of sight to the blind; Set at liberty the oppressed; v. 19, Proclaim acceptable year of the Lord.	v. 38, Jesus heals Simon's mother-in-law; v. 40, Jesus heals the sick, demons cast out; v. 43, Preach Good News.	v. 1, Preach and proclaim Good News to other cities; v. 2, Healing evils spirits and illnesses in women; examples of exorcism, e.g., Mary, cf. 8.4–15.

We can find something similar in Acts 2. Thus, we have an extended citation of the prophecy in Joel about the outpouring of the Spirit on a variety of persons—men and women, manservants and maidservants. It is no accident that thereafter we have narratives that demonstrate the Spirit changing the lives of men and women and inspiring them to speak God's word in various ways and settings. For example, not only does Peter preach various sermons, as do Philip and Paul, but there are also various unexpected men and women telling the truth and telling the Good News, such as the Ethiopian eunuch (Acts 8); Cornelius the centurion (Acts 10); Rhoda, the maidservant in the house of John Mark's mother (Acts 12); Priscilla, with her husband teaching the mighty evangelist Apollos (Acts 18); and on and on.

Note that it is not just that Luke believed that Scriptures were being fulfilled and coming to pass in the ministry of Jesus and his followers (which is true), but that he sees this as evidence of God's sovereign and saving activity in human history in an ongoing way. He does not wish to tell a narrative that has closure because salvation history was still going on in Luke's own era, from his point of view. Luke is striving for something quite specific in his two-volume work. He wants not merely to chronicle the saving work of God through Christ in human history of his period, but also to provide for the Christian movement a sense of direction, identity, and legitimation.

David Aune has put it this way:

> Christianity needed *definition* because, during the first generation of its existence, it exhibited a broad spectrum of beliefs and practices, sometimes manifest in splinter groups making exclusive claims. . . . Christianity needed *identity* because, unlike other ancient Mediterranean religions, it had ceased to remain tied to a particular ethnic group (i.e., it had increasingly looser relations to Judaism). . . . Christianity needed *legitimation* because no religious movement . . . could be credible unless it was rooted in antiquity. Luke provided legitimation by demonstrating the Jewish origins of Christianity and by emphasizing the divine providence that was reflected in every aspect of the development and expansion of the church.[17]

But there is more to it than that. Luke emphasized the fulfillment of Scripture, which is to say that he is not merely interested in the Jewish origins of the Jesus movement, but he also wants to make clear that it was an outworking of God's divine salvation plan since the beginning of salvation history and the writing of the ancient Scriptures at least, if not before. If ancient prophecies like Isaiah 61 and Joel 2 were coming to pass in the ministry of Jesus and his followers, then there was continuity between this movement and Israel, and also connection between this movement and the God of the Bible, the creator of the universe. It is not an accident that Paul emphasizes this point in the speech at the Areopagus in Acts 17. The history that matters is salvation history for Luke, and the culmination of that historical trajectory comes in the ministry of Jesus and his followers. All of this raises interesting questions about Luke's views of Jesus, to which we turn now in some detail.

LUKE'S VIEWS OF JESUS

Although it is clearly impossible to cover here all the **Christology** in Luke–Acts, one subject of special importance is Luke's use of the *Son of Man* sayings of Jesus. The phrase "Son of Man" was clearly important for the historical Jesus,[18] and it is equally important for Luke. Luke takes over 12 of the 14 occurrences found in Mark, and we find it 11 times in material he shares with Matthew (the First Evangelist only uses it 8 times in the parallel passages), and we find the phrase a further 2 times in material unique to Luke.

In addition, the material is also balanced in its appearance in relationship to important aspects of Jesus' ministry—7 times in relationship to Jesus' earthly ministerial work, once connected with a future but not final glory (Luke 22.69); 6 times in connection with the death of Jesus; and 10 times in connection with a future coming of Jesus. Jesus is not labeled Son of Man in the Infancy accounts of Luke; it is only when Jesus begins to assert his authority in regard to the coming of the Dominion of God and the way that changes the situation in early Judaism (including changing the way one views the Sabbath) that this title comes to the fore (cf. Luke 6.5, 22; 7.34).

At various junctures, Luke is capable of using the title *Christ* (which is not merely a name or a cipher for Luke) virtually interchangeably with *Son of Man* such that Luke can talk about the Son of Man suffering and coming in glory after death, but also the Christ coming in/into his glory after suffering (cf. Luke 9.22, 26 to Luke 24.26). This is all the more remarkable because Luke seems to realize very clearly, to judge from the fact that the phrase *Son of Man* only shows up once in Acts (Acts 7.56), that Son of Man was not a title regularly predicated of Jesus in earliest Christianity or viewed as a pregnant Christological title.

Luke the historian and theologian then has front-loaded the use of this key phrase between Luke 6 and 24 to make clear that although the later church did not find the phrase *Son of Man* so useful, the historical Jesus did, it being his preferred self-designation. This is once more a clear example of how Luke does his theologizing in what can be called a historically responsible manner—one that does not resort to anachronisms.

The one reference to Jesus as Son of Man in Acts 7.56 is remarkable and deserves a brief comment. Here for the only time in any Son of Man passage we hear about the Son of Man standing in heaven, at the right hand of God. This conveys the impression that Jesus is paying close attention to what is happening, and perhaps is standing to receive the first Christian martyr into heaven. Son of Man for Luke is a Christological phrase that can be used to refer to the present and future earthly work of Jesus, but intriguingly it can also be used, just here, to refer to the present work of Christ in heaven. It becomes then a term that Luke does not see as anachronistic past Easter, but it is only a term that apparently

CHRISTOLOGY

The study of the person, nature, and actions or deeds of Jesus Christ. This study is founded mainly on the gospel accounts of the New Testament.

works in a Jewish setting like Jerusalem where Stephen met his demise. Thereafter in Acts, the title never recurs.

Luke's Christology has been characterized by various scholars as an "exaltation Christology," focusing on the fact that Jesus has been exalted to the right hand of God and reigns from there. It is surely no accident that the ascension story appears in both Luke's Gospel and Acts (Luke 24, Acts 1)—in the former case used as a closure devise and in the latter to open the events of Acts and so make the transition to the Age of the Spirit (after Pentecost). Luke thinks not only temporally but spatially about such matters, and the ascension makes clear what happened to Jesus and his body after the resurrection—he left nothing behind but his followers. This is why the sending of the Spirit is so critical in the Lukan scheme of things. If Jesus is absent, then the church must have some other source of divine power and direction, and the Spirit provides both. It is instructive to compare and contrast this ascension motif with Matthew's Immanuel motif, the former stressing Christ's absence after the ascension, the latter stressing Christ's continual presence (although the means of that presence is not specified in Matthew).

Too much has been made of the claim that Luke alone presents us with the doctrine of the ascension, for in fact, we find essentially the same idea in John 14–17, a point reiterated after Easter in texts such as John 20.17; and we could point to the Christological hymns like Phil. 2.5–11, where we also find the notion of the return of Christ to heaven and a place of exaltation. Such an idea is implicit as well in 1 Cor. 15 (cf. Ephes. 4.8), which states that there was a definite time limit to Jesus' appearances on earth after Easter, as well as in Hebrews. If we ask the function of mentioning the ascension, it makes clear that Jesus is no longer a historical figure on earth.

This is why, for Luke the historian, this is an important doctrine; and some scholars have even spoken of the absentee Christology of Luke's second volume, where Jesus is off the historical stage in heaven but still appears occasionally as a character in the narrative through visions. Texts such as Acts 2.33, 3.21, 9.3, 22.6, and 26.13 hammer home the point that Christ is in heaven, and that is where the visions of him are broadcast from to Stephen or Paul (cf. Acts 7.9 and 23.11). It is the Spirit or an angel of God who acts for God and Christ on earth in Acts 8.26–39, 11.28, 12.7, 13.4, 15.28, 16.6, 20.23, 21.11, and 27.23. This may be fruitfully compared to the birth narratives, prior to the birth of Jesus, where again an angel or the Spirit is shown to be active in the lives of these Jewish people (particularly the women in Luke 1–2).

Again, the historical (temporal and spatial) approach to all this theologizing can be seen so very clearly in the use of the term *Lord* for Jesus. Jesus is called Lord in the narrative portions of both volumes (cf. Luke 7.13 and Acts 23.11), in a way that other Synoptic writers shy away from. Jesus alludes to himself as Lord once, obliquely in Luke 19.31–34, but here it means little more than "the master," or even "the owner." But no other being calls Jesus *Lord* in Luke's Gospel, unless the person is inspired (1.43, 76) or an angel (2.11). Of course, once we are past the resurrection of Jesus, various people call him Lord (cf. Luke 24.34 and Acts 10.36–38). This very same sort of phenomenon can be found in Luke–Acts with the use of sonship language applied to Jesus. In the Gospel, nonhuman voices call him son (Luke 1.32, 35; 3.22; 4.3ff.; 8.28); but in Acts 9.20 and 13.33, Paul openly calls Jesus son. Again, only super-humans call Jesus savior in the Gospel (Luke 2.11, 30; 3.6); but in Acts 4.12, 5.31, and 13.23, it is seen to be an essential part of a Christian confession about Jesus.

What all of this tells us is that Luke is supremely conscious of the difference the resurrection makes in the way Jesus was and should be viewed. The resurrection is the watershed event for Christology in Luke's view, and it is one of two watershed events (along with the pouring out of the Spirit) that are the crucial events for Luke's theology about the church. Had Jesus not been raised from the dead, he could not have fulfilled the various Christological roles he is said to fulfill in Acts; and had Jesus not been raised and ascended, the Spirit would not have been sent. Luke has clearly thought through all these matters in a careful historical way.

In light of all these sorts of reflections, it is not a surprise that we do not hear about the preexistence (i.e., his existence in heaven before taking on flesh) of Christ in Luke–Acts, although Acts 2.31 implies that prophetic David foresaw Jesus' resurrection coming in the future. Luke's concern is with the role Christ plays in human history from the time of his birth to his exaltation and beyond. Some scholars have stressed that Luke focuses on realized eschatology (or End Times theology) rather than future eschatology; and this is hardly surprising because in fact, Luke is a historian, not a prophet, but there are some references to the future coming of Christ as the judge (Acts 3.20ff., 17.31), although that is not Luke's primary concern in either of these volumes. Notice, for example, Peter's focus on the whole career of Jesus from his birth as a human being to his exaltation and coronation in Acts 2.22–36. Both in the Gospel and Acts, one of the ways Luke stresses the humanity of Jesus is by the appended phrase "of Nazareth," which interestingly continues in Acts after being prevalent in the Gospel (cf. Acts 3.6, 4.10).

There are various ways that Luke stresses that Jesus is both human and humane, often in his Gospel portraying his compassion in uniquely Lukan scenes. One immediately thinks of the widow of Nain story in Luke 7 or the dialogue with the penitent bandit on the cross in Luke 23. It is of one piece with this emphasis on his humanity that we still find the so-called low Christology at places in Acts—such as Acts 10.36ff., where the one who is called Lord over all "now" had God with him, and God anointed him with the Spirit and power while he was on earth. This is in no way a surprise after one looks at the genealogy in Luke 3 where Jesus is portrayed as the son of Adam, a striking contrast to the genealogy in Matthew 1.

Yet Luke does not neglect the fact that Jesus is the son of David, and so no mere mortal, even when appraising him as a human being. The connection between his being the Davidic Messiah and thus the Son of God is made through texts like Ps. 2.7 (cf. Acts 2.30, 13.33). This shows that even in Acts, Luke does not fail to portray Jesus as a Jew, indeed the Jewish Messiah. This is consistent with the material that portrays Jesus not only as the one who fulfills Isaianic prophecies (see Luke 4), but also the one who is the servant of whom Isaiah spoke (cf. Luke 22.24–30; Acts 3.13, 4.27–30, 8.26–40).

One of the traits of Luke–Acts is that we have a potpourri of Christological ideas without Luke trying to blend them all together. But this is what one would expect of a historian who is nonetheless a theologically oriented historian. Luke is simply trying to represent the variety he found in his various sources (see Luke 1.1–4). Sometimes, Luke's historical orientation has led to the suggestion that Luke has an Adoptionist Christology, that is, a Christology that suggests Jesus by means of the resurrection became more than he was before. So, for example, Acts 2.36 speaks of God having *made* Jesus Lord and Christ by means of the resurrection. This, however, simply reflects Luke's historical orientation. The resurrection changed the roles that Jesus could and did play in the life of his followers. Luke is not pontificating about the divine and human natures of Christ but about a career or role change, so to speak. The issue is not *who* Jesus is before and after Easter, but *what roles* he actively plays and when. Only as the exalted one could Jesus be savior and Messiah of all.

ATONEMENT

Within Christianity this term refers to the suffering and death of Jesus Christ which makes amends for sin and makes possible a relationship between humanity and God. In other words, the term draws a connection between the death of Jesus and the forgiveness of or release from sins.

Sometimes as well, Luke is accused of having no **atonement** theology; but not only does this neglect Luke 24 and Acts 2.38 and 13.38, which connect Jesus' death with the forgiveness of or release from sins, but Acts 20.28 should be mentioned as well. "The blood of his own" referred to by Paul surely makes evident that Luke thinks that the shed blood of Jesus is what dealt with sin and made the creation of a new community possible.

If there is one title that Luke most frequently likes to use to characterize the present role of Christ, it is clearly *Lord,* found some 210 times in Luke–Acts (275 in Paul, out of 717 total times in the New Testament). As Lord, Jesus exercises dominion over the world as well as over his own people. Of the some 104 references to Lord in Acts, only 18 are references to God the Father. Where the terms *God* and *Lord* are combined, it is always the father in view (Acts 2.39 and 3.22); but Luke has a penchant for combining *Lord* with Jesus, or using the phrase "the Lord Jesus Christ" (two titles surrounding one name, which matches up with the Roman nomenclature of emperors and others, e.g., Gaius Julius Caesar). We may compare Acts 1.21; 4.33; 8.16; 15.11; 16.31; 19.5–17; 20.24, 35; and 21.13 on the shorter phrase; and Acts 11.17, 15.26, and 28.31 on the longer one. It is also interesting that the phrase "Word of the Lord" is referring to words from or about Jesus (Acts 8.25; 13.44, 49; 15.35–36). The risen and exalted Lord then is the one a person must turn to not only to be saved (Acts 5.14, 9.35, 11.17), but also to be commissioned for ministry (Acts 20.24) or for "the Word of the Lord." Luke knows very well about the Jewish flavor of most of these titles. For example, Acts 3.18 and 4.26 show that he knows that "the Christ" is a title, not a name, for we find the qualifier "his" (**Christos**, like the Hebrew *Mashiach,* means "anointed one").

CHRISTOS

A Greek term that correlates with the Hebrew term *Mashiach* and means "anointed one."

It is a mistake to focus solely on one or another title or role that Jesus is said to play in Luke–Acts because it is Luke's intent to present us with a variety of images, some more dominant or central than others. We have not, for instance, mentioned that in the Gospel, Jesus is especially portrayed as the eschatological prophet (cf. Acts 4.27 and 10.38), who even calls himself a prophet and compares himself to Elijah and Elisha (Luke 4.24–27), a comparison others make as well (see Luke 7). In fact, Luke 7 should be compared with 2 Kings 5.1–4 and 1 Kings 17.17–24. In Luke 7, Jesus is acclaimed as "a great prophet whom God raised up." In Luke 13.33, Jesus himself alludes to the fact that he must die in Jerusalem as the other prophets did so. Stephen, in his speech in Acts 7.35–37, makes clear that Jesus is a prophet like Moses, giving God's people one more chance to be saved. But this is not all. He is also the one who inspires Christian prophets to speak through the Spirit, so the prophetic witness in Acts comes from the Spirit of Jesus (Acts 2.33, 3.13, 4.10, 13.30–33). This is very striking indeed and shows that Luke is capable of thinking synthetically about the relationship of the son and the Spirit.

R. H. Fuller has offered a useful summary of the Christology in Luke–Acts that shows so very well that Luke is thinking historically about these matters. At Jesus' birth, he is destined and made able by nature and pedigree to be the Messiah for God's people. At baptism, he is invested for ministry by the Holy Spirit and assumes the mantle of eschatological prophet. At death, he is King and suffering servant Messiah, although the latter is not revealed until after Easter, and by Jesus himself (Luke 24). Yet Jesus does not completely fulfill any of the major titles—Son of Man, Son of God, savior, or Lord—until he is exalted to the right hand of God and can truly offer both inspiration and salvation to those who accept him on earth. Then he assumes these roles fully and openly.[19]

Here is a good place to draw our discussion of Luke's thought world to a close. What we have seen is that Luke should certainly have never been accused of not being much of a theologian, which amazingly sometimes was the way he was viewed by scholars in the last century. In fact, he proves to be one of the theologians and ethicists in the New Testament who does the best job of integrating history, theology, ethics, rhetoric, and religious praxis in an intentional way. Luke is careful not to treat theology as if it were just a matter of articulating certain ideas. Theology in Luke–Acts, as in the other Synoptic writers, is grounded in God's saving acts in history, particularly through Jesus and his followers. Luke is the one Synoptic writer who offers us a considerable theology of the Holy Spirit, and not just in his second volume, as he strives to show the continuity between the ministry of Jesus in saving people and the ministry of his earliest followers thereafter, also empowered by the Spirit to preach, teach, and heal. His exaltation Christology is profound, as he believes that a historical series of events—the death, resurrection, and Pentecost—changed the world, formed a community, impelled a mission, fulfilled numerous prophecies, and challenged ancient religions ranging from Judaism to pagan religions of various sorts.[20]

SYNOPSIS OF THE CONTENT OF LUKE–ACTS

Luke is clearly using Mark as only one of his sources for his Gospel; while we find 90 percent or more of Mark's content in Matthew, we only find about 50 percent of Mark in Luke's Gospel. This is no doubt intentional because of the three Synoptic Gospels, Luke is the one who adds the most original content, beginning already in the birth narratives and continuing throughout with many unparalleled parables of Jesus, various episodes with women that we don't find in the other Gospels, a very interesting portrayal of Jesus' dialogue with the other two crucifixion victims on either side of him, and of course the unparalleled and much beloved Emmaus Road story. In effect, Luke tells us from the outset he will do something different. Like a detective reviewing a cold case, he says that many before him have attempted to tell the story (Luke 1.1–4) he is about to tell, but he has gone back and interviewed eyewitnesses and the original preachers of the Good News, and he has fresh material and a new ordering of the data that will bring a new perspective on things. It is clear he is trying to act as a good and careful first-century historian. He knows the narrative he is about to present is not a myth or a romance, it is history—salvation history—and so he must get his facts straight.

So where does he start? After having made up his mind that his first volume will have a "journeying up to Jerusalem, the city of Zion" orientation, not surprisingly he will start with a story about a priest in the temple—Zechariah, a very old priest, whose great day of honor has finally come when it is time to enter the holy of holies. But Zechariah has sorrow in his heart because after all these years of marriage, and well past the age for his wife Elizabeth to bear a child, he has no son to carry on his priestly line. The story then will begin in Jerusalem, and end in Jerusalem in the first volume, and begin in Jerusalem and gradually fan out west from Jerusalem to Rome in the second volume. We would never know from the first few paragraphs of Luke 1 that the narrative was going to be about good news involving a man called Jesus of Nazareth because Luke is writing as a historian, not as a biographer, and he wants to show how Jesus' story is the culmination of the story of Israel and its people. So we hear about Zechariah and Elizabeth first, who turns out to be a relative of Mary, the mother of Jesus. Luke is not satisfied with just telling us about one miraculous conception in a young girl named Mary, he also relates another one involving an old woman name Elizabeth. The story begins in miracle, continues in miracle, and ends with a huge miracle—the raising of a crucified man from the dead. God is intervening to save his people, ready or not. Throughout his account, Luke chooses to highlight the surprising role of women in God's plan—from Elizabeth to Mary, to Anna the prophetess in the temple, to the sinner woman who anoints Jesus' feet in the presence of an irate Pharisee (Luke 7.36–50), to Mary Magdalene and others who became traveling disciples of Jesus (Luke 8.1–3)—something unprecedented in early Judaism. God intends to turn things upside down—the least, last, and the lost will become the most, the first, and the found in God's eschatological Kingdom that is coming. Sinners, tax collectors, and women will make their way through the door first. In a hierarchical world that is male dominated, this message would not come across as familiar spiritual pabulum: it would come across as a threat to the existing status quo.

The birth narratives (plural) are concluded with a brief tale about Jesus in the temple at 12 already demonstrating he is remarkable and belongs there. He is the one the old sage Simon says will be set for the rising and falling of many (see Luke 2.25–52). All this transpires before we ever get to the point where Mark's account begins, namely, with John the Baptizer, and the baptism and temptations of Jesus (see Luke 3). Jesus' ministry begins with his baptism and takes off like a rocket emerging out of the water from a submarine into the stratosphere. Within only days or months, Jesus will be a name of promise, and a name spoken against in villages and towns all over Galilee. In a world without good doctors and medicine, the news of a healer spreads like wildfire throughout the land. But Jesus' focus was on the proclamation rather than the healing. Good News of everlasting life is more of a longer lasting remedy than a temporary healing. But salvation in all its dimensions physical and spiritual is coming through the hands of Jesus. And so Luke regales us with story after story of remarkable teachings—like the Sermon on the Plain in Luke 6; or the unique parables in Luke 10, 15, 16, and 18 about Good Samaritans, prodigal sons, bereft widows, repentant IRS agents (i.e., tax collectors). And if that were not enough, there are actual narratives about how these stories were coming true in the lives of people like Zacchaeus the tax collector, or Mary Magdalene, whom Jesus cast seven demons out of. Jesus isn't just reporting the Good News, he's bringing it to life. So the parables and miracles interpret one another, announcing salvation has once again returned to the land of promise.

By the time we reach the Passion Narrative in Luke's Gospel (Luke 19), Jesus has been aiming for Jerusalem for a long time, indeed ever since Luke 9—the city where the prophets die, the women cry, the sacrifices are offered, and God draws near. And as in Matthew and Mark, Luke tells us that Jesus knows all too well what his fate will be in Jerusalem, indeed he predicts his passion on various occasions, but understanding this is way above the pay grade of the disciples at that juncture. They could not conjure with the notion of a crucified messiah, indeed even less so when Jesus appeared about to take over Jerusalem riding into town as a king, being hailed as such, and then cleansing the temple. But alas, they did not understand that the road to triumph led through tragedy. You can't rise from the dead with an everlasting resurrection body unless you die first. Jesus, as it turns out, did not come to meet his disciples desires, he came to meet our needs—all of us.

It is worth highlighting a few of the touches that Luke the artist adds to the preexisting canvas of the Passion narratives that Mark and Matthew had sketched out. It is Luke alone who tells us in Luke 21.20 that Jerusalem will be surrounded by armies before the demise of the Temple once and for all; and so it was to be in A.D. 70 that Titus completed the siege of Jerusalem and destruction of the Temple. It is in Luke's account that we hear about a dispute among the disciples at the last supper as to who is the greatest, as if they were oblivious to what Jesus had just said about his own sacrifice (Luke 22.24ff.). There is in addition the word to Peter in particular that when he turned back around (after his denials) that he must strengthen his fellow disciples. Jesus had not given up on Peter leading his flock once He was gone. It is Luke alone, as well, who brings Herod Antipas into the Passion narrative in Luke 23, after Pilate has tried to pass the buck ("you're Herod's race, so you're Herod's case" to quote a famous musical about Jesus); but in the end, nothing comes of Jesus' visit to Herod who turns him back over to Pilate. Luke as well tells us that at the trial of Jesus before Pilate, someone accused him of being opposed to paying taxes to the emperor, which is false. Indeed, all of the accusations against Jesus are false.

The poignant conversation of Jesus with the revolutionaries on their crosses on either side of him in Luke 23.32ff. is also unique to this Gospel; and Jesus not only promises a place in Paradise (a Jewish term for heaven) for the penitent bandit or revolutionary, but in the end he forgives his tormentors before he passes away. We see a similar ending to the story of Stephen in Acts 7 where Stephen emulates Jesus' parting words. The shell-shocked disciples are left huddling, hiding in rooms in Jerusalem as the Passover feast ends, that is until women, and then Cleopas who was headed for Emmaus, come and report not merely an empty tomb, or a message of angels, but having seen the risen Jesus.

The story ends with Jesus eating with his disciples once more and with him providing the Bible study to end all Bible studies in which he demonstrated from the Law, the Prophets, and the Writings that it was necessary for the Messiah to suffer and on the third day be raised so repentance and forgiveness could be offered to all. The disciples are then tasked with staying in Jerusalem until the Spirit falls on them, empowering them and inspiring them and instructing them for ministry.

This is precisely where we find the disciples in Acts 1–2; and it is a great pity that in the assembling of the canon, Luke's Gospels was separated from Acts, so that all could see and realize this is two volumes of one work. Theophilus is still the audience in Acts 1, and a remarkable story emerges of changed men and women, the same ones who hid from the authorities behind closed doors shortly before then, who went out to change the world by proclaiming the breaking in of God's saving reign in their day and time. The cast of characters of course changes somewhat. Peter, who is the one main human figure who bridges the stories in both volumes, himself suddenly disappears from Jerusalem in Acts 12 and only makes a cameo appearance once more in the whole book at the council in Acts 15. James, the brother of Jesus, rises to the fore as the leader of the Jerusalem Church when Peter disappears, and we hear about the rise of others—Stephen (albeit only briefly, as he is the first Christian martyr), Philip, and of course Saul, who becomes the focus of the story from Acts 9 all the way to the end of Acts 28. If Peter dominates the first half of Acts, then Paul does so in the second half of the volume. The movement of the Gospel is ever west, and so eventually even the gravitational pull to Jerusalem gives way to the inexorable progress of God's work toward the very heart of the Empire in Rome. It is Paul and his coworkers who spread the Word through Syria, various of the provinces of what we call Turkey now, Greece, Macedonia, and then Italy, not to mention Cyprus as well. God's messengers could be detained, and even face their demise, one after another, but the Word of God and the work of the Spirit would not be stopped before it reached the then known world of Gentiles as well as Jews. Even trials and executions of Jesus, Stephen, and others become opportunities to witness to the very leaders and rulers of the world. As it turns out, they too have an expiration date, for only God's rule will last forever.

Sometimes Luke's account in Acts has been seen as an apologetic work that glosses over some of the problems the early church had within its own leadership in the race to display the great successes of the movement. This is not quite fair, as from Acts 1–15 we hear of disputes and struggles to iron out the message and the practices of the movement, climaxing in the compromises announced in Acts 15 in Jerusalem whereby Gentiles would not be required to become Jews to be followers of Jesus. And while undoubtedly Peter and Paul are lionized in Acts, at the same time their foibles and flaws are on display as well—Peter resists the vision from God in Acts 10, and Paul has to be told no by the Holy Spirit more than once when he tries to go in directions God was not leading him in western Turkey. These men may be depicted as saints, but they are not saviors. They too failed and had feet of clay at times.

Sometimes it has also been asked why it is that the Paul of Acts is not depicted as a letter writer. This is because Luke is portraying Paul the missionary, not Paul the discipler of those already converted. Paul's letters are written to those who are already Christians, dealing with their growing pains and problems. Acts is about the evangelization of the eastern Empire. Along the way of course, Paul regales us with stories about numerous interesting coworkers of Paul—Barnabas, Mark, Silas, Timothy (but oddly not Titus), Priscilla, Aquila, Apollos and more. In the end, we hear of the triumphant arrival of the Message and messenger of the Good News in Rome, courtesy of the Roman jurisprudence system that shipped him from Jerusalem to Rome. Paul is found under house arrest, likely chained to a soldier (talk about a captive audience for the Good News), debating with Roman Jews, and sharing with Roman Gentiles about Jesus.

Luke does not tell us how the trial of Paul in Rome turns out, perhaps in part because he is relating the history of the spread of a Message and a movement and not writing a biography of one man. It is the God-whispered words that were unstoppable, even if the tongues who told the tale were silenced one after another. In reality, because Paul was in Rome by A.D. 60; and the fire in Rome was yet four years off, at which point Nero began looking for scapegoats to blame for the fire; and as Luke says he was only under house arrest for two years, it is likely Paul was released and had several more years of ministry after A.D. 62. This is clearly enough the assumption of the Pastoral Epistles, and it is pointed to as well in the last of the Captivity Epistles, written about A.D. 62—both Philemon and Philippians relate that Paul expects to be released and to head back East. It was thus later in the A.D. 60s that Paul was retaken and executed by Nero, and the story is partially told in 2 Timothy, Paul's last will and testimony. Some scholars have rightly pointed to the Pastorals as telling "the rest of the Pauline story" after house arrest in Rome. I think this is surely right; and so, after exploring the latest of the four Gospels, the one called John, we must turn to Paul's famous letters, our earliest New Testament documents, to hear the rest of the Pauline story.

IMPLICATIONS

In some ways, it is a great pity that the assemblers of the New Testament collection decided to separate the Gospel of Luke from Acts, as they certainly belong together; and the current arrangement of Matthew, Mark, Luke, John, and Acts does not help us at all with recognizing this fact. If the church fathers wanted to keep all the Gospels together, they could have arranged them as Matthew, Mark, John, Luke, and Acts because the sequence was not decided on to follow chronological order (i.e., Matthew was not the earliest Gospel). The only problem with my suggestion is that Luke clearly belongs with the other Synoptics in its presentation of Jesus, and John stands apart from the other three in this regard.

So in the end, there is no solution to our problem of the severing of Acts from Luke. Perhaps, however, Luke intended his Gospel to be able to stand on its own if need be, although his desire was that the two volumes be read together in sequence. I suspect Luke would have been surprised that his volumes ended up separated from one another, but he would have been grateful they were both included in early Christianity's collection of sacred writings. We may be grateful in any case that there was one excellent historian among the Gospel writers who also took time to chronicle the story of the early church, or otherwise it does not appear that we would have ever known much about the first 30 years of growth and development of early Christianity apart from passing comments in letters such as those written by Paul.

KEY TERMS

Atonement   Muratorian Canon
Christology   p75
Christos   Polybius
Irenaeus

FOR FURTHER READING

Bock, Darrell. *Luke.* 2 vols. Grand Rapids, MI: Baker, 1996.

Johnson, L. T. *The Acts of the Apostles.* Edited by Daniel J. Harrington. Collegeville, MN: Liturgical Press, 2006.

Levine, A. J., and B. Witherington. *The Gospel of Luke.* Cambridge: Cambridge University Press, forthcoming.

Witherington, B. *The Acts of the Apostles: A Socio-Rhetorical Commentary.* Grand Rapids, MI: Eerdmans, 2001.

STUDY QUESTIONS

Why should or should we not see Luke and Acts as two volumes of one work?

Why was it important to Luke to emphasize the continuity between the ministry of Jesus and that of the earliest Christians after Easter?

What sort of ancient person could have made sense out of these two long books?

Why has Luke come to be called a theological historian?

What is the relationship between theology and history as Luke presents it?

What sort of images and ideas does Luke use to talk about Christ?

NOTES

1. E. P. Sanders, *The Historical Figure of Jesus* (London: Penguin, 1993), 1.

2. R. Tannehill, *The Narrative Unity of Luke–Acts: A Literary Interpretation*, 2 vols. (Minneapolis, MN: Fortress Press, 1989, 1991).

3. P. Borgman, *The Way According to Luke: Hearing the Whole Story of Luke–Acts* (Grand Rapids, MI: Eerdmans, 2006).

4. David Aune, *The New Testament in Its Literary Environment* (Louisville, KY: Westminster John Knox Press, 1987), 118.

5. C. K. Barrett, "The Third Gospel as a Preface to Acts?," in Festschrift Frans Neirynck, *The Four Gospels 1992*, ed. F. Van Segbroeck et al. (Leuven, Belgium: Leuven University Press, 1992), 1451–66, here 1453ff.

6. Especially because some of the material in Luke 24 and Acts 1 about Jesus' ascension overlaps.

7. I. H. Marshall, *Gospel of Luke* (Grand Rapids, MI: Eerdmans, 1978), 26, cf. 23.

8. B. Levick, *The Government of the Roman Empire: A Sourcebook*, 2nd ed. (New York: Routledge, 2000), 159–148.

9. For example, Clement of Alexandria, *Miscellanies* 5.12; Eusebius, *Church History* 3.4; Jerome, *Commentary on Isaiah* 3.6; Jerome, *Epistle* 53.9; Jerome, *Lives of Illustrious Men* 7.

10. See B. Witherington, *Paul's Letter to the Philippians: A Socio-Rhetorical Commentary* (Grand Rapids, MI: Eerdmans, 2011).

11. See B. Witherington, *Women in the Earliest Churches* (Cambridge: Cambridge University Press, 1988), 111–12.

12. See B. Witherington, *Philemon, Colossians, and Ephesians: A Socio-Rhetorical Commentary on the Captivity Epistles* (Grand Rapids, MI: Eerdmans, 2007).

13. J. B. Green, "Internal Repetition in Luke–Acts," in *History, Literature, and Society in the Book of Acts*, ed. B. Witherington (Cambridge: Cambridge University Press, 1996), 283–99.

14. Green, "Internal Repetition in Luke–Acts," 288.

15. Witherington, *Women in the Earliest Churches*, 128–57.

16. Some of what follows here can be found in fuller form in B. Witherington, *The Indelible Image: The Theological and Ethical Thought World of the New Testament*, vol. 1, *The Individual Witnesses* (Downers Grove, IL: Intervarsity Press, 2009).

17. David E. Aune, *The New Testament in Its Literary Environment* (Louisville, KY: Westminster John Knox Press, 1987), 137.

18. See the discussion in B. Witherington, *The Christology of Jesus* (Minneapolis, MN: Fortress Press, 1997).

19. R. H. Fuller and P. Perkins, *Who Is This Christ?: Gospel Christology and Contemporary Faith* (Philadelphia: Fortress Press, 1983), 81–95.

20. For a similar treatment of Luke in various ways, see the volume edited by C. G. Bartholomew et al., *Reading Luke: Interpretation, Reflection, Formation* (Grand Rapids, MI: Zondervan, 2005).

The glory of the incarnation. *"Christ our Light,"* Donald Jackson, Copyright 2002, The Saint John's Bible, *Order of Saint Benedict, Collegeville, Minnesota, USA. Used by permission. All rights reserved.*

8

The LAST WORD on JESUS— The BELOVED DISCIPLE'S TESTIMONY in the GOSPEL of JOHN

The Gospel of John is like a deceptively clear but deep lake fed by subterranean springs. In parts, it is shallow enough for a baby to wade in. In other parts, it is deep enough for an elephant to drown. Swim at your own risk, but not out of your depth![1]

AS STRANGE AS IT MAY SEEM, the only Gospel in the New Testament where there is direct mention *in the document itself* of who is responsible for its content is the fourth Gospel, known as the Gospel of John. In John 19.35, in a parenthetical

at a Glance

The fourth Gospel is probably the latest of the Gospels in the New Testament, and it is likely based on the testimony of a Judean eyewitness known as the Beloved Disciple, who may be someone named John but may even be Lazarus.

INTERNAL EVIDENCE

Evidence that is found internally or within a text itself.

EXTERNAL EVIDENCE

Evidence that is found externally such as in documents from the church fathers or other contemporaneous or later documents.

SYNOPTIC GOSPELS

The Synoptic Gospels include Matthew, Mark, and Luke. They are called the Synoptic Gospels due to the amount of similarity between the three gospels. Whereas John does have similarities with the Synoptic Gospels, John also contains many differences that do not cohere at the same level as the material or order of events in Matthew, Mark, and Luke.

remark in the third person, a man identified at John 19.26 as "the one whom Jesus loved" is said to be an eyewitness of Jesus' death. Similarly, in John 21.24, we hear again about this Beloved Disciple "who is testifying to these things and has written them down," but then we hear "and we know that his testimony is true." Who is the "we," and even more important, who is the "Beloved Disciple"? Inquiring minds want to know. If you love playing the role of Sherlock Holmes and enjoy getting to the bottom of a mystery about "who did it," then the fourth Gospel is the book for you.

FIRST THINGS

One of the basic principles that New Testament scholars rightly embrace is that the **internal evidence** in the Gospel itself, if there is any, must take precedence over the **external evidence** of later church fathers or later documents when trying to discern who wrote the document. One of the important reasons Christian scholars take this approach is because the inspired text of the Scriptures should be seen as the norm, and any later church traditions have less authority and should be evaluated on the basis of the earlier evidence in Scripture. Even for secular historians, the basic principle of "the earlier the source, the more likely it is to be conveying accurate information about historical events" is fundamental, especially if that source contains eyewitness reports. Because New Testament scholars are divided on who exactly is the testifier in this Gospel, and because early church fathers were not unanimous on this point either, and because we are not even sure the Beloved Disciple is the person who put together the final form of this document (recalling our earlier discussion about the Gospel of Matthew), it would be well to examine the internal evidence closely—especially because this Gospel seems to be written not, or not just, for insiders.[2]

In its unique purpose statement in John 20.31, we hear this: "But these things are written down in order that you might begin to believe that Jesus is the Messiah, the Son of God, and that through believing you may have life in his name." As we shall see, this purpose in itself may explain some of the many differences between this Gospel and the three **Synoptic Gospels**, all of which were written for those who were at one stage or another of being disciples of Christ already.

In the first place, there is no dispute among New Testament scholars that Irenaeus, writing in about A.D. 180, identified John the son of Zebedee as the author of this Gospel and as the Beloved Disciple, and many other church fathers followed him in this. It must be remembered, however, that Irenaeus was the great critic of Gnostic heresies and heretics, and certainly one of his reasons for insisting that an apostle like John wrote this Gospel was that the Gnostics especially liked the fourth Gospel and used it. Irenaeus was trying to rescue this Gospel for orthodoxy, and he succeeded. This does not mean that he was right in his assessment that John son of Zebedee must have been the author of this Gospel. For instance, Irenaeus only knew that someone called John the Elder had assembled this Gospel.

Second, based on the hints of Papias and **Polycrates** (both second-century A.D. church fathers), other scholars, including recently Richard Bauckham, have argued that the author of this Gospel and the Beloved Disciple are one and the same person, and that person is *not* John son of Zebedee but rather the one Papias calls "the elder John." But who is this person? Is he the same John that wrote the Book of Revelation? This seems very unlikely because the Greek style and vocabulary of Revelation are very different from that of either the Gospel of John, or 1 John; although one could conceive of a scenario in which the author of Revelation was also the author of 2–3 John, which are the only documents that speak of an "elder" or "old man" and that he edited someone else's documents. In other words, John the elder would be the author of Revelation and 2–3 John and the editor of the Beloved Disciple's testimony.

The problem with the traditional view that John son of Zebedee is the author is chiefly that it favors the external evidence *over* the internal evidence in the Gospel itself, as we shall see.[3] Although we must account for how this Gospel came to be labeled "John's Gospel," the truth is that the later label on the Gospel may merely refer to the person who was known to have edited and put the document together and not the person whose testimony is found *in* the document. There are a number of odd features in the Gospel itself that cry out for explanation and suggest that a distinction must be made between the Beloved Disciple and the final editor of the document. For example, the "we" in John 21 (mentioned previously) is clearly someone or several someones *other than the Beloved Disciple.*

Here is where we go back to one of our original observations made in the first couple of chapters in this study. The cultures in which these Gospels were written were largely oral cultures. The Gospels were written for ears that hear, to be read out loud in the order in which they appear, and to be read out in their entirety, in this case from John 1 to John 21. Obviously, ancient people must have had longer attention spans than some of us!

So let us suppose for a moment that we are Christians in a house church, say in Ephesus, and we are hearing this Gospel for the first time from beginning to end. Let us suppose as well just for a moment that we had heard another Gospel before—the earliest Gospel, namely, Mark's. This is certainly possible because the majority of scholars think John's Gospel was written in the A.D. 90s, well after Mark's Gospel was written and had been circulating in Christian circles for a couple of decades at least. With these provisos, we must ask, what would the *alert listener likely notice about the fourth Gospel?*

First, one would have noticed that the Gospel of John begins very differently than Mark's Gospel—with a dramatic theological prologue beginning at John 1.1. Second, after listening for 10 or so minutes, one might well be scratching

POLYCRATES

A second-century A.D. church father who was the Bishop of Ephesus.

one's head because the famous and unique Zebedee stories found in the Synoptics *are nowhere to be heard in the fourth Gospel:* (1) The story of the calling of the Zebedees from their nets at the Sea of Galilee is missing; (2) the story of the Zebedees being present when Jesus raised Jairus's daughter is missing; (3) the story of the Transfiguration, which Peter, James, and John alone saw, is missing; and (4) the story of the Zebedees requesting the box seats in the kingdom, one on the right side of Jesus and one on the left, when the Kingdom of God shows up, is missing, and on and on. The point is this—*all* of the special Zebedee stories, involving events that they could be unique eyewitnesses to, are *missing in this Gospel. This is very strange if John son of Zebedee is the author, as there is such an emphasis in this Gospel on eyewitness testimony.*

The next major thing our attentive listener would notice while mentally comparing this new Gospel to what was heard before in Mark's Gospel is that this Gospel has a very different character. In Mark, exorcisms are prevalent, but there is not one exorcism in the Gospel of John! In Mark, Jesus seems to be telling parables everywhere he goes, but there are few sayings that could really be called parables in the fourth Gospel. And if the reader of the fourth Gospel had said at the outset, "this is the eyewitness testimony of the Beloved Disciple," our hypothetical listener would have listened to 10 full chapters (for more than 30 minutes) and never once have heard any phrases remotely referring to what the Beloved Disciple said or did, or who he was. But this all changes when we get to John 11.

At the beginning of John 11, at about the halfway point through listening to this Gospel, our hypothetical listener would have heard these words: "Now a certain man was ill, Lazarus of Bethany. . . . So the sisters (of Lazarus) sent a message to Jesus, 'Lord, he whom you love is ill.'"

Now this alert listener will have realized that this is the first time in the whole Gospel that *one particular person* has been singled out as "the one whom Jesus loved." But after John 11.1–3, we hear this phrase off and on, in one form or another, throughout the rest of this Gospel all the way to the end of John 21. The natural conclusion a first-time listener would draw is that subsequent references to a particular person called "the Beloved Disciple" are surely references to the very same person because only one named person was singled out in this way beginning in John 11!

In other words, the internal evidence of this Gospel itself tells us that the Beloved Disciple is not someone named John but rather one named Lazarus. Even outsiders at John 11.36 who are mourners for Lazarus—who is now already four days dead—remark, "See how he (Jesus) loved him (Lazarus)." The Gospel writer could hardly have made the identification much clearer—both the family and the Jewish officials themselves called Lazarus "the one whom Jesus loves."

We have to let this sink in for a minute. We are being told on one hand that Lazarus is the Beloved Disciple, and on the other hand, he died, was thoroughly dead for three days, and Jesus raised the man that he loved so much from the dead.

Figure 8.1 Steps leading up to Caiaphas's house, where Jesus was taken. (© *Mark R. Fairchild, Ph.D.*)

Thereafter, this same Lazarus, the Beloved Disciple, wrote down his own memoirs, his eyewitness testimony about Jesus—including how he was present at a meal in Bethany after being raised from the dead (John 12), and was present as well, reclining on a couch with Jesus, when he chose to wash the disciples' feet (John 13). When Jesus was taken captive and led off to the high priest Caiaphas's house for questioning, he had access to that house (being known to the Jewish officials who attended his funeral no less—John 18); thereafter, he was at the foot of the cross, and Jesus turned the care of his mother over to this Beloved Disciple (John 19), and he witnessed the crucifixion. Then we are told in John 20 that he was the first male disciple to see the empty tomb, even ahead of Peter. After that, in John 21, we hear about his being on a fishing trip with Peter and five other disciples in Galilee, all of whom had breakfast by the sea together.

Finally, at the end of John 21, we are told a very odd story involving the Beloved Disciple. To set the stage, Jesus has just told Peter that he was going to be bound and taken away just as Jesus himself was, becoming a martyr; and at this juncture, Peter points to the Beloved Disciple and asks—"What about him?" The text then says, "If it is my will that he remain until I come, what is that to you? Follow me." But then the person who assembled this Gospel says, "So the rumor spread in that community that 'this disciple' [i.e., the Beloved Disciple] would not die, but Jesus did not say to him that he would not die, but rather 'If it is my will that he remain until I come. . . .'"

Figure 8.2 Dungeon
beneath Caiaphas's house
where Jesus was held. (©
Mark R. Fairchild, Ph.D.)

Now it is appropriate to ask why in the world we need this disclaimer. Everyone dies eventually. Then the light dawns. The community that the Beloved Disciple was a part of believed he would not die *a second time because Jesus had already raised him from the dead once! They believed that he would live until Jesus returned from heaven, in part based on the resurrection of Lazarus and in part based on the conditional statement of Jesus: "if it is my will."* It needs to be added that this saying by Jesus about the Beloved Disciple does not agree with the prediction by Jesus that the Zebedees would one day drink the same cup of martyrdom that Jesus did (see Mark 10.39). But this apparent contradiction is resolved if in fact the Beloved Disciple is definitely not one of the Zebedees.

But why now, as this Gospel is being put together, do we need this further odd explanation? Surely it is because the Beloved Disciple *has* indeed died once more, although not until he had written down his testimony about Jesus to some extent. Notice that although there is a suggestion in John 21 that Peter would be martyred, there is absolutely no such suggestion about the Beloved Disciple, who probably died a natural death in old age in Ephesus.

And this brings us to that "we" again at the end of John 21. The "we" is presumably the Johannine community who knows the full story of Lazarus and knows he is now dead. Some other member of that community has then assembled this Gospel after the death of the Beloved Disciple. Here perhaps is where John the elder or presbyter comes in—the fellow that Papias mentions, and indeed the fellow who *may* be responsible for 2–3 John (see the reference to "the elder" in 2 John 1 and 3 John 1). He is the person who assembled the fourth Gospel and wrote 2–3 John. He may be the same person as the author of Revelation who is John of Patmos, but it is unlikely that he is the same person as John son of Zebedee. We just have too many Johns in the New Testament (we have not even mentioned John the Baptizer or John Mark in this discussion), and it is not surprising that later church tradition fused and confused several of these Johns into one person.

To be clear then, 1 John and the Gospel of John may be attributed to the Beloved Disciple, a Judean eyewitness to the ministry of Jesus, but Revelation is definitely written by someone else; and 2–3 John, which speaks of an elder or old man, may also refer to the same person we know as John of Patmos. Thus, two persons composed all the Johannine literature (fourth Gospel, 1–3 John, Revelation)—the Beloved Disciple and John of Patmos, the elder John mentioned by Papias. The connection between them is that John of Patmos was probably part of the Beloved Disciple's community in Ephesus before he was exiled; and after exile, he returned to Ephesus and assembled the writings of the Beloved Disciple into the Gospel that bears his name.

If this theory about the Beloved Disciple is correct, it explains in detail why this Gospel is so different from the Synoptics: (1) It was written by a Judean

Figure 8.3 The traditional site of the tomb of Lazarus in Bethany. (© *Mark R. Fairchild, Ph.D.*)

disciple, and therefore it offers us some special Judean stories not found in Matthew, Mark, and Luke—the healing of the paralytic, the healing of the man born blind, and the raising of Lazarus, none of which are found in the Synoptics. (2) It also tells us special stories about Mary at the wedding feast at Cana and at the cross, which is understandable if Mary came to live in Bethany with Mary, Martha, and Lazarus after Jesus died (and Mary was present in Jerusalem thereafter according to Acts 1.14) and related such tales in Bethany. (3) It explains why the only Galilean miracle story found in John that is also in the Synoptics is the famous feeding of the five thousand story. The fourth Gospel does not focus on the Galilean ministry; it focuses on the Judean one and the Samaritan one (notice that John 3–4 involves fourth Gospel—only stories about Nicodemus and the Samaritan woman at the well). (4) It also explains why there are no exorcisms in John's Gospel. According to all four Gospels, Jesus did not do any exorcisms in Jerusalem or nearby.

Perhaps most of all, though, if we are wondering why in this Gospel alone there is such an emphasis on Jesus as God (John 1) and as the resurrection and life, it is because the testimony in this Gospel is by someone whom Jesus raised from the dead. If you are raised from the dead miraculously, this will change your worldview—drastically! This Gospel is written through the eyes of Easter or resurrection faith. So let us see what sort of Gospel this radically different fourth Gospel really is by examining its structure and some of its salient features: but first a disclaimer.

Other views of the authorship of this Gospel are certainly possible, and good scholars have come down in various places on this question. It is not *impossible* that John son of Zebedee had something to do with this Gospel. However—and it is a big however—one must account for the actual internal evidence in the Gospels, the clues to authorship there, and let that be the *primary* evidence and later church tradition be secondary evidence. When you do this, the concrete data in the fourth Gospel do not favor the Zebedee tradition in regard to authorship. The value of a good hypothesis is how much of the actual Gospel evidence and data it explains. No theory explains more of the unique features of this Gospel than the Lazarus = the Beloved Disciple equation, and no theory better explains the label John on the Gospel than that he is the one who assembled and arranged the material in this Gospel and was already an authority figure in the Ephesus Church, being the writer of Revelation and 2–3 John.

THE THEOLOGICAL STRUCTURE OF THE FOURTH GOSPEL

Compared to Matthew's or Luke's Gospel, the fourth Gospel has a very simple structure in four parts—there is a prologue at the beginning, an epilogue at the end, and in between are two major portions: a Book of Signs and a Book of Glory. Here is the outline.

OUTLINE OF JOHN 1.1–21	
Prologue	1.1–18
Book of Signs	1.19–12.50
1. Water to wine at Cana	2.1–12
2. Curing the official's son at Cana	4.46–54
3. Curing the paralytic at Bethesda	5.1–15
4. Loaves and fish multiplied in Galilee	6.1–15
5. Walking upon the sea in Galilee	6.16–21
6. Curing the blind man in Jerusalem	9.1–41
7. Raising Lazarus from the dead	11.1–53
Book of Glory	13.1–20.31
Epilogue	21*

*This outline we owe to Raymond Brown, *The Gospel of John*, vol. 1 (New York: Doubleday, 1966), cxl–cxli.

Nothing happens in the Gospel of John by accident, and none of the arrangement of the material is careless. There are seven sign narratives (as described above), seven "I Am" sayings (described in "A Closer Look"), and seven discourses tagged to the "I Am" sayings. Remember that seven is the symbolic number in early Judaism for perfection, so this Gospel is proclaiming over and over again that the Perfect One, the Savior of the World, has finally come, eclipsing all that has gone before. A further part of that motif is that in the early portions of this Gospel, we are being told that Jesus sums up and fulfills all the earlier institutions of Judaism—he is the Passover lamb; he is the temple (the place where God dwells on earth); he is the manna that came down from heaven ("I am the bread of life"); he is the Day of Atonement, atoning for the sins of one and all; he is the one who replaces Jewish purification water with the new wine of the Gospel; and so on. This in part explains why, in the Gospel of John, Jesus' cleansing of the Temple happens early in the story, not much later in the Passion narrative (cf. Jn. 2.13–22 to Mk. 11.15–19). All four Gospels agree—Jesus cleansed the Temple in Jerusalem only once. But the placement of the story in John's Gospel is theological, not chronological.

A CLOSER LOOK THE I AM SAYINGS

Let us first list the I Am sayings:
1) I am the bread of life. (John 6.35; cf. verses 41, 48, 51)
2) I am the light of the world. (John 8.12; cf. verses 18, 23)
3) I am the gate of the sheep. (John 10.7, 9)
4) I am the good shepherd. (John 10.11, 14)
5) I am the resurrection and the life. (John 11.25)
6) I am the way, the truth, and the life. (John 14.6)
7) I am the true vine. (John 15.1, 5)

These sayings, and the discourses that go with them, contribute to the uniqueness of this Gospel. You will notice that we find the first five in the Book of Signs portion of this Gospel, and the last two are in the Book of Glory. So they help link the two major parts of this Gospel together, and none of them appears before the sixth chapter of this Gospel.

The next thing to notice about this material is that almost every one of those predicates—light, life, bread, truth—had already been used to describe personified Wisdom in earlier Jewish Wisdom literature (in Prov. 3.8–9; see especially Prov. 8.35–36, 9.5; Wisdom of Solomon 7.25–26, 8.8, 11.4; Sirach; and 1 Enoch 42). The point here is that Jesus in person is the embodiment of these things that previously were only a personification, or at best were incarnated in the Torah, the Old Testament.

The fifth and sixth of these sayings are of the nature of summary statements. The essence of this is that Jesus is the true life and light revealed to humanity. He is both the revealer of everlasting life and the way to obtain it.

Besides these sorts of I Am sayings, there are other ones as well where the phrase "I Am" does not have a predicate. So, when Jesus walks on the water, he tells the disciples that they should not be afraid: "It is I" (6.20). More important is John 8.58: "Before Abraham was, I Am," a saying that confirms what John 1 told us—the son was present in heaven before he took on flesh and dwelt among us. All of these I Am sayings are meant to associate the son with the father so that we are not surprised when we also hear "I and the father are one."

When we raise the question of why none of this material is in the first three Gospels, there is a reasonable answer we can now give. This is the sort of teaching Jesus did in Judea; but he took a different approach, offering many parables, in Galilee. And indeed, as John 14–17 suggests, much of this was in-house teaching for the disciples as well. What is clear is that the Beloved Disciple has recast the teaching of Jesus in a wisdom idiom to make clear various things about Jesus being God come in person to his people as light and life and healing.

The one figure who is a constant throughout the fourth Gospel other than Jesus is Peter, who is called Cephas at the outset of the account in John 1.40–42, not later as in Mark 8. The emphasis in John 1.43–44 is that Peter is a fisherman from Bethsaida (rather than focusing on his Capernaum connections), a small fishing village on top of a hill overlooking the northwest corner of the Sea of Galilee, north of Capernaum and Migdal. Peter continues to be a prominent figure throughout the Johannine story, right to the end of the story, but notice how he is partially eclipsed by the positive portrayal of the Beloved Disciple from John 11–21.

That is, when the story focuses on Judaea and Jerusalem, the Beloved Disciple comes front and center. It is the Beloved Disciple who gains entrance into the high priest's house while Peter must wait outside. It is the Beloved Disciple who is the only male at the foot of the cross, with Peter nowhere in sight, indeed having already denied knowing Jesus. It is the Beloved Disciple who knows where the empty tomb is, beats Peter there, and believes something about Jesus on the basis of the empty tomb while Peter is left scratching his head. It is the Beloved Disciple who is spiritually in tune enough to recognize Jesus on the seashore in John 21; and at the end of that chapter, Peter himself is comparing his own fate to that of the Beloved Disciple.

Another feature of this Gospel that makes it stand out is what E. Kasemann once remarked on—Jesus bestrides the stage of this Gospel like a God.[4] There is nothing veiled about the presentation of Jesus as divine in this Gospel in contrast with Mark's Gospel. Indeed, the prologue tells us in the very first few verses that "the Word was God," and we hear Jesus say amazing things like "before Abraham was, I Am," which is perhaps an allusion to God's calling himself "I Am that I Am" in conversation with Moses (Exodus 3.14). At the same time, Jesus is clearly presented as mortal in this Gospel as well—he is thirsty (cf. John 4 and John 19 on the cross), he eats, he grows tired, and indeed he dies like humans do.

In fact, there is a V pattern to the telling of the story of Jesus in this Gospel. He came down from heaven, the divine Son of God taking on mortal flesh, he lived among us, and then he went back up to heaven. This pilgrimage is so important to the author of this Gospel that at various points it is emphasized that unless you know where Jesus came from, you cannot know who he is, and unless you know where he is going, you also will be impaired in your understanding of Jesus. Jesus comes from God the Father, as his only begotten Son, and returns to heaven after rising from the dead. So, for example, in John 9.29 the Jewish officials admit they do not even know where Jesus comes from. The idea of the heavenly Son of God taking on flesh is a theological explanation of the origins of Jesus that came to be called the Incarnation.

One of the key aspects of the storytelling in the Gospel of John is that this Gospel, perhaps more clearly than others, is building to a climax from the very

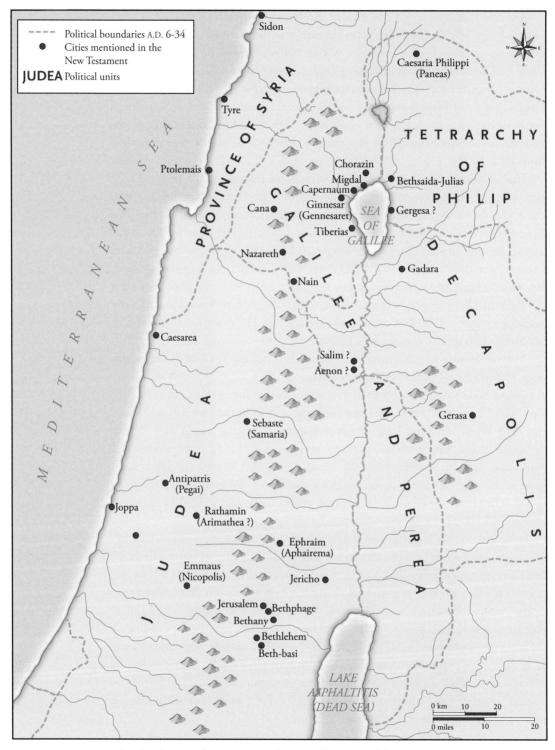

Map 8.1 A map of the Holy Land during the reign of the Herods.

beginning. We have a crescendo of the miracles. Look again at the list of the sign narratives in the Book of Signs. Turning water into gallons of wine is mere child's play compared to giving sight to a man born blind or raising a man from the dead who was four days dead. In early Judaism, there was a saying that because there are no stories in the Old Testament about a blind person miraculously receiving sight, when it happened, one would know the Messiah had come. And as for raising Lazarus from the dead, early Jews believed that after three days, the spirit of the deceased departed and returned to God. But Lazarus had been dead four days; and yet Jesus, who *is* the resurrection and the life, was able to bring him back to life in this world. And that final sign miracle in fact foreshadows the resurrection of Jesus himself. There are no more miracles between the raising of Lazarus and the raising of Jesus in this Gospel, as if to make clear the parallels.

You may have noticed that in the fourth Gospel, the miracles are called **semeion**, meaning "signs," whereas in the Synoptics, they are mostly called *dynamis,* which means "mighty works." That is, in John there is an emphasis on their symbolic quality, pointing outside themselves to Jesus; but in the Synoptics, the emphasis is on the power in the miracles, letting people know that God's powerful saving reign, his Kingdom, is breaking into human history.

There is also a crescendo of confessions of Jesus. Throughout this Gospel, we find people confessing Jesus to be the Passover lamb, or the Messiah, or this or that; but in fact, all these confessions, while true, are inadequate. The only confession that matches up with John 1's "big bang" statement that "the Word was God" is the confession of Thomas in John 20, where he calls the risen Jesus

SEMEION

A Greek word used in John to refer to "signs."

Figure 8.4 Tel Bethsaida, the home of Peter and his brother Andrew. (© *Mark R. Fairchild, Ph.D.)*

"my Lord and my God." This whole crescendo approach in the Gospel is not surprising in view of the purpose of this Gospel: "that you might believe Jesus is the Christ, the son of the living God, and have life in his name," as John 20 says.

Not surprisingly, if this Gospel is meant to be used for evangelistic purposes by Christian evangelists and teachers, the author realized it would be necessary to use what we call footnotes, or parenthetical or marginal explanations, just as in this book. In fact, there are more of these in the fourth Gospel than in the other three Gospels combined. Here is a look at some of them.

IN PASSING—MEANINGFUL ASIDES IN THE GOSPEL OF JOHN

You can tell a good deal about the audience of the Gospel of John from the passing explanations the author gives them, often in parenthetical remarks. First, there is the repeated translation of Hebrew or Aramaic words in this Gospel, which assumes the audience does not know those languages (see John 1.38, 41, 42; 9.7; 19.13, 17; 20.16). Second, there are explanations of Jewish and Samaritan customs (see John 2.6; 4.9; 5.16, 18; 9.14, 16; 19.31; 19.39–40). There are an astounding 50 examples of explanations of localities, times, or events (see John 1.28; 2.1; 3.23; 4.3–4; 5.2–3; 6.1; cf. 21.1; 11.18). In addition, there are a very few reminders from the Evangelist to Christians about key persons and stories (see John 3.24, 4.46, or 11.2). Sometimes, there are some remembrances of the Beloved Disciple of some small details about what happened (John 7.5 or 9.14), which are not included in any other Gospel.

There are also comments about the disciples' lack of understanding until after the resurrection (see John 2.12, 10.16, 20.9). There are asides about Scripture fulfillment (see John 12.14–15, 37–41; 19.24 or 19.28). There are, in addition, clarifying remarks (John 4.1–2: Jesus did not baptize anyone).

What these remarks suggest is that the audience certainly needs to be given lots of explanation! Looking at all these asides together, it also suggests that the audience lives outside of the Holy Land, does not know Hebrew or Aramaic, and needs some help with Jewish customs. All of this comports with the tradition that the locale of the Johannine community was outside the Holy Land, and it is thought to have been in Ephesus. Here would be where John the elder composed this Gospel out of the testimonies of the Beloved Disciple; and here is where John of Patmos also was involved with the church (see Rev. 2–3); and quite possibly, as we have earlier suggested, these two persons are in fact the same person. It is no wonder that John of Patmos or John the elder was confused with a further one, John son of Zebedee. Ironically, there is only one mention of the Zebedees under that name in the fourth Gospel—it is another passing reference at the very end of this Gospel in the epilogue in John 21.2.

A GLIMPSE OF GLORY—SPECIAL MOMENTS IN THE GOSPEL OF JOHN WITH NICODEMUS, THE SAMARITAN WOMAN, MARY MAGDALENE, AND PETER

The Gospel of John, although it is a form of ancient biography like Mark and Matthew, nonetheless takes a rather different approach to its source material than the three earlier Gospels. Our author has decided that regularly he will present us with longer stories than we find in the Synoptics, stories in which a dialogue leads to something else, sometimes to some action. Two regular features of this entire Gospel are the regular use of irony (saying one thing but meaning another—see, e.g., Caiaphas's prophecy—"it is necessary that one man die, so the nation may be spared" in Jn. 11) and two levels of discussion. Often, Jesus' dialogue partners are speaking on one level, but Jesus is speaking at a deeper and more spiritual level, as we shall see. For example, when Jesus says, "I have food that you do not know of" in John 4, the disciples think he means physical food, but in fact he means spiritual food. Our author clearly wants to present Jesus as addressing different sorts of inquirers or seekers.

One could call this the seeker Gospel because, for the most part, Jesus does not so much call disciples as attract them by some sort of spiritual gravity. And near the beginning of this Gospel, there is a neat pairing of a story about a pietistic Jewish teacher who comes at night to inquire of Jesus and a story of an immoral Samaritan woman who has her dialogue with Jesus at high noon. Clearly, Jesus is prepared to talk with almost anyone, friend, foe (Pilate), rival, or disciple—any time, any place.

The much beloved and much belabored story of Nicodemus has gotten the attention it has in modernity because it involves a discussion about "being born again," a topic near and dear to the heart of modern evangelists, teachers, and preachers. What we should notice from the beginning about John 3, however, is that this is a discussion between two pious Jews. Nicodemus is about as far from being a notorious sinner as my Sunday school pin-wearing grandmother. It comes as a shock to Nicodemus that Jesus says, even to this devout Jew, "you must be born again." It may come as a shock to us as well who have been raised in the church, but we too "must be born again."

The first thing to notice about Nicodemus is that he is a Pharisee. That means, among other things, that like Jesus he believes in resurrection (not all Jews did—for example, Sadducees didn't), and he believes in angels and demons as well. What he was not prepared to entertain, at least initially, is that good pious Jews themselves needed to be converted all over again to God through Jesus. Nicodemus comes to Jesus at night and addresses him as a teacher, using "rabbi," which was not a technical term in that day for an ordained rabbi—it was simply a term of respect for a teacher and means literally "my great one" or "my master." Nicodemus starts out in a flattering way: "We know you are a teacher who has come from God because no one can do these signs that you do apart from God's presence." In some ways, this is an odd remark because the signs are of course miracles, not teaching per se, but Nicodemus asserts that because of the signs, Jesus must be a teacher accredited by God.

Whether this was flattery or true praise, Jesus responds abruptly: "Amen, amen I say to you, no one can see the Kingdom of God unless they are born again / from above." Both in the fourth Gospel and in the Synoptics, Jesus regularly prefaces some teaching with the Hebrew word "Amen." This is odd because normally, then, as now, "Amen" is what someone else says in response to the teacher when he has heard some teaching he affirms. Jesus affirms the truthfulness of his *own* teaching in advance of offering it! In John, he uses two Amens up front when he is about to say something profound and in the Synoptics, just one.

Early Jewish teachers like Jesus often spoke in riddles, or veiled ways, and used double entendres, and we have one here. The Greek word **anothen** can mean either "again" or "from above." Jesus is indeed talking about a birth from above, but Nicodemus, as we shall see, takes him to mean a second birth after one's physical birth. Actually, Nicodemus thinks Jesus means *a second physical birth, which he deems impossible.* Nicodemus says flatly to Jesus, "An old man can't crawl back into his mother's womb and call for womb service!!" Nicodemus can give as good as he takes, and we are meant to think of a lively debate or dialogue here.

Jesus responds again equally directly and says, "Amen, Amen I say to you no one can enter the Kingdom of God unless he is born out of water, and out of Spirit. What is born of flesh is flesh and what is born of Spirit is spirit." These verses are some of the most closely scrutinized verses in the whole of the New Testament, and understandably so. But to understand them, we need to know something about early Jewish metaphors.

In early Judaism, water was a metaphor for semen and also for the amniotic fluid in the womb and for the "breaking of the waters" that pour out of a pregnant woman as she is about to give birth. In short, water has associations with the processes that lead to physical birth. Indeed, in Proverbs 5.15, we hear about how the wife is the cistern in which there is water (a cistern that the husband should confine himself to when he is sexually active, which is here called "drinking"). In an age before hospitals, babies were born at home, witnessed by one and all. They could see the waters break and the coming of the child. The phrase "born out of water" has nothing to do with the later practice of Christian baptism. Jesus is not debating later Christian sacraments with Nicodemus!

Jesus is saying that for a person to get into the Kingdom of God, he or she must first be physically born ("born out of water," born of flesh), and then be spiritually reborn (born out of or from the Spirit). What we have here is Semitic parallelism with "flesh is born of flesh . . . spirit of spirit" and just another way of talking about being born out of water and born out of the Spirit. We have discussed in the beginning of this book how ancient peoples had trouble with the idea that people could radically change, especially when they are old like Nicodemus.[5] But that is precisely what Jesus is asserting. Not only can Nicodemus change, but he must do so if he wants to see or enter the Kingdom of God. Jesus could have gone on to say that in addition, Nicodemus would one day need to be raised from the dead to enter the final kingdom, but that apparently was a subject for another day.

Nicodemus is thinking on the mundane level of a second physical birth, whereas Jesus is talking about a spiritual rebirth. This two-level discussion is characteristic of so many narratives in this Gospel. Eventually, the dialogue turns into a monologue, and it is hard to tell sometimes whether it is Jesus or the Gospel writer who is speaking. In any case, we have in John 3.16–17 a crucial statement that has become one of the most memorized verses in all the New Testament—"For God so loved the world that he gave his only begotten son, so that everyone who believes in him, shall not perish but rather will have everlasting life. Indeed, God did not send his son into the world to condemn the world but in order that the world might be saved through him." God, according to this Gospel, desires that none should perish but that all should have everlasting life.

Several things need to be stressed about the famous saying in John 3.16. First, it does seem to be a comment of the Evangelist because "the son" is spoken of in the third person. Second, this Gospel really does have its own theological vocabulary: "life" is a code word for salvation; "light," a code word for revelation; and "world" (*kosmos*), a code word for the fallen world of humanity organized against God, not just any kind of world. With this knowledge, we can now read John 3.16–17 with new understanding. It means "For God so loved even human beings who opposed him that he sent his only natural (begotten) Son so that everyone who believes in him shall be saved. For God did not send his Son into the world even to condemn human beings that opposed him tooth and nail, but in order that even those sorts of people could be saved." If you think this little dialogue is full of surprises, just wait until you see the next one in John 4.

There is a lot of contextual knowledge required to fully understand what is going on in John 4. Samaritans were not considered full-fledged Jews by most Galilean and Judean Jews. There was a long history of animosity between the two groups, both of which were of Jewish descent. In fact, so much were Samaritans seen as outside the proper bounds of the Jewish family that many Jews would go out of their way to avoid Samaria altogether. Some even said that the whole land had the uncleanness of a corpse (seven full days of ritual uncleanness). So the first really surprising thing about John 4 is that Jesus has parked himself next to Jacob's well right in the middle of Samaria and shows no signs of wanting to leave. His disciples are clearly bewildered. To them the phrase "Good Samaritan" would probably be seen as a contradiction in terms.

The second shocking thing about this story in John 4 is, as John 4.9 says, that Jews did not share meals or the common cup with Samaritans. This too is a shocking breach of etiquette because in the Ancient Near East, you were supposed to be hospitable even to your enemies if they needed drink or food. And yet Jesus asks this Samaritan woman for a drink of water from her cup, and he is prepared to be made unclean by doing so. This does not seem to bother Jesus at all.

The third shocking thing about this story is that in early Judaism, proper protocol suggested that men should not speak with foreign women, or strange women, or even women one was not related to or did not share village life with. And that brings us to the fourth shocking thing about this story, namely, that this is an immoral woman! She is an unknown woman (never named here), a Samaritan woman, and an immoral woman—three strikes against her from an early Jewish perspective.[6] And yet, Jesus, knowing all this, is still prepared to reach out to the woman, for this story is not primarily about Jesus' physical thirst but the woman's spiritual thirst.

We see the motif in this story in two ways. Jesus says to the woman that she should ask him, and he would give her "living water." The normal meaning of that phrase was "running water" (i.e., a creek). So the woman retorts, "if you know where the creek is nearer to town, then tell me so I don't have to come all the way out here to this well." But of course Jesus is talking about living water that slakes the thirst of the soul, not creek water! We see the two-level motif also when the disciples return from getting "takeout" in the Samaritan village. They offer Jesus food, and he says "I have food that you know not of," and they are thinking, "Was there another takeout place nearer to this well that Jesus went to?" But of course Jesus is talking about soul food, and what really satisfies him is seeing the transformation of the Samaritan woman's life through her encounter with Jesus.

There is clear irony in the story as well, for whereas the disciples were supposed to be Jesus' change agents and evangelists, the persons who actually plant the seeds of the Gospel in this story, leading people quite literally to Jesus, are Jesus and the Samaritan woman herself! Jesus' concern for women and his willingness to have them as his disciples is clear from all four Gospels. It was a characteristic trait of his ministry, and undoubtedly, it must have raised all sorts of eyebrows, especially when Jesus began to travel with women he was not related to, some of whom had been healed by exorcism (see Luke 8.1–3). We will say more about the famous Mary Magdalene in a moment.

Notice that there is a rather profound discussion between Jesus and this Samaritan woman about the nature of true worship. The Samaritan woman suggests that it is a matter of which holy mountain one worships on—Mt. Gerizim in Samaria or Mt. Zion in Jerusalem. Jesus replies by saying "you worship what you do not know, but we worship what we know because salvation comes from the Jews. But the hour is coming and is now here when true worshippers will worship the father in spirit and in truth, for the father seeks such as these to worship him. God is spirit, and those who worship him must worship in spirit and truth." Jesus is suggesting that true worship is about sincere, wholehearted worshipping of God. It is not a matter of sacred spaces or zones. Notice as well that Jesus grants that the Samaritans are indeed worshipping the right God, but in ignorance! This text could have some bearing on how Christians might relate to people who are part of other monotheistic religions, such as Judaism or Islam.

The theme of Jesus' relationship with key women plays out more fully in John 19–20, where we hear that women are last at the cross, first at the empty tomb, and first to see the risen Jesus. It is hard to doubt that these stories have historical substance because in that patriarchal world, you would not make women the chief witnesses of the cataclysmic and world-changing things that happened to Jesus at the end of his story. In fact, Miriam of Migdal (Mary Magdalene) is always listed first among the women disciples when we have lists like in Luke 8.1–3 (except once). She seems to have played a similar role to the one Peter played with the male disciples. And sure enough, she is right there at the cross with Jesus' mother and one or two other Marys. But that is not all. We must turn now briefly to John 20, the first Easter story.

According to John 20, Mary Magdalene and several other women went to the tomb of Joseph of Arimathea early on Sunday morning to change the linens and re-anoint Jesus' body. The normal mourning period was seven days, and the women did not want people to have to deal with foul odors when they came to mourn (cf. John 11.39). But what Mary discovered was an empty tomb! Now an empty tomb alone could be subject to all sorts of explanations, including grave robbing, and Mary does not immediately sing the Hallelujah chorus when she sees the empty tomb. Instead, she runs to report to the leader of the Galilean disciples (Peter) and the leader of the Judean disciples (Lazarus) that the tomb is empty. The men come and see the grave clothes, and the Beloved Disciple is said to believe something, but we are not told what. (Did he believe Jesus was raised just as he had been raised, or did he conclude God had taken Jesus up into heaven as he did Enoch and Elijah? We cannot tell.) What is clear is that no one is running around proclaiming Christ is arisen until they actually see him.

Figure 8.5 An ankle bone pierced by a Roman spike. This is how Jesus would have been nailed to the cross. (Ben Witherington)

After the men leave, Mary lingers at the tomb and has a vision of two angels. They sit like bookends at either end of the slab where Jesus' body had been laid. There is a void between them, but it is not devoid of meaning. Wherever in the Bible we encounter angels, they are God's messengers indicating that God is, or is about to be, at work in some dramatic way, and this story is no different. But it is not the angels that bring Mary out of her mourning and grief. It is when Jesus appears in the garden there and calls Mary by name.

As I have said, nothing happens in this Gospel by accident, and we are meant to hear an echo here of what Jesus said in John 10.3—that the sheep know the sound of the good shepherd's voice, he calls them by name, and they follow and obey him. When Jesus says "Miriam," Mary responds "Rabbouni!," which in Aramaic means "my master/teacher." You will notice she does not say "my husband!" despite the hysterical fiction of the *Da Vinci Code*. Jesus was not married to anyone, never mind to Mary Magdalene. He was more than a little busy bringing in the Kingdom of God and saving the world.

What happens next is amazing. Jesus tells Mary, "Don't cling to me, but rather go and tell the brothers. . . ." The first preacher of the Easter Jesus is none other than Mary Magdalene. This story is too improbable to be fiction! It is not the story early Christians would make up about Easter in a world in which women's witness was considered suspect. Unlike Peter and the other members of the twelve, Mary Magdalene did not deny, desert, or betray Jesus. She was faithful to the end and beyond. And she was rewarded by being the first to encounter the risen Jesus who, not incidentally, is tangible, hence Jesus' command "Don't cling to me." A resurrection body is not immaterial, it is just different—immune to disease, decay, and death (see the following on 1 Cor. 15).

One more remarkable story from this Gospel should be considered briefly: the story of breakfast by the sea with Peter and Jesus in the appendix found in John 21. The first thing we notice about this story is that it involves a charcoal fire. The only other place such a fire is mentioned in this Gospel in precisely those terms is the story of Peter denying Jesus three times in the courtyard of Caiaphas, where a brazier was burning (John 18.15–18). But here in John 21, we have a threefold restoration of Peter. Nothing happens by accident in this Gospel, and every detail matters. The threefold restoration is remarkable, but we can only appreciate it fully in the Greek.

In verse John 21.15, Jesus asks, "Simon do you *agape* me?" But Peter replies, "Yes, Lord you know I *philo* you." But that is not what Jesus asked. So Jesus asks again, "Simon son of John do you *agape* me." And once more Peter replies, "Lord you know that I *philo* you." But the third time the verb is changed. Jesus asks, "Do you at least *philo* me?" *Agape,* the first word for love that Jesus uses, refers to God's unconditional love. But *philo,* the word that Peter responds with the first two times, means brotherly love. The third time Jesus condescends to speak in a way that Peter can respond to, so he asks, "Do you at least love me as a brother?" This is too much for Peter. He breaks down and says, "You know everything Lord, you know I love you like a brother." Jesus accepts the level of love Peter was prepared to give then. And he gives Peter a threefold commission to "feed Jesus' lambs, tend his sheep, and feed his sheep." Peter is restored and becomes the shepherd of the disciple group, especially after Jesus returns to his Father.[7]

The Gospel of John is indeed a book that a person can dip into at whatever level he or she is ready to swim, like Peter with his response to Jesus in John 21. In later Christian tradition, this Gospel was symbolized by the eagle because it was said to give the God's eye view of Jesus and his story. We may be thankful we

Figure 8.6 Titulus on the cross. *(© Rick Danielson)*

have four different portraits of Jesus in our New Testament, for Jesus truly was
a man who fits no one formula, fits into no one's pigeonhole, and refuses to be
recreated in our own image. We need these four portraits even to begin to take
measure of the man who was also the Son of God.

SYNOPSIS OF CONTENTS

As we have seen previously, this Gospel follows the same general outline of the
three earlier Gospels (preliminary remarks or prologue, account of Jesus' ministry, Passion week account, stories about an empty tomb and a risen Jesus) with
the same heavy emphasis on explaining the last week of Jesus' earthly life leading to crucifixion and resurrection; nevertheless, this Evangelist feels free to tell
the story his own way, adding lots of Judean content and some unique material
from Galilee and Samaria as well. All four Gospels are Passion narratives with a
long introduction (each spending somewhere between 20 and 30 percent of their
verbiage on Jesus' last week). The Beloved Disciple and John's way of telling the
story is presenting us with seven remarkable miracle or sign narratives rising to
a crescendo and presenting us with seven remarkable I Am sayings rising to a
crescendo, and a series of confessions of Jesus—becoming increasingly on target
until finally "disbelieving Thomas" makes a confession that matches up with the
prologue where we heard "and the Word was God." Along the way, Jesus offers

PARAKLETOS

A Greek word used in John in reference to the Holy Spirit. The term refers to the Holy Spirit as another advocate for Jesus' message and person, just as Jesus was the Father's advocate when he came to earth. The term also means a counselor, one who instructs, gives advice, ministers comfort, and more.

long discourses, first in public, which are linked to each of the seven I Am sayings, and then in private in John 14–17 where they take the form of Jesus' final instructions to his disciples. It is also worth stressing that this Gospel uniquely indicates that Jesus must go away to send the Spirit, and the Spirit will be another ***Parakletos,*** that is, another advocate for Jesus' message and person, just as Jesus was the Father's advocate when he came to earth. The Greek word also means a counselor, one who instructs, gives advice, ministers comfort and more. Jesus is promising that God's presence will always be with them, he will not leave them bereft of comfort, counsel, advocacy, advice, direction, or inspiration; and furthermore, the Spirit is the lead actor as they try to convict, convince, and convert the world. He is God's secret agent on earth, and no one makes this clearer than the author of this Gospel. It is no surprise then that the risen Jesus breathes on his disciples in John 20 in another prophetic sign act, thus promising again he will send the Spirit to them after he ascends to the Father. The alert reader will note similarities with the Lukan account especially of what was to be the sequel to Jesus' ministry in the lives of his followers. This Gospel, like the others, presents us with a remarkable interpretive portrait of the most important figure in human history who was both truly human, and truly divine, and so capable of being what our author says he was—the Messiah, the Son of God, the Savior of the World.

IMPLICATIONS

The Gospel of John is profound, and yet the storytelling is beguilingly simple. It is not an accident that it was this Gospel that most sparked and spurred on the debates about the two natures of Christ, divine and human, when the ecumenical councils were held in A.D. 325 and afterward in places like Nicea and Chalcedon (both in modern-day Turkey). The author of this Gospel and subsequent readers were utterly convinced that Jesus, while being fully human, was much more than that; he was indeed properly called not just the Son of God, but God the Son. Although it has been characteristic of some New Testament scholarship to suggest that such a view of Jesus as both human and divine is something that was later applied to Jesus, like putting a royal robe on a peasant, when in fact the historical Jesus was no such person, the Gospel writers would beg to differ.

The problem with this conclusion is threefold: (1) The Synoptic Gospel writers also believe Jesus is both divine and human and present him that way through the son of Man material especially. (2) The same Son of Man material that draws on Daniel 7 is the very material most easily traced back to the historical Jesus as he explained himself during his ministry. (3) The very earliest Christian documents we have are Paul's letters; and already in these documents written within 30 years of Jesus' death, Jesus is proclaimed both risen Lord and God (see, e.g., 1 Cor. 8.6; Rom. 9.5; Phil. 2.5–11). It does not appear that the earliest Christians were guilty of imposing a fictitious divine halo on a not so divine human figure that managed to get himself crucified.

From the earliest days after Easter, Jesus was seen in transcendent categories, and as Paul reminds us in 1 Cor. 16, he was prayed to by his Aramaic-speaking Jewish followers using the term *Marana tha*. As has often been noted, a monotheistic Jew does not pray to a deceased rabbi to come back from heaven! What *Marana tha* meant was "come o Lord," for Jesus was viewed as a living Lord, part of the Godhead, and so a proper object of prayer and worship.

At the end of the day, the Gospel of John is not a testimony to Christological inflation, nor the attempt to remake the historical Jesus in the image of a God. The author of this Gospel was a monotheistic Jew, who was nonetheless prepared to call Jesus God. He claims to have had personal and firsthand evidence to support his conclusions. We are still trying to come to grips with the implications of the beloved testimony of the "the one whom Jesus loved." We can accept or reject the testimony of the Beloved Disciple, and we can debate who he actually was, but what we should not doubt is that he believed what he said about Jesus; and as an eyewitness of the life, death, and resurrection of Jesus, he was in a position to know the truth of the matter.

KEY TERMS

Anothen
External Evidence
Internal Evidence
Parakletos

Polycrates
Semeion
Synoptic Gospels

FOR FURTHER READING

Culpepper, Alan. *Anatomy of the Fourth Gospel: A Study in Literary Design.* Minneapolis, MN: Fortress Press, 1983.

Keener, C. *The Gospel of John: A Commentary.* 2 vols. Peabody, MA: Hendrickson, 2003.

Michaels, J. Ramsey. *The Gospel of John.* Grand Rapids, MI: Eerdmans, 2010.

Witherington, B. *John's Wisdom: A Commentary on the Fourth Gospel.* Louisville, KY: Westminster John Knox, 1995.

STUDY QUESTIONS

What should we make of the four-part structure of this Gospel, and why is there a crescendo of confessions and of miracles in this Gospel?

Point out some of the differences in this Gospel from the Synoptic Gospels. How would you explain these differences?

Why is the Beloved Disciple such an important, and yet mysterious, figure in this Gospel? When is he first mentioned, and who do you think he might be?

This Gospel has been called the seeker's Gospel? Why?

When there is reference to two levels of discourse in this Gospel, what is meant?

Why is it important to know where Jesus came from and where he is going to understand his story in this Gospel?

NOTES

1. Several commentators on John have made comments like this. This is a composite of what several have suggested.

2. For a recent argument that Lazarus may well be the Beloved Disciple, see A. T. Lincoln, *The Gospel According to Saint John* (Peabody, MA: Hendrickson, 2005).

3. There is the further problem that now there is a Greek papyrus fragment from the writings of Papias that suggests that John Zebedee, like his brother, was martyred early on, which Jesus himself predicted (Mk. 10.37–40). See Michael Oberweis, "Das Papias-Zeugnis vom Tode des Johannes Zebedäi," *Novum Testamentum* 38.3 (January 1996): 277–295.

4. E. Käsemann, *The Testament of Jesus: A Study of the Gospel of John According to John 17* (Minneapolis, MN: Fortress, 1968), 22ff.

5. For more on this line of interpretation, see B. Witherington, "The Waters of Birth: John 3.5 and 1 John 5.6–8," *New Testament Studies* 35, no. 1 (1989): 155–60.

6. There is another famous Johannine story about an immoral woman, the story about "the woman caught in adultery." Unfortunately, while many later manuscripts have this story at John 7.53–8.11, in other manuscripts, it is found in three other places in John, and even in one manuscript of Luke. It is a beloved story looking for a home. It was probably not part of the original form of John's Gospel, but I believe it may well be a true story about Jesus and this woman. It rings true as it presents a Jesus who balances justice and mercy, holiness and compassion.

7. Some scholars have suggested that these two different Greek words, "agape" and "philia," are just synonyms here; and although that conclusion is possible, it seems unlikely in this particular passage. On the other hand, the Beloved Disciple is called by both such Greek words, so perhaps they are right.

PART III

PAUL
and his
RHETORICAL
LETTERS

Ancient temple in Corinth, and Corinthian shop in the foreground like the one Paul made tents in. *(© Rick Danielson)*

PAUL— OUTLINES of the LIFE and LETTERS of the APOSTLE

Marcion [the heretic] was the only Gentile Christian who understood Paul, and he misunderstood him.
—APHORISM OF FRANZ OVERBECK, POPULARIZED BY ADOLPH VON HARNACK[1]

DOUBTLESS THERE WAS MUCH THOUGHT and wisdom involved in the decision to put the Gospels and Acts first in the New Testament, and indeed those books take up about half the space in the New Testament, even though these are not the earliest Christian documents we have. The early Christian movement was, after all, about the Good News of Jesus and its spread across the Mediterranean crescent. It was the early church's Christology more than anything else that distinguished the movement of Jesus from other movements that were spawned by early Judaism, such as the John the Baptist movement.

Figure 9.1 Perhaps the earliest image of Paul in a cave above Ephesus. *(Ben Witherington)*

Yet even a glance, at the Book of Acts reveals to us a person who, humanly speaking, had more to do with the spreading of that Good News than anyone else in the middle third of the first century A.D., namely, Saul of Tarsus, otherwise known as the apostle Paul. As you read through the Book of Acts from about Acts 9 on, Paul and his story increasingly become the focus of the book, so much so that the book ends rather abruptly in Acts 28 when Paul arrives in Rome—and we are not even told the outcome of Paul's wrestling with the Roman justice system!

When we look a little more closely at the New Testament, we discover a good 35 to 40 percent of it is attributed to Paul—13 documents in all, from Romans to Philemon. These documents are without question some of the very earliest Christian documents ever created, and indeed they originated before the earliest of the Gospels or Acts. This should not surprise us because all those cultures were basically oral cultures, and the emphasis in the early years was entirely on the oral proclamation of the Good News about Jesus.

Here, however, is a salient fact we must not fail to take account of—none of Paul's letters are written to non-Christians: *none of them*. Rather, they are responses to already existing Christian situations in Turkey, Greece, and elsewhere where Paul had previously evangelized or where his co-workers had evangelized (see Romans and Colossians). And this brings us to an important point.

Sometimes scholars have complained that the Paul of Acts seems to be a different person than the Paul of the letters. For example, it has been noticed that Paul's writing of letters is nowhere mentioned in Acts. At first blush, this may seem surprising until we realize that only one of the various speeches of Paul in Acts addresses Christians—the speech to the Ephesian elders in Acts 20. All the other speeches Paul makes in Acts are to non-Christians. And it is no accident that the speech in Acts 20 does indeed sound like the Paul of the letters. Again, we must stress that *all of the letters of Paul are written to Christians.* Acts thus is depicting Paul the evangelist, not Paul the pastor, by and large.

The letters, by contrast, are depicting Paul the pastor solving problems, encouraging the discouraged, rejoicing with those who are rejoicing, and mourning with those who mourn. *It is a mistake to assume that either the letters of Paul or the depiction of Paul in Acts tells the whole story or even reveals all the different aspects of Paul and his story.* Bearing that in mind, in this chapter, we are going to look at Paul's story, as we can reconstruct it from his letters, Acts, and other sources. In subsequent chapters (9–13), we will look at Paul's storied world, his letters, and their impact.

A PAULINE CHRONOLOGY

While dates and times are not the most important facts we need to know about Paul, it is important to have a sort of mental framework to be able to understand the historical context of Paul and his letters. Here is a basic chronology that will help us in this regard, though this is not the only way one could arrange the data.

PHASE ONE · PRE-CHRISTIAN SAUL

A.D. 5–10	Saul is born in Tarsus in Cilicia of orthodox Pharisaic Jews who are Roman citizens.
A.D. 10 (or so)	Saul's family moves to Jerusalem while he is still quite young (see Acts 26.4).
A.D. 15–20	Saul begins his studies in Jerusalem with Rabbi Gamaliel, grandson of Rabbi Gamaliel the elder.
A.D. 30 (or 33)	Jesus is crucified by Pontius Pilate.
A.D. 31(?)–34	Saul persecutes the church in Jerusalem, Judea, and Samaria; Stephen is stoned.

Figure 9.2 The Mt. of Olives where Jesus prayed in the Garden of Gethsemane. *(© Mark R. Fairchild, Ph.D.)*

PHASE TWO   CONVERSION AND HIDDEN YEARS

A.D. 33 or 34	Saul is converted on the Damascus Road and then travels on to Damascus (Ananias episode).
A.D. 34–37	Saul is in Arabia, the Nabatean region of Syria east of Damascus, and in the Transjordan (Gal. 1.17). Saul returns to Damascus and narrowly escapes the ethnarch of King Aretas IV, who may have controlled that city once Caligula became emperor in 37 (2 Cor. 11.32 and Acts 9.23–25).
A.D. 37	Saul makes his first visit to Jerusalem since conversion and has a private meeting with Peter and James (Gal. 1.18–20). Saul preaches to the Hellenists and escapes to his home region of Syria and Cilicia by way of boat from Caesarea Maritima (Acts 9.27–30).
A.D. 37–46	Saul preaches in his home region; results unknown or inconsequential (possibly great persecutions—see 2 Cor. 11.23–29). Sometime around A.D. 41–42, Saul has another visionary experience, receives thorn in flesh (2 Cor. 12.1–10), a physical malady likely involving his eyes (Gal. 4.13–16).

Figure 9.3 Petra. Paul may well have evangelized in this city, for King Aretas, who ruled there, tried to have Paul captured in Damascus. (© *Mark R. Fairchild, Ph.D.*)

Figure 9.4 Caesarea Maritima on the coast of Judea where Paul was held prisoner for 2 years.

Figure 9.5 Psidian Antioch aqueduct. *(© Mark R. Fairchild, Ph.D.)*

Figure 9.6 Cyprus Paphos House of Theseus. Where the palace of Sergius Paulus was whom Paul evangelized. *(© Mark R. Fairchild, Ph.D.)*

| A.D. 47 | Saul is found in Tarsus by Barnabas and brought to Antioch; preaches there for a year (Acts 11.25–26). |
| A.D. 48 | Saul makes his second visit to Jerusalem (the famine visit) with Barnabas and Titus (Acts 11.27–30, Gal. 2.1–10). Private agreement is reached between Saul and the other church leaders that he and Barnabas would go to the Gentiles, Peter and others to the Jews, and circumcision would not be imposed on Gentiles. Issues of food and fellowship between Jewish and Gentile followers of Jesus are unresolved (cf. Gal. 2.11–14). |

Figure 9.7 Forum Basilica, Pangaion Mountain, Philippi, Greece. (© *Mark R. Fairchild, Ph.D.*)

Figure 9.8 Acropolis, Athens, Greece. *(© Mark R. Fairchild, Ph.D.)*

Figure 9.9 Apollo Temple, Corinth, Greece. *(© Mark R. Fairchild, Ph.D.)*

JUDAIZERS

Pharisaic Jewish Christians who insisted that, to be true followers of Jesus and part of his community, even Gentiles must keep the whole Mosaic covenant, including circumcision, the Sabbath, and the food laws.

PHASE THREE   PAUL BEGINS HIS ENDORSED MISSIONARY TRAVELS AND EFFORTS

A.D. 48	First missionary journey is taken with Barnabas and Mark; Saul is commissioned by Antioch Church after basic endorsement from Jerusalem (Acts 13–14). He begins using his Greco-Roman name Paulos, visits Cyprus, Pamphylia, Galatia.
A.D. 48	Saul returns to Antioch. Antioch incident occurs with Peter and Barnabas withdrawing from meals with Gentiles due to pressure from **Judaizers**.
A.D. 49 (early)	Paul discovers the Judaizers had moved on to Asia Minor and were upsetting some of his converts made during his first missionary journey through south Galatia (Psidian Antioch, Iconium, Lystra, Derbe). Paul writes his letter to the Galatians shortly before going up to Jerusalem for the third time.
A.D. 49 (later)	Apostolic council takes place in Jerusalem. There is public agreement that Gentiles not be required to become Jews in order to be Christians, although Apostolic Decree (Acts 15) mandates that Gentiles must forsake idolatry, including forsaking dining in pagan temples where idolatry and immorality happens.
A.D. 50–52	Second missionary journey of Paul with Silas (Silvanus) instead of Barnabas and Mark. Silas is the apostolic delegate of James sent to explain the decree in churches with Gentiles, and he has independent authority from Jerusalem, not from Paul (Acts 15.22). Paul travels to Philippi, Thessalonica, Athens, and eventually stays at least a year and a half in Corinth before going on to Ephesus, Jerusalem, and finally Antioch (Acts 15.40–18.23). On this journey, he picks up Timothy in Lystra and Luke in Troas (Acts 16.1 and 16.10ff.).
A.D. 51–52	During his stay in Corinth, Paul writes 1–2 Thessalonians.
A.D. 51–52	The Gallio Incident (Acts 18.12–18) takes place, and there are increasing troubles from Jewish followers in Corinth, which precipitates Paul leaving after he had been there for 18–24 months. (This date we can fix firmly because we know when Gallio was governor of Corinth from external sources.)
A.D. 52	Second missionary period ends with a report to the Jerusalem Church (Acts 18.22) and a return to Antioch.

Figure 9.10 This Latin inscription reads, "Erastus, for the office of Aedile paved this." This is probably the same Erastus called the city treasurer in Romans 16. (© Mark R. Fairchild, Ph.D.)

LATER PAULINE CHRONOLOGY

A.D. 53–57 (or 58)   Third missionary journey. After an 18-month stay in Corinth (Acts 18.11), Paul sails to Syria, probably in the spring of A.D. 53, stopping briefly in the port of Ephesus and leaving Aquila and Priscilla to lay the groundwork for future missionary work. After preaching once in the synagogue and promising to return (Acts 18.19), he goes to Caesarea Maritima, visits briefly in Jerusalem, and returns to Antioch. After a stay there, he sets out on his last major missionary period as a free man, passing through the Galatian region and strengthening the churches there, but pressing on to Ephesus, where he stays for at least 2 and possibly 3 years.

A.D. 54 (or 55)   Paul writes 1 Corinthians from Ephesus; it is not the first letter he had written them, but the first one we still have (see 1 Cor. 5.9–10 on the previous letter). This letter addresses the many questions and problems raised by the Corinthians both orally and in writing in their communication with Paul since he had left there. First Corinthians fails to solve the problems in Corinth, as 2 Corinthians makes clear. News comes to Paul, perhaps from Timothy, of real trouble in Corinth after the writing of 1 Corinthians.

Figure 9.11 Celsus Library at night during a thunderstorm. This library was built in the early second century. (© Mark R. Fairchild, Ph.D.)

A.D. 55

The painful visit to Corinth (2 Cor. 2.1, not mentioned in Acts): This visit is a disaster, as opposition comes to a head. Paul's authority is questioned, and he leaves, feeling humiliated. As a result, Paul writes a stinging, forceful letter (the so-called severe letter), a fragment of which may or may not be found in 2 Cor. 10–13. Titus is the bearer of this severe letter. Paul begins to regret writing this letter, and after some missionary work in Troas, he crosses over into Macedonia, anxious to hear Titus's report on the result of the severe letter (this journey corresponds to the journey from Troas to Macedonia in Acts 20.1–16).

Fall A.D. 55 or 56

After hearing some good news from Titus, Paul writes 2 Corinthians (or at least 2 Corinthians 1–9) with some relief, although he realizes that there are still problems to be overcome. Shortly after, he journeys to Corinth, where he stays for 3 months; he then returns to Philippi in Macedonia at Passover.

Late A.D. 56 or 57

Paul writes Romans from Corinth (see Romans 16.1), shortly before setting out for Jerusalem for the last time (Rom. 15.25).

Figure 9.12 At the Celsus Library, there are statues of the virtues. This one is of Sophia, Wisdom. (© Mark R. Fairchild, Ph.D.)

Figure 9.13 An inscription about the Ephesian silversmiths mentioned in Acts 20 as causing Paul trouble. (© Mark R. Fairchild, Ph.D.)

Figure 9.14 A statue of a gladiator in the Ephesus Museum. (© Mark R. Fairchild, Ph.D.)

Fig 9.15 A statue of Nike the Goddess of Victory at the top of Curetes Street in Ephesus. (© Mark R. Fairchild, Ph.D.)

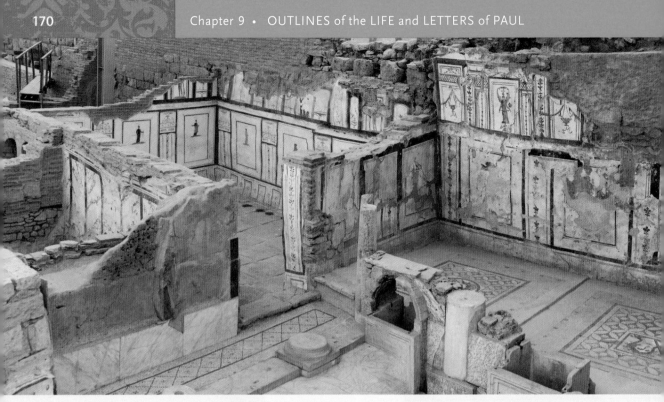

Figure 9.16 The slope houses in Ephesus. Wealthy homes on a hill in downtown Ephesus complete with frescoes, mosaics, and indoor plumbing. (© *Mark R. Fairchild, Ph.D.*)

Figure 9.17 Paul passed this way, by Assos, on the way to his meeting at Miletus. He would have seen this theater. (© *Mark R. Fairchild, Ph.D.*)

Figure 9.18 The Holy of Holies of the Herodian Temple in Jerusalem. (© *Rick Danielson*)

A.D. 57	Paul travels by boat from Philippi to Troas (where the famous Eutychus incidents happens, Acts 20.7–12) and then to Miletus, where he makes his farewell speech (Acts 20.18ff.). Finally, he hastens on to be in Jerusalem in time for Pentecost in May A.D. 57. Landing at Tyre, he strengthens Christians there and is warned not to go to Jerusalem, but he continues southward, stopping at Caesarea Maritima to visit with Philip and his prophesying daughters (Acts 21.8–9). Here, he encounters Agabus, who prophesies his being taken captive and handed over to Gentiles (note that Luke was with Paul on this entire journey and chronicled these events).
A.D. 57–59	An incident in the Temple court leads to Paul's being taken into custody by a Roman tribune. Paul asks to speak to his people and recounts his conversion and mission in Aramaic. A near riot breaks out. Paul is taken to the procurator's headquarters in Caesarea Maritima so Governor Felix can deal with him. He languishes under house arrest for 2 years until Festus becomes governor (probably in A.D. 59 or at the latest 60). Some scholars think Paul wrote the captivity epistles from here (Philemon, Philippians, Colossians, Ephesians) before departing for Rome.
A.D. 59–60	Seasonal data suggest that the journey to Rome took place in late 59 during the risky season for sea travel, and Paul probably arrived in Rome at least by February A.D. 60 (see Acts 27–28).
A.D. 60–62	Paul is under house arrest in Rome, during which time he writes the captivity epistles, with Philippians probably being the last of these letters, written in A.D. 62 shortly before the resolution of his judicial situation.[*]

A.D. 62	Luke knows Paul was under house arrest in Rome for only 2 years, and at no point in the accounts in Acts is Paul ever found guilty of anything, and certainly not of any capital offenses. If Paul's situation was resolved before the fire in Rome in A.D. 64, it is unlikely he was executed. Christianity did not really come under close imperial scrutiny until after the fire in Rome (July A.D. 64). Note that the Pastoral Epistles do not suggest a situation of house arrest but rather imprisonment (in the case of 2 Timothy) by Roman authorities. The following scenario is possible.
A.D. 62–64 or later	Paul travels back east in response to problems. This includes a possible summer visit to Asia Minor (perhaps Ephesus) and a summer and winter in Crete and Greece. Sometime after A.D. 64, Paul is arrested in Asia Minor and taken overland to Rome.
A.D. 64 (late) to 68	The years of the crackdown by Nero. If the Pastorals are by Paul, they were likely written during this period, perhaps 2 Timothy, while he was in Mamertine prison. He would have had to rely heavily on a scribe to do this, perhaps Luke.
A.D. 65–68	Paul is executed as a Roman citizen by beheading.

Figure 9.19 Paul would have walked down this street, perhaps on the way to visiting the temple. (© Mark R. Fairchild, Ph.D.)

* Note that everything after this point in time is largely inferential and conjectural because Acts ends with Paul in Rome. The Pastoral Epistles were presumably written after this time.

THE TRINITY OF PAUL'S IDENTITY

We will begin by talking about the most controversial aspect of Paul's identity—his Roman citizenship. There are some scholars who think Luke is wrong in indicating, more than once in Acts, that Paul was a Roman citizen. After all, nowhere in Paul's letters does he directly say he was a Roman citizen. There are, however, a variety of reasons to think that Luke knew what he was talking about on this point. First, there is Acts 16.37, where Paul's announcement that he is a Roman citizen gets him out of a sticky situation; and again in Acts 22.25–28, a similar announcement is made with a similar effect. The latter text even says Paul was born a Roman citizen. Indeed, we may well wonder how Paul ended up in Rome while under Roman arrest *if he was not a Roman citizen because only Roman citizens had the right of appeal to the emperor in such serious judicial matters. Then too, there is the later church tradition that he was executed by officials in Rome by beheading, a form of capital punishment usually reserved for Roman citizens.*

Furthermore, we do have evidence from before the middle of the first century of higher-status Jews who were indeed Roman citizens (e.g., Josephus the Jewish historian). We can also provide a rationale of how Paul became a Roman citizen. He and his family made tents of *cilicium,* goat's hair cloth. Roman legions were in the region and in constant need of tents made and tents repaired. Citizenship was regularly granted to those who had helped Rome by providing necessary goods and services. It is entirely plausible that Paul's family did so while living in Tarsus.

If we look more closely at the references to Paul as a Roman citizen in the two Acts texts, a plausible explanation arises as to why only on particular special occasions does Paul mention his citizenship. You will notice that Paul only discloses this status on an as-needed basis, that is, as a sort of trump card when his situation is getting out of hand.

If we ask why only then would Paul play that trump card, the answer is that Paul lived in an extremely status-conscious world, where much was accepted simply on the basis of a person's status. But Paul did not want his Gospel to be accepted, or received, or believed because of some special status he had. He wanted it to be accepted because it was a life-transforming truth. In other words, *he wanted the Gospel to be offered free of charge and to be accepted not because of the merit of who said it, but because of the value of what was said.* Then too, Paul believed that the forms and status hierarchies of this world were passing away, and the only status really worth mentioning or boasting about was "being in Christ" and being part of Christ's commonwealth (Phil. 3.20, and see 1 Cor. 7.31). Paul's status-hungry, status-conscious converts needed to rethink what they thought about human citizenships, and he did not want to reinforce what they already thought about the value of Roman citizenship. So Paul in his letters does not mention his Roman citizenship at all. The authority he has that he believes should carry weight in the church is his apostolic authority, and all

CLUES FROM THE CULTURE

Roman citizens can be recognized on inscriptions by their names. After the reign of Emperor Claudius (A.D. 41–54), Roman citizens had three names. The first was a given name, such as Gaius. The second was the family name, such as Julius, and the third was a personal name, such as Caesar. Paul, however, lived before, during, and after this period, so we should not be surprised that he does not identify himself by a triple name in his letters. He does not want his Gospel to be received by the audience on the basis of his elite social status.

CLUES FROM THE CULTURE

For all persons who have passed through their training I preserve intact their Alexandrian citizenship, with the exception of any persons who have insinuated themselves among you in spite of having been born of slave women.

—*Emperor Claudius to the Alexandrians*[2]

NEW PERSPECTIVE

A perspective or interpretation of Paul that typically interprets the key phrase "works of the law" in Pauline literature as boundary-defining rites of circumcision, food laws, and Sabbath keeping. These rites were used to distinguish Jews from other persons in the Greco-Roman world.

his letters are written to Christians. Only with outsiders who were Romans or worked for Rome, for whom Roman citizenship was the important thing in judicial matters, does Paul reveal this side of his identity.

A second aspect of Paul's interesting and complex social identity is that he was a Jew. Not surprisingly, this is the least controversial aspect of who Paul was. What sort of a Jew he was, though, has been heavily debated. Part of this scholarly debate hinges on how much change his believing in Christ really brought to Paul's life. Did he cease being a Jew after Damascus Road? Clearly, Paul does not think so. He views himself as a Jewish follower of Jesus, who was also a Jew. Some Jewish scholars today would say that Paul was an apostate Jew (Alan F. Segal); others call him a radical Jew (Daniel Boyarin); and some just see him as a peculiar and not fully observant Jew. The real bone of contention is whether a Jew can believe in Jesus and continue to be a full-fledged Jew. Also at issue is how Paul characterized himself. What kind of Jew says he can be all things to all people, at times being a Jew to the Jew, at times being the Gentile to the Gentile (1 Cor. 9)? The place to start and to frame this discussion is with what Paul said about himself.

There are several key texts in this discussion. Let us start with 2 Cor. 11.22 where Paul stresses not that he *was* a Hebrew of Hebrews, an Israelite, and a descendent of Abraham, but that he *is* these things. He still claims his Jewish heritage. Yet it is equally clear that he can sit lightly with some aspects of his Jewish heritage, as he is prepared to be with, and to eat with, and to fellowship with Gentiles on their own turf. First Corinthians 9.20–23 is Paul's explanation of his approach to mission and ministry in this regard. Paul tends to bring up his Jewish heritage and identity under pressure, as was the case with his Roman identity, and in polemical situations, as shown by the two texts mentioned earlier.

Galatians 1.13–14 is also a text found in a polemical context, but the important point about this text is the contrast Paul is prepared to make between "formerly" and "now." He says he was formerly advancing in Judaism, but is not now. There is also a clear contrast here between Judaism and the assembly of God (i.e., the church). Note that the term *Judaism,* found only in these verses in the New Testament (cf. 2 Macc. 2.21, 8.1, 14.38; 4 Macc. 4.26), refers not to geographical identity but focuses on the religious and social component of identity. Paul is indicating that he is now part of one sort of religious community, one he formerly persecuted, and not another. Paul affirms his Jewish heritage (see Rom. 9.4–5), and he affirms his ethnic identity (as an Israelite); but he is a sectarian Jew because he is a follower of Jesus.

Much debate has been engaged in lately about Paul's view of the Mosaic law. No one disputes that he saw it as a good thing that came from God (see Rom. 7.1–5). A **new perspective** on Paul has arisen that suggests that what Paul meant by "works of the law" are those boundary-defining rites of circumcision, food laws, and Sabbath keeping, which especially distinguished Jews from other persons in the Greco-Roman world. There are many problems with this view, and those problems come to a head in texts such as Romans 10.4, where Paul says that Christ is the end of the Mosaic law as a means of righteousness before God. Whether Christ is the fulfillment or simply the terminus of this law, Paul means that Christians are no longer obligated to it because of what Christ has done. Certainly, the Mosaic law was a means of living righteously for non-Christian Jews. What is often not taken into account in the debate about Paul and the law is that Paul views the law as a package deal because it is part of a covenant that is a package deal. It is the legal part of the Mosaic covenant.

Thus, in Gal. 4, Paul tells an allegory of two covenants, or actually three—the Abrahamic, the Mosaic, and the new covenant. In Paul's argument, the new covenant is connected to the Abrahamic covenant and distinguished from the Mosaic covenant by its law. The new covenant is seen as the fulfillment of the Abrahamic covenant in various ways. Paul likens the Mosaic covenant to a "pedagogue," that is, a child minder or nanny who only has a job until the child comes of age. But when Christ has come, a man born a Jew, born under the law, to redeem those under the Mosaic law out from under that law, the situation has changed. The old passes away and the new has come. In Paul's view, the Mosaic covenant played an important but temporary role in the life of God's people, but its day had passed once Christ came. Christ becomes not only the means of right-standing with God but also the means of living righteously before God, a role the Mosaic covenant had played before in the life of the believer. This is not to say that there are no commandments or laws that comes with the new covenant. Paul is comfortable with talking about the Law of Christ in Gal. 6 and 1 Cor. 9, by which he seems to mean the new commandments of Christ, plus only the portions of the Old Testament that Christ reaffirmed (e.g., no adultery), along with new apostolic teaching.

In short, in Paul's view, neither Jewish nor Gentile Christians were obligated to the Mosaic covenant any more. They were obligated to the new covenant with its "law of Christ" (see, e.g., the Sermon on the Mount). Terry Donaldson sums it up well: "The incompatibility of Christ and Torah [i.e., the Mosaic covenant as the factor defining the nature, limits, and shape of a religious community] was the constant element in the syllogism that on the one side of the conversion led to [Saul's] persecution of the church, and on the other resulted in [Paul's] fierce resistance to the Judaizers" (those Jewish Christians who insisted that everyone, including Gentiles, had to keep the Mosaic covenant to be Christ followers). Donaldson says that for Paul, there was a fundamental contradiction between the Mosaic law and salvation through faith in the crucified Christ as a means of defining the boundaries of the people of God.[3] Paul remained a zealot after conversion, just as he was before his conversion. Basically, he just changed sides in the argument.

But it is not as if he jettisoned all it meant to be a Jew and a Pharisee. He still affirmed the Old Testament as the sacred Scriptures—all of it. Christians could learn from all of it because it was God's word, even though they were not bound to the commandments in the Mosaic covenant unless they were reiterated in the new

CLUES FROM THE **CULTURE**

How fortunate he is, by Hercules, and blessed threefold! . . . for he was in a manner reborn and immediately engaged to the service of Isis.

—*Apuleius,* Metamorphosis, *11.16*

covenant. Paul still affirmed the Pharisaic notion of resurrection, although he applied it in fresh ways now to what had already happened to Jesus and what, one day, would happen to Jesus' followers. This leads us to a discussion of Paul as a Christian.

As my mentor, C. K. Barrett, once said in class: If Paul was not a convert to the following of Jesus, it would be hard to find anyone who had been converted in the first century A.D. so thoroughly had Paul become a follower, apostle, devotee, and worshipper of the Christ. It has sometimes been suggested that we should see what happened to Paul on Damascus Road as more of a prophetic calling than a conversion, but in fact it must be seen as a bit of both. Paul had previously been an enemy and persecutor of Christ and his people. Now he was an apostle of Christ and loved his converts and all Christians. Paul had come to view Jewish Christians as the true Jews and those who rejected Christ as temporarily broken off from the people of God—until they repented and turned to Christ, apparently at his second coming (see Rom. 11).

When a person goes through as thoroughgoing a change in worldview as Paul did, from enemy to friend of Christ and his people, when the whole way he viewed Christ and his fledgling movement changed after Damascus Road, one has to say his **symbolic universe** and worldview had been turned upside down in various ways. The insiders were now out, and the outsiders were now in. Notice how Paul talks about conversion. "If anyone is in Christ, behold he is a new creature (or there is a new creation), the old has passed away" (2 Cor. 5.17). Paul, it is true, does not use the term *Christianos* (Christian). But he does frequently speak of those who are "in Christ," and he distinguishes them from non-Christian Jews in various ways and places.

Paul was so completely a person "in Christ" that he not only emulated Christ but he also talked about suffering some of the sufferings of Christ. He was so completely a person in Christ that he was prepared to regard even all the good aspects of who he formerly was as rubbish compared to what he had gained in Christ (Phil. 3.4–11). Paul was so much a follower of Christ that he constantly talked about his life in the eschatological Spirit, who became a part of his life at conversion. He viewed himself as a prophet and tongue speaker (1 Cor. 14) and he saw himself as a person who performed miracles by that power of the Spirit (Rom. 15). There is so much more one can say, but this is enough to make clear that Paul was a Roman citizen, a Jew, and a Jewish follower of Jesus—and he was proud to say he was "in Christ," as part of the new Christian community of Jew and Gentile united in Christ.

PAUL THE MULTILINGUAL, MULTICULTURAL APOSTLE

In a world where perhaps only 1 or 2 out of 10 people could write or at least write at the level Paul did, Paul was clearly an exceptional person. But beyond basic literacy and knowing several languages (Greek, Aramaic, Hebrew, and

SYMBOLIC UNIVERSE

The sum total of fixed ideas and concepts in a person's mental world that are "givens," not debated, but taken for granted. To Paul, such concepts would be God and sin and redemption. These ideas are configured in relationship to one another through stories.

probably some Latin), Paul was also a well-educated man who knew some Greek philosophy and Greek **rhetoric** along with a wealth of knowledge of the Old Testament and early Jewish writings. He was, without doubt, along with the author of Hebrews and the author of Luke–Acts, one of the most well-educated men in all of early Christianity.

If we wonder where Paul got all this education, the answer may come as a surprise—probably in Jerusalem, where one could study all things Jewish and Greek, although Tarsus was also famous for having a good school of rhetoric. And as a Roman citizen and the child of a Roman citizen, he would have learned some things about Roman law as well, which would serve him in good stead when he was taken captive by Roman authorities.

To a degree that we perhaps cannot appreciate, oral cultures placed a premium on not just the content but also on the form of one's knowledge and how it was expressed. Oratorical skills were a key to advancing in a largely oral culture, and as Paul tells us in Galatians 1, he did indeed advance rapidly in early Judaism, surpassing many of his peers.

These oral skills, and the literary form of them when his words were put down in writing, were to become crucial when Paul took on the role of convincing the Gentile world that Jesus was the risen Lord of all in the Empire. The verbal art of persuasion, known as rhetoric, had long been a staple of ancient education since the time of Alexander the Great, thanks to the ongoing influence of people like Aristotle and his successors who wrote whole treatises on rhetoric and how it should be used. Letter writing as a literary vehicle for conveying more than mundane messages was by comparison a much more recent part of common practice and had far less impact as a part of ancient education. To really understand Paul the evangelist and persuader, we need to understand the essence of ancient rhetoric, which Paul uses again and again to convict, convince, convert, and indeed confirm and strengthen those already persuaded about Jesus the Christ.

RHETORIC

The verbal art of persuasion which had long been a staple of ancient education since the time of Alexander the Great. Alexander the Great was influenced by rhetoricians such as Aristotle and his successors who wrote treatises on rhetoric.

CLUES FROM THE CULTURE

Those who come before you claiming to be men of culture declaim speeches intended merely for display—and stupid ones on top of that!

—*Dio Chrysostom Or. 32.1*

RHETORIC IN THE GRECO-ROMAN WORLD

Mention the word *rhetoric* today, and you may see people wince. It conjures up images of political bombast and words "full of sound and fury, but signifying nothing." But in antiquity, rhetoric was a basic staple of ancient education at all levels precisely because, in an oral culture, speaking not merely eloquently but persuasively was crucial if one was going to make a success of one's life and climb up the hierarchal social ladder. Indeed, you may be surprised to learn that most higher education took the form of being trained or tutored by a rhetorician, and even elementary education involved rhetorical exercises from the outset. You could not escape rhetoric, even if you only had elementary education.

The basic staples of ancient education were reading, writing, and rhetoric. Rhetoricians were everywhere in the Greco-Roman world, including in the Holy Land; and by the time Paul arrived in Judea, it had been influenced by Greek culture and language for several centuries. In fact, there was no need to travel to a major university or university town in the empire to find a rhetorician. We have clear evidence that they permeated the empire, even on small Greek islands in the Aegean like Eretria (*Syllalogae Inscriptiones Graecae* 714).[4] Herod, with his strong **Hellenizing** agenda both in his building and educational schemes, would have made sure that there were several rhetoricians available to educate people in Jerusalem in the Greek art of persuasion.

One of the things we sometimes forget is just how stratified the ancient world was. By this I mean that life was based on all sorts of hierarchies, with a pecking order that placed women beneath men, the young beneath the old, Greeks beneath Romans, Jews beneath both Greeks and Romans, and so on. In fact, the divide between Greek speakers and non-Greek speakers was so fundamental to that world that the word for non-Greek speakers is still in use today (although with a different meaning)—*barbarians*! The whole of Paul's world could be divided into Greek speakers and barbarians (a word invented to indicate how some non-Greek speaking sounded to Greek ears—"bar . . . bar . . . bar . . .").

Education—especially rhetorical education—was one of the great equalizers in a society that prized eloquence and persuasion over almost everything else. Rhetoric became a major tool for "upstarts" like Cicero, who began life as a humble farm boy from Arpinum and advanced to become "the first man

HELLENIZING

The practice of spreading Greek culture, language, architecture, and habits first begun by Alexander the Great as he conquered the then-known world east of Macedonia.

Figure 9.20 The Parthenon from the lower Acropolis. (© Rick Danielson)

Figure 9.21 Cicero offering a rhetorical speech.

in Rome." So much was rhetoric the great equalizer that despite Cicero's lack of patrician blood, indeed his lack of pure Roman background, he rose to become the most important man in Rome during and after the time of Julius Caesar, all on the basis of his remarkable oratorical skills. We can thus begin to get a sense of how important rhetoric might be to a very evangelistic religious group like the early Christians. Above all else, their mission was to persuade non-believers about Jesus Christ.

There were three main types of rhetoric in antiquity—**forensic** (or judicial), which was the rhetoric of the law courts; **deliberative,** which was the rhetoric of public assembly; and **epideictic,** which was the rhetoric of funeral oratory and public speeches lauding some person, place, or event. To a degree we might not fully grasp, public speaking was seen as a major spectator sport. Speaking contests were a common staple of ancient games. Try to imagine a poetry contest being part of the modern Olympic Games today! Emperor Nero won his own poetry contest at the Isthmian Games in Corinth. (What a surprise!) Public speaking could draw huge crowds, especially if it took place somewhere it could be heard for free, such as the *agora,* or marketplace, in Athens (see Acts 17).

With the demise of Greek-style democracy and the rise of empire in the first century A.D., epideictic rhetoric (the rhetoric of oratorical display; pomp and circumstance; and inflated praise, blame, and entertainment) came to the fore. But at the same time, in a competitive culture like the Greco-Roman world (scholars call it an **agonistic** culture), lawyers were kept quite busy using the rhetoric of attack and defense, that is, judicial rhetoric (see 1 Cor. 6). There was, however, still a place for deliberative rhetoric, despite the loss of free assemblies—in political contexts such as ambassadorial speeches, negotiations between patrons and clients, when patrons were seeking votes, and especially in religious associations where persuasion about this or that religious rite or practice was at a premium.

Paul was quite capable of using all forms of rhetoric, but he much preferred deliberative rhetoric, as we shall see. It is interesting that Paul chooses the word *ekklesia* (literally, "the called-out ones," hence the "assembly") for his churches,

FORENSIC RHETORIC

The rhetoric of the law courts. Forensic rhetoric is characterized by attack and defense and focuses on past times. An example would include the arguments of attack and defense given by lawyers in a courtroom setting.

DELIBERATIVE RHETORIC

The rhetoric of the public assembly. Deliberative rhetoric is characterized by advice and consent and focuses on future events. For example, in Philippians we find an example of deliberative rhetoric that tries to persuade the Philippians to follow good examples and avoid bad ones. This sort of rhetoric involves persuading the audience about their future behavior.

EPIDEICTIC RHETORIC

The rhetoric of the funeral oratory and public speeches lauding some person, place, or event. Epideictic rhetoric is characterized by praise and blame and focuses on the present.

AGONISTIC

The Greek word *agon,* from which we get the word agony, refers to struggle and hence to a culture based on struggle and competitions of various sorts to get ahead. In such a culture, "honor challenges" (or as we might call them today, "spitting contests") would be engaged in by rivals to see who was best at one thing or another—speaking, wrestling, throwing the javelin, business, you name it. Winning was the way to gain honor, and with losing came shame. Competition and rivalries were such a part of ancient culture that whole tribes and kin groups would go to war with others over a simple challenge of honor (recall what prompted the Trojan War and the story of Helen of Troy).

as this was the term in earlier Greek life that referred to the democratic assemblies in Athens and elsewhere. This may suggest that Paul saw the church as the place especially where things should be accomplished by persuasion, not by authoritarian rule or decision-making in proverbial smoke-filled rooms behind the scenes. The Christian assembly was a place where freedom was to reign, where it was appropriate for discourse and dialogue to take place, so as to encourage people in regard to how they ought to believe and behave. Here is a chart to help us understand the three major species of rhetoric.

TYPES OF RHETORIC	CHARACTER	TEMPORAL FOCUS	VENUE
Forensic or judicial	Attack and defense	The past	Law courts
Deliberative or political	Advice and consent	The future	The "assembly"
Epideictic	Praise and blame	The present	The agora

It is not, however, just that there were different types of rhetoric, readily recognized by their character. Each rhetorical speech tended to have a certain skeletal outline it followed with some variations. There were certain essential elements that needed to be included. Here is a list of these elements:

EXORDIUM/OPENING REMARKS—The beginning of a speech was meant to establish rapport with the audience and make them well disposed to receive what follows.

NARRATIO/NARRATION—A narration of pertinent facts, explaining the nature of the disputed matter, or facts that needed to be taken into account as a basis for argument and persuasion.

PROPOSITIO/THESIS STATEMENT—The essential proposition or thesis of a discourse that the following arguments are to support.

PROBATIO/ARGUMENT PRO—The essential arguments *for* the proposition.

REFUTATIO/ARGUMENTS CON—Arguments intended to dismantle objections or the opposition's arguments against the thesis statement.

PERORATIO/FINAL EMOTIONAL APPEAL—The recapitulating of the main thesis statement, including a final emotional appeal to the deeper feelings of the audience to cap off the total act of persuasion.

The essence of the art of persuasion was offering persuasive arguments; but voice, gestures, tone, volume, and appearance all contributed or detracted from the goal of persuasion. Thus, first-century rhetorical handbooks, such as the one written by the Roman rhetorician and educator Quintilian, deal with all the factors that led to persuasion, both in form and content and in the "**ethos**" of the speaker, meaning the way the speaker comes across to an audience and his "authority." If an orator's hair piece blew off in the marketplace while he was waxing eloquent, he was having a bad ethos day; and once he was laughed at and shamed, he had little chance of persuading anyone about his thesis. Rhetoricians understood as well that not merely logic, but also emotions, contribute to persuasion; so it was normal for the more surface emotions of kindness, respectfulness, and friendliness to be appealed to in the exordium at the opening of the speech in order to get a fair hearing, with the deeper emotions of hate, love, fear, or grief being appealed to at the end to seal the deal in the peroration.

ETHOS

The way a speaker comes across to an audience especially in relation to his/her authority, character, or disposition.

In many ways, ancient rhetoricians were simply the ancient equivalent of preachers and evangelists. Because Paul set as his goal "that I might by all means win some for Christ" (1 Cor. 9.22), he quite readily used rhetoric to that end. It is a mistake to underestimate the importance of rhetoric in Paul's day and for Paul's tasks of evangelism.

Duane Litfin reminds us:

> Rhetoric played both a powerful and persuasive role in first century Greco-Roman society. [I]t was a commodity of which the vast majority of the population were either producers, or much more likely consumers, and not seldom avid consumers. . . . Oratory became more prevalent than ever. in both the Roman and the Greek setting the frequency with which speakers rose to address audiences, for whatever reasons, seemed to be on the rise during the first century. The quality of oratory may have declined but the quantity did not.[5]

If Paul was to be the apostle to the Gentiles, and he wanted to "take every thought captive for Christ," then rhetoric became a vital tool for accomplishing that aim. But it may be asked, of what relevance is all this when all we have are his letters, and we cannot hear Paul speak today? This is a fair question, and we devote some time to discussing the matter in the next section. We can say now, though, that ancient letters were forms of oral communication from a distance. That is, they were surrogates for an oral proclamation or verbal exchange. In fact, the epistolary elements found at the beginning and end of ancient letters (such as the name of the sender and the recipients, a greeting, a thanksgiving or prayer) help only to frame the speech that is contained within the letter. In other words, these letters are more than just mundane letters of request or instruction. Rather, they were sent from a distance as the best substitute for the presence of the author himself and meant to be read aloud in a rhetorically effective manner as if the author were present!

PAUL'S RHETORICAL LETTERS

When we actually examine Paul's letters closely, we discover that although they do have letter features at the beginning and the end of the documents, in between they do not much look like the vast majority of ancient letters, but rather they look like speeches or discourse or arguments. There is a good reason for this—they are! Had Paul been present with the audience to whom he was writing, this discourse is what he would have said to them orally in good rhetorical form. The bulk of each of these documents then is better analyzed following rhetorical analysis than following epistolary analysis. Let's take two good examples from the "undisputed" Pauline letters: first the simpler and shorter example in Philippians, then the longer and more complex example in Romans.

Here is a brief outline of the structure of Philippians:

RHETORICAL OUTLINE OF PHILIPPIANS	
Epistolary Prescript	1.1–2
Exordium/Opening Remarks	1.3–11
Narratio/Narration	1.12–26
Propositio/Thesis Statement	1.27–30
Probatio/Arguments Pro	2.1–4.3
Peroration/Final Emotional Appeal	4.4–9
Concluding Arguments	4.10–20
Epistolary Greetings and Closing	4.21–23

What we discover is that Philippians is an example of deliberative rhetoric urging the Philippians to follow good examples and avoid bad ones, the former being examples of self-sacrificial and unifying behavior and the latter being examples of disruptive and divisive behavior. As always, the thesis statement is crucial to understanding where Paul's arguments are going and how they function. In the case of Philippians, the thesis has to do with the Philippians, like Paul, living a life worthy of the Gospel, which is to say worthy of the story of Christ the servant as retold in Phil. 2. Paul's narration of his own recent situation, his arguments, his concluding peroration, and indeed the extra argument about support are all given in support of the basic thesis statement.

When we turn to Romans, we discover a much more lengthy and elaborate rhetorical discourse. What it shares with Philippians is that it is an example of a deliberative discourse, meant to aid in altering the belief and behavior of the audience in the near future. Here is the structure:

RHETORICAL OUTLINE OF ROMANS

Epistolary Prescript and Greetings	1.1–7	
Exordium/Opening Remarks	1.8–10	Establishing ethos and rapport
Narratio/Narration	1.11–15	Narration of facts pertinent to the arguments that follow
Propositio/Thesis Statement	1.16–17	Thesis statement about the righteousness of God and the setting and making righteous of human beings
Probatio/Arguments Pro	1.18–8.39	Arguments for the thesis statement
Refutatio/Arguments Con	9.1–11.36	Arguments against the theory that a righteous God would abandon his first chosen people
Arguments for Unifying Praxis and Religion for Jews and Gentiles	12.1–21	
Arguments for Unifying Behavior and Witness	13.1–14	
Arguments for Unifying Behavior in House	14.1–15.13	
Peroratio/Final Emotional Appeal	15.14–21	For Gentiles especially
Epistolary Reference to Travel Plans and Doxology	15. 22–33	
Concluding Greetings	16. 1–16	
Reinforcing arguments about Praxis	16. 17–20	Second Peroratio for Jewish Christians
Concluding Greetings from Pauline Coworkers	16.24	
Final Benediction	16. 25–27	

This structure involves more epistolary elements toward the close of the document; and not only at the end but along the way, we have little doxologies and benedictions that remind us that this reading out of the document was to be done in the context of worship, perhaps playing the role as the sermon or address. The "assembly" (*ekklesia*) Paul is addressing is an assembly at worship.

Rhetorical analysis of all 13 Pauline letters has been undertaken by many fine Pauline scholars, and they all submit to such an analysis quite readily. Rhetorical analysis is not merely another form of literary analysis, more or less helpful, but an indispensable tool to understanding what Paul is doing, that is, *making arguments to try to persuade his converts of various things.* Especially helpful is pinpointing the thesis statement that helps us see where the rest of the discourse will be going. It is easy to get lost in the maze of Paul's arguments unless we see their purpose, rhetorical structure, and trajectory, and then it begins to make better sense. Knowing rhetoric also helps us to read the signals to the audience better—when Paul is being irenic, ironic, sarcastic, bombastic, hyperbolic, or deadly serious.

Rhetoric reminds us also that Paul's discourses are arranged quite carefully. They are not haphazard or random. While it is generally true that Paul speaks about ethical and practical subjects more often toward the end of the document, and theological ones more toward the beginning, in fact there is no hard and fast division of the documents in this way. Theology and ethics are intertwined in Paul's discourse.

But rhetoric helps us understand Paul as well. He was a missionary, a preacher, and a persuader par excellence, and he uses all the rhetorical tools at hand to help him in these tasks. Paul's rhetoric also reminds us that Paul was a man of considerable education and, as a Roman citizen, a man of considerable social status as well. One gets the impression he was constantly stepping down the social ladder and acting as a servant to others for the sake of Christ.

Rhetoric also tells us that Paul was very much at home in the Greek-speaking and rhetorical world of the Empire. Although he was most certainly a Jew, he would not have been seen as a total stranger by Gentiles, a good thing because he was an apostle to the Gentiles! Paul's use of rhetoric also reminds us that Paul was prepared to live in his world and use its best elements in the service of Christ. He says in one of his last letters that Christians should reflect on whatever is true, honorable, just, pure, aesthetically pleasing, commendable, excellent, and praiseworthy (Phil. 4.8). Clearly, rhetoric was seen as one such part of culture that could be used in service to Christ. Culture was to be sifted, not simply rejected. Whereas Paul could command his converts, his letters make clear, he would far rather treat them as adults and try to persuade them to accept his advice freely and without coercion. In our next sections, we must briefly consider Paul the thinker and his storied world.

PAUL'S NARRATIVE THOUGHT WORLD

> The grace of God is not, for Paul, an idea, or even primarily an attribute of God, but the action of God in history. God's grace is always, and inevitably, "storied," working in history (though often also concealed within it) to bring life out of death, power out of weakness, salvation out of sin. Thus Paul's stories convey the Gospel inasmuch as they carry the pattern of grace, justification of the ungodly, and God's critical judgment on human pretensions. Paul does not tell his stories and *then* transmit their meaning: That meaning is embodied in the shape of the stories themselves.
>
> —JOHN BARCLAY[6]

Oral culture is by and large a culture of storytellers. When only 10 to 20 percent of the population can read or write, most people learn aurally through stories, parables, proverbs, maxims, and the like. It is easy enough to place Jesus in his oral and aural context and see why his pedagogy took the shape it did, but what about Paul? On the surface of things, Paul's letters do not appear to be collections of stories or maxims. They contain some stories and maxims, but they do not appear to be largely composed of them.

Occasionally, we find Paul retelling old stories, particularly Old Testament stories in a rather full form (see 1 Cor. 10 or Gal. 4); but by and large, such stories function at the subsurface level in Paul's letters. Like a tune always playing in Paul's head, which occasionally we find the apostle humming or singing out loud, his storied world provides the inspiration for his life and thought processes, including both his theologizing and ethicizing in particular congregational situations.

Just as we might easily overlook a tune someone was humming as we walked and talked with them, in the past, scholars often overlooked the importance of Paul's narrative thought world as the fount from which his challenging rhetoric sprang. This fortunately has been remedied lately, in part because we have begun to listen to cognitive science: the science of the mind. This science is insistent in telling us that *story is the fundamental organizational principle of the mind.* Indeed, there is a narrative structure of human identity, a before and after; and this sense of movement, direction, progress or regress, and growth or atrophy is thought of in a *processive* way such that the story or narrative is the medium in which a human being's identity and sense of identity is formed. Human existence is experienced in *narratival* ways. It may be debated whether this is because reality has a narrative and goal-oriented structure or whether human beings merely perceive reality that way.[7] What seems beyond debate, however, is that because human beings in general have always perceived reality in terms of story or stories, it is reasonable and right to assume that Paul did so as well.[8]

Thus, I believe N. T. Wright is absolutely correct when he says of ancient persons like Paul that "human writing is best conceived as . . . the telling of stories which bring worldviews into articulation." Thus, he says that the right question to ask about Paul's thought world is, "What were the stories which give narrative depth to Paul's worldview, which formed an irreducible part of his symbolic universe?"[9]

This whole approach to Paul's theology and ethics may at first seem odd to you if you have been taught to think in abstract ways about Paul's thought world. For example, if you have been taught to think in abstract concepts like *justification, sanctification, grace,* or *salvation,* and then have been taught to link those ideas in a particular way (justification leads to sanctification, which eventually leads to glorification), the notion that such ideas in fact are grounded and grow out of stories may seem foreign to you. But I assure you, such thinking was not alien to the oral cultures in which Paul lived; and if we really wish to understand the thought of the man who has been called the greatest Christian theologian ever, we must come to grips with this sort of approach to studying Paul's thought.

I want to be clear that this does not merely mean that we need to have a good grasp on the Old Testament stories that helped generate Paul's thought, although that is the main component of things. But we also need to realize that Paul was not merely influenced by Biblical stories, as it were, or even by Biblical and Christian stories; he was also influenced by stories from the wider culture, and perhaps none more widespread than the growing mythology accompanying the development of the emperor cult. Consider, for example, the following inscription, which was found in fragments in five cities in what is now Turkey, indeed, in the very region Paul apparently spent his most time evangelizing:

> Providence has filled Augustus with divine power for the benefit
> of humanity, and in her beneficence has granted us and those
> who come after us [a savior] who has made wars to cease . . . And
> Caesar, when he was manifest, transcended the expectations of [all
> who had anticipated the good news] . . . and the birthday of our god
> signaled the beginning of the good newses [*euangelia*—here the
> word is plural] for the world because of him.
> —*Priene Inscription*

There were competing narratives striving to win the hearts and minds of the people of the Greco-Roman world. We need to keep in mind that during the first century A.D., there were only two historical persons who were also worshipped in that same era—the emperor and Jesus of Nazareth. The story just recounted in that inscription is a story making both a political and religious claim. In another sense, so did the Jesus story because if Jesus is the risen Lord, and there is only one God, then Caesar can only be a pretender, a parody of the real God or the real Lord. Let us consider not the story of the antihero but the main stories that shaped Paul's theological and ethical thought world.[10]

FIVE STORIES THAT SHOOK AND SHAPED PAUL'S WORLD AND WORLDVIEW

There are some five major stories or formative narratives that Paul's thought is grounded in, which he reflects on and uses, often interweaving these stories together: (1) the story of God, the one who existed before all worlds, including all thought worlds, and made them; (2) the story of the world gone wrong in the first Adam; (3) the story of God's people, Israel, in that world, from Abraham to Moses and beyond; (4) the story of the Jewish Messiah, Jesus, which arises out of these previous stories but reconfigures them all; and (5) the story of Christians, including Paul himself, which arises out of stories 2 through 4.

The stories of Christ and Christians are closely knit together, constituting the beginning of the tale of how the world is being set right again. Christ's story is the hinge, the crucial turning point, bringing to a climax the previous stories and determining in advance how the rest of the story will turn out and play out. The climax only comes, however, by an interruption of the downward spiral of the previous stories. Thus, the story of Christ can be called a divine interruption by the original creator of the story in the first place. The story of God's own people, in Paul's way of thinking, contracts to that of Christ, the seed of Abraham, but expands once more to include Christ's followers. This concept is best relayed by the term **incorporative personality.** Christ is the seed, but his offspring are also present in him, and so they become Abraham's heirs through being in the seed who is Christ. Thus the term *seed* in Gal. 3.16 has both an individual and a collective sense, just as it did with Abraham, for "in Abraham," Isaac and subsequent descendants also received the promise. We will be able to say a good deal more about these various stories as we investigate Paul's letters one by one in their probable chronological order beginning in Chapter 10.

IMPLICATIONS

When the author walks on the stage the play is over. God is going to invade, all right . . . something so beautiful to some of us and

---

INCORPORATIVE PERSONALITY

A phrase that reflects the realities of a collectivist culture, a culture where the group identity is primary and individual identity is secondary. What happens in such a culture is that some illustrious ancestor is seen not merely as the group's forefather but also as acting for them, as their representative, such that in some sense they were present with, say, Abraham or in the Greco-Roman world with brave Odysseus. Thus, people in these cultures can see themselves as being "in" their ancestor, part of his doings in the past. Thus, for Paul, Christ can be said to be "the seed" of Abraham, summing up and representing all Abraham's descendants and acting for them all. In addition, Paul sees Christ as incorporating all those who are his followers, and in this case, Christ is viewed as God the Father in that regard.

so terrible to others that none of us will have any choice left. For
this time it will be God without disguise . . . it will be too late then
to choose your side. There is no use saying you choose to lie down
when it has become impossible to stand up.
—C. S. Lewis[11]

On any showing, Paul was a complex person, with various facets to his identity. One thing he was not was insincere. Even his opponents could sense this
fact. He was a man of strong passions and strong views, and he was not afraid
to share them with the world. In part, this was because Paul believed that he
was a called, converted, and indeed an inspired and prophetic figure, conveying the word of God, the Good News about Jesus, to a lost world. Humanly
speaking, without the efforts of Paul, the church may well have not become
the predominantly Gentile-dominated community that it was by the second
century A.D.

John Donne, the great English cleric, once said about Paul's letters, "whereso-
ever I open St. Paul's letters I hear thunder, a thunder that rolls throughout the
earth." As the Corinthians had said much earlier, Paul's letters or discourses are
weighty, profound, and deep, both in terms of their theological and their ethical
ideas. But Paul was not interested in being yet one more talking head, one more
rhetorician or philosopher of his age. He was interested in saving persons from
their self-centered and sin-drenched lives. His letters, like his preaching, were
constantly demanding his audience to make decisions, change direction, and
embrace the good and the true as he saw it.

Paul showed that Christianity as an intellectual enterprise could stand toe
to toe with any philosophy of life or religious orientation put forth in the
ancient world, and it is fair to say that this is still true. We are still trying to
take the measure of Paul's thought world and his contribution to human society, including our own Western society. Paul was certainly not the inventor of
Christianity, but he was probably, after Jesus, its first great thinker, evangelist,
and persuader—and we have yet to take the full measure of the lettered man
and his rhetorical letters.

As Paul tells all his stories, he keeps uppermost in mind that he lives in the
"end of days," that is, in the eschatological age. He is ever mindful of the sort
of thing C. S. Lewis says in the preceding quote. That is, Paul fervently believes
that Christ will indeed return, like a thief in the night, although no one knows
the timing of the event. What this means above all is that now, in this life, is the
time to make a decision about what one thinks about the story of Christ. This
gives a definite urgency to Paul's storytelling, and the theologizing and ethicizing
he does on the basis of the stories.

There is always a danger, when one talks about Paul's thought world in terms of stories, that someone may say, "well that's only a story, and Paul has a vivid imagination." The problem with that is Paul had vivid experiences that fed his imagination. It's like the old joke of when someone asks, "Do you believe in infant baptism?," to which I would reply, "Believe in it, I've seen it!" To the question, "Do you believe in the risen Christ?," Paul would reply, "Believe in Him? I've seen him."

Paul's stories don't just come from a hyperactive imagination reflecting on the ancient tales in the Old Testament, although that is part of what is happening. They also come from the facts of Paul's life, the encounters he has with other Christians like Peter and James, the miracles that happened in the course of Paul's ministry, and so on, including especially the miracle of his seeing Christ on Damascus Road. In other words, Paul is able to testify that the amazing things recorded about God's people in the Old Testament kept happening in his lifetime, and indeed even to him and his fellow Christians. They have become part of the grand sweep of the story of salvation history, and the rescue of God's people, and indeed of the world. When story becomes history, it becomes more than just a good yarn: it becomes the script for one's own life.

KEY TERMS

Agonistic	Narratio/Narration
Deliberative Rhetoric	New Perspective
Epideictic Rhetoric	Peroratio/Final Emotional Appeal
Ethos	Probatio/Argument Pro
Exordium/Opening Remarks	Propositio/Proposition
Forensic Rhetoric	Refutatio/Arguments Con
Hellenizing	Rhetoric
Incorporative Personality	Symbolic Universe
Judaizers	

FOR FURTHER READING

Gorman, M. J. *Cruciformity: Paul's Narrative Spirituality of the Cross.* Grand Rapids, MI: Eerdmans, 2001.

Longenecker, B., ed. *Narrative Dynamics in Paul: A Critical Assessment.* Louisville, KY: Westminster John Knox, 2002.

Murphy-O'Connor, J. *Paul the Letter Writer: His World, His Options, His Skills.* Collegeville, MN: Liturgical Press, 1995.

Witherington, B. *New Testament Rhetoric: An Introductory Guide to the Art of Persuasion in and of the New Testament.* Eugene, OR: Cascade, 2009.

————. *Paul's Narrative Thought World: The Tapestry of Tragedy and Triumph.* Louisville, KY: Westminster John Knox, 1994.

————. *The Paul Quest: The Renewed Search for the Jew of Tarsus.* Downers Grove, IL: InterVarsity Press, 1998.

STUDY QUESTIONS

What is the main difference between the image of Paul in Acts and in his letters?

Explain the threefold nature of Paul's identity. Which part of his identity seems most dominant to you?

What was Paul's view of the Mosaic law after his conversion? Explain the difference between a covenant and the laws within a covenant.

What is rhetoric? Why was it important in an oral culture?

What were the three R's of ancient education?

Which most shaped ancient communication—letter conventions or rhetorical conventions? Why?

Why do you think human beings tend to make sense of life by using stories?

What were the major stories Paul assumed and drew on in his theologizing and ethicizing?

How does the story of Christ change and redirect the human story?

NOTES

1. See Todd Still's article and the notes that explain the derivation of this saying: "Shadow and Light: Marcion's (Mis)Construal of the Apostle Paul," in *Paul and the Second Century*, ed. M. Bird and J. Dodson (Dorset, England: T & T Clark, 2011), 91–107.

2. Cited in B. Levick, *The Government of the Roman Empire,* 2nd ed. (London: Routledge, 2000), n124.

3. T. Donaldson, "Zealot and Convert: The Origin of Paul's Christ-Torah Antithesis," *Catholic Biblical Quarterly* 51, no. 4 (1989): 655–682.

4. See B. Witherington, *The Paul Quest: The Renewed Search for the Jew of Tarsus* (Downers Grove, IL: InterVarsity Press, 1998), 115.

5. D. Litfin, *St. Paul's Theology of Proclamation: 1 Corinthians 1-4 and Greco-Roman Rhetoric* (Cambridge: Cambridge University Press, 1994), 132.

6. J. Barclay, "Paul's Story: Theology as Testimony," in *Narrative Dynamics in Paul: A Critical Assessment*, ed. B. Longenecker (Louisville, KY: Westminster John Knox, 2002), 133–156.

7. In my view, humans perceive it that way because reality is that way; it is going somewhere, and it has purpose, a goal, and the like.

8. See B. W. Longenecker, "Narrative Interest in the Study of Paul: Retrospective and Prospective," in *Narrative Dynamics in Paul: A Critical Assessment*, ed. B. Longenecker (Louisville, KY: Westminster John Knox, 2002), 4.

9. N. T. Wright, *The New Testament and the People of God*, vol.1, *Christian Origins and the Question of God* (Minneapolis, MN: Fortress Press, 1992), 65, 404.

10. For the reader who wants much more of the sort of material in this chapter, see B. Witherington, *The Indelible Image: The Theological and Ethical Thought World of the New Testament*, 2 vols. (Downers Grove, IL: InterVarsity Press, 2007–2008).

11. From C. S. Lewis, *Mere Christianity* (San Francisco: Harper, 2001), 65.

Pillars in the sea at the man-made port that Herod built—Caesarea Maritima. *(© Mark R. Fairchild, Ph.D.)*

10 PAUL the LETTER WRITER PART ONE: The EARLIER LETTERS

THAT PAUL WAS A LETTER WRITER no one disputes. Indeed, he was one of the great letter writers of the first century A.D. and certainly one of the most literate and well-educated persons of his era, and we are fortunate to have so many documents attributed to him in the New Testament. Paul's social level and the way he steps down the ladder of social status to serve others shines through in all his writings. It is, however, an interesting and curious fact that we have no correspondence from Paul's pen from the time of his conversion somewhere in the A.D. mid-30s until about A.D. 49 or even later. If Galatians is Paul's earliest letter (and many would dispute this), it still cannot be dated until *after* Paul's first missionary journey when he visited and converted some of the people in the Roman province of Galatia. If, on the other hand, we take 1 Thessalonians to be the earliest extant document from Paul, it can be dated no earlier than the early A.D. 50s at best. What does this mean?

For one thing, it means we have no letters from Paul the new convert to Christ. A gap of 15 or more years lies between Paul's conversion to Christ and the earliest document we have from his hand. By the time he began writing his letters, he was already a mature Christian person with a fully developed thought world (see Chapter 9), and he was well into his missionary work as apostle to the Gentiles.

The letters, then, give us a glimpse of Paul when he was already in the middle of things, not a neophyte at all, and not just beginning his missionary work. In this chapter, we will focus on the earliest Pauline letters, bearing in mind that none of these letters reflect "Paul in his early days as a Christian." We will take a brief walk through Galatians and 1 and 2 Thessalonians in this chapter, hitting the highlights. This chapter is followed by Chapter 11, dealing with the so-called capital Pauline letters 1 and 2 Corinthians and Romans (Galatians, if dated later, is also considered one of the capital Pauline letters). Next comes Chapter 12 on the Captivity epistles (Colossians, Ephesians, Philemon, and Philippians). Last, in Chapter 13, we will discuss the Pastoral Epistles (1 and 2 Timothy and Titus). In these four chapters, we will survey the content and intent of Paul's letter writing.

PAUL'S FIRST SALVO—GALATIANS

The Epistle to the Galatians is my Epistle: I have betrothed myself to it. It is my wife.

—*Martin Luther*

Even on a cursory reading, it is hard to miss the polemical, even frantic, tone of much of Galatians. Paul writes in a combative mode and mood from beginning to end. But what had so set him off, what had made him so upset, even angry? What prompted him to even call his beloved converts idiots (Gal. 3.1)?! The answer is this—he believed he was dealing with a fundamental betrayal of a nonnegotiable, namely, the very character of the Gospel, especially as it applied to Gentiles. Paul's opponents are not the Galatians themselves but the *Judaizers,* or Jerusalem Jewish Christians who were arguing that all followers of Jesus of whatever ethnic extraction, in order to be full-fledged Christians, needed to be circumcised and keep the whole Mosaic covenant. Paul utterly rejects their view and minces no words in saying so. In fact, Paul, ever with a flair for the dramatic, even suggests that if the Judaizers were so keen on circumcision, he wishes they would just let the knife slip and dismember themselves (Gal. 5.12)! One is unlikely to hear a sermon on that text anytime soon.

Figure 10.1 Creation as described in Genesis. *"Creation," Donald Jackson, Copyright 2003,* The Saint John's Bible, *Order of Saint Benedict, Collegeville, Minnesota, USA.*

Figure 10.2 Moses will have seen some pyramids during his stay in Egypt, perhaps passing this on his way to see the Pharaoh. After Moses and the Israelites escaped Egypt, they went to Mt. Sinai, where the heart of the Mosaic covenant, the ten commandments, was given to them. (© *Mark R. Fairchild, Ph.D.*)

What is it that Paul is combating in Galatians? Is he, as Luther thought, mainly fighting over "justification by grace through faith"? If so, he does it in a peculiar way because all of his audience are already converts to Jesus. In regard to right-standing with God, they already have it. Paul's concern is actually about the issue of how those who are already Christians can grow in Christ, remain faithful to God, and carry on with their Christian life. He does not think any Gentile needs to add observance of the Mosaic covenant to their already Christian practices and beliefs. The question he is actually addressing is, *How then shall we live now that we are Christians?* Nevertheless, the reason he says that Christians should keep the law of Christ rather than the Mosaic law, and follow Christ rather than Moses, is precisely because he does believe that the audience has been saved by grace and through faith in the crucified savior Jesus. It is just that the Judaizers apparently had not drawn out the proper implications of that truth so far as it affects ongoing Christian belief and behavior.

Galatians, like Paul's other letters, has a rhetorical structure and argues in a deliberative fashion; that is, it attempts to convince the audience about matters of belief and behavior so they will not make a dreadful mistake and follow the urgings of the Judaizers. Paul is trying to head off a train wreck by means of this passionate discourse. Here is the structure of the discourse, and we will pay special attention to its thesis statement.

at a Glance

Galatians was authored by Paul not long after he had visited Galatia on his first full missionary journey. Probably written from Antioch, this document is a circular letter (i.e., written to Christians in several places in Galatia—Psidian Antioch, Iconium, Lystra); and if Paul's letters can be divided into problem-solving letters and progress-oriented letters, this one is the former, and not surprisingly involves polemics. Although some scholars think this document was written in the A.D. 50s after the so-called Apostolic Council mentioned in Acts 15, it seems far more likely to have been written just

continued

continued

prior to that council in A.D. 50 and so reflects no knowledge of the outcome of that Council, which Paul could certainly have appealed to in order to fend off the Judaizers. The problem that generates the letter is the probable infiltration of Judaizers into the Pauline churches in Galatia. The whole purpose of the document is to prevent the Galatians, who are mostly Gentiles, from submitting to circumcision and the full-blown keeping of the Mosaic covenant. For quite some time, scholars have debated the location of the audience to whom Paul was writing. Two main theories are known as the North Galatia theory, indicating that Paul was writing to the northern part of the province, and the South Galatia theory, which suggests that he was writing to the southern part where the Roman road was already established. Those who take into account historical and archaeological facts conclude that the South Galatia theory represents the most plausible view.

MOSAIC COVENANT

The covenant that God made with Moses on Mt. Sinai concerning Israel. The covenant outlines the way of life for the Israelite people and the way they will be in relationship with God and other peoples.

OUTLINE OF GALATIONS

Epistolary Prescript	1.1–5	
Exordium/Introduction	1.6–10	Two Gospels?
Narratio/Narration of Facts	1.11–2.14	A narrative of surprising events
Propositio/Thesis Statement	2.15–21	Saved by the faithfulness of Christ, not by works of the Mosaic law
Probatio/Arguments Pro	3.1–6.10	Seven arguments to support the thesis
Paul's Autograph	6.11	
Peroratio/Emotional Summing Up	6.12–17	
Epistolary Closing	6.18	

SYNOPSIS OF CONTENTS

Unlike some of Paul's longer letters, Galatians, rather like Philippians, accomplishes its aims in a shorter amount of time and space. Normally, after the initial greetings (Paul . . . to the Galatians, "grace and peace"), Paul would give a prayer or thanksgiving report (cf. 1 Cor. 1), but apparently he can't think of anything to be thankful for about the situation in Galatia, so instead he launches right into his polemics. In fact, Paul even adds important content to the opening greetings! He begins by asserting his apostolic authority (Gal. 1.1–2), making clear his authority is not derived from the Jerusalem church or from any mere human source but rather directly from Christ; and then, after the initial greeting, he reminds the audience that Christ gave his very life to rescue the world from its sin and from "the present evil age," that is, the fallen world in which we live.

At this juncture, already at Gal. 1.6, Paul gets right to the point of the problem. Paul accuses the audience of abandoning the One who called them (by which he could mean himself or Christ) and turning to a very different Gospel, which he characterizes as no Gospel at all! Paul was not an early advocate of the "you have your religious views and I have mine and they are equally valid" theory. Paul then places the blame directly on "some people" (v. 7) who are trying to pervert the true Gospel of salvation by grace through faith without the requirement of keeping the **Mosaic covenant**. Paul says whoever it is who is preaching this false Gospel should be seen as under God's curse! These are strong words, and the intent of them is to warn the Galatians off from believing or receiving the message of the Judaizers who were insisting that all true Christians must get themselves circumcised and keep the Mosaic law. Apparently, according to Galatians 1, verse 10, Paul had been accused by these conservative Jewish Christians from Jerusalem of being a smooth-talking people pleaser, offering up a Gospel that was Gospel lite!

It is at Gal. 1.11 that Paul goes on a long narration of important events in his life that carries on until Gal. 2.15. This is the longest such narration of auto-biographical details by Paul in any of his letters, and the reason for it seems to be twofold: 1) there seem to have been some accusations against Paul that suggested that his Gospel was humanly derived, not from God, and that it did not have the approval of the pillar apostles, Peter, James, and John, in Jerusalem; and 2) this narration sets up and supports the arguments that Paul will launch in the rest of the letter, after he makes clear his essential thesis in Gal. 2.15–21.

Figure 10.3 The serpent and the apple. (© Rick Danielson)

In sum, Paul maintains in Gal. 1.11–2.15 that his Gospel had come to him directly from Christ, through his conversion experience on Damascus Road, after which he went away for some years to Arabia, by which he probably means Nabatea, the capital of which was Petra (in Jordan today). He then visited the leaders of the Jerusalem church to lay before them the Gospel he derived from Christ, and they did not in any way object to his Gospel—indeed, they also gave him the right hand of fellowship so he could be recognized as "the apostle to the Gentiles" in the same way Peter was designated as the main apostle to the Jews. Finally, he makes clear that when Peter and Barnabas withdrew from table fellowship with Gentiles under pressure from the Judaizers who had come to Antioch from Jerusalem, he opposed this betrayal of the Gospel for Gentiles, even opposing Peter in public and shaming him in the assembly meeting there. This then leads to Paul's essential thesis statement, which is the most crucial text for understanding what follows in this letter. We need then to look closely at what he is trying to accomplish by considering his basic thesis statement. Here is a literal translation of Gal. 2.15–21, bearing in mind that this is presented as part of Paul's argument with Peter after he withdrew from table fellowship with Gentiles in Antioch due to pressure from the Judaizers.

> *We by nature are Jews, and not sinners from the Gentile nations, and seeing that a human being is not acquitted from works of the Law except through the faithfulness of Jesus Christ even we began to believe in Jesus Christ, in order that we might be set right/justified by the faithfulness of Christ, and not by works of the Law, because "by works of the Law will no flesh be set right." But if seeking to be acquitted by*

Christ we ourselves were found to be at the same time sinners, then is Christ a servant of sin? Absolutely not! For if I build up again what was destroyed, I show myself to be a transgressor. For I, through the Law, died to the Law in order that I might live to God. I have been crucified with Christ, I no longer live, but Christ lives in me. But now living in the flesh, I am living in the faith—that of the Son of God who loved me and gave himself for me. I do not render invalid the grace of God, for if through the Law [there is] righteousness/right-standing, then Christ died for nothing.

What Paul is arguing toward and arguing for is a tale of two covenants, told in metaphorical fashion in Galatians 4. In that tale, Paul will directly connect the **Abrahamic covenant** with the New Covenant and explain that the Mosaic covenant was temporal and temporary until Christ should come to redeem those under the Mosaic law. We need to understand that Paul's argument is not basically a "faith versus works" argument in which faith is seen as good and works as bad. Indeed, Paul will argue that it is the work of Christ on the cross, which he colorfully calls "the faithfulness of Christ" in the preceding translation, that has made human attempts at doing the works of the Mosaic law unnecessary and unhelpful when it comes to the matter of right-standing with God and righteousness or sanctification that comes from God.

Furthermore, in Galatians 6, Paul will go on to say that Christians are expected to keep "the Law of Christ," by which he means several things (the portions of the Old Testament Law reaffirmed by Christ, the new teaching of Christ, and some apostolic teaching as well). *Just as Paul is not contrasting works with faith, nor is he contrasting all Law with faith either.* What he is doing is saying that right-standing and the obtaining of the Holy Spirit comes to us by grace and through faith and not through the keeping of the Mosaic law (see Gal. 3.1–3), either prior to faith in Christ or thereafter. He is telling his Galatians that they will gain nothing by getting circumcised and keeping the Mosaic

> **ABRAHAMIC COVENANT**
>
> The covenant God made with Abram described in Genesis 15:18–21. God promises that Abram's descendants would inherit the land of many other nations. Genesis 12:1–3 also describes the promise that God made to Abram, namely that he would be the father of many nations. In Genesis 17:9–14 God directs Abraham to circumcise all males as a sign of the covenant.

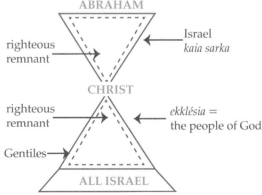

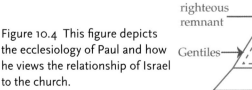

Figure 10.4 This figure depicts the ecclesiology of Paul and how he views the relationship of Israel to the church.

law, for they already have the benefits in Christ, through the Spirit, and in the Law of Christ, which the Judaizers are promising comes with full keeping of the Mosaic covenant.

Notice in the thesis statement translated previously the use of forensic language of acquittal more than once. It was necessary for Paul to die to the Mosaic law and its keeping in order to be exonerated or acquitted of its guilty verdict on his belief and behavior. In other words, the Mosaic law is obsolete now that Christ and his death and the new covenant and the Holy Spirit have shown up. The basis for right-standing with God is objectively "the faithfulness of Christ" (his death on the cross) and subjectively our faith in his finished work on the cross. Christians thereafter live in the freedom of the Spirit and with the guidance of the Law of Christ, and are no longer obligated to the Mosaic law.

The astounding thing is that Paul thinks this is true not just for his Gentile converts but also for Jews like himself and Peter. They are no longer required to be circumcised and keep the 600+ commandments of the Mosaic law. Among other things, this means they are free to have table fellowship with Gentiles without any fears of becoming ritually or morally unclean. But when Paul made this argument we find in Galatians 2, it appears he was standing in splendid isolation, without the support of either Peter or his good friend Barnabas, and he accuses them both of hypocrisy for withdrawing from table fellowship with Gentiles.

When Paul says his old self was crucified with Christ on Golgotha, he means not merely the sinful part of his old self but indeed, his whole old self—even the Pharisaic-Law-keeping self that at one time had led to his advancing in Judaism beyond many of his peers as he claims in Galatians 1. In 2 Cor. 5.17–18, he puts it this way: "If anyone is in Christ, he is a new creature, everything old has passed away; see everything has become new." The tension in the Christian life, according to Paul, is not old self versus new self, with the old self still hanging around and dragging the person down. No, the tension in the Christian life according to Galatians 5 is flesh versus Spirit, by which Paul means the sinful inclinations in the human body still tug a person one way while the Holy Spirit pulls and guides them in another direction. When Paul says triumphantly to his converts in Galatians "for freedom Christ has set you free," he means not just that they have avoided the burden of the Mosaic law, but also that they have been liberated from the bondage of sin. Although sin remains, it no longer reigns in the Christians because of the powerful presence and work of the Spirit in that life. This in practical terms means that Christians can resist and overcome temptation and the inclinations of the flesh. In the case of the young Christians in Galatia, it also means that they need not give in to the pressure of the Judaizers to become full-fledged Jews. Some of these same sorts of ideas occur again in Paul's later letter written largely to the Gentile Christians in Rome, which we will discuss in Chapter 11.

1 AND 2 THESSALONIANS

Whereas 1 and 2 Thessalonians are certainly shorter and easier to read than Paul's more complex letters, such as Romans and 1 Corinthians, when it comes to the discussions of **eschatology** or the end times, they are no less complex than Romans. What we especially need to keep in mind in this case is that these are pastoral letters, letters of concern and pastoral care to a group of Christians who have been persecuted and some of whom have died! Paul is not dealing with abstract subjects in these documents but trying to minister to his fledgling Christians in Thessalonica at the point of their need.

It is one of the interesting features of Paul's letters that, apart from Galatians, Paul always begins the discourse proper with some sort of wish prayer, blessing prayer, or at least a report of what he has been praying for them (as in 1 Thess.). Sometimes it is more a matter of informing the audience, sometimes more a matter of praying for the audience, or sometimes more a matter of blessing the audience; but in all cases, Paul's discourses tend to open in a manner meant to establish rapport with the audience and good feeling between the apostle and that audience.

If one examines 1 Thessalonians closely, it becomes clear that it is like funeral oratory, and so is a form of epideictic rhetoric, the rhetoric of praise and blame. It has no thesis statement and does not directly argue for some verdict or change of behavior, but rather it tries to spiritually form the audience through consolation, consultation, and clarification of the audience's confusions over eschatology and other things. Here is a brief rhetorical outline of 1 Thessalonians.

RHETORICAL OUTLINE OF 1 THESSALONIANS

Epistolary Prescript and Greeting	1.1
Thanksgiving Report/Exordium	1.2–3
Narratio of Relevant Facts	1.4–3.10
Concluding Wish Prayer	3.11–13
Exhortation to Holy and Hopeful Living	4.1–5.15
Peroratio/Final Emotional Appeal	5.16–21
Concluding Wish Prayer	5.23–24
Closing Greetings and Charges	5.25–27
Benediction	5.28

SYNOPSIS OF CONTENTS

Paul will urge the Thessalonians to realize that their fellow believers have not died in vain, so they should continue to live in hope until the Lord returns.

Resurrection was a difficult idea for pagans to wrap their minds around. They were used to thinking at most of the immortality of the soul, and that is definitely not what Paul is talking about in 1 Thess. 4–5. We will focus on that part of 1 Thess. because it is the most discussed and debated portion even today of that discourse.

First, if you read 1 Thess. 4.13–5.11 carefully, you will notice Paul's use of the metaphor of a "thief coming in the night" to describe the character of Christ's return to raise the dead and save his people. This metaphor actually is something Paul seems to have gotten from the teaching of Jesus himself (Mt. 24.43), and it connotes the idea that Christ will come back suddenly at an unexpected time, so the believer must always be ready for his return.

Sometimes, even scholars make the mistake of thinking that Paul is suggesting a timetable for the return of Christ—sooner rather than later and indeed during the apostle's own lifetime, in which case Paul was wrong about this matter. In fact, Paul's declarations in 1 Thess. 4.13–5.11 indicate that he puts himself in the only category he could put himself in, given the fact that there are two unknown dates—the date of his own death and the date of Christ's return. Because Paul did not know the timing of his own death or of Christ's return, he could not say, "we who are dead when Jesus comes back." No, he had to put himself in the category of the living because he believed it was possible (not certain, but possible) Christ *might* return soon. What Paul knows for sure is that there are some Thessalonian believers who are already dead, and he speaks about their resurrection. What he says about everyone else including himself is, "we who are left, who are living when Christ returns. . . ." Paul has great expectations but no calculations about the timing of Christ's return.

This explanation helps us to see that there is no contradiction between what Paul says in 1 Thess. 4.13–5.11 and what he says in 2 Thess. 2 about the second coming of Jesus. In the latter text, he talks about events that lead up to the return of Christ, including dealing with some sort of evil world leader, as well as something involving the temple in Jerusalem. The way prophecy works in the Biblical tradition is that the prophets saw the future as being like a range of mountains viewed from a distance. They juxtapose the nearer and further mountains together, the nearer events and the more distant ones, because what *mattered* is God's keeping his word about final justice and final redemption for God's people, not the timing of these events, nor, for that matter, the gap in time between the preliminary and the final eschatological events. We have to bear in mind that Paul and most early Christians believed they already lived in the end times, which were inaugurated by the coming, the death, the resurrection, and the Spirit giving of Jesus.

One other aspect of the material in 1 Thess. 4.13–5.11 deserves discussion. Is Paul talking here about some sort of rapture of the faithful entirely out of this world and into heaven, so they may avoid the final tribulation on earth? The answer to

CLUES FROM THE CULTURE

You are devoted to oratory . . . and you tolerate as speakers only those who are very clever.

—*Dio Chrysostom Or. 35.1*

at a Glance
1 AND 2 THESSALONIANS

These documents are written by Paul (see 1 Thess. 5.27 and 2 Thess. 3.17) with the consultation and help of his coworkers Timothy and Silas. The first of these letters seems to have been written from Corinth in about A.D. 51, with the second one coming later in the A.D. 50s. The audience is the same for both letters, but the situation has changed, and so the rhetoric changes. First Thessalonians is consolatory, using eschatology to reassure the Thessalonians that their deceased brothers and sisters will not be left out of the final resurrection; whereas 2 Thessalonians focuses on the problem of converts who apparently are still too pagan and will not work, and who are bearing bad witness to their city.

this question is definitely not. Paul is talking about meeting the Lord in the air (not in heaven) with both the dead in Christ and the living going forth to meet and greet the Lord as he returns, and then returning with him to reign upon the earth.

To give a little more detail, Paul is actually using the language and metaphors of a royal visit to a walled city to describe the return of Christ. During such a visit, the king's herald would go before him toward the city gate and walls; blow the trumpet (see the reference to the angel with a trumpet in 1 Thess. 4), alerting the watchman on the wall that the king was returning to his city; and then give the cry of command: "Lift up your gates so the glorious king may come in" (see Psalm 24). Being the good watchman that he was, he would ask which king the herald was referring to, in other words, "stand and identify." Once the watchman was satisfied with the identification, then and then only would the gates open, and the city greeting committee would go out to meet the king and his entourage and welcome him back into the city.

In Paul's vivid description, the dead in Christ and the living will go out to meet King Jesus in the air and then welcome him back to reign on the earth. Paul, in other words, describes the believers as the greeting committee. The final locale of this reunion is not outside the city or up in the air but down on terra firma (firm ground) within the city. Thessalonica was indeed a walled city that had been visited in living memory by Augustus himself before he became emperor, and even more recently by other royal dignitaries. They would have caught the nuances of Paul's metaphorical description here quite nicely. It was only in the 17th century that Christians began to make the mistake of thinking 1 Thess. 4 might be about some sort of rapture out of trouble on earth.

Think about the whole drift of 1 Thessalonians, though. Paul is consoling living Christians about their martyred fellow believers! He is not telling them, "Don't worry, you will avoid martyrdom by being raptured." He is telling them that, whatever happens, God will have the last word because Christ will return and raise the dead in Christ to live with him when he returns to reign on earth. The consolation offered involves resurrection, not rapture, and glorification, not escape from earthly troubles.

There is an interesting array of subjects that Paul touches on in both 1 and 2 Thessalonians, and one of these is work. Here is a brief list of some of the parallel passages:

Perseverance in Tribulation	1 Thess. 1.6–8	2 Thess. 1.4
The Calling of Sanctification	1 Thess. 2.12–13	2 Thess. 2.13–14
Parallel Prayers	1 Thess. 3.11	2 Thess. 2.16
Requests	1 Thess. 4.1	2 Thess. 3.1
Instructions for Right Living	1 Thess. 4.1–2	2 Thess. 3.6–7
Continue Loving/Working	1 Thess. 4.10	2 Thess. 3.10–12
Benediction	1 Thess. 5.23	2 Thess. 3.16

We could say that 1 and 2 Thess. are two peas from the same pod. In fact, 2 Thess. is just a continuation of the same discussions, a little later in time, with the same author and the same audience. One of these subjects is work, so we say a little more about Paul's perspective on work here.

Attempts by scholars to connect the issue of idleness and work to the presentation of eschatology in 1 and 2 Thess. have on the whole failed. Paul deliberately separates these issues, especially in 2 Thess., where it is bracketed off by prayers. Here is the rhetorical outline of 2 Thess:

RHETORICAL OUTLINE OF 2 THESSALONIANS	
Epistolary Prescript	1.1–2
Exordium/Thanksgiving Prayer	1.3–10
Propositio/Thesis Statement	1.11–12
Refutatio/Arguments Con—Prelude to the Parousia	2.1–12
Thanksgiving/Firm Living	2.13–15
Another Wish Prayer	2.16–17
Final Request	3.1–5
Probatio/Arguments Pro	3.6–12
Peroratio/Final Emotional Appeal	3.13–15
Wish Prayer/Benediction	3.16
Epistolary Closing/Autograph	3.17
Closing Wish Prayer/Benediction	3.18

It is no accident that Paul set an example of working when he was in Thessalonica. He did not do this just to make a living; as on other occasions, he had no problem with being supported by converts in other congregations, for example, the church in Philippi (see 2 Cor. 8–9). Paul worked to set an example for the men in his congregation who tended to seek to be clients of wealthy patrons and in general took little or no initiative to work unless called upon by their patrons. Paul knew that what would carry the greatest weight when trying to change others' behavior was to set a good example himself. Paul also knew that the heart of ancient religion was *praxis* (behavior); and with the majority of the audience in Thessalonica being former pagans, he knew that he had to do at least as much teaching on ethics and practice as on beliefs.

I would suggest that in 2 Thess. 3, and to some degree in the parallel material in 1 Thess. on work, Paul is drawing on the traditional discussions about work and community ethos found in Aristotle and other sources familiar to the audience (see Aristotle's *Politics* 3.13.1284a, a saying Paul quotes in the similar discussion on work in Galatians 5.23). Paul's basic principle is "let those who will not work, not eat." Idleness is not merely the devil's playground according to Paul; it is a bad example for a Christian to set because each person should be encouraged to "carry his own weight" and each worker is "worthy of his hire" and should be properly paid. If one works with one's hands, as an artisan would do (Paul busily making and mending tents), then one is not indebted to a patron. Plato wrote that people should "take care of their own business" (i.e., needs; *Republic* 433A–B). Paul then is not trying to impose an alien Jewish work ethic on a largely Gentile crowd.

This explains an otherwise puzzling passage in Gal. 6.2–6 where Paul says both "we should bear one another's burdens" and also "each one should carry his own load," and then he also goes on to say that teachers deserve to be supported by those whom they have taught! Although this might seem like a series of contradictions on a superficial reading of that text, in fact it is not. The second saying, "each one should carry his own load," is directed against those who were relying on patronage to supply their needs and were not prepared to take the initiative and find and do work to support themselves. The first of the sayings refers to helping bear the burdens of those who need such help. It refers to helping those who are not entirely able to help themselves—especially widows, orphans, and the destitute. And finally, Paul will argue in 1 Cor. 9 that a workman, in this case, an apostle, has the right to be supported by his converts, but he also has the right to refuse such support if it would be misconstrued as some kind of patronage and reciprocity relationship that would restrict Paul's travel and ability to offer the Gospel free of charge. Paul did not want to become some Christian patron's paid in-house teacher!

We need to stress that typically, lower- or middle-status males in the Greco-Roman world would seek to attach themselves to some patron so they could avoid what they viewed as bone-crushing menial and demeaning labor. The problem was, this put them into a reciprocity spin cycle as clients of the patron in which they owed their souls and bodies to the patron, had to jump when he snapped his fingers, and could not get out of the payback relationship unless the patron terminated it. Paul does not want newly minted Christians to be sycophants, hangers-on, or sponges. He wants them to set a good example by working. Unlike some Greco-Roman higher status persons, Jews did not have a problem with hard work and manual labor. They saw it as a means of self-sufficiency.

In short, patron–client relationships created entangling alliances. You cannot be your own person as a client, and such relationships are often ethically compromising. You end up saying or doing the dirty work of the patron. Indeed, a client might even be expected to dine in pagan temples with their patron from time to time and be dragged into religiously compromising situations. As a result, Paul makes known his own work among them and encourages his audience to avoid establishing patron/client relationships that come with strings attached. Instead, Paul's message is to work to please God by following the in-structions given to them that came by the authority of Jesus.

It appears from 2 Thess. 3 that things have gotten worse since the time when Paul wrote 1 Thessalonians, so he must now instruct the audience to shun those who are idle so as to shame them into better patterns of behavior. In an honor and shame culture such as we find in the Greco-Roman world, shunning actu-ally was an effective strategy, as one could not afford to be publicly shamed by one's inner circle or friends. That was not just bad for one's image, it was also bad for business. A slacker got a reputation for being undependable. Paul offers as an alternative "do not grow weary in doing well." Yes, there is a strong work ethic in the New Testament: call it the Pauline work ethic, not the Puritan work ethic. Finally, Paul was a person who believed, as did Jesus, that God did reward the faithful and diligent servant. He did not suggest that working was its own reward, he suggested that self-sacrificial behavior like that of Christ would not go unnoticed or unrewarded by the Almighty.

IMPLICATIONS

One of the things that is so winsome and appealing about Paul is his whole-heartedness and genuineness. As we have seen in Galatians and 1 and 2 Thes-salonians, Paul does nothing by half measures. He is a walking and talking bundle of outrageous extremes, and one never has to ask him—How do you really feel about this or that matter (say, for instance, circumcising Gentiles)? You get the sense that you always knew where you stood with Paul. He does not mince words. He seems almost incapable of playing his cards close to his vest, especially when he is so invested in the lives of his fledgling converts in Galatia or Thessalonica.

We have emphasized in this chapter that Paul's letters are situation specific, dealing with the particular problems and promise of his new converts at the time when these letters were written. In the case of Galatia, the problem was outside interference by conservative Jewish Christians. In the case of Thessalonica, the problem was persecution by non-Christian outsiders, which had resulted in the death of some Christians there and the deep grieving and confusion that fol-lowed among those still loyal to Christ. In both circumstances, Paul is operating as a pastor who loves his converts and wants to steer them in the right direction, wants them to not give up hope or their faith, wants them to continue to have a close relationship with their apostle. The poignancy of Paul's self-description as the "mother" who gave birth to the converts in Gal. 4, or the midwife or nurse who delivered and fed them in the Thessalonian letters, shows just how intimate a relationship Paul felt he had with his converts. He is a pastor, and his theology and ethics are pastoral in character. He never brings up subjects simply for debate or discussion. He is always trying to persuade, always trying to offer a word on target to help his audiences along their Christian way.

There are indeed some practical implications for what Paul says in Galatians and the two Thessalonian letters, and we can mention a few of them here. Obviously, Paul believes that salvation is a gift of God's grace, not something one can earn or deserve. Equally obviously he thinks that salvation is a work in progress, by which I mean he thinks conversion is only the beginning of salvation and that thereafter, we are supposed to work out our salvation with fear and trembling as God works in our midst to will and to do, as Paul says clearly in Philippians. Paul is concerned about some of his converts abandoning their faith due to pressure or persecution (in Thessalonica) or perverting the Gospel under pressure from the Judaizers (in Galatia). These letters are written in part to forestall such an outcome.

Paul also believes that genuine faith leads to good works of various sorts (or, to coin an aphorism, genuine faith works), but it does not lead to going back and keeping the Mosaic covenant and doing the works of the Mosaic law. Instead Christians according to Gal. 6 are to follow the Law of Christ, which refers to 1) the example of Christ, his life, and lifestyle; 2) the teaching of Christ; and 3) the portions of the older teachings in the Old Testament that either Christ or his apostles reaffirmed as valid for Christians, such as "don't commit adultery." There is plenty of place in Paul's Gospel for good works and hard work, and he believes that each person should carry their own weight and help others who are unable to do so. In Chapter 11, this will become clearer when we deal with 1 and 2 Corinthians and Romans in some detail.

KEY TERMS

Abraham Covenant   Mosaic Covenant
Eschatology

FOR FURTHER READING

Fee, G. D. *The First and Second Letters to the Thessalonians.* Grand Rapids, MI: Eerdmans, 2009.

Moo, D. *Galatians.* Grand Rapids, MI: Baker, 2013.

Witherington, B. *1 and 2 Thessalonians: A Socio-Rhetorical Commentary.* Grand Rapids, MI: Eerdmans, 2006.

————. Witherington, B. *Grace in Galatia: A Commentary on St. Paul's Letter to the Galatians.* Grand Rapids, MI: Eerdmans, 1998.

STUDY QUESTIONS

If you had to assess these three letters as representative of Paul's teaching, would you say he puts more stress on belief or on behavior? Why does he seem to see both as important for one's faith and salvation?

What sort of work ethic do these letters reveal Paul had? How did he view people who sponged off of others and did not carry their own load?

Why was Paul so adamant that his Gentile converts not get circumcised and not try to keep the Mosaic covenant? What does this tell you about Paul's views of the new covenant and its differences from the Mosaic one?

NOTES

1. Cited in R. MacMullen, *Paganism in the Roman Empire* (New Haven, CT: Yale University Press, 1983), 98–99.

The Roman bath at Hierapolis. (© Mark R. Fairchild, Ph.D.)

11 PAUL the LETTER WRITER PART TWO: The CAPITAL PAULINE EPISTLES

ALTHOUGH IT IS TRUE THAT WE CAN SEE Galatians and 1 and 2 Thessalonians as examples of Paul the troubleshooter solving belief and behavior problems, this is all the more so in 1 and 2 Corinthians where, without question, there are major problems of a variety of sorts in the Corinthian house churches.

1 AND 2 CORINTHIANS

First and Second Corinthians are some of the most beloved and belabored of all the Pauline documents, and no one disputes that they show just how many problems and how many different kinds of problems—theological, ethical, practical—Paul could have with his largely Gentile converts. When we catch up with Paul in 1 Corinthians, we are listening in to a conversation in progress, and a vigorous one at that. Paul would plead, cajole, exhort, command, persuade, and in short do whatever it took to try to get his Corinthians back on track with their Christian lives.

One of the interesting features about both these long discourses (1 and 2 Corinthians) is that they involve what can be called mixed rhetoric. In 1 Corinthians, we find largely deliberative rhetoric, with an epideictic digression in praise of love in 1 Cor. 13. In 2 Corinthians, we see both deliberative (2 Cor. 1–9) and forensic (2 Cor. 10–13) rhetoric, as Paul pulls out all the rhetorical stops to accomplish his aims with his audience. What 1 and 2 Corinthians demonstrate is that Paul is not writing abstract theological or ethical treatises. These are **ad hoc** letters or discourses, by which I mean, these are documents written to address specific issues with specific audiences at a specific point in time. Unless we understand the historical, social, and rhetorical contexts, we are unlikely to get the meaning of these texts right.

Here is the rhetorical structure of the largely deliberative discourse we call 1 Corinthians:

RHETORICAL OUTLINE OF 1 CORINTHIANS	
Epistolary Prescript	1.1–3
Epistolary Thanksgiving/Exordium	1.4–9
Propositio/Thesis Statement	1.10
Narratio/Narration of Pertinent Facts	1.11–17
Probatio/Arguments Pro	1.18–16.12 (Nine arguments with epideictic digression in 1 Cor. 13)
Peroratio/Final Emotional Appeal	16.13–18
Closing Epistolary Greetings and Blessing	16.19–24

SYNOPSIS OF CONTENTS

If we pause to examine the thesis statement, it becomes clear that 1 Corinthians is an attempt to produce unity, harmony, concord, and peace in a very factious situation where Christians were behaving like immature children indulging in sibling rivalry. At the same time, the Corinthians appear to have had many valid spiritual gifts, which just goes to show that the level of one's giftedness has little to do with the level of one's spiritual maturity. Paul, one issue at a time, addressed the things that were causing divisions, arguments, and splits in the house churches in Corinth.

Figure 11.1 A view from the Acro-Corinth near the temple of the Aphrodite ruins. (© *Mark R. Fairchild, Ph.D.*)

Paul was correcting *specific* problems, and this includes those famous passages in 1 Corinthians 11 and 14 about women and their roles in the house churches (more on that later in this chapter). It is a mistake, for example, to think that Paul would expect all women in all centuries in all cultures to wear head coverings just because he exhorted the Corinthian women prophetesses to do so in Corinth. In addition, one has to distinguish between principles and practices. Principles are universal, but practices are culturally variable, and a head covering is a cultural practice.

Furthermore, at important junctures, Paul is answering specific questions written or spoken to him by Corinthian Christians. For example, when we read in 1 Cor. 7.1 the saying "it is good for a man not to touch a woman," we cannot afford to ignore the connection of these words with what comes immediately before them: "Now about the things which *you* wrote"—the "you" are the Corinthians, and Paul is quoting one or another of them who seems to be an ascetic and thinks sexual contact is unclean or immoral. This is clearly *not* Paul's own view because he goes on in 1 Corinthians 7 to say that each man should have his own wife, and vice versa, *unless* one has a special charisma or spiritual gift to remain single for the sake of the Lord. Paul was neither a prude nor a monk. Probably he had been married as a Pharisee before his conversion, but now as a Christian apostle, he was single (having likely been shunned by his family when he converted); and his calling, work, and travel probably made it necessary for him to stay single. Paul does believe that because Christ died and rose, the eschatological clock has been set ticking, and one would be unwise to live without realizing that "the form of this world," including institutions like marriage, which God gave us for our earthly good, was passing away.

A CLOSER LOOK

Unfortunately, during the course of the 20th and 21st centuries, Paul has become something of a whipping boy for everything from male chauvinism to the prevention of women from assuming ministerial roles to the repression of normal sexual desires. On all such counts, Paul is not guilty. What is true of Paul is that he is a wise pastor, so he must start with his converts where they are—even with all their prejudices and problems and even with the social arrangements they are already enmeshed in. Paul believes in persuasion, and that is a subtle solvent for change. He believes that the yeast of the Gospel must be allowed to do its work gradually, and the people themselves must become convinced of what Christ-like behavior and belief really are. Thus, when we find Paul dealing with messy marriage and ministry situations such as in Corinth, it is a mistake to assume that a work in progress is necessarily Paul's endgame. In regard to Paul and women, it is especially important to take the ad hoc nature of Paul's remarks into account.

Let's be clear from the outset that Paul had a variety of female coworkers who did ministry with him. There were folk like the wife-and-husband team of Priscilla and Aquila (see Acts 18, 1 Cor. 16, and Rom. 16); the apostles Andronicus and Junia, Euodia and Syntyche in Phil. 4; or Phoebe the deacon in Rom. 16. Furthermore, in 1 Cor. 11, there are Paul's specific instructions that it is fine for women to pray and prophesy in the house church worship service so long as they wear a head covering. We will say more about that shortly. The point is, Paul did not believe that Christian women should not assume a wide variety of ministerial roles in the church, and their marital status did not seem to affect the matter one way or another. Roles in the church were not determined by gender but by calling and gifting. The reason for this was obvious—it was the Holy Spirit who gave Christians a variety of gifts, and the Spirit bestowed these gifts regardless of gender, social status, race, age, and the like.

What then should we make of passages like 1 Cor. 14.33b–36 or 1 Tim. 2.8–15, passages that so often have been used to stifle if not stop the ministry of women in the body of Christ? Both passages are correcting problems. This should be obvious from reading the first part of 1 Corinthians 14, or by reading 1 Timothy 2.8, where Paul first corrects men, then tells them to stop grumbling and lift up holy hands in prayer. In the case of 1 Cor. 14.33b–36, the problem being corrected is clearly caused by married women who are asking questions during the time of the prophecies, the speaking in tongues, and the interpretation of tongues. Paul says these women should ask their "man" at home if they have questions. Why would they be asking questions? Because that is exactly what Gentiles did when they went to visit the nearby oracle at Delphi.

Prophets were seen as providing a consulting service, so you went to see them and ask the fundamental questions of life: Should I marry this person? Will I ever be well? Will I have children? Should I buy property? These women assumed that Christian prophecy worked like Greek prophecy, but they were wrong, so Paul tells them to consult someone at home.

That, of course, is not all he says. He also says that all the church people, including women, ought to be silent when the word of God is being spoken or taught. Indeed, believers are called to be in submission to God and the holy teaching "as even the law" says. In 1 Cor. 14, Paul is not talking about women being in submission to men. Nothing whatsoever is said about that in 1 Cor. 14. The silence he commands is a specific one when the inspired words are being spoken, as is clear from the earlier part of 1 Cor. 14.

In 1 Tim. 2, the situation is a bit different. Here, Paul is addressing high-status women with bling and fancy clothes. He sees these things as a distraction. What we know about ancient women of Paul's era is that those of high status tended to have long hair piled up on their heads and were known to weave jewels and precious stones into their hair to draw attention to their hair. When Paul says in 1 Cor. 11 that a woman's hair is her glory, many in antiquity would have agreed; but in a worship service, only God's glory should be in evidence, not woman's or man's. But there is another factor as well. Christians mainly held their meetings at night after the workday was done, in rooms where there would be a myriad of lit oil lamps. If a woman walked into a worship service with that sort of hairdo and with her head uncovered, it would have reflected a lot of light and been rather like a walking disco ball—a total distraction. Hence, for two good reasons, Paul says women should not dress ostentatiously or have bejeweled hair. But there is more. In 1 Tim. 2, Paul adds, "I am not now permitting (such a) woman to teach or to usurp authority over the male (teachers). They are to be quiet and remain in submission."

The scenario begins to become clear. Higher-status women in Ephesus (which is where the audience of 1 Timothy lived) were educated women, and educated women regularly played a variety of religious roles in temples in Ephesus—not because they had been instructed by anyone, but simply because of their rank, status, and ability to read. It would be natural for such women to expect immediately to be teachers in their new chosen religion—Christianity. Paul says to such well-dressed articulate women, you need to learn first. He was not at that time permitting them to teach. Again, Paul says nothing here about women in general being in submission to men. The submission clause here has to do with submitting to the teaching, not to the male teachers. Furthermore, the Greek verb "I am not permitting" never has the meaning "I would never allow." Paul is concerned that these higher-status women need to be patient and learn.

Apparently, some had even tried to usurp the place of one or more of the official teachers in Ephesus, perhaps one of the Ephesian elders, and it was causing a problem. Paul then is correcting an abuse of a possible privilege, not ruling out women from ever teaching, even teaching men.

As for Paul and sex, it is clear enough in 1 Cor. 7 that although Paul believes that sex should be reserved for heterosexual, married relationships, he has no problems with couples making love as husband and wife. Indeed, he goes so far as to say that the only real reason to abstain would be for a time of prayer, and then the couple should come back together and continue to conjugate the verb "to love." As we can see from all this, Paul has been poorly served by some interpreters regarding the issues of women and their roles in the church and, for that matter, even the basic matter of sex.*

* For much more on this subject, see B. Witherington, *Women and the Genesis of Christianity*, ed. A. Witherington (Cambridge, England: Cambridge University Press, 1990).

First Corinthians is an interesting document that begins its first argument by talking about the cross of Christ (1 Cor. 1) and ends its last argument by talking about the resurrection. In between, there are numerous arguments about sexual aberrations, taking fellow believers to court, eating meat offered to idols in pagan temples, behaving badly at the Lord's Supper, and misusing the gifts of prophecy and speaking in tongues. As 1 Cor. 13 stresses, all such spiritual gifts are to be used in a loving manner, which is to say not in a self-centered or egotistical manner.

Paul begins his arguments in 1 Cor. 1 by explaining what counts as wisdom in God's view of things, and then he hands out sage advice on a whole host of subjects, some of which the Corinthians had asked him about in a letter and some of which he had heard about from oral reports of Christians coming from Corinth to Ephesus. Because of its great importance to Christian thought, we will examine Paul's climactic argument about resurrection in 1 Cor. 15 briefly here.

SYNKRISIS

A rhetorical device used to compare and contrast two things. For example, Paul contrasts the earthly bodies we have now and the resurrection bodies we shall obtain at the resurrection.

If we ask the question, "What does Paul mean by resurrection?," the answer seems clear enough. He means something that happens to or involves a physical body such that either it comes back to life or somehow the person is reconstituted in a body, whatever state of decay he or she had been in before. Resurrection does not refer to dying and going to heaven, nor does resurrection, according to Paul, refer to immortality of the soul. Furthermore, when Paul talks about resurrection, he does a *synkrisis*, a rhetorical comparison and contrast between the bodies we have now and the bodies we shall obtain at the resurrection.

On one hand, says Paul, there is continuity between the body we have now and the eschatological body. The continuity is this: the same person is involved, life is involved, and a body that is sustained by that life is involved. Paul believes in individual identity and personality that is preserved in the afterlife. In other words, he is no advocate of reincarnation (the notion that, in some previous life, one may have been a bug or a flower, and in some future life, one may go further up the chain of life). He does not believe "all life is one"; he believes all life is distinct, particularly in the case of all human life. Paul will be Paul, Mary will be Mary, Joseph will be Joseph, and so on, in the resurrection. Here, however, are the differences seen by Paul between this body and the resurrection body:

PRESENT BODY	RESURRECTION BODY
Mortal	Everlasting
Weak	Powerful
Inglorious	Glorious
Enlivened by Life Breath	Enlivened by the Holy Spirit

In short, Paul believes that a person in a resurrection body is immune to disease, decay, and death and immune to suffering, sin, and sorrow. What Paul means when he calls a resurrection body a "spiritual body" is not a body that is immaterial or "made out of spirit" but rather a body totally energized and sustained by the Holy Spirit.

Why is this idea of resurrection so important to Paul? Why not just talk about dying and going to heaven, which in fact Paul does believe in, as 2 Cor. 5 shows? The reason is in part because Paul believes that God wants to redeem all of creation and all that we are—not just our spirits or minds but our bodies as well. The God who is the creator God made it all and desires to redeem it all, which is in part why the Bible as a whole ends not with a nice story about dying and going to heaven but rather a story about how the heavenly city comes down and takes up permanent residence in a newly restored earth—a new creation (Rev. 21–22). Apparently, most early Christians believed this. What they also believed was that Christ's history, in particular his resurrection, was their destiny—they too would be raised and conformed even in the flesh to the image of the risen Christ.

From this celestial high point of Paul's persuasion, it would be nice to never have to come down; however, when we turn the page to 2 Corinthians, we come back down to earth with a thud. Apparently, all of that great rhetoric in 1 Corinthians did not solve all the Corinthians' problems, and we are right back in the thick of them for 13 chapters in 2 Corinthians. This is a sobering reminder that the early church was just as flawed as the church is today, and just as full of promise as well.

Here is the rhetorical outline of this diverse document we call 2 Corinthians:

RHETORICAL OUTLINE OF 2 CORINTHIANS	
Epistolary Prescript	1.1–2
Epistolary Thanksgiving/Exordium	1.3–7
Narratio/Narrative of Pertinent Facts	1.8–2.16
Propositio/Thesis Statement	2.17
Probatio and Refutatio/Arguments	3.1–13.4 (Five arguments Pro and Con with subdivisions)
Peroratio/Final Emotional Appeal	13.5–10
Closing Epistolary Greetings and Remarks	13.11–13

SYNOPSIS OF CONTENTS

The thesis statement in 2 Corinthians 2.17 makes clear the combative air that exudes from this discourse: "For we are not peddlers of God's word like so many, but in Christ we speak as persons of sincerity, as persons sent from God and standing in his presence." This discourse really is about Paul comparing himself to those he calls the pseudo-apostles in 2 Cor. 10–13. The Corinthians had apparently become enamored with false teachers who claimed apostolic status.

Paul had been downgraded to someone about whom it was said, "While his letters are rhetorically powerful, his personal presence is weak and offensive." Paul was having an ethos problem—a problem of authority and identity in Corinth. He was being misrepresented and critiqued unfairly. He appears to have even been accused of being "on the take," that is, preaching the Gospel in order to make money, hence the term "peddler." You can sense how deeply wounded Paul was when he wrote 2 Corinthians 1–9 especially. When one has led various people to Christ, and then they unfairly begin to treat you as a peddler and a meddler, all is not well. And so it is that Paul pulls out all the rhetorical stops in this discourse, even finishing with a flourish of forensic rhetoric in 2 Cor. 10–13, the rhetoric of attack and defense, in order to reestablish his authority and apostolic place in the lives and hearts of his dearly beloved, but also bedeviled, Corinthians.

Early in the letter, Paul explains what prompted his previous painful letter (namely, his being attacked by one of the Corinthian Christians), which we no longer have, and why it was he had not returned to Corinth as promised one additional time before the writing of this letter. Clearly Paul is on the defensive, and his ministry is under attack, so he must defend his authority and his behavior.

One particularly poignant portion of 2 Corinthians can be found in 2 Cor. 3–5 where Paul explains that the Mosaic covenant came with glory, but its glory has been eclipsed now by the new covenant and the glory of Christ himself. Even the Ten Commandments, written with a divine finger, according to Exodus, pales in comparison to the new life and instruction in and by the Spirit of God now available to those who are in Christ. Then Paul talks about how outwardly the believer is wasting away, but inwardly the Holy Spirit is renewing their minds, hearts, and wills day by day. They are like fragile clay lamps, but with a great light shining out of them and through them, the light of God. Paul then explains in 2 Cor. 5 that this body is temporary, and is like a tent; and when one dies, one is "absent from the body, and present with the Lord" until it is time for the new resurrection body when Christ returns.

Paul reminds his converts in 2 Cor. 6.14–7.1 of what he had said previously in 1 Cor. 8–10, namely, that Christians should not get involved with pagans in their pagan worship activities and meals. This is in turn was followed by detailed instruction about the collection for famine relief for the church in Jerusalem in 2 Cor. 8–9, which Paul had mentioned in passing in 1 Cor. 16.

It is useful to look at one remarkable section in 2 Cor. 10–12 to see how Paul uses irony and mock boasting to shame his converts back into line and back into a better relationship with their apostle. Although there is much that could be said about this rich material, we will mention only a few things here. Paul engages in mock boasting, or what Plutarch calls "inoffensive self-praise." He does this as a shaming device. And so he boasts about things people in antiquity would never ever boast about—his sufferings, the number of times he had been beaten, his

Figure 11.2 Hand lamps from Thyatira, used by people when they went out at night or walked through a dark house. The ancient equivalent of a flashlight. (© Mark R. Fairchild, Ph.D.)

shipwrecks, how he had been pursued by his enemies, and the number of times he had been humiliated in the service of Christ. One can imagine the audience getting more and more embarrassed the more Paul brags about all of the ordeals he has gone through for their sake and the sake of other converts.

But that is not all. Paul boasts of his personal weaknesses! He had already done some of that in 2 Cor. 4, but it crops up again here. Notice how in 2 Cor. 11.30–33 he applies this inverted sort of boasting to the time when he was lowered in a basket over the wall in Antioch so he could escape the Nabatean authorities. What makes this so ironic is that in the Roman world, there was a custom of giving a soldier a medal for being first up the wall and into the city that was being conquered. Paul says it was his honor to be first down the wall in a basket under cover of night! No one would brag about that—unless of course one was trying to show how ridiculous the inflated bragging of the false apostles and the Corinthians themselves was. But even this is not all.

In 2 Cor. 12, Paul tells a tale about himself in the third person. He says he was caught up into the third heaven in a visionary experience. But then, with tongue in cheek, he says, "I heard things . . . *that I can't tell you about*" (contrast the claims of his opponents). And then he even says, "And to prevent me from getting a big head because I had had a vision, God gave me a stake in my flesh, a messenger of Satan." Paul is talking about some sort of physical malady or problem that he prayed would go away but never did. Indeed, what God told him goes completely against the idea that if you have enough faith, you will always be healthy and wealthy. God told him, "My power is made perfect in your weakness, my grace is sufficient for you." That is, God allowed Paul to remain physically weak to prevent him from becoming an egomaniac or a spiritual snob because of his visions. God kept him in a state whereby he would need to rely on the grace of God every day.

This tour de force argument in 2 Cor. 10–13—so full of irony, surprise, and deflation devices critiquing all the things people regularly bragged about in antiquity—is remarkable. It shows the lengths to which Paul would go, rhetorically speaking, not merely to get the audience's attention but to humble them and lead them in the paths of obedience. In the end, Paul strongly urges his audience to test themselves and see if they are true to their Christian convictions; and he warns his converts that he is coming back to Corinth and he would rather not come as a judge, sorting them out, but rather as their friend. It is hard not to hear 2 Cor. 10–13 as a strong critique of the flattering rhetoric of those Paul calls the pseudo-apostles, who apparently have beguiled the Corinthians, the sort of rhetoric one often heard in Corinth when one was trying to win the favor of someone. When we turn to Romans next, we find Paul addressing very different situations and problems, which call for very different and more deliberative rhetoric as Paul tries to establish some common ground with a Roman audience he has yet to visit.

CLUES FROM THE CULTURE

You are devoted to oratory . . . and you tolerate as speakers only those who are very clever.

—*Dio Chrysostom Or. 35.1*

ROMANS—THE RIGHTEOUSNESS OF GOD AND THE SETTING RIGHT OF HUMAN BEINGS

Scholars and lay people alike have often noticed the similarities between Galatians and Romans in terms of the theme Protestant Reformers labeled "justification by grace through faith." There are certainly some themes shared in common in these two documents, but they are also different in many ways. Whereas Galatians, like Romans, seems to be written to a largely Gentile audience, the Galatians are Paul's converts, whereas the Romans are largely not Paul's converts. At the time of writing Romans, in about A.D. 57, Paul had not visited the city yet, and he did not found the church there. He was not, practically speaking, the apostle of *these* Gentiles—yet. And there is a second difference between Galatians and Romans. In Galatians, Paul is trying to get his converts to avoid or kick out the Jewish Christians who came from Jerusalem who are troubling them. In Romans, Paul is trying to get the majority Gentile Christian audience to treat the Jewish Christians in Rome better, to embrace them and be hospitable to them. Finally, in Romans, Paul's rhetorical strategy is to use the rhetorical technique called ***insinuatio***, by which is meant that in the first eight chapters, he says nice things and tries to establish rapport with the audience before getting to the bone of contention in Rome in Romans 9 and following. By contrast, in Galatians, Paul takes off the kid gloves and starts the polemics in the very first chapter. One has to believe that these two differing rhetorical moves and approaches are dictated by the fact that the Galatians are Paul's spiritual offspring, but the Romans are largely strangers. If you want to see the difference in rhetorical approach, even when using similar material, compare and contrast what Paul says about Abraham in Galatians 3 and in Romans 4:

at a Glance

Written about A.D. 57, before Paul went to Jerusalem for the final time and then on to Rome, and written before Nero became the persecutor of Christians, but after Jewish Christians had returned to Rome following their being exiled by the Emperor Claudius until his death in A.D. 54, Romans seeks to put Jewish and Gentile Christians on equal footing and on better terms with each other, making clear that they are all set right by God by grace through faith, and therefore the Gentile believers need to treat the Jewish believers, to whom they are indebted for the Bible and many other things, with more love, respect, and hospitality.

INSINUATIO

A rhetorical technique by which the author first says nice things in order to establish rapport with the audience before getting to the bone of contention. The technique attempts to soften up the audience before matters of contention are approached.

GALATIANS 3

(verses 6ff.) Abraham trusted God and "it was credited to him for righteousness" so you believers are also descendants of Abraham. The Scripture foresaw that God would set right the Gentiles by faith, and it declared the Good News to Abraham in advance saying "the Gentiles will be blessed in you."

(verse 9) Therefore, those who believe are blessed with believing Abraham.

ROMANS 4

(verse 1) What was gained by Abraham our ancestor according to the flesh? Was he set right by works? No, the Scripture says, "Abraham trusted God and it was credited to him as righteousness" (explanation of the difference between something credited and something earned as wages by working).

In both of these passages, Gen. 15.6 is quoted and the story of Abraham is drawn upon. But in Galatians, Paul is stressing how the Gentiles were included on the same basis as Abraham, by faith, and indeed were included in the chosen people due to a promise made to Abraham himself. Works of the Mosaic law did not enter into the discussion at all; they came later in the time of Moses. In Romans, the point is somewhat different on several scores. Notice first the reference to Abraham, our ancestor according to the flesh. Here Paul, probably ironically, is reminding the largely Gentile audience that they are not Jews and not Abraham's descendants by heredity. They have no such claim on Abraham, unlike the Jewish Christians in Rome. They only have a claim through faith to be Abraham's offspring. Paul is trying to put the Gentiles in their place and elevate the status and honor rating of Jewish Christians in Rome, as Romans 9–11 will go on to make very clear. Paul has no such concern in Galatians. Indeed, he is trying to make the Gentile converts in Galatia see what an exalted status they already have in Christ and thus have no need to get themselves circumcised and keep the Mosaic covenant. The differing audiences and situations lead to differing rhetorical usages of the Abraham story in these two texts and reveal some of the differences between Galatians and Romans.

So what is Romans really all about? Paul tells us in his thesis statement in Romans 1.16–17: "For I am not ashamed of the Good News, because it is the power of God for salvation to everyone who believes, for the Jew first, and also for the Gentile, for in the Good News the righteousness of God is revealed, a righteousness that has been revealed from the faithful one [i.e., Christ] to those who have faith, just as it is written, 'the righteous from faith shall live.'"

Romans has as its theme righteousness, both God's righteousness and human beings' right-standing and righteousness before God. The Greek word group that Paul rings the changes on in this most discussed of all human documents are the words *dikaios, dikaiosune, dikaioo:* righteous, righteousness, to set right, and other variants. Paul wants to make clear God's righteous and just character. We can see this already in Romans 1.18–32, where Paul talks about God's righteous wrath against sin and degradation. That side of the equation involves God's justice, and justice is one face of God's righteousness. But there is another side to God's righteousness: his faithfulness. God will do right by his people by keeping the promises he made to Abraham and other Jews long ago. And, in fact, there is a third dimension because God wants to set right his fallen creatures, put them back into right relationship with himself; and further, he wants to help them be righteous persons, having the same moral character as God has.

The problem with the traditional language about Galatians and Romans that we owe to Luther, Calvin, Wesley, and others is that it was assumed this language was simply forensic, or legal, in character. As it turns out, this is not true. Although God is concerned about setting things right between us and himself, he is not interested in perpetuating legal fictions—that is, the idea that, while we are in fact sinners and scoundrels, nonetheless God is going to just credit us as righteous now and forever because of what Jesus did on the cross for us. This approach *adds* the idea that Christ's righteousness is imputed to us because we never *become* righteous in God's eyes or in actuality.

Here are the problems with this whole approach: 1) God's righteousness has to do with both his justice and his saving intent. God actually wants his holy moral character replicated in his creatures. Although this begins by God giving us right-standing with him purely by grace and with no merit on our part, it does not end there. 2) When Paul actually discusses Abraham, he does not use the language of the law court to explain Gen. 15.6; rather, he uses the language of business—of credits and debits and work and wages. 3) In fact, Paul says that it was Abraham's own faith that was credited as Abraham's righteousness. Nothing is said about Christ's righteousness standing in the place of our own righteousness. God expects his children to actually be born again, then sanctified and finally glorified, a process in which they actually become righteous through the work of the Holy Spirit. 4) This is why the thesis statement in Romans says that it is "the righteous" who shall live and have everlasting life, although the means by which a person becomes righteous is through faith in the Faithful One—Jesus.

Human righteousness, in Paul's view, involves both right-standing and inward transformation (both one's position in relationship to God and one's condition) being conformed in due course to the righteous character of Christ. But this righteousness of believers only comes to them by grace through faith and through the internal working of the Spirit. It is not a human work or achievement; it has to be believed, received, and then worked out with fear and trembling as God works in the believer to will and to do. We have already noted the rhetorical outline of Romans[1] so we will not repeat that here, but we must say at this juncture that the better one understands Paul's rhetorical purposes in Romans, the better one understands his theological and ethical arguments here. Romans is a challenging read because of its dense and complex content. By contrast, reading 1–2 Thessalonians seems much easier. Let us walk through Paul's magnum opus and unpack some of its major ideas.

SYNOPSIS OF CONTENTS

The letter prescript shows that Paul is dealing carefully with his audience because the majority of them are not his converts. From the very outset, one of his goals in this letter is to defend the marginalized Jewish Christians in Rome and work to have them reconciled with the majority Gentile Christians before Paul arrives in the Eternal City; Paul emphasizes that the Gospel of God is about a Jewish messiah foretold in the Jewish Scriptures—a Messiah who was a descendant from David, but also was demonstrated to be Son of God in power by means of and from the time when the Holy Spirit raised him from the dead. Paul says he received the task of bringing about "the obedience of faith" among the Gentiles, including his audience. Thus, he makes a claim to be their apostle as well, even if they have never met him.

The exordium that follows in Rom. 1.8–15 seeks to establish rapport with the audience by commending his audience for their renowned faith and by telling them he often prays for them. Lest they think he was intentionally neglecting them, he tells them he has often intended to come to them, but the time simply wasn't right. His intent was to come and share the Gospel with them and others in Rome, but then he corrects himself a bit and says his intent was so they could mutually benefit each other. He will go on to tell them he intends to go on beyond Rome to Spain and is hoping they will help provide the resources for doing so.

The essential proposition or thesis statement occurs at Rom. 1.16-17 announcing that the major topic of this entire discourse will be the righteousness of God in all its senses (see previous text). Faith and the obedience of faith will be the keys to unpacking this righteousness so far, as it involves the audience and their beliefs and behaviors.

Paul then launches into his first argument, a scathing critique of the fallenness of the world in Rom. 1.18-32, perhaps especially of the Gentile world; and Paul says that God's righteous wrath against all ungodliness and wickedness is already revealed, perhaps especially in the cross of Christ. Paul then explains that God is not unknown to anyone on earth, for the reality and power of God is evident in all of his creation. Thus, the issue for the lost is not whether they have heard about God or not, but rather what they have done with what they do know about God. On that score, Paul is clear enough that fallen human beings have exchanged the truth about God for a lie. They know the true God, but they will not acknowledge Him.

Because of this rejection of what they do know about God, this rebellion against their Creator, God has handed them over to their own desires, and Paul is clear enough that one form that those sinful desires have taken is sexual relationships that are against nature—by which he means both male and female forms of homosexual behavior. If we ask why Paul begins his discourse in this stern fashion, the answer is he is trying to level the playing field and make clear, especially to the Gentiles in his audience, that they have no grounds at all, in terms of their moral and spiritual heritage, for vaunting themselves over Jews. Paul will go on to suggest that both Jews and Gentiles have fallen short of God's highest and best for them, so both groups need to be saved by grace through faith in Jesus. These leveling arguments continue in Rom. 2.1–3.20 in which Paul has a dialogue with an imaginary Gentile teacher or philosopher, and an imaginary Jewish one as well, to make clear that neither have any grounds for boasting before God.

In Rom. 3.21–31, Paul revisits and further unpacks the thesis statement found in Rom. 1.16–17. The righteousness of God is not just displayed in his righteous judgment on sin, it is also displayed through the faithfulness of Christ who died on the cross atoning for human sin and satisfying the just requirement of the Law in regard to condemnation of sin. Thus right-standing with God, or justification, comes through faith in the faithful One, Jesus, who was obedient to God's will even to the point of death on the cross. God himself put forth Jesus as an atonement for sin: this did not happen by accident, nor was it a mere human tragedy. Notice that Paul adds that God did this because he could not pass over sin forever. God is both just and merciful, both righteous and compassionate, both holy and loving; and because he cannot simply ignore his holy nature, sin eventually has to be dealt with. If you think it is easy for a holy God to forgive sin, look at the cross. God will be both righteous, vindicating his own character, and the one who sets right fallen human beings through the saving acts of Jesus.

Both Jews and Gentiles then are set right with God by the same means— through faith in Christ and his redemptive work. These concepts, of course, would be difficult for Gentiles especially to grasp. The notion of a just God was familiar enough, but the notion of grace, of a loving and merciful God who saved us in spite of our sins was something new, as was the very nature of grace—unmerited favor or benefit, unconditionally given. This was difficult to grasp in a payback world that knew the mantra "you don't get something for nothing," even from a deity.

To illustrate how this all works, Paul turns in Romans 4 to the example of Abraham who trusted God, and it was credited or reckoned to him as righteousness. Again there is nothing here about the imputing of Christ's righteousness into Abraham; rather, when the ledger is opened, in the credit column is Abraham's trust in God, and in the debit column is his lack of actual righteousness. Abraham then is seen as a paradigm for how Christians should view their situation with God. The surprising part of the discussion is not what we have just mentioned but the fact that the righteous God has set out to set right and make righteous the ungodly, even God's enemies.

In the Old Testament, and especially in the Psalms, one hears a great deal about God vindicating the just or the righteous, or those who keep the Law; but here we have the scandalous news that God has set out to vindicate the ungodly, the unrighteous, the unclean. What this demonstrates is that clearly enough God's righteousness doesn't just involve vindicating the faithful. In other words, it is not just about God's covenant faithfulness to his promises to faithful Jews. The same sort of reckoning of trust as righteousness applies to us, says Paul in Rom. 4.23–24, because we have believed that God has raised Jesus from the dead to set us in right relationship with God.

But what are the benefits of being set back in right relationship with God? Paul says in Romans 5 that it involves many things, including being at peace with God, gaining access to God's grace and blessings, and having hope of sharing in God's glory—by which Paul may mean sharing in the resurrection—when we get the same glorious, Spirit-empowered body the risen Jesus had from Easter onward. Lest we think, however, that being in right relationship with God makes one bulletproof from the harm that a wicked world can do, Paul adds that we may expect suffering. But God can use this suffering to improve our endurance, which in turn improves our character, which in turn gives us hope because in all of this, God has lavishly poured out his love into the believers' hearts through the indwelling Spirit that has been given to the believer.

Lest there be any thought that a fallen human being could deserve or earn Christ's atonement and its benefits, Paul, in Rom. 5.6–20, makes clear that is quite impossible. It is all a gift from God. This leads to the important rhetorical comparison of Adam, the founder of the race, and Christ, the last Adam who refounded the race in Rom. 5.12–21. Paul is operating with the notion that the actions of the head of a race affect all those who are descendants of the founder. So it was that the single trespass of Adam, a willful violation of a direct command of God (noting the difference between the broader term "sin," which can include failing to do the right thing, or sins of omission or ignorance, and the term "trespass") is what set the world in retrograde motion. And the result of deliberate sin in the world was in fact death. As Paul would later put it, "the wages of sin is death."

Death was the punishment for sin. Death hovered over the human race, exercised dominion over it, as though the Grim Reaper ruled the world—that is, until Jesus, the Life and the Resurrection, entered the world and made clear that God's Yes to life is louder than Death's No! So just as those who were in Adam all received the fallen tendencies and punishment for sin, so all those who are in Christ receive the free gift of right-standing, salvation, and forgiveness of sins. This argument is based on the clear ancient notion of dyadic or corporate personality (see the previous discussion). One's group identity was seen as primary and most shaping who you are; one's individual identity was seen as secondary. It is not an accident that Paul talks about believers being "in Christ," that is, in the body of Christ, with our group identity norming and forming our individual identity.

In view of what Paul has said thus far in Romans, almost any Jew would have raised this question—well what about the Mosaic law, what was its function if it wasn't life giving but rather turned out to be death dealing for those who broke the Law, for fallen human beings? Paul, on one hand in Rom. 6–7, will say that the Mosaic law was holy, just, and good; but on the other hand, although it could tell God's people what to do, it couldn't enable them to do it because they were fallen creatures. Christ and the Spirit had to intervene to enable people to keep God's Word and Laws. Paul elsewhere in Gal. 4 and 2 Cor. 3 had made clear that the Mosaic covenant was temporary, intended to keep God's people in line until the coming of the Messiah Jesus, whom Paul calls "the seed of Abraham."

The most debated of all portions of the whole New Testament is Rom. 7.6–25. Who is the "I" talking here? Is it Paul, speaking autobiographically, is it Paul using a rhetorical device and speaking as someone else? In light of what Paul says both before this disputed passage in 7.5 and afterward in Rom. 8.1–3 where he contrasts those who are in bondage to sin with those who are in Christ and have been set free from the rule of sin and death in their lives, it is likely Paul is retelling the tale of Adam, in Rom. 7.6–13, and then the tale of all those who are in Adam and not yet in Christ in 7.14–25. In other words, this chapter is describing how things look to a Christian when he considers the plight of the world. The key clues in the chapter are that in Rom. 7.6–13, the speaker says he was once alive apart from God's Law, and that would only have been true of Adam and Eve. In a dramatic statement, Paul vividly says "but when the single commandment came the snake (Sin personified) woke up and I died." Thus, in Rom. 7.14–25, we hear of the plight of the person who knows better, knows what he ought to do but is not able to do it. Someone must deliver this person from his bondage to sin. Paul intercedes and says that Jesus Christ has and can do this! Rom. 7.6–13 is Paul speaking as Adam, and in 7.14–25 as all those in Adam and outside Christ.

Romans 8 is a chapter full of references to what the Christian life is like—it is Spirit filled, free from the bondage of sin, it is a prayerful life. The lively Spirit is the down payment, the preview of coming attractions of the new life of the resurrection that will one day transform our very bodies. And not just believers but the whole of creation (Rom. 8.19) is eagerly awaiting its renewal—the day of resurrection will also be the day of the renewal of the earth as well and all its creatures. One day it will obtain the same freedom and glory as God's children. Paul is rising to a dramatic climax in Romans 8 before he has to turn to the bone of contention, which he has put off discussing until Rom. 9–11. He tells us that "for those who love God and are called according to choice or purpose," God not only works all things together for good for them, he has also destined them in advance to be conformed by resurrection to the image of his Son, Jesus. The discussion in Rom. 8.28–30 is not about God picking persons to be Christians in the first place; it is rather a message of hope and joy for those who are in Christ—we have a great destiny. One day we shall be like Christ, and God has promised this. Indeed, he has even promised that no outside forces, not the Devil, not demons, not life not death, not things to come, not anything in all of creation, can separate us from the love of Christ. The one thing missing in this list of things that cannot separate us from God is ourselves. Paul certainly does believe that, however unlikely, apostasy can be committed by true believers. We are not eternally secure until we are securely in eternity. But we do not need to worry about other powers, forces, persons, and circumstances ripping us out of the hands of God. God will not allow us to fall against our will.

Picture for a moment a wise and kind parent with a firm grip on their child crossing the busy and dangerous highway of life. The parent has a firm grip on the child, and unless the child makes a herculean effort and wrenches itself free from the grasp of the parent, the child will make it safely to the other side of life's highway. Paul doesn't believe that one can lose one's salvation, like one might lose car keys or glasses. He does believe that by a conscious effort of rebellion, one can "make shipwreck of one's faith," as he will say in the Pastoral Epistles. One can't make a shipwreck of something one never had. Thus, trust in the love and firm grip of God on one's life is a must, and Paul has been stressing this ever since telling the tale of Abraham in Romans 4.

Romans 9–11 is one long, Scripture-saturated, complex argument. When the Jewish Christians were allowed back into Rome in A.D. 54 after banishment under Claudius ended with his death, they clearly were the stepchildren of the Roman Christian community. Roman anti-Semitism was rife in the capital city, and it seems to have infected the church. It would appear that the Gentile Christians were not even meeting with the Jewish Christians, and there was talk that God had replaced his first chosen people with a second chosen people—namely, Gentile Christians. Paul writes Rom. 9–11 to make clear especially to the Gentile audience (see Rom. 11.13) the following things: 1) God has not forsaken his first chosen people, he has a plan to incorporate them into Christ, even though at present the majority of them have rejected Christ and have been temporarily broken off from the people of God. 2) Had God reneged on his numerous promises to Israel (by which Paul means non-Christian Jews), then there is no reason why Gentiles should think God would keep promises made to them, for instance, to be the heirs of Abraham. 3) Paul, through a revelation from God, has discovered that God is operating in a way that is the opposite of what Jews expected. They expected that when Messiah came, God would gather all the Jews, including the ones in countries other than the Holy Land, back together; and that after that, Gentiles would come into the fold and believe in the one true God. Paul says in fact, God has chosen to do it the other way around—through the Gospel he is mostly saving Gentiles at present; but when the full number of Gentiles has been saved (see Rom. 11.25) by grace through faith in Jesus, then *in the same manner* God will turn around and save Israel, by grace through faith in Jesus. 4) This last saving of Israel will not transpire until Jesus returns and turns away "the impiety of Jacob." So God's breaking off of some Jews who had hardened their hearts against Jesus was only temporary, to make room for the inclusion of Gentiles in the present; but the day would come that the mercy of God through Christ would reincorporate those Jews back into the people of God. 5) Because all this is true, Paul says, there is no grounds for Gentiles to be boasting about having replaced Jews in God's favor; indeed, God has made it impossible for anyone to boast because all are now and will be part of the people of God by grace through faith in Jesus, and not by any other means.

As if this tour de force argument were not enough, Paul rolls right on to dealing with the practical implications of all this theologizing in Rom. 1–11. In Romans 12, Paul says that in view of the mercies of God, all God's people should present themselves to God as living sacrifices, living holy and acceptable lives, and realizing that this is their real worship. True belief in and love of Christ should lead to Christ-like behavior. This means also de-enculturating one's self from the world and its values. As one translator puts it, "don't let the world squeeze you into its mold."

Then Paul, in the rest of Romans 12, will give his own exposition of various of the teachings of Jesus in the Sermon of the Mount—including the call to love one's enemies, pray for those who persecute you, be generous in giving to those in need, never repay evil for evil, leave vengeance in God's hands, live peaceably with one's neighbors, and exercise one's spiritual gifts including prophecy and teaching according to the grace given one and according to the measure of one's faith (Rom. 12.6–8). It is always a good thing to know what one's gifts and grace are and aren't and what one's limits are as well.

It is no surprise that Paul, in Romans 13, addressing Christians who live in Rome and having already told them to live peacefully among their pagan neighbors, tells them they should be subject to the governing authorities who have a right to administer justice (indeed, are even the agents of God in such tasks when they do it rightly) and a right to collect taxes as well. We must remember that in A.D. 57, Nero had not yet become a persecuting tyrant, and Paul is speaking on the assumption that the government is functioning as it ought to do and is not functioning like later Nero and then Domitian did (and on the latter, we hear John of Patmos' judgment in Revelation).

In Romans 14, Paul addresses the fact that the Roman Jewish and Gentile Christians are not getting along. The Gentile majority seems to be passing judgment on the Jewish minority that is following food laws, and perhaps keeping the Sabbath, and other things. Paul says quite clearly in Rom. 14.14 that he believes that no food is unclean and that Christians don't have to keep such Jewish laws, not even Jewish Christians; but at the same time, no one should act in a fashion to cause one's weaker brother or sister to stumble. It is interesting that Paul here, and in 1 Cor. 8–10, agrees with the strong but seeks to protect the weak who, in his view, *have too many Jewish scruples about food and other aspects of the ritual law.* The ruling principle is to always act in love and patience and kindness toward others, whatever their views on such matters that do not impinge on their salvation.

This theme of the strong making concessions for the sake of the weak continues into Romans 15, and then Paul makes a bold direct command—"welcome one another as Christ has welcomed you." He will continue these sorts of commands in Romans 16 where he tells the Gentiles to embrace all the listed Jewish Christians in Rome with every show of affection, welcoming them into their homes and their fellowship meetings. He reminds in Rom. 15.8 that Christ became a servant of the Jews in order that he might confirm the promises made to Abraham and the other patriarchs. God has not reneged on those promises. Paul cites a series of Old Testament texts, all of which speak of Gentiles praising God for his mercy, in this case not only on them but also on the "circumcised." In the end, it's all grace and all mercy for all of us if we are to be saved. Justice is what happens when we get what we deserve; and because we've all sinned, that is not good news for us. Mercy is when God passes over our sin and lays the blame and cost on Jesus. Grace is when we get something positive we never earned or deserved—a new relationship with God, including right-standing, reconciliation, peace, and the gift of God's love and Spirit in our lives.

Later in Romans 15, Paul explains his travel plans, which in fact go awry when he is taken captive in Jerusalem and is in a holding pattern for 2 years until he is shipped to Rome. Paul has apprehensions of what will happen when he journeys from Corinth to Jerusalem with the collection for famine relief for the saints in Jerusalem (see Rom. 15.30–33). It turns out his concerns were justified.

Finally, in Romans 16, Paul commends Phoebe to the audience. She is a deacon (the first person called a deacon in the New Testament) who is coming to Rome to do ministry, and probably is the bearer of this letter and the one who would read it out to the house churches there. Paul wants the Roman Christians not just to welcome her but to support her ministry while she is there. Then Paul provides a long list of greetings of Jewish Christians, and note this is different from his normal pattern—he does not greet them, he tells the Gentile Christians in Rome to embrace and greet them!

These include his longtime coworkers Priscilla and Aquila who have helped the church in Corinth and Ephesus and now in Rome. It also includes another Christian couple, Andronius and Junia, who are called apostles of note and about whom it is said that they were in Christ before Paul and had even been in jail with Paul. This means they were some of the earliest Christians, and the fact that Paul calls them apostles suggests they had seen the risen Lord (see 1 Cor. 9.1–2). Toward the end of the greetings, we find a humorous note in which an individual interjects himself into Paul's letter—"I Tertius greet you in the Lord" (Rom. 16.22). He is the one who is Paul's scribe and has written this massive missive for Paul. He certainly had a right to interject himself here at the end after working so hard to write down the 16 previous chapters on papyrus.

Thus ends Paul's masterpiece, his most influential letter, and the most commented on book in the whole of the New Testament—and not without good reason. Here we learn about Good News for everyone—for the Jew first, and also for the Gentile, news that comes from a righteous God who wants a righteous and holy people; God has managed to find a way by sending Jesus the Righteous One to die for our sins and set us right and sanctify us as we go on the long journey to be conformed to the image of the risen One.

IMPLICATIONS

There are such riches and depths to the Pauline discourses that it was quite impossible to do more than give one a taste of Paul's most familiar writings in this chapter. It is far too easy for those who study Paul's letters for all their rich theologizing and ethical reflection to forget, or at least neglect, the fact that Paul was a pastor, deeply concerned about his converts and coworkers. It is actually hard to read any of these letters and miss the level of emotional investment Paul had in his converts. He rejoiced when they rejoiced, he mourned when they mourned, and he experienced all sorts of anxieties when he was apart from them and could be no direct help to them.

I like what Gordon Fee says at this juncture: "The NT was written in the context of real people in a very real world. Biblical texts are too often the scholar's playground and the believer's rule book, without adequate appreciation for the truly human nature of these texts—texts written by one whose speech was ever informed by his theology, but who expressed that theology at a very personal and practical level."[2]

KEY TERMS

Ad Hoc Document   *Synkrisis*
Insinuatio

STUDY QUESTIONS

Why do you think it is that Paul wrote letter discourses that were so much longer than almost all other ancient letters?

If you had to assess Paul's emphases in his discourses, would you say he put more emphasis on belief or on behavior? Why did he see both as very important to one's faith and salvation?

How would you explain Paul's use of rhetoric, and why does he do it?

FOR FURTHER READING

Keener, Craig. *1–2 Corinthians*. Cambridge: Cambridge University Press, 2005.
Witherington, B., with D. Hyatt. *Paul's Letter to the Romans: A Socio-Rhetorical Commentary*. Grand Rapids, MI: Eerdmans, 2004.

NOTES

1. See previous pages.
2. G. D. Fee, *Paul's Letter to the Philippians* (Grand Rapids, MI: Eerdmans, 1995), 284.

What's left of the Temple of Artemis in Ephesus, now in a miry swamp.
(© Mark R. Fairchild, Ph.D.)

CHAPTER 12
PAUL the LETTER WRITER PART THREE: The CAPTIVITY EPISTLES

THE CAPTIVITY EPISTLES ARE THOSE LETTERS written while Paul was chained and under house arrest, probably in Rome, although some scholars have argued for Ephesus as the locale. The letters in question are Colossians, Ephesians, Philemon, and Philippians; it is well to bear in mind that Paul continued to suffer for Christ most of the time during the latter years of his life as these letters make clear.

The captivity epistles are certainly interesting in their own right, and they have received more attention from scholars on the whole than the Thessalonian correspondence. There is, in fact, an interrelationship among three of these documents—Colossians, Ephesians, and Philemon—but Philippians is a different story. If you examine Col. 4.7–9 and Ephes. 6.21–22, it seems very clear that there is some sort of literary relationship between these two passages. In addition, there are numerous parallels between the **household codes** in Colossians 3–4 and Ephesians 5–6, not to mention many similar turns of phrase and ideas in the two documents in general. The question then becomes, which is the chicken and which the egg? Most scholars seem reasonably sure that Colossians is earlier and Ephesians draws on it. I agree with this judgment. There is, furthermore, a similarity of Greek style, syntax, and phrasing in Colossians and Ephesians, which makes them stand out to some degree from the earlier Paulines. This is because a certain kind of rhetorical style is being employed

at a Glance: The Captivity Epistles

Colossians, Ephesians, Philemon, and Philippians are usually viewed by scholars as some of the later letters of Paul. About the authorship of Philemon and Philippians there is really no debate. The majority of commentators accept Colossians as written by Paul, and the scholarly verdict on Ephesians is about evenly split. Although some scholars have of late suggested that Philippians may be from an earlier period in Paul's life, most still ascribe all these letters to near the end of Paul's life, somewhere between A.D. 60 and 62. Most also still think they were written from Rome, although some have suggested Ephesus; but why would Paul be under house arrest in Ephesus, something he never suggests? A very small number of scholars think these letters may have been written when Paul was under house arrest in Caesarea Maritima, which was in the late A.D. 50s, but this is doubtful. The letters should not be called prison epistles, as there is no evidence that Paul was in jail when they were written. He was simply in chains, and as a Roman citizen, that normally meant under house arrest at his own expense.

in these two documents—**Asiatic rhetoric**, the preferred form of style and diction in the region to which these documents were sent, which was the Province of Asia and its neighboring areas. Yet with all this in common, Colossians and Ephesians are quite different in some respects.

For one thing, Colossians is a situation-specific discourse, written according to the conventions of deliberative rhetoric. It has a thesis statement, arguments, and the usual features of a Pauline letter, including greetings and the autograph of Paul. Ephesians, however, is a sermon and thus epideictic rhetoric. It gives us lots of prayers and blessings and discussions but not really any arguments or a thesis statement; however, neither was required in an ancient sermon—a "word of exhortation" (*logos protreptikos*).

The Asiatic rhetoric is especially noticeable in Ephesians, which contains very long sentences, one of which goes on for more than 20 lines! Ancient preachers tended to be expansive and at times hyperbolic for dramatic effect, and Paul was such a preacher. Ephesians is also a general or generic document, and so has been suspected of being a circular letter or discourse. This is probably right, especially when we realize that the words "in Ephesus" in Ephes. 1.1 are missing from some manuscripts and seem awkward where they are in the sentence as well. Ephesians has been called "the quintessence," or most supreme expression,

Figure 12.1 Tarsus area Roman road. (© *Mark R. Fairchild, Ph.D.*)

of Pauline thought, and certainly it is a powerful and poignant discourse capped off by the best peroration in the New Testament, in Ephes. 6.10–20.

Although sometimes it has been thought that Philemon is a private letter, as it turns out, this is not the case. The closest thing to private letters in the New Testament, rather than group communications, are the Pastoral Epistles and 3 John. Philemon is written not just to Philemon but to members of his family and to the church that meets in his house as well. Philemon is being called out on the issue of his runaway slave before his house church and being urged to manumit the slave Onesimus, whom Paul has converted and whom Paul wants back as a coworker.

As for Philippians, this is perhaps Paul's most beloved small letter; and unlike many of Paul's letters, it speaks a lot about joy and seems on the whole to be a progress-oriented rather than a problem-solving discourse. Paul wants the converts in Philippi to continue to build their unity, solve what minor differences they may have, and follow the good, self-sacrificial examples of Christ, Paul, and Timothy. Whereas in Colossians and Ephesians there seems to be no hint that Paul might soon be free, in both Philemon and Philippians there are such hints along the way. Rhetorically speaking, all these documents, except Ephesians, are in the form of deliberative rhetoric.

An important further issue that needs to be raised because Colossians and Philemon seem likely to be written to the same house church (or at least Philemon's house church, which is one of the house churches in Colossae) is the issue of levels of discourse. If we take the issue of slavery as discussed in these three discourses, it seems that we have a progressively more "Christian" and frank discussion of the issues of slavery as we move from Colossians to Ephesians to Philemon.

Colossians is **first-order moral discourse**—the kind of thing Paul would say when he first broached the difficult subject of slavery—whereas Ephesians is **second-order moral discourse** in which Paul is prepared to push a little harder to make the situation between masters and slaves more humane and Christian in character. And finally, in Philemon, there is **third-order moral discourse** in which Paul is able to be frank with someone who is a close associate and coworker of his, whom he asks to manumit his slave Onesimus.

One of the things we learn from studying the slavery material in these three documents is that we should never take any one letter of Paul's to be telling us all of his most important thoughts on any one particular subject. One might not have guessed that Paul saw any sort of incompatibility between being a slave master and being a Christian if we only had Colossians. But when we get to Philemon and the phrase "no longer as a slave, but as he really is—a brother in Christ," then it begins to dawn on us that Paul does indeed believe what he said back in Gal. 3.28—that in Christ there ought to be no slave or free, whatever the case might be in the fallen pagan world.

It is not, however, just in the comments on slavery that we see some progression of thought because when Paul talks about the relationship between husband

HOUSEHOLD CODES

Ancient household codes included details about how the head of the household was to treat and engage with the other members of the home. It was also common to find discussions of how husbands related to wives, fathers related to children, and masters related to slaves.

ASIATIC RHETORIC

Rhetoric that employs a preferred form of style and diction in the province of Asia and neighboring areas. Common features include very long and ornate sentences and fanciful style.

FIRST-ORDER MORAL DISCOURSE

The type of discourse one would use when addressing an audience for the first time. The goal is to begin the discussion and meet the audience where they are at before persuading them to move in a different direction.

SECOND-ORDER MORAL DISCOURSE

Discourse that attempts to move the audience to a position that is further from what was presented at the first-order level.

THIRD-ORDER MORAL DISCOURSE

A type of discourse that one has with a person or audience that he/she has an intimate relationship with. The discussion is more frank and to the point.

and wife in Col. 3.18–19, it is possible to conclude that Paul only refers to wives submitting to their husbands. But one cannot draw this conclusion from Eph. 5.21–24, where Paul first talks about mutual submission of all Christians to one another, and then uses the example of the relationship of husband and wife to explain what this looks like. Again, Paul's thought in one particular passage or discourse on some subject should not be seen as Paul's last word or the full expression of his mind on such difficult subjects. Paul believed that in the body of Christ, with the use of persuasion more than commands, and by the help of God's grace and the Spirit's work, it was possible for a new sort of community to arise or emerge free from the worst excesses of human fallenness, free from things like the repression of women or the enslavement of other human beings.

SYNOPSIS OF COLOSSIANS AND EPHESIANS

The church in Colossae seems to have arisen through the evangelism of one of Paul's converts, Epaphras (Col. 1.7, 4.12), who seems also to have planted the churches in Hierapolis and Laodicea, all in the Lycus valley 90 or so miles east of Ephesus. As in Romans then, Paul is not writing to those he was the spiritual father of directly, but only indirectly. Paul writes to give them some guidance on both belief and behavior, including how to run their households. We may outline Colossians as follows:

RHETORICAL OUTLINE OF COLOSSIANS	
Prescript and Greetings	1.1–2
Exordium/Thanksgiving Prayer	1.3–14
Narratio/Narration of Pertinent Facts/The Pattern of Christ	1.15–20
Propositio/Thesis Statement	1.21–23
Probatio/Arguments for the Thesis	1.24–2.5
Exhortations Based on the Arguments	
A. Continue to Live in Christ, Forsaking Other Knowledge, Philosophies, Principles, Rituals	2.6–23
B. Forsaking Other Lifestyles, Filled with the Word and Wisdom of Christ	3.1–17
C. Submission and Obedience in the Christian Household	3.18-4.1
Peroratio/Final Emotional Appeal/A Call to Prayer and Other Forms of Wise Speech and Action	4.2–6
Closing Greetings and Instructions	4.7–18

As the thesis statement in Col. 1.21–23 makes clear, Paul is concerned about the audience defecting from the true Gospel. His point will be that they already have both the wisdom and the salvation they need in Christ, and they do not need to add to that some esoteric Jewish practices such as "the worship of/by angels," which seems to refer to being caught up in some sort of visionary experience of heavenly worship. The problems in Colossae are different from those in Galatia, but the prescription of Paul is similar—namely, you don't need to do that because you already have such benefits through faith in Christ. They have already been rescued out of darkness and transferred into the Kingdom of Christ, so there was no point in turning aside now to other tempting options. In Col. 1.15–20, we probably have a fragment of a Christ hymn that exalts Christ as our Wisdom, using the language that had previously been used of the personified wisdom of God in books like the Wisdom of Solomon.

Paul's point is that it is in and through the heavenly Christ that all things are held together, and even the angels are dependent on him; so there is no point in focusing on lower supernatural beings when one has direct access to Christ and all his benefits. In Christ all the fullness of God dwells, and not one ounce of it can be found in the angels. If the goal is drawing closer to God, it's one-stop shopping in Jesus. You don't need saints or angels to get there.

The word wisdom keeps coming because apparently the Colossians have become fascinated with esoteric Jewish speculations about angels and heaven. Paul says that's pointless, for all the treasures of God's wisdom and knowledge are hidden in Christ himself (Col. 2.3-4). Notice the contrast between Christ

Figure 12.2 Theater at Ephesus. (© Mark R. Fairchild, Ph.D.)

STOICHEIA

A Greek term that refers to elementary religious traditions or sometimes to the basic elements believed to make up the world—earth, air, fire, water.

and the *stoicheia* of the universe, that is, the elementary religious traditions that Christians don't need to be dabbling in. We find as well the claim in Col. 2.14–15 that Christ disarmed the principalities and powers through his death on the cross, and they don't even deserve lip service or the time of day from Christians. They are spent forces. Col. 2.16–19 makes clear just how Jewish this alternate teaching Paul is rebutting was—it involves celebrating new moons, and Sabbaths, and dealing in visions, and "the worship of angels." Christians have died to the elementary religious teachings of this sort, so they should not continue to live by them (Col. 2.20–23). As that paragraph continues, it seems clear that the Colossians were being allured by the claims about some sort of ascetical practices including severe treatments of one's body all for the purpose of piety, of drawing closer to God. But of what value are such practices when it is already true that the Christian has "Christ in you, the hope of glory"?

In Col. 3.12–17, Paul rehearses some general Christian ethical teaching inculcating humility, patience, love, and true worship—which involves singing hymns and psalms and spiritual songs to God. Paul is promoting virtues that will bind the congregation together in the bond of love. He then turns to the more difficult issue of the patriarchal household structures and the household codes used to regulate them. Here it will be useful to look a bit more closely at both the household codes in Col. 3–4 and those in Ephes. 5–6, especially because the latter seems to be an expansion of and further Christianization of the former.

COLOSSIANS 3.18–4.1/EPHESIANS 5.21–6.9— THE HOUSEHOLD CODES

COL. 3.18–4.1	EPH. 5.21–6.9—THE HOUSEHOLD CODES
All: Be subject to one another out of reverence for Christ (5.21—only in Eph.).	
Wives: Be subject to your husbands, as is fitting in the Lord (3.18).	*Wives:* Be subject to your husbands, as you are to the Lord, etc. (5.22–24).
Husbands: Love your wives and never treat them harshly (3.19).	*Husbands:* Love your wives, just as Christ loved the Church, etc. (5.25–33).
Children: Obey your parents in everything . . . your acceptable duty in the Lord (3.20).	*Children:* Obey your parents in the Lord, for this is right, etc. (6.1–3).
Fathers: Do not provoke your children, or they may lose heart (3.21).	*Fathers:* Do not provoke your children to anger; bring them up in the Lord (6.4).
Slaves: Obey earthly masters in everything . . . fearing the Lord (3.22–25).	*Slaves:* Obey your earthly masters, as you obey Christ (6.5–8).
Masters: Treat your slaves justly and fairly; you also have a Master in heaven (4.1).	*Masters:* Stop threatening your slaves; you have the same Master in heaven (6.9).

The first thing to notice about these parallels is the assumption that the normal or average ancient Greco-Roman household included slaves, unlike modern homes. Second, notice that the head of the household plays three different roles—husband, father, and master—whereas no other member of the household plays more than two roles (i.e., the wife is also a mother). What really makes these household codes stand out from non-Christian codes from the same era are the instructions about and the restricting of the roles of head of the household. *In other household codes by non-Christian writers, only the subordinate members of the patriarchal household are told what they must and must not do.* Therefore, these household codes balance assigned responsibilities and try to make sure that the head of the household does not abuse the power and authority he has. Equally distinctive is the command to the husband to love his wife (not usually the advice given to a husband in that era) and the stress on not relating to his children or slaves in an impersonal or abusive way. He is reminded that he must be accountable to God for the way he relates to the other members of his family.

What we see in Colossians and Ephesians is a progressively more Christian approach to these matters. Colossians reflects Paul's first attempt to inject Christian values into the existing male-dominated family structure, and Ephesians takes things a step further. This is especially evident in Ephes. 5.21 where Paul calls for mutual submission among all members of the church, regardless of whether they are males or females. In other words, Paul is not reaffirming unilateral submission of women to men or wives to husbands.[1] He thinks the implications of Christian ethics lead to mutual submission and service of all Christians to all other Christians. This was a revolutionary idea in a male-dominated world. Notice as well that Paul suggests in Ephes. 5 that the husband's self-sacrificial service and love should be modeled on Christ, recalling what Paul says about this matter in Phil. 2.5–11 (described later). The husband is expected to be the head servant of all its members in the family.

Although much can be said about Paul's view of slavery, it should be clear from the household codes that Paul treats these members of the family as persons, not as property, persons who have moral potential and the ability to make ethical choices. Turning to Philemon, we see that Paul is working not only to deconstruct the patriarchal structure of the family but also working to eliminate slavery altogether. He says in Philemon that Philemon should accept his runaway slave back "no longer as a slave but as more than a slave—a beloved brother" (chapter 1, verse 16).

Thus, Paul is not baptizing the existing household structures and calling them good in these household codes; rather, he is modifying them from the inside out and working toward the day when his baptismal formula ("for in Christ there is neither Jew nor Gentile, neither slave nor free, no male and female for all are one in Christ"—Gal. 3.28) is more than a hope—it is a reality. We must turn to Ephesians now recognizing that it is a circular document, a sermon sent to Ephesus and other Pauline churches; and it is not dealing with one specific situation but with the general ethos and milieu of these churches and what their worship and family life and beliefs and behaviors ought to look like. Here is the outline of Ephesians:

RHETORICAL OUTLINE OF EPHESIANS	
Epistolary Prescript	1.1–2
Exordium/A Eulogy of Sorts	1.3–14
Thanksgiving Prayer	1.15–23
Narratio/Narration of Pertinent Facts/Gentiles Then and Now and Their Apostle	2.1–22; 3.2–13
Concluding Prayer and Doxology	3.1, 14–21
Exhortation Based on the Homily	4.1–6.9
Peroration to Stand Firm	6.10–20
Epistolary Postscript	6.21–24

SYNOPSIS OF CONTENTS

What we have in Ephesians is a sermon that summarizes some of the main elements in Paul's theological and ethical teaching. The material is repetitive and at times deliberately hyperbolic, but that is the very nature of epideictic rhetoric. Paul is praising the Christian life, the Christ, the church, and then explaining about behavior that comports with those things. The discourse begins with a 26-line-long sentence in the Greek that leaves one breathless. Paul explains in Eph. 1.3–23 that God has already blessed us with every spiritual blessing in Christ and then he speaks of the fact that we were "chosen in Christ before the foundation of the world." Of course we did not exist then, and what Paul likely really means is that Christ, who did exist then, was chosen before the foundation of the world to be the Elect One, and we are elect to the extent we are in Him. The means by which we get into Him, as Paul goes on to say in this passage, is by grace through faith. It is in Him we have the adoption as sons and daughters, and have our redemption, not in ourselves. God's plan for the fullness of time was to gather up all things in Him, to unite all things in Him. When the audience first believed, at that very time they received the Spirit, which is the promise and foretaste of their eternal inheritance.

Paul in Ephes. 2 reminds the largely Gentile audience of the before and after of their story. Formerly they were dead in trespasses, following the ways of this world, and in thrall to the ruler of this world, by which Paul likely means Satan. But God, rich in mercy, saved the audience by his grace through faith. Paul goes on in this chapter to stress that Christ has broken down the barriers between Jews and Gentiles, in part by fulfilling and thus making obsolete the Mosaic covenant.

Ephes. 2.15 is pretty clear on this point—he has abolished that law with its commandments. This does not mean that Paul thinks we have a right to be lawless. Rather, we follow a different covenant and it has the Law of Christ, the law of love. Those who had once been strangers and aliens to God and his people have been joined together with them in Christ—Jew and Gentile united in Christ. The point is, as Ephes. 4.1–6 makes evident, that there be one body, one Spirit, one hope and one Lord, one faith, one baptism, and one God and Father of us all. It rather quickly becomes clear that this somewhat generic sermon is trying to take these already existing congregations forward toward a deeper relationship with Christ, and a deeper union with one another, without the differences between Jews and Gentiles getting in the way.

We have already spoken of the overlap between the end of Colossians and the end of Ephesians, and this includes a verbatim in the Greek of the following words—Col. 4.7–8 and Ephes. 5.21–22. It appears clear then that Ephesians is based on Colossians and can be said to be an expanded homily based on some of the themes in Colossians, taking them a step further and not dealing with a specific problem of Jewish esoteric ascetical practices.

PHILEMON

This short and poignant little letter, so full of pathos and pleas, is Paul's attempt to get a coworker who is a slave owner, Philemon, to accept back his runaway slave Onesimus not only without punishment but as a brother in Christ and no longer as slave. This was a lot to ask, and so Paul pulls out all the rhetorical stops in this brief deliberative discourse to persuade Philemon to "do the right thing." There is more than a little arm-twisting and appeal to the emotions in this little document, and it shows us what was considered within the bounds of propriety in an ancient rhetoric-saturated environment; it might look like heavy-handed manipulation today.

The chapter is so brief, the shortest of Paul's letters, it doesn't require an outline; but it definitely follows the regular rhetorical structure—first, the ex-ordium where Paul butters up Philemon calling him a dear friend and coworker and someone who has love for all the saints and shows great faithfulness to Christ (verses 2–7). Paul testifies he has received much joy from Philemon's love "because the hearts of the saints have been refreshed through you." Paul will build on this opening by later calling Onesimus his spiritual child and asking Philemon to "refresh Paul's heart" (v. 20) by manumitting and sending the slave back to Paul recognized as a "useful" brother in Christ. Throughout, Paul will be punning on Onesimus' name, which means "useful," only he has become useless to Philemon by running away; so Paul pleads for some "use" from Philemon in verse 20a.

Notice the pull on the heartstrings when Paul says in verse 9 that he is appealing to Philemon rather than commanding him "as an old man, and in chains for Christ's sake." You can hear the violins playing in the background. Paul will appeal to reason, emotion—and remember he is doing all of this in front of the church that meets in Philemon's house where the letter is being read out, perhaps even delivered by Onesimus himself! Philemon is being put on the spot.

Were all that not enough, Paul, after offering an IOU to Philemon for anything Onesimus might have pilfered or owed his master (at the very least his time and service for a good period of time), then reminds him "not to mention that you owe me your very spiritual life!" Apparently, Philemon was converted by Paul. Then in verse 17, he tells Philemon if you value our partnership— "welcome him as you would welcome me!" And then he finishes with a flourish by saying, "I'm confident of your obedience in this matter" (v. 21—noting how previously he said he was just appealing to him). Finally, there is the real coup de grâce—"I'm expecting to be free soon, so prepare a guest room for me in your house. I'm planning on coming to make sure this all turns out right!" (v. 22).

This deserves a wow. This is full-blown rhetoric with no holds barred, meant to persuade Philemon that he really has no other options than to do what Paul has told him in this letter. And of course, it could have gone in the completely opposite direction because a slave was mere property in the empire, and his life could be taken for running away with no repercussions at all. The fact that we have this letter at all likely makes clear that all went well in the end. Then too, there is the tradition that Onesimus went on to be a bishop and leader in the church, so all's well that ends well. The journey from slave to servant of Christ to bishop is a short one when God's grace is at work through apostles like Paul.

PHILIPPIANS

Probably, Philippians is the latest of the Pauline Captivity letters, written somewhere around A.D. 62, and not long before Paul was released from house arrest and headed back east to deal with congregational problems. The basis for this conclusion is simple: First, Paul was a Roman citizen, and Roman law was already heavily tilted in their favor when non-Roman citizens like the high priest in Jerusalem were making accusations. Second, the requirement of Roman law when someone appealed to Caesar is that the accusers had to come in person to bear witness against the accused and make their case. This of course was onerous because the high priest was not about to leave volatile Jerusalem in the early A.D. 60s when the Jewish war was about to erupt against Roman authority. Nor is it likely that he would have been able to send emissaries that had seen Paul allegedly defile the Temple in Jerusalem. Remember the accusations came much earlier in the A.D. 50s, and the accusers might well be long gone because they appear to have been Diaspora Jews who didn't live in Jerusalem. Anyway, the accusations were false. Paul did not take a Gentile into the forbidden Jews-only zone of the Jerusalem temple. Third, when your accusers fail to show up before the emperor, the case is dismissed, which in all likelihood did happen. It was a different matter when Paul was taken the second time, after a fire transpired in Rome itself. Thus, Paul's belief that he will soon be restored to his converts back east, including in Philippi, was a reasonable belief. Here is the structure of this deliberative discourse, which exhorts the audience to follow the good examples of Christ, Paul, and Timothy when it comes to living out the Christian life and living in harmony with each other.

RHETORICAL OUTLINE OF PHILIPPIANS

Epistolary Prescript	1.1–2
Exordium/Introductory Remarks	1.3–11
Narratio/Narration of Pertinent Facts	1.12–26
Propositio/Thesis Statement	1.27–30
Probatio/Arguments for the Thesis	2.1–4.3
Peroratio/Final Emotional Appeal	4.4–9
Additional Argument (by way of P.S.)	4.10–20
Epistolary Greetings and Closing	4.21–23

Philippians is in many minds Paul's most winsome and joyful letter, despite the suffering Paul has been going through. It is clear enough that if there was one congregation that Paul had a deeply personal relationship with, it was the church at Philippi. This letter is full of heartfelt sentiments talking about the love and the joy Paul and his audience share in Christ and in the spreading of the Good News. Paul from the outset makes clear that God can even use difficult and painful circumstances to spread the Good News; for instance, Paul's house arrest has led to the spreading of the Good News "throughout the whole Praetorium," a reference to the Imperial guards who have been taking

Figure 12.3 Herod's palace at Caesarea Maritima where Paul appeared before Festus and Herod Agrippa. (© *Mark R. Fairchild, Ph.D.*)

turns watching Paul, chained to him day after day (Phil 1.12–13). Talk about a captive audience. At the end of this letter, Paul sends greetings from the Christians who work in the Emperor's household, probably slaves, but high-ranking ones (Phil 4.22). Both of these references favor the notion that Paul is writing from Rome, not somewhere else.

Although this letter is basically a progress-oriented letter, there are a couple of sticky issues he will address: 1) squabbles among the female leadership in the house churches in Philippi (Euodia and Syntyche—Phil. 4.2–3). The discourse is pleading for them, and indeed the whole congregation, to "be of one mind," or as Paul puts it in Phil. 2—to have the same mind that was in Christ Jesus, which leads to servant leadership, not squabbles. 2) Paul has been in a relationship of "giving and receiving" with the Philippians (something he mentions as well in 2 Cor. 8–9 where he speaks of them sending him monetary support); and in his argument that serves as a kind of P.S. in 4.10–20, Paul gently tells his beloved Philippians they can stop sending such gifts. Paul is saying they have done enough—indeed, they have been exceedingly generous and he is grateful—but it was time for them to direct their generosity elsewhere. In that same passage, Paul says only the Philippians had this sort of relationship with Paul, and this is because they did not see it as a matter of their becoming Paul's patrons—no, it was about sharing God's grace between them, and Paul had already given them the Gospel and plenty else too.

The very heart of the letter involves a piece of exalted prose, or perhaps a Christological hymn fragment. Paul is not adverse to using various ritual elements from worship as teaching tools, whether it is a baptismal formula like we find in Gal. 3.28 or the early Christian hymn material in Colossians 1 and in Philippians 2, both of which involve hymns of praise to Christ. Paul was perfectly happy to use such Christian traditions in his discourses, and not surprisingly he mainly uses material regularly used in worship—creedal fragments (see Romans 1.3–4 or Ephes. 4.4–5), benedictions or doxologies (see the end of most of these letters), Scripture quotations or allusions, and finally the aforementioned hymnic material. This is only to be expected because Paul's discourses seem to have been read out loud to the congregation as part of their worship service, as the preaching of the service so to speak.

In Phil. 2.5–11, the story of Christ is most ably and beautifully summed up in a Christological hymn:

> In your relationships with one another, have the same mindset as
> Christ Jesus:
>
> *Who, being in very nature God,*
>   *did not consider equality with God something to be used to his own advantage;*
> *rather, he emptied himself*
>   *by taking the very nature of a servant,*
>   *being made in human likeness.*
> *And being found in appearance as a man,*
>   *he humbled himself*
>   *by becoming obedient to death—*
>   *even death on a cross!*
> *Therefore God exalted him to the highest place*
>   *and gave him the name that is above every name,*
> *that at the name of Jesus every knee should bow,*
>   *in heaven and on earth and under the earth,*
> *and every tongue acknowledge that Jesus Christ is Lord,*
>   *to the glory of God the Father.*

Notice from the outset that although we have some exalted theological language in this passage, its function is to hold up Christ as an example of self-sacrificial love, with a not so subtle added point to allow God to do the exalting of a person rather than engaging in the sort of self-congratulatory behavior and boasting so typical of the Greco-Roman world. Paul says we are to have the same mind in ourselves about humbling ourselves and being faithful even unto death as Christ had. Having just said in Phil. 2.4 that we are to think not of ourselves but rather of the well-being of others, he further explains what he means in the Christ hymn.

If we ask where this hymnic material comes from, there can be little doubt that some of it comes from Paul's, or his source's, reflections on Christ and his career of preexistence, earthly existence, and exalted existence in heaven (a V pattern to the career) in light of material from Isaiah 40–55. Here are some of the parallels scholars note:

Phil. 2.7—Emptied himself.	Isaiah 53.12—Poured himself out.
Form of a slave/human likeness.	Isaiah 52.14, 53.2—Form/appearance.
Phil. 2.8—Humbled himself.	Isaiah 53.7—He was brought low.
Obedient to death.	Isaiah 53.12—To death.
Phil. 2.9—Therefore God exalted Him to the highest place.	Isaiah 53.12—Therefore I will allot him a portion with the great. Is. 52.13—Exalted and lifted up and shall be very high.
Phil. 2.10—Every knee bow; every tongue confess.	Isaiah 45.22–23—"To me every knee will bow; every tongue swear."

One of the implications of the parallels is that Paul is perfectly happy to speak of Christ as both divine and human, not merely one or the other. Whereas it is Yahweh in Is. 45.22–23 to whom every nation is to bow, in Phil. 2, it is to Christ, who is God the Son. The hymn then begins, telling us that Jesus is in very nature God and left heaven to add a human nature to his divine nature; and that in the end, everyone will recognize Christ as God and worship him as he is and deserves. It is hard to ignore, however, that the *function* of presenting this hymnic material is ethical. Paul is arguing for Christians, in a culture full of hubris and boasting, to humble themselves and act as servants. In the Greco-Roman world, humbling oneself was not seen as a virtue but rather as the appropriate behavior of slaves. Paradoxically, Paul stresses that it is the behavior of the savior of the world, who behaved so very differently than the other persons in that age who claimed to be the world's savior—the emperor. Christ and his humility and servant nature, not Caesar and his propaganda and arrogance, are held up as the template for Christian behavior.

This narrative is not a contrast between the story of the first Adam and the last one, namely, Christ. In contrast to the language of 1 Cor. 15.45–49 or of Rom. 5.12–21—both of which texts speak of Christ as the final founder of the human race, the eschatological Adam—no such language is used here in Phil. 2.5–11. A monotheistic Jew like Paul could in any case never have talked about the worship of a mere human being like Adam, but clearly this is how Christ is spoken of in this text. Adam would be an unsuitable parallel to the glory and

Figure 12.4 Sepphoris synagogue. (© *Mark R. Fairchild, Ph.D.*)

divine status and advantages Christ is said to have given up in order to become fully human. Furthermore, Genesis says nothing about Adam and Eve desiring absolute equality with God, something that God's Son already had by nature during his preexistence. Then too, Phil. 2.5–7 speaks of Christ making choices that affected his earthly form and condition, something that Adam was never able to do. The phrase "being found in human form" becomes inexplicable if Christ had never been anything other than a human being.

Thus this synopsis of the Christ story tells of a person who existed prior to taking on human form and continued to exist beyond death in heaven. Phil. 2.5–11 is a story divided into three parts—the story has a V pattern with the death on the cross being the nadir or the bottom of the V. There is preexistence, earthly existence, and then a return to heavenly existence after both death and resurrection (not just at or after death). Christ is the actor who thinks, considers, chooses, and lives out this trajectory according to Paul. It is interesting that whereas the verbs in the first half of the hymn are mostly active verbs telling us what Christ did, the verbs in the second half are passive, telling us what God did for Christ as a result of his attitudes and actions leading up to and including death.

Christ as it turns out is both divine and human, both humble and wise, both servant and Lord according to this story, but at varying stages of his career. It is fascinating as well that here especially we see the harmonic conversion of Paul's theologizing and ethicizing because this passage begins in verse 5: "have this mind in yourself which was also in Christ Jesus, who. . . ." Here the theologizing actually has an ethical function, meant to lead believers to imitate Christ (which of course shows that Paul presupposes that such is possible).

Christ deliberately stepped down, he deliberately did not draw on his divine prerogatives, he deliberately took a lower place, he deliberately submitted even unto death on a cross. Of course the analogy here between Christ's behavior and that of Christians is just that—an analogy. Nevertheless, it is a potent one, making clear that believers can and ought to follow the self-sacrificial example of Christ to the benefit of others. The crucified conqueror's story is to be recapitulated on a lesser scale in the life of his followers, including in the life of Paul himself.

In this same Philippian letter, Paul says, "I want to know Christ and the power of his resurrection and the sharing of his sufferings by becoming like him in his death, if somehow I might attain the resurrection of the dead" (Phil. 3.10–11). Paul then sees himself as modeling Christ so that others will do so as well. Thus, he says in Phil. 3.17, "Brothers and sisters, join in imitating me" (cf. 1 Cor. 11.1). This is not a reflection of Paul's hubris but rather of his humility, stepping down and imitating the behavior of the servant Christ. Paul is not claiming to be *the* pattern, only a good example of how to follow Christ's pattern. The right-standing obtained through faith in Christ (Phil. 3.9) was not meant to allow the believer to be left standing doing nothing. Indeed, it is the right-standing with God that is the platform for the believer to be able to imitate Christ, no longer having to earn or striving to obtain right-standing with God through their deeds or good works. To "gain Christ" (Phil. 3.8) is not merely to gain right-standing with God, it is to ultimately gain full conformity to Christ's image at the resurrection (Phil. 3.10–11).

The Christ hymn in Phil.2.5–11 reveals important clues explaining how it was that Christ was able to carry out his "mission (seemingly) impossible." He was in very nature God, and he could have taken advantage of his equality with the Father but chose not to do so. By right and by nature he had what God the Father had. But instead of taking advantage of his divine perks and prerogatives and glory, he set them aside in order to take on the very nature of a human being, and the very role of a servant or slave among human beings. What this seems to mean is *not* that he set aside his divine nature in exchange for a human one, but rather he set aside his right to draw on his divine attributes (omniscience, omnipresence, omnipotence) while on earth. He submitted to the normal human limitations of time, space, power, knowledge, and mortality.

In other words, the **incarnation** meant a divine being deliberately self-limiting in order to be truly and fully human. This did not include the necessity of becoming a sinner. This is why Paul in Rom. 8.3 says that he came in the "likeness of sinful flesh." He appeared like any other human being, and

INCARNATION

A term used to refer to Jesus as a divine being who deliberately limited himself in order to also become fully and truly human. In other words, the term points toward Jesus' assumption of full humanity while also remaining fully divine.

yet he was not a sinner. This of course implies a lot about Paul's view of true human nature. He did not believe that to be truly human, one must sin. Sin is seen as an aberration and not an essential trait of being truly human, unlike the limitations of time, space, power, and knowledge. Christ then is viewed as one who lived among humans as a true human being would and should, drawing on the same resources a normal godly person should and would—the Word of God and the Spirit of God and prayer.

Christ not only stripped himself of divine glory, he also shunned any normal human accolades and honors, taking on the form of a servant or slave. He did not get caught up in the boasting and honor challenges of his day, striving for ever more public recognition. Yet in the end he was honored, for God gave him the divine name, in fact the name for God in the LXX, namely, "Lord." Isaiah 45.21–25 lies in the background here. Here then in Phil. 2.5–11 as in 1 Cor. 8.5–6, we see Paul affirming a transformed definition of Jewish monotheism, which includes Christ within the definition of God. Christ is not given a purely honorific title or name after his resurrection, like an honorary degree. To the contrary, the name Jesus is given connotes the nature that he has—he is the risen Lord God Almighty. The name matches the nature, and that is why the worship by everyone, angels and demons included, of Jesus is appropriate.

Now of course the story of Christ has a sequel without equal that we have not talked about—the glorious return of Christ for final judgment and redemption (1 Thess. 4–5). There is an already and not yet dimension to the Christ story. Already the climax of the story has happened and not yet has the consummation devoutly to be wished arrived. We stand between D-Day and V-E day, as Oscar Cullmann once said, when it comes the Christ story, with D-Day being the death and resurrection of Jesus, the turning point in the war against the dark lords, and Christ's return being Victory Day. And of course because this is true, there is an already and not yet dimension to the story of Christians as well, including Paul.

IMPLICATIONS

How difficult it must have been for Paul the pastor when he was not a free man as was the case when he wrote the Captivity Epistles, and indeed did not know for sure whether he ever would be a master of his own time and travel plans again. Paul, ever the man of action, had to do something, indeed several somethings to help his fledgling converts populating small house churches in countries we today call Turkey, Greece, and Italy. We may be eternally grateful that one of those things was that he wrote numerous letters to those he loved while he was apart from them.

One of the things most appealing about Paul is his wholeheartedness and genuineness. He does nothing by half measures. He is a walking talking bundle of outrageous extremes. You never had to say to this man "tell me how you really feel about X." You get the sense that you always knew where you stood with this apostle. He seems almost incapable of playing his cards close to the vest for long.

And sometimes in our very different and very much later cultural settings we may find Paul's emoting and arm-twisting and rhetoric a bit too manipulative for us to be fully comfortable with. But if we think this, we have forgotten that Paul lived in a very different cultural setting with a very different emotional climate. **Pathos** was the stock in trade of much communication that was intended to persuade, and people of that rhetoric-saturated culture were not merely used to it, they knew how to read it. They knew when it was deliberate hyperbole and when it was not. They knew when it was genuine and when it was for rhetorical effect, whereas we do not always pick up the rhetorical signals. It is our job to learn to hear Paul's letters as if we were part of one of his original congregations. Then we may well do more than just hear them, we may understand and be persuaded by them.

PATHOS

The emotional response of the audience when the author appeals to their emotions in order to persuade.

KEY TERMS

Asiatic Rhetoric

First-Order Moral Discourse

Household Codes

Incarnation

Pathos

Second-Order Moral Discourse

Stoicheia

Third-Order Moral Discourse

FOR FURTHER READING

Bockmuehl, M. *The Epistle to the Philippians.* Peabody, MA: Hendrickson, 1998.

Capes, D. B., R. Reeves, and E. Randolph Richards. *Rediscovering Paul: An Introduction to His World, Letters, and Theology.* Downers Grove, IL: InterVarsity Press, 2007.

Donfried, Karl, and I. H. Marshall. *The Theology of the Shorter Pauline Letters.* Cambridge, England: Cambridge University Press, 1993.

STUDY QUESTIONS

Why do you think Paul wrote letter discourses that were so much longer than almost all other ancient letters?

If you had to assess Paul's emphases in his discourses, would you say he put more emphasis on belief or on behavior? Why did he see both as very important to one's faith and salvation?

How would you explain Paul's use of rhetoric, and why does he do it? Why does Paul say in Philemon that he would rather persuade than command Philemon to do something? What implication does this have for leaders today? Why is persuading better than demanding in most cases?

What sort of problems did Paul's largely Gentile congregations have? Why do you think that so many of Paul's letters are troubleshooting or problem-solving letters? What sort of image does this leave in your mind about Paul's churches? Are they much different from churches today?

NOTES

1. In fact, there is no verb in the Greek phrase in Ephes. 5.22—it simply says "wives to husbands . . . ," and the Greek structure assumes that whatever "be subject" means in verse 21 (where it is applied equally to men and women) is the same as what it means in verse 22.

The synagogue ruins in Capernaum. Jesus preached at the earlier form of this synagogue.
(© Rick Danielson)

13 PAUL the LETTER WRITER PART FOUR: The PASTORAL EPISTLES and the PROBLEM of PSEUDONYMOUS LETTERS

IN MANY IF NOT MOST INTRODUCTIONS to the New Testament, it is often taken for granted that we have documents in the New Testament that are attributed to persons who actually had nothing to do with the composition of those documents. And because this suggestion comes up more often in discussions of some of the Pauline documents and the so-called general epistles than elsewhere in the New Testament, it is appropriate for us to talk about this matter here, although this also applies to the discussion of documents such as 2 Peter as well.

Let us first define terms. The word *pseudonymous* means a falsely attributed author. It is a very different term than the word ***anonymous***, which means an unknown author. The document we call Hebrews is an anonymous document. Nothing in the document nor from later external discussion tells us clearly who wrote Hebrews. We are not concerned here with anonymous documents. None of the Pauline documents are or claim to be anonymous. They are all attributed to Paul. The question is—are they from Paul?

In part, this discussion has been made more complicated than it needs to be because modern scholars have sometimes imposed modern notions of authorship on ancient documents. To some of them, *authorship* means "did this particular person *compose* this document?" We have already seen, however, that the composition of documents in the first century A.D., especially long and complicated documents, was mostly a job for specialists. Such documents were composed by scribes at the request of a person wanting to communicate something to other persons, whether near or far (see Chapter 2). A better definition of authorship in the first century would be a document that comes from the mind and thought world of X, with X being the catalyst and brain behind the composition, even though X may not have written a single Greek letter in the document.

But there is another dimension to this whole matter too seldom considered. Many ancient documents were in fact compilation documents, like modern collections of essays from a variety of authors. Scribes would often make compendiums, for example, of the wisdom of a variety of sages. We absolutely see this practice in the book of Proverbs, where besides Solomonic wisdom, we also clearly have wisdom from other men (e.g., the saying of Agur in Proverbs 30 and wisdom from King Lemuel in Proverbs 31). I would suggest that there are compilation documents like that in the New Testament as well (described later) but not in the later Pauline documents. With these caveats, we are ready to have the rest of the discussion.

WHY THE AUTHORSHIP ISSUE MATTERS

What difference does it make whether some of these New Testament documents are pseudonymous or not? As it turns out, the answer matters greatly in several ways. To start, as David deSilva rightly says, it makes an enormous difference in the way one reconstructs the history of early Christianity and the development of its theological and ethical thinking. Second, it makes a great deal of difference when it comes to honesty and truth as well.

For example, if the so-called epistles of James and Jude come from the A.D. 50s and are responding to issues that existed then, including issues arising from the Pauline communities about faith and works, then we have a window into some of the differences in the earliest forms of the Christian faith and in the views of their leading figures. If, on the other hand, these documents are pseudepigrapha (meaning falsely attributed to the named author) from the A.D. 80s or 90s, then James should be seen as a Jewish Christian document reacting to, rather than being in dialogue with, the Pauline legacy. Further, relating to honesty and truth, if the Pastoral Epistles are not by Paul, then we cannot conclude that Paul himself chose to structure the leadership of his communities, as he was about to die, in the way we see elders and deacons discussed in these letters. These are but two examples, but it should be clear that the authenticity question matters in terms of history, theology, **ecclesiology**, and ethics, to mention a few relevant topics.[1]

The question of pseudonymity should be evaluated on a genre-by-genre basis. It is quite clear that there were pseudonymous apocalyptic works both in early Judaism (e.g., portions of the Enoch corpus) and in early Christianity (the Apocalypse of Peter). Indeed, one could even argue that pseudonymity was a regular feature of the apocalyptic genre of literature.

One cannot, however, demonstrate that about ancient ad hoc letters. By ad hoc, I mean situation-specific letters written to a particular audience. Although one could make a case for circular letters of a very general sort accommodating or comporting with the practice of writing pseudepigraphical letters, it is certainly more difficult to make such a case for a particularistic letter. I have elsewhere given various reasons why I do not think one can make a convincing case for 2 Thessalonians or Ephesians (or Colossians) as pseudepigrapha, although the strongest case has been made for Ephesians, precisely because it is likely to be a circular document and more of a homily than a letter.[2] Without rehearsing those arguments here, I will stress that each document must be examined on a case-by-case basis.

The truth is, the more one studies this issue, the more complex it becomes. For example, we may ask what counts as authorship. Could a document that contained a source document from a famous person (perhaps at the beginning of a composite document) be attributed to that person? The answer is yes.

In fact, we see this in two very different sorts of documents in the New Testament. In 2 Peter, we clearly have a composite document, borrowing much of Jude, but also using a Petrine source, in its first chapter.[3] We also see this phenomenon in the Gospel of Matthew, which uses one or more special Matthean sources, which I would argue goes back to the apostle Matthew.[4] The former of these two documents is a composite letter of sorts and falls within the parameters of this chapter. This reminds us that we must not import into this discussion various modern notions of authorship and intellectual property. The question must be what was the scope or flexibility of ancient conceptions of authorship and intellectual property? Were there in fact ancient notions of intellectual property and plagiarism? We will speak to these two questions in a moment.

Let us consider briefly another issue that might affect this matter. We know that Paul used secretaries, as Rom. 16.22 makes evident; and in addition, he tells us at the end of Galatians and 2 Thessalonians that he is taking up the pen, which likely means he only actually wrote down or penned a minority of the words in some of his genuine letters.

ECCLESIOLOGY

A term used to refer to the study of the church.

This raises the pertinent question of whether he might have done something other than just dictate to a secretary. Might he have had a secretary compose a draft, to which he would make alterations? Might he have allowed scribes considerable latitude in composing with plans to revise or correct later? Multiple stages of composition are not all that likely for several reasons: (1) Paul was a man on the move, and he was often in a hurry. (2) Frequently, he had to respond quickly to urgent and emergent circumstances. His letters bear the mark of this in various places. For example, sometimes there are incomplete sentences, suggesting that the scribe could not keep up with the pace of dictation. (3) Paper was expensive, paying a scribe was very expensive, and there are enough infelicities and gaps in the genuine Pauline letters to suggest that these documents were never revised, and thus they often bear the marks of initial dictation. Incomplete sentences are a dead giveaway.[5]

What is more plausible is that, if Paul was in prison, he might well have conveyed his thoughts orally to a trusted colleague or coworker who would then write them down and send them off. This seems to have certainly been within the parameters of ancient views of genuine authorship rather than pseudepigraphy. We do not find this happening in letters like Philemon or Philippians, where Paul was still able to dictate letters to those present and send them off while he was under house arrest.

The Pastoral Epistles, however, are perhaps a different story. One could argue that if Paul was under duress and not far from the time of execution, there would be no leisure or setting where he would likely have been able to dictate letters, nor would many people have free access to him. Perhaps only one trusted friend or colleague who could bring food and convey messages orally (and later write them down) could come to him at a time if he were under close supervision in the Campus Martius, the military camp at the edge of Rome. This *might* be the case with 2 Timothy, and if so, we might well expect the style to be rather different from the earlier Paulines. However, this does not explain why the pastorals *all* manifest a rather uniform style that in some important respects distinguishes them from the earlier Pauline letters. Furthermore, it does not explain the character of 1 Timothy and Titus at all, both of which were written while Paul was still apparently a free man and not in Rome. We must look elsewhere for an answer to these sorts of questions.

In my judgment, the real dividing line between a genuine letter and a pseudepigraphical one is whether the material comes from the mind of a particular person or not, *not* whether it fully reflects his grammar and syntax and vocabulary. I would add that *a genuine letter not only comes from the mind of the person, but it is written down by him, by his request, or on his behalf.*[6] This seems to have been well within the scope of ancient views of what counted as authorship.

In the case of the Pastoral Epistles, I would argue that the "voice is the voice of Paul, but the hands are the hands of Luke." Luke wrote these documents while Paul was alive, but, in the case of 2 Timothy, in prison. Luke composed the

Figure 13.1 Here on the Acropolis was the original library of Pergamum, much of which ended up in the library in Alexandria as a lovesick Marc Antony shipped off some 200,000 scrolls to Egypt as a wedding present to Cleopatra. (© *Mark R. Fairchild, Ph.D.*)

documents in his own style (there are over 40 words in the pastorals found elsewhere in the New Testament, only in Luke–Acts, not to mention corresponding turns of phrases and key terms). There is a reason why some scholars have seen the pastorals as the sequel to Acts. In a sense, they are a sequel, and ironically, they were probably composed by the same man. What we see in the pastorals then is the cooperative effort of two important early Christians who also contributed other documents to our present New Testament.

In short, the Pastoral Epistles do not have falsely attributed authorship any more than the earlier Paulines. What we do have is more contributions from Paul's colleague and secretary, Luke, in the case of these three documents. We will talk more about this toward the close of this chapter, but first we must consider a bit more closely the writing environment in which the pastorals were composed.

THE PASTORAL EPISTLES—WHAT SORT OF RHETORIC IS THIS?

Bearing in mind the discussions earlier in this chapter, we now turn to the Pastoral Epistles and consider briefly what we find there. The first important point to make is that these really are personal, even private, letters, and only 3 John is

at a Glance

The Pastoral Epistles are surely the latest of all the Pauline documents, likely composed in the A.D. mid-60s shortly before the death of Paul, and with much help from a coworker, probably Luke. The three documents manifest a rather uniform style and phraseology that distinguish them in several important ways from the earlier Paulines. They offer us Paul's parting advice and a sort of last will and testament in 2 Timothy from the apostle to the Gentiles.

comparable. That the church later thought this mail was suitable to be read by all Christians does not change the fact that Paul intended these letters as instructions and encouragement for two of his closest coworkers—Timothy and Titus.

It is clear enough that skillful scribes and writers were able to alter their Greek style according to the content and audience they were dealing with. The fact that the pastorals use more elementary rhetoric than we are accustomed to finding in Paul's letters and the fact that the style better resembles Luke's style of grammar and vocabulary really do not count against the notion that what is being expressed in these documents is the mind of Paul, near the very end of his life. We will consider two small samples of the sort of argumentation that goes on in these documents.

Enthymemes are by definition incomplete syllogisms, a form of rhetoric or argumentation in which the hearer is expected to understand the logic of the argument and supply the missing member in it. What we have in the Pastoral Epistles is lots of enthymemes, and those who have not read the pastorals with a knowledge of rhetoric have understandably found the logic of various passages confusing or, even worse, incoherent. Our first small example comes from probably the earliest of these three letters, the one to Titus, and the passage we are looking at is Titus 1.10–16. Here is the rhetorical structure in the form of an enthymeme.

ENTHYMEMES

A form of rhetoric that employs incomplete syllogisms in which the hearer is expected to understand the logic of the argument and supply the missing member of the argument.

PRIMARY ARGUMENT ABOUT FALSE TEACHERS

1. Elders must rebuke those who oppose the right teaching . . .

2. . . . because there are many who rebel against it, engaging in idle chatter and deception.

3. . . . especially those of the circumcision [who use Jewish myths and commandments to persuade].

4. They must be silenced . . .

5. . . . because they have already turned whole families in the community away from the truth, for the sake of their own profit.

6. Their own Cretan prophet warned against such teachers—"all Cretans are liars, cruel animals, lazy gluttons."

7. We can confirm that this testimony is true.

8. They must be sternly rebuked also for their own good, to strengthen their own faith.

In this primary argument, Paul uses the maxim as a major premise to make his case that the false teachers' mouths must be stopped because they are spreading lies and are doing it for personal gain. He backs up the force of the maxim with his own authority, confirming that what the maxim says is true; and because it is true, it provides justification for the stern rebuke, refutation, and silencing of such people. He adds that it is also for their own good, and not just because of the havoc they are wreaking in the church, leading whole families astray. The implied premise or step in the first **syllogism** that the audience must supply is something like this: The false teachers are serving up Jewish myths and commandments (perhaps including the command to be circumcised). If a modern reader does not know that in ancient practice a premise is implied, he/she is not likely to understand fully the intended meaning of the enthymeme. This is one reason why it is helpful to gain knowledge of such rhetorical devices.

SYLLOGISM

A form of argumentation that builds an argument using a major premise and a minor premise. The audience must employ deductive reasoning in order to extract the conclusion of the argument, which is based on the major and minor premise.

SECONDARY ARGUMENT ABOUT FALSE TEACHERS

1. Those who have pure minds and hearts can listen to such teaching without pollution and can participate in many things without harm.

2. But to the corrupt and unbelieving, nothing but trouble comes from listening because their minds and consciences are already defiled.

3. Unfortunately, it is these same people who claim to truly know God.

4. But clearly their lifestyle makes it obvious that this is not so.

5. Notice that they are incapable of good works and instead engage in abominations.

6. [Therefore it is evident that they neither know God nor are they pure.]

The Pastoral Epistles are loaded with small quotations or maxims that are expanded and expounded in the incomplete syllogism or enthymeme. This is a very different kind of argumentation than we find in Paul's earlier letters, but perhaps he uses this here because (1) it is the kind of rhetorical argument Timothy and Titus were capable of offering their converts based on their prior rhetorical training, and (2) it was a sort of simple rhetoric, drawing on familiar maxims that were most effective with certain Cretans and residents in Ephesus. Paul and Luke were clearly both skilled enough in Greek and rhetoric to alter their style and mode of argumentation to suit the occasion and audience. In short, these sorts of differences from the earlier Paulines do not really count against their

Pauline character. Only if the pastorals could be shown to be un-Pauline or even anti-Pauline in content would a conclusion of pseudonymity become more probable. But a convincing case for this view has yet to be made. The balance of probabilities still favors the pastorals being Pauline in character.

OUTLINES AND SYNOPSES OF CONTENTS OF THE PASTORALS

Titus

What we have in Titus is a sort of rhetorical mandate letter, a letter from a superior to an inferior giving instructions telling him how to set things up in a new setting and establish good order and control of the situation. Here is the breakdown offered by C. J. Classen.[7]

OUTLINE OF TITUS	
Epistolary Prescript	1.1–4
Mandate to Appoint Elders of Good Reputation with the Necessary Qualities (and the Opposite of This is Described in Verses 10–13)	1.5–9
More General Directives to Show Christians the Path to Sound Belief (with Specific Orders for Old Men, Old Women, Young Women, Young Men, Slaves)	1.13b–3.7
Special Instructions for Titus	3.12–14
Final Greetings	3.15

We have already seen that our author is using incomplete syllogisms in these three letters, but he is also using rhetorical comparisons and contrasts (*synkrisis*) in Titus 1–2 showing what positive leaders look like in contrast to opponents and false teachers. What one needs to understand about this entire letter is that Paul is dealing with a missionary or church plant situation, and it is necessary to start with people where they are. Where they are is in a male-dominated cultural environment, so of course if one wants to win friends and influence people, you start with the leadership structures that already exist and then modify them over time in a more Christian direction.

This explains the instructions about appointing male elders in the various towns in Crete where the Gospel has been shared successfully. They should be men who have been married only once, men of good character, not given to drunkenness and other vices of the Greco-Roman world—arrogance, quick temper, greed. Because Christianity is an evangelistic religion, he also needs to

Figure 13.2 The Celsus Library in Ephesus. Paul would have lectured near here. (© Rick Danielson)

model hospitality, prudence, goodness, self-control, and trustworthiness so that when he preaches the belief and behavior called for in the Gospel, he will come across as genuine—not as a peddler of a message he doesn't actually believe.

Titus 1.12 is a classic example of how context matters to interpretation—Paul, quoting a Cretan prophet commenting about Cretans, says "Cretans are always liars, vicious brutes, gluttons." Now of course, this is a hyperbolic generalization, it is the kind of thing a native who knew his countrymen well could get away with saying; but Paul uses it to instill caution in Titus in regard to not being naïve about how people respond to the Gospel, and sometimes say positive things but don't mean them. Paul has seen his share of liars, deceivers, corrupt people, and people on the take.

The great concern in a senior-dominated culture is for the older men and women who have accepted the Christian faith to present examples of good character to the unbelievers, as Titus 2 stresses. When there are young women whose husbands are not Christians, they are to be submissive to their husbands so that they will have opportunities to bear good witness to the Gospel. Sharing the

Good News to a family member was more important than insisting on equality or freedom. When you are a minority religion, people are always looking for excuses to discredit your faith, so Paul is saying to these women they are not to make waves—be good managers of their households, be chaste and self-controlled, and help their spouses. Likewise the young men are to be known for their good works in public and their sound and wise speech. All of this advice is given with one eye on the effect on pagans and with the concern of how to witness indirectly and win some for Christ. The same goes for slaves who should be honest and not rebellious or given to talking back to their owners. Again, this is first-order moral discourse. This is not by any means what Paul would say if the slave's owner was *also* a convert to Christianity already, as we have seen in Philemon.

Paul gives no hint in Titus of being in distress yet, and he has coworkers with him when he writes this (Tit. 3.12–15). The style of the document is Lukan, but we must see these instructions as examples of Paul trying to prepare his main coworkers, Titus and Timothy, for the transition to the period when he will be with them no longer. They must establish the Christian structures of leadership and police the behavior and beliefs of the converts, and they must appoint leaders in every town to carry out such mandates.

There can be little doubt that as far as leadership structure goes in the early church, it was hierarchical in character—apostles at the top, and then their itinerant coworkers like Titus and Timothy, and then the local church leaders—overseers, elders, deacons, teachers, prophets. The behavior of such leaders and other key converts is the burden of this document because Paul wants to give no offense, and set no stumbling block before potential converts, unless it is the Gospel message itself. Sometimes we do not realize what a hard sell proclaiming a crucified and raised Jewish savior figure was in a pagan world. Most pagans did not believe in resurrection at all (see Acts 17), and they thought crucifixion was the most shameful way to die possible, possibly even a sign the person had been repudiated or cursed by a deity. With this message as the Good News, there could be zero tolerance for misbehavior by Christian witnesses and leaders, and zero tolerance of bad teaching either.

1 Timothy

Without much doubt, Timothy was by far Paul's closest coworker: indeed, Paul was given to calling him his spiritual son. Paul greatly loved this young man, but he also knew the young man was not the outgoing, boisterous, courageous person that Paul himself was. Timothy, in a word, was timid, and apparently soft-spoken as well. One of the main concerns and burdens of all three of the Pastoral Epistles is for the teaching of sound beliefs and good behavior—not Jewish myths, genealogical speculations, and esoteric teachings. There are some "trustworthy sayings" in all three of these letters, which seem to be maxims that

Paul expected either Timothy and Titus to memorize or already know. Here are the five sayings found in these three letters:

1. "He saved us through the washing of regeneration and renewal of the Holy Spirit, who was richly poured out for us through Jesus Christ our Savior, in order that having been set right by his grace we might become heirs according to the hope of eternal life. Trustworthy is this saying."—Titus 3.5–8a

2. "Trustworthy is the saying and worthy of full acceptance: Christ Jesus came into the world to save sinners."—1 Tim. 1.15

3. "Trustworthy is the saying: 'If anyone aspires to the office of overseer, he is desiring a good work.'"—1 Tim. 3.1

4. "Physical discipline/training is useful for a few things, but godliness is useful for everything being the promise of life now and in the future. Trustworthy is the saying and worthy of full acceptance."—1 Tim. 4.8b–9

5. "Trustworthy is the saying: 'For if we died together, we will also live together. If we endure, we will also reign together. If we deny Christ, he will also deny us. If we are faithless, he remains faithful, for he is unable to deny himself.'"—2 Tim. 2.11–13.

Considered together, these sayings show that these three letters are concerned with the practical matters of what is entailed in being a good leader—namely, knowing the core beliefs, modeling Christ-like behavior, remaining true and trustworthy even when suffering or persecuted, remembering how one was saved and graced by God and called to the tasks now being undertaken.

The structure of 1 Timothy may be outlined as follows:

OUTLINE OF 1 TIMOTHY

Epistolary Prescript	1.1–2
The "Other" Gospels of Laws, Myths, Genealogies	1.3–20
Prayer and Praxis in Worship	2.1–15
Oversight and Service in Ephesus	3.1–16
Future Shock, Present Service	4.1–16
Ordering the House Church	5.1–6.2a
False Teaching	6.2b–10
Peroration (Final Emotional Appeal) for an Apostolic Coworker	6.11–21

The rhetoric in the Pastoral Epistles is more elementary than in Paul's earlier letters and does not involve the full structure of arguments, probably because Paul is dealing with coworkers who already know his teachings and lifestyle very well and so only need instructions and reminders on how to implement their leadership roles. This also explains the pragmatic character of these three documents as well.

Another feature of both 1 and 2 Timothy is Paul's candid personal remarks. Paul freely admits that he was formerly a blasphemer of Christ, a persecutor of the church, a violent man, but that he received mercy because he acted in ignorance (1 Tim. 1.12–15). Although Paul does not seem to be in total distress when 1 Timothy is written, by the time 2 Timothy is written, it appears we are close to the end of the apostle's life.

It is striking that in the Pastoral Epistles, Paul emphasizes the universal scope of God's plan of salvation, just as we find in Luke–Acts. Jesus is the Savior (again language we do not much find in the earlier Paulines but frequently in Luke–Acts) who came to provide a ransom for all, and be the mediator between God and humanity for all (1 Tim. 2.5), but this salvation is only efficacious for those who believe and receive the Good News. It does not work automatically or unilaterally. Paul believes there are three tenses to salvation—I have been saved, I am being saved, and I shall be saved when Christ returns and transforms the believers. This is why there are exhortations, even to a leader like Timothy, to avoid heresy and apostasy and moral lapses and instead "fight the good fight, take hold of everlasting life to which you were called, and for which you made the good confession in the presence of many witnesses. . . . Timothy guard what has been entrusted to you" (1 Tim. 6.12–20). Paul knows that "the game is still afoot," that one must persevere in the faith to the end, despite rejection, abuse, suffering, failure, and the numerous temptations of the heart and the flesh. Paul understands that the character of Christianity will change as the apostles die out, and so as he passes the baton to the next generation of Christian leaders, he strongly stresses the issue of preserving orthodox teaching about both belief and behavior and apostolic practice as well. Last instructions of an apostle to those who will lead thereafter are critical. They are not afterthoughts but carefully thought out plans to carry the church forward into its life in the post-apostolic era.

2 Timothy

2 Timothy is perhaps the last chance to hear the Pauline voice, the last epistle he had written by Luke, while he was in the Mamertine awaiting likely beheading. It returns to the normal rhetorical structures of Paul's earlier letters, as follows:

OUTLINE OF 2 TIMOTHY

Epistolary Prescript	1.1–2
Thanksgiving Prayer/Exordium	1.3–5
Propositio/Thesis Statement—2 Tim. 1.6–7, "Stir up the Gift, Draw on the Power"	1.6–7
Argument One: Prepare to Testify, Suffer, Guard the Deposit	1.8–14
Narratio/Transition	1.15–18
Argument Two: Entrust, Endure, Remember	2.1–13
Argument Three: Warn the Opponents, Avoid Quarrels	2.14–26
Argument Four: Apostasy and Corruption in the Last Days	3.1–9
Argument Five: Continue in My Apostolic Teaching and in the Scriptures	3.10–17
Peroration/Final Emotional Appeal/Do the Work of an Evangelist	4.1–8
Travel Plans for Timothy/Personal Remarks	4.9–18
Closing Greetings/Benediction	4.19–22

This letter, unlike Titus and 1 Timothy, definitely has an argumentative character, and displays not just minor rhetorical devices but the full rhetorical outline of a speech, an act of persuasion. Clearly Paul had a final exhortation for his closest associate. We don't just have maxims (trustworthy sayings), rhetorical comparisons, and incomplete syllogisms, as in the other two Pastoral Epistles. Here we have something closer to what we saw in the earlier Paulines (compare, e.g., Philippians, which is about the same length and the same deliberative sort of rhetoric).

This letter is full of pathos. Paul has been abandoned, except for his doctor, Luke. He desperately wants to see Timothy one last time before he dies so "my joy might be full" (2 Tim. 1.4). Paul is full of reminiscences in this letter, and even reminds Timothy of his Christian grandmother and mother's faith that now resides in him. Already we have an example of three generations of Christian faith in one family. In 2 Tim. 1.6, Paul urges Timothy to rekindle the flame of his gifts and reminds that God did not give us a spirit of fear or cowardice. As I said before, Timothy was not naturally a bold person, but rather the opposite, so he required some jump-starting. Paul is not asking Timothy to be just like his spiritual father and mentor Paul. He is asking him merely to preserve the sound teaching and practice he heard from Paul. Paul doesn't expect Timothy to be a creative theologian or ethicist; he expects him to be a faithful leader and pastor. He reminds Timothy that when the fires of trial grow hot, even the formerly faithful may run away. So it seems was the case with Onesiphorus, who visited

Figure 13.3 A wealthy person's home in Ephesus next to the Library of Celsus.
(© *Mark R. Fairchild, Ph.D.*)

Paul in Rome while he was previously under house arrest, but now like others, has abandoned Paul (and Paul prays for mercy for him; 2 Tim. 1.16–17).

As in 1 Timothy, there is a strong emphasis on salvation not being complete unless one perseveres to the end; so we hear in 2 Tim. 2.10–13 again about how even the elect still have not yet fully obtained final salvation in Christ Jesus. Election is one thing, salvation is another. Even members of the elect may commit apostasy under pressure and trials. Thus, he adds "if we endure we shall reign together, but if we deny, he shall deny us," with the us being Paul himself and Timothy.

In an oral culture that was also an honor and shame culture, there were many verbal sparring contests seeking to win honor challenges over another person and so establish one's own honor. Paul in 2 Tim. 2.14 warns Timothy against getting involved in "word battles." Rather, he is to "cut straight the word of truth," which I take to mean "offer them the unvarnished truth." Don't resort to flattery or deceit as some rhetoricians would. Godless chatter, says Paul, eats away at your inner parts like gangrene! On one hand, Paul is encouraging Timothy to contend for the faith. On the other hand, "Avoid foolish and uneducated speculation. . . . it is not necessary to quarrel but to be kind toward all, having the gift of teaching, forbearing with gentleness, instructing even the opponents"

(2 Tim. 2.23–25). It is clear enough that in Ephesus, where Paul had been for over 2 years earlier in his life and where Timothy was now doing ministry, that there were both Jewish and pagan rival teachers and rhetoricians; so in the competitive marketplace of ideas, Timothy needed to know how to handle himself and best present the Gospel. But it is not as though Timothy is without guidance. As 2 Tim. 3 will say, he has the example and teachings of Paul, which he knows very well, and he has the Old Testament Scriptures, which are "god-breathed, and profitable for teaching, for refutation, for correction, for training in righteousness." What is interesting about this description is that starting with the word *profitable*, it could also be a description of the effect of good deliberative rhetoric, good acts of persuasion that seeks to instruct, provide advice, correct, and rebuke where necessary.

By the time we get to 2 Tim. 4.6–8, we will have already sensed that this is a discourse with lots of urgency and pleading involved. But here finally, Paul says directly—"For I am already being poured out as a libation and the time of my departure has come, I have run the good race, finished the course, I have kept the faith. Finally reserved for me is the laurel crown of righteousness, which the Lord the righteous judge, will award me on that day, and not only me but also all those who have loved his appearing."

The imagery of the Olympic race was used by Paul and other early Christians to describe the course of the Christian life. What the analogy emphasized was (1) it required training and discipline to run the whole race; (2) that one's life was going somewhere, there was a goal; (3) however arduous the race, one must persevere to the end and finish the race; (4) having done so, it would be Jesus himself the fair and righteous Judge to determine the winners; and (5) there would be rewards for running and finishing properly. Paul talks more about this notion of rewards for serving the Lord well throughout life, and doing good ministry along the way, in 1 Cor. 3. Let me be clear that Paul is not saying that salvation itself is the reward but that there would be rewards for those who passed through successfully all three tenses of salvation—I have been saved, I am being saved, and I shall be saved to the uttermost (by full conformity to the image of Jesus by resurrection when he returns). Christians are runners who need to keep their eyes on the goal and the prize and not fall short of finishing well.

At 2 Tim. 4.9–18, it becomes clear that Paul thinks he still has a bit of time. He has already gone through the "primo actio" or first hearing—which is to say the first phase of his trial—and absolutely no one came to his defense; but it's not over yet. He was rescued from instant judgment and being sent off to the lions or being beheaded on the spot. But the situation looks grim; so Timothy, bringing Mark as well, must hurry. Paul tells him as well to bring the parchments, which are likely what we would call Paul's own personal copies of all those letters he sent to his churches. It was normal for a scribe to make one papyrus copy for sending and one more permanent copy to be kept by the sender. I suspect this is what Paul is talking about. With this, we hear from Paul no more. What we know is that his coworkers carried on, perhaps without all the fanfare and turmoil that surround Paul the trailblazer; but nonetheless, they carried on, and the church grew and prospered in all the regions of the Empire where Paul had been. And indeed, humanly speaking, we Gentiles who may be reading this very book might not be doing so were it not for herculean labors of the Apostle to the Gentiles.

IMPLICATIONS

It is not possible in a study of this sort to treat each of Paul's 13 letters in detail. What we can say here is that a very good case can be made that they all come from the mind of Paul, whatever scribes Paul may have used, and whatever degree of literary license he gave them to compose in their own style. Style, in any case, was no good indicator of authorship because really skilled people would vary their style according to the subject matter and the rhetorical intent, as we can clearly see Luke doing within Luke–Acts.

The issues of resolving the authorship of the contested Paulines: 2 Thessalonians, Ephesians, possibly Colossians, and the pastorals must be left to detailed discussions I have undertaken in my commentaries on all these documents. Here, it must suffice to say that I see no good reason to doubt that any of these documents come ultimately from the mind of Paul. The writings of such a central and seminal figure as Paul, who was so well known across so many geographical boundaries and in so many Christian communities, were deemed so important that they were some of the first documents to be collected together into a group, as 2 Peter 3 attests. Because this happened already in the first century A.D. while some of Paul's coworkers and friends were still alive, we may assume that those very people were available to exercise quality control if they knew that some of the documents did not come from the mind of Paul.

The fact that *none of these 13 letters were disputed in regard to their Pauline authorship,* so far as we can tell in the whole period of the first four centuries of Christian history, means that the church was quite sure about them all along. So far as I can see, we are in no position, at this great a remove in time, to provide any sort of compelling evidence against this judgment.

Most of the usual objections to the disputed Paulines can be explained as (1) a result of false notions about what authorship meant in antiquity (vis-à-vis the use of scribes or companions to compose documents); (2) on the basis of misreading Pauline texts without proper contextual understanding (e.g., early Jews were quite capable of talking about both events leading up to the end and the possible imminence of the end in the same breath); (3) a failure to recognize that Paul had rhetorical skills and could vary his style according to his audience (e.g., using Asiatic rhetoric in Ephesians); and (4) failure to recognize that, toward the end of Paul's life, he would indeed have been concerned to leave behind a leadership structure like the one described in the pastorals, as the age of the apostolic figures waned and disappeared altogether.

There are such riches and depths to the Pauline discourses that it was quite impossible to do more than give one a taste of Paul's writings in these chapters. It is far too easy for those who study Paul's letters for all their rich theologizing and ethical reflection to forget, or at least neglect the fact, that Paul was a pastor, deeply concerned about his converts and coworkers. It is actually hard to read any of these letters and miss the level of emotional investment Paul had in his converts. He rejoiced when they rejoiced, he mourned when they mourned, and he experienced all sorts of anxieties when he was apart from them and could be no direct help to them. How much more difficult for him must it have been when he was not a free man as in the case when he wrote the Captivity Epistles, and indeed did not know for sure whether he ever would be a master of his own time and travel plans again? And how much higher must his anxiety level have been when, even later, he had Luke write the Pastorals for him, while he was actually facing his demise through the judicial system in Rome? And yet even to the very end, Paul was still exercising his apostolic office, still summoning his coworkers, still exhorting his converts, until he could utter the God-whispered words no more. Yet he need not have feared that even death would silence him, for his letters live on and continue to speak for him even today.

KEY TERMS

Anonymous	Enthymemes
Ecclesiology	Syllogism

FOR FURTHER READING

Bauckham, R. J. "Pseudo-Apostolic Letters." *Journal of Biblical Literature* 107, no. 3 (1988): 469–494.

Metzger, B. M. "Literary Forgeries and Canonical Pseudepigrapha." *Journal of Biblical Literature* 91 (1972): 3–24.

Richards, E. *Paul and First Century Letter Writing: Secretaries, Composition and Collection.* Downers Grove, IL: InterVarsity Press, 2004.

Witherington, B. *Letters and Homilies for Hellenized Christians.* Vol. 1, *A Socio-Rhetorical Commentary on Titus, 1-2 Timothy and 1-3 John.* Downers Grove, IL: InterVarsity Press, 2006.

STUDY QUESTIONS

Why do you think these three letters have been called Pastoral Epistles? What do you make of Timothy and Titus as Paul's coworkers? Why do you think Paul felt he needed to exhort them as he does even to the end of his life?

Thinking about the principle of starting with people where they are, and then gradually trying to change their worldview and behavior, do you think this approach, which involves persuasion rather than coercion, is a good one? Why or why not when it comes to religious faith?

At the end of his life, Paul expresses regrets about his previous sins against Christians when he was a persecutor of them before his conversion. Do you think this is one of the reasons he emphasized God's grace and mercy so much, because he himself had needed and experienced it?

NOTES

1. See the helpful discussion in D. deSilva, *An Introduction to the New Testament: Contexts, Methods & Ministry Formation* (Downers Grove, IL: InterVarsity Press, 2004), 685–689.
2. See B. Witherington, "Introduction" in *1 and 2 Thessalonians: A Socio-Rhetorical Commentary* (Grand Rapids, MI: Eerdmans, 2006); and B. Witherington and D. Hyatt, "Introduction" in *The Letters to Philemon, Colossians, and Ephesians: A Socio-Rhetorical Commentary on the Captivity Epistles* (Grand Rapids, MI: Eerdmans, 2007).
3. See B. Witherington "A Petrine Source in 2nd Peter," pages 187–92 in *Society of Biblical Literature 1985 Seminar Papers.* Edited by K. H. Richards. (Atlanta, GA: Scholars Press, 1985).
4. See B. Witherington, "Introduction" in *Matthew* (Macon, GA: Smyth and Helwys, 2006).
5. One should, however, consider the careful study of E. Richards, *Paul and First-Century Letter Writing: Secretaries, Composition and Collection* (Downers Grove, IL: InterVarsity Press, 2004).
6. I owe this helpful supplemental point to Dr. Jan van der Watt.
7. *Rhetorical Criticism of the New Testament* (Tubingen, Germany: Mohr Siebeck, 2000), 66.

PART IV

LETTERS and HOMILIES for JEWISH CHRISTIANS

The mixture of Jewish and Greek images in a synagogue mosaic floor is not uncommon in a highly Hellenized city like Sepphoris. (© *Mark R. Fairchild, Ph.D.*)

The SERMON of JAMES the JUST—JESUS' BROTHER

GENERAL EPISTLES?

One of the major problems with some conceptions about early Christianity is that because so much of the New Testament is taken up with Pauline letters or stories about Paul (most of Acts 9–28), this has sometimes left the impression that already during the lifetime of Paul, Christianity had become an overwhelmingly Gentile-dominated religion. This perception is likely wrong, for a whole host of reasons.

First, by A.D. 64, the followers of Jesus were not yet distinguished from Judaism as a separate religion, at least not in official quarters. And whatever else one says, the real leaders of early Christianity—whether we think of Peter, James, Paul, John, Philip, or Barnabas—were all Jews who were in agreement with what Paul says in Romans 1— that the Good News about the Jewish Messiah Jesus was for the Jews first. Even Paul, the apostle to the Gentiles, pursued a "go to the synagogue with the Good News first" strategy, as Acts and Paul's own references to the number of times he suffered the 39 lashes (an exclusively Jewish punishment) demonstrate this fact (2 Cor. 11.24).

The second reason this must be doubted is because in Galatians 1, it is clear enough that Peter has been assigned the task of being the missionary to the Jews in the Diaspora as well as in the Holy Land, and we know in fact he did this. Paul mentions in 1 Corinthians that Peter has been to Corinth and has some adherents there. He may even have baptized some Jews there. The division of labor between Paul and Peter was *not geographical,* not least because many more Jews lived outside the Holy Land than inside it. The division of labor was ethnic—Paul to the Gentiles, Peter to the Jews, wherever and whenever. But even this division could not be a hard and fast one because of the God-fearers. They were Gentiles, but they were attending the synagogue—whose responsibility were they? Both Paul and Peter seem to have targeted this group for evangelism. There is a good reason we have the story in Acts 10–11 of Cornelius, the Roman soldier and synagogue attender. It makes clear that Peter was evangelizing such people, and this meant that the evangelism of Gentiles was not only endorsed by the leader of the Jerusalem disciples but also that it was not simply left to Paul and his colleagues.

The third reason we must doubt this theory is that we have a variety of documents written to Jewish Christians in the New Testament in various places, and we must take seriously that the audience of these documents was in fact mainly Jewish Christians. I am referring to James, Jude, 1 Peter, Hebrews, 1–3 John, and possibly Revelation, which are most of the remaining books of the New Testament!

What we need to envision is that Jewish Christian missionaries to Jews established their own congregations in many of the cities of the empire where there were *also* Pauline congregations—Ephesus, Sardis, Laodicea, and Corinth, to mention a few. In addition, they established Jewish Christian congregations in places like Galilee and other Jewish centers where Paul never went. Rome, for example, had both largely Jewish Christian congregations and Gentile Christian congregations. Paul's Letter to the Romans bears witness to this dual reality and is in part a discourse with the intention of getting these two Christian groups together, to be reconciled with one another before he arrives. As it turns out, Peter may have gone to as many places as Paul did, to judge from the list of congregations and their geographical locations in 1 Peter's **prescript** (1 Pet. 1.1).

Some of these Jewish Christian groups, particularly the ones located in or near the Holy Land, were more traditionally Jewish (e.g., the audience of Matthew or Jude), and some were more Hellenized (as we shall see, this applies to the audience of 1 Peter and the Johannine epistles); but it is certainly something of an irony that documents such as Hebrews, James, Jude, the Johannine epistles, and 1 Peter got lumped together under the heading "Catholic Epistles." Nothing could be further from the truth than the suggestion that these documents were a bunch of general encyclicals written to all Christians everywhere in the Empire.

The label "Catholic Epistles," which means universally directed epistles, was not placed on these diverse documents until long after they were written. It does

Figure 14.1 Just as there were Jews in many cities in the Roman Empire, so there came to be Jewish followers of Jesus in these cities. James is addressing them in his sermon. Here, we see the lintel for the synagogue in Corinth, which reads "Synagogue of the Hebrews." *(© Mark R. Fairchild, Ph.D.)*

not reflect how the original authors or audiences viewed these documents. It appears to have been Eusebius who first called seven of these letters the "general epistles" (Eusebius, *Ecclesiastical History,* 2.23.35). Hebrews was not included in the general or catholic epistles group because it was thought to be by Paul and was grouped early on with the Pauline corpus.

The near total refusal by some scholars to take seriously the spread of non-Pauline Christianity at the hands of people like Peter and his coworkers leads to a lopsided and distorted vision of how Christianity grew and spread in the first century A.D. and to a misreading of many of the documents in the last third of the New Testament.

Our discussion of these Jewish Christian documents begins in this chapter and continues in the following four: Chapters 15, 16, 17, and 18. We start with documents likely written by the brothers of Jesus—James—and, in Chapter 15, Jude. We will spend a good deal of time with these New Testament documents because (1) they are often neglected or ignored, and (2) they are just as often misunderstood or even maligned.

JAMES—A WISDOM SERMON IN ENCYCLICAL FORM

Although fresh winds have been blowing now for a couple of decades in the scholarly discussion of James, and there is renewed interest in the document,

at a Glance

The document attributed to James the brother of Jesus was probably authored by him in the early A.D. 50s in part in response to some problems in Jewish Christian congregations outside the Holy Land, and in part in response to some misunderstandings about Paul and his Gospel. The document is more of a sermon than a letter meant to circulate through various churches.

the "epistle" of James, ever since the Protestant Reformation, has existed under a cloud of suspicion as to its authorship and authenticity, and thus its rightful place in the canon. Luther proclaimed this document "a right strawy epistle, since it has in it no quality of the Gospel" in his 1522 Preface to the New Testament portion of the German Bible. Subsequent Protestant scholars have also looked askance at it as well. Many have been willing to see it as a sub-Christian or non-canonical text. J. H. Elliott says it has even been ranked among the "junk mail" of the New Testament in the modern era![1] This is more than a little unfortunate, as James is a rich source of material to help us understand the ethical ethos of early Jewish Christianity.

Although the early church had a few questions about this document, real suspicions about James largely arose in a much later era of church history, and they specifically originated with Luther and continued after him. What were the reasons for these suspicions and problems?

1. There was thought to be an apparent contradiction between this document and those of the dominant theologian of the early Christian Church, Paul. James 2 was thought to proclaim something other than justification by faith alone, and this is the main reason for Luther's problems with this letter (cf. James 2 and Galatians 3).

2. This document *on the surface* seems to have little or no specifically Christian content with the exception of James 1.2 and 2.1, which have been seen by some scholars as Christian additions to a non-Christian document of Jewish origins.

3. There is also the problem that this document hardly seems like a letter at all. It mentions no one specifically by name to whom it is written, makes no personal remarks, sends no greetings or directions to or from anyone, appears to have little continuity from one verse to another, and gives no indication that the author is interacting with specific church problems in any specific place. As we will see, these complaints have some merit if this document is read as a letter—which it is not. In fact, it is a homily or sermon, like 1 John.

4. Finally, the document is said to give no appearance of being by the Lord's brother, James, as it makes no reference to this at all and reflects no personal knowledge of the earthly Jesus.

All of this has led various scholars to argue the following:

1. The epistle was not written by James the brother of the Lord.

2. It is a late first-century epistle at the earliest.

3. It is not really a letter at all but a collection of ethical remarks strung together by catchwords or possibly an adaptation of the Hellenistic **diatribe** form, or even a theological catechetical tract. Especially in the German form-critical tradition, as characterized by M. Dibelius, this document has not been treated as a coherent, or even really a very Christian, document.

These views have had influence out of proportion to their merits. In fact, James is a rich, rhetorical document deeply indebted to both the sayings of Jesus and the LXX, the Greek translation of the Old Testament.

THE LANGUAGE, WISDOM, AND RHETORICAL STYLE OF JAMES

The Greek of James has perhaps been underappreciated. L. T. Johnson is even prepared to go so far as to say it rivals the polish and occasionally the eloquence of Hebrews.[2] I would stress that the language is very *Septuagintal,* by which I mean only 13 words in James are not found in the Greek translation of the Old Testament (the LXX). This gives the Greek a **Semitic** feel in places. The valuable detailed examination of the Greek of James in J. B. Mayor still stands up to close scrutiny. His conclusion that our author wrote this document originally in Greek shows familiarity with the LXX and seems especially indebted to Jewish wisdom books like Sirach; and Wisdom of Solomon (as well as the LXX of Proverbs) is important for discerning the "voice" and character of this document, to which we turn next.[3]

The enthymeme was a frequent rhetorical form of argumentation used by early Christians, a form that involves an incomplete syllogism. In Chapter 13, we talked about its frequent use in the Pastoral Epistles, and we find it here in James as well. By *incomplete,* I mean that one of the premises is missing, and the audience is expected to be able to supply it and thus make the connections. This form of argumentation was frequently used in exhortations of hortatory speeches, and we find this style of argumentation in James with some frequency.

In James's 108 verses, there are some 59 imperatives (i.e., commands or demands), most of them in the second person (46)—and 10 are found in 4.7–10 alone, where the tone becomes strident. What is notable about these imperatives is that they usually do not stand in isolation but are accompanied by explanations (using "because": James 1.12, 23; 2.10; 3.1; 4.3; 5.8, 11), warrants (using "for": James 1.6, 7, 11, 13, 20, 24; 2.11, 13, 26; 3.2, 16; 4.14), or purpose clauses (James 1.3; 5.8). Notice as well that there are clear signals that these imperatives do not stand alone but are part of a larger argument, as is shown by the use of "so then" (James 4.4, 7; 5.7, 16), "therefore" (James 1.21;

DIATRIBE

A form of rhetorical writing that often involves an imaginary debate partner, speech in character, and the use of rhetorical questions. The goal is to confront or debate in an imaginative way for an instructive purpose.

SEMITIC

When used as an adjective and in reference to a language, the term denotes the characteristics or features of the Semitic languages such as Hebrew or Aramaic. So, if a Greek phrase or passage has a Semitic feel, this means that it bears the influence of a Semitic language such as Aramaic or Hebrew.

4.6), and even "thus" (James 1.11; 2.12, 17; 2.26; 3.5). Thus, although it is true that there are relatively few longer sentences (but see James 2.2–4; 3.15–16; 4.13–15), it is important to realize that by and large *what we do not have in this document is isolated exhortations.* Instead, it uses the sort of enthymematic argumentation, or ethical arguments in shorthand, that we also found in the Pastoral Epistles in Chapter 13. It is interesting that although our author is prepared to persuade, he is also not afraid to command, and he does so regularly as part of the persuasion.

The question then becomes how proverbs, maxims, and various sorts of wisdom speech *function* in this sort of discourse. Generally speaking, we can say that they function to make a point that is then supported by a brief argument, purpose clause, or explanation or analogy. At times, James even breaks into what could be called *diatribe* style involving an imaginary debate, and even speech in character, for example, when our author allows those Christians who practice discrimination in the Christian community (James 2.3), or those who refuse to help the needy (James 2.16), or those who have faith but no deeds (James 2.18), or those who boast of future plans (James 4.13) to speak briefly for themselves. This is not surprising in a piece of deliberative rhetoric such as we find in James.

Not only is there the imaginary dialogue partner in the diatribe style in James, but also the typical posing of pithy direct questions that are instantly answered (James 3.13; 4.14; 5.13–14) as well as the posing of numerous rhetorical questions to draw the audience into thinking as the author does; often these occur in clusters, served up one right after the other for maximum effect (James 2.4, 5–7, 14, 16, 20; 3.11, 12; 4.1, 4–5; 5.6). The voice of the author begins to emerge in such material, and it is clearly the voice of an authority figure who is pushing the audience to change their behavior. Sometimes, he even becomes rather impatient with the audience. Thus, we have short warnings or chiding remarks like "don't be deceived" (James 1.16); "you know this" (James 1.19); even "do you know?" and "do you see?" (James 2.20, 22); the admonitory "this ought not to be so" (James 3.10); and the impatient "come now!" (4.13; 5.1).

Equally clearly, this discourse is one that was meant to be heard, drawing on a full range of oral and aural rhetorical devices. For example, rhythm and rhyme are readily used (rhythm: James 3.6–7; rhyme: James 1.6, 14; 2.12; 3.16; 4.8), and James has a strong penchant for alliteration, particularly the "p" sound (James 1.2, 3, 11, 17, 22; 3.2), the "d" sound (James 1.1, 6, 21; 2.16; 3.8), and the "k" sound (James 2.3; 4.8), to mention but a few examples. Alas, most of this is lost in an English translation.

This is a document meant to be read aloud to good rhetorical effect, or better said, it is meant to be delivered or performed in a rhetorically effective manner. Of the some 560 words in this discourse, 60 are not found elsewhere in the New

Testament. Our author certainly is not just repeating what he has heard before, or simply passing on early Christian tradition. He is a master of his source material; and considering how much of the document reflects these sorts of rhetorical devices in Greek, it becomes nearly impossible to imagine this homily as being a translation from Aramaic rather than composed originally in Greek.

Our author is known for his vivid language, especially his vivid comparisons, using the rhetorical device known as *synkrisis,* a comparison of two unlike things or persons that are alike in some particular way. Here, however, the comparison serves the purpose of urging the audience to change their behavior; and so, not surprisingly, our author is not satisfied with comparing and contrasting what is good to what is "better." His use of analogies is most frequently brought forth to show what behavior is bad or forbidden or even evil—a wave whipped up by the wind (James 1.6), foliage that withers in the sun (James 1.10–11), a raging fire in a forest (James 3.5–6), fresh or brackish water (James 3.11), and the like. But our author uses examples not only from nature but also from human behavior—for instance, the taming of wild animals (James 3.7), the reining in of a horse (James 3.3), or steering a ship (James 3.4).

Sometimes, in his comparisons or implied comparisons, James also draws on exemplary figures from antiquity such as Job (cf. James 2.21–25; 5.10–11, 17–18), but notice how differently they function than the examples cited in Heb. 11. The use of vivid language in James sometimes serves as a sort of rhetorical wake-up call to the audience, warning them about misbehavior; and sometimes, it is clearly used for its shock value, for example, when our author speaks of the tongue being a world of wickedness. We need to know how such wisdom language works to understand its intended effect.

Wisdom rhetoric is often compressed into pithy or even paradoxical maxims with brief support so that they will be both memorable and memorizable. The implications require a certain unpacking, and the density of the ideas is deliberate, meant to force meditation and reflection. The analogies, of course, cannot be taken literally, but their bite should not be taken out of them by modern warnings about not overpressing figurative language. James is more than a clever wordsmith or pundit; he is an authoritative teacher who wants to change the behavior among the Jewish Christian communities in the Diaspora. This brings us to the issue of the rhetoric in James. It is deliberative in character, as James is trying to change the behavior of his audience in the near future.

If there were any doubts about the Christian nature of this document, once the use of the Jesus tradition is taken into account, those doubts disappear. The use of Jesus' sayings in this document is anything but a reiteration of conventional Jewish wisdom material. It rather reflects a combination of conventional and counter-order wisdom for a particular subset of the Christian community, namely, the Jewish Christians. As such, it is addressed to Jewish Christians throughout the empire but outside of Israel. There is traditional Jewish wisdom

Figure 14.2 Christian graffiti. (© *Mark R. Fairchild, Ph.D.*)

material here about the taming of the tongue, but it is juxtaposed with Jesus' own critique of wealth and the wealthy. What makes this document so remarkable, and so like the teaching of Jesus, is that it offers both old and new material drawn from Jewish wisdom material. In this regard, it is much like the Gospel of Matthew. It is useful to set out a brief list of comparative texts from the LXX and the Jesus tradition insofar as they relate to James:

DRAWING ON EARLIER WISDOM

Prov. 3.34	James 4.6
Prov. 9.30	James 3.18
Prov. 10.12	James 5.20
Sir.* 15.11–20	James 1.12–18
Sir. 19.6–12; 20.4–7, 17–19; 35.5–10; 38.13–26	James 3 in general

* Sir. = Sirach (Ecclesiasticus)

More extensive are the parallels with the Matthean form of the Q sayings of Jesus that we find in the Sermon on the Mount:[4]

Matt. 5.11–12/Lk. 6.22–23	James 1.2
Matt. 5.48	James 1.4
Matt. 7.7	James 1.5
Matt. 7.11	James 1.17
Matt. 7.24/Lk. 6.46–47	James 1.22
Matt. 7.26/Lk. 6.49	James 1.23
Matt. 5.3, 5/Lk. 6.20	James 2.5
Matt. 5.18–19 (cf. Lk. 3.9)	James 2.10
Matt. 5.21–22	James 2.11
Matt. 5.7/Lk. 6.36	James 2.13
Matt. 7.16–18/Lk. 6.43–44	James 3.12
Matt. 5.9	James 3.18
Matt. 7.7–8	James 4.2–3
Matt. 6.24/Lk. 16.13	James 4.4
Matt. 5.8	James 4.8
Matt. 5.4/Lk. 6.25	James 4.9
Matt. 7.1–2/Lk. 6.37–38	James 4.11
Matt. 6.19–21/Lk. 12.33	James 5.2–3
Matt. 7.1/Lk. 6.37	James 5.6
Matt. 5.11–12/Lk. 6.23	James 5.10
Matt. 5.34–37	James 5.12

It is right to conclude that "while James ultimately has wisdom material as his background, this is refracted . . . through the pre-Gospel Jesus tradition."[5] These parallels rule out the earlier suggestions that this was not originally a Christian document or was not very Christian in character.

We notice four things when analyzing these parallels more closely: (1) James rarely cites the sayings of Jesus directly; rather, he weaves various ideas, themes, and phrases into his own discourse; (2) the material is then presented as the teaching of James, not the sayings of Jesus, although the audience would probably recognize the passages; (3) it does not appear that Matthew is drawing on James, or vice versa, but rather both are drawing on common source material; and (4) this in turn suggests, although it does not prove, that the Matthean form of the sayings of Jesus are closer to the original form than the Lukan form (see Appendix A).

THE AUTHORSHIP AND PROVENANCE QUESTION

James 1.1 mentions a man called James—but which James? There are several possibilities:

1. James the brother of the Lord

2. James the Less

3. James the son of Zebedee

4. James the son of Alphaeus

5. Some otherwise unknown early Christian named James.

We may dismiss James son of Zebedee because he died in A.D. 44 before he would likely have been involved in any literary activity (cf. Acts 12.2). The problem with arguing that it is by James the Less, James of Alphaeus, or an unknown James is precisely that they were not sufficiently well or widely known to have identified themselves in a general epistle simply as James, nor could they have assumed the authority this document assumes without further identification because of their lack of widespread recognition. As W. G. Kümmel rightly states

> In fact in primitive Christianity there was only one James who was well known and who occupied so significant a position that he is designated by the simple names James the Lord's brother.[6]

This James died in A.D. 62, a martyr.

Many features of this sermon in fact suggest a Judean origin and a pre–A.D. 70 date for this epistle:

1. The obvious Jewish wisdom flavor is of the same ilk as some of Jesus' teachings.

2. There are references to conditions of weather typical of Palestine, but not elsewhere except in southeastern Asia Minor (James 5.7).

3. The use of such phrases as "into our synagogue" (James 2.2) and the reference to the elders in James 5.14 suggest an early date before there was a clear separation of the church from the synagogue and before there were bishops.

4. The Christology of the letter is simple, and the allusions to the Sermon on the Mount are of a preliterary sort, that is, before the Gospels were likely written.[7]

Perhaps the most serious objection to the authenticity of this epistle is the supposed contradiction of James 2.14ff. with Pauline teaching. Against this view are several important considerations:

1. Too often, James the Just is portrayed as an extreme Pharisaical legalist on the basis of the later church father Hegesippus. However, Hegesippus is not to be trusted on many points, and this document suggests a James that was mediating in his views. This is a view supported by the portrayal of James in Acts 15.

2. Acts 15.19ff. suggests that James was especially sensitive about not offending Jews and strict Jewish Christians, and wishing that Moses' teaching on certain ethical things be upheld to prevent strife in the Christian community. If we look closely at 2.14ff. in James, we do not see a teaching that denies justification by faith but one that insists that real faith will produce real work, that is, good works. This, of course, Paul himself argued for, weighing in against those who had an allergic reaction to law in general on various occasions (see the core sample following).

The real question is, does knowledge of Paul's teaching necessitate a post-James the Just dating? The answer is no because Paul says he met with James early in his Christian ministry, and we may be sure they did not discuss the weather (Gal. 1.19). Further, Acts 9 and 15 support the idea that there were various opportunities for James to hear, or hear about, Paul's Gospel, and perhaps even to have read some of his letters if James the Just did indeed die as late as A.D. 62, a martyr. Indeed, one wonders if Gal. 2.9 does not make explicit that Paul had been thoroughly checked out by James and perhaps was monitored on an ongoing basis if a bad report came to James (James 2.22). Thus, the conditions existed for James (the document) to reflect a knowledge of Paul and correct a misunderstanding of Paul and his doctrine as early as the A.D. 50s. This he does in James 2.14ff., as we shall see in a moment. Kümmel is right in seeing James as correcting a misunderstanding, not asserting any new anti-Pauline doctrine. Kümmel puts it this way:

> If the distinctions in the terminology and the divergent polemical aims of Paul and James are taken into account appropriately, . . . a considerably larger area of commonality can be established than Luther saw.[8]

Some, however, have objected to James being written by Jesus' brother because of the quality of the Greek. The Greek in James is good Greek, even to an extent literary Greek; however, it is also *simple* Greek and does not rise to the heights of eloquence of various Greek masters. In short, it is the kind of Greek that someone who has learned it well and is proficient, although not usually eloquent, in it would produce. The Semitic tinges suggest an author who has another native language or at least knows such a language.

We must remember however that, in Jerusalem, James would have had access to Jewish or Jewish Christian converts who were likely very proficient in Greek and whose aid in writing James could have enlisted. There is plenty of evidence for the saturation of Palestine with Greek and Greek culture by the first century, and we may well ask why such a letter would be put out after A.D. 70, when the situation had changed so drastically that this letter would hardly address any pressing or non-Jewish, Christian kind of concerns. The language factor then cannot be decisive against the authenticity of the epistle, and the content is consistent with such a view.

WHAT KIND OF DOCUMENT IS JAMES?

James the document does not have many of the usual features of an ordinary first-century personal letter. Rather, it is mainly a series of moral exhortations, as no one doubts. It includes both brief sayings (proverbs) and more extended discourses. Diatribe (i.e., debate with an imaginary opponent) as a genre term is not fully applicable except to a part of the letter (cf. James 2). Besides, Jewish sermons have that same form and elements of the diatribe. If James is attempting to refute in part a misunderstanding of Paul's thought, then it can be called a polemic against such misunderstandings. But, as Peter Davids adds

> In Acts, James the Just is portrayed as a mediator, a moderator. . . . The book fits this picture. Against the rich, James levels stinging eschatological denunciation in line with the strongest words of Jesus (Lk 6:24–26). His church is the church of the poor [who have] fervent eschatological expectation. Yet for all his sympathy for the poor, James refuses to join the Zealots. He demands that Christians give up the world. The desire to find financial security is in fact demonic, a test. Furthermore, he calls for the rejection of hatred and strife (4.1–3), abusive words (3:5b–12), and anger (1:19–20). No oaths are to be taken (5.12), including those to the Zealot cause.[9]

We thus conclude that this document was written at least by the A.D. 50s, by one who we know as James, brother of the Lord, as a hortatory sermon. As such, it may be seen as in some respects like Matthew's Sermon on the Mount but only to the extent that both draw on the sayings of Jesus. Thus, the reference to the twelve tribes in James 1.1 may be to Jewish Christians already in the Diaspora, although a wider audience may also have been implied and included.

We must take seriously that James is addressing Christians at some distance from himself, which is why he chooses typical but known examples of the problems to illustrate the social praxis he wants to instill in these congregations. We should not expect, because this is a document meant to circulate through various congregations, that James would be addressing some *particular* problem of a specific region or church. Notice too that he assumes he has authority over *all* these largely Jewish congregations as well. He assumes that the charitable and communal practices (as outlined in Acts 2–6) of the mother church should be emulated by the other Jewish Christian congregations in the Diaspora. Partiality to the rich was always a deadly thing, as it created stratification in a congregation, with some having second-class status. This ruined the **koinonia** of such a small community.

L. G. Perdue has stressed that the social function of this document is to reinforce the socializing process for Jews who have recently become Christians and, due to pressure, persecution, or hardship, are wavering in their faith. In order for the group to continue to exist as a distinct entity, separate from Judaism, certain boundaries for the in-group needed to be clearly defined over against the larger culture and, to a lesser degree, over against the Jewish subculture. The teaching in James presents a group ethic designed to maintain rather clear boundaries between the in-group and the out-group.[10] What the document implies is that the Jews who have converted to Christianity were quite Hellenized Jews who struggled with conforming to the ethos of the larger culture and needed to be drawn back to a more Jewish ethical lifestyle.

Our author is deeply concerned with issues of moral purity, and he addresses this concern by indicating ways to control speech, limit behavior, and properly relate to others. This is the very sort of minority ethic that we find other Jews like the author of Wisdom of Solomon or Jesus ben Sira setting out to help Jews survive in a hostile and foreign environment.[11] Here, the issue is correct practice rather than orthodoxy, which makes this sermon in some respects different from 1 John. James wants to nip in the bud tendencies that lead to the disintegration of Jewish Christian communities. He does this not simply by criticizing various sins but by attempting to inculcate an ethic that he had seen exhibited in the Jerusalem community as described in Acts 2–6. There is one further implication of the social analysis of James. As Johnson puts it, "James reflects the social realities and outlook appropriate to a sect in the early stages of its life."[12]

KOINONIA

A Greek word literally meaning a sharing or participation of something in common by various persons, although sometimes translated as "fellowship." The word, however, speaks more to the process of sharing than the result of a close-knit community.

OUTLINE OF JAMES'S SERMON		
Epistolary Prescript	1.1	
Exordium/Introductory Remarks	1.2–18	The Wisdom/Word from Above
Propositio/Thesis Statement	1.19–27	
Rhetorical Arguments and Elaborations of Various Sorts Using Comparisons and Enthymemes	2.1–5.6	
Peroratio/Final Emotional Appeal	5.7–12	Recapitulation of Major Themes and in 5.13–20, Final Exhortation/ Emotional Appeal

CLUES FROM THE **CULTURE**

"Out you go! For shame!" says the marshal. "Out of the equestrian seats, you whose wealth does not satisfy the requirement!"

—*Juvenal*, Satires 3.153–55

Notice that there are no epistolary elements of any sort at the conclusion of the discourse. In other words, we have just the opposite here of what we find in the homily to the Hebrews. There, we have some epistolary closing elements such as greetings, but not an epistolary opening; here, we have the epistolary opening, but otherwise the document conforms to rhetorical structures. It would have taken about 25 minutes, depending on the pace of the orator, to proclaim the sermon we know as James. It will be useful to examine a synopsis of the contents and one famous core sample of this sermon in more detail.

SYNOPSIS OF CONTENTS

The sermon begins with the name James who is called a servant of God and of the Lord Jesus and the word "greetings," followed by a reference to trials, which can produce endurance if reacted to properly, counting it all joy. This theme seems very similar to what Paul says in Rom. 5.3–5. James then encourages petitionary prayers for wisdom and reminds the audience that faith, rather than doubt, should be their approach to prayer and life. Doubt unsettles things and leaves people in two minds as to what to do or say. The theme of eschatological reversal, the rich brought low, and the lowly exalted is announced in James 1.9–11. James will have some very stern things to say about the rich in this sermon.

In James 1.12–16, the subject of temptation and how to deal with it is broached, and James is emphatic that temptation never comes from God—and in any case, God himself can't be tempted. Then James brings up the issue of generosity, in particular the generosity of God, because every good gift comes from above. This theme is crucial for James, as it makes clear that the rich should

Figure 14.3 Wealthy woman with gold earrings. (© *Mark R. Fairchild, Ph.D.*)

not see what they have as their own private property. No, it is a gift from God, and God will hold them accountable for what they do with the gift.

The thesis statement comes in James 1.19–27, which involves two major thrusts—Christians must be teachable, and so quick to listen and slow to speak, especially when it comes to words fired in anger. They must tame their tongues. James says that God's Word, implanted in the heart of the believer, has the power to heal a person. Lest we think, however, that listening is all that James wants of his audience, he quickly adds that they must be doers of the Word and not merely hearers of it. A strong emphasis on doing God's Word will resonate throughout the rest of this discourse, including, as it says in James 1.27, taking care of widows and orphans.

The first section of the two major sections of James Chapter 2 (2.1–13 and 14–26) deals with the matter of showing partiality especially vis-à-vis the rich and the poor. In the background is the idea that God is no respecter of persons with the implication that neither should his people be. Our author is picking up earlier discussions in wisdom literature against favoritism and that stress God's impartiality (see Sir. 7.6–7 on the former and Sir. 35.10–18 on the latter). James addresses his audience as "my brothers" once more so we may be sure he considered them Christians. However, they are Christians under construction and requiring instruction from James's point of view. James is particularly incensed when favoritism to the rich is shown in the Christian meeting in terms of seating and the like. Dishonoring the poor in worship is showing favoritism that goes against God's own approach to such people. Not to mention that such favoritism toward the rich violates the general command to love one's neighbor, whoever they are, as one's self. What good is it if you stringently keep some of the laws, such as "don't commit adultery," but you neglect all the Old Testament commandments about care for the poor, especially the widows and orphans. You become accountable for violating the Law if you only selectively keep it.

James 2.14–26 may be called the storm center of this sermon, or certainly the portion that has drawn the most attention and most fire, and not just from Luther. That it has been troublesome in Protestant circles, more than in Catholic, is of course because of the vital aspect of the concept of justification by faith alone in Protestant thinking.

James begins in Chapter 2, verse 14, by asking his Christian audience whether or not a faith without works is useful or useless. To ask about the profit, use, or benefit of something is a common question in deliberative rhetoric. The nature of the conditional sentence here shows he thinks this question might well arise. The second remark is also a question. "Is your faith able to save you?"—a rhetorical question, to which the answer implied is "no"—*if by faith is meant that type of faith that James is attacking.* James has here broadened the previous discussion to the more expansive topic of faith and works and not just the keeping of the Law. Crucial to understanding this verse is recognizing the use of the definite article before the word "faith." The question should be translated as "*Can that sort of faith save him?*" Notice that the discussion here has moved on from talking about visitors to the assembly of faith to "brothers and sisters." Christian treatment of fellow Christians is at issue here. Apparently there were those Christians who would offer warm words to their fellow indigent Christians but not lift a finger to alleviate their poverty.

To this behavior James rejoins, "if you say you have faith and fail to help—of what use is it? What good does it do you or anyone else?" James has thus made two key points: (1) living faith necessarily entails good deeds; and (2) faith and works are so integrally related that faith by itself is useless or dead unless coupled with works, or as one scholar puts it, the sort of "faith" James is critiquing is "not merely outwardly inoperative but inwardly dead."[13] Davids summarizes well:

> For James, then, there is no such thing as a true and living faith which does not produce works, for the only true faith is a "faith working through love" (Gal. 5:6). Works are not an "added extra" any more than breath is an "added extra" to a living body. The so-called faith which fails to produce works (the works to be produced are charity, not the "works of the law" such as circumcision against which Paul inveighs) is simply not "saving faith."[14]

To the believer who prides himself on right belief (and clearly in James 2, verses 18 and 19, faith means something else than what it usually means for James, not trust in or active dependence on God but rather mere belief that

God exists), James says to such a mere believer—"so you say you believe God is one. Good for you, however so do demons and they are shuddering in their belief—fearing the wrath of God to come. A lot of good that faith did them." The sarcasm in James 2, verse 19, is hard to miss.[15] The demons are the ultimate example of faith divorced from works, or right confession from right living. In James 2, verse 20, James becomes even more sarcastic: "So you want evidence, O empty headed one (cf. Rom. 2.1, 9.20), that faith without works is useless/without profit—let's turn to the Scriptures." Another way of translating the Greek word here would be "workless"—faith without works is workless, or as I would prefer to put it, *faith without works won't work*!

The two examples from Scripture that James cites were very standard examples of true faith among the Jews. He is choosing the most stellar example (Abraham) and in some ways the most scandalous example, Rahab the harlot. James knows how much Abraham was idolized in the Jewish tradition. For example, a Jewish writing, The Book of Jubilees 23.10, says "Abraham was perfect in all his deeds with the Lord, and well-pleasing in righteousness all the days of his life." Sir. 44.19 says "no one has been found like him in glory." More important is 1 Macc. 2.51–52, which says Abraham was reckoned righteous not on the basis of his faith but as a result of passing the test and remaining faithful and obedient when he was asked to sacrifice his son. Clearly James does not push his use of the exemplary Abraham to these extremes, but he stands in the tradition of seeing Abraham as the example par excellence. The use made of Gen. 22 here is closely similar to the use made in Heb. 11.17–19, which says that it was by faith that Abraham, when tested, brought forth Isaac and offered his son.

The point of James's argument, then, has nothing to do with a forensic declaration of justification; the argument is simply that Abraham did have faith, which here, unlike other places in James, means monotheistic belief. For this Abraham was famous in Jewish tradition—but he also had deeds flowing from that faith. Thus, James is not dealing with works of the law as a means to become saved or as an entrance requirement. Notice he never speaks of "works of the law." He is dealing with the conduct of those who already believe. He is talking about the perfection of faith in its working out through good works. "Work out your salvation with fear and trembling" was how Paul put it; or better in Gal. 5.6, Paul speaks of faith working itself out through love, whereas James speaks of faith coming to mature expression or its perfect end or goal in works. These two ideas are closely similar.

In James 3, there is the warning that not many Christians should become teachers because teachers have to do a lot of talking, and the issue of making mistakes in speaking is a critical one because no one is perfect in all they say. So teachers especially have to be able to bridle their tongues. A loose tongue can do major damage to the listeners, like the old adage "loose lips sink ships." How can the same instrument, the tongue, be used to both bless and curse God? The warning here about the dangers of loose talk, and even wicked words, is strong.

Even the teacher must not settle just for good words but must practice works with a gentleness born of wisdom. A teacher above all should model wise, righteous, gentle, merciful, impartial conduct.

James 4 deals with the disputes and arguments that arise among Christians, and he suggests that one of their major causes is cravings for things that other people have that you don't have. And even when one asks God for things, if you spend what he gives you just on selfish pleasures, then you are no better than worldly non-believers. James offers the good news that if the Christian will resist the Devil and his temptations, that he will flee; and if one draws near to God, God will do likewise. The chapter ends with a call to remorse over and repentance for sins, particularly repentance for speaking evil of one's fellow Christians.

James 5 continues the strong rebuke to the rich, with the warning that their day of judgment is coming when their expensive clothes will rot, their gold will be tarnished, their bank accounts will vanish, and their selfish hearts judged. Having said that, he adds, however, that it is not our job to judge one another, for Jesus the judge is coming to take care of the matter. He concludes with practical advice to avoid oaths, as Jesus said; to pray over the sick and anoint them, for God can use such prayers for healing; and he adds that believers should confess their sins to each other. Transparency in the community will bind it together. And if anyone goes astray, the community should go after them and bring them back into the fold.

The sermon by James is a lively one, which should not be pitted against Paul's notions of right-standing with God by faith alone. James is dealing with the belief and behavior of those who are already Christians, not with how one becomes a Christian. And Paul agrees with James that an inherent part and manifestation of Christian faith is good works. We must next spend some time with Jesus' other brother who wrote something found in the New Testament—Jude.

IMPLICATIONS

Without doubt, there were differences of opinions within the circle of the earliest Christians. It is incorrect, however, to say that there were *major* differences of views between James and Paul on the issue of faith and works. Paul's discussion of salvation by faith alone has to do with how one obtains right-standing with God. James is not discussing that issue at all in his sermon. He is discussing how Christians should behave toward others after their conversion. Both James and Paul would agree that genuine faith manifests itself in deeds of piety and mercy. While Paul says, "You were created in Christ for good works," James says more bluntly that faith without good works is useless. It is unfortunate that James's interesting sermon has suffered both neglect and abuse in the Protestant tradition, and undeservedly so as well.

Figure 14.4 The likely burial box of James, the brother of Jesus. The inscription reads "James son of Joseph, his brother was Jesus." *(Ben Witherington)*

The differences in early Christianity had far more to do with *praxis* than with belief; the challenge had to do with how to incorporate Gentiles into what was then a largely Jewish collection of believers in Jesus. While James probably did believe that Jewish Christians should be observant Jews when they were in Jewish settings at least, he did not impose such rules on Gentiles. The decree in Acts 15 is a warning that Gentile Christians must stay out of places, like pagan temples, where the four things—meat offered to idols, blood, things strangled, and sexual immorality—could be found together. The issue was one of spiritual venue, not menu. We can see Paul himself implementing this decree in 1 Cor. 8–10, where he says the same thing—Gentiles must stay out of pagan temples where eating is believed to be done in the presence of a pagan god. But there was no problem with eating such meat at home or in a different spiritual **milieu**.

The sermon called James then is not a polemic against Paul or against justification by grace through faith. It is an urgent appeal to Jewish Christians to live out their faith through deeds of charity and piety, and along the way some misunderstandings of Paul's Gospel are corrected in James 2. There is no evidence here, or in Paul's letters, that James and Paul had a fundamental disagreement on the basis of salvation in Christ or the necessity of good works as part

MILIEU

A term used to refer to a social and cultural setting.

of normal Christian behavior. What they may have disagreed on, although even this is not clear, is whether Jewish Christians should continue to keep all the Mosaic covenant or not. Certainly, this sermon we call James does not present us with a person who was some sort of legalist or someone who insisted that the Mosaic law be kept by all Christians, unlike the Judaizers whom Paul combated in Galatians.

KEY TERMS

Diatribe   Prescript

Koinonia   Semitic

Milieu

FOR FURTHER READING

Brosend, W. *James and Jude.* Cambridge: Cambridge University Press, 2004.

Hartin, P. J. *James and the Q Sayings of Jesus.* Sheffield, England: Sheffield University Press, 1991.

Witherington, B. *Letters and Homilies for Jewish Christians: A Socio-Rhetorical Commentary on Hebrews, James and Jude.* Downers Grove, IL: InterVarsity Press, 2007.

———. "Not So Idle Thoughts about *Eidolothuton,*" *Tyndale Bulletin* 44, no. 2 (1993): 237–254.

STUDY QUESTIONS

Why has James been such a neglected or criticized document? Do you think the criticism is based on a good or a poor understanding of the contents of the sermon itself?

In the Old Testament, God has a chosen people. James tells us that God plays no favorites. How would you reconcile these two ideas?

James says, "Faith without works is dead." How would you understand this aphorism?

Do you think that James and Paul had significant differences of opinion about how a person is saved? How about a significant difference of opinions about how Christians should live after they are saved?

NOTES

1. J. H. Elliott, "The Epistle of James in Rhetorical and Social Scientific Perspective. Holiness and Wholeness and Patterns of Replication," *Biblical Theology Bulletin* 23 (1993): 71–81; here 71.

2. L. T. Johnson, *The Letter of James* (New Haven, CT: Yale University Press, 2005), 7.

3. J. B. Mayor, *The Epistle of St. James* (Ithaca, NY: Cornell University Press, 2009), cclxiv–cclxv.

4. On Q, see Appendix A. These parallels have been laid out convincingly in P. J. Hartin, *James and the Q Sayings of Jesus* (Sheffield, England: Sheffield University Press, 1991), 144–45.

5. P. H. Davids, "The Epistle of James in Modern Discussion," *Aufsteig und Niedergang der römischen Welt* 25.5 (1988): 3622–3684, here 3638.

6. W. G. Kümmel, *Introduction to the New Testament*. Translated by Howard Clark Kee (London: SCM Press, 1975), 412.

7. P. Davids, *The Epistle of James: A Commentary on the Greek Text*. New International Greek Testament Commentary (Grand Rapids, MI: Eerdmans, 1982), 13ff.

8. Kümmel, *Introduction to the New Testament*, 415.

9. Davids, *The Epistle of James: A Commentary*, 34.

10. L. G. Perdue, "Paraenesis and the Epistle of James," *Zeitschrift für die Neutestamentliche Wissenschaft und die Kunde der älteren Kirche* 72 (1981): 241–256.

11. See B. Witherington, *Jesus the Sage: The Pilgrimage of Wisdom* (Minneapolis, MN: Fortress Press, 1994), 246.

12. L. T. Johnson, *The Letter of James* (New Haven, CT: Yale University Press, 2005), 119. By "sect," Johnson means a small religious group that is a recognizable and distinct subset of a larger religious group, with stricter views on some things.

13. Mayor, *The Epistle of St. James*, 126.

14. Davids, *The Epistle of James: A Commentary*, 122.

15. See W. Brosend, *James and Jude* (Cambridge: Cambridge University Press, 2004), 75.

Fresco of apostle Saint Jude Thaddeus on the wall of Basilica di Santa Prassede in Rome.

15

The OTHER BROTHER and his ESCHATOLOGICAL THINKING—JUDE

WHEN WE GLANCE AT THE VERY SHORT DOCUMENT attributed to Jude the brother of Jesus, we may be tempted to see it as just another New Testament letter and evaluate it as a letter. This would be a mistake because letters in antiquity do not function like modern letters. **Cicero**, a Roman philosopher and orator, is very blunt about the matter. He says that a letter is in effect a speech in written medium (*ad Atticum* 8.14.1; cf. Pseudo-Demetrius De elocutione 223). As the document had to be sent, one would add epistolary elements at the beginning and the end of the speech. Otherwise, we are most often dealing with the transcript of a speech, composed with the long ingrained rules of rhetoric in the mind of the author.

So then, Jude offers us a particular kind of speech, although it begins with epistolary elements. It is a sermon or speech in rhetorical form that has only an epistolary opening to indicate that it came to the audience in a written form, even though it was likely delivered orally at the point of destination. We must think constantly in terms of the oral majority of the culture and how literate persons like Jude were trying to speak into their situations.

at a Glance

The letter of Jude is probably written by the brother of Jesus and it is possibly the earliest document in the New Testament. It was likely written in the A.D. 50s rather than in the 40s because it speaks of congregations founded by apostles before Jude visited them. This document is very different from James in its eschatological flavor and its interest in non-canonical Jewish traditions.

JUDE—THE MAN

The brother of Jesus we know as Jude was in fact named Judas. This particular name occurs in one form or another some 36 times in the New Testament, of which 23 are references to Judas Iscariot and thus are of no relevance to this study. Our Judas/Jude is mentioned quite clearly as Jesus' brother in Mk. 6.3 and Mt. 13.55, but he is mentioned third in the earlier Markan listing and fourth in the Matthean listing. This may mean that he was not the next brother in line after James to be the head of Jesus' family, as these things were determined by age. This may in turn explain why he did not succeed James as head of the Jerusalem church. In the New Testament, the only brothers mentioned whose names are James and Jude are the brothers of Jesus, the very same ones said to be present in the upper room at Pentecost according to Acts 1.14, after having not been followers of or believers in Jesus during his ministry (John 7.5).

The fact that the canonical document bearing the name Jude begins with the identification "brother of James" (verse 1) establishes the connection with the holy family beyond a reasonable doubt. The fact that the author calls himself a servant of Jesus, as does James in Jam. 1.1, does not count against his blood kinship with Jesus, as it simply reflects his humility and his use of a common title, which Christian leaders used in that era to establish or make a claim to authority in a church setting (see, e.g., Phil. 1.1). As Richard Bauckham stresses, the connection of this Judas and this document to the holy family is secure because "the only man in the whole early church who could be called simply James without risk of ambiguity was James the Lord's brother."[1]

If we consider 1 Cor. 9.5 briefly, keeping in mind that we have no evidence that James was itinerant, we must then conclude that it is likely that Jesus' brother Jude was an itinerant Jewish Christian missionary who was married and traveled with his wife. Because Paul does not suggest that these brothers were missionaries to Gentiles as Paul was, and because Jude's discourse likely is addressing a Jewish Christian audience using various interesting Jewish traditions, even extra-canonical ones, it is very likely he was a missionary to Jews as Peter was. In fact, Julius Africanus at a later time tells us that the family of Jesus spread the Gospel throughout Israel, starting from Nazareth and a nearby town named Kokhaba (quoted in Eusebius, *Hist. Eccl.* 1.7.14). This likely confirms that apart from James, the family of Jesus was based in Galilee after Easter, which is perhaps another reason Jude did not succeed James as leader of the Jerusalem church.

Can we say more about Jude's activities? The Book of Acts says very little about missionary work in Galilee after the Pentecost events. It was only after persecution and in the wake of the scattering of the Greek-speaking Jews that the Jerusalem church truly began to do mission work outside of Jerusalem and its environs (Acts 8.14–25, 9.32–10.48). Even then the missionary activity seems to have been confined to Judea and Samaria, although Acts 11.19 suggests travel

Figure 15.1 This reconstructed first-century fishing boat was found in the mud when the sea of Galilee was at a low ebb over a decade ago. (© *Mark R. Fairchild, Ph.D.*)

Figure 15.2 Fish from the sea of Galilee. (© *Mark R. Fairchild, Ph.D.*)

Figure 15.3 Galilee, Israel Sea. *(© Mark R. Fairchild, Ph.D.)*

further afield. One must take into account Acts 9.31, however, which indicates plainly that there was a well-established church in Galilee at that time, presumably in the mid to late A.D. 30s. I suspect that this is another example of Luke not wanting to go beyond his source material. He had contacts with the Jerusalem church and its vicinity and learned about the mission work done that radiated out from that locale. He was simply not well informed about what happened to the relatives of Jesus other than James, nor about missionary activity in Galilee and its immediate vicinity.

Eckhard Schnabel concludes that a mission based in Galilee could easily have reached southern Syria, Damascus, Phoenicia, various places in the Decapolis, and other places east of the Jordan (perhaps Pella?). Both he and Bauckham conclude that there was likely extensive missionary activity in Galilee and its surrounding areas, which did not result from missionaries sent out from Jerusalem. What we also should note is that because it is Symeon, a cousin of Jesus and not Jude the brother of Jesus, who took over the leadership of the Jerusalem Church upon the death of James in A.D. 62, this suggests that Jude was no longer based in Jerusalem and that his missionary work took him elsewhere.[2]

Bauckham concludes: "From the beginning, the Jewish Christian mission was not only to pilgrims in Jerusalem, but also extended throughout Palestine through the travels of missionaries among whom the younger brothers of Jesus and other members of the family were prominent. It is as missionaries engaged in preaching Jesus the Messiah to their fellow-Jews that the relatives of Jesus are primarily to be envisaged."[3] What Jude (the discourse) suggests is that there is controversy and competition on this mission field, particularly from some more libertine Jewish teachers of some sort. But we must stress once more that 1 Cor. 9.5, written in the early 50s A.D., shows that Paul takes it for granted that his audience *knows* that Jude and other brothers of Jesus are both married and are traveling evangelists of a sort. This then raises important questions about the provenance of the canonical document that bears Jude's name.

One verse of Jude the document is germane to our discussion at this point. Verse 17 is sometimes thought to exclude Jude from the apostolic era, for he seems to refer to "apostles" as part of a previous generation. This, however, is a misreading of this verse because what it actually says is that our author was not among the apostles who founded the churches he was currently addressing in this discourse.[4] One more historical fact of interest and possible relevance bears mention.

Figure 15.4 Galilee was a Hellenized region, as this synagogue floor in Sepphoris (only 6 miles from Jesus' home) shows with signs of the Zodiac on it. (© *Mark R. Fairchild, Ph.D.*)

EUSEBIUS

A Roman historian who later became the Bishop of Caesarea Maritima. Eusebius is referred to as the "Father of Church History," as he chronicled much of the church's history in his work called *Ecclesiastical History*. His historical writings span three centuries.

HEGESIPPUS

A second-century Christian who chronicled some events of the early church. He also wrote apologetically against the Gnostics and Marcion. What remains of his writings is quoted by Eusebius.

According to **Eusebius**, quoting the earlier material of **Hegesippus**, the two grandsons of Jude were brought before Emperor Domitian (which if true would have transpired in the late A.D. 80s or early 90s) on the basis of the accusations of some Jews that they were relatives of the condemned Jesus and descendants of the Davidic line.[5] These accusations, however, failed to produce a guilty verdict, and these descendants of Jude are thought to have been set free. For our purposes, two things are important about this tradition: (1) Hegesippus, in the account quoted by Eusebius, says of Jude that he was "the Savior's brother after the flesh" and that this was the ground of the accusation of Jude's grandsons; and (2) the mention of such grandsons confirms what 1 Cor. 9.5 already suggested, that is, that Jude and other brothers of Jesus were both actual brothers of Jesus and were in fact married. From *Hist. Eccl.* 3.19.1–3 and 3.20.1, 7, then, we learn that he had children and grandchildren. If this tradition is based in fact, it also suggests that, by this time, Jude, along with the other brothers, was already deceased, or else the accusations would have been made against him personally, not against his grandsons. This in turn suggests we must look for a date for Jude the document somewhere in the early or middle part of the first century A.D. Last, in light of the infamous character that the name Judas was to take on for Christians (because of Judas Iscariot), still to this day, it is unlikely that anyone in the first or second century A.D. would have made up the notion that someone named Judas was both the brother of Jesus and the author of this document.

But what do we really know about the history of Jude's Galilee, particularly in the first 60 years of the New Testament era? Is it really plausible that a manual worker from Nazareth could have received enough education to write a document like Jude? What would the social situation of his audience be like? Here we can say that yes indeed it was possible for a Jew to get an education in Greek and in rhetoric in Galilee. In the supplemental materials on the accompanying website, we reflect in more depth on the basis for this conclusion.

JUDE THE BOOK

Jude, like most of the so-called general epistles, has suffered from a distinct, if not intentional, neglect in the Christian world. Tucked away behind 3 John and before Revelation, most people do not even know where the book is, never mind what it is about. As it only fills up a page of text, it hardly deserves to be called a book. It is a rather brief sermon following the conventions of deliberative rhetoric with an epistolary opening and a doxological conclusion.

If indeed this document was written by the brother of James, it is no surprise that there is some reason to think that our author knows not only of James but perhaps also of his writings. J. Daryl Charles has pointed out that these two homilies share the following elements: (1) a general address (James 1.1; Jude 1–2); (2) a hortatory conclusion (James 5.20; Jude verses 22–23); (3) a sizable presentation of deliberative proofs (James 2.1–4.12; Jude verses 5–11); which is followed by (4) a series of admonitions (James 4.13–5.18; Jude verses 12–23), which are grouped into two pairs—the first aimed at opponents (James 4.13–17 and 5.1–6; Jude verses 12–13, 14–15), the second aimed at believers (James 5.7–12; 13.1–18; Jude verses 17–19, 20–23). (5) Both documents have an *exordium* or introduction that hints at the problems (James 1.2–8; Jude verses 3–4); (6) both frequently use catchwords, especially at strategic junctures; (7) both use hymnic or doxological material (James 3.13–18; Jude verses 24–25; and (8) both conclude with an exhortation to turn the sinner from his way (James 5.20; Jude verse 23).[6]

Charles reminds us that the verbal correspondence between James and Jude is quite striking. There is a higher degree of this sort of correspondence between these two documents than any other two documents in the New Testament, with the exception of Colossians and Ephesians, and Jude and 2 Peter. "All told there are 93 cases of verbal agreement which occur in the two letters, with 27 terms occurring two or more times in both. Astonishingly, *each* of the 25 verses of Jude averages approximately four words found in the epistle of James—an extraordinary rate of verbal correspondence."[7] In addition to all this, as Charles remarks, there are thematic overlaps between these documents; and "while both James and Jude are strongly motivated by ethical concerns each assumes a doctrinal foundation already laid with the readers."[8]

The most important of the theological correspondences is that both writers refer to Jesus as Lord who performs the functions at the second coming previously predicated of Yahweh (i.e., God the Father), including execution of judgment on the ungodly (cf. James. 5.7–11; Jude verses 3–5). "Thus Old Testament theophany [i.e., an appearing of God] and New Testament Christology merge in the view of the writer."[9] Although this is not enough to suggest direct literary dependency of the homily of Jude on that of James, it is enough to suggest that they have drunk from the same Jewish well and perhaps also to suggest that Jude is aware of and is writing in the wake of, although he is not directly borrowing from, the homily of James. Both of these writers show some real skill in using Koine Greek, and we may assume they both gained this skill in Jerusalem after Easter, although it may have been gained earlier in Galilee.

One of the interesting differences between Jude and James is that, whereas James is drawing on the teachings of their brother Jesus, Jude is busy doing commentary on other early Jewish literature of various sorts, as the outline following will indicate. Jude, however, not only bears some kind of "family" resemblance to James, but he almost certainly bears some sort of literary relationship to 2 Peter. In the first place, 19 out of 25 of Jude's verses appear in some form in 2 Peter. Most scholars, rightly in my judgment, think that 2 Peter is drawing on the more primitive material in Jude rather than the reverse. We will say a bit more about this when we discuss 2 Peter.

RHETORICAL OUTLINE OF JUDE'S DISCOURSE	
Epistolary Salutation	1–2
Exordium/Introduction, Narratio/Brief Statement of Facts, Proposition (intruders, marked out for judgment are in your midst)	3–4
Three Proofs from Sacred Tradition (Exodus, Angels, Sodom v. 7)	5–10
First summation (dreamers defile and blaspheme)	8
Example of judgment (Michael vs. the Devil over Moses' body)	9
Second summation (blasphemers are destroyed)	10
Three More Proofs from Sacred Tradition (Cain, Balaam, Korah)	11–16
Third summation (verses 12–13, blemishes on love feast)	12–13
Example of judgment (Enoch's prophecy)	14–15
Fourth Summation (grumblers and troublemakers)	16
Final Peroration/Emotional Appeal—Exhorting the Faithful	17–23
Remember the words of the apostles	17–19
Build yourself up and pray	20
Keep yourself in the love of God	21
Have mercy on some, save others	22–23
Benediction*	24–25

* See D. F. Watson, *Invention, Arrangement, and Style: Rhetorical Criticism of Jude and 2 Peter* (Atlanta, GA: Scholars Press, 1988), 29–79; and W. Brosend, *James and Jude* (Cambridge: Cambridge University Press, 2004), 166.

JUDE'S AUDIENCE

One thing that is immediately apparent in Jude is that the boundaries of the community he addresses are porous enough that outside Jewish teachers can enter and stir up the audience. This surely suggests a time prior to the Jewish war in the A.D. 60s, and well before the major separation of Jews and Jewish Christians after the fall of Jerusalem in A.D. 70, a divide probably reflected in the rhetoric in Matthew against the Pharisees.[10]

 Another social dimension that we need to consider in analyzing Jude is the use of purity language to reinforce boundaries that are porous. Although I am rather skeptical of some of the cultural anthropological analysis applied by Jerome Neyrey and others to Jude (as the concepts often need to be more firmly grounded in the actual social values and behavior of persons in the Greco-Roman world), in regard to the issue of purity language, he is on to something. Neyrey puts it this way:

> Ancient Jews and Greeks alike thought of the universe and all in it as a *kosmos,* an organized and structured whole. This general sense of order and appropriate classification is what is meant by "purity" on a general, abstract level. . . . Something is "pure" or "clean" when it is in accord with the social expectation of order and propriety; conversely, things are "polluted" or "unclean" when they violate the common assumptions of the way the world is structured. . . . All attempts to classify, to hierarchize, to draw boundary lines and the like indicate a strong sense of "purity" or order.[11]

Notice the language about "pollution" in verse 8, or "blemishes" in verse 12 or "shame" in verse 13. The false teachers are thus portrayed as "out of bounds" and violating the order and rules and ethics of the community. What Neyrey fails to say is that our author's sense of order is not grounded merely in the "way things always have been" or the creation rules of the cosmos. His sense of order and his ethics are actually grounded eschatologically in the way God has reoriented things in Christ's first coming and will continue to reorient things in the eschatological judgment, not in the way things always have been since the Fall.

This use of purity language, coupled with the use of both canonical and apocryphal early sacred Jewish traditions, makes as clear as it can be that Jude is addressing other Jewish Christians in a way that would most effectively persuade them to divest themselves of the influence of the false teachers. Jude the document becomes a word on target when one recognizes that the author and audience share a universe of discourse that is eschatological, esoteric, text-based, and early Jewish Christian in various respects. We must take seriously then that the false teachers have some clout, some authority within the audience Jude addresses, and they have been wielding it in self-serving ways, to judge from what Jude says about them.

Perhaps the most surprising, and in some minds disturbing, feature of this piece of early Jewish Christian eschatological exhortation is its use of non-Biblical materials, for example, from earlier Jewish documents called Enoch, or the Assumption of Moses, which refers to wrangling between the angel Michael and the Devil over the body of Moses. It is certainly this dimension of the text that has raised the most eyebrows and caused the most comment. Here it is sufficient to say that those who believe that the Bible is God's Word should not find this problematic. Not all of God's truth is found within the canon of Scripture; and all truth, wherever it is found, is God's truth. So the fact that a New Testament writer cites an early Jewish document or two should not trouble us. The assumption would be that he believed that, in some sense, what he was citing was also an expression of truth in some form.

This document then manifests an ethos that suggests that Jewish Christians are freely mingling with non-Christian Jews and that the boundaries of the Christian community are very porous, hence the need for this discourse warning against false teachers and false prophets. If we ask when such a community likely existed, a community familiar with various kinds of arcane Jewish lore, the most logical explanation is before A.D. 70 and before the real parting of the ways between Jews and Jewish Christians—and perhaps the most likely locale is in Galilee itself. Let's then briefly review the contents of this very short sermon.

SYNOPSIS OF CONTENTS

From the outset, Jude is proud to announce both that he serves his eldest brother Jesus, as does James, and that he is the brother of James. This suggests he was less widely known than either of his brothers. Jude writes to a situation in which some false teachers have managed to worm their way into the congregation Jude is addressing, and although he was going to write another sermon for their listening, when he learned of this intrusion, he felt he must address it. These teachers may not even be claiming to be followers of Jesus, but in any case, Jude says they turn the grace of God into an opportunity for misbehavior and deny the Lord Jesus.

Verses 5–7 involve a review of how God had previously dealt with disbelievers and troublers of the community of faith, citing the example of the destruction of the grumblers in the wilderness wandering period and of the angels mentioned in Gen. 6 who violated the creation order by mating with human women. To this he adds the notorious example of what happened to the sinners in Sodom and Gomorrah who pursued "unnatural lust" in the form of sexual immorality.

Verses 8–13 can be called a form of invective, meant to make the audience shun such people, and colorful metaphors abound—the intruding false teachers are like waterless clouds or trees without fruit, twice dead and even uprooted! They are like wind-tossed waves, or wandering stars "for whom the deepest darkness has been reserved." Verse 12 even says they are blemishes on your community meals, called love feasts. But Jude promises that his brother will return and judge such people.

Thus, in the final peroration and conclusion and benediction in verses 20–25, Jude urges the audience to stand firm in their faith, to stop listening to the false ones, to have mercy on the wavering who perhaps have begun to believe the false teachers, and that they need to snatch from the fire those who are about to leap into the bonfire lit by the false teachers. The homily ends with the reassurance that God is able to keep them from falling prey to such deception and wickedness.

IMPLICATIONS

When you enter the thought world of Jude, you enter a world that is foreign to most 21st-century Christians, especially regarding a story he tells about a wrestling match over the body of Moses, something you will find nowhere in the Old Testament. Jude, however, was addressing Jewish Christians who lived in a world of Jewish lore and traditions. Further, they could readily relate to his quoting a tradition from the book named after Enoch. More important, Jude, the discourse, bears witness to the hard struggles for the Jewish Christian community in Galilee and elsewhere to survive in an environment where there were both internal and external critics of the Jesus movement.

It is entirely possible that Jude is chronologically one of the earliest, if not the earliest, document in the New Testament, and it shows how very Jewish the communities of Jesus were as they struggled to establish their own sense of identity and independence from the synagogue. One also gets the sense that whatever authority structure that may have existed in the Jerusalem Church, elsewhere leadership structures were more catch-as-catch-can; and it was always possible for a false teacher or prophet to slip into a house church, even during a love feast where the Lord's Supper was shared, and create mayhem.

Two reasons that this was possible were (1) Christians had always been encouraged to welcome strangers and offer them hospitality in their homes, and (2) the Jesus movement was an evangelistic movement, so even strangers with strange beliefs were seen as potential converts and might be allowed to show up in worship meetings. The results sometimes could be chaotic. As Paul once said in 1 Cor. 14, "if an uninitiated person [using the Greek word from which we get the word "idiot"] shows up in your assembly, will he not think you mad if there is no order to your worship?"

One wonders just how much authority Jude actually had over congregations founded by other apostolic figures. Was it an authority based on his being a brother of James, the head of the Jerusalem Church? If so, that was a very different sort of authority from what Paul claimed came from his having seen the risen Lord and been commissioned by it. Whatever the case, the discourse known as Jude opens a surprisingly revealing window on the messiness of early Jewish Christian church life. It is a good cautionary reminder that we should not think that the early church had its act together, and the church today is much more problematic. No, the church has always had its struggles, precisely because it is made up of people who all have their own issues, viewpoints, and commitments.

Jude's word to his audience and to us is that we must continue to care about the purity of the Gospel and character of Christ's community lest we become indistinguishable from the world itself.

KEY TERMS

Cicero

Eusebius

Hegesippus

FOR FURTHER READING

Bauckham, R. "Jude, Epistle of," in *The Anchor Bible Dictionary*. Vol. 3. Edited by D. N. Freedman. New York: Doubleday, 1992.

Charles, J. Daryl. *Literary Strategy in the Epistle of Jude*. Scranton, PA: University of Scranton Press, 1993.

Watson, D. F. "The Letter of Jude." In *New Interpreters Bible*. Vol. 12: *Hebrews; James; 1 & 2 Peter; 1, 2, & 3 John; Jude*. Edited by L. E. Keck, F. B. Craddock, C. C. Rowland, & L. T. Johnson. Nashville, TN: Abingdon, 1998.

Witherington, B. *Letters and Homilies for Jewish Christians: A Socio-rhetorical Commentary on Hebrews, James and Jude*. Downers Grove, IL: InterVarsity Press, 2007.

STUDY QUESTIONS

What do we know of Jude, the brother of Jesus, and James from the Gospel of Mark?

John 7.5 tells us that the brothers of Jesus did not believe in him during his ministry. What do you imagine changed their minds?

What seem to be Jude's main complaints about the false teachers or prophets? What sort of negative impact were they having on the Jewish Christian groups Jude is addressing?

Jude seems to see some strong analogies between his own day and Old Testament times. Are there any similarities that you think Jude would see between our own day and Old Testament times if he were here to tell us?

How hard do you think it was for Jude to have Jesus as his older brother?

NOTES

1. R. Bauckham, "Jude, Epistle of," in *The Anchor Bible Dictionary,* vol. 3, ed. D. N. Freedman (New York: Doubleday, 1992), 1098–1103, here 1101.
2. See E. Schnabel, *Early Christian Mission*, vol. 1. *Jesus and the Twelve* (Downers Grove, IL: InterVarsity Press, 2004), 749–50.
3. R. J. Bauckham, *Jude, 2 Peter, Word Biblical Commentary*, vol. 50 (Waco, TX: Word Books, 1983), 375.

4. See D. F. Watson, "The Letter of Jude" in *New Interpreters Bible*, vol. 12, *Hebrews; James; 1& 2 Peter; 1, 2, & 3 John; Jude,* L. E. Keck, F. B. Craddock, C. C. Rowland, & L. T. Johnson (Nashville, TN: Abingdon, 1998), 474.

5. On this, see Bauckham, *Jude, 2 Peter,* 94–95.

6. J. Daryl Charles, *Literary Strategy in the Epistle of Jude* (Scranton, PA: University of Scranton Press, 1993), 75–76.

7. Ibid., 77.

8. Ibid., 79.

9. Ibid., 79.

10. See the helpful discussion by Martin Hengel, "Early Christianity as a Jewish-Messianic, Universalistic Movement," in *Conflicts and Challenges in Early Christianity*, ed. Donald Hagner (Harrisburg, PA: Trinity Press, 1999), 1–41.

11. Neyrey, "Jude and 2 Peter," in *The Anchor Bible*, vol. 37C, ed. D. N. Freedman (New York: Doubleday, 1993), 10–11.

Here at Caesara Phillipi, outside the Holy Land, is where Peter made his famous confession that Jesus was the Christ, the Son of God. (© *Mark R. Fairchild, Ph.D.*)

16 The SUFFERING SERVANT— 1 PETER

SCHOLARS' RECONSTRUCTION OF EARLIEST CHRISTIAN HISTORY is to a significant degree dependent on how they arrange the data and what assumptions they make about the authorship of various documents. There are not too many scholars today who think that there are a bunch of documents composed in the second century A.D. in the New Testament itself, but this assumption was pretty prevalent in the first half of the 20th century, especially in Germany. Scholarly trends shift as the evidence mounts in one direction or another. Certainly, one of the trends in the last 20 or so years has been to reevaluate the last third of the New Testament canon, and in the process, reevaluate early Jewish Christianity and its documents. In general, there has been a growing appreciation of these documents (with recognition that all or almost all of them come from the first century A.D.) and a growing recognition that they do not reflect a tiny minority of early Christian life but rather one of the two major streams of early Christian life.

Jewish Christian congregations founded by the Beloved Disciple, Peter, Jude, emissaries of James, the author of Hebrews, and others seem to have had a life of their own when compared to the Pauline churches. Often, these churches were in the same regions as various churches founded by Paul and his coworkers, and they may well have had considerable interaction with the Pauline churches. There is no evidence that the Jewish and Pauline churches would have regarded each other as heterodox, but nonetheless they each had their own existence. The Jewish Christian Churches were not likely amalgamated with or incorporated into the Pauline ones before late in the first century or at the beginning of the second century A.D. at the earliest. In fact, many of these Jewish Christian Churches appear to have continued to have their own existence well beyond the era in which the New Testament itself was written.

This powerful discourse—
1 Peter—is a reflection on
suffering for the sake of
Christ and was probably addressed to Jewish Christians
in various parts of northern
and western Turkey, although
a significant number of
scholars have suggested it
was written largely to Gentile
Christians (see the discussion that follows). It is likely
from Peter the apostle, with
the help of Silas, and was
written sometime in the A.D.
mid-60s in Rome prior to Peter's martyrdom in that city.

EBIONITE

A term literally meaning
"the poor," used as a
reference to a small but
important sect of Jewish
Christians who seem to
have had issues with Paul
and his Gospel and also
had a low Christology,
believing that Jesus was
not part of the Godhead.
The Ebionites should not
be confused with James or
Jude, who do not reflect
that sort of low Christology. It is possible they
were a continuation of a
group called the Judaizers
in the New Testament—
Pharisaic Jewish Christians
believing in strict adherence to the Mosaic law for
all followers of Jesus (see
Acts 15.1–3). They seem to
have nonetheless claimed
James the brother of Jesus
as their first leader.

The ongoing viability and vibrancy of Jewish Christianity is shown not just by the existence of the **Ebionites** or documents like the Hebrew Gospel of Matthew, which continued to support and educate these groups, but also by the continued warnings of some of the church fathers well into the fourth century A.D. about "Judaizing." In other words, we have done a disservice to Jewish Christianity if we think it quickly disappeared due to the rising tide of Pauline and Gentile Christianity, even as early as the first century A.D. This is simply not so, and the very number of documents in the New Testament canon that originally addressed groups that were largely, if not wholly, composed of Jewish Christians eloquently testifies to their ongoing existence.

THE SOCIAL WORLD OF EARLY CHRISTIANITY

It has been said that Christianity in the first century A.D. was a social world in the making.[1] This is true, but the question is what sort of social world was being constructed by the external evangelistic program and the internal order-ing of Christian communities based in house churches? Was it an ordering that baptized various forms of the social status quo and called it good? Was the aim to make clear that Christianity was *not* a revolutionary new religious sect in the Roman Empire? Was it an attempt to extend largely Jewish values and beliefs to a wider audience? And what role was 1 Peter meant to play in this social con-structing of a "new world," or at least a new Christian society and subculture? These are relevant and crucial questions to consider as we introduce ourselves to 1 Peter, which has in some circles been taken to be the least revolutionary and most socially conservative of all the New Testament documents.

Often missed in such a sociological study of 1 Peter is the fact that the author is also busily constructing a rhetorical world, a world of advice and consent, persuasion and dissuasion, where certain beliefs and behaviors are inculcated not merely for social reasons but also for theological or ideological ones as well. When we analyze 1 Peter as rhetoric, what do we learn about the aims and purposes of this document, broadly speaking? Is it meant to steel the audience for persecution by persuading them about the value of Christ-likeness? Is there some considerable rhetorical problem this discourse is meant to overcome? And what do we make of the use in this document not only of the Old Testament but also material from Jesus' rhetoric, James's rhetoric, and Paul's rhetoric?

Carl Holladay remarks:

> For all its Pauline echoes, however, 1 Peter also has close affinities with the synoptic tradition and to a lesser extent with the Gospel of John, Hebrews, and James. There are remarkable convergences with Peter's speeches in Acts. Since 1 Peter resonates with such a wide

> spectrum of early Christian witnesses, some scholars have suggested,
> only half-jokingly, that its author knew the whole New Testament! . . .
> Part of 1 Peter's enduring appeal stems from the breadth and depth
> of common tradition on which it draws and its appropriation of the
> earlier, apostolic consensus in giving authority to its distinctive voice.[2]

Where was our author placed, geographically, socially, temporally, and rhetorically that he would have known all of this material; and does such evidence provide clues to the authorship of this document? Could 1 Peter really be the masterpiece and last grand act of the great apostle who had known (and known the rhetoric of) Jesus, James, and Paul and now was making their contributions serviceable for his own audience? Was our author at the fount from which the apostolic tributaries flowed forth, and so in touch with the origins of Jewish and Gentile Christianity and its leaders, or was he at the place where all those tributaries came back together at the end of the first century and the beginning of the second? All of these sorts of questions are intertwined in a study of 1 Peter. For now, it is enough to note that even though 2 Peter is a **composite document** deeply indebted to its predecessors, it also characterizes 1 Peter, although in a very different way. The Petrine legacy in the canon is tradition rich.

COMPOSITE DOCUMENT

A document that collects material from other sources and depends on them.

THE AUTHORSHIP, AUDIENCE, AND SOCIAL MILIEU OF 1 PETER

1 Peter itself is part of an ongoing social relationship between the author and the audience. As such, it has a certain social dynamic to it. We may ask what this tells us about the state of the relationship between the author and the audience. Does he see them as peers ("fellow elders"), followers, friends, or converts? Does he view them as largely Jews, largely Gentiles, or a balanced mixture of the two ethnic groups? What is the social level of the author and the audience? Is it commensurate? Is there disparity?

What is the social strategy of our author to help the audience cope with its now alien world from which they are increasingly alienated by their faith? 1 Peter can be said to be the only New Testament document that systematically addresses the issue of Christians being resident aliens within the macro-structures of the larger society.[3] Why does 1 Peter have this character and peculiar distinction within the canon? It is these sorts of questions that lead to a deeper understanding of the social dimensions of this document, particularly its ethical and practical content, but also its theology.

One of the real contributions of John Elliott to our study of 1 Peter is that he has demonstrated that the language in this document about being resident aliens and visiting strangers should not be treated in a purely spiritual sense.

Figure 16.1 In a highly stratified culture, different labels were used to put people in their place and identify their proper status. Here, we see a bench from the theater at Miletus reserved for "God-fearers," that is, for Gentiles who are adherents of the Jewish religion. (© Mark R. Fairchild, Ph.D.)

DIASPORA

A term used in reference to Jews who were dispersed outside of the Holy Land.

MACRO-CULTURE

The dominant culture within a certain context.

MICRO-CULTURE

A subculture that exists under the umbrella of a macro-culture. Those who are part of a micro-culture may speak a different language or may define identity or rules differently than those who are predominantly a part of the macro-culture or culture at large.

The spiritual interpretation refers to the traditional suggestion that all believers are labeled with an exile or sojourning status until they are united with Christ. Rather, Elliott argues that the terminology has a clear social and political sense in 1 Peter, whatever else we may want to say. In light of the highly Jewish character of 1 Peter, it would seem logical to conclude that it is the **Diaspora** Jews and God-fearers who are called resident aliens in 1 Peter as it is in other Jewish literature. Therefore, we should surely conclude this is likely in 1 Peter as well. And there is further good reason to do so.

The prescript in 1 Pet. 1.1 refers to God's elect, who are then called visiting strangers in the world, scattered throughout the western part of what we now call Turkey. The language of the Jewish Diaspora is used here, in similar fashion to what we found in James 1.1. Furthermore, our author, writing from a foreign capital where there is a pagan ruler, calls his locale Babylon (1 Pet. 5.13), coded language that alludes to the exilic status of Jews.

Babylon here, as in the Book of Revelation, refers to Rome. The author then is indicating to his audience that he shares their resident alien and exilic condition where he is. Indeed, he is at the epicenter of the Diaspora in his day, for it was the Romans who displaced so many of the Jews who lived in Asia Minor and its neighboring regions. One can even say that the social function of this discourse is to encourage the sense of alienation from the **macro-culture** and thereby aid the integration with the **micro-culture** of early Christianity. Their dual identity is that they are resident aliens in the empire, but they are "in Christ" in the kingdom!

Look closely at the language of 1 Pet. 2.12. The audience is to live Christian lives among the "nations," more specifically, the Gentile nations. Notice that Peter does not use religious language here (e.g., the term *pagans,* or idolaters). He simply uses ethnic language here. Now it would be very strange to advise an audience of Gentiles (or largely Gentiles) to live like Christians among the Gentiles. Gentiles do not talk about themselves as "the other nations."[4] This is Jewish language, and it best suits the theory that the audience consisted largely of Jews, in this case Jewish Christians, with perhaps some Gentiles who had previously been connected to the synagogue (called "God-fearers"). The Jewish Christians are to live as resident aliens or visiting stranger Christians among the overwhelmingly Gentile majority in each of these regions. Are there other reasons to affirm not only the sociological conclusion that these terms should not be spiritualized, but also that they refer to actual Jews in the Dispersion?

That there was a very sizable Jewish population in the provinces listed at the beginning of 1 Peter (Pontus, Galatia, Cappadocia, Asia, and Bithynia) in the first and second centuries of the common era few scholars today doubt. One estimate says that of a population of about 4 million in Asia Minor in the A.D. 60s, some 300,000 were Jews, and there were perhaps 5,000 Christians as well.[5] The evidence is equally clear that the Jewish Diaspora in Asia Minor dates from at least the third century B.C., when Antiochus III sent some two thousand Jews from Babylon to colonize various places in the region, including the kingdoms of Lydia and Phrygia.[6] Paul Trebilco has shown just how sizable, and indeed influential, this population had become in many cities in the region by the early part of the first century A.D.[7]

The evidence we have, both literary and archaeological, also suggests that Jews (perhaps particularly in Asia Minor) were well integrated into the social ethos of the region, having become quite Hellenized. This is particularly evident in a place like Sardis, where a remarkable Diaspora synagogue was built right next to the gymnasium at the center of the town and also abutting a series of shops where Jewish merchants sold their wares. Just how Hellenized some Jews could become in such an environment is shown by the evidence of the attempts by Jewish athletes to have the evidence of their circumcision removed by the re-attaching of the foreskin so they could work out in the gymnasium and compete in Olympic-style games as well.[8] Rodney Stark concludes that many of the Jews of the Diaspora were indistinguishable from Gentiles unless one sought them out in the synagogue or in the home.[9]

For Hellenized Jews living for a long time in the Hellenistic milieu of Anatolia, accepting invitations to dinner parties, sometimes held in dining rooms attached to Greek or Roman temples, must have seemed far less problematic than for Jews in Judaea. Although still wanting to be part of the Jewish subculture, nevertheless, such Hellenized Jews sought to have the sort of business and personal relationships with non-Jews that were cemented at such dinner parties.

Having spent considerable time at archaeological sites in Asia Minor over the last several years, it has become clearer and clearer to me that we must not imagine that Jews in the cities of Asia Minor and the neighboring regions lived in some sort of Jewish cultural ghetto. To the contrary, the picture, for example, of Saul of Tarsus and his family being citizens of a great city like Tarsus (Acts 21.39) is by no means uncommon. This meant that they were thought to model some of the civic virtues and participate as fully as they could in the life of the city, presumably without, in their own minds, crossing the line over into idolatry and obvious violations of the Ten Commandments.[10] I would suggest that it is against this sort of highly Hellenized backdrop of Diaspora Jews in this particular region that questions of audience and authorship should be adjudicated regarding a document like 1 Peter.

Lest we think it unlikely that our author would consider Jews outside of Christ as just as lost as Gentiles, I point to Ephesians 2.3, which says of both groups, "All of us who also lived among them at one time (i.e., the powers and principalities and the devil) gratifying the desires of our sinful inclinations and following its cravings and thoughts. Like the rest we were by nature objects of wrath." In other words, our author takes a sectarian view of all his contemporaries outside of Christ, whether they are Jews or Gentiles—they are lost. We must pay close attention to the recent work of Rodney Stark on these matters:

> Another link between Hellenism and early Christianity was through the Jews of the Diaspora, who like the early Christians also worshipped in Greek. Many of them chafed at the ethnic barrier their religion placed between them and their full participation in Hellenic society—the Law made it difficult for them even to eat with their Gentile associates. . . . When Paul stripped the Jewish prerequisite from Christianity, he not only made the faith open to Gentiles, but offered the Hellenized Jews an attractive religious option, which many of them took.[11]

Figure 16.2 This large gymnasium complex is right next to the Hellenized synagogue in Sardis. (© *Mark R. Fairchild, Ph.D.*)

This is exactly right, and in my view Peter in his missionary work simply followed Paul's lead and offered Hellenized Jews the same Gospel of salvation by grace through faith without the restrictions of the law that hindered their fuller participation in society in some respects. Christianity offered such Hellenized Jews a form of ethical monotheism that did not set up the same barriers to participation in the wider culture as the full practice of Judaism itself. The result is what we find in 1 Peter—Peter writing largely to Hellenized Jewish Christians.

Our author writes with a conversionist and sectarian mentality assuming that those who are outside the Christian circle are to one degree or another religiously in the dark, whether they are formerly Jews or formerly Gentiles. But even more to the point, looking at 1 Pet. 1.14–16 carefully, (1) our author is quoting from Lev. 11.44–45, which of course is directed quite specifically to Jews alone; and (2), in this context, we hear about the audience of that Leviticus passage being God's chosen children. Again, this is most naturally taken to be a reference to Jews in 1 Peter as well.

Thus, the question becomes whether our author has something of a completionist reading of the earlier history of Israel or not, that is, the idea that Jew and Gentile united in Christ is the continuation of God's people Israel. I do not think that such a view can be lightly dismissed because other New Testament authors seem to reflect it. In fact, I would suggest that this is precisely how our author thinks. For example, in 1 Pet. 2.5, he exhorts his audience to let themselves be built into a new spiritual house, to be a new holy priesthood, and to offer new spiritual sacrifices acceptable to God through Jesus Christ. Here, he is certainly taking up the language of the Hebrew Scriptures and applying it now to Christians engaged in a very different sort of worship, the worship of Jesus as Lord. Clearly enough, our author feels that he can make such an intellectual leap in the way he handles the Hebrew Scriptures, and he is comfortable applying terms previously reserved for non-Christian Israel to his audience.

It is no accident that our author uses the Greek term **Christianos** (which means adherents of Christ, or those belonging to Christ) in 1 Peter 4.16. This is the Greek term from which we get the word *Christian.* Christians were now distinguishable from Jews in general, and if they were thought not to be Jews, they did not have the protective umbrella of being part of a legal religion. They were now subject to even more marginalization as "resident aliens" who were viewed as part of a superstition rather than part of a historically rooted religion. Remember that in ancient contexts, religions that could be established as age-old were given more credibility. This loss of a thoroughgoing connection to an ancient religion subjected them to legal abuse, especially when they refused to worship the emperor. I suspect that Peter adds this warning in light of what has just happened in Rome—the Christians had been called out by name, by the emperor, as responsible for the horrible fire in A.D. 64 that gutted whole areas in Rome. He is then anticipating this may well happen in Asia Minor as well.

CHRISTIANOS

A Greek term that means adherents of Christ or those belonging to Christ.

The social upheaval described in the document must correlate with something going on or potentially happening soon where the audience is. It cannot simply be a description of what is happening where the author is, in Rome. As Elliott also says, "all the pertinent terms refer to verbal rather than physical abuse or legal action" (see 1 Pet. 2.12, 3.3, 3.16, 4.14).[12] These terms refer to social pressure and persecution not yet ending in governmentally inaugurated legal action. This surely makes it more likely that this document was written *before* the persecution of Nero had reached its zenith, resulting in the martyrdoms of Peter and Paul. Had it been written after that time, it is hard to imagine there not being clear references to martyrdoms, as there is in Revelation, especially considering how much emphasis there is on suffering in 1 Peter, noting the various allusions to the Suffering Servant of Isaiah in this discourse. Peter is still urging respect for governing authorities, whereas in Revelation, the central government is seen as an instrument of Satan (contrast 1 Pet. 2.13–17). As in the book of Hebrews, we see in this document a social situation in which the audience (and the author of course) has not yet suffered to the point of loss of life, but there has been abuse of various sorts.[13]

The division of labor between largely Gentile missionaries (the Pauline circle) and largely Jewish missionaries (the Petrine, Jamesian, and Johannine circles) led to basically separate communities of Christians in various cities in the empire, including cities in Asia Minor and its surrounding provinces. Peter is writing to churches, some of which are in areas where Paul has set up house churches, and some of which are not. And yet Peter is exercising authority over the churches to which he is writing. The obvious conclusion to be drawn from this is that the division of missionary labor had to do with the ethnic target audience, not regions of the empire, and that Peter is addressing largely Jewish Christians (perhaps with some God-fearers) in this discourse and not addressing communities founded by Paul or his coworkers.

I thus concur with Elliott when he suggests the "letter's geographical destination offers neither evidence nor reason for regarding 1 Peter as intended for Pauline churches or for areas of the Pauline mission field. . . . 1 Peter is best read on its own terms, as an independent though complementary witness to the diversified growth of early Christianity in Asia Minor."[14] Various of these provinces were so huge that we may envision Peter being involved in eastern Galatia on his way north to Pontus, while Paul is involved in southern Galatia. The order of the regions mentioned in the beginning of the document (1 Pet. 1.1)—Pontus, Galatia, Cappadocia, Asia, and Bithynia—suggests the planned route through which this encyclical (a letter written for several audiences) would be taken.[15] In other words, this document, like Revelation, mentions cities or regions in the order in which the circular document will reach them.

The discourse thus far naturally leads to a discussion of what can be said about the identity of the author of this document. That he is a Jew few if any scholars would dispute, and a Jew who has a special affinity for the Psalms and some Isaianic material as well. That he is in addition a Jewish Christian is clear enough from the content of the document, and again this is rarely disputed. The next question of import is how one should take the reference to Babylon in 1 Pet. 5.13. That it is coded language few would dispute today. The actual region of Babylon went by another name during the Greco-Roman era. It is natural to compare this usage to Rev. 18, where there is a woe oracle about the fall of Babylon, and the reference there is clearly Rome.[16] But now we must ask, if Babylon = Rome in 1 Pet. 5, what does it tell us about the social situation of the author that he would use such language? The most reasonable answer is that he himself is in a marginalized condition, as a Jewish follower of Jesus, and he views his locale as the source and center of the oppression and persecution. One has to ask—why?

Why does the author of 1 Peter speak of a king (*Basilea*), rather than the emperor, when he talks about governing authorities? My suggestion is that (1) the document is written during a period of persecution, hence the coded language both about the city and the emperor (although the author may in addition be thinking of client kings elsewhere in the empire); and (2), only two periods best suit that description, namely, the latter years of the reign of Nero (cf. Romans, written about A.D. 57, during the early Neronian period) or the time of **Domitian**, that is, either in the mid-60s or the early to mid-90s A.D. Our author expects the persecution to go on and to affect Christians both where he is and perhaps where the audience is as well. This helps explain the strong stress on the resident alien sort of language. Obviously, when you are persecuted, you feel alienated from the existing governance and social structures in your region. Clearly, our author too is some sort of major religious authority figure; he calls himself an apostle and an elder in relationship to the audience.

Another piece of the puzzle comes in realizing the implications of the echoes of earlier Pauline material (e.g., the phrase "in Christ"), earlier material from the homily of James, some of the sayings of Jesus, and finally perhaps echoes of some of the material in the pastorals as well. In my view, 2 Timothy was written from Rome by Paul and a cowriter (Luke) in the A.D. mid-60s after the fire and likely before Paul's death. I suggest that 1 Peter is a document that comes from the very same place and likely during the very same time period, although for a very different audience—Jewish Christians.

E. G. Selwyn is quite right that the reception of this document as authentic and, indeed, as a sacred text is early, clear, and widespread.[17] In fact, it and 1 John are the only documents from among the so-called catholic epistles whose authenticity was uncontested in both the eastern and western parts of the church.

The character of the discourse favors the suggestion that these congregations have been founded for some time. In my view, it is likely that Peter began evangelizing these regions in the 40s and returned to these areas after the Jerusalem Council in A.D. 50. This means he covered a lot of ground, and he and his coworkers had considerable success with the Jews in these areas. Among other things, this also suggests a date not earlier than the A.D. 60s for this document. Based on Acts 2.9–11, I suggest that Peter followed up on the initial success he

DOMITIAN

A Roman emperor who ruled from A.D. 81–96. Christians experienced another persecution under Domitian.

had with Diaspora Jews at Pentecost by literally following them to their home regions in due course and building on those social networks. Notice the mention of both Pontus and Cappadocia in the list in Acts 2.

Finally, we may also stress at this juncture that it is a mistake to underplay the potential danger Christians were in, in the regions addressed, once it was recognized that they were not simply Jews. Peter was right to be concerned about the effect of pressure, persecution, and prosecution and the resultant suffering of Christians from this region he had evangelized.

THE RHETORICAL OUTLINE OF 1 PETER

This discourse reflects a sort of Greek and rhetoric that was suitable for the audiences addressed in this document. It was called Asiatic Greek and Asiatic rhetoric because it reflected the style of the region. This style tended to involve long sentences and the use of metaphors and rhetorical hyperbole. We certainly find these kinds of elements in 1 Peter. The function of this discourse is to get the audience to embrace a more holy lifestyle, which indeed will make them stand out from the crowd in terms of their religion and ethics. The author wants to remind these Jewish Christians of what they had already been told and promised in the Old Testament—that as a group, they were the household or temple of God; the place where God especially dwelt on earth; and on top of that, they were a royal priesthood, offering the world up to God. Here is a brief outline giving a sense of the structure and subject matter of the discourse:

RHETORICAL OUTLINE OF 1 PETER		
Epistolary Prescript	1.1–2	
Exordium/Introductory Remarks	1.3–12	Thanksgiving for so great a salvation
Proposition/Thesis Statement	1.13–16	You are holy and have a hope, so you should live like it.
First Argument	1.17–2.10	Living as redeeming resident aliens
Second Argument	2.11–3.12	Submission to authority figures
Third Argument	3.13–4.11	Suffering and self-control
Fourth Argument	4.12–19	Sharing the sufferings of Christ
Fifth Argument	5.1–5	Appeal to the elders and the youth
Peroration/Final Emotional Appeal	5.6–9	Humility and self-control in suffering, with closing doxology (5.10–11)
Epistolary Postscript	5.12–14	

The question to be raised about this outline is, whose rhetoric is this? Is Peter capable of such rhetoric? According to church tradition that goes back to Papias and is probably reliable, Mark wrote down the Petrine remembrances about Jesus in his Gospel (see Chapter 5), and there is some evidence that there was an Aramaic original for some of that document.[18] If there is truth in this tradition, it suggests that Peter needed some help in communicating in Greek, at least in written form. Thus, 1 Pet. 5.12 becomes crucial.

Unlike in 1–2 Thess., 1 Peter makes no claims about the authority of Silvanus. In 1–2 Thess., Paul indeed is the speaker, but he wants to make it known that two other authority figures involved in founding the church in Thessalonica (Silvanus/ Silas and Timothy) are also standing behind him and are in agreement with what is said in the discourse. 1 Peter makes no such claims about the authority of Silvanus. He is not mentioned until the end of the document; at the beginning stands Peter the Apostle alone. In deliberative rhetoric, the assertion of one's authority was crucial at the outset, establishing one's ethos and indeed the tenor of the document. This discourse is presented as an authoritative word from Peter, presumably to his various converts.

Figure 16.3 If Peter traveled by land from the Holy Land to the provinces listed in 1 Peter 1, he would have had to cross these formidable mountains in Turkey, the Taurus Mountains.
(© Mark R. Fairchild, Ph.D.)

What then was the role of Silvanus? It is true that some scholars have attempted to see 1 Pet. 5.12 as claiming that the letter was sent to these various churches through Silvanus the letter carrier. There is a problem with this conclusion. If one diagrams the Greek sentence in question, leaving out the subordinate clauses, it reads: "through Silvanus . . . I wrote to you briefly." Silvanus may well have carried this document through these regions, just as he carried the letter from the Jerusalem Council meeting (see Acts 15), but this Greek sentence surely claims more.

Notice that we do *not* have the verb "send/sent" in 1 Pet. 5.12, unlike what is in Acts 15.22–23, where it seems clear that the reference is to a letter carrier rather than a letter writer. This is also the case in Ignatius's letters to the *Philippians* 11.2 and to the *Smyrnaens* 12.1. It was the normal practice for an author who used a scribe to take up the pen toward the end of the document and add a few words of his own. We see this in various Pauline letters (e.g., see the end of Galatians or Romans), and there is no reason to think the situation is different in

Figure 16.4 Sheep are a traditional image for God's people, as God is imaged as a shepherd. (© Rick Danielson)

this case, considering where Silvanus's name is mentioned. It is difficult to judge how much Silvanus contributed to 1 Peter, but because he is not claimed as an author *even at this point* (Peter says "I wrote . . ." here), we may assume that he simply played the role of scribe at most, as far as the composition of the document is concerned. He may also have been its deliverer and interpreter.[19]

Like Paul, Silvanus may well have received good training in Greek and in rhetoric in Jerusalem, a training Peter would probably not have gotten growing up in Galilee before following Jesus. Because there is some evidence of Hebrew influence in the ways of phrasing things in 1 Peter, it may well be that Peter dictated in Aramaic and Silvanus wrote in Greek, looking at and transcribing from his own copy of the Greek translation of the Old Testament (the LXX) when quoting. Or it may be that Silvanus was himself bilingual but more literate that Peter, so he framed Peter's words in better Greek and better rhetorical style. Peter's spoken Greek may well have been better than his written Greek, as is so often the case in such oral multilingual cultures.

That being so, we may conclude that the voice is decidedly the voice of Peter if we trust the rhetorical claim of the document itself, even if the hands are the hands of Silvanus. Indeed, there are hints in the text that the author has a direct knowledge of the trial of Jesus (1 Pet. 2.21–24), the Transfiguration of Jesus (1 Pet. 5.1), the specific command of the risen Jesus in John 21.17 (see 1 Pet. 5.2), and the foot washing by Jesus (1 Pet. 5.5 in which "cloth yourself with humility" is an allusion to Jesus taking off his main garment, wrapping a towel around himself, and taking on the role of the slave who washes people's feet!). When we couple this with some 10 echoes of Jesus' sayings, no author better fits these facts that Peter himself.[20]

SYNOPSIS OF CONTENTS

Let us start with a fresh translation of 1 Pet. 1.1–2.

> Peter, apostle of Jesus Christ, to the elect sojourners of the dispersion (in) Pontus, Galatia, Cappodicia, Asia, and Bithynia, according to the foreknowledge of God the Father in sanctification of the Spirit unto obedience and sprinkling of the blood of Jesus Christ. Grace to you and peace be multiplied.

Here we have one of the richest greetings in all of the New Testament in terms of theological content, and we must comment on certain key words. First, Peter calls himself an apostle, unlike James or Jude. The word apostle comes from the Greek verb meaning to send. An apostle is thus, strictly speaking, a sent one, and in the New Testament one sent by Christ or His church to perform some specific task—usually evangelizing or related activities. The background of the term *apostle* probably lies in the Jewish concept of Shaliah, one who was an authorized agent or representative appointed to carry out a specific mission (cf. Jn. 13.16, Mt. 10.40, 2 Cor. 8.23, Mark 3.13ff, Mt 10.5–40).

For Paul it appears that the qualification for being an apostle is "having seen the Risen Lord" (cf. 1 Cor. 9.1 to 1 Cor. 15). Luke, in Luke–Acts, seems to use the term more broadly (Lk. 6.13, Lk. 24.9–13; Acts 1.2, 8, 14.4, 14; cf. Acts 13.1–3). It can include such people as Barnabas. There may perhaps be a distinction between being an apostle of *a* church sent on a specific mission (i.e., a sent one of a church) and an apostle of Jesus Christ sent more broadly by Him and the church to be involved in a larger and ongoing work. There is evidence to suggest that a *Shaliah* could not pass on his authority or commission in a Jewish context. Did this also apply to Christian apostles?

C. K. Barrett has pointed out that "If they (Peter and his colleagues) had been appointed . . . Shalihim by the Lord, this naturally means that he regarded them as officials and administrators in his stead for the community, the escha-tological Israel, that he had brought into being."[21] If the Spirit plays a vital role in singling out people for church leadership since Pentecost (cf. 1 Cor. 12), then the Twelve cannot be seen, at least by Luke, as paradigms of leadership for the Spirit-filled community after apostolic times. This is so because (1) the Twelve had a special task of helping to found the community of Christ in the world, and (2) they received their commission and re-commission *before* the Spirit was given. Notice how the Twelve are filled up prior to Pentecost in Acts 1 and are *not* filled again thereafter. Therefore, we must distinguish between the Twelve as The Twelve and their unique roles at the beginning and at the end of salvation history (cf. Mt. 19.28; Lk. 22.30, judging the Twelve tribes) and apostles.

This does not mean that the Twelve are outmoded by Pentecost or are of no historical purpose after Acts 1.15ff. Indeed, it is Peter in Acts 2 who takes charge of matters at Pentecost and becomes the spokesman for the Christians. Further, it is the Twelve, as Apostles, who must have been responsible for distributing charity until the responsibility became too much, and they had to ordain seven others chosen by the people to assume this role (Acts 2.42–47, 4.32–37, 6.1–7).

Here we see the Twelve, especially Peter, in leadership roles during the transition period. They have one foot in the life of Jesus and the other in the life of the church—they are able to relate the one to the other. Notice that their witness in Acts has also changed from the days of the earthly ministry. Whereas in Luke, they witness *for* Jesus *about* the Kingdom, in Acts, they witness *about* Jesus *and* the resurrection.

After the early days of the community, the Twelve do not seem to have been in the forefront of Church expansion; and Luke, for the most part, leaves them behind after Acts 6. This is undoubtedly good history and does not give the Twelve more prominence than they actually had. Still, there is surprisingly little about them in Acts.

We must conclude, however, that it is apostles as apostles who, if any leadership or guidance was given on choosing leaders, gave such guidance. Further, if Paul's definition of apostle is the one that prevailed (i.e., one who has seen and been commissioned by the Risen Lord), then necessarily we cannot talk about apostolic succession—the passing on of the apostolic office. We can, however, talk about the passing on of the apostolic faith or traditions and also in some regards the parceling out of various apostolic functions and latter church leadership (deacons, elders, bishops; notice how it is the Twelve as apostles who act even like deacons distributing charity until it was necessary to ordain the seven: Acts 2.42ff.).

One may suspect, in view of other Pauline influences evident in 1 Peter, that when we hear the phrase in Chapter 1, verse 1, that Peter is an "apostle of Jesus Christ," he means the same thing as Paul does—an emissary commissioned by the risen Jesus; and thus, this is an implicit claim to having seen the risen Lord after Easter. It is noteworthy as well that the author identifies himself by his nickname—Peter—rather than as Simon. Simon may have been the first person ever to have the nickname Peter, which later became a proper name.

Peter in 1 Peter, Chapter 1, verse 1b, calls his audience "sojourners" (i.e., a foreigner who is currently staying in a place where he has little or no legal status), which may imply both the transience of their life here on earth but also suggest that their home lies elsewhere—that is, heaven. That is how many have taken these words. They are God's vagabonds by election, with the election alienating them from their non-Christian neighbors.

The problems with spiritualizing this language, however, are twofold: first, this term had a social and legal meaning in its day, and there is nothing in this prescript here to suggest that the term "elect" should carry more weight in understanding this word than the word that follows it. The term "Diaspora," especially when we then have a list of actual locations in the Diaspora that follows this terminology, likely connotes both a physical place and a social condition. Second, nothing at all is said here about heaven being the home of believers. The term Diaspora had a specific social sense for Jewish Christians—it didn't mean being on earth as opposed to being in heaven. It meant being outside of Israel as opposed to dwelling in the Holy Land. This is perfectly clear from noting its use in the LXX (cf. Deut. 28.25, 30.4; Neh. 1.9; Ps. 147.2; Is. 49.6; Jer. 15.7, 34.17; Dan. 12.2).

Dispersion here seems to mean as it did in James, those outside Palestine, but here even more narrowly defined to refer to certain provinces or regions in western Turkey. It is interesting that Josephus, quoting Strabo, notes the widespread perception that "This people [i.e., Jews] has already made its way into every city, and it is not easy to find any place in the habitable world which has not received this nation" (Josephus's *Ant.* 14.115). This did not mean that Jews were the majority in most of these places; it only meant that the majority of these places had some Jews. We might have expected a west to east listing of the provinces because this document is coming from Rome, but perhaps Peter is thinking of the order in which he visited these places.

Perhaps Peter, like Paul, began his evangelization of the region from Antioch. After all, this is where we find Peter in Gal. 2 in about A.D. 49–50. We may assume then that he went from Antioch overland, passed through the Cilician Gates, the pass in those formidable mountains in the province of Syria and Cilicia, and then began evangelizing the region, perhaps in Pontus. This region involves some 129,000 or more square miles, so we are talking about an enormous amount of territory. The route followed, which ended in Bithynia, may suggest that Peter kept heading west from Bithynia across the Hellespont (perhaps down to Corinth in the early A.D. 50s; see 1 Cor. 1.12, 9.5). From Corinth, perhaps he went back east and did more work in the provinces mentioned in 1 Peter.

This enormous amount of territory covered in part by Peter, but not by the Pauline mission, would certainly explain why Peter falls entirely off the Lukan radar after Peter's appearance at the Jerusalem Council in A.D. 50 in Acts 15, and indeed had already been mostly off Luke's radar since the early A.D. 40s (see Acts 12) when Peter escaped jail in Jerusalem, said goodbye to the church there, and "went to another place."

We may envision then Peter's ministry in the listed provinces of Turkey in the 40s and perhaps in the A.D. 50s as well. By A.D. 57, when Paul writes to the churches in Rome, Peter has not yet arrived. This may have transpired in the late 50s or more likely the early A.D. 60s. By then, he is being assisted by Mark in Rome, and notice that there is no mention of Paul at all in 1 Peter. This can be either because Paul has gone back east after being released from house arrest in Rome in A.D. 62, in which case this document is written some time during A.D. 63–64, or more likely it is written after the fire in 64 but before Paul is dragged back to Rome in chains, and so perhaps about A.D. 65–66. This chronology of the later life of Peter is of course speculative, but it meets the facts of the New Testament and certain early church traditions about Peter and Paul being martyred in Rome. It has the added advantage of explaining the silences both in Acts and in 1 Peter, as well as in the Pastorals.

Peter also calls his audience the "elect"—or if you prefer, the chosen—and they are chosen according to the foreknowledge of God, which is a way of saying they were not chosen arbitrarily or without foresight and insight into how they would respond. The term "elect" was used of Israel in the Old Testament [cf. Deut. 30.4; Neh. 1.9; Ps. 147.2; 1 *QS* (*The Community Rule*) 8.6, 11.16].

He proceeds to state that they are chosen by God, by means of or "in" the sanctifying work of the Spirit, and for obedience and sprinkling of the blood of Jesus Christ. Note the reference to Father, Spirit, and Christ in that order in these three phrases about the choosing. The implication is clearly that all three are in some sense God and involved in the divine choosing. The order of reference is interesting—Father, then Spirit, then Son. I would suggest this makes sense if the audience is Jews. As Jews, they already had a relationship with the Father, and indeed with the Spirit of God (see, e.g., 1 Pet. 1.10–11), but the relationship with Jesus Christ came last. Had the author been addressing pagans here, we might have expected a reference to the sprinkling of the blood and the coming to faith in Christ first. This may also explain why Jews in Acts are said to be baptized in the name of Jesus. This was the new thing for them—they already had pledged allegiance to God the Father.

The concept of election and God's foreknowledge is found also in Paul and in other early Jewish sources before that. Here as elsewhere in the New Testament, this terminology functions as a reassurance device for Christians under pressure—don't worry—God has chosen you and he will protect you even through your trials and sufferings. The concept entails the idea that no outside force such as suffering can separate a believer from Christ (cf. Rom. 8.28ff). It will be noted that Peter is talking here about the people who made up the churches in this area, that is, the Christians. He is addressing an elect and select *group*, not an elect individual.

It could, for instance, be argued that Peter (like Paul in Rom. 8) is talking about God choosing a destiny and a way of living for Christians, not God electing individuals to *become* Christians. Clearly the focus here and in Romans 8 is on what Christians must do *after* they believe—that is, persevere, obey until Christ returns. The Greek term **prognōsin**, from which we get the term *prognosis*, makes clear that God's choice is based on His foreknowledge (cf. the other uses in Acts 2.23; Rom. 8.29, 11.2; and only once in the LXX, Judith 9.6).

Notice that not just these Jewish Christians but also Christ himself is said to be the object of God's foreknowledge (1 Pet. 1.20). The emphasis in this language is stressing the divine initiative in choosing and the divine plan of salvation. What is the content of God's foreknowledge? Strictly speaking, of course, God simply knows all things—we call it foreknowledge because from our perspective in time, in relation to us, God knew it beforehand. If 2 Tim. 2.19 is a clue, it refers to God knowing the ones who are his, *in advance*. It is, of course, true that God knows everything *about them* as well, but the focus here and in Romans 8 seems to be on knowing *them*, knowing who would be His.

We can thus conclude that although Peter does not explain, he does mean, first, that God's choosing is on the basis of His knowledge. God knew who would be His and He chose them; He even chose them before they responded and enabled them to respond through the prevenient work of the Spirit in them. Second, if, however, God's choice is based on God's knowledge, then it cannot be said to be arbitrary or capricious. God chose those whom God knew were and would be His, those He knew would respond. There is a clear contradiction to the idea that God's knowledge is based on what He first antecedently willed,

PROGNŌSIN

A Greek term from which the English term "prognosis" is derived and means foreknowledge.

in which case Peter would have said, "He (fore) knew them *because* He had first chosen them." The church father Origen puts it this way: "Foreknowledge means no more than seeing what is inside a person. It is now no longer foreknowledge in effect, but knowledge of something real that has been foreseen. Those to whom Peter is writing were chosen according to foreknowledge."[22]

The point is to reassure all those individual believers that God has a destiny for them and He will protect them, but they must respond in obedience. Indeed, they were saved in the first place due to their responding to the divine initiative. They are only elect as part of the elect group, not in isolation. Peter is addressing a group of people as a group and assumes the collectivistic identity they share. Peter shares with Paul the notion that Christ was the foreknown and destined savior, or as He will be called in 1 Peter, the elect stone, which if believers are joined to Him by faith, they also can become living and elect stones. In other words, this election took place "in Christ," a phrase our author borrows from Paul as well.

It should not be a shock that Peter could speak of his audience of Jewish Christians as sojourners and resident aliens, and that the discussion carries both a theological and a sociological referent. It is true enough that the two key terms can be virtually interchangeable (cf. Gen. 23.4; Ps. 39.12) to refer to foreigners living in a foreign land, but the lack of technical specificity in 1 Peter should not lead us to think that there was no social significance to the terminology. The issue in the social usage is not the "homelessness" of the audience. They certainly had and could own homes as resident aliens. The issue is whether they were treated as citizens by outsiders, and whether they viewed themselves as in some sense marginalized due to their Jewishness and Christian faith, or not. On both counts, they were like foreigners in these provinces.

We notice from 1 Peter, Chapter 1, verse 2, that the purpose of the Spirit's sanctifying work is twofold, and the first half is easier to explain—obedience. This means we are not to see the Spirit's work in the believer as an end in itself as if the experience were the whole purpose. Rather, the experience and cleansing work of the Spirit are to enable and equip the believer to respond positively and obey God. It is unlikely that this phrase refers to the consecration of the messengers who conveyed the Gospel to the audience or even the consecration of the Gospel message itself, as that is not the subject here—rather the chosen ones are. This becomes even more likely an interpretation when we notice the second phrase, "and the sprinkling of blood of Jesus," which seems to refer to Ex. 34.1–11, about which Vincent Taylor says the following:

> In this narrative (Ex. xxxiv. 1–11) a distinction is drawn between the blood sprinkled upon the altar and that which is sprinkled upon the people. The former is the symbol of the people's obedience; it is their offering to God, confirmed by the words: "All the words which Yahweh hath spoken will we do" (cf. the "obedience" in St. Peter's phrase). The latter, the blood sprinkled upon them, is dedicated blood which

> Yahweh has accepted, and the sprinkling means that the people now
> share in the blessings and powers which it represents and conveys. It
> is this blood which is described as "the blood of the covenant."[23]

Thus, in this case, it means that the Spirit works in the believer for the purpose of applying the benefits of the sprinkled blood, that is, presumably cleansing and perhaps forgiveness and reconciliation are in view. It may be that this is a reference to the "obedience of faith," that is, the initial obedient response of faith at which time one receives the benefits of Christ's shed and applied blood. However, more likely it refers to the life of obedience and cleansing that begins at the initial response of faith.

Peter wishes these believers grace and peace in abundance, both of which they will definitely need in abundance to persevere and obey through suffering. Obedience is only possible due to the sanctifying work of the Spirit seems to be the drift of the sentence. We have similar language to what we find at Qumran— "For it is through the Spirit of true Counsel concerning the ways of humankind that all his sins shall be expiated. . . . He shall be cleansed from all his sins by the Spirit of holiness uniting him to his truth. . . . And when his flesh is sprinkled with purifying water and sanctified by cleansing water, it shall be made clean by the humble submission of his soul to all the precepts of God" (1 *QS* 3.6–8). The subject in both texts is sanctification by the Spirit, not consecration or predetermination. I thus agree with L. Goppelt's translation here: "the sanctification accomplished by the Spirit" (i.e., internally, not by water sprinkled on the body).[24] We may compare a similar discussion in Heb. 9.18–21 and Heb. 12.24.

The third clause about Christ probably alludes to Ex. 24.7–8, and therefore has nothing to do with Christian baptism at all. It is referring to the establishment of the covenant—in this case, the new covenant inaugurated by means of the shed blood of Jesus himself—and note here that the language about becoming a royal priesthood and a holy nation in 1 Peter 2.9 is also the language of covenanting (cf. Ex. 19.5–6). The purpose of God's choosing, of the Spirit's sanctifying, and indeed of Jesus' shedding of blood is not merely that the believer may be saved but also that he may obey God's commandments. He has been chosen, empowered, and cleansed so he can do so, says Peter. This emphasis at the end of the sentence sets up the following discourse that is loaded with imperatives. The imperative so very clearly grows out of the indicative of what God has done for the believer, as 1 Pet. 1.2 so aptly demonstrates. That is, God's action is the basis of and enables the believer's response.

The final clause of this opening segment of the discourse involves the traditional Christian or at least Pauline greeting—Grace and peace (cf. Rom.1.7; 1 Cor. 1.3; 2 Cor. 1.2; Gal. 1.3). The unique feature of this particular greeting is the addition of a verb that means "be multiplied" (cf. Dan. 4.37c LXX). Here ends the opening prescript, but already the audience had been encouraged to view themselves as special in various ways, deeply loved by God, and given the power and strength to persevere in the faith despite persecution. In fact, no document in the New Testament offers a more rich and developed understanding of Christian suffering, and how it is like Christ's suffering, than this document.

Because the major themes of this discourse have already been largely announced in the opening salvo just discussed, we can give a more cursory treatment to the rest of the discourse at this point. The exordium, which begins in 1 Peter, chapter 1, verse 3, provides us with the usual attempt to establish rapport with the audience. Peter explains that the new birth has been given to believers as a gift as a result of the resurrection of Jesus, and not only so but a great inheritance is also part of the gift. In the meantime, while Christians are still being persecuted, prosecuted, and executed, God is protecting them and their faith and keeping them on track for "a salvation ready to be revealed in the last time" (1 Pet. 1.5). Notice the future character of this salvation. Their trials should be seen as simply testing and strengthening their faith. Also notice that Peter, like Paul, also refers to salvation that the believer already has (1 Pet. 1.9).

In 1 Peter, chapter 1, verses 10–12, a remarkable claim is made that the Old Testament prophets prophesied by means of the spirit of Christ within them, and so, not surprisingly, prophesied about Christ and his coming sufferings and subsequent glory. Even more surprising is that those prophets were informed that they were not serving themselves but God's people in the eschatological age, namely, Christians that Peter is in part addressing.

The thesis statement, found beginning with 1 Peter, chapter 1, verse 13, makes clear the real intent of this discourse, namely, Peter is calling the audience to holy living and a good witness in spite of the suffering they are undergoing. They are to be holy as God is holy, and this requires ethical discipline and intentionality. They need to remember that they have been ransomed by Christ, God's sacrificial lamb who poured out his life blood as the price of that ransom. The idea here is of buying someone out of slavery—in this case, the bondage to sin—not of paying a ransom to a kidnapper, say Satan. Peter reassures the audience that their obedience to the truth is purifying their inner self regardless of the difficulties their outer selves are experiencing.

1 Pet. 2 reminds the audience of the great heritage they have. Just as Christ is the living stone, so the audience are stones being built into a temple, for God's people are His temple, and they all are to be a holy priesthood, a holy nation. Peter is not talking about a class of priests that we might call clergy; he is speaking about the priesthood of all believers. Even though times are difficult, for the Lord's sake (1 Peter 2.13) the believers are to accept every genuine authority, whether the emperor or the provincial governors. Everyone is to be honored, including the emperor, but the true God is to be feared, or better said revered. The example of Christ who endured abuse, suffering, and even death on the cross is set up as the example of "nonresistance," even for Christian slaves when they suffer unjustly. The motivation for such advice becomes clear in 1 Pet. 3, when Peter urges wives to submit to their husbands so that they might be won

to Christ "when they see the purity and reverence of your lives" (1 Pet. 3.2). Christian husbands are commanded to show honor and consideration to their wives. The repeated refrain of these chapters is be prepared to suffer, but make sure you follow the example of Christ when you do. The difference, of course, is made clear in 1 Peter, Chapter 3, verse 18—Christ's suffering was once for all, and once for all sins, so the suffering of believers does not provide, or need to provide, that kind of benefit. The last portion of 1 Pet. 3 we will say more about when we get to similar material in 2 Peter, but here it will suffice to say that Peter is talking about Christ dying, and rising from the dead, and then going to bear witness on His way to heaven to the fallen angels now incarcerated in a cosmic jail. The angels are those referred to in Gen. 6. The text is not about Christ descending into hell, or bearing witness to the human dead. 1 Pet. 4.6, however, may refer to the dead receiving the Gospel.

Peter continues to deal with the issue of Christian suffering throughout the rest of 1 Pet. 4, and he stresses that Christians must not be reactive but proactive even in such difficult circumstances. For example, they must continue to love one another "for love covers a multitude of sins" (1 Pet. 4.8), they must continue to be hospitable, they must not return abuse when they are abused. Finally, in 1 Pet. 5, Peter exhorts the leaders of the communities he is addressing—the elders—to do their work of shepherding well, not lording it over the believers but rather serving them, and in a way that amounts to seeking personal gain. The Devil may be on the loose, like a lion looking for someone to devour (1 Pet. 5.8), but God's Spirit is on the move, and Christ's return is certain, although the timing is unknown. Therefore, the audience must remain vigilant and steadfast, as the thesis statement suggested.

It is not an accident that it is in this document that the clearest picture is painted of Christ as the Suffering Servant referred to in Isaiah 52–53. Nor is it an accident that Peter himself was looking forward to his own end in all likelihood, for Christ had warned him of this very thing (John 21).[25] Thus, Christ and his apostle Peter, and his various Jewish followers, were united in calling, in election, in suffering, and in glory. Peter calls his audience to count it all as gain that they may get to follow not only in his footsteps in suffering for Christ but also in the very footsteps of Christ who opened not his mouth against his tormentors, even when he was being sacrificed. Indeed, as Luke 23 indicates, he forgave his tormentors from the cross.

IMPLICATIONS

The legacy of Peter to the early church is considerable, and certainly one of the more enduring and endearing contributions he made is this fine letter called 1 Peter. In one sense, because he is addressing highly Hellenized Jewish Christians and some God-fearers, it is doubtful that he would have said much differently had he mainly been addressing Gentile Christians. The fact, however, that he addresses these Jewish Christians as resident aliens in those Roman provinces would have been a not-so-subtle reminder of the tenuousness of their situation and their vulnerability to suffering for their faith, to one extent or another. Regardless of how long they had lived in one or another of the cities in these provinces, their religion did indeed make them stand out in a polytheistic environment and in a world where politics, religion, and social reality were all profoundly intertwined. These converts needed precisely what Peter gives them in this discourse—a theology of suffering, a realizing of their tenuous situation, and a strong hope for their future.

At the same time, 1 Peter absolutely provides its audiences with the sort of instructions about living in, although not being of, the Greco-Roman world that would have been helpful. They were to present no offense to anyone, except the offense of the Gospel, and so they were to honor governing officials, pay their taxes, and "seek the welfare" of their cities to the degree and in ways they could do so.

What we have here is not a baptism of the pagan culture writ large but a call to careful sifting of the culture, affirming those aspects that were good and honorable and could glorify Christ. The tension between appropriate participation in society and inappropriate participation was already a familiar one for Jews before they became Christians, and Peter continues to remind them of holding such things in tension.

Like a good pastor, Peter deals with his audiences where they are, but seeks to help them do a better job of Christianizing their households and social situations so that, at least in the Christian community, a new vision of society could be glimpsed. In the end, this letter, even if only written for Peter by Silas, gives the lie to the suggestion that Peter was not an able theologian and ethicist, not able to offer the same sort of powerful persuasion and guidance we find in the letters of Paul. It is a pity we do not have more such documents from Peter, but then we can be thankful that he stands behind the Gospel of Mark, contributes, as we shall see, a personal testimony to 2 Peter, and authored 1 Peter. Between these sources and the portrayals of Peter in the Gospels, Acts, and other early Christian literature, we are able to take the measure of the man and the enormous contributions he made to planting Christianity throughout the Greco-Roman world.

KEY TERMS

Christianos	Macro-culture
Composite Document	Micro-culture
Diaspora	Prognōsin
Domitian	
Ebionites	

FOR FURTHER READING

Elliott, John H. *A Home for the Homeless: A Sociological Exegesis of 1 Peter, Its Situation and Strategy*. Philadelphia, PA: Fortress Press, 1981.

Harner, P. B. *What Are They Saying about the Catholic Epistles?* New York: Paulist Press, 2004.

Hillyer, N. *1 and 2 Peter, Jude*. Peabody, MA: Hendrickson, 1992.

Trebilco, P. L. *Jewish Communities in Asia Minor*. New York: Cambridge University Press, 1991.

Winter, Bruce W. *Seek the Welfare of the City: Christians as Benefactors and Citizens*. Grand Rapids, MI: Eerdmans, 1994.

Witherington, B. *Letters and Homilies for Hellenized Christians*. Vol. 2, *A Socio-Rhetorical Commentary on 1–2 Peter*. Downers Grove, IL: InterVarsity Press, 2009.

STUDY QUESTIONS

When Jesus said, "Take up your cross and follow me," do you think he meant it literally? What sort of theology of suffering do we find in 1 Peter?

What did you learn about Peter that you did not know before by studying 1 Peter?

Which do you think would have been more difficult—to be a Gentile or a Jewish convert to Christianity in the cities Peter is addressing?

What do you think it means today for Christians to be "in the world" but not "of the world"?

What do you think Peter means when he says believers are "elect" and "a royal priesthood"?

NOTES

1. See John H. Elliott, *A Home for the Homeless: A Sociological Exegesis of 1 Peter, Its Situation and Strategy* (Philadelphia, PA: Fortress Press, 1981), 2.

2. Carl R. Holladay, *A Critical Introduction to the New Testament: Interpreting the Message and Meaning of Jesus Christ* (Nashville, TN: Abingdon Press, 2005), 485.

3. Leonard Goppelt, *A Commentary on 1 Peter* (Grand Rapids, MI: Eerdmans, 1993), 3–41.

4. It could be countered that in 1 Thess. 4.5 Cor. 5.1, and Ephes. 4.17, Paul, speaking to Gentiles, does refer to the audience in distinction from the *ethnesin* (nations). However, Paul's use of the word there is not merely ethnic, it is religious and is rightly translated "pagan" in these places.

5. See Elliott, *A Home for the Homeless*, 45.

6. See S. Mitchell, *Anatolia: Land, Men, Gods in Asia Minor*, vol. 2, *The Rise of the Church* (Oxford: Clarendon Press, 1993), 32.

7. P. L. Trebilco, *Jewish Communities in Asia Minor* (New York: Cambridge University Press, 1991), 32.

8. See B. Witherington, *Acts of the Apostles: A Socio-Rhetorical Commentary* (Grand Rapids, MI: Eerdmans, 1998), 210–213.

9. R. Stark, *Cities of God: The Real Story of How Christianity Became an Urban Movement and Conquered Rome* (San Francisco: Harper Collins, 2006), 78.

10. Remember that at least for many Jews, eating unclean food was a rather normal problem in the Diaspora, which could be remedied after the fact by going through rites of purification. Many Jews apparently would not have seen such eating as some sort of major violation of their Jewish faith and practice.

11. Stark, *Cities of God*, 78.

12. Elliott, *Home for the Homeless*, 80.

13. And my explanation of this is that these documents are both written at about the same point in time—the A.D. mid-60s.

14. Elliott, *Home for the Homeless*, 64–65.

15. C. J. Hemer, "The Address of 1 Peter," *Expository Times* 89 (1978), 239–243.

16. See B. Witherington, *Revelation* (Cambridge: Cambridge University Press, 2003).

17. E. G. Selwyn, *First Epistle of St. Peter* (London: Macmillan, 1946), 38.

18. See B. Witherington, *The Gospel of Mark: A Socio-Historical Commentary* (Grand Rapids, MI: Eerdmans, 2001).

19. On this latter point, see E. Randolph Richard, *Paul and First Century Letter Writing: Secretaries, Composition, and Collection* (Downers Grove, IL: InterVarsity Press, 2004).

20. See P. B. Harner, *What Are They Saying about the Catholic Epistles?* (New York: Paulist Press, 2004), 30.

21. C. K. Barrett, *The Signs of an Apostle* (London: Epworth Press, 1968), 7–8.

22. Quoted in *Ancient Christian Commentary on Scripture*, vol. 11, *James, 1–2 Peter, 1–3 John, Jude*, ed. G. Bray (Downers Grove, IL: InterVarsity Press, 2000), 69.

23. V. Taylor, *Jesus and His Sacrifice: A Study of the Passion-Sayings in the Gospels* (London: Hodder and Stoughton, 1943), 137.

24. Goppelt, *A Commentary on 1 Peter*, 73.

25. See the discussion previously.

This famous coliseum was built by Vespasian and Titus, not Nero. Christians were not persecuted here in the A.D. 60s. (© *Rick Danielson*)

17

The SERMON of the FAMOUS ANONYMOUS PREACHER— HEBREWS

Faith needs a generous and vigorous soul, one rising above all things of sense and passing beyond the weakness of human reasonings. For it is not possible to become a believer otherwise than by raising oneself above the customs of the world. . . . For when a soul finds one that shares its same sufferings, it is refreshed and recovers it breath. This we may see both in the case of faith and in the case of affliction, "that we may be mutually encouraged by each other's faith."

CHRYSOSTOM—*HOM.* 22.1–2 ON HEBREWS

THE AUTHORSHIP, AUDIENCE, AND PROVENANCE OF HEBREWS

It is clear enough that the document we call Hebrews is anonymous and written to a first-century Christian audience. The latest possible date for this composition is the A.D. 90s, for the good reason that Heb. 1.3–15 is clearly alluded to and drawn on in 1 Clem. 36.1–6, a Christian document from the A.D. 90s. One of the telling indicators

at a Glance

Written mainly for Jewish Christians and perhaps some Gentile God-fearers in Rome who were considering abandoning their Christian commitment, the author seems to be writing at a time when Christians in Rome are being persecuted, jailed, and having property taken but not yet executed. No time better suits this scenario than the mid-60s after the fire in Rome of A.D. 64. The author is capable of elegant Greek and has considerable rhetorical skill and knowledge of the Greek Old Testament. He is probably a Diaspora Jewish Christian from the Pauline circle, possibly Apollos, but clearly not one of the original eyewitnesses of Jesus.

PANTAENUS

A Greek theologian and philosopher from the second century who converted to Christianity and was a key thinker and head of the Catechetical School of Alexandria. Pantaenus was a teacher of Clement of Alexandria.

CLEMENT OF ALEXANDRIA

A second-century church father and theologian of the Christian faith who taught in the Catechetical School of Alexandria.

that 1 Clement is directly dependent on Hebrews 1 is not only that Clement quotes Ps. 110.1 as a direct address of God to His son, as at Heb. 1.13, but he also uses the same introductory formula in 1 Clem. 36.1–6 as we find in Heb. 1 (and at Heb. 1.5–13; 3.5–6; 7.17, 21), whereas elsewhere Clement uses other formulae.

Pointing in the direction of the Pauline orbit is the fact that one of our very earliest manuscripts of a portion of the New Testament, Papyrus 46 (p46), which dates to the late second or early third century, places Hebrews among the Pauline letters (in fact, right after Romans and before 1 Corinthians). In the canonical lists of the fourth and fifth century, Hebrews is placed either after the Paulines written to whole churches and before the more personal letters (1 and 2 Timothy, Titus, Philemon) or, more frequently, at the end of the whole Pauline corpus. Origen famously said that "God only knows" who wrote this document (see Eusebius, *Hist. Eccles.* 6.25.13).

The simple title "To the Hebrews" (without any authorial ascription) is first attested at the end of the second century A.D. by **Pantaenus**, **Clement of Alexandria**, and **Tertullian**. The letter, in fact, was first accepted as Scripture (and as Pauline) in the whole Greek and Syrian churches in the third century A.D. and finally in the western part of the Church in the second half of the fourth century A.D., when probably most accepted it as the 14th Pauline letter. Much later, Calvin, **Melancthon**, and **Beza** all regarded it as non-Pauline; and Luther was not even sure it was canonical, much less Pauline. It should thus be clear that Hebrews has traveled a rather rocky road to get into the canon, and even once in the canon, neglect or doubts have plagued it.

Regarding the provenance of the document, we have a small clue in Heb. 13.24, where we hear "those from Italy greet you," and a second clue in Heb. 13.23 that tells of the release of Timothy, surely the same one referred to in the pastoral epistles who is known to the audience of this document. Our author also says that he and Timothy will come to see the audience if possible. If we put these things together with the echoes of earlier Pauline letters in this document, I suggest that this document is written to Christians in Rome (hence the reason Clement knows of and draws on this document already before the end of the first century) by someone who is part of the larger Pauline circle. In support of this conclusion, the phrase "from Italy" in Acts 18.3 refers to those who are outside the Italian peninsula, in this case Priscilla and Aquila, and "Italy" means Rome in that same text as the context makes clear.

Of course, the conjectures have been endless as to (1) why the document is anonymous and (2) who in the larger Pauline circle could have written this document. Certain conjectures can be ruled out, including the notion that Paul wrote this document, although there were many in the early church who assumed so. I say this with some confidence because not only does our author not identify himself either as Paul or as an apostle anywhere in this lengthy sermon, but Heb. 2.3 strongly suggests the author was a second-generation Christian. Notice how the author refers there to the message of salvation first being spoken by the Lord and only later "confirmed *to us by those who heard him.*" Paul *did* claim to hear personally from Jesus, at least on Damascus Road, and he absolutely repudiated the notion that his Gospel about Jesus came to him from others (see Gal. 1.11–12). Our author of Hebrews has been in touch with eyewitnesses, or, more accurately, *ear*witnesses of the Lord, but he was not among them.[1]

But why is this document anonymous? Is it because the author is neither an eyewitness nor an apostle? This hardly seems likely to be the cause because we have other documents in the New Testament attributed to non-eyewitnesses and non-apostles such as Luke's two volumes and the Revelation of the seer John of Patmos. Is it because the author is a woman? This is perhaps possible, but elsewhere women who played important ministry roles are named in Christian circles without any reservation. It is of course possible that the author is so well-known to the audience that there was no need for an identification here. I would suggest, however, that although that may be true, there is another primary reason for the anonymity of this document.

This document, like 1 John, is a homily[2]; in fact, D. J. Harrington has called it "arguably the greatest Christian sermon ever written down."[3] It does not partake of the qualities of a letter except at the very end of the document (Heb. 13.22–25), and these epistolary features are added because this sermon had to be sent to the audience rather than delivered orally to them by the author. In fact, H. Thyen, after studying all the evidence for early Jewish homilies, has argued that Hebrews is the only completely preserved Jewish homily of the period, but this is overlooking 1 John as well as James.[4]

Sermon manuscripts, ancient or modern, do not conform to the characteristics of the beginning of a letter with addressor or addressee expected at the outset. Neither do other rhetorical forms of speaking, and we should make no mistake this document involves rhetoric of considerable skill. It is then an oral document, and in fact a particular type of oral document—a homily in the form of a "word of exhortation" as Heb. 13.22 puts it. It is not an accident that *this is the very same phrase used to characterize Paul's sermon in Acts 13.15.*

Hebrews is not a haphazard discourse but a piece of polished rhetoric that has been variously categorized as either epideictic or deliberative rhetoric, or some combination of the two (see later in this chapter). Here, the point is that the document's authority rests in its contents and not in its author's claims to apostolic authority. To judge from the end of Heb. 13, it is assumed, but not argued, that this author has some authority over his audience, who know very well who he is, and can anticipate a visit from him and Timothy before long. The oral and sermonic character of the document cannot be stressed enough. Here is how one professor of preaching puts it:

TERTULLIAN

Tertullian, a church father of the second to third century, was one of the first Christian theologians and writers to compose documents in the Latin language. He wrote many apologetic works in order to defend the Christian faith against heresy.

MELANCTHON

Philip Melancthon (1497–1560) worked alongside Martin Luther as a German Reformer. Together, they started the Lutheran movement.

BEZA

Theodore Beza, a Frenchman, was involved in the Reformation of the sixteenth century. Beza was mentored by John Calvin.

Hebrews, like all good sermons, is a dialogical event in a mono-logical format. The preacher does not hurl information and arguments at the readers as if they were targets. Rather, Hebrews is written to create a conversation, to evoke participation, to prod the faithful memories of the readers. Beginning with the first sentence, "us" and "we" language abounds. Also, the Preacher employs rhetorical questions to awaken the voice of the listener (see 1.5 and 1.14, for example); raps on the pulpit a bit when the going gets sluggish (5.11); occasionally restates the main point to insure that even the inattentive and drowsy are on board (see 8.1); doesn't bother to "footnote" the sources the hearers already know quite well (see the familiar preacher's phrase in 2.6: "Someone has said somewhere . . ."); and keeps making explicit verbal contact with the listeners (see 3.12 and 6.9, for example) to remind them that they are not only supposed to be listening to this sermon, they are also, by their active hearing, to be a part of creating it. As soon as we experience the rise and fall of the opening words of Hebrews, the reader becomes aware that they are not simply watching a roller coaster hurtling along the rhetorical tracks; they are in the lead car. In Hebrews, the gospel is not merely an idea submitted for intellectual consideration; it is a life- embracing demand that summons to action.[5]

Although we certainly cannot know for sure, a little detective work with Hebrews and other parts of the New Testament leads us to a plausible conclusion as to who is speaking in this document. In favor of Apollos, the well-known preacher from the Pauline circle, are the following factors: First, 1 Cor. 1–4, coupled with Acts 18–19, suggests that Apollos did circulate in Pauline communities and could well have been known to Timothy, as well as to Paul, Aquila, and Priscilla. Second, Acts 18.24–26 tells us that this man came from Alexandria and was learned in the Scriptures. Certainly, the author of this document is learned in the Greek Old Testament, perhaps on a par with Paul's depth of knowledge of the Old Testament. He does not, however, know the Hebrew Old Testament. From the content of this sermon, it is highly likely that our author is also a Jew, but he is apparently a Diaspora Jew who seems to know something of Platonism, not unlike that other famous Jew from Alexandria, Philo.

But what was the focus of Apollos's ministry? To judge from Acts 18 especially, he was someone who evangelized in synagogues, which is to say his focus was on Jews and Gentile synagogue adherents. This theory also helps explain little conundrums about Hebrews. For example, our author speaks of instructions about "baptisms" (plural) at Heb. 6.2. This has often puzzled commentators, but it becomes more self-explanatory in light of Acts 18.25, which tells us that Apollos knew only of the baptism of John, even though he was a Christian, until he met Priscilla and Aquila in Ephesus. Quite naturally, he would have included instructions about the differences between these two forms of baptism for his audiences, having learned the importance of distinguishing them sometime in the A.D. 50s. There is one more factor that needs to be considered. Our author is not merely a local church leader. He can distinguish himself from his congregation and call for their support in Heb. 13.7, 17, and 24, but he can also assume authority over the entire audience, apparently including these leaders (see Heb. 13.17). He seems then to be an itinerant Pauline coworker with authority over local congregations and leaders.

All we have said thus far comports well with the ascription placed on this document: "To the Hebrews," by which is meant "to the Jewish Christians" (cf. 2 Cor. 11.22). We do not have other early Christian documents with this sort of attribution from the first or early second century A.D., so we can hardly conclude that it was a common generic label frequently used by Christians during that period. Especially in view of the increasingly Gentile character of the movement, it is hardly likely that this label would be picked out of thin air even though it was not likely originally a part of this document.

Furthermore, we know that there was a synagogue in Rome quite specifically called a "synagogue of the Hebrews" in the latter half of the first century A.D., and we may note the archaeological evidence from Corinth with the use of the very same phrase, perhaps from the early second century A.D.

Because the term "Hebrews" is quite specifically used in such instances to distinguish Jews from Gentiles, we must assume that whoever put this label on the document was convinced that it was for Jewish Christians. In addition, p46 already has this attribution of this document, which is our oldest document that contains this work.

Although it is true that what we have in Hebrews is Jewish Messianism, not an attack on Judaism or Jewish leaders, nevertheless when one says, "God has made old the first covenant" (Heb. 8.13), it seems clear enough that there is an obsolescence argument in this sermon. Hebrews is not like the epistle of Barnabas, which suggests that non-Christian Israel never had a place among the elect(!). Nevertheless, to admit that the story of Israel has been typologically taken up into a new whole that consummates in the Christ event is to admit that our author has a completionist schema in mind.

One is not complete, perfect, or saved to the uttermost without faith in Christ, according to this sermon. Especially telling in this regard is Heb. 13.10, 15–16, where our author tells us that "we" Christians have an altar from which those who officiate in the tent have no right to eat! And the "him" in Heb. 13.15–16 is Christ, about whom it is said "through Him let us offer a sacrifice of praise to God." Clearly enough, our author distinguishes Christians and their sacrifices from those who still "minister in the tent." Our author even speaks of Moses suffering for Christ (Heb. 11.26), so committed is he to taking up the heritage of Israel into his Christological and typological schema. We must conclude then that this discourse is in no way a polemic directly attacking Judaism but rather a completionist argument. It is an argument directed to Jewish Christians to make clear that going back to non-Christian Judaism is not an option for them any more than going forward into paganism is.

Clearly, the audience of this sermon is in some social distress and under some pressure to renege on their commitments to Christ and his community. Craig Koester chronicles three stages in the social life of this community: (1) proclamation and conversion, which is well in the past; (2) persecution and solidarity, which is in the more recent past; and (3) friction and malaise, which is ongoing.[6] Particularly revealing is Heb. 10.32–34 in which the author stresses "remember those earlier days after you received the light, when you stood your ground in a great contest in the face of suffering. Sometimes you were publicly exposed to insult and persecution, at other times you stood side by side with those who were so treated. You sympathized with those in prison and joyfully accepted confiscation of your property."

There were two periods of suffering for Jewish Christians in Rome in the middle of the first century A.D. The first came at the hands of Claudius in A.D. 49, when various Jews and Jewish Christians were expelled from Rome until the end of Claudius's reign in A.D. 54. As we have pointed out elsewhere, this led to a fragmented and divided congregation of Christians in Rome, to whom Paul wrote Romans, in A.D. 57 or 58, trying to get the Gentile majority of Christians to embrace the Jewish minority there, some of whom had only recently returned to Rome.[7] There had certainly been disenfranchisement of various Jewish Christians and confiscation of their property in A.D. 49, which was a regular legal action when sending someone into exile under Roman law and practice. But our author also knows of some arrests and apparently some martyrdoms, which more probably places us in the later A.D. 60s.

A factor that must count against placing this document as late as the A.D. 70s is that there is no mention of the demise of the temple in this document. The usual rebuttal to this observation is that our author does not mention the temple at all but only the Old Testament institution of the Tabernacle. This is not an adequate response because it would have served our author's obsolescence argument enormously well if he could have said, "and further proof that the Old Testament system has been superseded by the sacrifice and priesthood of Christ can be seen from the recent demise of the temple in Jerusalem." This he does not do, even though our author is clearly a Jew who is passionate about the Old Testament and its institutions, as well as the greater benefit and glory now to be found in Christ's life, death, and advocacy as the heavenly high priest.

Figure 17.1 Circus Maximus: Ruins of the Domus Augustana on the Palatine Hill in Rome, Italy.

Our author speaks not only of confiscation of property but also of suffering and imprisonment. He suggests that only "some" of their number suffered these ill effects, presumably the leaders of the group. In fact, Heb. 13.7 probably alludes to the martyrdom of some of their leaders. No time frame better suits this entire description than sometime after the Neronian crackdown when even Paul and Peter were arrested and executed along with various others in various venues, including the Circus Maximus in Rome, for all to see.

Christians were subject to public ridicule, suffering, torture, confiscation of property, and even execution for being part of a horrible ***superstitio*** (superstition), which was illegal and led to accusations by Nero, in an attempt to find a scapegoat, that they had caused the fire in Rome. Under such conditions, and with Jewish Christians like Peter and Paul being especially singled out for these punishments, it is not at all surprising that various other Jewish Christians were thinking of giving up their commitment to Christ and the Christian community, perhaps even going back to the Jewish synagogue community, which was

SUPERSTITIO

A Greek term from which the English term "superstition" is derived. The term delineated a form of unsanctioned, unauthorized, or illegal religion.

protected as a recognized religion. This rhetorical problem produced this re-markable discourse written to Jewish Christians in Rome that was meant to stave off further defections and apostasy and meant to make clear that, after all, the Old Testament Institutions and rituals offered only the shadow of which Christ and His work are the substance and fulfillment.

Written in the later A.D. 60s after the death of Peter and Paul, and indeed after the pastoral epistles that found Timothy in Ephesus, I suggest this docu-ment was probably produced at about the time the Gospel of Mark was also written to the church in Rome, right at the end or just after the end of Nero's reign of terror. The mention of Timothy is important. He was the chief apostolic delegate of Paul in Ephesus, a community also frequented by Apollos. We have now learned in Heb. 13 that Timothy had been under arrest for some time but had just been released. This must have transpired after Paul wrote 2 Timothy. This again points us to a time not earlier than about A.D. 67–68. Finally, there are the affinities between 1 Peter and Hebrews in various regards. 1 Peter is a docu-ment written from Rome (1 Pet. 5.13) to Jewish Christians outside of Rome before Peter's death in the late A.D. 60s. Yet our writer seems to know of this document. Could he have been one of the recipients of this pastoral letter from Peter or part of a congregation that received it? This is possible.

Weighing all the social factors cumulatively, we can say that we need a social situation where some local Christian leaders have lost their lives in the recent past, but that the current audience being addressed has not yet suffered unto death. That no authorities are addressed or even mentioned by name in this document is perhaps a sign that the community had lost its greatest and most well-known leaders. No time better suits all these factors than the late A.D. 60s. near the end of Nero's reign.

Figure 17.2 Coin of Nero.

THE RHETORIC OF HEBREWS

We are now well served in regard to the rhetorical discussion of Hebrews, and the consensus of opinion is not only that this document reflects macro-rhetoric (the various divisions of a rhetorical speech) and micro-rhetoric, but also that its species is either deliberative or epideictic, or some combination of the two. In other words, there is agreement that it is definitely not judicial or forensic rhetoric, and also that the recognition of individual rhetorical devices, which certainly are plentiful in Hebrews, does not take the full measure of the way our author uses rhetoric.

There are rather clear clues in the document itself as to what sort of rhetoric it is. Consider the following statements in the discourse: (1) Heb. 2.1—"We must pay more careful attention therefore to what we have [already] heard, so that we do not drift away." (2) Heb. 3.1—"Therefore holy brothers and sisters who share in the heavenly calling fix your thoughts on Jesus." (3) Heb. 3.12—"See to it, brothers and sisters, that none of you . . . turns away from the living and true God." (4) Heb. 4.1—"Therefore, since the promise of entering his rest still stands, let us be careful that none of you be found to have fallen short of it." (5) Heb. 4.14—"Therefore . . . let us hold firmly to the faith we profess." (6) Heb. 6.1, 11—"Therefore let us leave the elementary teachings about Christ and go on to maturity . . . we want each of you to show this same diligence to the end . . . we do not want you to become lazy but to imitate those who through faith and patience inherit what has been promised." (7) Heb. 10.22–23, 35—"Let us draw near to God with a sincere heart. . . . Let us hold unswervingly to the hope we profess. . . . Do not throw away your confidence." (8) Heb. 10.39—"We are not of those who shrink back and are destroyed." (9) Heb. 12.1—"Let us throw off everything that hinders . . . and let us run with perseverance the race marked out for us." (10) Heb. 12.14–15—"Let us make every effort to live in peace . . . see to it that no one misses the grace of God." (11) Heb. 13.1—"Keep on loving each other as brothers and sisters." (12) The discourse as a whole is called a word of exhortation in a brief (!) letter (Heb. 13.22). As G. H. Guthrie has rightly pointed out, the alternating back and forth between exposition and exhortation, with the latter being the punch line, provides evidence that this discourse exists *for the sake of the exhortation that directly addresses the issue of concern. Thus, "the expositional material serves the hortatory purpose of the whole work."*[8]

If we look at all of this carefully, it seems very clear that this discourse is not about urging a change in direction or a new policy, nor is the author correcting obvious new problems in belief or behavior. Further, the author is not trying to produce concord or reconciliation in the audience; he is rather trying to shore up their faith in the face of pressure, suffering, and the temptation to defect.

He is trying to confirm the audience in a faith and practice they already have, urging them to stand firm against the dangers of apostasy and wandering away.

He is urging them instead to stay the course with perseverance, continuing to run in the direction they are already going and have been going since they first believed, thus going on to perfection and exhibiting their faith and perseverance. This sort of act of persuasion is surely epideictic in character, appealing to the values and virtues the audience has already embraced in the past. One may likely conclude that for the author of Hebrews, apostasy is a real danger for these believers, and thus it could be argued that one is not eternally secure until securely in eternity.

The focus of the rhetoric in this document is, furthermore, clearly in the present. Our author focuses on what Christ is now doing as the heavenly high priest and what the audience is and ought to continue to be doing in the present. There is also the appeal to continue to imitate the forbears in the faith and Christ himself. The appeal to imitation can be found in either deliberative or epideictic rhetoric; in the latter case, it is an appeal to continue to imitate the models they already know and have looked to. When we couple all this with the doxological beginning of the discourse in Heb. 1 and the worship climax in Heb. 12.18–27, it seems clear that this discourse maintains an epideictic flavor throughout. Most rhetorically adept homilies, in any case, fall into the category of epideictic rhetoric.

Also comporting with this conclusion is that we do not have formal arguments in this discourse but rather one long act of persuasion that involves comparisons, enthymemes (incomplete syllogisms), repetition, amplification, use of catchwords, and a toggling between exposition of texts and application. Furthermore, after the exordium (an attempt to make the audience more open to what follows) in Heb. 1.1–4, it was not necessary to have a *narratio* (narration) or *propositio* (thesis statement) because in effect, there is only one long argument or act of persuasion in various parts throughout the discourse. The **encomium** of faith in Heb. 11 does not stand out from its context as if it were some sort of digression or different type of rhetoric, or a rhetorical anomaly in the midst of a nonrhetorical document. Rather, it fits in nicely with the remainder of the homily that also exhorts the audience to specific aims. Also comporting with the conclusion that this is epideictic rhetoric is the enormous amount of honor and shame language used in this discourse to make sure that the audience will continue to be faithful in their beliefs, behavior, and life trajectory, not slipping back into pre-Christian forms of religion, in this case non-Christian Jewish ones.

In a rhetorical encomium, there are standing aspects of a person's life that will be praised—noble birth, illustrious ancestors, education, fame, offices held and titles, wealth, physical virtues (e.g., strength), moral virtues, and death. Without question, many of these topics surface in the praise of Jesus in this sermon. We may also point out that the comparisons (*synkrisis*) we have in this discourse follow the conventions of epideictic rhetoric in regard to such comparisons, for example, between Jesus and the angels, or Jesus and Melchizedek,

ENCOMIUM

A rhetorical style in which certain aspects of one's life are praised. Elements that are typically praised are noble birth, notable ancestry, titles, offices that are held, economic status, and morality among others.

or Jesus and Moses—or the believers' current life and what will be the case if they commit apostasy or go in a retrograde motion into a form of religion that will not save them. The function of such comparisons in an epideictic discourse is to demonstrate the superiority of that one person or thing that is being praised (see Aristotle, *Rhetoric,* 1.9.38–39; *Rhet. Alex.* 1441a27–28). Andrew T. Lincoln ably sums up how "comparison" functions in Hebrews:

> *Synkrisis* [is] a rhetorical form that compares representatives of a type in order to determine the superiority of one over another. It functions as a means of praise or blame by comparison and makes the comparison in terms of family, natural endowments, education, achievements and death. In Hebrews various earlier figures or types of Christ are seen as lesser by comparison with him and family relations (Christ as divine Son), education (learning perfection through suffering), and death (the achievement of Christ's sacrificial death) all feature in the comparison. This sort of argument structures the discourse because, as in an encomium, a discourse in praise of someone, the *synkrisis* is used for the purpose of moral exhortation. So in Hebrews, the comparison of angels and the Son, of Moses and Christ, of Aaron and Christ, of the Levitical priesthood and Christ, of the old covenant and the new covenant, is in each case followed by paraenesis.[9]

In this discourse, it is Christ's superiority and the superiority of faith in Christ and following his example that are being praised, and this is contrasted with falling away, defecting, avoiding shame, and suffering. Christ is the model of despising shame and maintaining one's course in life faithfully to the end, and indeed of being "perfected" through death—sent directly into the realm of the perfect.[10] Although the emphasis in this discourse is mainly on that which is praiseworthy, our author does not hesitate to illustrate blameworthy behavior; for example, he highlights the unfaith and apostasy of the wilderness-wandering generation (Heb. 3.7–19). In fact, rhetorical comparison can be said to be the major structuring device for the whole discourse right to its climax in the peroration at the end of Heb. 12 as our author exalts the better mediator, the better sacrifice, the better covenant, the better example of faith, and the better theophany—all by means of rhetorical comparison not with something that is bad but rather only with something that is less glorious or adequate or able to save people.[11]

One more thing can be stressed at this point. Epideictic rhetoric characteristically would use a lot of picture language, that is, visual rhetoric so that "you seem to see what you describe and bring it vividly before the eyes of your audience" and thus "attention is drawn from the reasoning to the enthralling effect of the imagination" (Longinus, *On the Sublime*, 15.1, 11). Epideictic rhetoric persuades as much by moving the audience with such images and so enthralling them, catching them up in love, wonder, and praise. The appeal to the emotions is prominent in such rhetoric, stirred up by the visual images.

Consider, for example, the beginning of the peroration in Heb. 12.22, containing the last harangue, the final appeal to the deeper emotions of these Diaspora Jewish Christians who have been pressured and persecuted and, in many cases, may have never had the joy of making the pilgrimage to Mt. Zion: "But you have come to Mt. Zion, to the heavenly Jerusalem, the city of the living God. You have come to thousands upon thousands of angels in joyful assembly, to the church of the first born, whose names are written in heaven. You have come to God . . . to Jesus the mediator."

These are Christians who, like the author, have likely never seen or heard Jesus in person. But now before their eyes is portrayed the climax of their faith pilgrimage, the same sort of climax that Jesus reached when he died, rose, and then ascended into heaven. And the discourse ends with worshipping God with reverence and awe, a clearly epideictic topic meant to create pathos (emotion). Our author knows very well what he is doing in this epideictic discourse, and he does it eloquently and brilliantly from start to finish. He has made Jesus and true faith so attractive that it would be shameful to turn back now and shameful to defect. Rather, he urges and stirs them up to carry on with the beliefs and behaviors they have already embraced. Following is a fuller breakdown of the structure of this sermon.

RHETORICAL OUTLINE OF HEBREWS

Exordium/Introductory Remarks 1.1–4   Partial revelation in the past, full revelation in the son

PROBATIO/ARGUMENTS PRO

SECTION	THEME	OLD TESTAMENT TEXT	PARENESIS
Part One (1.5–14)	Christ's Superiority	Catena (1.5–13)	2.1–4
Part Two (2.5–18)	You Crowned Him	Ps. 8	(2.6–8)
Part Three (3.1–4.13)	Today	Ps. 95 (3.7–11)	3.12–4.13
Part Four (4.14–7.28)	Priest Forever	Ps. 110 (5.6)	4.14–16; 5.11–6.12
Part Five (8.1–10.31)	New Covenant	Jer. 31 (8.8–12)	10.19–29
Part Six (10.32–12.3)	By Faith	Hab. 2 (10.37–38)	12.1–2
Part Seven (12.3–17)	Don't Lose Heart	Prov. 3 (12.5–6)	12.3–16

PERORATIO/FINAL EMOTIONAL APPEAL

Pilgrim's End	12.18–29	Theophany at Sinai texts (Ex. 19; Deut. 4.9, 31; Hag. 2.6)
Final Summary Exhortation	13.1–21	
Epistolary Closing	13.22–25	

There is overlap, repetition, amplification, and reinforcement in the argument, but this is precisely what one would expect in an epideictic discourse, as we will see with the case of 1 John. One of the interesting differences between these two sermons is that 1 John is topically driven, not textually driven, and so is less of an expository sermon in that sense, whereas Hebrews is certainly textually oriented and is far more expository in character. We begin to see the remarkable range of the Christian rhetoric of praise and blame in 1 John and Hebrews; and in both cases, the sermons are directed in the main, if not almost exclusively, to Jewish Christians in two different major cities in the empire (Ephesus and Rome) that were seedbeds for the early Christian movement.

We need to keep steadily in view that the function of praise and blame of any topic is to motivate the audience to continue to remember and embrace their core values (involving both ideology and praxis) and avoid slipping into blameworthy beliefs and behaviors (see Aristotle, *Rhetoric,* 1.9.36; Quintilian, *Inst. Or.* 3.7.28; *Rhet. Ad Herrn.* 3.8, para. 15). In other words, even when using complex concepts and ideas, the ultimate aim of the rhetoric is practical and ethical in character. The practicality of the document, however, does not mean that the document lacks profundity.

CORE SAMPLINGS

Hebrews 12.1 turns to the more direct form of exhortation, based on what has just been set forth as examples in Hebrews 11. The climax of the "hall of faith" chapter in Hebrews 11 actually comes here at the beginning of Hebrews 12, where Christ is depicted as the paramount example of true faith and faithfulness. It was typical of eulogies or encomia to conclude with an exhortation to imitate the person who was the subject of the encomium. The use of "consequently" in Heb. 12, verse 1, shows that what follows is based on what has come before in Heb. 11 and that these verses should never have been separated from Heb. 11 by a chapter division.

Although our author has mentioned numerous examples of faith in Heb. 11, he has purposely left till last the most important of all—Jesus the trailblazer/pioneer and completer/perfecter of faith, a subject that he introduced already at Heb. 2.10. Jesus himself suffered greatly for the sake of the joy he saw beyond the suffering, indeed, as much or more than any of the previous examples. Like the patriarchs, then, he lived in forward motion looking forward to the fulfillment of the promises later, which is here called the joy set before him. Thus, finally, it will be Jesus who is set forth as the ultimate and final example of faith in this argument. Here, Christology and exhortation are truly wed in the closing argument of the homily, and notice that athletic imagery unites the entire subsection of Heb. 12.1–13 (cf. especially verses 1–3 and 12–13). But the metaphors shift here, the marathon has entered the stadium for the finish of the ordeal, and now the faithful are asked to sprint, following the example of Jesus and in the presence of the "witnesses" who have run before them and are now in the stands, presumably cheering them on.

MARTUS

A Greek term often translated as "witness." It is the term from which we get the English word "martyr."

The word *martus* ("witness") has an interesting history. Originally, it had the sense of someone who saw something and so a spectator at a game, or someone who bore witness to something they saw. But in the course of time, it came to have the more technical and specifically religious meaning of one who died for one's faith and thereby witnessed its validity.[12] It is the Greek word from which we get the word *martyr*. The real question is, where do we stand in the development of the word when our author uses it? In view of the fact that Heb. 12.1 is retrospective, and our author has just given us a long list of those who have died for their faith and will give us one more in the case of Jesus, it is not impossible that the Greek word already has the more specialized meaning of those who have died for their faith.

But in view of the running metaphor, our author may be thinking of a crowd of spectators watching the race. On the other hand, who are these spectators? They are those who have passed on, being faithful witnesses to God. Our author says there is a great cloud of these witnesses. Thus, he wants his audience to see themselves as surrounded by friendly and encouraging witnesses from the hall of faith, not hostile and violent neighbors wishing them ill. The idea is perhaps being surrounded by a multitude, much like a fog or cloud engulfs everything that goes into it. Here sin is seen as a hindrance to the successful running of the race of faith.

The running metaphor begins and ends this section (Heb. 12, verses 1–2, 12–13). We picture the runner casting off all weights, excess clothing (of course, in antiquity, especially in the Greek games, they ran naked). But this is a metaphor for spiritual endurance until one reaches the goal, and so the burdens to be put off are especially sin that so easily tempts and besets the believer. The believer is to concentrate on the task at hand and run the course that lies before him with perseverance, showing endurance in the face of opposition or competition.

The verb for looking here is an interesting one. It means a definite looking away from other things and a fixing one's eyes on only the goal or one object. The image is the familiar one, for if runners look over their shoulders or are distracted, they may well lose the race. They must fix their gaze on the finish line and ignore all distractions, however interesting. Here, believers are to fix their eyes on the one who has already run this race of faith from start to finish successfully, persevering to the very finish line, namely, Jesus. Notice the use of the human name of God's son and the reference to His human activities. He is seen here as the first faithful one to actually achieve faith's goal, and hence He is the paradigm. The verb here literally means looking away from everything else and fixating one's gaze on one particular object. As C. Koester says, it was common for a runner in a Greek race to fix his gaze on the one sitting in the seat of honor that would be halfway down the track in a special box near to the field.[13] This comports with the earlier imagery of Jesus seated in the seat of honor on the right hand of God the Father.

In regard to the meaning of the phrase "Jesus the originator/trailblazer and finisher or completer of faith," here we note that the word *our* is nowhere to be found in the text. Rather, Jesus is seen as the primal and primary example of faith and how to run the race of faith and ignore the shame and taunting heaped on the runner (cf. Heb. 13.13); and as such, Esau in Heb. 12, verses 16–17, becomes the counterexample of how not to go forward. Jesus fought the good fight and finished the course and so kept faith with the Father's plan for his life—obedient even to death.

Only here, in dramatic fashion, does our author use the word *cross* in this discourse to refer to Jesus' suffering and death. As such, Jesus is being held up here to his audience as the great example of persevering faith. Thus, he is called the originator/trailblazer and finisher/perfecter of faith. Here alone in Scripture do we have the Greek noun meaning perfecter/completer. He is the first and last word on the subject; he is the primary and final example of it. "When we see the disciplined, loving, strong, merciful, and faithful way that Jesus ran the race, we are motivated to lace up our running shoes, to grasp the baton, and to sprint for the finish line."[14] What is seen as being brought to perfection in Jesus here is *faith,* not believers, or even Jesus himself in this case. He is the perfecter of faith, just as He is its pioneer, boldly going to the finish line that no one before Him had yet reached. "The predicates express the conviction that from first to last Jesus exercised faith in an essential sense and brought it to a triumphant conclusion."[15]

Thus, our author in Heb. 12, verse 2b, shows that Jesus was that good runner, who, regardless of the obstacles and opposition endured to the end, even endured the cross, thinking nothing of the shame. Despising shame here is much the same as despising public opinion of one's actions. Now it may be our author is thinking of what was shameful from a Jewish perspective—being naked in public, which not coincidentally was the normal condition of both runners and those hanging on crosses. In fact, Cicero calls the cross "the tree of shame" (*Defense of Rabirius* 4.13).

We must bear in mind that it would be a major reversal of opinion and a rhetorical coup if one could turn shame about a crucifixion into a noble death. "A shameful death was the most feared of evils among many ancients since it left one with no opportunity to regain one's honor. The last word on one's life was a judgment of worthlessness" (cf. Epictetus, *Diss.* 2.1.13).[16] There was a reward for Christ's perseverance to the end. He would have the joy of becoming the author of our salvation, and for himself of regaining his rightful seat beside the Father. These were prizes worth looking forward to, working for, even dying for, and so Jesus did. At the end of Heb. 12, verse 2, this later joy of exaltation is specifically mentioned.

In Heb. 12, verse 3, we are told that Jesus endured the hostility of sinners so that we would not grow faint in faith or be worn out by life's trials. He did it so believers might make it as well, so that believers might persevere as well. It is not just that he set an example, it is that he enabled believers to follow such an example by giving them the Spirit and power to persevere. Chrysostom, an early Church Father, indicates the way Christ's example is being used here: "If then he who was under no necessity of being crucified, was crucified for our sake, how much more is it right that we should endure all things nobly! . . . But what is 'despising the shame'? He chose, he means, that ignominious death. For suppose that he died, some wonder why he should die so ignominiously? For no other reason than to teach us to make no account of glory from the human sphere" (*Homilies on Hebrews* 28.4).

Figure 17.3 Abraham Sacrificing Isaac, relief on portal of Saint Petronius Basilica in Bologna, Italy.

IMPLICATIONS

For many readers of the New Testament, the sermon called Hebrews comes as something of a surprise. All of a sudden, one is launched into ancient debates about angels and Christ and Moses and Abraham, and priests and tabernacles and sacrifices, complete with Scripture citations in abundance. The early Jewish atmosphere of this book is off-putting to some Christians not used to swimming in a Scripture-saturated lake, and a good-sized lake at that.

Sometimes, this book has mistakenly been read as an example of what goes wrong when one tries to amalgamate Platonic thought with Jewish afterlife teaching. In fact, the character of this sermon has more to do with its epideictic rhetorical nature than with the vagaries of Platonic speculation about worlds of shadow and substance, with heaven being the blueprint of temples and tabernacles on earth. Our author has his feet firmly planted on earth and is looking forward to the return of Christ and the great transformation that will happen to the world at that juncture. But like a good apocalyptic thinker, he believes that the realities that are in heaven will one day be on earth when Christ returns. In the meantime, he is basically urging his audience to keep the values they already embrace, including keeping the Christian faith and following the examples of all those in the "hall of faith" in Heb. 11–12, especially Christ, the climactic example of faith and faithful living to the end.

Our erudite author presents us with an image of Christ as a heavenly high priest interceding for the faithful in heaven, which we have almost no hint of elsewhere in the New Testament, and his message to his Jewish Christians in Rome is "better than." Although the Mosaic covenant was good, it is "becoming old," and is being replaced with the new covenant that is "better" in so many ways. Christ has provided a once-and-for-all sacrifice, for all sins, for all persons, for all times. Because this is so, Christians no longer need priests, temples, or sacrifices, other than the sacrifices of prayer and praise and self they are to always offer to God. And the good news is that Christians do not have to keep paying for their sins; and because of this, they can enter into a divine rest and peace about life and living that only God in Christ can offer. It is a great pity that this book has been so neglected by the church through the centuries. Perhaps in this century, this powerful sermon will finally receive the loud *amen* it deserves from its hearers.

Figure 17.4 *Transfiguration* by Giovanni Bellini.

KEY TERMS

Beza	Melancthon
Clement of Alexandria	Pantaenus
Encomium	*Superstitio*
Martus	Tertullian

FOR FURTHER READING

deSilva, D. *Perseverance in Gratitude: A Socio-Rhetorical Commentary on the Epistle "to the Hebrews."* Grand Rapids, MI: Eerdmans, 2000.

Hagner, D. A. *Encountering the Book of Hebrews: An Exposition.* Grand Rapids, MI: Baker, 2002.

Lincoln, A. T. *Hebrews. A Guide.* London: T+T Clark, 2006.

Witherington, B. *Letters and Homilies for Jewish Christians: A Socio-Rhetorical Commentary on Hebrews, James and Jude.* Downers Grove, IL: InterVarsity Press, 2007.

STUDY QUESTIONS

Why do you think this document is anonymous?

What kind of sermon is Hebrews? Have you ever heard a sermon quite like this one?

Why is it so important to the author to stress how much better the new covenant and Christ are compared to Moses and the Mosaic covenant?

Do you believe the author is right in being concerned that some of his Christian audience are in real danger of committing apostasy by renouncing Christ?

What do you make of the image of Christ as a heavenly high priest, having offered a perfect sacrifice on the cross and now dwelling in the heavenly sanctuary, where he intercedes with the Father on our behalf?

NOTES

1. See the discussion by K. Schenck, *Understanding the Book of Hebrews: The Story Behind the Sermon* (Louisville, KY: Westminster John Knox Press, 2003), 89.

2. D. A. Hagner, *Encountering the Book of Hebrews: An Exposition* (Grand Rapids, MI: Baker, 2002), 29.

3. D. J. Harrington, *What are They Saying about the Letter to the Hebrews?* (New York: Paulist Press, 2005), 1.

4. H. Thyen, *Der Stil der judisch-hellenistichen Homilie* (Gottingen, Germany: Vandenhoeck and Ruprecht, 1955), 106.

5. T. Long, *Hebrews: Interpretation: A Bible Commentary for Teaching and Preaching* (Louisville, KY: Westminster John Knox Press, 1997), 6.

6. C. R. Koester, *Hebrews* (New York: Doubleday, 2001), 64–72.

7. B. Witherington with D. Hyatt, *Paul's Letter to the Romans: A Socio-Rhetorical Commentary* (Grand Rapids, MI: Eerdmans, 2004).

8. G. Guthrie, *The Structure of Hebrews. A Text-Linguistic Analysis* (Grand Rapids, MI: Baker, 1998), 143.

9. A. T. Lincoln, *Hebrews: A Guide* (London: T+T Clark, 2006), 19.

10. D. deSilva, *Perseverance in Gratitude: A Socio-Rhetorical Commentary on the Epistle "to the Hebrews"* (Grand Rapids, MI: Eerdmans, 2000), 34–35.

11. As is so clearly demonstrated by C. F. Evans, *The Theology of Rhetoric: The Epistle to the Hebrews* (London: Dr. Williams's Trust, 1988).

12. For a detailed word study, see B. Witherington, *Revelation* (Cambridge: Cambridge University Press, 2003), 67–68.

13. Koester, *Hebrews*, 522.

14. Long, *Hebrews*, 129.

15. Long, *Hebrews*, 129.

16. deSilva, *Perseverance in Gratitude*, 432.

of Israel that I am bound with this chain." ²¹ They
replied, "We have received no letters from Judea
about you, and none of the brothers coming here
has reported or spoken anything evil about you.
²² But we would like to hear from you what you think,
for with regard to this sect we know that everywhere
²³ it is spoken against." ❡ After they had set a day to
meet with him, they came to him at his lodgings in
great numbers. From morning until evening he explained the matter to them, testifying to the kingdom
of God and trying to convince them about Jesus
both from the law of Moses & from the prophets.
²⁴ Some were convinced by what he had said while
others refused to believe. ²⁵ So they disagreed with
each other; and as they were leaving, Paul made
one further statement: "The Holy Spirit was right
in saying to your ancestors through the prophet
Isaiah,
²⁶ 'Go to this people and say,
    You will indeed listen, but never understand,
    and you will indeed look, but never perceive.
²⁷ For this people's heart has grown dull,
    and their ears are hard of hearing,
        and they have shut their eyes;
    so that they might look with their eyes,
    and listen with their ears,
    and understand with their heart and turn —
    and I would heal them.'
²⁸ Let it be known to you then that this salvation of
God has been sent to the Gentiles; they will listen."
³⁰ ❡ He lived there two whole years at his own expense
and welcomed all who came to him, ³¹ proclaiming
the kingdom of God and teaching about the Lord
Jesus Christ with all boldness & without hindrance.

YOU WILL BE
MY WITNESS
IN JERUSALEM
AND IN ALL
JUDEA AND
SAMARIA AND
TO THE ENDS
OF THE EARTH

The great cloud of witnesses as depicted in the St. John's Bible. *"You Will Be My Witness,"* Donald Jackson, Copyright 2002,
The Saint John's Bible, *Order of Saint Benedict, Collegeville, Minnesota, USA. All rights reserved.*

A BELOVED SERMON and TWO ELDERLY LETTERS — 1–3 JOHN

IN THE CANON OF THE NEW TESTAMENT, the Johannine epistles are included in the cluster of documents known as the catholic or general epistles. But what accounts for the ordering and arrangement of these epistles? The collection begins with James, attributed to a brother of Jesus, and it ends with Jude, attributed to another brother of Jesus. We can assume then that the principle of organization of the entire collection was not based on the author's closeness of relationship to Jesus. John Painter suggests that perhaps the collection is arranged, at least for the most part, on the basis of who were the pillar apostles in the early church—James, Peter, and John (see Gal. 2).[1] This may be correct because the order of these documents is indeed James; 1 and 2 Peter; then 1, 2, 3 John; and concluding with Jude. But it also appears that originally there were smaller collections put together because the Johannine letters, like the Pauline letters, are basically arranged according to length.

Consisting of 2,137 words, 1 John is the longest of all the catholic or general epistles, and 2 John (245 words) and 3 John (219 words) are the two shortest documents in the New Testament. Also, 2–3 John are, in length and to some degree in character, the New Testament documents most like ancient letters of the period. When these

at a Glance

The three documents called the Johannine epistles are of varied origins and character. 1 John is actually not a letter, but a sermon, and can be attributed to the Beloved Disciple, who was also responsible for the materials found in the Gospel of John. However, 2–3 John are likely by John the Elder, a different person, who may also have been responsible for collecting and assembling the memoirs of the Beloved Disciple into a Gospel. These documents were written for Jewish Christian congregations in the Ephesus area, probably in the A.D. 80s.

three documents were combined with James, Jude, and 1 and 2 Peter, they were placed after three out of four of these documents, *even though* 1 John was slightly longer than James or 1 Peter.

This means that length itself was not the sole or primary criterion that determined the ordering of these documents in the canon. In other words, there were several different criteria in play that determined the arrangement of books in the canon. Even authorship itself was not the dominant criterion. This is clear from the separation of these Johannine letters from both the fourth Gospel and the Book of Revelation, even though it was widely believed during the canonizing period that at least the fourth Gospel and 1 John were by the same author.

That there is some sort of relationship between theses epistles and the Gospel of John is the opinion of the vast majority of New Testament scholars, although what precisely that relationship is, and how we should answer the chicken-or-egg question (which came first—the Gospel or the letters?), is not agreed on by scholars. We must consider these issues together at this juncture.

THE AUTHORSHIP ISSUES

It is my view that the Beloved Disciple is a different person from John of Patmos, the Beloved Disciple is responsible for writing 1 John, and he is the *source* of the material in the fourth Gospel—although those memoirs were collected, edited, and made available to the community of faith by another person, whom I will call the *Fourth Evangelist.* He is probably the same person as John the Elder (which might account for the name of the Gospel), and he may also be the same person as John the prophet of Patmos.[2] In other words, I think we must reckon with *two if not three* writers involved in the composition of the final form of the Johannine corpus (counting Revelation as part of the Johannine literature), although one of them, John the Elder, plays the role of a collector and final editor of the memoirs of the Beloved Disciple in the fourth Gospel. None of these conclusions, however, call for the supposition that we are dealing with a Johannine *school* of some sort. Neither Revelation nor the letters suggest anything of the kind; and it is likely that no more than two persons were involved with the Gospel—the Beloved Disciple and the collector and editor of the material, John the Elder, the man Papias once encountered.

Although it is possible that John of Patmos might be John son of Zebedee, this seems unlikely because he identifies himself as a seer/prophet in Rev. 1, and in 2–3 John as an elder, rather than as either an apostle or one of the original twelve (see Chapter 20). It is unlikely, as we have seen in our study of the fourth Gospel, that the Beloved Disciple is the same person as John son of Zebedee either, being rather an eyewitness disciple of the Judean portion of

Jesus' ministry; and it seems likely he is the same person as Lazarus, who is the first person called "the one whom Jesus loved" in the Gospel of John (Jn. 11.3), although this can be debated.

The letters themselves (1–3 John) are formally anonymous, by which I mean that they do not identify the author by name *within* the course of the documents themselves, and so these documents do not raise the issue of pseudonymity (a falsely attributed author) in the way the pastorals or 2 Peter do. At some point, these documents were attributed to someone named John, although which John was not specified; and in fact, there was no little debate about whether John the Elder was a different person from John son of Zebedee, with various early church fathers thinking this was the case.

Because the author of 2–3 John identifies himself as *ho* **presbyteros***,* which could mean either "the elder" or "the old man" or even "the older man" (of two Johns?), even as late as the time of Eusebius in the fourth century A.D., 2–3 John were debated books regarding whether they should be included within the canon (see Eusebius, *Hist. Eccles.* 3.24.17, 3.25.2–3). The fourth Gospel and 1 John were not disputed in this way, it being assumed by most that they were penned by John the Apostle. I suggest that John the Elder is the author of 2–3 John, and he is the one who edited the fourth Gospel as well. The author of 1 John, however, was the Beloved Disciple.

In fact, well after the time of Eusebius, we hear Bede in the eighth century still saying this about 2–3 John:

> Some think that this and the following letter are not of John the Apostle but of a certain John the Presbyter, whose tomb has been pointed out in Ephesus up to the present day. Indeed, Papias, a hearer of the apostles and bishop in Hierapolis, frequently mentions him in his works. But now the general consensus of the church is that John the Apostle also wrote these letters.
> —*Expos. on the Second Epistle of John*[3]

The problem with this entire debate is that it is hard to deny that the vocabulary and style of the two "letters" is similar enough to suggest a common author, and at the same time there is enough similarity between the Gospel and especially 1 John to suggest a common author or source for those two documents as well. The Book of Revelation clearly enough was not seen, and should not be seen, as having the same style and literary character as these other Johannine documents. I would attribute what little evidence there is of similar vocabulary shared by 2–3 John with 1 John and the Gospel to the influence of the Beloved Disciple on John the Elder. Here then is a chart of those who created the Johannine literature, noting that *they are all involved in the same Jewish Christian communities in Asia Minor.*

PRESBYTEROS

A Greek term that may mean either "the elder," "the old man," or even "the older man."

Figure 18.1 Ephesus was the great jewel of Asia Minor, and probably the city where the Johannine community had several congregations. (© Mark R. Fairchild, Ph.D.)

Beloved Disciple	John the Elder	John of Patmos
Lazarus, who wrote down his memoirs found in the fourth Gospel and wrote 1 John	Who wrote 2–3 John and collected and edited the fourth Gospel after the death of the Beloved Disciple	A prophet who wrote Revelation to Johannine churches (perhaps he is also John the Elder)

As with the Pastoral Epistles, we have a genre issue to consider as well, for 1 John is not a letter at all but rather a homily or rhetorical exhortation, whereas 2–3 John are the documents in the New Testament that are most like other ancient letters in length and scope. Either of those documents could have fit on one sheet of papyrus, and 3 John is in fact the shortest document in the New Testament.

There has to have been some good reason why such brief letters as 2–3 John have been preserved and indeed included within the canon. Only 3 John is a personal or private letter to an individual, whereas 2 John is written to a congregation at some distance from the author. It is not an accident that only 3 John mentions the names of persons the author is concerned about. It alone is a truly personal letter in this collection. The letters to Timothy and Titus, with the exception of 2 Timothy, are more like pastoral letters from an apostle to his apostolic delegates.

The issue of the style of the Johannine epistles is a complicated one when it comes to the Greek because it was not always true that "style reveals the person" in that world. L. T. Johnson makes this point very effectively:

> In the Hellenistic world, the rhetorical ideal was expressed by . . . "writing in character" whether in speeches, drama, or narrative. The same ideal applied to the writing of letters in antiquity. Style was a matter of being rhetorically appropriate to circumstances and followed definite conventions. . . . In Paul's time [and later], style was less a matter of personal expressiveness and more a matter of social presence and rhetorical craft. Writers of such differing gifts as Luke the Evangelist and Lucian the Satirist display a dazzling variety of "styles" that are controlled by a single writer in the service of "writing in character."[4]

Whereas what Johnson says is true for writers with considerable skill in writing Greek such as Luke, the truth is that the Greek of the epistles and the Gospel of John do not display a dazzling array of styles or skills. It is rather simple and straightforward Greek, sometimes even wooden Greek (particularly in the epistles), the sort one would give to first-year Greek students to read. By the same token, it is more than sufficiently different from the Greek of Revelation to have been noticed by the earliest commentators on Revelation, especially Dionysius of Alexandria.

In my view, it does not appear that the style of the Johannine epistles would place these letters into the category of an assumed higher style chosen for some particular rhetorical aim or end. That there is rhetoric, and indeed rhetoric of some finesse, involved in these letters is clear. What is not the case is that they should be seen as examples of "speech in character" as if the writer were speaking in someone else's voice.

No, the "Elder" is here speaking for himself quite clearly and directly. This John sees himself as an authority figure who can address both local and more remote congregations in an authoritative way. It is my view that these letters provide us with a window in time on the author and his view of his audiences *probably sometime in the* A.D. *80s, addressing congregations that are experiencing some serious internal difficulties*. These communities are already familiar with many of the Gospel traditions later enshrined in the fourth Gospel, perhaps in the early A.D. 90s. The problem is that the Elder does not seem to have the same authority the Beloved Disciple did, and he is having difficulty dealing with a local leader at some distance from him. At a still later date, John of Patmos, who may also be John the Elder, was to address some of these same communities, drawing on the Johannine tradition in some respects, but making his own modifications, in the middle A.D. 90s and during the reign of Domitian.

Here will be a good point to say more about the author of 2–3 John as *presbyteros*. First, it does not seem likely that we should take this term in a comparative sense (the older of two or more persons) because we find no such comparisons in these documents. The term then is used in a positive rather than a comparative sense. Second, as R. E. Brown points out, this man seems to disavow the teaching office associated with local church elders at 1 Jn. 2.27.[5] If he was the elder in a local congregation, then why would he assume he had the authority to address congregations even in a remote location some distance from his own? By the same token, if he was one of the Twelve, why would he never suggest this?

Notice by contrast that the author of 1 John is an eyewitness of some sort, but the elder in 2–3 John does not make any such claim. At the same time, the pastorals tell us that elders could be appointed over whole areas, such as a city, and I suspect this is what we are dealing with in 2–3 John. So once more, Papias was right to call the man John the Elder. Unlike the Beloved Disciple, he is neither an eyewitness nor an apostle but an appointed person authorized probably by the Beloved Disciple himself after he wrote the sermon called 1 John and before he passed away.

THE SOCIAL CONTEXT OF THE JOHANNINE EPISTLES

Having said this much, it is a good time to discuss the social context of these Johannine letters. It would appear, if Rev. 2–3 is a clue, that 1–3 John were all written for congregations in western Asia, including in Ephesus and its vicinity. This of course raises interesting questions. Were the Johannine epistles written for some of Paul's former churches, or was there a separate "Johannine" community? One should not simply assume either of these conclusions. But several factors suggest that although there was likely cross-fertilization and communication between the Johannine communities and the Pauline ones, these epistles were likely separate entities and not simply successive stages in the development of the same communities.

I come to this conclusion for the following good reasons: First, in Gal. 2.7, Paul states very clearly that it was the will of the Jerusalem leadership that he be the apostle to the Gentiles, whereas Peter would be the apostle to the Jews. This division of labor did not mean that there would not be Jewish Christians in Paul's churches, or vice versa with Peter's churches, but it did mean that Paul would primarily concentrate on converting Gentiles and forming communities for them, and Peter on converting Jews and forming communities primarily for them. Second, so far as I can see, neither John the Elder nor the Beloved Disciple was a part of Paul's collegial network of co-laborers working on the Gentile mission. We do not hear anything about them working with any of the Pauline group of coworkers who frequented this same territory in western Asia—Timothy, Titus, Priscilla, Aquila, Apollos, Tychicus, Onesiphorus, and so on. We hear instead only of Diotrephes, Gaius, and Demetrius in 3 John being associated with the Elder, which are not necessarily names that ring any Pauline bells, nor is there any

Figure 18.2 This Herculaneum villa shows the sort of setting early Christian worship took place in—a home. Obviously, for a Christian meeting to take place in this setting, it required having a convert of higher social status. (© Mark R. Fairchild, Ph.D.)

appeal to earlier names who might have planted these churches being addressed in 1–3 John. I think then we must conclude these are *not* Pauline congregations that were being addressed. Third, the social character manifested in 1–3 John is so very different from the captivity epistles written to this same vicinity (Colossians, Ephesians, Philemon) and the Pastoral Epistles that it seems unlikely they could have been written for the same communities. Although it is true that all of these documents primarily are dealing with internal problems, problems within the Christian communities themselves rather than problems with "the world," the character of 1–3 John is such that it could be said they bear witness to an **isolationist sect**. Missing entirely is the concern we see in the pastorals (and could also find in the captivity epistles, e.g., Philippians) for limited accommodation to and conversion of the larger society of which these congregations were a part. The world, in these Johannine letters, is not something to be borrowing values and taking one's cues from.

The Greek term ***kosmos***, translated loosely as "world," in Johannine literature has the sense of humanity organized against God and God's people. There is in short far more of a dualistic quality to the Johannine literature compared to the Pauline corpus, even more evident in Revelation than in the Johannine epistles but not absent from the epistles. One important explanation for this difference is that our author is addressing a different kind of audience—a largely Jewish one—and addressing them in a fashion familiar from Jewish wisdom literature. In none of the Johannine documents is apostolic status an issue.

The twelve are only once spoken of as the Twelve in the fourth Gospel, and they are not identified as apostles and neither is the Beloved Disciple. In the Johannine letters (2–3 John), it is an Elder (and not a merely local church elder), and in Revelation, a prophet/seer, who are the surviving authority figures for this community at the time when those documents were written; and unfortunately, the prophet John was in exile! In other words, *these documents were written after*

ISOLATIONIST SECT

A very inwardly oriented religious community that works hard to preserve its boundaries with the world, which of course makes real evangelism difficult.

KOSMOS

A Greek term that is loosely translated as "world" in Johannine literature. The English cognate is cosmos.

there were no longer any apostles on the scene (indeed, the apostles are seen as something in the past and/or future in Rev. 21.14). There is also no emphasis in these documents on passing along apostolic traditions, identified as such. In other words, we are in a very different social milieu than that of the Pauline letters, but a milieu that is nonetheless Christian.

But is it mostly Jewish Christians or Gentile Christians who inhabit and live in this Johannine world? If we are primarily dealing with highly Hellenized Jewish converts from Asia along with some Gentiles, this may be a distinction without much of a difference. What we can and must say about the book of Revelation is that it was written by someone who had a Scripture-saturated mind, and he seemed to assume that at least some of the audience would pick up the allusions and Scriptural signals he encoded into his work. This, coupled with the polemic about the synagogue found in Rev. 2–3, may also suggest a predominantly Jewish Christian community. But there is another factor at work as well that points in this direction.

The Beloved Disciple and John the Elder seem clearly to be Jewish Christians, and the Beloved Disciple began his Christian pilgrimage in Judea and somehow made his way to Asia. His Gospel traditions, and also 1 John, reflect a particular kind of Jewish literature—wisdom literature. What we do not find in 1–3 John are quotes from Cretan poets, citations of the popular maxims Gentiles might know, and the like, which we do find in the pastorals. There is no attempt here to appeal to the wider scope of knowledge, values, or ethos of the Gentile world in these documents (cf. James on this point). It is rather a Hellenized Jewish sectarian worldview that is drawn on, a worldview we also find in documents such as Sirach and Wisdom of Solomon, although here all that earlier Jewish wisdom is filtered through the life and teachings of Jesus.

In the Johannine community, we find ourselves in the middle of conversations about two ways of living, believing, and behaving in a world of darkness and light that sound more nearly like Qumran discussions than Pauline ones. Notice, for example, how in 3 John 7 the author refers to the "Gentiles" or "pagans" in a way that suggests that (1) the author certainly is not from this ethnic group, and (2) the missionaries referred to are not from this category either. It seems unlikely the author would speak in this rather pejorative way about Gentiles if his audience was predominantly Gentile.

But what about the reference at the end of 1 John to stay away from idols (5.21)? Is this not like the warning by James to Gentile believers in Acts 15? In fact, this is probably not an association we should make, for the social setting in 1 John is very different. Consider what D. Watson says about this last verse of 1 John: "'Little children, keep yourselves from idols' . . . is a command to denounce the secessionists' false Christology and ethics and an implicit plea to remain faithful to the values of the Johannine Community."[6] Exactly so, and thus this verse has nothing to do with Gentiles in the audience feeling tempted to go back to dinner parties in pagan temples or the like (cf. 1 Cor. 8–10). The term *idol* is a Jewish polemical term, and one frequently used in earlier Hebrew literature in the Old Testament to critique non-Jewish gods and their cults. In other words, *idol* can be an in-house term used among Jews, in this case Jewish Christians. It need not signal that the Johannine audience is predominantly Gentile any more than the absence of citations from the Old Testament suggests this.

The type of literature rather than the audience has more to do with the presence or absence of Scripture citations here and often elsewhere. Wisdom literature does not tend to cite the Hebrew Scriptures (cf. Proverbs; Ecclesiastes; Wisdom of Solomon; and the aphorisms, maxims, and parables of Jesus). It is also irrelevant that Jews are not mentioned in these letters, as these letters were written to and for an isolationist sect whose leader was dealing with internal, not external, problems.

Notice also the lack of focus on future eschatology in the Johannine epistles (it is not entirely absent, but it is not at all a focal point of these documents), which makes them unlike the pastorals, never mind the earlier Paulines, while still having an eschatological flavor (there are antichrists already afoot in the area). The Beloved Disciple in 1 John is interested in serving up counter-order wisdom and some "traditional" wisdom about Jesus and the Christian life to help keep these sectarian communities intact. He shows no concern for how this will appear to outsiders who do not lurk even on the periphery of the discussion here, unlike in the pastorals.

THE DATE AND PROVENANCE OF THE JOHANNINE EPISTLES

If we are concerned about a date before which these documents could have been written, there are some key points for us to consider. It seems very unlikely that these letters were written in the second century for the very good reason that **Polycarp**, writing in the first quarter of that century, already knows at least 1 John and perhaps also 2 John (see his *Letter to the Philippians* 7.1–2 and cf. 1 Jn. 1.1–4, 4.2–3; and 2 Jn. 7). Eusebius tells us that Papias knew 1 John in the first decades of the second century as well (*Hist. Eccles.* 3.39.17). It is hard to know when to date the epistle of Barnabas, surely no later than the mid-second century, and it references 1 John as well (5.9–11).

We must stress that 2–3 John are real ad hoc letters and must be treated as such, whereas 1 John seems very clearly not to be a letter at all. It is rather a very rhetorically effective discourse or homily. There is considerable debate about how to order these documents, chronologically speaking; but in my view, it does not matter a great deal. The theology and ethics of 1 John seem to be presupposed in 2–3 John, whether the audience heard these things previously in an oral form or 1 John circulated in these churches prior to the writing of 2–3 John.

POLYCARP

A church father who was the Bishop of Smyrna. According to Irenaeus, Polycarp was a disciple of John the Apostle. He lived in the second half of the first century and into the second century. Polycarp died as a martyr and was burned for his faith.

I do think it is clearly right that some of the ideas in the Fourth Gospel were developed a little further in 1 John, but this does not require that the Gospel was written first, and there is a very good reason to dispute this. In Jn. 21.20–24, we have a story that alludes to the death of the Beloved Disciple before the return of Christ. It seems that at least one of the reasons John the Elder put that Gospel together, full of the memoirs of the Beloved Disciple, is because the Beloved Disciple died before the Gospel could be collected and edited.

But 1 John is clearly written by a living person! You notice, however, that the author of that sermon never uses the phrase "Beloved Disciple." It was those who loved and have learned from him in his community, people like John the Elder, who called him the Beloved Disciple. Certainly, the sermon and probably 2–3 John were written before the final form of those Gospel traditions appeared in the form they are now in the Gospel of John. S. Smalley, who compares ideas from 1 John and the Gospel, shows they are likely from the same mind, that of the Beloved Disciple.

I. THE GODHEAD AND THE CHRISTIAN

Love of the Father	1 Jn. 4.15; Jn. 14.21
Abiding of the Son	1 Jn. 3.24; Jn. 15.4
Gift of the Spirit	1 Jn. 4.13; Jn. 14.16–17

II. THE CHRISTIAN AND THE GODHEAD

Mutual Indwelling	1 Jn. 3.24; Jn. 14.20
Forgiveness	1 Jn. 1.9; Jn. 15.3, 13.8
Eternal Life	1 Jn. 2.25; Jn. 17.2
Righteousness	1 Jn. 2.29; Jn. 16.10

III. CONDITIONS FOR CHRISTIAN DISCIPLESHIP

Renounce Sin	1 Jn. 1.8, 3.4; Jn. 16.8
Be Obedient	1 Jn. 2.3, 3.10; Jn. 14.15
Reject Worldliness	1 Jn. 2.12, 4.1; Jn. 15.19
Keep the Faith	1 Jn. 2.18, 5.5; Jn. 17.8[7]

What is especially interesting about this comparison is that 1 John could be said to be a homiletical development of certain themes found in the farewell discourses (Jn. 14–17). In fact, that is the one section of the fourth Gospel that is most like our letters.

In 1 John, our author uses "we" and "us" language. He is writing to an audience he is part of, although apparently not currently with. In 2 John, the author is clearly at some distance from the audience. Notice as well that, in 2 John, the church is addressed rather formally as "the Elect Lady" (probably not a reference to an individual person). I thus conclude that the 2–3 John documents were written in that order chronologically to two different but related house churches over which the elder had some jurisdiction.[8] Neither of these letters suggests the same intimacy between author and audience that we hear of in 1 John.

The picture one gets from both Paul and the later writings of Ignatius is that Ephesus had numerous house churches, as did the outlying cities. But are the congregations addressed in 2–3 John merely in Ephesus's suburbs? Probably they were not. The writing of these letters suggests that these churches are far enough away that letters needed to be written to them. Perhaps they were in the Lycus Valley, or at least several days journey away, so that our author could assume it would take some time for the false teachers to get there and establish themselves—so these letters could serve as effective warnings.

It is not certain, but certainly possible, that the congregation discussed in 3 John is the same one referred to in 2 John. Indeed, I think this is likely. Keep in mind that 3 John is actually a brief personal letter to one Gaius, a good friend of John the Elder, whereas 2 John is written to a congregation. Gaius is a member of the congregation that the Elder has written to in 2 John, but this congregation seems to be run by a man named Diotrephes, who apparently does not acknowledge or accept the Elder's directives and may well have turned away the missionaries that he sent their way (hence the urging of Gaius to help them and give them funds so they may continue on their way).

There is no locale that better suits this description of the congregations than Ephesus. Notice that early church tradition told various tales about the Beloved Disciple having contact with various false teachers in this very region.[9] Notice as well that, in these documents, it is not the Jews in the synagogue who are making the trouble but rather false teachers who were within but have gone out of the community (at least out of the Beloved Disciple's congregation addressed in 1 John).

What were the false teachers teaching? This is difficult to discern because these documents are both rhetorical and polemical in character. There is nothing to suggest they were Gnostics (no discussion of aeons, emanations, matter-spirit dualism), although they may have been **docetics**, that is, those who denied that the Son of God actually took on flesh instead of merely appearing to do so. The issue is what does denying "Jesus Christ come in the flesh" mean? Or what does denying "Jesus is the Christ, the Son of God" mean? Their errors are seen to be both theological and ethical in any case. They seem to have claimed some sort of inspiration or charismatic authority, but they do not seem to have been libertines or immoral per se. Two cautionary words are in order: (1) the rhetorical force of these documents must be taken into account in assessing the issue of the

DOCETIC

A person who denies that Jesus, the Son of God, actually took on human flesh. Instead, the belief is that Jesus merely appeared to take on human flesh. Docetism is the formal name of this heresy.

opponents; and (2) these opponents seem to be a thing of the past for the church in 1 John, but perhaps a worrisome presence on the horizon in 2–3 John. We should neither under- nor overestimate these opponents.

Fresh winds are blowing in the study of the Johannine Epistles and two things have been coming to the surface: (1) the Jewish sapiential (i.e., wisdom) character of these documents and (2) the likely Jewish audience of these documents, as well as the Jewish extraction of those who left the congregations. On the former point, it is good to remind ourselves of *the way the rhetoric of wisdom literature works. It provides general principles or "truths" often in colorful or memorable and figurative wording and it presupposes a rather specific religious and social context for it to hold true. Sometimes it deliberately involves rhetorical hyperbole, for instance, in the maxim "the love of money is a root of every kind of evil."* If this is the correct translation, and it may well be in view of the emphatic position of the word "root," then it is in order to point out that the rhetorical function of **hyperbole** is to dramatically emphasize something, drawing attention to it and trying to inculcate a strong positive response in the audience, in this case to urge them to avoid avarice. Such polemical maxims are not meant to be taken absolutely literally. They are rather general rules of thumb that are applicable in many circumstances and in a particular kind of ethos or social environment.

On the Jewish character of the author, audience, schismatics, and discourse in these letters, we may profit from interacting briefly with T. Griffith's monograph.[10] Here is how Griffith sums up his own views:

> My specific proposal is that 1 John is the product of a continuing debate between Jews and Jewish Christians over whether Jesus was the Messiah at a time when some Jewish Christians belonging to Johannine Christianity had reverted to Judaism. . . . 1 John has primarily pastoral, rather than polemical aims. The letter thus represents a sustained effort to prevent further apostasy among Johannine Christians by strengthening their identity and cohesion.[11]

> Once the need to interpret the letter in the light of later heresies has been removed, the case for arguing that the letter must be later than the Gospel looks much weaker.[12]

It seems to me that the scenario we must envision, which prompted these documents, is as follows: (1) The Johannine community was a Jewish Christian community that largely reached out to Jews in the area of Ephesus. The boundaries of these congregations were rather porous early on, and various Jews came to visit in the house churches in question. (2) Some of these Jews stayed for a long time, long enough to be recognized as members of the community, and in some cases even become leaders, teachers, or prophets in the community. (3) However,

HYPERBOLE

A form of exaggeration that functions rhetorically to emphasize something or draw attention to it in order to inculcate a strong positive response from the audience. Hyperbole is not intended to be taken literally.

Figure 18.3 A golden image of the god Dionysius. (© *Mark R. Fairchild, Ph.D.*)

there came a point when it became clear that their views of Jesus and those of the Beloved Disciple differed. There was a considerable schism, with the schismatics leaving and apparently taking with them a goodly number of the members of the home congregation and perhaps some of the satellite churches as well. (4) 1 John and the later Johannine letters are written as a response to this crisis, attempting to do damage control in various ways. (5) One of the rhetorical strategies in 1 John is that the author will shore up the boundaries of the community by insisting on a particular Jewish view of Jesus—that he is Messiah, Son of God, and savior, and that he died for the sins of the world. (6) He insists on the ethic of Jesus, especially as it was to be later elucidated in Jn. 14–17, as the ethic the community must adhere to in repairing its wounds and going forward.

THE RHETORIC OF THE JOHANNINE EPISTLES

We are far better served with the Johannine Epistles than with the Pastoral Epistles when it comes to rhetorical analysis, mainly due to the work of D. F. Watson and several European scholars.[13] There is not only detailed rhetorical analysis of these documents but also clear statements can be made on their species—2–3 John are probably deliberative discourses (although 3 John could also be seen as epideictic in character), whereas 1 John is epideictic in character, being a sermon. This explains some of the differences between 1 John and 2–3 John. D. L. Stamps has rightly noted that at some 13 junctures in 1 John, our author uses the phrase "I write" to signal his form of communication ("I write to you" or "I am writing to you").[14] This means that 1 John is not likely just a transcript of an oral message given to the Beloved Disciple's own congregation. However, this is not the end of the story.

Written documents in antiquity were read out loud to or by the audience. They often served as surrogates for oral communication, the culture being primarily an oral culture and not a culture of the literate or of texts. Perhaps only 10 to 15 percent of the Greco-Roman world could really read or write. Thus, although this document seems to have begun life as a written document, this neither means it was intended to be a letter nor does it in any way rule out that it could be seen as a homily, meant to be effectively delivered orally to an audience.

What it does mean, however, is that this is not likely a document delivered to our author's "immediate" audience, or an audience where he is currently present or in residence, unless of course the author is ill. Whereas this character of 1 John also does not necessarily make this document an encyclical, I incline to the theory that this sermon was intended to circulate in the Johannine churches and may well have been known in the church addressed in 2 John, as some of the themes and ideas of 1 John reappear in 2 John. The content is not intended to be of a broadly generic but rather of a wisdom nature and is viewed as suitable for this cluster of churches that have interrelated problems and draw on the same Christian tradition.

S. Stowers reminds us that

> Greco-Roman culture regarded the well-delivered and persuasive speech as the most characteristic feature of civilized life. In contrast to our own culture, linguistic skill focused on oral speech; the written word was secondary, derived from primary rhetoric. Letter writing remained only on the fringes of formal rhetorical education throughout antiquity. It was never integrated into the rhetorical systems and thus does not appear in the standard handbooks. This means *there were never any detailed systematic rules for letters, as there were for standard rhetorical forms. The rules for certain types of speeches, however, were adapted for use in corresponding letter types.* So, for example, a letter of consolation written by a person with rhetorical training may more or less follow the form of the consolatory speech.[15]

What Stowers's remarks make perfectly clear is that rhetoric was the dominant communication force in the culture, and letter writing was influenced by that paradigm. Indeed, the budding epistolary theorists were always looking over their shoulders at the rhetoricians and examining rhetorical handbooks for guidance. We must keep all this in mind when we read 1–3 John.

THE RHETORICAL STRUCTURE OF 1 JOHN

First John is a far more complex piece of material than we find in 2–3 John, and it is also clear enough that we have no obvious epistolary elements in this discourse. It begins without an epistolary prescript, and it ends with a bang with an exhortation about staying away from idols. We have already noted its similarity, and perhaps indebtedness, to John 14–17.

Watson argues that the *exordium,* or introduction, is in 1 John 1.1–4; the *peroration,* or final emotional appeal, is in 1 John 5.13–21; and the *probatio,* or arguments for, essentially involve everything in between.[16] He sees the entire discourse as an example of epideictic rhetoric. Here, I find very little to quibble with either in terms of the rhetorical arrangement (or "invention") or the species of the rhetoric, though I would suggest that the peroration is in fact 5.18–21.

Epideictic rhetoric is the rhetoric of praise and blame. This form of rhetoric deals with values the audience already affirms, in an attempt to enhance or intensify the adherence to those values. This clearly seems to be the character of the rhetoric here as can be seen, for example, in 1 Jn. 2.7, where our author says he is writing not a new command to the audience but rather an old one that they are long familiar with and affirm. He will draw out the new implications of that old command that they already adhere to and adapt it to their current situation. The message throughout will have to do with love, life, and light as things to praise and treasure, and their opposites (including sin) as things to condemn. In epideictic rhetoric, neither a proposition nor a narration is required, for the author is not trying to prove some key thesis statement or mount a series of arguments in favor of that thesis statement. Rather, he is trying to increase adherence to values already held.

Epideictic rhetoric is the rhetoric of sermons and other sorts of hortatory addresses, and what we find in this particular sermon in 1 John is a series of interlocking themes or topics, developed over the course of the sermon, that are stated, amplified, and reiterated but not debated. D. Watson is absolutely right that throughout this discourse, our author uses the rhetorical technique of amplification, ringing the changes on certain key themes over and over with slight variations in order to stress the need for the adherence to the basics. Like a musical round, these themes keep coming up with slightly different permutations and combinations, praising values already affirmed, and condemning vices to be avoided (cf. Aristotle, *Rhetoric* 1.9.1368a.38–40; *Rhet ad Alex.* 3; Quintilian, *Inst. Or.* 3.7.6). How very different is the discourse here from the sort of dialogical argument patterns we find in Romans or James, for example. We have here only the voice of the author, and he does not engage in debate with opponents or anyone else. He simply exercises his authority in the form of an epideictic discourse.

THE RHETORICAL STRUCTURE OF 2 JOHN

Although 2 John is very succinct, it nonetheless has rhetorical form. A formal *propositio,* or thesis statement, was not required if the argument was brief and would require only one proposition (see Cicero, *Inv.* 1.23.33; Quintilian, *Inst. Or.* 4.5.8). It certainly could be included, however, and verse 5 looks like a proposition. We may lay out the epistolary and rhetorical elements in this document as follows:

Epistolary Opening	verses 1–3
Exordium/Opening Remarks	verse 4
Propositio/Thesis Statement	verse 5
Probatio/Argument for Thesis	verses 6–11
Peroratio/Final Emotional Appeal	verse 12
Epistolary Closing	verse 13

It will be seen from this analysis that four of the verses will submit to epistolary analysis and fall into the category of epistolary elements, whereas nine of the verses do not submit to such analysis and are better described as following rhetorical paradigms.

THE RHETORICAL STRUCTURE OF 3 JOHN

This document, even more than 2 John, seems to be responding to a serious problem that prompted its writing.

> The exigence [or problem] prompting the Presbyter to write is the refusal of Diotrephes, a new and ambitious leader of a Johannine church, to extend hospitality to traveling missionary brethren of the Johannine community. This exigence is not only the passive withdrawal of hospitality but the active refusal to allow others of the church to extend hospitality under threat of expulsion.[17]

Accordingly, our author has written Gaius to remedy this situation, so he will provide hospitality and traveling funds for these missionaries and so see them on their way. Because our author is arguing for a change in the situation, and he is offering persuasion to accomplish that change, it seems best to see this letter also as an example of deliberative rhetoric, as the call for imitation in verse 11 also suggests.

Gaius is being persuaded to engage in hospitable behavior in the near future when the missionaries (and Demetrius?) arrive on his doorstep. This is shown to be both advantageous and expedient, which is the essence of deliberative appeals. The appeal does not need to engage in strenuous acts of persuasion because presumably Gaius is already prepared to be hospitable, although perhaps, if he was part of Diotrephes's house church, he might need some persuading to accept those his church leader had or would reject.

After the preliminary epistolary elements and introductory remarks, verses 5–6 serve to provide us with the proposition (that Gaius must help the missionaries make it to their next destination), with verse 5 making Gaius favorably disposed and verse 6 indicating the action the author wants to undertake in the near future. The balance of the discourse has the rhetorical function of persuading Gaius to do what verse 6 suggests. He is not to follow bad examples but rather good ones, and thus Gaius is to "send the missionaries on their way." This is technical language, and it does not refer to hosting the missionaries. To send them on their way in a worthy manner means to provide supplies and traveling funds for these missionaries as they are going on to another locale. It seems to me then that the epistolary and rhetorical structure of 3 John is as follows:

Epistolary Prescript	verse 1
Exordium	verses 2–4
Propositio	verses 5–6
Narratio	verses 7–8
Probatio	verses 9–12
Peroratio	verses 13–14a
Epistolary Postscript	verse 14b

There is not a mixing of the epistolary and rhetorical elements, but rather the epistolary elements frame the rhetorical discourse because this is set down in writing using the framework of a letter.

CORE SAMPLINGS—1 JOHN 4

In the ongoing flow of the sermon we call 1 John, the subject of love comes to the fore, love not only as a test of true Christianity but also as a witness of God's true character. And this love is not seen as an alternative to true confessions about Jesus but as part of the package of right confession and right living, which should characterize any true Christian. Amplification as a rhetorical technique,

CHIASM

A literary device in which one uses a sort of parallel construction to focus on key points, such that three topics are mentioned and then brought up again in reverse order in the passage in question, but the focus of the passage is on its center, in this case the D element, 1 John 4.17–18.

CLUES FROM THE CULTURE

Epicurus, himself the father of truth commanded wise persons to be lovers, and said that this is the goal of life.

—*Petronius, Satire 132*

if anything, increases in this section over what has preceded it, especially in regard to the topic of love. W. Loader has discerned a **chiasm** in this section as follows:

A. 4.1–6 Right confession of Christ and true discernment

B. 4.7–11 God's children love one another

C. 4.12–16 The unseen God dwelling in the believer

D. 4.17–18 The love which casts out fear of judgment

C'. 4.19–21 Loving the unseen God and the seen believer

B'. 5.1–4a God's children loving God's fellow believers

A'. 5.4b–12 Right confession of Christ and its evidence.[18]

We are going to focus on the center of that chiasm. The second portion of this segment of the discourse begins with a variety of forms of the word *love*. In fact, in 1 John 3.1–5.12, we have the largest clustering of love language anywhere in the New Testament, and notably in no book of the New Testament except the fourth Gospel does the Greek verb *agapao* occur half so many times as here. "No wonder that the writer of this epistle has been known in the Church as 'the Apostle of Love.'"[19]

Here, for the third time in this discourse, our author will speak about brotherly love and also its connection with God's love (see 1 John 2.7–11 on love as a sign of walking in the light; and, in 1 John 3.10–18, as a form of righteousness and a mark of being a child of God). One can argue that 1 John 4.7–21 is a rhetorical unit, with verse 7 as the theme verse, and verses 7–11 as the first subunit where our love for the brothers and sisters is grounded in God's character as love and in God's loving action demonstrated by the sending and propitiatory death of the son.[20] 1 John 4, verse 7, begins with the author calling the audience "beloved," which is followed by the verbal form "let us love," by the noun *love,* and by the Greek participle that means *loving*. This may be the most love-filled verse in the Bible. "Love constitutes the foundation of the author's thinking about God and Christian community."[21]

It also involves the rhetorical device of alliteration on the letter "a" to make it striking to the ear. The ability of Christians to love one another comes from God, for we are told that "love is of God," and God has an unending supply, however short our human supply may run. "Anyone who enters into a real relationship with a loving God can be transformed into a loving person."[22] The author here is saying more than just that we love in gratitude for the fact that God first loved us. In fact, he also says that if we are sharing such love, then in the process of loving, "we know God."

Loving is a way of getting to know God or getting to know what God is really like better. By contrast, our author says in 1 John 4, verse 8, that those who do not love know nothing of God. Our author is not suggesting that being loving is in itself a sufficient sign that someone is born of God.

> Human love, however noble and however highly motivated, falls short if it refuses to include the Father and the Son as supreme objects of its affection. It falls short of the divine pattern, and by itself cannot save a [hu]man; it cannot be put in the balance to compensate for the sin of rejecting God.[23]

The subject of love—godly, godlike, and God's love—has come up before in this discourse, but it will be dealt with more thoroughly here as the main portion of the sermon draws to a close. If we ask why it is stressed so much in 1 John, the answer surely must be, at least in part, because our author is trying to heal the wounds of schism and get the remaining faithful Christians to redouble their efforts to create true Christian community. They must pull together after the crisis of schism. This fraternal love, if exhibited and expressed, will shore up the boundaries and wounds of the community. Our author does not speak to the issue of loving the world or non-Christians, although some of the things he says could be applied by extension to that relationship as well.

It is a fact that in Greek literature before New Testament times, the verb *agapao,* which means "to love," has nowhere near the importance, or even the connotations, that it has in the New Testament.[24] How can we explain the usage in the New Testament? C. H. Dodd puts it this way:

> The noun is scarcely found in non-Biblical Greek. The verb generally has such meanings as "to be content with," "to like," "to esteem," "to prefer." It is a comparatively cool and colourless word. It is this word, with its noun, that the translators of the Old Testament used by preference for the love of God to man and man's response, and by doing so they began to fill it with the distinctive content for which paganism, even in its highest forms, had no proper expression. In the New Testament this fresh content is enlarged and intensified through meditation upon the meaning of the death of Christ.[25]

It is interesting, in addition, that when pagan religious writers do speak of a loving god, they usually use the word *eros,* which normally refers to sexual desire and sexual love. This is precisely what the New Testament writers *do not want to say* about God's love for humankind or God's character. From the Jewish point of view, a deity is not merely a human being writ large with a whole lot more power and life. The God of the Bible is the creator God who is wholly other, not a being who takes his cues from human behavior. God is the definition of what goodness, truth, life, light, love, and holiness mean. God does not conform to human definitions of these things.

Here, we learn that "God is love," which is in fact the second attempt at defining God in this discourse, the first coming at 1 John 1.5, where we heard "God is light," and we may also rightly compare John 4.24, where we are told God is spirit, a statement about God's metaphysical nature, whereas the two other predications are about God's character.

Although we might be tempted to think that this phrase means that God is loving, and so defined by his loving activities (which is true), it would seem that this phrase means something more. God not merely possesses or expresses love, but love is a term that seems to embrace all God is. Yet still, God is not really being defined here by an abstraction, nor is it a claim that the reverse of this statement is true (i.e., that "love is God"). What may be meant by "God is love" is in part that "if the characteristic divine activity is that of loving, then God must be personal, for we cannot be loved by an abstraction, or by anything less than a person . . . But to say 'God is love' implies that *all* his activity is loving activity. If he creates, he creates in love; if he rules, he rules in love; if he judges, he judges in love. All that he does is the expression of his nature, which is—to love."[26] One more thing—the definition of love proceeds from God and works its way down to us: "not that we loved God but that God loved us and sent his son" (1 John 4.10).

Exhibit A of the loving character of God, paradoxically enough, is that he sent his son to die for a sinful and ungrateful world. 1 John 4, verses 9–10, stress first that Jesus was sent so that we might have life through him and second that God sent his son as a sacrifice of atonement to propitiate divine anger about sin. If God is love, then it is hardly a surprise that God is supremely and righteously angry with our sinning because it destroys the love relationships we have with God and with each other as well. We have here statements that are akin to what we find in John 3.16–17. Love and life are the polar opposites of hate and death, and yet the substitutionary and atoning death of Jesus is the prime example of God's love for us. J. Denny long ago put it this way:

> So far from finding any kind of contrast between love and propitiation, the apostle can convey no idea of love to anyone except by pointing to propitiation—love is what is manifested there. . . . For him to say "God is love" is exactly the same as to say "God has in his son made atonement for the sin of the world." If the propitiatory death of Jesus is eliminated from the love of God, it might be unfair to say that the love of God is robbed of all meaning, but it is certainly robbed of its apostolic meaning. It has no longer that

meaning which goes deeper than sin, sorrow, and death, and which recreates life in the adoring joy, wonder, and purity of the first epistle of John.[27]

Again in 1 John 4, verse 10, it is stressed that it is not that we have first generated this love that creates community in Christ but that God has loved us and so "our loving is a participation in the loving which first came to us and enabled us to love."[28] Having said all of this, he rounds off this subsection by ending in 1 John 4, verse 11, where he began—with the command to the beloved ones to love one another—only now the context, the content, and the character have been made much clearer having been linked to the character and actions of God, especially God's actions in and through his son. Thus, this verse is yet another example of amplification, for our author has already said this in similar terms in 1 John 3.16 and has referred to the sacrifice of Christ there to do so as well. This way of ending this short section on love is something of a surprise; we might have expected the author to say that because God has loved us in this way, we should reciprocate such love to God. But in fact, our author is more concerned about the spreading of God's love throughout the community intravenously, so to speak; and in any case, we are meant probably to hear an echo of what Jesus has said in Jn. 13.34, where brotherly and sisterly love is grounded in Jesus' love for his followers.

Instead of physically seeing the Father, our author stresses that if we fulfill the commandment to love one another, then we will know and experience the presence of God in our midst and God's love is thereby made complete, or brought to perfect expression or had its full intended effect (cf. 1 John 2.5 and 3.17). The circuit of God's love is brought to completion when we love each other. If we take the several statements about perfect or complete love together (1 John 2.5 and 4.17–18), the net effect is this: "Obedience, active love, confidence, these three point to the same fact. Where the one is the other is. The source of all is the full development of the divine gift of love."[29] The possible discussions of this divine love are of course inexhaustible, but hopefully, this sample will give the reader a sense of the substance of this sermon. *Theology and ethics are closely intertwined here, for if God is love, and the great commandments are to love God and one another, then love is not merely a noun describing God, it is a verb describing the very behavior God intends to replicate in us.*

IMPLICATIONS

The epistles 1–3 John are fascinating documents, and they remind us that the early church had just as many problems and as many possibilities as the church does today. There were people coming to and leaving the churches with disputes, issues of authority, leadership problems, and doctrinal problems. It is interesting that in all three of these documents, the basic approach of the writer is to emphasize love and community instead of engaging in long arguments about doctrine or dogma. As a pastoral approach, we could learn a good deal from this because the spectacle of Christians constantly bickering with each other is a bad witness to the world, which just further divides the body of Christ. If we are looking for wisdom for the Christian life, and a guide to growing into Christian maturity, we could hardly do better than to follow the advice we are given in 1 John. If God indeed is chiefly characterized by love, so should we be.

FOR FURTHER READING

Brown, Raymond. *The Community of the Beloved Disciple: The Life, Loves and Hates of an Individual Church in the New Testament.* Mahwah, NJ: Paulist Press, 1979.

Furnish, V.P. *The Love Command in the New Testament.* Nashville, TN: Abingdon Press, 1972.

Griffith, T. *Keep Yourselves from Idols. A New Look at 1 John.* Sheffield, England: Sheffield Academic Press, 2002.

Painter, John. *1, 2, and 3 John.* Collegeville, MN: Liturgical Press, 2008.

Witherington, B. *Letters and Homilies for Hellenized Christians.* Vol. 1, *A Socio-Rhetorical Commentary on Titus, 1-2 Timothy and 1-3 John.* Downers Grove, IL: InterVarsity Press, 2006.

KEY TERMS

Chiasm

Docetic

Hyperbole

Isolationist Sect

Kosmos

Polycarp

Presbyteros

STUDY QUESTIONS

There seem to be at least two persons, or possibly three, involved in the composition of the Gospel of John, 1–3 John, and Revelation. Who are they, and how would you view their interrelationship?

Why is 1 John not a letter? What makes it a sermon?

What do you think it actually means to say "God is love"? What is the difference between divine love and human physical love? What does the term *agape*/love mean to you?

Why were divisions so difficult and devastating to a small-minority religious group like the earliest Christians?

What do you make of the fact that it appears that there were largely Jewish and largely Gentile congregations, founded by two different sets of missionaries (some Pauline and some focusing on the evangelism of Jews)? In what ways is this like the ethnic divisions in the church today?

NOTES

1. John Painter, *1, 2, and 3 John* (Collegeville, MN: Liturgical Press, 2008), 35.

2. From a very early date, there was doubt (for a variety of reasons) that the fourth Gospel was written, at least in its final form, by the same person as these epistles. Isho'dad of Merv, for example, says this of 1 John (the document most like the fourth Gospel): "About this epistle many have erred, supposing that it was written by the apostle John, yet if they had investigated the matter, they would have seen that the thought, shape and authority of this letter are greatly inferior to the sound words of the Evangelist." *Commentaries 40*, cited in *Ancient Christian Commentary on Scripture: New Testament XI: James, 1–2 Peter, 1–3 John, Jude*, ed. G. Bray (Downers Grove, IL: InterVarsity Press, 2000), 167.

3. See the discussion in J. Lieu, *The Second and Third Epistles of John: History and Background*, ed. J. Riches (Edinburgh, Scotland: T+T Clark, 1986), 5–7.

4. L. T. Johnson, *The First and Second Letters to Timothy*, Anchor Yale Bible Commentaries (New Haven, CT: Yale University Press, 2001), 60.

5. R. E. Brown, *The Epistles of John* (New York: Doubleday, 1982), 14–35.

6. D. F. Watson, "Amplification Techniques in 1 John: The Interaction of Rhetorical Style and Invention," *Journal for the Study of the New Testament* 16, no. 51 (1993): 120.

7. S. Smalley, *1, 2, 3 John* (Waco, TX: Word, 1984), xxx.

8. It is clear to me that Gaius is in a separate household from where the church that is under Diotrephes's sway meets, but it is not clear that there is a separate church that meets in Gaius's house, although that is not impossible.

9. Brown, *The Epistles of John*, 14–35.

10. T. Griffith, *Keep Yourselves from Idols. A New Look at 1 John* (Sheffield, England: Sheffield Academic Press, 2002).

11. Ibid., 1.

12. Ibid., 209.

13. I am thankful to have been able to read through Watson's forthcoming commentary for Cambridge University Press on 1–3 John as the editor of that series. See Duane F. Watson, "Amplification Techniques in 1 John: the Interaction of Rhetorical Style and Invention," *Journal for the Study of the New Testament* 51 (1993): 99–123; D. F. Watson, "An Epideictic Strategy for Increasing Adherence to Community Values: 1 John 1:1-2:27," *Proceedings of the Eastern Great Lakes and Midwest Biblical Societies* 11 (1991): 144–152.

14. D. L. Stamps, "The Johannine Writings," in *Handbook of Classical Rhetoric in the Hellenistic Period 330 B.C.-A.D. 400*, ed. S. E. Porter (Boston/Leiden: Brill Academic Publishers, Inc., 2001), 609–632; here see 622.

15. S. Stowers, *Letter Writing in Greco-Roman Antiquity*, ed. W. A. Meeks (Philadelphia, PA: Westminster Press, 1986), 33–34, italics added by me for emphasis.

16. Watson, "Amplification Techniques," 118–123.

17. D. F. Watson, "A Rhetorical Analysis of 3 John: A Study in Epistolary Rhetoric," *Catholic Biblical Quarterly* 51 (1989): 481.

18. W. Loader, *The Johannine Epistles* (London: Epworth, 1997), 47.

19. A. Plummer, *Epistles of St. John* (Memphis, TN: General Books, 2010), 101.

20. D. M. Scholer, "1 John 4.7–21," *Review and Expositor* 87 (1990): 309–314.

21. Loader, *Johannine Epistles*, 51.

22. Smalley, *1, 2, 3 John*, 238.

23. I. H. Marshall, *The Epistles of John* (Grand Rapids, MI: Eerdmans, 1994), 212.

24. There is a huge body of literature on this subject. See especially A. Nygren, *Agape and Eros* (New York: Peter Smith, 1983); C. Spicq, *Agape in the New Testament*, 3 vols. (New York: Herder, 1963–1966); and V. P. Furnish, *The Love Command in the New Testament* (Nashville, TN: Abingdon Press, 1972).

25. C. H. Dodd, *Johannine Epistles*, The Moffat New Testament Commentary (London: Hodder & Stoughton, 1946), 111–112.

26. Dodd, *Johannine Epistles*, 109–110.

27. J. Denny, *The Death of Christ* (London: Tyndale Press, 1956), 152.

28. Loader, *Johannine Epistles*, 53.

29. B.F. Westcott, *The Epistles of St. John* (Eugene, OR: Wipf and Stock, 2001), 153.

PART V

In the END—
APOCALYPSE—
and
THEREAFTER

Doric columns that are part of a wealthy person's tomb. (© *Mark R. Fairchild, Ph.D.*)

CHAPTER 19

PICKING up the PIECES, FORMING up the CANON— 2 PETER

PRELIMINARY CONSIDERATIONS

There is a remarkable passage from the Babylonian Talmud, a collection of early Jewish writings of relevance to our discussion of 2 Peter. Here is what it says:

> Moses wrote his book, the portion of Balaam, and Job. Joshua wrote his book and [the last] eight verses of the Torah. Samuel wrote his book, and Judges, and Ruth. David wrote the book of the Psalms at the instruction of the Ten Elders, namely Adam, the first human being; Melchizedek; Abraham; Moses; Heman; Yeduthun; Asaph; and the three sons of Korah. Jeremiah wrote his book, the Book of Kings, and Lamentations. Hezekiah and his associates wrote Isaiah, Proverbs, Song of Songs, and Qohelet. The men of the Great Assembly wrote Ezekiel and the Twelve, Daniel, and the Scroll of Esthers. Ezra wrote his book and the genealogies of Chronicles up to his time. . . . Who then finished it? Nehemiah the son of Hachaliah.
> —B.T. B. Bat. 14b-15a

Notice that this passage is sometimes referring to authorship in the modern sense, but sometimes it is just referring to who finally wrote down or copied the final form of the text, as in the case with the reference to Hezekiah and the book of Isaiah. What this points to is that there was a collectivist rather than individualist view of authorship in antiquity, perhaps particularly in Jewish communities. Traditions and prophecies that began with a prophet would be transcribed by scribes, edited and amplified over the course of time, and put into something like an official form by royal officials for the sake of the use of the rulers.

Clearly, however, none of the New Testament documents come out of a royal archive or palace situation, and we cannot assume that all such practices and concerns apply in the case of the New Testament. The New Testament is clearly minority literature, which is one of the things that makes it so interesting. But what this quote does make clear is that edited documents (i.e., composite documents compiled by scribes) not merely existed, but such documents would normally be ascribed to their most famous contributor. Recall once more what was said in a recent landmark study on scribes and scribal culture, particularly Jewish scribes:

> Our concept of the author as an individual is what underpins our concern with authenticity, originality, and intellectual property. The Ancient Near East had little place for such notions. Authenticity is subordinate to authority and relevant only inasmuch as it underpins textual authority; originality is subordinate to the common stock of cultural forms and values. . . . To us it would seem wrong to credit an editor with the work of an author. The author in our mind, is the intellectual source of the text, whereas an editor merely polishes; the former is the creative genius, the latter merely the technician. This distinction was obviously less important to the ancients. They did not place the same value on originality. To them, an author does not invent his text but merely arranges it; the content of the text exists first, before being laid down in writing.[1]

This last sentence of the quote applies all the more to material believed to be inspired by God. A prophet, such as Isaiah, would never claim authorship of prophecies he believed God gave him. The words, concepts, and message came first from God, before the prophet spoke or the scribe wrote it down. We must bear these things in mind when we examine 2 Peter.

THE MYSTERY THAT IS 2 PETER

If you love a good mystery, welcome to 2 Peter—a mystery wrapped in an enigma cloaked in a conundrum, to coin a redundant phrase that gives one a feel for the florid nature of the Asiatic Greek used in 2 Peter. One really has to put on one's detective hat and pick up one's magnifying glass to solve the puzzle that is this document. Just how different this book is is shown by the fact that out of a total vocabulary of 401 different words (total word count 1,103), there are some 57 words found *nowhere* else in the New Testament—half of these do not occur in the LXX (the Greek translation of the Old Testament), half of the rest are unknown in early Jewish literature, and at least three words occur nowhere else in all of Greek literature before or during this period.

Second Peter repeats only 38 percent of its vocabulary, which amounts to less than some 21 books of the New Testament; however, there are more than enough examples, at least 25, of wordplays and synonyms to make parts of this discourse sound quite repetitive.[2] Add to this that there are no, or almost no, Semitisms in this work—but there certainly are in 1 Peter. If style expresses the individual personality, the person who assembled this document is not much like the other New Testament authors. But it is not just the language issues that make 2 Peter difficult. Without question, 2 Peter is the most difficult New Testament book to deal with in terms of the basic authorship, date, and composition issues. In a remarkable statement, James Dunn opines, "I would want to insist that not a few compositions of Martin Luther and John Wesley, for example, were as, if not more, inspired than the author of 2 Peter."[3]

Furthermore, there is a strong consensus among most scholars, even many evangelicals (such as Richard Bauckham), that 2 Peter *cannot* have been written by Peter, and certainly not by the Peter who was responsible for 1 Peter. In terms of perspective, Greek style, theological content, language, dependency on Jude, and a host of other factors, 2 Peter is said by some to be a clear example of a New Testament pseudepigraph, a letter with a falsely attributed author (see Chapter 13). It is also true that 2 Peter has been something of the stepchild, or even the whipping boy, of New Testament studies, especially in Germany. This has led to the conclusion that the letter must have been written in the post-Apostolic era, reflecting later concerns, and some have been willing to say that it comes from the mid-second century, if not later.

Along with Jude, 2 Peter was regarded as of doubtful value, if not spurious altogether. It is listed by Eusebius as one of the "disputed" books (i.e., of uncertain apostolic authorship and canonical value). Jerome resorts to the view that Peter uses a different secretary in 2 Peter, and perhaps his authority led to its eventual acceptance. Jerome recognizes that for the most part, the style and vocabulary of 2 Peter betrays "another hand." Even the Reformers had serious doubts. Erasmus saw 2 Peter as spurious or written by Silvanus. Luther only thought it *might* be written by Peter. Even Calvin resorted to the view that it was written by a disciple at Peter's direction. None of this inspires confidence in the apostolic and Petrine nature of 2 Peter.

There are obvious affinities between our letter and certain other letters and documents that came from Rome between A.D. 80 and 100, for example,

1 Clement, 2 Clement, and the Shepherd of Hermas. As R. Bauckham shows in his commentary, these letters and their content bear the closest resemblance to 2 Peter among non-canonical works, while Jude and 1 Peter are its nearest canonical relatives. The non-canonical material might suggest a date in the period A.D. 80–100.

In regard to sources, there are several views: (1) Jude used 2 Peter;[4] (2) both Jude and the author of 2 Peter used a common source; or (3) 2 Peter definitely used Jude. In regard to the last view, Ralph Martin[5] provides the following table:

JUDE	2 PETER	JUDE	2 PETER	
4	2.1–3	11–12a	2.15, 13	
5	2.5	12b–13	2.17	19 out of 25 of Jude's verses seem to exist in some form in 2 Peter!
6, 7	2.4, 6	16	2.18	
8, 9	2.10, 11	17	3.2	
10	2.12	18	3.3	

In short, almost all the significant material in Jude is taken over, used, and expanded on or adapted in 2 Peter 2. And just as impressively, the material is found *in exactly the same order* in both documents, covering the same themes and topics. This is not a case of just borrowing an idea or two, or a term or phrase or two. The argument here for literary dependence is very strong indeed. Why not conclude that they used a common source? Because both of these authors seem to arrange their material according to their own purposes, we would not necessarily expect to find all of this material in the very same order in the two documents, and why would they have borrowed the exact same material from the third source, and not other material?

There are very good reasons for not concluding that it is Jude borrowing from 2 Peter: First, the non-canonical books referred to in Jude are deleted from the common material in 2 Peter. This indeed suggests that 2 Peter was written later, and for a broader audience than the Jewish sectarian one Jude is addressing. Second, Jude looks to be composed freely and without any such copying of sources, whereas 2 Peter is pretty clearly a composite document. The false teaching combated in 2 Peter can be argued to be of a somewhat different and perhaps later variety from what we find in Jude. We must give due weight to Duane F. Watson's very detailed demonstration of the dependence of 2 Peter on Jude (and not vice versa).[6] In my view, his arguments are compelling, and there has been no successful refutation of it since it was put forth in 1988. It is confirmed by the detailed comparisons in the landmark commentary by Richard Bauckham as well.[7] "Scholarship is on solid ground in postulating a literary relationship between 2 Peter and Jude; the evidence is best explained by the hypothesis that 2 Peter was dependent on Jude."[8]

This means that 2 Peter can certainly not be earlier than Jude and thus not earlier than A.D. 50–60. More helpful, however, is the likelihood that 2 Peter was written after 1 Peter and is possibly in part dependent on it, or at least knows of its content. The reference in 2 Peter 3.1 is most naturally taken as an allusion to 1 Peter because this letter purports to be by Peter and we know of no other Petrine letters in the first century. On the surface of things, 2 Peter 1 appears to be Peter's last words and personal testimony to the church, and as such, it could not have come earlier than A.D. 64–66 because this is when 1 Peter was likely written and when Peter died.

We have thus narrowed the time gap to A.D. 64–100. Roughly, this makes it a first-century document, but it does not make it by Peter in its final form. We should mention at this point a key factor that may suggest that at least part of 2 Peter depends on something Peter wrote or said. 2 Peter, section 1.12–21, reads like Peter's personal and final testimony, and linguistically this section of the letter has various phrases and words in common with 1 Peter. Mayor notes two phrases in particular: 2 Peter 1.16 (cf. 1 Peter 2.12) and 2 Peter 1.21 (cf. 1 Peter 2.15).[9] More impressive are the 18 words this small section of 2 Peter shares with 1 Peter. In so short a segment of text, so many common words cannot be ignored—they are not accidental. Nor can it be said that 2 Peter, section 1.12–21, exhibits especially grandiose Asiatic Greek or any significant number of Hellenisms, but the rest of 2 Peter does! Our testimony section in general does not have the heavy, cumbersome sentences we find at 2 Peter 1.3–4, 2.4–10, and 3.5–6. This is significant because the rest of 2 Peter does definitely reflect Asiatic Greek. It is fair to say that what we have elsewhere in 2 Peter is rather pompous, bookish Greek that is different from 1 Peter in many ways and words. Thus, Bauckham says the following:

> As Bo Reicke points out (146–7), 2 Peter must be related to the "Asiatic" style of Greek rhetoric which was coming into fashion in 2 Peter's time, and which, with its love of high-sounding expressions, florid and verbose language, and elaborate literary effects, was an artificial style which Reicke aptly compares with European baroque. If 2 Peter's language can seem bombastic and pompous to us, it must be judged by the taste of its age and circle, and we should not too quickly decide that the writer overreached himself in his literary ambition.[10]

In fact, the matter needs to be characterized a bit differently. 1 Peter reflects to some degree the Asiatic style, but not in nearly the pronounced fashion we find in 2 Peter. The difference is immediately apparent to anyone who is familiar with New Testament and Asiatic Greek. It is unlikely that Peter the Fisherman had picked up such bookish Greek, and nowhere are we told in 2 Peter that a secretary is being used.

I would suggest that 2 Peter is a document that can truly be said to be one of the first Christian attempts at "mass communication." It is written to all Christians in the empire, unlike 1 Peter. Asiatic Greek was (especially in the middle of the empire where Christianity was beginning to flourish) the most popular form of Greek. This is persuasion for the masses speaking in the people's language; and only more traditionalist patricians, upper crust Romans, and other well-educated members of society were likely to turn up their noses at it. Like modern musical snobs who love classical music but look down their noses at pop or country or rap music, Greek style in the empire was often a reflector of class, education, and ambitions as well. But in our case, it tells us most about the audience 2 Peter addresses. And this audience is Christians, both Jews and Gentiles, throughout the empire who needed to be galvanized to continue to embrace the apostolic values and virtues, beliefs and behaviors of the previous generation of believers. Both the style and the content of the document suggest we are addressing Christians considerably after the end of Peter's and Paul's lives.

Figure 19.1 The famous Knossos Palace on the island of Crete. It was from places like this that "mass communication" tended to go forth to broad audiences within a ruler's domain. Early Christian literature like 2 Peter is distinctive among minority literature in its attempt to address an audience all over the empire, albeit an audience of Christians. (© Mark R. Fairchild, Ph.D.)

Certain other factors also make it very likely that the letter in its present form comes from a time after the death of Peter:

1. The reference to Paul's letters in 2 Peter 3.14ff. Here, Paul's letters are spoken of as "all his letters" and as Scripture. This strongly suggests a time after the death of Paul when his letters or at least several of them had been collected, or were at least known of by the writer of 2 Peter and had come to be regarded as Scripture. This likely happened in the period A.D. 70–100. Further, the person behind the *present* form of 2 Peter shows little dependence on the thought and theology of 1 Peter. He writes in his own way and uses different terms for common concepts (e.g., 1 Peter calls the second coming, "the revealing of Jesus Christ," whereas 2 Peter speaks of the **parousia**). Whoever wrote 2 Peter knew *about* Paul and his letters but had formulated his thoughts independently, and this is true also in regard to the thoughts of Peter by and large (although 2 Peter 3.6ff. suggests he had read 1 Peter).

2. Perhaps as important is the reference to *your* apostles in 2 Peter 3.2, which suggests that the writer is not one of them and certainly not his audience's apostle. The words of "your apostles" are being called to memory, suggesting perhaps they are of a previous era. It is uncertain as to whether "our fathers" in 2 Peter 3.4 is a reference to early Christian fathers, namely, the apostles, or to the Old Testament saints. If it is the former, then here is more evidence that we are in the post-apostolic era. The problem of perceived "delay" of Christ's coming may also be a sign of the lateness of 2 Peter.

3. We may distinguish the author from Jude in that he edits out Jude's use of extra-canonical material, by and large, although he does share some Jewish apocalyptic thought with him. More clearly, he also, like those of the apostolic age, maintains and speaks of the second coming and its vital importance for and effect on Christians and their behavior. He does not write like one who lived when their hope had faded, as some authors of the second century did. Indeed, it is his purpose to stress it in this letter.

It is surprising that many scholars today do not seem to realize that there are other options besides declaring this document either a pseudepigraph or a letter composed by Peter himself. I would put this down to the fact that most New Testament scholars do not know **sapiential literature** as well as they should, and they especially seem unaware of the scribal practices found in early Judaism and early Christianity where scribes would not merely copy but also edit together collections of valuable sacred traditions, just as we see happening in 2 Peter. These are not exercises in pure creativity nor in forgery (see the K. van der Toorn extract on p. 378). There are ways of preserving sources and traditions

PAROUSIA

A Greek word that can mean "arrival" or "coming," or even sometimes "presence." It was a term like *epiphania* ("appearing") used by early Christians to talk about the second coming of Christ the King because this very same language was used for the "coming" or "appearing" of the so-called divine emperor to a city. Christ was seen as the divine reality, of which the emperor was just a pale parody.

SAPIENTIAL LITERATURE

A form of literature that discusses wisdom.

from the past and applying them in later situations, with the editors neither claiming authorship nor trying to deceive anyone about the sort or sources of their sources.[11]

PUTTING TOGETHER THE PIECES

Here is a summary of what we can say about the sources in 2 Peter:

1. At least 2 Peter 1.12–21, perhaps also 3.1–3, must be seen as the testimony of Peter, perhaps orally passed on to the Church at Rome shortly before his martyrdom. This testimony draws on some of Jesus' own teaching about false prophets (cf. Mk. 13), as well as Peter's own experiences (at the Transfiguration).

2. It has been somewhat edited and written up to fit into a larger document that draws heavily on Jude in 2 Peter 2, but its style is not as bombastic or Hellenistic as what we find elsewhere in the epistle and suggests use of a source, possibly even a written source, with more Hebraisms and Semitic Greek.

3. 2 Peter 1.3–11 is to be seen as a summary of apostolic teaching, or better said, Peter's apostolic preaching, which comported with general apostolic teaching. It is written in Asiatic Greek and suggests that the author relied on memory or an oral source, composing it himself for the first time.

4. 2 Peter 2.3b–22 must be seen as a recasting of Jude into Asiatic Greek to address a different situation. Here again, there is a reliance on authentic tradition from a church leader of the first generation. The scribe editing 2 Peter is not intending to offer his own doctrine but to combat certain opponents by using authoritative Christian material and adopting and adapting it. Even his reference to Paul must be seen as an appeal to previous apostolic authority that his audience is called on to heed.

5. 2 Peter 3.1–18 may be a mixture of Petrine testimony (3.1–3) and Petrine and Pauline ideas about the *parousia*. There is nothing particularly original here except the idea of the final conflagration of the world, an idea with some precedent in Hellenistic sources.

6. It is likely that this document was drawn up after Peter's death (and Paul's?) by someone in the Petrine circle—a colleague, however, probably *not* an understudy. Bauckham's guess of Linus, the second great leader and Bishop of Rome (cf. 2 Tim 4.21; Eusebius, *Hist Eccl.,* 3.13, 21–5, 6, 1), is plausible. Linus, if he is the compiler and writer of 2 Peter, did not intend for anyone to see this

document either as a forgery or as his own composition. Rather, it is in part Peter's last testament and as such bears Peter's name. The affinities with 1 and 2 Clement, 1 Peter, and Hermas suggest that it was sent from Rome to at least some of the same audience as those who had been evangelized by Paul and received his letters and who may have read 1 Peter.

In conclusion, we may quote Ramsey Michaels:

> Posthumous publication in Peter's name does not necessarily imply any intent to deceive. If the tradition behind Second Peter is genuinely Petrine [at least in part], then the only kind of compiler of this material who might be guilty of deception would be one who presumptuously signed his own name to the apostle's teaching. This testament, however, frankly calls itself a "second" or "secondary" epistle (3:1), a designation that perhaps glances back not at First Peter or at a lost epistle but precisely at the traditional Petrine teachings out of which Second Peter is built.[12]

Second Peter may well be the latest New Testament document, with the possible exception of Revelation. Possibly reflective of the late date of the document is the elimination of the extra-canonical material found in Jude but not in the directly parallel portion of 2 Peter. Because the Roman Church seems to be the destination or point of origin for many New Testament documents, including various letters of Paul, 1 Peter, Hebrews, and presumably the encyclical homily of James, there is no location more likely for the composition of 2 Peter than the growing church in Rome, drawing on its apostolic resources.[13]

THE RHETORIC OF 2 PETER

The rhetorical discussion of 2 Peter is not nearly as advanced as it ought to be because after the discussions of Watson and Neyrey in the period 1988–1993, very little has been accomplished since that time. Thomas J. Kraus's work on the style of 2 Peter is helpful in distinguishing this discourse from most of the rest of the New Testament and showing it has a more cosmopolitan style, but he fails to compare 2 Peter to other Asiatic rhetorical discourses.

Kraus suggests that 2 Peter is reacting to some degree to the circulation of the Pauline corpus. One could have wished for a careful comparison with Ephesians—that other epideictic rhetorical piece that *is* in the form of Asiatic rhetoric.[14] Furthermore, Ephesians, like 2 Peter, is an **encyclical**, a document meant to circulate through various churches, and so there is a general character to it as well. The difference is that 2 Peter is heavily indebted to source material,

ENCYCLICAL DOCUMENT

A document meant to circulate throughout various churches. Encyclical documents often have a general character, as they are intended for a larger audience.

being composite, whereas Ephesians is a fresh composition, although it too has at least one partial source or parallel text—Colossians.[15]

More helpful is the study of L. Thuren. He shows that "change of style" is a central editorial and rhetorical feature of this discourse.[16] Too often, we forget that, for those adept at Greek, style could be a matter of choice of form of expression, not merely a reflection of personality. Also quite helpful is the detailed essay by Terrance Callan, who lays out the basic case that here the Greek is in the grand or more ornate style, specifically in the Asiatic style and with a cogent understanding of rhetoric.[17] He finds this style in inscriptions of the period, particularly the Nimrud-Dagh inscription found in Turkey.[18] What this demonstrates is that this style was quite popular with the public and used especially in the honorific inscriptions that people wanted to sound at least grand, if not grandiose.

To moderns like ourselves, on first glance, the style of 2 Peter seems to be an example of a person overcome with the exuberance of his own verbosity, loving rare words, the coining of terms, and solemn and sonorous and grandiloquent language and phrasing. Cicero tells us that, in terms of ornament, one should use rare words only rarely, new words more frequently, and metaphors and tropes the most frequently of all (de Oratore, 3.153–55). We certainly find all this and more in 2 Peter. There are some 26 metaphors in play in 2 Peter and a barrage of rhetorical devices—hyperbole, onomatopoeia, and other devices. This reminds us that this document was meant to be heard, not read silently, in the main. It is an oral document. There are several long sentences that characterized Greek in the grand style: 2 Peter 1.3–7, 2.4–10a, and 2.12–14.

Lack of a knowledge of Asiatic Greek and its great popularity in the first century and anachronistic applying of modern tastes to 2 Peter have led to the conclusion that the style is too elaborate, grandiose, baroque, or even artificial. Callan is clearly right when he stresses, "We can see that many negative assessments of style of 2 Peter are not evaluations of it according to the canons of style recognized by its author and readers. Instead, they are implicitly expressions of preference for a different style, like the criticism of Asianism in its own time."[19]

Turning the matter around, Callan asks, what does the choice of the grand style tell us about our author's rhetorical purposes? He highlights several good points: (1) The use of the grand Greek style indicates that the author sees himself as expressing powerful and important thoughts. The style suits the lofty subject

Figure 19.2 The statues of the rulers on top of Mt. Nimrud in Turkey. It was here that the famous Nimrud-Dagh stele inscription was found, reflecting the sort of Asiatic Greek also found in 2 Peter.

matter. (2) Writing in the grand style implies that the author is primarily seeking to appeal to the emotions of his audience, not to inform them of things they do not already know. This comports well with the epideictic nature of this discourse. (3) The author wishes to arouse the audience to continue to develop their Christian virtues in light of the return of Christ.[20]

We are dealing with a polemical rhetorical document in 2 Peter, at least in 2 Pet. 2–3. The rhetoric begins immediately after the briefest possible of epistolary introductions in 2 Pet. 1.1–2. There is no epistolary conclusion at all—no personalia (biographical information), no travel plans, no concluding farewell—only a final doxology that is not really an epistolary feature but rather a feature of early Jewish and Christian worship, as this discourse will have been delivered in worship. In other words, epistolary conventions explain next to nothing about this discourse, whereas rhetorical conventions explain the vast majority of it.

2 Peter can be outlined as follows:

RHETORICAL OUTLINE OF 2 PETER

Epistolary Prescript	1.1–2
Exordium/Opening Remarks	1.3–11 (including a catalog of virtues in 1.5–7 in *sorites* (i.e., additive list) form
Quoted Testimony	1.12–21
Beguilers Past and Present—A Rhetorical *Synkrisis* (Comparison) of the Blameworthy	2.1–22 (including a treatment of vices)
Eschatological Reminders	3.1–13
Peroration/Final Emotional Appeal	3.14–18a
Concluding Doxology	3.18b

Here, then, I think we find part of the rhetorical problem, the bone of contention, that prompted the assembling of 2 Peter and its dissemination. More than just the issue of false teachers who were scoffing at early Christian eschatology, our author is worried about losing the Petrine and early Jewish legacy, in the wake of the Pauline one sweeping across the church. He thus writes this encyclical to the whole church. I would suggest that *this may well be the very first document, the very first encyclical, ever written to the entire extant church.* This makes it a very important document indeed in terms of the history of the development of the Christian movement.

Something had to have happened before Ignatius of Antioch comes along early in the second century A.D. and addresses Jewish and Gentile Christians alike in his letters and assumes authority over them. In 2 Peter, we get a little glimpse of what led to that development. It is possible that Linus was one of Peter's converts in Asia Minor who came to Rome, possibly with Peter, in the A.D. 60s. This would explain why he was not present in the Roman churches when Paul wrote Rom. 16 in about A.D. 57, and so is not greeted then.

Finally, it is time to lay to rest the whole theory of "early Catholicism" as supposedly represented in a document like 2 Peter (or for that matter the Pastoral Epistles). That theory of early Christian development argued that, beginning with the second generation of Christians, there was a movement toward the institutionalization of offices in the church and toward treating the "faith" as a body of orthodox doctrine and praxis to be believed and received, with less emphasis on the centrality of Christian experience. In other words, this was seen as a movement toward formalization and more formality as orthodoxy began to take a more definite, and even rigid, form. It was supposed that this movement was nurtured by the waning of early Christian eschatological belief in the possible imminence of Christ's return and the rise of heresy in various forms, which necessitated both centralization of authority and clear articulation of doctrine. The not-so-implicit message was that we should see such texts as 2 Peter not as preserving the earlier legacy but as a fall from the original grace of the early apostolic Gospel and movement. But do we find anything like "early Catholicism" in 2 Peter? Actually, the answer is no. What we find is not a foreshadowing of the second-century church here but a reflection on the apostolic past. We must consider one example of this—the testament of Peter in 2 Pet. 1.

CORE SAMPLINGS—2 PETER 1.12–21

Peter is presented as a prophetic figure pointing to Christ, just as the Old Testament prophets were viewed as doing. There are true prophets and false prophets, true teachers and false teachers, and Peter is being ranked with the former just as the false teachers will be compared with the latter. This is said to be a reminder, and so the audience is being nudged in the direction of praising the good prophets and teachers who point to Christ and blaming the false ones who do not.

We have chosen this portion of 2 Peter because it appears to be Peter's last words to other Christians. "Final words are very important, carefully chosen, not to be forgotten."[21] This is all the more the case when we are dealing with genuine last words, not just a fictive testament masked as someone's last words. But why were these words so important to our author at his time of writing in the A.D. 60s? The answer is not hard to find: "Tradition has replaced the living voice, and the legacy of the past must be preserved. This urgent need put pressure on the church to choose its leadership carefully, to teach its membership thoroughly, and to define 'the true faith' precisely."[22] Just so, and if we can judge by the length of the treatment of false teachers in 2 Pet. 2, our author believes that the church is facing a leadership crisis in his day, and there is danger of losing the essence and character of the apostolic teaching due to the influence of false teaching.

Our author responds to this crisis by dusting off a piece of Petrine tradition, a piece of material from Jude, the Lord's brother. He also alludes to the Pauline tradition that needs to be properly interpreted as well, weaving these things together like a student putting together a good term paper using excellent sources. "Obviously, the author is not an advocate of the church's continual reassessment and reinterpretation of the positions held by a previous generation. The apostolic tradition is for him a package of truth to be handed on."[23]

To good rhetorical effect, our author will contrast truth versus **myth**, with the latter being said to be the character of the false teaching and the former being the character of the apostolic tradition. Nothing less is at stake. And he will trot out a threefold cord of testimony—Peter's, the Old Testament's, and the Holy Spirit's—that bears witness to the truth of the apostolic tradition. Our author clearly thinks, as did Peter, that he lives in dark days, and that the apostolic tradition is a lamp to guide the church in transition along the way as it walks carefully into the post-apostolic era.

It is hard for us, in an age when innovation and change are so highly valued, to enter into the mindset of a culture where tradition was much more highly valued than it is today, and innovation and change, especially in religion, were viewed with great suspicion. If a religion was not ancient, with a hoary pedigree, it qualified as a "superstition," something that would be looked on with great skepticism by the ancients.[24] Our author then uses his rhetoric to play off this cultural dynamic by setting forth the apostolic tradition and contrasting it with the innovations of the false teachers.

2 Peter 1, verse 13, essentially indicates that Peter feels that it is his apostolic responsibility to remind his audience of that proper foundation for Christian living as long as he is living, and indeed beyond (2 Peter 1.15). The last part of 2 Peter 1, verse 14, says literally "as long as I am in this tent." Although this may be an allusion to 1 Pet. 2.11, more likely Peter is either drawing on a common image of the body as a somewhat flimsy and mobile outer shell of the human personality, or perhaps he is thinking of what St. Paul said about his own departure in 2 Cor. 5.1–4. In 1 Peter, there is evidence that Peter knew and was definitely influenced by some of Paul's letters and his thoughts, unlike the author of 2 Peter who shows little Pauline influence. Not only the reference to the body as a tent, but in 2 Peter 1, verse 14, the "putting off" (the language used for taking off clothes) of it seems to recall 2 Cor. 5.1–10. Peter, like Paul, says nothing about a body/soul dualism, but there is no doubt some sort of body/personality or body/life dualism is here as in 2 Cor. 5. The point in our text, however, is not to teach about such matters. Nonetheless, the words of a hymn convey the image well: "Here in the body pent, absent from heaven I roam, yet nightly I pitch my

MYTH

Greek myths, the stories about the gods, could be seen as stories that were not literally true or grounded in history. However, these myths expressed religious, moral, or philosophical truth in pictorial form.

moving tent, a day's march nearer home." If this idea is in Peter's mind, then indeed 1 Pet. 2.11 may be in the back of his mind.

In 2 Peter 1, verse 14, Peter says he knows that it will be time to divest himself of this tent "soon." Perhaps there had been a recent prophecy of Peter's death, but the second half of 2 Peter 1, verse 21, adds an additional reference to a prophecy by Jesus of Peter's death ("just as also Jesus said. . . ."). John 21.18 is likely in view where it is implied that, when Peter is old, he will die by crucifixion. Most likely, 2 Peter 1, verse 15, refers to Peter making every effort to ensure that his testimony is written down and conveyed to the same audience that received 1 Peter and, in addition, to a much wider audience, as things turned out. In this, he succeeded, and no doubt this discourse had a special poignancy for those who did receive it after Peter's death and heard his words speak to them after he had met a violent death. Note the connection between Peter's talking about his own "exodus" or departure here and the connection with at least one tradition of the Transfiguration story. Luke 9.31 uses the exact same word, *exodus,* to describe what Moses and Elijah were talking to Jesus about during the Transfiguration experience (cf. Wis. Sol. 3.2 and 7.6, where it is also used of death; and especially Josephus, *Ant.* 4.189, where Moses in his farewell message uses this term).

There is a remarkable tradition found in the much later apocryphal document called the Acts of Peter in which Peter has a *Quo Vadis* experience. The legend relates that Peter is leaving Rome to escape arrest by Nero's men, and he is met and confronted on the road by Jesus himself. Peter asks Jesus, "Where are you going?" (*Quo Vadis* in Latin). Jesus replies that he is going into Rome to be crucified again. Peter thus turns back and submits to crucifixion. We can date this story no earlier than about A.D. 180, and so we really cannot see this as the backdrop to these verses in 2 Peter, but it shows the trajectory of one way the Petrine tradition could go when not constrained by historical evidence.

2 Peter 1, verse 16, begins the defense by Peter of the Gospel he preached to his hearers. Notice that he does not accuse the opponents of following myths, but rebuts the charge that he had done so. The "we" no doubt refers to the apostle(s), presumably those who preached in or wrote to the churches in Asia Minor. What was a myth in New Testament times? What did the term mean?

> The old Greek myths, the stories about the gods, could be seen as stories which were not literally true but expressed religious, moral, or philosophical truth in pictorial form. They could be subjected to allegorical interpretation, as by the Stoics. The Hellenistic age was in many respects one which showed a "growing preference for . . . [myth] over . . . [rational argument] as a means of expressing truth. . . ." on the other hand, there was a strong tradition of criticism and repudiation of myths, as morally unedifying, or as childish, nonsensical or fabulous. Here *mythos* can come, like "myth" in much

modern English usage, to mean a story which is *not true,* a fable or fairy story (again in the derogatory senses).[25]

In short, a "myth" was something that was not grounded in history, although it may have some philosophical or moral truth content (cf. 1 Tim. 1.4; 2 Tim. 4.4; Josephus, *Ant.* 1.22).[26] Diodorus Siculus puts it this way: "For it is true that the myths which are related about Hades, in spite of the fact that their subject matter is fictitious, contribute greatly to fostering piety and justice amongst human beings" (1.2.2).

Peter sets about the task of refuting the idea that there would be no future *parousia* and judgment in space and time. These false teachers apparently saw Christianity as a matter of totally realized eschatology (perhaps not unlike the problem in Corinth: cf. 1 Cor. 15, "How can some of you say there is no resurrection from the dead?")—the resurrection or new life being seen as either what happened at baptism or perhaps present spiritual life was constituted by ecstatic experiences leading to (false) prophecy. The opponents thought such stories about the *parousia* were clever but in fact were fabrications of an overheated Christian mindset. In Plato's *Republic* 2.364–66, Plato complained that tales about future divine judgment were being used by both nannies and rulers to enforce morality. This complaint was still being made much later by Epicureans like Lucretius (*Nature of Things* 3.966–1023). Something like this seems to have been the complaint of the false teachers about the apostolic tradition about the *parousia.* Philo made the same sort of contrast between a "myth" and a sacred oracle or testimony on more than one occasion (*Flight,* 121 and 152), using the formula "not a myth invented . . . but a sacred oracle."

One of the small indicators of the character of the rhetoric here is that, whereas Peter uses the term *revelation* to refer to the second coming in 1 Peter, here he uses *parousia,* or royal arrival/visit (see 1 Thess. 2.19). The emphasis thus is on the appearing of the glorious king in the future as he appeared in the past on the Mount of Transfiguration. Thus, the future, like the past, is related to the present of the speaker and present issues, as is usual in epideictic rhetoric.

Beginning in 2 Peter 1, verse 16b, Peter rebuts this charge. Not only had he not followed myths, he had also made known to his audience the power and *parousia* of the Lord. Probably here, as elsewhere in this discourse, we have a **hendiadys**, meaning "powerful coming" or "coming in power," instead of two separate matters. Far from concocting myths, Peter and other apostles had been eyewitnesses of and about the Transfiguration. The Greek word used here is a crucial one, meaning literally "observers" or "spectators." In 1 Pet. 2.12, it refers to being witnesses/spectators of a believer's good deeds, but this is connected to glorifying God at Christ's *parousia,* a clear connection to our present text. Further, this terminology is used nowhere else in the whole New Testament in any form of the word, so the connection can hardly be accidental here. We must take this as strong evidence that 2 Peter 1.12–21 is from Peter himself.

HENDIADYS

A figure of speech that expresses one idea with two words (typically joined by a conjunction). For example, the words "coming in power" express one major idea. A hendiadys is interchangeable with the use of an adjective and a noun such as "powerful coming."

What is it that Peter had seen at the Transfiguration? He says here that he had seen Christ's majesty, a majesty or "glory and honor" (cf. Heb. 1.3, 8.1 as descriptors of God and Ps. 8.5 of humans crowned with glory and honor). Christ had received these things from God the Father on that occasion. We are unable to go into detail about that here, but it appears rather clear that this description of the Transfiguration is independent of the Gospel accounts. Peter himself is likely giving his own remembrances here that would quite naturally not conform to any secondhand formulations of the event.

It is probable that we should see Psalm 2 in the background here (especially Ps. 2.7b–12), which is an enthronement psalm that contains the line, "You are my son—today I have become your father." The importance of this allusion to Psalm 2 is this: Peter sees in the Transfiguration a depiction of Jesus being installed as eschatological king and judge over all the earth, an office he does not assume until the *parousia.*

It is quite probable that the Synoptic evangelists (especially Mark) also saw the Transfiguration as a foreshadowing not of resurrection or ascension but of *parousia.* In fact, in Matt. 16.28, there is a direct reference to the coming of the son in/into his kingdom just before the Transfiguration story. And interestingly, later Christian tradition also wanted to connect the Transfiguration with the *parousia.*[27]

Presumably, the reason Peter wanted to set up booths is because he thought that the great and final day of eschatological celebration was at hand (see Mk. 9.5ff.). If this is a correct interpretation of our text, it explains why Peter refers to the Transfiguration to refute the notion that there would be no *parousia.* Peter is saying "at the Transfiguration, which I saw personally, Christ was given in token an office that he will not fulfill until his *parousia.* Therefore, there must be a *parousia,* or else the Transfiguration was pointless."

2 Peter 1, verse 17b, is a reverential way of avoiding two things: saying God spoke directly and saying God's name. The "majestic glory" referred to at the end of the verse is simply another Semitic way of saying God (cf. 1 Clem. 9.2). Notice that Peter intends to focus only on the investiture (2 Peter 1, verse 17a) and what the voice said (2 Peter 1, verse 17b). The literal rendering here would be "a voice was conveyed from the Majestic Glory." There is probably sufficient evidence to suggest that "my Beloved" was in fact a separate Messianic title for Christ (see Eph. 1.9), meaning "my Elect One."

The last phrase in 2 Peter 1, verse 17c, is "with whom/in whom I am well pleased." The point of this is clearly that the Transfiguration and that which it foreshadows (*parousia*) are part of God's eternal plan involving the election of Jesus as king and judge over the world. It is thus hardly a humanly contrived myth. Peter stresses that he was with Jesus then and heard all this, so he can vouch for it personally. It happened on the holy mountain. Here, we may again see an allusion to Ps. 2.6: "on Zion my holy hill." Peter then has cast his own experience in scriptural language, investing it with such language to indicate that this event was a fulfillment of Messianic prophecy in the Psalms. This prepares us for what follows in 2 Peter 1, verses 19–21.

Possibly, 2 Peter 1, verse 19, should be seen as an allusion to the prophetic word in Ps. 2. Peter is probably not suggesting here that it has greater certainty than his own personal experience but that it has very great certainty and it is something on which one can firmly rely. The prophetic word then is seen here as a second witness to the truth of the *parousia's* historicity. The debate has been about whether Peter is saying that Scripture confirms his experience or that the apostolic witness fulfills and thus authenticates Scripture. But the meaning "made more sure" is doubtful. Probably, we should translate the term as a superlative—"made very firm."

Nor is there likely a comparison between the value of prophecy vis-à-vis the value of personal experience. The point rather seems to be that Peter is introducing a second and objective witness here that people can check out for themselves. The drift of the argument seems to be, "if you do not believe me, check out the Old Testament Messianic prophecies, here especially Ps. 2.9. The prophetic word has unquestionable clarity and certainty, you can rely on it." 2 Peter 1, verse 19b, indicates that the audience must heed this word, for it is their only light in an otherwise dark and murky world—it can guide them through the darkness as nothing else can. 2 Peter 1, verse 19c, must be seen as a reference to the *parousia,* which causes no problems if the author had said only "when the day dawns."

Notice he says that these prophetic words: guide us *until then.* There is a time-conditioned element even in Scripture. To be sure, it is eternal truth, but it is only applicable in and to situations in time, and when time expires, we will no longer need a guide book to walk through the dark; believers will have in fact the day star in their very hearts to illumine them (cf. 1 Cor. 13.8–13—prophecy and knowledge cease—and the general thought of Jer. 31 about God's Word written on the heart).

The reference to the "light-bearer" should not puzzle us for long because Num. 24.17 (LXX) seems to be in the background here—"a star shall rise out of Jacob," and the reference is to the Messiah. The point then is that Christ will illumine the believer not just from the outside in but from the inside out on the day of *parousia,* because his day of revelation will be their day of transformation. Hence, the phrase "in your hearts" is natural and understandable. It is not a reference to believers being currently and slowly illuminated by God's presence or word. F. Craddock puts it this way: "'in your hearts' reminds us that the day of the Lord will not only be cosmic in its immensity but also personally transforming in its effect."[28] We may wish to compare the references to Christ as morning star in Rev. 2.28 and 22.16.

2 Peter 1, verses 20–21, express why we may so firmly rely on Old Testament prophecy, or why it has such great certainty. Verse 21 gives the reason for verse 20,

and we will tackle it first. In fact, we have here a short-form syllogism, otherwise known as an enthymeme.[29] We can outline it as follows:

1. No real prophecy simply comes from the prophet's imagination and interpretation.

2. Rather, all genuine prophecy like that found in the Old Testament is inspired by the Spirit.

3. Therefore, those prophecies in the Old Testament about the *parousia* are inspired and true.

Biblical prophecy was never brought about by the will of a human being, but rather humans borne (carried) along by the Holy Spirit spoke from God. We find in these words a definition of inspiration and how the prophetic Scriptures came to be. First, the author insists that true prophecy never is a purely human product that results from mere human will. The "not" in 2 Peter 1, verse 21a, contrasts with verse 21b's "but." Instead, these persons were borne along, carried, and compelled by the Holy Spirit so that they spoke not merely human words but "from God." The key verb here "carried along" can be used of the wind moving something along or driving it in a certain direction, or it can be used figuratively of God's Spirit moving or motivating human beings (cf. Job 17.1 LXX).

The phrases here suggest that God is the primary author of prophetic Scripture. These prophets, although they spoke in their own words, spoke from God. What does "carried along," "borne along," "impelled," and "moved" by the Holy Spirit mean? We should probably not see any mechanical dictation theory (a word for word dictation). Rather, it is intended to indicate that the human authors were guided, directed, and motivated by the Holy Spirit so that what they said was not their own creation or imaginings but the very word of God himself—the truth. Thus, the Spirit is the motivator or originator, the guide or guard, of the words of the human author so that what he says is actually spoken from God.

Now we must ask what 2 Peter 1, verse 20, means. Do we read "no prophecy is a matter of one's own interpretation" or "no prophecy arises from the prophet's own interpretation"? Either one of these is possible, but most likely it means, "It is not a matter of one's own interpretation, because it derives from God and is objective truth, not subjective opinion." J. Neyrey rightly reminds us that we are dealing with a collectivist culture where the group was primary, the individual secondary, and "the right of private interpretation" was not even remotely on the horizon.[30] Perhaps then Peter is refuting an argument of his opponents that said, "So he says there is going to be a *parousia* and that the Old Testament says so. Well that's just his interpretation of the matter."

Peter has thus left us on the high ground at the end of his testimony—with the witness of Scripture. Both Scripture and apostolic experience and testimony are on the side of the teaching in this discourse. It is interesting that Paul, in texts like Gal. 3 and 1 Cor. 11, also appeals to experience first and then to Scripture to support his argument. And he has stressed that when it comes to interpreting Scripture, it is not just a matter of my opinion versus your opinion. The Holy Spirit was viewed as the one who interprets the words in and for the prophet. Teachings that were at variance with apostolic teaching and interpretation of Scripture were to be rejected. All of this suggests a time when the church had begun to think about what counted as Scripture, where its own genuine experiences fit into the picture, and what it meant to live in the eschatological age. These reflections would have special import at the end of the apostolic era when the living voice of someone like Peter, an eyewitness, had been stilled, except through the medium of the words he left behind—his personal testimony.

IMPLICATIONS

Second Peter is perhaps *the* document in the New Testament that most reveals how documents functioned very differently in the first century than they do today. In the first century A.D., most people could not read and write. Often, things written down were just scripts for some oral proclamation that was going to happen later by an ambassador, a sage, a philosopher, or a preacher. Second Peter is not only a composite document, it is also an oral document reflecting a Greek oral and rhetorical style popular especially in what we today call Turkey.

Second Peter presents us with a document that challenges our modern notions of what counts as "authorship," for it includes only an eyewitness source from Peter, but it is a document put together by someone else. It also includes most of Jude in an edited form. What this document, assembled in the post-apostolic age, testifies to is how highly valued the writings and sayings of the apostles still were in that era—whether from a Peter or a Jude or a Paul. Indeed, 2 Peter 3 indicates that Paul's writings are already being treated as if they were Scriptures. Second Peter then becomes an important testimony about the transition to the post-apostolic age, and how those who lived then realized they were not apostles nor creators of Holy Writ. Rather, they realized that Holy Writ and true prophecy came largely from an earlier time, and the editor lived when false prophets needed to be distinguished and critiqued on the basis of the earlier apostolic traditions. This would continue to be the practice of the church of the second and third centuries.

KEY TERMS

Encyclical

Hendiadys

Myth

Parousia

Sapiential Literature

FOR FURTHER READING

Barrett, C. K. "Myth and the New Testament: The Greek Word *Mythos.*" *Expository Times* 68 (1957): 345–348.

Neyrey, Jerome. "The Apologetic Use of the Transfiguration in 2 Peter 1.16–21." *Catholic Biblical Quarterly* 42 (1980): 504–519.

Watson, D. F. "2 Peter." In *New Interpreter's Bible,* vol. 12. Nashville, TN: Abingdon, 1988.

Witherington, B. *Letters and Homilies for Hellenized Christians.* Vol. 2, *A Socio-Rhetorical Commentary on 1-2 Peter.* Downers Grove, IL: InterVarsity Press, 2007.

———. "A Petrine Source in 2 Peter." In *Society of Biblical Literature 1985 Seminar Papers,* edited by K. H. Richards, 187–192. Atlanta, GA: Scholars Press.

STUDY QUESTIONS

Why do you think Peter would choose the Transfiguration as an event to especially leave a testimony about for future generations?

Reflect on the role of scribes as opposed to the role of authors in the first-century world. What was the difference between the two roles?

Peter has some interesting things to say about the nature of inspiration and prophecy. What sort of view of these things is espoused in 2 Peter 1?

Why do you think this book was included in the New Testament when the canon was closed in the fourth century A.D.?

NOTES

1. K. van der Toorn, *Scribal Culture and the Making of the Hebrew Bible* (Cambridge, MA: Harvard University Press, 2007), 47–48.

2. T. Callan, "The Style of the Second Letter of Peter," *Biblica* 84 (2003): 202–224; here 209, nn. 37 and 38.

3. J. D. G. Dunn, *Unity and Diversity in the New Testament: An Inquiry into the Character of Earliest Christianity* (Philadelphia, PA: Westminster John Knox Press, 1977), 285–286.

4. Douglas Moo, *2 Peter, Jude* (Grand Rapids, MI: Zondervan, 1996), 16–18.

5. R. P. Martin, *New Testament Foundations: A Guide for Christian Students,* vol. 2, *The Acts, the Letters, the Apocalypse,* rev. ed. (Eugene, OR: Wipf and Stock, 2000), 385.

6. D. F. Watson, *Invention, Arrangement, and Style: Rhetorical Criticism of Jude and 2 Peter* (Atlanta, GA: Scholars Press, 1988), 163–187.

7. R. J. Bauckham, *Jude, 2 Peter,* Word Biblical Commentary, vol. 50, (Waco, TX: Word Books, 1983), 141–143.

8. Michael J. Gilmour, *The Significance of Parallels between 2 Peter and Other Early Christian Literature* (Leiden, The Netherlands: E. J. Brill, 2002), 120.

9. cf. G. H. Boobyer, "The Indebtedness of 2 Peter to 1 Peter," in *New Testament Essays: Studies in Memory of Thomas Water Manson,* ed. A. J. B. Higgins (Manchester: Manchester University Press, 1959), 44–51. I have argued this

case at length in B. Witherington, *Letters and Homilies for Hellenized Christians*, vol. 2, *A Socio-Rhetorical Commentary on 1-2 Peter* (Downers Grove, IL: InterVarsity Press, 2008).

10. Bauckham, *Jude, 2 Peter* , 137.

11. Take, for example, the book of Proverbs, attributed to Solomon, which contains only some material that likely goes back to Solomon and various other sources of wise sayings as well, some of which Solomon may have collected and some of which was collected later. Similarly, in Ecclesiastes, we have the sayings of Qoheleth; but this book is put together, as its last chapter manifests, by a later scribe or tradent. The same seems to be the case with 2 Peter, which is edited by a scribe, perhaps Linus.

12. Glenn W. Barker, William L. Lane, and J. Ramsey Michaels, *The New Testament Speaks* (San Francisco: Harper & Row, 1969), 352.

13. On the use of Petrine material in 2 Peter, see B. Witherington, "A Petrine Source in 2 Peter," in *Society of Biblical Literature 1985 Seminar Papers*, ed. K. H. Richards (Atlanta, GA: Scholars Press, 1985), 187–192.

14. Thomas J. Kraus, *Sprache, Stil und historischer Ort des zweiten Petrusbriefes* (Tubingen, Germany: Mohr-Siebeck, 2001).

15. B. Witherington, "Introduction," in *Letters to Philemon, Colossians, and Ephesians* (Grand Rapids, MI: Eerdmans, 2007), 1–36.

16. L. Thuren, "Style Never Goes out of Fashion: 2 Peter Re-Evaluated," in *Rhetoric, Scripture and Theology: Essays from the 1994 Pretoria Conference, Journal for the Study of the New Testament Supplement Series*, 131, ed. S. E. Porter and T. H. Olbricht (Sheffield, England: Sheffield Academic Press, 1996), 329–347.

17. T. Callan, "The Style of the Second Letter of Peter," *Biblica* 84 (2003): 202–224.

18. Ibid. 217–218.

19. Ibid. 223.

20. Ibid. 223–224.

21. F. B. Craddock, *First and Second Peter and Jude, Westminster Bible Companion* (Louisville, KY: Westminster John Knox Press, 1995), 103.

22. Ibid. 102.

23. Ibid. 104.

24. J. H. Neyrey, *2 Peter, Jude,* Anchor Yale Bible Commentaries (New Haven, CT: Yale University Press, 1994), 166.

25. Bauckham, *Jude, 2 Peter*, 213.

26. C. K. Barrett, "Myth and the New Testament: The Greek Word Mythos," *Expository Times* 68 (1957): 345–348.

27. Jerome Neyrey, "The Apologetic Use of the Transfiguration in 2 Peter 1.16–21," *Catholic Biblical Quarterly* 42 (1980): 504–519.

28. Craddock, *First and Second Peter*, 107.

29. Watson, *Invention, Arrangement, and Style*, 105.

30. Neyrey, *2 Peter, Jude,* 182.

The view from the summit on the island of Patmos. It was here that John the prophet was exiled, probably working in a penal colony, and here where he received his revelations, which were compiled in the Book of Revelation sometime in the A.D. 90s. (© Mark R. Fairchild, Ph.D.)

20 APOCALYPSE LATER— The BOOK of REVELATION

IF YOU HAVE EVER BEEN TO A 4TH OF JULY CELEBRATION, you quickly discover that they always save the best fireworks display for last. The New Testament is rather like that. Revelation is full of sound and fury—gnarly dragons, damsels in distress (see Rev. 12), all heaven breaking loose in the form of three sets of seven judgments, and Jesus hip deep in blood when he returns. If any book in the New Testament was meant to produce "shock and awe," it is this one. Whatever else one may say about it, the Book of Revelation is scarcely boring. The New Testament ends with a bang, not a whimper.

The problem is that Revelation is the most complex book (besides 2 Peter) in the New Testament and the one most difficult to understand. If you are a new student of the New Testament, whatever you do, don't start your odyssey through the New Testament with this book! And if, when you first read Revelation, you are more than puzzled, don't feel bad. In fact, most of the Protestant Reformers did not understand it, and that great commentator on every other book of the New Testament, John Calvin, did not attempt a commentary on this book. Indeed, to judge from the comments of

at a Glance

This last visionary book of
the New Testament comes
from the mind and imagi-
nation of John, a Christian
prophet marooned on the
island of Patmos 40 miles
off the coast of western Asia
Minor. He is probably not the
same person as John the son
of Zebedee, although that
cannot entirely be ruled out.
More likely, he is the same
person as the one called "the
Elder" in 2–3 John. Likely
written in the last decade
of the first century during
a period of pressure and
persecution of Christians
under the reign of Domitian,
it provides us with the only
full book of prophecy in the
New Testament and, in this
case, apocalyptic prophecy.
Its message is that Christians
need to be prepared to follow
their master, bearing witness
even unto death, for justice
and judgment must be left
in the hands of the only
one worthy of judging the
world—the lamb who un-
seals the seals and sees all.

ARNION

A Greek word for "lamb."

AMNOS

A Greek word for "lamb."

some of the church fathers, you might think we would need to hang a sign out in front of this book saying "Abandon hope, all ye who enter here!" Fortunately, we do not really need to be that skeptical about comprehending this book. The question is—Where do we *begin* to understand it?

WHO, WHAT, WHEN, WHERE, AND WHY?

The Book of Revelation was written by a man we call John of Patmos. He identifies himself clearly in Rev. 1.1. This book then is not *pseudonymous,* that is, not
falsely ascribed to someone who did not in fact write it. But who is this John? If
you do a close reading of this text in its original language, Greek, you learn the
following things. First, the author does not claim to be one of the original apostles or eyewitnesses of the life of Jesus, unlike the Beloved Disciple. In fact, texts
like Rev. 21.14, which talks about the 12 apostles whose names are inscribed on
the walls of the new Jerusalem, suggest that the author is distinguishing himself
from these important figures from the past. John claims to be a seer—a visionary prophet—and what we have in the Book of Revelation is something very
different from the material we have in either the Gospel of John or the Letters of
John. Second, the Greek of Revelation is of a whole different ilk from the Greek
in the Gospel of John and 1 John. Although the Greek style of a particular writer
can change some over time, we are talking about a dramatically different style
and sort of Greek in Revelation compared to the Gospel and 1 John. Third, in
fact, you would have to argue that the author of Revelation got a vocabulary and
grammar transplant to explain some of the differences. For example, take the
word for lamb in Revelation, **arnion**. It is used some 29 times in Revelation. By
contrast, *arnion* is never used for lamb in the Gospel John; **amnos** is. Or take the
Greek spelling for Jerusalem in Revelation compared to the Gospel: *Ierosalem* in
Revelation, but *Ierosoluma* in the Gospel. Or take the Greek word **ethnos/ethne**,
which always means the Gentile nations in Revelation. In the Gospel of John,
it refers always and exclusively to the *Jews*! And even when John and the author
of the fourth Gospel use the same Greek word, they mean different things by it.
Take the word **alethinos**, which means true as opposed to false in Revelation: in
the Gospel, it means authentic or genuine as opposed to phony.

I could go on and on giving examples, but the point is that the same person
did not write all these "John" documents. John of Patmos is a prophet who has
authority in at least the seven churches he addresses in Asia Minor in Rev. 2–3.
He does not claim to be an apostle or an eyewitness of the historical Jesus, but
he does claim to be an eye- and *ear*witness of all sorts of visions of Christ and
many other things in heaven and on earth. He is perhaps also the person who,
as an old man, penned 2–3 John and, after he returned from exile, collected and
edited the testimony of the Beloved Disciple into the fourth Gospel.

Figure 20.1 The Artemis Temple at Sardis, another city of Revelation.
(© Mark R. Fairchild, Ph.D.)

The *where* of this book is easy. It was written in the first century A.D. from the island of Patmos, which is about 40 miles off the west coast of Turkey (ancient Asia Minor). It was written to seven churches, which, to judge from the letters in Rev. 2–3, had existed for some time, probably some decades. Because there is evidence of pressure, prosecution, and even martyrdom in these churches, the document has been usually dated either to the period of Nero's persecutions in the A.D. 60s or to the time of Domitian's persecutions in the A.D. 90s The latter times make much more sense, considering not only the age of the congregations addressed but also a variety of other clues in Revelation: (1) Calling Rome Babylon makes best sense after the destruction of Jerusalem in A.D. 70 and not before it. Rome would be seen by this Jewish Christian prophet as doing to Jerusalem the same sort of thing Babylon did in the sixth century B.C. (2) The author seems to know some of the content of Paul's letters. (3) Jerusalem is likened to two previously destroyed cities, Sodom and Gomorrah. This does not fit pre- A.D. 70 Jerusalem, but it makes sense if the author is writing long after the destruction of Jerusalem. (4) The allusions to the worship of the emperor in this book better suit the time of Domitian's reign. All in all, it is likely this book was written during that megalomaniac emperor's brutal rule in the A.D. 90s.

As for *why* this book was composed, it seems clear that it was written to comfort and inspire beleaguered Christians under pressure and persecution in Asia Minor. This book presents the audience with a profound theology of suffering and bearing faithful witness even unto death. Indeed, the very word *martus,* meaning witness, in this book begins to have its later sense—someone who bore faithful witness even unto death, like Antipas (see Rev. 2–3). It is not an accident that the dominant image of Christ in this book is the image of the slain but

ETHNOS/ETHNE

A Greek word that may be used to refer to either Gentile nations or to the Jewish nation. Context will help to determine the correct usage. For example, in Revelation, the term refers to the Gentile nations. In John, it refers to the Jewish nation.

ALETHINOS

A Greek word that means true. In certain cases, it may also mean authentic or genuine.

triumphant lamb. It is an image meant to inspire Christians and encourage them to believe there would be triumph beyond tragedy, victory beyond death. This book was written so the saints in Asia Minor would lift up their eyes not just to heaven, whence comes their help, but to look forward to the time of Christ's return for judgment and redemption.

Although there are many images of destruction and judgment in this book, the constant theme beginning in Rev. 5 is "judgment is mine says the Lord, I will repay." That is, the message for Christians in Asia Minor is not "get ready to fight or retaliate for persecution," but rather "be prepared to die for the sake of Christ and your faith, and leave judgment in the hands of the Lord." Indeed, Revelation 5 says that only Christ is worthy of punishing or judging the world. No one else is worthy of unleashing the three sets of seven judgments on the world and then coming in person to finish the job. This book is not a call to arms for Christians; it is a call to say "a farewell to arms" and be prepared to be martyred. It is the earliest Christian "book of martyrs." We have raised as many questions as we have answered, and so we need to consider some of these issues in a bit more detail now because of their complexity.

THE PARTICULARITY OF REVELATION

We must take seriously the evidence in Rev. 2–3 that we are dealing with a document addressed to the actual congregations with which John had contact, congregations on the western edge of the province of Asia. In fact, all of these congregations are on the main road or roads out of Ephesus that connect this region. Early Christianity was an urban phenomenon by and large, a fact to which Revelation bears witness. If we probe more closely into the social situation of these Christians, then we need to bear in mind that only two letters—that to Smyrna (Rev. 2.8–11) and that to Pergamum (Rev. 2.12–17)—address the issue of the relationship of the church to a social reality outside itself. In both cases, we discover that "the only references to the wider Roman Asian milieu are to the repression of Christians,"[1] including the martyrdom of a man named Antipas. To this may be added the unremittingly negative portrait of the powers that be, including the emperor, in various parts of Revelation.

It is perhaps misleading to point out that we have no evidence of *systematic* persecution of Christians by Roman officials in this period, when in fact we do have clear evidence of suffering, oppression, repression, suppression, confisca-tion of property, and occasional martyrdom. On the whole, it appears to be on target to conclude that we are dealing with "a socio-religious setting for the Revelation of John in which Asian Christians experienced local harassment, ridicule, discrimination and oppression in the early 90s for their religious be-liefs and customs."[2] A careful examination of the use of the word *martus* shows

Figure 20.2 Laodicea was one of the seven cities mentioned in Rev. 2–3 that had churches. This city, as this picture of its agora indicates, was a city on the rise with considerable wealth. This created problems for the church there. (© *Mark R. Fairchild, Ph.D.*)

that in each occurrence in Revelation (five cases—1.5, 3.14 [of Jesus], 2.13, 11.3, 17.6), the violent death of someone who was a faithful witness is referred to. Indeed, the term that is translated as "faithful" (*pistos*) in Rev. 2.10 and 13 and perhaps also in 1.5 seems to mean faithful unto death. This does not mean that *martus* in Revelation is already a technical term for martyr—because Rev. 15.5 shows it can be used to just mean "witness"—but rather that it regularly carries the connotation in this document of a witness who is faithful even unto a violent death.[3]

What does this mean in regard to the particular circumstances of John himself? Domitian, like other emperors and with the aid of those who served under him, regularly used the form of punishment known as *relegation*. There were two forms this could take: *relegatio in insulam* or *deportatio ad insulam*. The former meant confinement within an island, and the latter was deportation to an island—but thereafter, one had freedom within the island context. In either case, banishment for life was involved. This was, indeed, under any normal circumstances, a permanent ban of persons from the regions where they had previously lived, at least until that emperor died and his decrees ceased to be binding.

It is very possible that John was suffering such a lifetime ban from the western coast of Asia Minor, hence the urgency to write to his converts. Note that he nowhere states that he hopes to come to them soon. Indeed, he only speaks of Jesus coming quickly. Patmos, some 40 miles off the coast of Asia Minor (modern Turkey), was indeed no prize to live on. Like other islands, it was likely used as a penal colony by the Romans. It is not clear from our text whether John

CLUES FROM THE
CULTURE

Then comes a Jewess . . . a
high priestess of the tree,
a trusty go-between of the
highest heaven. She too fills
her palm, but more sparingly,
for a Jew will interpret dreams
of any kind you please for the
minutest of coins.

—Juvenal Satire 6.42

was merely deported, or whether he was also confined and subjected to hard labor while on Patmos, but in either case, he could not hope to visit his converts again. In light of this, one can see Revelation as an attempt to provide the whole apocalyptic picture to the Johannine audience in one effort because John himself would be unable to come and explain these matters to these churches through conversations over a period of time.

If it is true that John had suffered banishment from Asia Minor, from a sociological point of view, this strongly suggests that he was someone important, a leader in the churches in Asia Minor, and not merely a peripheral prophet. This would explain why he took it upon himself to exhort these various churches as he did on the basis of some intimate knowledge of their spiritual and social conditions. Writing before the time of the monarchial bishops, but probably after the time when the apostles were present in the region, John sought to assert his prophetic authority in order to help these churches get through a dark period of oppression and suppression that could and sometimes did lead to martyrdom. What sort of person was this John of Patmos, and how did he think and write?

THE RHETORIC AND RESOURCES OF REVELATION

Revelation is full of allusions to and partial quotations of the Old Testament. Usually, it is maintained that John used the Old Testament and other early Jewish (and Greco-Roman) sources in the same way a miner goes after gold, digging around for what he is looking for without much regard for the setting in which the precious material was originally found. It is also urged that in this reappropriation of earlier material, John shows little interest in the original significance or meaning that a verse or an image or an idea originally had. This view has of late been challenged.[4] R. Bauckham and J. Fekkes have both argued that John has engaged in meticulous exegesis of his source material, largely the Old Testament prophetic books, and they appear to be largely right.[5]

John the prophet draws his materials directly from the Hebrew or Aramaic prophecies in the Old Testament and not from the Greek Old Testament, the LXX.[6] This suggests that while Revelation may not be an example of translation Greek, it may well be an example of second-language Greek; that is, the author's primary language is Aramaic.[7] Sometimes, too much stress has been placed on John's use of apocalyptic traditions and not enough on his self-understanding as a prophet. This is a matter of proper balancing because this work needs to be seen as a work of apocalyptic prophecy. The apocalyptic symbols and ideas serve the cause of prophetic interpretation of numerous Old Testament texts, and clearly the Old Testament is John's primary nonvisionary source of material. *John believes wholeheartedly that he and his audience live in an age when various of the prophecies have and are coming true, and so there is a definite concern on his part about the relationship between promise/prophecy and fulfillment, although he approaches the matter somewhat differently than the first or third evangelists.*

Instead of pretending to be an ancient luminary, while actually writing history in the guise of prophecy, John grounds his work right from the outset in his own quite particular historical situation by beginning the work addressing particular congregations dealing with specific issues. The "attachment of a epistolary format to the visions, along with the personal identification of John, lifts the book out of the realm of the pseudonymous apocalypses and places it within the context of real churches with specific problems in a fairly limited local setting."[8] John knows his audience and their issues, and he reflects a detailed knowledge of their geographical, historical, political, and religious circumstances.[9]

But what we find in this book should hardly be called mere prophetic letters. The epistolary form that frames this work involves too little of the document to be seen as the defining feature of it. No, John wishes to unveil some of the Revelation, in particular the revelatory visions he has received from God, and do so in a manner that will serve as exhortation and comfort for his audience. The initial phrase "revelation of Jesus Christ" in Rev. 1.1 is not some technical term for the genre of the work or the manner of the revelation or even a claim to some specific sort of vision experience but rather an indication that all that follows ultimately comes from God and thus is divine revelation.

It is no accident that Revelation is the only book in the New Testament that, like what we often find in Old Testament prophetic works, includes first-person oracles in the name of the deity. John sees himself, like many other prophets, as God's mouthpiece, and he would repudiate the notion that what he unveils is his own prophecy that he dreamed up. No indeed, it is the revelation of Jesus Christ that this book contains. This is why John stresses that these prophecies should not be altered or deleted (Rev. 22.18–19).

It is important to recognize that John is talking about a sort of prophecy that, unlike some other New Testament prophecy referred to by Paul (in 1 Cor. 14, cf. 1 Thess. 5.21), does not require sifting and weighing or testing or evaluating, but rather like the prophecies in the Old Testament is by and large meant to simply be received and applied.

> John not only takes up *where* the prophets left off, but he also takes over *what* they left behind. He is not only part of a prophetic circle, but also stands in a prophetic continuum that carries on and brings to final revelation the living words of God entrusted to the care of the brotherhood (Rev. 10.7).[10]

It is in this context that one must evaluate John's use of the Old Testament, including especially its prophetic portions.

Perhaps the main reason John does not quote the Old Testament very frequently is because he approaches that material not as a scribe or sage or apostle but as a prophet. "He does not commend his visions on the basis of apostolic authority conferred by the *earthly* Jesus. Nor is his book a personal word of exhortation which derives its authority from quoting divine revelation. . . . His commission gives birth to a new prophecy—a fresh revelation—which is authorized simultaneously by God, the *risen* Christ, and the divine Spirit."[11] This new revelation can entail quoting the Old Testament, but because John sees himself as on a par with Old Testament prophets, or among their number, he does not very often feel the need to quote it (but compare Rev. 2.26b–27 to Ps. 2.8a, 9). The vast array of allusions and quotes of the Old Testament (at least 278 allusions in the 404 verses in the book) serves a variety of purposes, one of which is that it bolsters the authority of the entire work and the *ethos* of the speaker John.

Like the prophets of old, John uses prophetic diction and first-person style, as well as prophetic phrases, images, and ideas. John does not borrow Old Testament material merely for its poetic effect or metaphorical force; he "wants the readers to appreciate the prophetic foundation of his statements."[12] Fekkes shows in great detail how in the vast majority of cases, John's use of an Old Testament text goes beyond similarities of language and imagery to a similar use of themes, and the correspondence even extends "to the setting and purpose of the original biblical passage" when compared to its reuse in Revelation. John seems to choose his texts on the basis of theme and the issue he wishes to address rather than on the basis of canonical source, although clearly he favors apocalyptic material such as that in Ezekiel, Daniel, and Zechariah as well as material from Isaiah 40–55, Jeremiah, and Joel. It is untrue that John "simply uses the Old Testament as a religious thesaurus to pad his visions with conventional symbolism and rhetoric."[13]

Fekkes is also helpful in formulating how the Book of Revelation may have come to be composed. He recognizes that John had actual visionary experiences, yet this work is not a mere transcript of such experiences but rather the literary presentation of them. One must also take into count John's previsionary influences, as well as his postvisionary editing of his source material. It is neither a purely literary product nor merely an exercise in exegesis of the Old Testament texts but some combination of revelation, reflection, and literary composition.[14] "Revelation is visionary, it is not *ad hoc*. And for all that its use of Scripture is implicit, it is not superficial."[15]

There has been considerable debate about the relationship between the letters in Rev. 2–3 and the visions that follow them. Some have even suggested that whereas the letters address first-century audiences, the rest is addressed to some future Christian audience. This argument, however, does not work because the letters serve as a particularized preamble so that Rev. 4–22 comprises the apocalyptic prophecies the Spirit is addressing to all the churches, whether during or after the time of John.

These prophecies, including the visionary material, make up what we would call arguments presented by the seer meant to persuade the audiences to heed the exhortations given in the letters in Rev. 2–3. Basically, he is offering an eschatological and otherworldly sanction for those exhortations, showing what the rewards are for faithfulness and "conquering" and what the punishments are for failing to do so. John will reveal what is happening in heaven and what will happen beyond the present (see Rev. 4.1), not merely as a preview of coming attractions to comfort the faithful, although it serves that purpose as well, but as an eschatological sanction for the initial exhortations given to each church. The "rhetorical function of these assertions [i.e., the visions] is to change the audience's mind in the present."[16] *Among other things, what this means for the interpretation of Revelation is that all of this book was meant to make sense to John's first-century audience.* I would add that whatever the text meant to those first Christians is also what it means for believers today. The meaning of the text has not changed over time because the meaning is in the text, in its choice and arrangement of words, sentences, paragraphs.

Figure 20.3 The Coliseum did not exist in the time of Nero, but during the time of Domitian, when Revelation was written, it may well have been a place where Christians were martyred. (© *Mark R. Fairchild, Ph.D.*)

One of the more helpful treatments of the rhetoric of Revelation is that of R. Royalty, who stresses the performative character of the work. He stresses that this is a work that was meant to be heard by the audience, by those who want to hear.[17] He reminds us that in forensic or judicial rhetoric, external proofs, such as the testimony of witnesses or court documents, are crucial. In John's context, where there is a fundamental trust in sacred Scripture as well as in the living prophetic word, John chooses in relating his visions to draw on both the Old Testament and the living voice of Jesus, perhaps the two highest authorities he could appeal to, to try and persuade his audience to heed his exhortations. Christ is obviously the most compelling living witness, but notice how John also appeals to other witnesses, including other prophetic figures in Rev. 11.[18] His audience stands before the heavenly court and hears compelling testimonies (including from the martyrs), which reminds them that earthly courts and judgments do not have the last word on their lives.

Official documents are at the heart of the revelations in Rev. 4–21, which is only appropriate in a forensic rhetorical setting. It is in court that official documents were unsealed and read. The audience is comforted by the fact that the divine verdict is a foregone conclusion, the faithful will one day conquer, and the wicked will one day be judged; but in the meantime, the audience must remain faithful and must repent of their sin and lethargy and cowardice. The unsealing of the official scrolls that chronicle the coming redemptive judgments is meant to facilitate this outcome.

Revelation clearly follows the basic rhetorical pattern for persuasion. First, the speaker's authority is established with the audience (in the introduction, the report of the commissioning vision, and the letters that demonstrate that John has the authority to address this audience), then the authority of his arguments in the form of visions is established through making clear that they ultimately come from ultimate authorities—the living word and the written word.

Finally, there is the authority of the emotional appeal at the end where pathos comes into play. Redemption is then unveiled to the audience members, who are under duress and crisis, and a promise of the end of disease, decay and death, suffering, and sorrow is made (see Rev. 20–22). Ethos (establishing of authority), followed by **logos** (arguments based on the authority), and then pathos (final emotional appeals), are all found in the rhetorically appropriate places in Revelation.

How has our author structured, or better-said *restructured,* his source material? Is the main section of this book intended to be a chronological account of the events leading up to the end of the world, or is the arrangement of materials topical and thematic? It is important to point out first that this document must be taken as a unity, for its major symbols and themes are used consistently throughout. Furthermore, the letters in Rev. 2–3 are introduced by the

LOGOS

The logical arguments of a rhetorical discourse. The arguments are based on the authority of the speaker (*ethos*).

vision in Rev. 1, and there is little dispute that Rev. 4–5 introduces the main body of Revelation.

The storm center of the debate about the structure of Revelation centers on Rev. 6–19. Is this a continuous chronological series of revelations, or do we have a two- or threefold repetition of the same sequence of judgments in these chapters? Put another way, are the seven seals, the seven trumpets, and the seven bowls or cups describing the same reality, perhaps with some variation? One can compare Rev. 11.15ff. with 16.17 and argue that both of these visions seem to climax at the end of the age.

Yet on first blush, it appears that the seventh seal is opened in order to usher in the events heralded by the seven trumpets. Against this, however, is the fact that the opening of the sixth seal in Rev. 6.12ff. *seems* to involve a graphic description of the end of the world. The three sets of seven judgments do not merely repeat what has been said in the previous set of seven judgments. They evolve and expand on what was previously said. They then could be seen as increasingly precise or intense disclosures of the same reality, like a cameraman getting a closer and closer focus on the same canvas. Or, one could say that these sets of seven overlap, with the second set beginning before the end of the first and then carrying things further, and the third picking up in the midst of the second set and carrying things even further.[19] This last suggestion seems to make the best sense of the three sets of seven judgments.

Another of the major talking points in the debate about the structure of Revelation is what to do with the scenes of heavenly worship found in Rev. 7 and in 10.1–11.13. There is an inherent problem with seeing these sections as pregnant pauses in the chronological account, or interludes, much less seeing them as diversions. The hymns clearly comment on and complement the visions and auditions of the book, and perhaps they function as a sort of divine commentary, rather like a court reporter putting things in perspective. In fact, there are many more hymns than those in Rev. 7 and 10–11; see Rev. 12.10, 14.1–5, 15.2–4, 19.1–9, and 20.4–6. These hymns serve not only as commentary but also as praise of the apocalyptic actions being taken.

Perhaps precisely because of the complexity of the structure of Revelation, some have sought overly simplistic answers to the structural questions. For example, some have suggested that Rev. 1.9–3.22 is about the things that are, and Rev. 4.1–22.5 is about the things that are to come hereafter. This is not wholly satisfactory, not only because of the threefold pattern of seven judgments and overlapping figures and ideas found in Rev. 3 and 4; but most tellingly, in Rev. 11, the author seems to be discussing a past event—the destruction of the temple. Notice too that the first trumpet voice at Rev. 4.1–2 is the same as the voice like a trumpet in Rev. 1.10–12.

One of the more compelling demonstrations of the author's use of parallelism in general has been offered by C. H. Giblin, who shows that Rev. 17.1–19.10

needs to be seen as parallel to Rev. 21.9–22.11, dealing with mirror opposite great cities: one wicked, one wonderful.[20] But this particular example of parallelism or recapitulation of a structure does not indicate duplication. These two passages are not alternate discussions of the same reality. The book concludes with a tale of two contrasting cities—the all-too-earthly Babylon (aka Rome) and the heavenly Jerusalem.

Perhaps the most helpful discussion of the structure and composition of Revelation is that of R. Bauckham.[21] He stresses at the outset that the structure of the book, which is crucial to understanding its meaning, must have been recognizable on the basis of an oral performance (Rev. 1.3).[22] This requires clear linguistic markers, which is to say it requires repetition of certain key terms and phrases. In Bauckham's view, the key to interpreting the book's structure is the phrase "in the Spirit" found at Rev. 1.10, 4.2, 17.3, and 21.10. Rev. 4.2 is an exact reproduction of 1.10 ("I was in the Spirit"), whereas the latter two references are basically the same in the form "[the angel] carried me away in the Spirit." On this showing, Rev. 1.9–10 begins the inaugural vision; 4.2 provides a second beginning of the visionary experience; and 17.3 and 21.9–10 introduce the listener to two final parallel visionary experiences.[23] Rev. 17.11–19.10 and 21.9–22.9 present us with the visions of the two cities portrayed as women.

The entire book has been pressing forward toward the conclusion revealed in these two sections involving the destruction of Babylon and its replacement by the new Jerusalem. "The intimate connection between the two parallel sections is further indicated by the announcement of the lamb's marriage to his bride at the end of the rejoicing over the fall of Babylon ([Rev.] 19.7–9a)."[24] Bauckham goes on to argue that Rev. 22.6–9 is in fact a transitional passage that concludes the last major section and introduces the epilogue. The recognition of the two parallel passages in Rev. 17 and 21 means that the material between these two sections (Rev. 19.11–21.8) must necessarily be about the transition from the demise of Babylon to the descent of the new Jerusalem.[25] It cannot be about the time before the demise of Babylon.[26]

Bauckham is also able to demonstrate the interlocking nature of the book's motifs. For example, the voice heard in Rev. 1.10–11 is the same as the voice in 4.1; and the angel who introduces John to the visions beginning in Rev. 17.1 and 21.9 is one of the seven angels who pours out the bowl or cup judgments in Rev. 6–16.[27] Furthermore, he provides an extra structural foundation for the conclusion that the threefold seven judgments are basically describing one reality (although perhaps in progressively more intense or complete ways), for they all conclude with the same final judgment reached in the seventh of each of the three series. This is demonstrated by the repeated use of the terms *thunder, lightning, earthquake,* and *heavy hail* in varying order at Rev. 4.5, 8.5, 11.19, and 16.18–21. This phrase is an echo of Ex. 19.16. "The seven seal-openings are linked to the seven trumpets by the technique of overlapping or interweaving."[28]

For Bauckham, the whole sequence of bowls is a development of the seventh trumpet, and the three woes are identical with the judgments inaugurated by the last three trumpets.

One of the great structural puzzles of Revelation is what to make of Rev. 12–14, which is a section that begins abruptly. Bauckham rightly indicates that the fresh start was needed because this section involves a flashback to a time chronologically earlier than anything up to Rev. 12. The series of seven bowls (Rev. 16) then becomes a continuation of the narrative begun in Rev. 12. The seven bowls are a fuller version of the seventh trumpet. There is a provisional conclusion at the end of the seven-bowls sequence with a further conclusion in Rev. 19.11–21.8.[29] These conclusions led Bauckham[30] to see the following as the structure of the work:

RHETORICAL OUTLINE OF REVELATION

1.1–8	Prologue
1.9–3.22	Inaugural Vision of Christ and Seven Messages to Churches
4.1–5.14	Inaugural Vision of Heaven Leading to Three Series of Sevens and Two Intercalations
6.1–8.1; 8.3–5	Seven Seals
8.2; 8.6–11.19	Seven Trumpets
12.1–14.20; 15.2–4	The Story of God's People in Conflict with Evil
15.1; 15.5–16.21	Seven Bowls
17.1–19.10	Babylon the Harlot
19.11–21.8	Transition from Babylon to New Jerusalem
21.9–22.5	The New Jerusalem, the Bride
22.6–21	Epilogue

One further feature of Bauckham's analysis deserves comment. Bauckham notes how carefully the sevens have been structured into the text, with seven representing completion. There is thus a complete set of judgments, a full set of the title Lord God Almighty (Rev. 1.8, 4.8, 11.17, 15.3, 16.7, 19.6, 21.22); but there is also a complete set of beatitudes, and the seven beatitudes provide a sort of summary of Revelation's positive message to believers and also encapsulate the adequate response to the prophecies (cf. Rev. 1.3; 14.13; 16.15; 19.9; 20.6; 22.7, 14). The majority of these beatitudes cluster at the end of the work, where the events of final redemption are recounted. If the believers are characterized by hearing, keeping, faithfulness, and readiness, they will obtain the fullness of these blessings (rest from labors, invitation to lamb's supper, participation in the first resurrection, sharing in the tree of life, and entry into the new Jerusalem).[31]

REVELATION IN ITS SOCIAL SETTING IN WESTERN ASIA MINOR

EMPEROR CULT

The Emperor cult was an organized form of religion that worshipped the emperor or dynasty of emperors. Emperors were divinized and worshipped as gods. The cult is also referred to as the Imperial cult.

It has become commonplace in recent commentaries on Revelation to point out that part of what John is reacting against is the growing influence of the imperial cult and the worship of Emperor Domitian, especially in the province where these seven churches are located. I believe this observation is correct. Asia Minor seems to have been a place where the **emperor cult** thrived in the A.D. 90s, not least because the emperor had bestowed on Asia many perks and benefits and benefactions.

In this situation, the cities mentioned in Revelation competed with one another for recognition, honor, and benefits bestowed by the emperor. One form

Figure 20.4 The tree of life (Rev. 22) as depicted in the St. John's Bible. (Detail from "Vision of the New Jerusalem," Donald Jackson, Copyright 2011, *The Saint John's Bible* Order of Saint Benedict, Collegeville, Minnesota, USA. All rights reserved.)

this took was the building of temples for the sake of furthering the emperor cult. Because the emperor was seen as the ultimate benefactor, protector, and provider of peace and order in society, there needed to be a way in a reciprocity culture for the residents and citizens to repay the emperor. This was largely accomplished through the deference, loyalty, and even worship offered through the emperor cult. Because the emperor seldom toured the provinces (no emperor visited Asia in the first century), and the vast majority of residents seldom, if ever, went to Rome, in an age long before television, the chief way locals had contact with and knew their emperor was through the emperor cult, which involved temples, statues, public festivals, honor columns, inscriptions, coins, and holidays.

It must be remembered that Temples were the banks of antiquity, not merely because they provided storage for valuable property, but they also loaned money at interest, provided mortgages, and the like. In temples, one experienced the convergence of political, economic, and religious life, and this was especially the case in the temples dedicated to the emperor. Asia was perhaps the first province to really generate an emperor cult, with Pergamum building a temple to Rome and Augustus only 4 years after Augustus pacified the empire (27 B.C.).

This temple was in fact the meeting place of the provincial assembly of Asia and the place where decrees and letters from Rome would be read out. It is possible that John, knowing full well about Pergamum, conceived of heaven as the Christians' assembly hall, where the divine decrees would be read out and justice would finally be done by Christ, who is truly "our Lord and our God," in contradistinction to Emperor Domitian.[32] If so, John's high Christology is hardly just a religious statement but a political one as well. This explains why Christians are warned to expect stern reprisals for their allegiance to a very different Lord from Caesar. Their faith, because it involved exclusive devotion to only one God, would be seen as dangerous and unpatriotic, for Christians would not participate in the emperor cult.

> The imperial cult was a *religio* in that it bound the residents of the cities together in the broader context of empire. All members were expected to participate in the imperial cult. . . . there was a social expectation that one would voluntarily participate as a demonstration of one's "faith" in the empire.[33]

This is why the topic of eating meat sacrificed to idols is such an issue in Revelation, as well as in 1 Corinthians and Acts 15. To fail to fellowship with one's neighbors in the temple feasts was antisocial and, if it was an emperor cult feast, unpatriotic. The following chart provided by W. Howard-Brook and A. Gwyther shows how pervasive the influence of the imperial cult would have been in the cities to which John wrote.

ASIAN CITY	IMPERIAL CULT	IMPERIAL ALTAR	IMPERIAL PRIEST
Ephesus	X	X	X
Smyrna	X	X	X
Pergamum	X	X	X
Thyatira		X	X
Sardis	X	X	X
Philadelphia	X		X
Laodicea		X*	

*W. Howard-Brook, A. Gwyther, with a foreword by E. McAlister, *Unveiling Empire: Reading Revelation Then and Now* (Maryknoll, NY: Orbis Books, 1999), 104.

> No other province [than Asia] is known to have had more than one provincial cult of emperors at this time, and several provinces appear to have had none. Clearly, Asia was on the cutting edge of imperial cult activity. And John was denouncing the entire institution as coming from the devil.[34]

John's revelation came to him at a time when the imperial cult was increasingly being used as the social glue to bind each major Asian city, but also the province, together.

> John's vision excoriated this system. It declared invalid the increasingly successful social contract of late first-century Asia. That contract according to Revelation, was based on blasphemy, maintained by violence and dedicated to the destruction of those who sought to live a godly life. To those of like mind, John's visions were prophetic. To most of the inhabitants of Asia, however, they would have seemed like sedition.[35]

Texts such as Rev. 13.4, 15–16; 14.9–11; 15.2; 16.2; 19.20; and 20.4, which refer or allude to the worship of the Beast, likely reflect the impact of the emperor cult on John and other early Christians.

Was John then only speaking to his own quite specific situation and his own time? Clearly, the church did not think so, or they would never have included this book in its canon of Scripture. I would suggest John's Revelation was right on target for his Asian audience, but the symbols he uses are flexible enough that they could and would be appropriately used to address many other situations of crisis in church life; and in fact, they were used that way in every generation of church history, and rightly so. The symbols used by John are universal and multivalent (meaning with multiple possible referents). We will talk more about the particular genre or type of prophetic aspect of Revelation in a moment.

THE CHRISTOLOGY OF REVELATION

Revelation is presented from the outset as a "revelation of Jesus Christ," which among other things reminds us that John's Christology is the heart of the matter for him when it comes to theology. It is Christ's vision that John conveys, and the vision is about Christ, in whose hands are all the scrolls that are to be unsealed and all the truths to be revealed. Christ is the one who sets in motion the eschatological judgments and provides the final redemption. It thus behooves us to consider carefully John's reflections on the Christ, as it is a key to understanding the work as a whole.

There are a lot of primitive, and also some highly polished, images of and ideas about Christ in this book.[36] Because Revelation is a document meant to address Christians in physical and spiritual danger, we should not be surprised if it concentrates on images and ideas of Christ that would be helpful to address that situation. It is natural then for the author to stress the sovereignty of God, the power of Christ, Christ's judgment of the wicked for the saints, and the like. In short, it is natural for the author to stress forensic images of Christ as both judge and one who redeems the faithful from judgment (as the Lamb of God).

It is not surprising that we do not really find a gentle Jesus, meek and mild, in this book but rather one who sits on the judgment seat with his Father, one who rides forth in judgment with a sword proceeding from his mouth, one who even when he can be seen as a lamb can be seen at the same time as a lion. Here is a mighty and fearsome Christ indeed, with most of the emphasis on what Christ in heaven now is (an exalted Lord) or will be for believers when he returns. There is little attention given to the ministry of Jesus or the merely human side of Jesus, except by way of emphasizing his death and its benefits.

A rapid survey of the various titles applied to Christ in Revelation reveals the following: Christ only appears seven times, Son of God once, Son of Man twice (but each case as part of an analogy not a title), *logos* or word once, but Lord 23 times (and also used interchangeably with God and Christ) and lamb 28 times. In this work, none of the merely human titles of Jesus, such as teacher, rabbi, servant, prophet, or man, are used. It is equally interesting that some of the more Hellenistic titles, such as savior or God, are also notably absent. In other words, in terms of terminology and titles, this book is very different from

John's Gospel, where Son of God and Son of Man dominate the landscape, and the Johannine epistles, where Christ and Son of God are prominent.

The extreme Jewishness of this document and its different Christological terms provide further evidence that this book was not written by the same person who wrote either the Gospel or 1 John or both. This document has a very high Christology stressing Christ's heavenly exaltation and roles since and because of his death and resurrection.

The Christological tone for the whole book is set in the very first chapter with the first Christological vision of John of Patmos. The book begins with the assertion that this is "the revelation of Jesus Christ," and it is probably no accident that it is only in this chapter that the title Jesus Christ appears (three times). "The first Christian readers would need to be led from Jesus Christ to the lamb, the name which dominates the second part of the book."[37] Jesus is the faithful witness, the firstborn from the dead, the ruler of the kings of the earth (Rev. 1.5), and also the one who will come on the clouds in the future for judgment (Rev. 1.7). Rev. 1.5 also mentions Jesus' redemptive death and blood. It is also in this chapter that we have the first of only two references in this book to Jesus as one like a Son of Man, only here his garb makes clear his divinity.

What is interesting about this is that the author begins here a trend that will continue throughout the work of applying Old Testament images and names formerly used of Yahweh (i.e., God the Father) but now applied to Christ or both the Father and Christ. Whereas it was the "ancient of days" in Dan. 7 that has such raiment, here it is Christ who is both divine and one like a Son of Man (Rev. 1.13). It is not clear whether the person referred to as **Alpha** and **Omega** in Rev. 1.8 is God or Christ (cf. Rev. 21.6), although it is probably God; but more clearly, at Rev. 1.17–18, Christ is referred to as the First and Last (and at Rev. 22.13, he is the Alpha and Omega), the one who was dead but is now alive forever and has in his hands the keys of death and Hades and also holds the churches in the palm of his hand, something a Christian under fire might find comforting. From this lofty Christological height, the book never descends.

It is worthwhile to consider for a moment the significance of calling both God and Christ the Alpha and Omega. It conveys the idea that the person in question "precedes and originates all things, as their Creator, and he will bring all things to their eschatological fulfillment. The titles can not mean anything else when they are used of Christ in 22.13."[38] Furthermore, when Jesus is called the first and the last, this seems to be grounded in Is. 44.6 and 48.12, where it is a divine self-designation of Yahweh's. Not only so, but it is used in a context where it aids in stressing the exclusive monotheistic proposition "besides me there is no God." Here in Revelation, "First and Last" probably does not mean anything very different from what Alpha and Omega mean.

ALPHA

The first letter of the Greek alphabet. The letter is also used to refer to the beginning of something.

OMEGA

The last letter of the Greek alphabet. The letter is also used to refer to the end or culmination of something.

This interpretation comports with what we hear at Rev. 3.14 in which Christ is called "the origin (*arche*) of God's creation," which likely does not mean he is the first created being or the firstborn from the dead (for which other terminology is used), but rather it is another way of saying about Christ what is said clearly in Rev. 22.13. In other words, Christ is seen as preceding all things and as in part the source or creator of all things, along with the father (as in John 1). By saying he is the Omega or Last, we are probably meant to think of Christ's assumption of the role of the coming final judge on the eschatological day of the Lord (see Rev. 19). This First/Last and Alpha/Omega language is used "as a way of stating unambiguously that Jesus belongs to the fullness of the eternal being of God, this surpasses anything in the [rest of the] New Testament."[39] It is not then surprising that, in Revelation, perhaps more than in any other New Testament book, Jesus is the object of worship and adoration, which in this same book is said not to be appropriate of mere angelic supernatural beings (cf. Rev. 19.10, 22.8–9).

Because Jesus is included in John of Patmos's definition of God, he is seen as a very appropriate object of worship. In Rev. 5, we are introduced to the image of Christ as the lamb, which is to become the dominant image in the book thereafter. Notice, for example, how in Rev. 5.8 the lamb—who has triumphed through his death and resurrection—is the focus of the circle of worship in heaven, which includes the worship of the living creatures and the elders, the representatives of all kinds of creatures both animal and human (cf. Rev. 5.6 and 7.17).[40]

It is precisely as slain lamb that this lamb conquers and judges with righteous wrath (Rev. 6.16). The worship of the lamb is not somehow separate or distinct from the worship of God but is seen as a part of it in Rev. 5.13. If a doxology is a clear indication of the object of worship, then the one offered to Christ alone in Rev. 1.5–6 surely indicates that he is being approached as God. This doxology should be compared to two other such doxologies offered to Christ alone at 2 Tim. 4.8 and 2 Pet. 3.18, which suggest that the practices described in Revelation of worshipping Christ were not somehow an aberration but rather a widespread practice in a variety of Christian communities.[41]

Consider what it means to say that the slaughtered lamb is seen on the throne and is worshipped for his overcoming through death and resurrection the powers of this world. It must surely include the notion that God was in Christ reconciling the world to himself, but more to the point, the way God rules the world is by and in the slaughtered and exalted lamb. Christ's suffering and death are seen as the act of an eternal being, thus having eternal efficacy and making evident how God has chosen to overcome evil and rule the world. Only God saves, and he has done this as the Lamb.

The one who is called ruler of God's creation in Rev. 3.14 is also in that same chapter called the one who holds the key of David (Rev. 3.7) and thus is the Jewish Messiah. Just because John thinks he is more than the Jewish Messiah does not mean he leaves behind this notion as unimportant. In Rev. 5.5, Christ is seen as lion of the tribe of Judah and also the root of David. The lamb image is also thoroughly Jewish, and a slaughtered lamb the ultimate symbol of atonement for sins in a Jewish context. But John has transformed this image to speak not only of a lamb slain but of something else no early Jew who was not a Christian spoke of—a lamb once slain but now glorified and powerful. Here, the story of Jesus has transformed this Jewish image into something unexpected, paradoxical, new. It is no surprise that the slain lamb image arises repeatedly in a document written to Christians who are being persecuted. They, too, are lambs for the slaughter, but like Jesus, they in the end will have victory over death and their human tormentors.

Another image transferred from God to Christ is the image of Jesus being the one who has the book of life and also the one who opens the scrolls that disclose God's future plan and will. Only he is said in Rev. 5 to be worthy enough to open not only the scroll but all the seals upon it. We see here the notion of Christ as the implementer of divine justice upon the earth.

The concept of redemptive judgment may seem foreign to us, but it is a prevalent concept in the Old Testament, especially in Joshua and Judges. The idea in a nutshell is that God redeems his oppressed people by judging their enemies, hence the term *redemptive* judgment. Thus, our author is not saying anything novel by predicating both judgment and redemption of his deity; the only novelty is that Christ is said to be assuming these divine roles. He is both savior of the saved and judge of the wicked. Notice how the end result of the battle of good and evil will be, and indeed, in John's view, already is, "the kingdom of the world has become the kingdom of our Lord and of his Christ, and he will reign forever and ever" (Rev. 11.15). "Lord" in these verses refers to God rather than Christ, and Christ is used in its titular and Jewish sense. Our author clearly includes Christ within his description of God alongside the Father. This way of putting things in Rev. 11.15 suggests that our author was in touch with the earliest Jewish Christian ways of confessing their monotheism, such as can be seen in 1 Cor. 8.6.

Thus, the lamb will triumph and one day invite his own to a wedding feast (Rev. 19.9). He will also come as the pale rider, grim reaper, or executioner spoken of in Rev. 19. The lamb is also the lion. As Christ, he will reign for a thousand years with his martyrs (Rev. 20.4ff.), which may refer to his present reign in heaven with the martyrs already there; but in view of the discussion of resurrection in Jn. 20, it probably refers to a future reign on earth at the close of the age. Christ is the one who began and will bring to a close God's plan for humanity.

At the end of Revelation, we are told in Rev. 21 that Christ and the Lord God (here the Father) will be the temple and glory of God's people and they will dwell together forever—beyond disease, decay, death, sin, suffering, sorrow, tears, and torment. For now, our author sees Christ as one who stands at the door of human hearts and knocks, but one day he shall burst on the human scene as a ravaging lion destroying, or at least judging, the wicked and thereby rescuing the righteous. Thus, believers are urged at the close of the book to urge him to come—the one who is daystar dawning on history's horizon. Both horizontal and vertical eschatology fuse in the final vision of things such that heaven and earth in effect merge. The new Jerusalem descends from above, making a new earth to go along with a new heaven. The one who lies at the center of this vision, indeed the one who turns this vision into reality, is, according to John, none other than Jesus—who is at once lamb, lion, and Lord. We should have expected this Christocentric and theocentric conclusion because we were told at the outset of the book that this is "the revelation of (and about) Jesus Christ."

THE GENRE OF REVELATION

The debate about the genre of Revelation continues to rage on, with most scholars now convinced that Revelation is some sort of apocalyptic literature. The question is—What sort? I have argued elsewhere that the apocalyptic genre is a type of hybrid literature that reflects the combining of the Jewish prophetic and wisdom traditions, and this is as true of a book like Daniel as it is of Revelation.[42] But Revelation, in view of its audience, must also be set in the context of Greco-Roman prophecy. The short answer to the genre question is that this is visionary prophecy using apocalyptic images, that is, highly metaphorical hyperbolic images to convey its truth, rather as political cartoons do sometimes. Here is a scholarly definition of apocalyptic literature:

> A genre of revelatory literature with a narrative framework, in which a revelation is mediated by an otherworldly being to a human recipient, disclosing a transcendent reality which is both temporal, insofar as it envisages eschatological salvation, and spatial insofar as it involves another, supernatural world.[43]

Present, mundane reality is interpreted in light of both the supernatural world and the future. For the Book of Revelation, this entails beginning with the present experiences of the churches and trying to help them interpret and endure those experiences in the light of the larger perspective that John's visions of what is above and beyond give them. This is clearly minority literature written in a coded way for persons enduring some sort of crisis.

Eschatological ideas are not necessarily the heart of what apocalyptic literature is all about, for such ideas are found in many types of early Jewish and Christian literature; and for that matter, there are apocalypses that do not really focus on the final form the future will take. Apocalyptic literature then is primarily a matter of the use of a distinctive form—visions with often bizarre and hyperbolic metaphors and images. Some apocalypses focus almost entirely on otherworldly journeys without saying much about the end of human history, and others do the reverse. In other words, historical apocalypses are not the pattern for the whole genre. The very heart of the apocalyptic genre is the unveiling of secrets and truths about God's perspective on a variety of subjects including justice and the problem of evil, and what God proposes to do about such matters.

Apocalyptic literature is the dominant form of prophecy in Jewish contexts from the second century B.C. to the second century A.D., and it reflects the fact that its authors believed they lived in the age when earlier prophecies were being fulfilled, and therefore it was right to contemplate what God's final answer and solution would be to the human dilemma. This dominance of the apocalyptic view also reflects the deeply held conviction that God's people lived in dark times when God's hand in matters and God's will for believers were not perfectly evident. God's plan had to be revealed like a secret, for matters in human history were mysterious and complex.

It is my view that the major cause of the shift from traditional to apocalyptic prophecy during that era was not because there weren't still traditional style oracular and sign prophets abroad (e.g., John the Baptist), but the shift came because of the conviction that God's people were living at the dawn of or actually in the eschatological age and also because they saw themselves as in some sense in exile (this is particularly clear in Daniel and Ezekiel). The final things had already been set in motion, and under such circumstances, it was appropriate to talk about the end of the end times.

One of the major points I have made in my earlier study of prophecy is that it is important to distinguish between prophetic experience, prophetic expression, and the prophetic tradition. The Book of Revelation is certainly not simply a transcript of a prophetic experience, as its epistolary framework makes clear. Rather, the seer has incorporated into a complex literary whole a report of his vision or visions reflected on in light of the Hebrew Scriptures and a variety of other sources. John had visions and then fashioned an apocalyptic prophetic work to express not merely what he had seen but what bearing that vision had on his audiences. This means that we might well not have an apocalypse at all had John not been some distance from his audiences. Rather, he might have just shared most of his visions orally with his churches as they came, without resorting to a literary creation.

We probably should not imagine John on the island of Patmos poring over Hebrew Scripture scrolls and then creating a literary patchwork quilt. The visions that came to John came to a Scripture-saturated mind, but also to a mind well acquainted with popular and mythical images of the larger Greco-Roman world. What John heard he may well have transcribed almost verbatim, but what he saw he had to describe, and thus he drew on his existing mental resources to do so.

When what one sees are images and symbols in odd combinations, one must grope for analogies to describe the experience (hence the repeated use of the phrase "it was like. . . ."). One must resort to metaphorical, mythological, and sometimes multivalent language. By this I mean the seer describes some aspect of what he sees and does so in metaphorical language that is generic enough in character that it could refer to several persons or events at once. The seer must resort to somewhat universal symbols that explain why such works have been able to communicate across time, which in itself also helps explain why these works were preserved. But paradoxically, it is also true that apocalyptic prophecy always requires interpretation or explanation. It is indeed a coded form of language, and those not knowing the universe of discourse will be in the dark.

Whatever the content of these spiritual experiences ("I was in the Spirit on the Lord's day"—Rev. 1.10), the book as it now exists is a literary attempt to use such materials to persuade and exhort several groups of Christians who were apparently badly in need of some reassurance and encouragement and instruction. The rhetorical dimensions and function of the book must not be overlooked.

It cannot be stressed enough that one of the rhetorical functions of a work like Revelation is to give early Christians *perspective, especially in regard to the matters of good and evil, redemption and judgment.* Revelation seeks to peel back the veil and reveal to the audience the underlying supernatural forces at work behind the scenes that are affecting what is going on at the human level. *In short, a certain limited dualism is evident in this literature.* The message is often, "Though it appears that evil is triumphing, God is still in his heaven, and in due course, all will be right with the world." It is stressed that the goal of life is ultimately beyond death in either the afterlife or the afterworld on earth or both. There is also usually a strong sense of alienation and loss of power in these documents, and thus a major stress on God's sovereignty and divine intervention in human affairs. The stress is on transcendent solutions to human dilemmas, although human efforts have not been rendered either meaningless or pointless.

Here is a good place to say a bit more about the use of multivalent symbols in Revelation. *It is true that the wounded beast in Rev. 13 and 17 probably does allude to Nero, but with the help of mythological imagery, Nero is portrayed as but a representative example of a higher supernatural evil—the anti-Christ figure. The author knows that Nero does not exhaust the meaning of the beast, but he certainly exemplifies it well.* There could be other such figures as well, for the author is dealing with types. These symbols are plastic, flexible, and on the order of character analysis rather than literal descriptions. Christ can be depicted in Revelation as the blood-drenched warrior or a lamb who was slain, or a lion, or an old man with snow-white hair. All these descriptions are meant to reveal some aspect of his character and activity. In this respect, these symbols are very much like some modern political cartoons.

Apocalyptic literature is basically minority literature and often even sectarian literature, the product of a subset of a subculture in the Greco-Roman world. Although it is not always true that such literature is written in a time of crisis or for a people experiencing crisis or persecution at that specific point, it is certainly written for people who feel vulnerable in a world that largely does not concur with their own worldview. In the case of Revelation, there is enough internal evidence to suggest that there had been some persecution and even martyrdom, and more was expected.

It is not surprising then that apocalyptic prophecy often has a political dimension, dealing with the dominant human powers that appear to be shaping the destiny of God's people. Whether it is Revelation portraying Rome as a modern-day Babylon or Daniel portraying a succession of beastly empires, there is frequent discussion of these matters in such literature, but always under the veil of apocalyptic symbols and images. One must be an insider to really sense the referents and the drift of the polemic and promises. This aspect of apocalyptic literature grows directly out of the classical Jewish prophetic material where nations and rulers, including Israel's, are critiqued: but here this is carried out by *outsiders* (those who do not have controlling access to the political process) using *insiders*' language. From a psychological point of view, one might wish to consider the suggestion that having been cut off from their spiritual center in Jerusalem (or in John's case, in the Christian communities in western Asia Minor), revelation was expected to come to God's people in less clear and more enigmatic ways, for they were further from the perceived central locale of the divine presence.

GEMATRIA

A system or code that assigns symbolic values to numbers. For example, the number seven is significant as it is often referred to as the number of perfection. A fascination with symbolic numbers is commonly present in apocalyptic literature.

There is certainly a great fascination in apocalyptic literature with symbolic numbers, the use of which by early Jews was called **gematria.** There are some oft-repeated numbers: 4, 7, 10, 12, and their multiples. Knowing that seven means completion or perfection helps one to understand not only why there are seven seals in Revelation (a complete and comprehensive set of judgments), but also why the anti-Christ figure is numbered 666, which signifies chaos and incompletion. There is also a tendency in this literature to speak of time elusively or elliptically—such as Daniel's "a time, a time and a half, and a time" or his famous interpretation of Jeremiah's 70 weeks. Yet it is surprisingly rare to find in either Jewish or Christian apocalypses any sort of precise calculations about how many days or years are left before the end.

Scholars have often puzzled over two different numbers that apparently refer to the same time period in Dan. 12.11–12, but it need not be a case of recalculation or later editorial emendation. If the numbers are symbolic in nature (e.g., multiples of 7, or half of 7), they should probably not be taken as attempts, much less failed attempts, at precise calculation.

What such numbers do suggest when they describe periods of time is that matters are determined or fixed already by God, and thus God is still in control so that evil and suffering will at some point in time cease. The message of such numbers is "this too will pass," or "this too will come to pass." They were not meant to encourage ancient or modern chronological forecasting.

But what if justice is indeed deferred or not seen to be done in a reasonable amount of time? *Certainly, a major impetus for producing apocalyptic literature is this sense of justice deferred for the minority group, which has led to a robust emphasis on vindication both in the afterlife and, more important, the end times.* It is not an accident that apocalypses often manifest interest in justice and political issues on one hand and the otherworld and the afterlife on the other. There is a relationship between these two things—if there is no life to come, then many of the wrongs done in this life will never be rectified, and God's justice will be called into question.

Apocalyptic literature, especially apocalyptic prophecy, is often an attempt to deal with the issue of theodicy (the problem of evil and of the suffering even of good people). For instance, Revelation reassures the saints not only about personal individual vindication in the afterlife, but also about justice for God's people in the end. Indeed, it is at the point where cosmology and history meet, when heaven comes down to earth in the form of the Messiah and the new Jerusalem, that there is finally both resolution and reward for the saints and a solution to the human dilemma caused by suffering and evil. Suffering and death are overcome by resurrection and everlasting life, and evil is overcome by the Last Judgment.

Obviously, the persuasiveness of this schema depends entirely on the audience's belief in not only a transcendent world but also a God who actually cares enough to intervene in human history and

Figure 20.5 The image is from Is. 11.6, a picture of Eden restored. (© Rick Danielson)

set things right once and for all. But the very fact that this sort of information is only conveyed through visions, dreams, and oracles makes clear that without revelation, without the unveiling of divine secrets and mysteries, humans would be in the dark about such matters. *It is the message of apocalyptic literature that the meaning and purpose of human history cannot finally be discovered simply by an empirical study or analysis of that history.* This does not mean that the author has given up on history, as is sometimes asserted, but that he is placing his trust in what God can finally make of history rather than what humans can accomplish in history.

CORE SAMPLINGS: REVELATION 11

As we draw this chapter to a close, it will be well if we examine one sample of the book in more detail to show how what has been said thus far helps us properly interpret the book of Revelation. Scrutiny will be given to two consecutive sections—Rev. 11, which presents the tale of the two witnesses, and Rev. 12, the story of the woman and the dragon. It is possible to see Rev. 11 as a continuation of Rev. 10, but this may be debated. In any case, there is no debate about the indebtedness of Rev. 11 to Ezek. 40–48. In the vision, John is given a staff and told to rise and measure the temple of God and its surroundings. There have been at least four basic suggestions as to what this measuring means: (1) It is the preliminary to rebuilding and restoring the temple. This is certainly true in the case of Ezek. 40–48, and it is understandable how a Jewish Christian prophet after A.D. 70 who is in exile might see himself as being in the same position as Ezekiel. How then would this square with the fact that John seems to see the church as the new temple of God such that any restoration of the old temple would be superfluous? (2) The temple is being sized up for destruction. This makes especially good sense if this book was written in the 60s rather than the A.D. 90 as is usually thought, and if our author was familiar with the Jesus tradition on this subject (see Mk. 13). On the whole, the arguments for a date in the A.D. 60s do not convince. (3) The measurements are taken to indicate the parts to be protected from physical harm. This does not seem to fit with the theme found earlier in Revelation of partial judgments even on God's people. (4) Measuring refers to protection from spiritual rather than physical harm.

One clue to unraveling this mystery is found at Rev. 11.14 where one discovers that what is recounted as happening to the temple and to its worshippers (the latter being a point against this being a retrospective remark about A.D. 70) is said to be the second woe, not the last woe. Notice that this event is clearly identified as happening in Jerusalem, for there is mention of the place where the Lord was crucified.

One must now broach the subject of the two witnesses. Whoever they are supposed to represent, it is clear enough that they are presented here as being at least *like* Moses and Elijah, the two witnesses who stood with Jesus on the mount of transfiguration according to the Synoptic tradition found in Mk. 9. Notice that these witnesses bring the fire-breathing word of God to earth, including plagues and the like, but they are also taken back up into heaven. If this is a prophecy of Jerusalem's fall, why has it been placed in this locale in Revelation and called the second woe? If this is a prophecy about the final preservation of the Jewish people, why then are the witnesses identified with the figure used in the letters to identify the church?

A more probable explanation than that this is about Jerusalem or Jews is that this is about the universal church and its task of witnessing, or more specifically about the churches at Smyrna and Philadelphia who were undergoing persecution and perhaps enduring instances of martyrdom as John wrote. This would explain why the number two is used of the witnesses here, rather than the earlier seven of all the churches John is addressing. Some have seen here an allusion to Deut. 19.15 where it is said that the verification of the truth of anything requires the validating testimony of two witnesses. But if John believed this was still true, would this not imply he would need a second witness to validate his own testimony, something this prophet doesn't appear to think he needs? His words appear to have independent authority for the seven churches, and he expects them to be unchallenged. It is surely easier to see here a reference to two of John's churches undergoing persecution. This fits with the reference in the text to the lamp stands (cf. Rev. 2–3).

If John could cast his own role in the light of the prophet Ezekiel, there is no reason why he could not cast the role of two of his churches in the light of the experiences of Elijah and Moses.[44] The implication is that not only John's life but that of his churches bears prophetic witness to God's revelation or truth. On this view, the idea of outward harm and even physical death is meant to suggest that even such extreme persecution cannot harm such witnesses spiritually.

The witnesses are called olive trees, for they carry within them the fuel they need to light their candlesticks. The reference to Daniel's three and a half years suggests the church will go through such persecution, not be raptured out of it. One must also see the reference to Sodom and Egypt as a statement about the spiritual status of Jerusalem—a city occupied and trampled under foot by Gentiles in the last decade of the first century. In other words, it is a place of oppression, slavery, and immorality. That the bodies of the witnesses are not allowed to be buried was considered one of the utmost indignities or crimes that could be perpetrated against a people in that culture (cf. Ps. Sol. 2.30ff).

Again Ezekiel is drawn on in Rev. 11.11 to speak of the resurrection of the two witnesses, possibly alluding to the resurrection of the martyrs, which will be referred to in Rev. 20.2. According to Rev. 11, verse 13, once the witnesses were vindicated by being taken to heaven, judgment fell upon a tenth part of the unholy city, during a supernaturally induced upheaval, and 7,000 are said to be killed. Perhaps not coincidentally, this would have been about a tenth of the non-festival season population of Jerusalem. The upshot of this is that John is suggesting that Jews, symbolized by Jerusalem, are the persecuting agents troubling the churches in this case. There is here a coded message of great relevance to the present and future situation of at least two of John's churches, offering them future hope of vindication despite present difficulties.

In this chapter, there is a rich intertextual feast with echoes of both Biblical and non-Biblical, both Jewish and Gentile traditions. The author hears oracles and songs, and sees visions, but he chooses to relate these visions in language his mostly Gentile audience can understand and apply to themselves. The language is definitely referential, although it is also symbolic and metaphorical and even mythic in character. It cannot be taken literally, but it must be taken seriously, for the author believes he is depicting in apocalyptic language some truths and realities his audience needs to know about. This is not merely heavenly language with an earthly meaning but rather apocalyptic language about the interplay of heaven and earth, time and eternity, history and the supernatural. Had this study pressed on further to investigate Rev. 19–22, one would have seen that our author can indeed offer predictions about the future in apocalyptic form, as well as descriptions of the past and present in that same visionary form. The eschatological as well as the otherworldly, the horizontal as well as the vertical dimensions of this author's vision of the final solution, are prominent throughout.

It is not the case that Revelation is purely about the transcendent. It is rather about providing a transcendent perspective on the interface between the transcendent realm and the historical realm, showing the underlying and overarching supernatural forces at work in human history, guiding and goading human beings and human institutions. There is indeed in this work a passionate concern about how history will ultimately turn out, and the earliest recorded reflections by second- and third-century Christian commentators certainly took the book as referential and historically focused in nature. For example, it was assumed that Rev. 20 was indeed speaking about a millennial kingdom of Christ coming upon the earth at or near the end of human history.

Thus, whatever our level of discomfort or comfort with this fact, due attention must be given to the referential nature of John's symbols. He seems to have fervently believed that Justice and Redemption would not both be finally accomplished, nor be seen to be accomplished unless such matters were finalized in space and time, "when the kingdoms of this world shall become the kingdoms of our Lord and of his Christ." None of us are in the position to say that John was wrong about the final climax of human history because we have not arrived at such a climax thus far in 2,000 plus years of church history. The language of imminence in this work is a clarion call to be prepared for that end, whenever it may come. The church is called to be the church expectant, the church prepared for "what will yet come." Like the saints under the altar in Rev. 6, it is more appropriate for the church to cry out "how long O Lord" than to simply wish to join those saints in their present location.

By this I mean this book does not encourage us to have a purely other-worldly view of eternal life, it does not encourage us to focus on heaven rather than history as the final goal or terminus of Christian life, it does not encourage us to abandon the eschatology of the earliest Christians such as Paul. The saints in heaven are impatient for the end of history and final vindication, they are not basking in everlasting peace believing they have reached the end. Thus the book of Revelation has much to tell us about "what was, and is, and is to come."

It is our job to have ears capable of hearing what John says on all of these matters. If we do so, we will learn that God's yes to life is louder than evil and death's no to it, that justice and redemption will one day prevail on earth, and that this is indeed Good News coming in the form of a "revelation from Jesus Christ," which is to say coming from one who both experienced death and triumphed over it. It is He who knows what is above and beyond our present mundane historical concerns and situation. He alone is worthy and is able to reveal such profound truths and to deal with issues of justice and redemption once and for all.

IMPLICATIONS

I had taken some of my students on a tour of Egypt, and they had been on the go for several days. We were at the temple in Luxor looking at statues of pharaohs and colorful hieroglyphs. To the left was a Japanese tour group taking lots of pictures, and to the right a German tour guide with some Europeans. Over a loudspeaker just outside of the temple was a call to prayer blasting from a minaret in Arabic. My students were getting cultural vertigo at about this point. They felt like strangers in a strange land. My Egyptian guide sensed what was happening and said to them, "Don't worry, we will get you out of here soon, and take you to the American Cultural Embassy." When they looked puzzled, he said "McDonald's," and they all cheered. They had had a bit too much of Egyptian food and were longing for something familiar. Studying the Book of Revelation with no tour guide or road map can leave you with a strong sense of cultural vertigo for sure. You might be tempted to throw up your hands and say, "Who can figure this out?"

My response to this dilemma is that if you persevere in studying Revelation in light of its original contexts, the light will eventually dawn. It will all be worth it, not least because John still has a major message for the church today, and not just for those suffering oppression or even facing martyrdom. His word to Christians is to bear witness and leave your lives in the hands of a sovereign God, for He (not we) is the judge of the world. Although it may appear now that the times are out of joint and the powers of darkness are winning, in the end God will have the last word, and new creation will come to pass. It will be worth waiting for.

KEY TERMS

Alethinos	*Ethnos/Ethne*
Alpha	Gematria
Amnos	Logos
Arnion	Omega
Emperor Cult	

FOR FURTHER READING

Bauckham, R. *The Theology of the Book of Revelation.* Cambridge: Cambridge University Press, 1993.

Collins, John. *The Apocalyptic Imagination: An Introduction to Jewish Apocalyptic Literature.* 2nd ed. Grand Rapids, MI: Eerdmans, 1998.

Witherington, B. *Jesus the Seer: The Progress of Prophecy.* Peabody, MA: Hendrickson, 1999.

————. *Revelation.* Cambridge: Cambridge University Press, 2003.

STUDY QUESTIONS

When you read through the Book of Revelation, what strikes you most about the various visions, images, and metaphors? Does it sometimes remind you of political cartoons or even some of the more apocalyptic graphic comic books?

What do you think John's main aim was in writing this book? How was it intended to help the seven churches in Asia Minor?

Does John promise the Christians in these seven cities that if they are just faithful enough, they won't have to suffer? If not, what is he promising them? Is it just "pie in the sky, by and by" or something also in the historical future?

There is a myriad of colorful images used to describe Christ. List several of these and contemplate their symbolic significance. Why do you suppose John thinks that so many images, even radically different ones (e.g., he is the lion of the tribe of Judah, but he is also and more frequently in this book the pierced lamb), help him convey the identity and roles of Christ?

How does the Christ of this last book of the New Testament seem similar to and also different from the Christ of the Gospels?

NOTES

1. T. B. Slater, "On the Social Setting of the Revelation," *New Testament Studies* 44 (1998): 232–256; here 241.
2. Slater, "On the Social Setting," 254.
3. The technical sense of martyr and martyrdom is found for *martus* and its cognates already in the late second century A.D. in *The Martyrdom of Polycarp* (see especially 2.iii, line 397). On this whole matter, see A. A. Trites, "Martyrs and Martyrdom in the Apocalypse," *Novum Testamentum* 15, no. 1 (1973): 72–80.
4. A useful survey of the entire discussion pro and con about these matters can be found in G. K. Beale, *John's Use of the Old Testament in Revelation* (Sheffield, England: Sheffield Academic Press, 1998).
5. Also see R. Bauckham, *The Climax of Prophecy: Studies on the Book of Revelation* (London: T&T Clark, 1993), especially pp. 38–91.
6. J. Fekkes, *Isaiah and the Prophetic Traditions in the Book of Revelation: Visionary Antecedents and Their Developments: Visionary Antecedents and Their Development* (Sheffield, England: Sheffield Academic Press, 1994), 17.
7. Which places in doubt the suggestion that the author's Greek style is deliberately prolix because of his apocalyptic subject matter. John's interest is in unsealing the seals. His concern is for revelation, not deliberate obfuscation.
8. Fekkes, *Isaiah and the Prophetic Traditions*, 39.
9. C. Hemer, *The Letters to the Seven Churches of Asia in Their Local Setting* (Sheffield, England: JSOT Press, 1986); and cf. R. H. Worth, *The Seven Cities of the Apocalypse and Roman Culture* (Mahwah, NJ: Paulist Press, 1998) and *The Seven Cities of the Apocalypse and Greco-Asian Culture* (Mahwah, NJ: Paulist Press, 1999).
10. Fekkes, *Isaiah and the Prophetic Traditions*, 58.
11. Ibid. 66.
12. Ibid. 69.
13. Ibid. 288.
14. Ibid. 289–290.
15. Ibid. 290.
16. R. Royalty, *The Streets of Heaven: The Ideology of Wealth in the Apocalypse of John* (Macon, GA: Mercer University Press, 1998), 128.
17. Ibid. 127.
18. Ibid. 132: "The function of the visions in Revelation [is] as external proofs."
19. To use a mundane analogy, it's rather like the old refrain at summer camp when the song leader said, "second verse, same as the first, a little bit louder and a little bit worse."
20. C. H. Giblin, "Recapitulation and the Literary Coherence of John's Apocalypse," *Catholic Biblical Quarterly* 56 (1994): 81–95.

21. Bauckham, *The Climax of Prophecy*, 1–37.
22. Ibid. 1–2.
23. Ibid. 3–4.
24. Ibid. 5.
25. Ibid. 5.
26. This in turn means that if one takes Babylon as a multivalent symbol not merely referring to Rome (although in the first instance, that is its referent), but referring more universally to humanity organized against God, then the suggestion of Augustine and others after him of an amillennial reading of Rev. 19.11–21.8 simply will not work.
27. Bauckham, *The Climax of Prophecy*, 6–7.
28. Ibid. 8–9.
29. Ibid. 16.
30. Ibid. 21–22.
31. Ibid. 29–30.
32. See, e.g., Royalty, *The Streets of Heaven*, 242: ". . . the introduction (Rev. 1.1–20) challenges Roman authority and power by casting God and Christ as the wealthy patrons of the Christian communities with more power and status than Caesar . . . [O]pposition to the dominant culture in the Apocalypse is not an attempt to redeem that culture but rather an attempt to replace it with a Christianized version of the same thing" (246).
33. W. Howard-Brook, A. Gwyther, with a foreword by E. McAlister, *Unveiling Empire: Reading Revelation Then and Now* (Maryknoll, NY: Orbis Books, 1999), 103.
34. S. Friesen, "Ephesus: Key to a Vision in Revelation," *Biblical Archaeology Review* 19 (May/June 1993): 34.
35. Friesen, "Ephesus," 37.
36. What follows is found in a somewhat different form in B. Witherington, *The Many Faces of the Christ: The Christologies of the New Testament and Beyond* (New York: Crossroad, 1998).
37. D. Guthrie, "The Christology of Revelation," in *Jesus of Nazareth: Lord and Christ: Essays on the Historical Jesus and New Testament Christology*, ed. J. B. Green and Max Turner (Grand Rapids, MI: Eerdmans, 1994), 397–409, here 398.
38. R. Bauckham, *The Theology of the Book of Revelation* (Cambridge: Cambridge University Press, 1993), 55. In the next few paragraphs, I shall be echoing and amplifying various of Bauckham's arguments with which I am in agreement.
39. Ibid. 57.
40. Even as a lamb, Christ is not seen as weak but rather as powerful and fully capable of overthrowing enemies not unlike the lamb symbol in the Testament of Joseph. There is perhaps some indebtedness of John to the author

of this work, for in *The Testament of Joseph* 19.8–9, we hear of the twofold Messiah who is presented as both lion and lamb.

41. Does it say anything to us that these three texts may all have been addressed to Christians in Asia Minor in areas where emperor worship was prevalent?

42. B. Witherington, *Jesus the Seer: The Progress of Prophecy* (Peabody, MA: Hendrickson, 1999), 216–245.

43. J. J. Collins, ed., *Apocalypse: The Morphology of a Genre: Semeia* Vol. 14 (Missoula, MT: Society of Biblical Literature, 1979), 9. To this definition D. Helholm added the suggestion that it is literature intended for a group in crisis with the intent of exhortation or consolation by means of divine authority.

44. See D. Aune, *Revelation 1–5, World Biblical Commentary, Vol. 52a* (Nashville, TN: Thomas Nelson, 1997), 600.

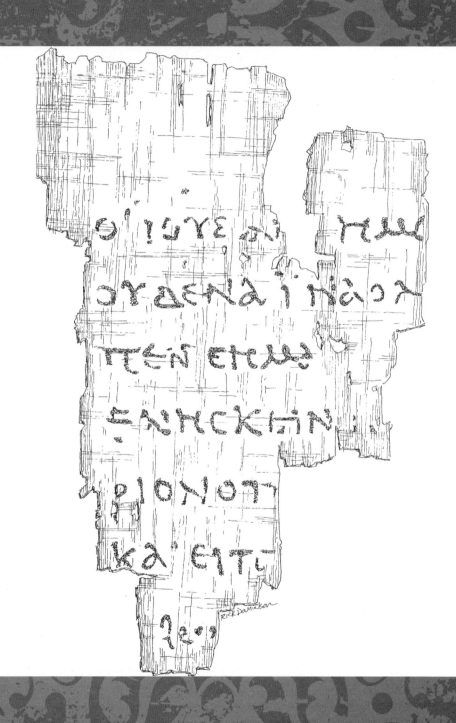
Papyrus fragment of the 4th Gospel. (© Rick Danielson)

The MAKING of the NEW TESTAMENT— Did the CANON MISFIRE?

*Put another way, instead of suggesting that certain books were acciden-
tally included and others were accidentally excluded from the New
Testament canon—whether the exclusion be defined in terms of the
activities of individuals, synods, or councils—it is more accurate to say
that certain books excluded themselves from the canon . . . it is a clear
case of survival of the fittest.*
—BRUCE M. METZGER[1]

A CANON, BY DEFINITION, IS A MEASURING DEVICE, like a ruler. The
term came to refer to a limited collection of authoritative books, in this case Christian
books. When we talk about the **canon** of the New Testament, we are talking about
those books considered to be sacred Scripture, inspired by God and authoritative for
the faith and practice of Christians.

CANON

A measuring device, like a rule. In reference to the Christian canon, the term refers to a limited collection of authoritative books. These books are considered to be sacred Scripture, inspired by God and authoritative for the faith and practice of Christians.

CONSTANTINE

A Roman Emperor from A.D. 306–337. Constantine is known especially as the first Roman Emperor to become a convert to Christianity and to promote the Christian faith within the Empire.

COUNCIL OF NICEA

A meeting of church bishops in A.D. 325 that established a doctrine of the nature of the relationship between the Son and the Father. The Nicene Creed was also a product of this council.

at a Glance

In this chapter, we recount the story of how we came to have our New Testament as a collection of 27 early and apostolic Christian books. The church did not determine, but rather recognized, using historical and theological criteria, which were the earliest and apostolic documents. It was not the case that there were Gnostic or

continued

The New Testament documents as a collection of 27 books were not formally recognized until the fourth century A.D. by churches in the East, the West, and North Africa. Of late, it has been fashionable in some scholarly circles to suggest that, before that time, there was nothing that one could call orthodoxy (because it is assumed that the canon determines orthodoxy). To this is added the claim that there were numerous forms of equally legitimate Christian groups that had their own sacred texts with equal claims to being truth before **Constantine** and the **Council of Nicea** squelched or excommunicated these other interesting Christian groups and texts. This picture of the process of canon formation of the New Testament, and indeed the formation of orthodoxy in the early church, is so historically inaccurate that it can only be called *revisionist history based on a myth about Christian origins and early Christian theology.*

As we will discuss later in this chapter, it is not an accident that the New Testament consists of documents that were *all* written in the first century A.D. There was, and had always been, criteria for what might be considered a sacred text for Christians. To qualify, a sacred text needed to be (1) by an apostle or original eyewitness of the life of Jesus and earliest Christianity or draw on the original testimonies or memoirs of eyewitnesses; (2) by a coworker of such an apostle or one who had direct contact with the original eyewitnesses; and in addition, (3) it had to comport with the original teaching of the apostles and eyewitnesses as well. *All of the documents in the New Testament meet these criteria in one way or another.* When the original eyewitnesses, apostles, and their coworkers died out, the period in which such documents could be composed was over. The apostolic tradition could be passed on, but the period for creating foundational, truly apostolic documents had come to a close.

CANON CONSCIOUSNESS AND SCRIPTURE CONSCIOUSNESS

The canonizing process seems to have begun, regarding what we call the Old Testament, before the time of Jesus. There were various factors contributing to this, most obviously the desire to translate the sacred texts into Greek from Hebrew, which formed what came to be called the LXX or Septuagint. In the preface to the book written by Jesus ben Sira in Jerusalem (but then somewhat later translated by his grandson somewhere around 130 B.C.), there is mention already of three major groups of the Old Testament text—the law, the prophets, and the writings, although we are not told all of what would be included in the third category in particular.

The point of mentioning this is that we see already the rise of what can be called "canon consciousness"—the awareness that certain collections of early Jewish books should be seen as unquestionably inspired, authoritative, and truthful, whereas other books might not be viewed that way. But before there ever was canon consciousness, there had to already be what can be called Scripture consciousness—the awareness that this or that book should be seen as inspired by God. This sort of thinking already existed well before the New Testament era; and it should therefore not surprise us when we hear claims, like this one in 2 Tim. 3.16, that "all Scripture is God-breathed," by which is meant all the Hebrew Scriptures, the Old Testament.

We can examine closely the evidence of how early Jews were thinking about these matters by considering what has been found at Qumran or the Dead Sea community. We find every single Old Testament book, with the possible exception of Esther, carefully copied and kept at their community site near the Dead Sea. We find other early Jewish books as well, such as Jubilees and Enoch, but there is no evidence that they were deemed to be part of the Old Testament collection or were treated as having the same authority as the books that became part of the Old Testament.

Sociologists have long pointed out that groups that believe they live, in some sense, in the end of days, the eschatological age, have a propensity to have their own awareness of what counts as sacred texts and what doesn't, precisely because they believe they are in an age when the prophecies and promises of God are coming true and thus the need for clear definition of the books in which these prophecies and promises are found. The fulfillment mentality presses such people to define what counts as sacred texts or the Word of God and what does not. This sort of eschatological and fulfillment mentality clearly describes the mentality of the earliest Christians, as we have seen again and again in this book. I suspect that the reason we have only one real book of prophecy in the New Testament, Revelation, is because the writers were all convinced that they lived in the age of prophecy fulfillment, and there was less interest in or desire to have new books of prophecy compared to the situation in Old Testament times.

It is not an accident that Luke goes out of his way to depict the risen Jesus as providing the befuddled disciples on the road to Emmaus with a Bible study in which it is shown from the law, the prophets, and the psalms the foreshadowings and predictions that the Son of Man must suffer, be killed, and rise again (Luke 24). Jesus himself is the instigator for his own movement of (1) recognizing what are the sacred texts and (2) realizing they are being fulfilled in the age in which these persons lived. But it was not only Jesus who had the mentality to realize that there was a definite group of sacred texts, which collected together, should be seen as the inspired Word of God. We find this very same mentality in the person of the famous Jewish historian Josephus. Here is what he says toward the end of the first century A.D.:

> We do not have innumerable writings that disagree and contradict,
> for only 22 books which are truly reliable and contain the account
> of this whole period [i.e., of Jewish history]. Of these the first five

continued

other heterodox documents originally in the canon of the New Testament that were later excluded. They were never included in any canon list or in the New Testament canon at all. In the chapter, we also chronicle the rise of apostolic, word of God, and canonical consciousness.

> books of Moses contain the laws in addition to the tradition of the
> origin of humanity up to Moses' death. This period encompasses
> almost 3,000 years. From Moses' death to Artaxerxes the Persian
> king after Xerxes, the prophets have recorded the events of their
> times in 13 books. The remaining four books contain hymns to God
> and didactic poems for human life.
>
> —*Against Apion 1.37–43*

Here, we see not only the threefold division of the Old Testament but a specific number of books mentioned, which indicates that Josephus is thinking in terms of a closed or closing canon. In this same passage, he calls the material in this collection "the decrees of God" (Josephus's *Against Apion* 1.42). Whereas we have 39 books in our Old Testament today, we must not forget that early Jews viewed various books that are now separated in our Old Testament as in fact parts of one chronicle. For example, Ezra-Nehemiah was definitely considered part of one account, and this may have been the case with 1–2 Samuel, 1–2 Kings, and 1–2 Chronicles as well. What were Josephus's 13 books of the prophets? It is not clear whether or not he is referring to both the earlier and the later prophets—both what we call the historical books (1 Samuel through 2 Chronicles) and what we call the major (e.g., Jeremiah and Isaiah) and the minor (e.g., Hosea and Amos) prophets. This distinction of major and minor refers to the length of the documents and not their importance.

There is a further Jewish canon list found in the Babylonian Talmud (a collection of Jewish writings) at Baba Batra 14b–15a, and it is usually dated somewhere between A.D. 70, when the temple fell, and A.D. 200. This list clearly identifies the 24 books that today make up the Hebrew Bible. (Note that the Hebrew Bible has the same books as the English Bible, only they are 24 in number in the Hebrew Bible and have been further divided into 39 books in the English Bible. The content, however, is the same.) This canon of the Old Testament was basically the one early Christians came to work with.

For example, Melito of Sardis in about A.D. 189 made a pilgrimage from Sardis to the Holy Land on a fact-finding mission to be sure what books belonged in the Old Testament. He lists them all clearly and completely, and his list is identical to the list from the Talmud, except that he leaves out Esther (which was still a debated book in the first century A.D.) and includes Wisdom of Solomon (Nehemiah also seems to be included with Ezra in his list). Now what this suggests is that, both for the rabbis and for some Christians, the Old Testament canon was basically closed by the end of the second century A.D. Melito shows us that Christians in the second century were indeed already manifesting a clear canon consciousness.

There is, however, another remarkable testimony to the Scripture and canon consciousness of early Christians found in the New Testament itself. Whenever the phrase "Scripture says" or "God says" or "it is written" appears in the New Testament, with only one possible exception (from Jude), it *always refers to books we find in our Old Testament today. It never refers to* **extra-canonical books***!* Now this is remarkable when compared to what we find for example at Qumran. If indeed what counted as Scripture was a wide open question for Christians in the first century A.D., this fact is inexplicable.

I think we can explain this phenomenon by the fact that all the writers of the New Testament were Jews, with two possible exceptions: Luke and the compiler and editor of 2 Peter. As such, they already had a theology of sacred Scripture. Also, the way both Jesus and Paul handled and used the Old Testament provided a legacy regarding what counted as a sacred text. And in regard to Luke and the compiler of 2 Peter, they also have a sense that there is a living Word of God to be heard in their compositions. In the case of 2 Peter, some sort of collection of Paul's letters was already viewed as Scripture. *You have to explain the lack of diversity in what is used as Scripture in earliest Christianity, as the New Testament shows, not merely the presence of more speculation later, when the church was largely Gentile in character.*

What about that one exceptional text in Jude, verse 14? It is quoting from the early Jewish book of Enoch, and here is what it actually says: "Enoch the seventh from Adam, prophesied about them: 'See the Lord is coming . . . '" This text does not use a Scripture quotation formula like "it is written." In fact, it talks about what Enoch said or prophesied. It is the prophetic person of Enoch who is mentioned here and his words that are cited, not an entire book of prophecy that might be regarded as Scripture. *Authority is ascribed to Enoch, not to a book here.* For all we know, Jude is quoting some oral tradition here that he trusts is true. But even if he were quoting from 1 Enoch, it does not follow from this that he deems the whole book true, much less Scripture, any more than when Paul quotes a Greek poet that he deems everything such a poet said as true or trustworthy. In other words, Jude verse 14 does not appear to provide us with clear evidence that any early Christian in the first century quoted extra-canonical Jewish texts as if they were Scripture.

THE RISE OF NEW TESTAMENT SCRIPTURE AND CANON CONSCIOUSNESS

Among the earliest followers of Jesus, there was already a Scripture and canon consciousness and, in addition, a belief that persons like Paul and the author of Hebrews (among others) were speaking not merely human words but prophetic words of God (1 Thess. 2.13) when they preached and taught (see Chapter 1). Therefore, we should not in any way be surprised that early Christian documents, including Paul's letters, began to be regarded as Scripture, on a par with the Old Testament, very early on, indeed before the first century A.D. concluded.

EXTRA-CANONICAL BOOKS

Books that not only Protestants exclude from the Old Testament canon, but also Catholics and Orthodox in the case of books like 1 Enoch or the Testament of Abraham. In addition, Protestants exclude some books (e.g., Sirach, Wisdom of Solomon) that are counted as having secondary or deuterocanonical status by some non-Protestants.

In an illuminating study of Luke–Acts, C. K. Barrett, my mentor of blessed memory, once wrote the following:

> The author accepts the Old Testament, and provides, to accompany it, an explanatory and interpretive parallel book—we may call it, although Luke did not, a New Testament. It was the only New Testament Luke's church had, and this was the first church to have one. Throughout the development of the New Testament canon, New Testaments (including . . . Marcion's. His Gospel and Apostle must have made it very difficult for those who wished to beat him at his own game to use any other form. And it was intrinsically right) had the same basic form: Gospel and Apostle. In his first volume Luke supplied the teaching and action of Jesus which provided the foundation on which the whole Christian movement rested, and he was careful to show at the beginning of the book that Jesus was born within Judaism and in fulfillment of prophecy, and to underline the same point at the beginning of Jesus' ministry: "Today has this scripture been fulfilled in your ears" (Lk. 4.21). His second volume provides the guarantee that what followed was the intended and valid outcome of what had been narrated in the first and also contained specimens of the teaching of the apostles—sufficient to show . . . the content of the Gospel and the unity of representative leaders in preaching it. What more did a church such as Luke's need? This was their New Testament; and as far as we know it was the first.[2]

From a historical point of view, it would be hard to exaggerate the significance of these remarks, if Barrett is correct. It would mean that not only was there an awareness of writing the word of God on the part of some New Testament writers, but there was also a canon consciousness, not just about the Old Testament, but in the case of Luke, about the beginnings of a New Testament as well. This development did not begin after or in reaction to Marcion. It began in the first century A.D., even while some of the eyewitnesses and original apostles were still alive.

Let us now turn to the end of the New Testament era. The discussion of the understanding of inspiration in early Judaism and early Christianity, particularly in eschatological, prophetic, or Messianic sects, should be broached at this point. What determined whether something should be seen as sacred text or not was whether it was believed to be an inscripturated form of the word of God, in this case, the word of God proclaimed and then written down in the first century. This belief is crucial to understanding why there was so much emphasis on the apostolic source documents, viewing them in a more hallowed light than a second-century figure like Bishop Papias or Bishop Ignatius viewed their own writings. They understood the crucial nature of apostolic and eyewitness testimony[3] long before there were any canon lists at all, so far as we know.

But where do we find the origins of the idea that what the earliest Christians were proclaiming and writing was itself the word of God and thus suitable to be viewed as Scripture if written down? Recall that 1 Thess. 2.13, perhaps the earliest of all Christian documents, already presents us with evidence that Paul's proclamation of the Gospel was considered inspired, indeed the word of God, by Paul himself and not merely the opinions of a human being.[4]

In other words, the issue was not just whether Paul had the Spirit, which was true of all early Christians, but rather was he an apostle of Jesus Christ commissioned for proclaiming the living Word of God to various people? Not all Christians were given such a gift or a task, as the gift lists in the Pauline epistles make clear. Apostles are seen as gifts to the church distinguishable from other inspired figures such as prophets (see 1 Cor. 12). First Corinthians 14.36–37 makes clear Paul's own thinking about this matter, for in the same breath he affirms he has the Spirit, that he is authorized to give his converts the command of the Lord (which refers to what he is writing at that moment in 1 Cor. 14), and that he speaks the word of God. In other words, we already see a mentality here that affirms not only that the apostle proclaimed the word of God orally but also that what he wrote was "the Lord's command" for that audience, not distinguishing his own teaching from that of Jesus in terms of inspiration or authority. In other words, we already see in our earliest Christian writer, Paul, the beginnings of Scripture consciousness about Christian writings of the apostles and their coworkers as well as a connection between that idea and the apostolic proclamation.

The process of collecting and circulating apostolic documents in groupings had already begun by the end of the New Testament era, if not before, as is evidenced by 2 Pet. 3, which most commentators do indeed think comes from the turn of the era, not much later.[5] Not surprisingly, the earliest New Testament documents are the first ones to make it into a circulating collection—Paul's letters. More important, we learn from 2 Pet. 3.16 that the letters of Paul could be ranked with "the other Scriptures." Now this implies that the author is thinking of a collection of Paul's letters as a known entity and also assuming that the audience will know what "the other Scriptures are." We are thus dealing with the beginnings of *Christian* canon consciousness here, and Paul's letters are already seen, despite their difficulties, as part of the collection of sacred texts for Christians. You do not refer to "the other Scriptures" unless you are implying that Paul's letters were considered as that by at least this author and his Christian audience.[6]

I would be among those who agree with Graham Stanton and Martin Hengel that the label "according to Matthew" (et al.) did not become widely used until there was a grouping of these documents together, no later than early in the second century.[7] If these documents had been previously anonymous, which is not likely, they certainly were not by Papias's day because he calls them by their canonical names already in 125 A.D. or so. It seems likely that there was already a **codex** of Gospels, perhaps the canonical four, early in the second century. We thus have already in play, perhaps as early as A.D. 125, collections of texts of the

CODEX

The precursor to modern books, being pages of texts, sometimes on papyrus, sometimes on parchment, in book rather than roll form. The great codexes, such as *Vaticanus,* include all or almost all the New Testament in one codex, but they come from the fourth century and later.

large majority of what was to become the New Testament (four Gospels in one codex, Paul's letters in another), collections made well before the end of the second century A.D.

How were these early inspired Christian texts viewed? Were they thought to be just like the writings of Ignatius, Justin Martyr, or Papias? There is absolutely no evidence they were. Those three writers all cite the earlier apostolic documents in ways that distinguish their own writings from them, even when *they see their own writings as in some sense inspired,* as Ignatius seems to have done. Why? Because, although there may not have been what could be called a full canon consciousness on their part, there was a strong apostolic writings consciousness as the source documents of the movement. In fact, we already see this in the A.D. 90s with Clement of Rome in the way he treats Paul's letters.

Thus, the Muratorian fragment and also Irenaeus at the end of the second century should not be seen as anomalies out of due season prior to the fourth century. They are rather reflecting this earlier apostolic tradition and even canon consciousness, if I can put it that way. The argument that the Muratorian list is anachronistic in the second century is questionable at best, especially when *this list does not match up with later canon lists.* Were it a later list, we might expect it to be more like one or another of the fourth-century lists surely, and perhaps we have shortchanged the impetus Marcion provided in the direction of composing such a list. Clearly enough, Irenaeus is reacting to Marcion and the Gnostics. There is no reason why the composer of that Muratorian list might not have done so as well. Here is what this late second-century list gives us, bearing in mind that the beginning and end of this document are missing:

> . . . at which nevertheless he was present, and so he placed [them in his narrative]. (2) The third book of the Gospel is that according to Luke. (3) Luke, the well-known physician, after the ascension of Christ, (4–5) when Paul had taken with him as one zealous for the law, (6) composed it in his own name, according to [the general] belief. Yet he himself had not (7) seen the Lord in the flesh; and therefore, as he was able to ascertain events, (8) so indeed he begins to tell the story from the birth of John. (9) The fourth of the Gospels is that of John, [one] of the disciples. (10) To his fellow disciples and bishops, who had been urging him [to write], (11) he said, "Fast with me from today to three days, and what (12) will be revealed to each one (13) let us tell it to one another." In the same night it was revealed (14) to Andrew, [one] of the apostles, (15–16) that John should write down all things in his own name while all of them should review it. And so, though various (17) elements may be taught in the individual books of the Gospels, (18) nevertheless this makes no difference to the faith of believers, since by the one

sovereign Spirit all things (20) have been declared in all [the Gospels]: concerning the (21) nativity, concerning the passion, concerning the resurrection, (22) concerning life with his disciples, (23) and concerning his twofold coming; (24) the first in lowliness when he was despised, which has taken place, (25) the second glorious in royal power, (26) which is still in the future. What (27) marvel is it then, if John so consistently (28) mentions these particular points also in his epistles, (29) saying about himself, "What we have seen with our eyes (30) and heard with our ears and our hands (31) have handled, these things we have written to you"? (32) For in this way he professes [himself] to be not only an eyewitness and hearer, (33) but also a writer of all the marvelous deeds of the Lord, in their order. (34) Moreover, the acts of all the apostles (35) were written in one book. For "most excellent" Theophilus's Luke compiled (36) the individual events that took place in his presence—(37) as he plainly shows by omitting the martyrdom of Peter (38) as well as the departure of Paul from the city [of Rome] (39) when he journeyed to Spain. As for the epistles of (40–1) Paul, they themselves make clear to those desiring to understand, which ones [they are], from what place, or for what reason they were sent. (42) First of all, to the Corinthians, prohibiting their heretical schisms; (43) next, to the Galatians, against circumcision; (44–6) then to the Romans he wrote at length, explaining the order (or, plan) of the Scriptures, and also that Christ is their principle (or, main theme). It is necessary (47) for us to discuss these one by one, since the blessed (48) apostle Paul himself, following the example of his predecessor (49–50) John, writes by name to only seven churches in the following sequence: To the Corinthians (51) first, to the Ephesians second, to the Philippians third, (52) to the Colossians fourth, to the Galatians fifth, (53) to the Thessalonians sixth, to the Romans (54–5) seventh. It is true that he writes once more to the Corinthians and to the Thessalonians for the sake of admonition, (56–7) yet it is clearly recognizable that there is one church spread throughout the whole extent of the earth. For John also in the (58) Apocalypse, though he writes to seven churches, (59–60) nevertheless speaks to all. [Paul also wrote] out of affection and love one to Philemon, one to Titus, and two to Timothy; and these are held sacred (62–3) in the esteem of the church catholic for the regulation of ecclesiastical discipline. There is current also [an epistle] to (64) the Laodiceans, [and] another to the Alexandrians, [both] forged in Paul's (65) name to [further] the heresy of Marcion, and several others (66) which cannot be received into the catholic church (67)—for it is not fitting that gall be mixed with honey.

(68) Moreover, the epistle of Jude and two of the above-mentioned (or, bearing the name of) John are counted (or, used) in the catholic [church]; and [the book of] Wisdom, (70) written by the friends of Solomon In his honor. (71) We receive only the apocalypses of John and Peter, (72) though some of us are not willing that the latter be read in church. (73) But Hermas wrote the *Shepherd* (74) very recently, in our times, in the city of Rome, (75) while bishop Pius, his brother, was occupying the [episcopal] chair (76) of the church of the city of Rome. (77) And therefore it ought indeed to be read; but (78) it cannot be read publicly to the people in church either among (79) the prophets, whose number is complete, or among (80) the apostles, for it is after [their] time. (81) But we accept nothing whatever of Arsinous or Valentinus or Miltiades, (82) who also composed (83) a new book of psalms for Marcion, (84–5) together with Basilides, the Asian founder of the Cataphrygians. . . .

This document, which is important on many counts, reveals the following key points: (1) Given that it was written in the second century during the same era when Hermas was written, the author knew a canon list that seems in the first instance to be responding to the heretic Marcion's truncated list, which involved only the Gospel of Luke and some Pauline letters; (2) it seems from the last couple of lines as well to be responding to the Gnostics; (3) it knows a list in this order— Gospels, Acts, Pauline letters (all 13 of them), three letters by John, one by Jude, and the Revelation of John and it also mentions Wisdom of Solomon and the Apocalypse of Peter as accepted; (4) clearly, from the fragmentary beginning, there is one or more Gospels mentioned before Luke in this list; (5) notable by their absence are 1–2 Peter and James; (6) it contains important early testimony about Luke's writings to Theophilus in which it is plainly stated he is not an eyewitness but is a physician and that his second volume does not chronicle the demise of Peter or Paul; and (7) it continues the tradition that Paul was set free after house arrest in Rome and went on to Spain. Perhaps the most important thing about this list is that, like later canon lists, *no Gnostic documents and no Ebionite documents were ever included in any canon list. It is thus historically false to say that such documents were later expelled from the New Testament canon. They had never been included in such lists and thinking about the New Testament canon at any time.*

By the end of the second century, the church was overwhelmingly Gentile, and it had largely begun to adopt the LXX as its Old Testament Bible, for better or worse. As the Gnostic movement was to show, there was a growing anti-Semitism in early Christianity and in its fringe or split-off sects, witnessed both by Marcion and the Gnostic literature. This brings us to the so-called canon debate about the catholic epistles and Revelation. It should be noted that the only documents that *were* even debated by the church between the second and

Figure 21.1 Papias was the second-century church father who first commented at length on the authorship of the Gospels. He was bishop in Hierapolis, the main street of which we see in this picture. (© *Mark R. Fairchild, Ph.D.*)

fourth centuries were documents that were from orthodox writers or early Jewish documents like Wisdom of Solomon; and most of the former sorts of documents ended up in the canon.

The real problem with documents like Jude or James is that, by the third and fourth centuries, when the vast majority of the church truly was Gentile, they were deemed far too Jewish and too unlike the favored Pauline collection. The same was especially the case with Revelation. Eusebius could hardly contain his animus against the "chiliasts" (believers in a millennium) and Judaizers within Christianity. The same is sadly true of other church fathers. Second Peter came under the same rubric because it cites so much of Jude. And even Hebrews was suspected by some not merely because it is anonymous, but because it is too Jewish. Probably 2–3 John, especially if bundled with some of these other documents, raised problems for the same reason.

If we ask why it was so difficult to see these documents as genuine and apostolic in the third and fourth centuries (and even beyond), the answer is not hard to figure out. They are too unlike the more "Gentile" documents. They thus had an uphill climb into the hearts of many Christians in those centuries. In other words, it is not hard to figure out why the church of post-apostolic times took so long to figure out what was already known by some in the first century—the general apostolic limits of their sacred texts. The truth is that the church had a different character and mentality, a largely non-Jewish one by the end of the second century. This is why the recognition of some of the apostolic documents took so long in various quarters in the church.

We do not need here to retell the tale of Athanasius and his Festal Letter mentioning just 27 New Testament books in about A.D. 367 or the concurrence of Pope Innocent with that limitation or the agreement to the same number by the African councils of the late fourth century. Nor do we need to rehearse the canon lists themselves. What we need to note is that, from at least three very different segments of the church, the word went out that there were definite boundaries to not only the Old Testament, but also the New Testament at that time. It is not surprising that some of the lists are not precisely identical given that the church was not united. What is remarkable is that both in the East and the West there was an ecclesiastical voice that said the New Testament had these 27 books and not others.

What all such lists were saying is that the canon was closed, even if different segments of the church had a slightly different contents list for the closed canon of the Bible as a whole. *In all of this, it was not a matter of the church defining, but rather of the church recognizing what were and weren't the apostolic books.* This process of recognition inherently ruled out Gnostic and other post–New Testament era books, even books written by orthodox post-apostolic Christian figures such as Clement of Rome or the author of the Didache.

In my judgment, it is a mistake to take the great codexes, and what is included in them, as canon lists. Nowhere in those documents is there a preface or addendum that says, "These are our Christian Scriptures." What we may assume is that the books in the great codexes were all viewed as important and valuable Christian texts, and thus where there was room in the codex more might be included than just the apostolic ones. Indeed, they might even go backward and include favorite earlier works like Wisdom of Solomon. These were approved books for Christian study. We do not know that such codexes were taken out of the scriptorium and used as pulpit Bibles, so to speak.

What closed the canon was not the church but rather the dying out of the apostolic and eyewitness figures whose pens were laid down once and for all, which happened in the first century. It took a growing and increasingly Gentile church a further three centuries to fully recognize the importance of what had happened in the first century, not just in terms of the *regula fidei* (rule of orthodox faith), but also the *regula canona* (rule of canon). The issue was not merely whether a writer had the Spirit. The church continued to have the Spirit. This was not the sole or whole basis for what was to be considered Scripture. What was also required was proximity to the Christ event and its first eyewitnesses and apostles. What was required was being part of the earliest and most ancient apostolic circles of Peter, Paul, James, and others.[8]

Even secondary figures, like Luke or Mark, who had direct contact with and had learned from the apostles and eyewitnesses, were able to write these new

Christian source documents, something later generations, not privy to interviewing or being eyewitnesses, could not do. Luke 1.1–4 makes quite clear what the mentality was, particularly of those in the wider apostolic circle. The eyewitnesses and original preachers of the word had to be sought out and consulted. If earlier accounts had been written, they had to be consulted by the likes of a Luke. Papias reflected this whole attitude very clearly. He wanted to hear what the apostles had said, at least from those of the second and third generation who had met and heard them. The apostolic testimony was all important, and in the end its pedigree would be the decisive issue. Why?

Because Christianity, like early Judaism, was a historical religion; and in historical matters, antiquity, eyewitness testimony, and authoritative original witnesses were crucial.[9] Even in Paul's day, this was understood. He tells us, writing in about A.D. 52, that he passed on to his Corinthian converts what he had already received of the Gospel story of the passion and burial and resurrection that had happened "according to the Scriptures" (1 Cor. 15.1–4). Not, mind you, according to one or another text of Scripture, one or another prophetic scroll; the Scriptures were all seen as testifying to Jesus. Paul had received this testimony as a sacred trust and tradition handed on to him probably, as Gal. 1–2 suggests, from Peter himself, who helped him get the *historia*/historical facts straight. Early Jews handled their sacred traditions with care and reverence. Paul was no different in handing on the Gospel tradition.

Margaret Mitchell, in her seminal essay, "The Emergence of the Written Record," says this:

> The earliest gospel message had texts in it as central to it—in this case the holy scriptures of Israel. The first followers of Jesus of Nazareth had turned to their "scriptures," the sacred texts of Judaism in the Hebrew and Greek languages, and sought to explain the Jesus whom they had come to know by what they found there. Paul could only have confidently summarized the message that these things were "according to the scriptures" if he was certain his audience was already familiar with the key supporting texts.[10]

Just so, and this implies there was an enormous reason for the earliest Christians to have in hand, and be sure about, what their sacred texts were and what they contained. They after all had to demonstrate some remarkable things from Scripture—including the idea of a crucified Messiah that would have seemed sheer folly to early Jews not expecting such.

I am thus understandably dubious that there was not considerable clarity about the general boundaries of the sacred Scriptures of Israel for early Christians like Paul. If even texts like Job, Malachi, Ezekiel, Zechariah, Jeremiah, Isaiah, and Daniel could be seen as crucial sources for explaining the Christ event, then it is clear enough that the corpus of sacred texts was viewed as much more than the Torah alone, or even the Torah plus the former prophets and the later pre-exilic ones. And most remarkably, neither those who relied on the Hebrew text nor those who relied on the Greek text cite as Scripture anything that does not eventually end up in the Hebrew canon. Not once. This speaks volumes, and it needs to be taken into account by those who want to see the earliest period of the canonizing process as nothing but flux and great uncertainty.

What did the author of 2 Tim. 3.16 mean when he said, "Every passage of Scripture (or all Scripture) is God-breathed and profitable"? Notice the use of the singular for Scripture. It reflects an assumption of a bounded collection that has plenary inspiration (divine inspiration of the concepts and ideas contained within). Yes, there was already in the New Testament era a reasonably clear sense on the part of some Christians of what counted as the Old Testament Scriptures and what did not.

So let me reiterate that the canonizing process not only began before the first century for the Old Testament and in the first century for the New Testament (as witnessed by Luke and 2 Pet. 3), but also its limits were de facto defined by the nature of the historical reality of early Christianity in the first century, with its reliance on the apostolic and eyewitness testimony to provide it with its sacred tradition.

Canon consciousness is not, of course, the same as apostolic consciousness or awareness of writing Scripture. Canon consciousness regarding the New Testament as a full collection is something that was a matter of the later recognition by the church of final limitations or hard boundaries of the whole collection. It is possible, many would say probable, that some of the writers of the New Testament may well have been unaware that they were writing *canonical* documents, documents meant for a specific collection; but to judge from the case of our earliest Christian writer Paul, they *were* aware that they were speaking "the word of God" when they spoke the Gospel, and not merely the words of human beings, as that very early document 1 Thess. already tells us (1 Thess. 2.11–13).

They were aware of speaking inspired speech, and the written residue of such speech was likewise seen as inspired, authoritative, important, and true. In the case of Luke, they were also aware that a "New Testament" would include some combination of Gospel plus apostle—the stories and teachings of Jesus and of his immediate apostolic followers and successors. Of course, there was no reality or cognizance of a full New Testament in the New Testament era as a collection. Such a full collection would come at a later time. For the very earliest Christians, there was the Old Testament (see 2 Tim. 3.16) and the apostolic tradition. As things turned out in regard to the New Testament books, apostolic documents were all that were going to end up in the Christian canon 300 years later.[11]

The recognition and final definition of the canon took centuries. It is thus all the more remarkable that only apostolic books, and not those of the worthies of later centuries, were included in the New Testament canon. In the end, even the highly Gentile fourth-century church did not want to break faith with their Jewish Christian apostolic forebears, and so both *regula fidei* (the rule of faith) and *regula canona* (the canon) were grounded in the earliest, apostolic testimonies, which became our New Testament. Canon lists are only the after-the-fact residue of this affirmation of faith in the original apostolic witness. They should not be the main focus or bête noir of canonical criticism or canon studies today.

THE ORGANIZING OF ORTHODOXY AND ORTHOPRAXY

If we ask how orthodoxy was taught during the time when the canon was surfacing or how orthodoxy was taught before there was a functioning New Testament, there is a reasonable answer that can be given. Darrell Bock, at the end of his important study, *The Missing Gospels,* addresses this very question. In essence, he reminds us that our earliest New Testament documents show that orthodoxy and orthopraxy were taught through *Scripture* (Hebrew Scripture and what was read in the church from the new community); *singing* (hymns like Phil 2 and Col. 1 that have theology in them); *summaries* (doctrinal summaries like 1 Cor. 8.4–6; 11.23–25; 15.3–5; Rom. 1.2–4; and the several summaries in the pastorals); *sacraments* (the core theology embedded in the practice of baptism and the Lord's Supper); and *supervisors of the traditions* (the apostolic oversight of the teaching and the eyewitnesses and servants of the word from Jesus [Luke 1.2]). All of these were means of teaching that were a part of the core life of the community and not the result of some secret teaching. By and large, it was by these various means that theological and ethical norms were conveyed until we get to the time of Irenaeus and others, when a more fully formed and expressed canon consciousness shows up in the writings.[12]

IN THE END

In the end, having introduced ourselves to the whole New Testament, the following can be said: *There are probably no pseudonymous books of any kind in the New Testament.* There are books written by two brothers of Jesus; books written by apostles; books written by eyewitnesses; books written by coworkers or those who could and did consult eyewitnesses and original apostles; and, of course, compilation documents like 2 Peter that follow the conventions of earlier scribes, attributing the work to its most famous contributor or source—Peter.

The reason there are no pseudonymous books is precisely because these are all documents that come from the first and second generations of early Christianity and from a very small circle of authoritative voices, perhaps only 11 of them (Mark, Matthew, Luke, the Beloved Disciple, John of Patmos, Paul, Peter,

James, Jude, Apollos, and the compiler of 2 Peter). Their social networks were reasonably tightknit, and it is clear that they shared common and each other's material, so we can say with some confidence that they shared a common vision of the basics of orthodoxy and orthopraxy, especially regarding what they believed about Christ and what they believed Christian discipleship should entail. Orthodoxy did not have to wait on the canon to emerge because the rule of faith already existed in the first century, and its adherence to apostolic and eyewitness testimony was a guiding principle for recognizing what ought and ought not to be included in the canon of the New Testament in due course.

At this great remove in time and space from these historical events, we have no sound historical basis or just-unearthed evidence for rewriting the story of earliest Christianity in a radically new way. We have no basis for affirming the existence of lost Christianities, which in the case of Gnosticism, for example, have been known about ever since the time of the early church and were not even considered truly Christian in their own day. We also have no basis for suggesting that the church began with a huge and contradictory array of beliefs and practices and only later imposed orthodoxy and orthopraxy in the fourth century, banishing previously acceptable forms of Christianity into outer darkness.

In fact, the story of the New Testament and earliest Christianity is much less like a novel about a conspiracy theory and a later church cover-up, and more like a story of a group of people who followed the example of their master and quietly faced persecution, prosecution, and even execution for their new-found faith in Jesus. If you read the New Testament with an open mind, you will realize that people like Peter and James and Paul would not and did not quietly give up their lives to execution for beliefs that they knew in their hearts were never true. They paid with their lives for their convictions that what they believed about Jesus was too firmly grounded in history to ignore, too true to betray, too good to lie about, and so important it was worth dying for.

There is a reason why the Bible, and in particular the New Testament, is the best-selling book of all time. It is because millions and millions of people in the last 2,000 years of almost every race on earth have found in it a historically grounded truth that not merely informed them but transformed them. They found in it not merely a new concept of freedom, but someone who could set them free. It is my hope that those reading this textbook would soon find themselves right at home and in good company with those who wrote the New Testament, and that they would begin to appreciate it on its own terms.

IMPLICATIONS

When you think about the amazing process by which we came to have these 27 books in the New Testament, you can see why Bruce Metzger once said that the church did not so much determine the canon as come to recognize after long reflection what books had always been the earliest, apostolic, eyewitness Christian books. No books from the time of Tertullian or later ended up in the New Testament. Indeed, no books from after the time of Ignatius of Antioch or Papias became part of the New Testament. Not a one.

As Metzger went on to say, the more you study the New Testament, the more you can see how the Spirit guided the process of the canonization of the New Testament. Thank goodness anti-Semitic books from the second century and later did not make it into the New Testament. Thank goodness Gnostic documents with their un-Jewish dualistic philosophies (spirit is good, matter is evil) did not make it into the New Testament. Thank goodness Marcion, who wanted to forget the whole Old Testament and just have a canon of Luke's Gospel and some Pauline letters, was not listened to.

Although it is important to study all early Christian literature, we can be thankful that applying apostolic and eyewitness criteria to the canonizing process helped us to focus on the earliest and best of early Christian literature. We may also be grateful that the church fathers at the church councils around and before A.D. 367, when there was general agreement on the 27 books, did not agree with the myth of origins of some modern scholars who want to suggest that Biblical orthodoxy and orthopraxy only showed up after Constantine. *This is both historically false and theologically unhelpful.*

Figure 21.2 The harbor at Knidos, one of the many ports Paul stopped at on his way to share the Good News in Rome. *(© Mark R. Fairchild, Ph.D.)*

It is interesting that the Council of Nicea, which helped us to understand Christian theology about Christ's relationship to God the Father more clearly, drew its conclusions some 40 years before Athanasius or Pope Innocent or the pronouncements of the African church about the 27 books. In other words, even formal conciliar orthodoxy existed before the recognition of the canon of the New Testament. The canon of the New Testament did not determine orthodoxy; it simply enshrined and encapsulated what the apostolic church had long believed about Jesus and many other subjects.

KEY TERMS

Canon	Council of Nicea
Codex	Extra-Canonical Books
Constantine	

FOR FURTHER READING

Bauckham, R. *Jesus and the Eyewitnesses: The Gospels as Eyewitness Testimony.* Grand Rapids, MI: Eerdmans, 2006.

Bock, Darrell. *The Missing Gospels: Unearthing the Truth Behind Alternative Christianities.* Nashville, TN: Thomas Nelson, 2006.

Witherington, B. *The Living Word of God: Rethinking the Theology of the Bible.* Waco, TX: Baylor University Press, 2007

————. *What's in a Word: Rethinking the Socio-Rhetorical Character of the New Testament.* Waco, TX: Baylor University Press, 2009.

STUDY QUESTIONS

Why do you think it took so long for the church to figure out which 27 books should be viewed as apostolic and belonging in a New Testament?

What is wrong with the theory that there was no such thing as orthodoxy in the earliest church in the first century A.D.?

What does it tell us about the early church that most of its New Testament appears to have been composed and/or compiled by Jewish Christians— indeed almost all of it, except Luke–Acts and 2 Peter?

Why was it important for the church to recognize a closed or limited group of documents as its foundational documents? What would have been the problem with including a Gnostic document like the Gospel of Judas in a canon with the 27 books of the New Testament?

NOTES

1. B. M. Metzger, *The Canon of the New Testament: Its Origin, Development, and Significance* (New York: Oxford University Press, 1987), 286.
2. C. K. Barrett, "The First New Testament," *Novum Testamentum* 38 (1996): 94–104, here 102–103. His note on Marcion is in the text of the quote in parentheses.

3. Regarding the Papias traditions, see especially R. Bauckham, *Jesus and the Eyewitnesses: The Gospels as Eyewitness Testimony* (Grand Rapids, MI: Eerdmans, 2006).

4. For more on this theme, see B. Witherington, *The Living Word of God: Rethinking the Theology of the Bible* (Waco, TX: Baylor University Press, 2007).

5. Although I would not go as far as he does, I do think that David Trobisch is on the right track in suggesting that apostles like Paul may well have already themselves reflected a sort of canon consciousness and so made collections of their writings for wider audiences than they originally intended. See D. Trobisch, *Paul's Letter Collection: Tracing the Origins* (Bolivar, MO: Quiet Water Publications, 2001).

6. B. Witherington, *Letters and Homilies for Gentile Christians*, vol. 2, *A Socio-Rhetorical Commentary on 1-2 Peter* (Downers Grove, IL: InterVarsity Press, 2008).

7. G. N. Stanton, "The Fourfold Gospel," *New Testament Studies* 43 (1997): 317–346; M. Hengel, *The Four Gospels and the One Gospel of Jesus Christ: An Investigation of the Collection and Origin of the Canonical Gospels*, trans. John Bowdon (Harrisburg, PA: Trinity Press, 2000). See also T. C. Skeat, "The Oldest Manuscript of the Four Gospels?," *New Testament Studies*, 43 (1997): 1–34.

8. B. Witherington, *What Have They Done with Jesus?: Beyond Strange Theories and Bad History—Why We Can Trust the Bible* (San Francisco: Harper, 2006).

9. Bauckham, *Jesus and the Eyewitnesses.*

10. M. Mitchell, "The Emergence of the Written Record," in *The Cambridge History of Christianity*, vol. 1, *Origins to Constantine,* ed. M. M. Mitchell and F. M. Young (Cambridge: Cambridge University Press, 2006), 178.

11. By apostolic, I mean those written by apostles or their coworkers. The author of 2 Peter seems to have had some contact with apostles, and he certainly draws on apostolic documents like Jude.

12. For much more on this, see D. L. Bock, *The Missing Gospels: Unearthing the Truth Behind Alternative Christianities* (Nashville, TN: Thomas Nelson, 2006).

APPENDIX A

Right on Q?
Are the SYNOPTICS a PROBLEM?

Christian piety sometimes has imagined that the Gospel authors were secretaries of God. Medieval paintings often show Matthew or one of the other Gospel authors seated at a desk with an angel standing behind him and whispering in his ear. [But] . . . the matter was a bit more complicated . . . (indeed, the author of the Gospel of Luke says that he has done some research. . . . [1.1–4]). As [Luke's] comment implies, the Gospel authors did not have to start from scratch. They had . . . sources.
     —MARK ALLAN POWELL[1]

Possibly even before Mark's Gospel was written, although this is by no means certain, there began to be collections of "Jesus' Greatest Hits," by which I mean some of the essential teachings of Jesus. The fact that Mark does not seem to have had access to much of this material suggests that this process of collecting the sayings of Jesus only came to full fruition in the last 20 or so years of the first century A.D. when the eyewitnesses who had seen and known and heard Jesus began to become very few in number. Perhaps, however, the process of collection had actually begun considerably earlier in the Holy Land. Whenever it began, both the author of the first Gospel, called Matthew's Gospel, and the author of the third Gospel, called Luke's, seem to have had access to one form or another of this collection of mostly the sayings of Jesus that amount to more than 225 verses of material. In scholarly jargon, this collection of non-Markan material has been called Q, from the German word *Quelle,* which means source.

WAS THERE EVEN A Q COLLECTION?

Although the majority of scholars believe there was a collection or even several collections of the sayings of Jesus in earliest Christianity, there is yet to be any external evidence of such a document. Sometimes, scholars have pointed to the Gospel of Thomas, which is a compendium of mostly sayings of Jesus that probably dates to the latter part of the second century A.D., as proof that there must have been a Q document. When one examines the Gospel of Thomas, however, one sees a theological reason why that sort of document was compiled, namely, that it was believed that the teachings of Jesus were of paramount importance; and the deeds of Jesus, including his miracles and death on the cross, were of less or no importance. The earliest Christians did not agree with that view, as is shown not only from the letters of Paul but also from the speeches of Acts, the sermon we call the letter of James, the Gospels themselves, and other New Testament documents. In any case, the Gospel of Thomas also has some narrative material, so the notion that it consists only of sayings is not true.

Nevertheless, there is evidence from early Judaism that famous first-century Jewish teachers you may never have heard of, like Gamaliel or Hanina ben Dosa or Honi the Circle Drawer, did have their more memorable sayings preserved in writing and collected into some sort of compendiums. We find some of this material in later collections of Jewish literature called the Talmuds.

There is no reason why the earliest followers of Jesus might not have done so as well, *not to supplant the basic Gospel story of the life, ministry, death, and resurrection of Jesus, but to supplement that story,* going deeper into the teachings of Jesus for the purpose of discipleship. There is no real historical evidence of early Christian communities in Galilee or elsewhere that *simply* focused on the sayings of Jesus and not the larger Gospel story that included Jesus' teachings. For the writers of the New Testament, a Gospel without reference to the death and resurrection of Jesus was not a true or full *Gospel.* In this appendix, we talk about the so-called Q source, but if we are going to do that, we must first discuss the issue of the so-called Synoptic problem.

IS THERE A SYNOPTIC PROBLEM?

The word *synoptic* comes from two different words that mean "with one eye." The first three Gospels in the New Testament are called the Synoptic Gospels because, in many ways, they take the same approach to the story of Jesus, tell many of the same stories, and have the same viewpoint about Jesus as the Son of Man and Son of God. They stand together when compared with the very different portrait of Jesus we find in the Gospel of John. But why exactly are the first three Gospels so similar? Are they independent witnesses to the life of Jesus, or do they depend on a common source of materials? For instance, do the later Gospels—Matthew and Luke—depend on the earlier Gospel Mark and use it as a source? Let us approach this issue by using an analogy.

Suppose I am teaching a seminary class, as I regularly do, and suddenly one semester I receive two term papers from two different students, only I discover that more than 90% of the first term paper also appears in the second student's term paper, and of that 90%, more than 50% of it is a verbatim copy of the other paper. What should I conclude? I must conclude that there is some sort of *literary* relationship between these two documents.

Scholars have long noticed that what I have just described is exactly the case between our earliest Gospel, Mark, and the Gospel we call Matthew. Matthew contains more than 90% of the material we also find in Mark, and of that 90%, more than 50% is a verbatim, word-for-word copy of that material in the Greek. We can also point out that some 55% of Mark's Gospel recurs in Luke's Gospel, and of that 55%, there is a 53% verbatim or word-for-word correspondence. It is these facts about Mark, Matthew, and Luke that have caused scholars to debate what the relationship was between these three Gospels. The chart at right shows exactly what we find in the three Synoptic Gospels when compared to one another in detail.

This chart depicts the Gospel of Mark in the second column, whereas Matthew's Gospel is in the first column on the left, and Luke's Gospel is in the third column on the right. What you immediately notice from even a casual glance at the chart is (1) how much shorter Mark's Gospel is than either Matthew's or Luke's and (2) that Luke's is the longest of the three Synoptic Gospels. The color purple in this chart represents the material we find in Mark that is also found in Matthew or Luke, or both. If you look very carefully, you will discover a few small green bits in the Markan column that are not found in either Matthew or Luke, but this represents 5% or less of Mark's material. The green represents the tiny amount of Mark not found in the other Gospels.

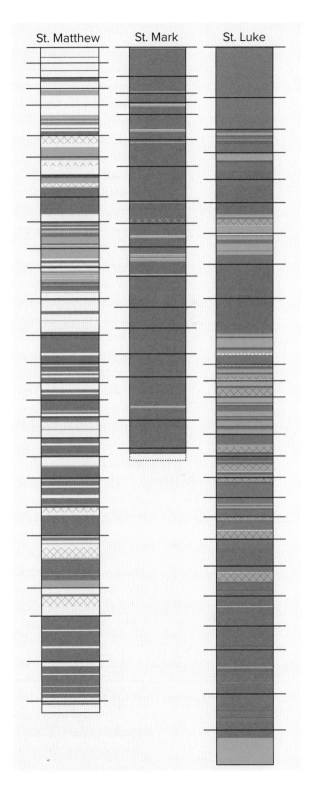

Figure Appendix.1 This chart is a variant on the one found in Allan Barr, *Diagram of Synoptic Relationships* (New York: Continuum, 1995). This chart was republished first by T+T Clark at my recommendation, and then by Continuum.

The second thing you notice from close study of this chart is that there is a lot more purple (or Markan material) found in Matthew's Gospel than there is in Luke's. Luke takes over far less of Mark's material than does the First Evangelist, perhaps in order to make room for a lot of the unique material he has found in other sources (remembering that Luke 1.1–4 tells us that Luke consulted and used oral and written sources that were produced before he wrote his Gospel).

The next thing to notice about this invaluable chart is that the color white in the Matthean column indicates material found only in Matthew's Gospel. You can see that this material is especially prevalent at the beginning of Matthew's Gospel but that it is also found elsewhere throughout that Gospel. Similarly, orange is the color in the third column of the chart, which represents Luke's unique material, and even at a glance, it is evident that he has more unique material in his Gospel than Matthew does in his Gospel, who is more closely following Mark's substance and ordering of things.

Finally, although it is harder to see in the Lukan column, there is light blue material in both Matthew and Luke. Notice that this material is found in the middle section, or ministry section, of both these Gospels, not at the beginning or end of those Gospels. *This is the so-called Q material—some 250-plus verses common to Matthew and Luke and not found in Mark. Sorting out the Synoptic Gospel relationships helps us understand the need for a concept such as Q.*

The way most New Testament scholars sort out the interrelationships of the first three Gospels is that Mark came first and was used by both Matthew and Luke. Matthew and Luke also used another common source, which is called Q. On top of that, both Matthew and Luke had a special source or sources of material that the other did not have access to.

There are some scholars who have suggested that there was no Q source, but rather that Luke simply used Matthew for the sayings material. Most scholars have been unpersuaded by this suggestion, but it definitely remains possible. Even fewer scholars have thought that Matthew was the earliest Gospel and that Mark and Luke drew on Matthew. But this theory raises more questions than it answers. For example, why would Mark leave out all of the Sermon on the Mount in order to make room for longer miracle stories also found in Matthew, when Mark wants to emphasize that Jesus was a teacher? Or again, if Luke had access to Matthew's Gospel, why in the world would he leave out all of Matthew's rich material in Mt. 1–2 about the birth and infancy of Jesus? When you read Luke 1–2, it is clear he does not know many, if any, of the stories and sayings in Mt. 1–2, or else he would have incorporated some of that material, for example, about the wise men, in his Gospel. Accordingly, at left is the source diagram most New Testament scholars of all sorts of faith postures or no faith accept as likely.

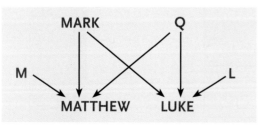

The M and L in the diagram refer to the unique material in Matthew and Luke, respectively. Thus, Mark and Q are taken to be the earliest sources used by Matthew and Luke. With this in mind, we can now turn to the issue of the scope, character, and nature of the early sayings collection called Q.

THE WISDOM OF JESUS

One of the major overlooked aspects of the presentation of Jesus in the Gospels is that, with regularity, Jesus is presented as a sage, indeed as the wisdom of God come in person. This is one of the reasons why the focus in early Judaism was on a source of wisdom, Torah, but the focus in early Christianity was on Jesus himself. The Q collection attempts to give its recipients an overview of some of Jesus' wisdom, and in the process demonstrate that Jesus is greater than the two greatest sages of the Old Testament—Moses and Solomon. Indeed, Jesus is God's instructions (which is what Torah means) come in the flesh. One of the things that becomes apparent is that the so-called Sermon on the Mount is likely a collection of things Jesus said on various occasions, assembled topically. The reason to draw this conclusion is that the material found in Mt. 5–7 in one place is found in several places in Luke's Gospel. The following is an outline of the Q material in the order in which it seems to have been compiled.

A.   **THE STORY OF JESUS THE SAGE/WISDOM**
1. The Forerunner and the Announcement of the Sage's Coming by John—Mt. 3.1–12/Lk. 3.2–9, 15–17
2. The Anointing of the Sage with the Spirit—Mt. 3.13–16/Lk. 3.21–22
3. The Testing of the Sage—Mt. 4.1–11/Lk. 4.1–13
4. The Sermon of the Sage—Mt. 5–7/Lk. 6.20–49
5. The Miracles of the Sage—Mt. 8.5–10/Lk. 7.1–10
6. The Questioning of the Sage by John—Mt. 11.2–6/Lk. 7.18–23
7. The Response of the Sage—Mt. 11.7–11/Lk. 7.24–28
8. The Rejection of the Sage by This Generation—Mt. 11.16–19/Lk. 7.31–35

This section of Q concludes with "Yet Wisdom is vindicated by her deeds" ("Wisdom" being Jesus himself, who is revealed as such at the end of this first section).

B.   **DISCIPLESHIP TO JESUS THE SAGE—ITS CHARACTER AND MISSION**
9. Discipleship's Cost—Mt. 8.19–22/Lk. 9.57–62
10. Discipleship's Mission—Mt. 9.37–38; 10.5–16; 11.20–24; 11.25–27; 13.16–17/Lk. 10.1–24 (including the Mission Speech, Woe on Galilean Villages, Authority of Missionaries, Thanksgiving, and Blessing)

11. The Disciple's Prayer and Praying—Mt. 6.7–13; 7.7–11/
Lk. 11.2–4; 11.5–

This section of Q ends with the disciples being urged to seek wisdom from above.

C.   THE WARS AND WOES OF WISDOM

12. Struggling with Satan—Mt. 12.22–30; 43–45/Lk. 11.14–26

13. Signs of Trouble—Mt. 12.38–42/Lk. 11.29–32

14. The Light of One's Life—Mt. 5.15; 6.22–23/Lk. 11.33–36

15. The Woes of Wisdom—Mt. 23.4, 6, 7, 13, 22–23/Lk. 11.42–52

This section ends with the saying "The Wisdom of God said . . ." recounting the seventh woe on would-be sages.

D.   THE REVELATIONS OF WISDOM

16. Hidden and Revealed—Mt. 10.26–27/Lk. 12.2–3

17. Wisdom's Persecuted Followers—Mt. 10.28–31/Lk. 12.4–7

18. Acknowledging the Sage and the Spirit—Mt. 10.19, 32–33/
Lk. 12.8–12

19. Wisdom in Nature—Mt. 6.25–33/Lk. 12.22–31

20. The Treasures of Wisdom—Mt. 6.19–21/Lk. 12.32–34

21. Preparation for Wisdom's Feast—Mt. 24.43–44/Lk. 12.35–40

22. Preparation for Wisdom's Return—Mt. 24.45–51/Lk. 12.42–48

23. Wisdom's Second Baptism—Lk. 12.49–50

24. Divisions over Wisdom and Wisdom's Demise—Mt. 10.34–36/
Lk. 12.51–53

25. Signs of Trouble II—Mt. 16.2–3/Lk. 12.54–56

26. Time to Settle Accounts—Mt. 5.25–26/Lk. 12.57–59

27. The Lament of Wisdom for Jerusalem—Mt. 23.37–39/ Lk. 13.34–35

This fourth section of Q ends with Wisdom rejected in Jerusalem, and Jerusalem's "house" forsaken by God. Wisdom will not be seen again in Jerusalem until a beatitude is pronounced on Wisdom (i.e., Jesus).

E.   THE NARRATIVE PARABLES AND APHORISMS OF JESUS, GOD'S WISDOM

28. Seed and Leaven—Mt. 13.31–33/Lk. 13.18–21

29. Gate and Door—Mt. 7.13–14; 22–23/Lk. 13.23–27

30. East and West, Last and First—Mt. 8.11–12; 20.16/Lk. 13.28–30

31. Wisdom's Banquet—Mt. 22.1–10/Lk. 14.15–24

32. The Cost of Discipleship (Cross Talk)—Mt. 10.37–38/Lk. 14.5–27

33. Old Salt—Mt. 5.13/Lk. 14.34–35

34. Lost Sheep—Mt. 18.12–14/Lk. 15.3–7

35. Lost Coin—Lk. 15.8–10

This section of Q ends with Wisdom's search for the lost.

F.   DISCIPLESHIP AT THE TURN OF THE ERA

36. Choose Whom You Serve, God or Mammon—Mt. 6.24/Lk. 16.13

37. The End of Torah's Era?—Mt. 11.12–13; 5.18/Lk. 16.16–17

38. The End of a Marriage—Mt. 5.32/Lk. 16.18

39. Sins and Forgiveness—Mt. 18.7, 21–22/ Lk. 17.1–4

40. Mustard Seed Faith—Mt. 17.20/Lk. 17.5–6

This section of Q ends with the assurance to the disciples that even little faith can work great miracles.

G.   THE END OF THE AGE

41. Against False Hopes—Mt. 24.26/Lk. 17.22–23

42. Like Lightning—Mt. 24.27/Lk. 17.24

43. Like Vultures—Mt. 24.28/Lk. 17.37

44. Like Noah and Lot's Time—Mt. 24.37–39/Lk. 17. 26–30

45. No Turning Back—Mt. 24.17–18/Lk. 17.31–32

46. Find Life by Losing It—Mt. 10.29/Lk. 17.33

47. Division of Laborers—Mt. 24.40–41/Lk. 17.34–35

48. Parables of the Tenants—Mt. 25.14–30/Lk. 19.11–27

49. At Table and on Thrones in the Dominion—Mt. 19.28/Lk. 22.28–30

The last part of Q is a reflection on the end times and the roles Jesus and the disciples will play at the end.[2]

What you see in the above list is *all* of the material that is contained in Q. Although it is mostly sayings material, there is some narrative, for example, the stories of Jesus' baptism and temptations. Most scholars think, and they are likely right, that Luke preserves the order of this sayings collection more closely than does Matthew. You will notice that in fact from 1 to 49, they are in numerical chapter order in Luke's Gospel (from Luke 3–Luke 22). You will also notice that there are exactly 49 sayings, and they are divided into seven sets or groups. Seven was an important symbolic number in early Judaism, conveying the notion of completion, perfection, or even fulfillment. The not-so-subliminal message of the Q collection is that Jesus is the perfect teacher, revealing the perfect wisdom of God for God's people. It should also be noticed that this collection of materials contains both wisdom and eschatological teachings of Jesus, with Jesus being presented as some sort of eschatological sage or embodiment of God's wisdom come in person to God's people. Notice that the sections in Q alternate between focusing on Jesus and focusing on his disciples and their discipleship, with the last section focusing on both and the roles they will play when Jesus returns.

Although a good number of scholars have thought that Luke more often preserves versions of Jesus' sayings that are closer to his exact original words, I have become increasingly unconvinced that this is so because Luke is adapting and adopting the teaching of Jesus for a more Gentile audience than was the likely audience of Matthew's Gospel. In that process, Luke tends to de-emphasize the future eschatological teaching of Jesus. There is much more that could be said about this important source of material that both Matthew and Luke use, but enough has been said here to introduce you to the subject.

IMPLICATIONS

We learn from these reflections that (1) the Gospel writers used sources to write their Gospels, and (2) they often depended on one another to do so. The proper thing to conclude from these two facts is that in broad strokes the first three Gospels writers were in strong agreement about what Jesus said and did. The second important insight one can gain from this material is that Jesus was a famous teacher and that his teaching was both memorable and probably memorizable, or at least it was written down not long after the death of Jesus, as we find a considerable amount of it in these Gospels. On a closer look at Jesus' teaching, there are some distinctive features to it:

A. Jesus taught without footnotes and spoke on his own authority. By this, I mean that many early Jewish teachers would use the formula, "I say on the authority of Rabbi Gamaliel, who says on the authority of Rabbi Shammai . . . ," citing human traditions. Jesus never does that. He speaks on his own authority. Notice that Mk. 1.27 tells us that one of the earliest clear reactions to Jesus is that he was offering new teaching and with independent authority.

B. The newness of Jesus' teaching was remarked on more than once. Jesus was not just explaining the Old Testament; he was on various occasions offering new teaching. No one in early Judaism spoke quite like Jesus did, and no other teacher suggested that he was God's final wisdom come in person as Jesus did.

C. The profound conviction of Jesus that he was bringing in God's final work of salvation and judgment for God's people, and indeed on God's people, is a repeated theme in these sayings. But equally clearly, Jesus did not come to tell early Jews that God was going to choose a different and purely Gentile people of God. This is especially clear in Matthew's Gospel, which was written for Jewish Christians.

FOR FURTHER READING

Barr, A. *Diagram of Synoptic Relationships.* New York: Continuum, 1995.

Black, David Alan, and David R. Beck, ed. *Rethinking the Synoptic Problem,* Grand Rapids, MI: Baker, 2001.

Witherington, B. *Jesus the Sage and the Pilgrimage of Wisdom.* Minneapolis, MN: Fortress Press, 1994.

STUDY QUESTIONS

What is Q?

What is the Synoptic problem?

Why do scholars think Matthew and Luke used Mark's Gospel as a source?

What does the high degree of similarity in Matthew, Mark, and Luke in their portraits of Jesus tell you about their views about Jesus and about the Gospels reliability?

NOTES

1. M. A. Powell, *Introducing the New Testament: A Historical, Literary, and Theological Survey* (Grand Rapids, MI: Baker Academic, 2009), 92–93.
2. For much more on this subject, see B. Witherington, *Jesus the Sage and the Pilgrimage of Wisdom* (Minneapolis, MN: Fortress, 1994).

APPENDIX B

EPISTOLARY PSEUDEPIGRAPHA AND INTELLECTUAL PROPERTY IN ANTIQUITY—FRAMING THE DISCUSSION

First, we may ask, were there pseudonymous letters in early Judaism and early Christianity during the first two centuries A.D.? The answer is surely yes. We have documents like 4 Ezra from the Jewish side of things and the Epistle to the Laodiceans from the Christian side, although the latter is surely a second-century document created on the basis of the hint that there was such a letter in Col. 4.16. These examples make it clear that such documents existed. Neither of these *documents* ended up in the Jewish or the later Christian canon, so we may ask why they were not considered for inclusion in those canons. In any case, we cannot deny that there were at least a few such documents in play in the New Testament era or a little after it in the relevant religious communities.

This fact raises the important question of whether such pseudonymous documents created any ethical questions for early Jews or early Christians, or was the creation of such documents simply accepted *as part of the literary conventions of the time*? We are plagued in part with inconsistent definitions within the scholarly community of what might amount to a pseudonymous document. As a result, answers to the ethical question have often varied.

For example, Richard Bauckham attempts to divide such documents into various categories. He immediately excludes documents that would have been written within the lifetime of an apostolic figure, but not by him. He concludes it is very unlikely that any such documents exist in the New Testament.[1]

Bauckham helps us in various ways to see how difficult it would have been to pull off a pseudonymous letter that was situation specific. For one thing, as he says, not only does the "I" in a pseudonymous letter not refer to the named author, but also the "you" likely does not refer to the named audience, not least because that named audience would likely have recognized that the document was a forgery![2] He concludes, "But in no indubitably pseudepigraphical letter known to me are the supposed addressees and the real readers identical."[3] The actual author can only address the actual audience under a literary fiction that involves not only his but also the audience's real identity!

There is then the issue of distance in time and space. For a pseudonymous document to work effectively, it needs to be written in the name of a famous enough person *at a great enough remove from its putative author and audience* that its authority and authenticity would be less likely to be challenged. This presents a serious problem for claims about New Testament letters, all of which, with the possible exception of 2 Peter, were written before the end of the first century A.D.—that is, before the apostolic eyewitnesses or those who had contact with the eyewitnesses had all died out. In summary, if these documents were falsely attributed to popular authors, the audiences could have easily spotted them as a fraud.

Second, a more precise definition is offered by I. H. Marshall: "A text is pseudonymous when it is not by the person whose name it bears in the sense that it is written after his death by another person or during his life by another person who was not in some way commissioned to do so."[4] We may further refine this discussion by pointing out, as David Meade has done, that we should probably distinguish between pseudonyms that are fictitious and those that are borrowed from real human beings.[5] We may also wish to bracket out the use of actual names of ancient or legendary worthies (e.g., Abraham and Isaac), as no one in the first century would have been deceived into thinking they were still composing documents during the canonizing era.

The issue has to do with the use of real names of contemporary or near-contemporary persons who were known religious authority figures in that era. The motive for pseudonymity would in fact vary from genre to genre; for example, in a pseudonymous apocalypse, the motive might be to pass off history writing as prophecy retrojected into the mouth of an ancient famous religious figure. The issue of prophecy does not necessarily arise in this way with pseudonymous letters.

Third, it has sometimes been argued that the canonical documents given the names James and Jude are not pseudonymous, for although they were not written by *the* actual brothers of Jesus, they were written by some other unknown early Christian figures who really had such names. This theory is very problematic, precisely because these are documents that present themselves as being written by Jesus' actual brothers, and they were certainly viewed in that light in subsequent centuries by Christians. Indeed, they would not likely have been included in the canon had they not been viewed in that light. So, it is doubtful that the issue of these documents and pseudonymity can be resolved with that artful dodge. This has been lately emphasized in a study by B. Ehrman, who makes a strong case against the notion that pseudonymity was an accepted literary practice in the New Testament era, which had no negative ethical implications and no attempt to deceive an audience, at least when it comes to the composition of situation-specific letters.[6]

Fourth, there is another consideration from an ancient educational standpoint. There was a rhetorical exercise called "impersonation" (*prosopopoeia*). This exercise was even taken on by schoolboys, where they would try to write a speech as if they were a famous person speaking—Caesar or Alexander, for instance.

This rhetorical technique is in fact found in the New Testament in Rom. 7.7–13 when Paul speaks in the first person as Adam, a figure introduced in Rom. 5.[7] However, this rhetorical exercise was limited in scope, and to my knowledge it involved only speeches or discourses, not the composition of written documents, particularly letters, using a famous person's name. In addition, in the use of this rhetorical device there was no attempt to deceive nor to use someone else's authority to achieve some nefarious aim in these rhetorical exercises. It was always, furthermore, a famous person from the past who was being impersonated.

Our concern is with documents that could actually be called forgeries because there was at least some attempt to deceive some audience, near or far.[8] Deceit is deceit, whether it is for political, financial, personal, or spiritual gain. The issue is whether we have documents in the New Testament purporting to be by one person—a famous person—but really written by another who had not been authorized by the famous person to write. It is interesting that it was not until 1792 that an English scholar, E. Evanson, first suggested there might be pseudonymous documents in the New Testament. Prior to that time, this had not been an issue of real debate in the church when it came to canonical books.

Fifth, it has often been suggested by scholars in the modern era that whereas on one hand, we definitely have pseudonymous documents in the New Testament, on the other hand, there was no attempt to deceive. It has also sometimes been added by such scholars that the writers were writing in the Spirit, or as part of the legacy or school of Paul or Peter or James, or even that they were pneumatic persons who could speak for others or in others' names.

If we consider, for example, 2 Timothy or Titus, these letters contain many personal details and appear to be addressing a particular historical situation. So, it is hard to avoid the conclusion, if they are pseudepigraphical, then there is an intent to deceive the audience, trying to make it appear as if they are by Paul's own hand, not merely written in the spirit of Paul.[9] We also have no sound historical evidence that Paul or Peter or James ever had "schools" in the sense that we may talk about Greco-Roman schools where people were trained to speak and write like famous persons. Discipling certainly went on, but the sources are quite silent as to whether apostolic coworkers or disciples of apostles were trained to imitate *the writings* of their apostolic figures.

Furthermore, it is perfectly clear that non-apostles or those who were not even eyewitnesses of much of what they wrote, like Luke or Mark, felt free to write in their *own* names, and their works were included in the canon under their own names. We also have anonymous New Testament documents that were deemed to have integrity and authority that were included in the canon (e.g., Hebrews, 2–3 John).[10] In addition, we have composite documents like 2 Peter that do have a link with the reputed author. These things are all demonstrable, and they make it unlikely that there would have been a felt need for pseudepigraphy in the New Testament era, *unless* someone really did have the desire to deceive and did not have the authority to speak in his or her own voice or anonymously.

There are further problems with facile reasoning that pseudepigraphy would not have been a problem in the first-century church. Sometimes, this reasoning takes the form that we find in J. D. G. Dunn's work, in which he argues that because pseudepigrapha were not a problem for early non-Christian Jews, they would not have been a problem for early Christian Jews. Dunn, of course, points to writings such as 1 Enoch and 4 Ezra or the Letter to Aristeas.[11] The problem with using those examples, as E. E. Ellis has shown, is that the former is an apocalyptic work attributed to an ancient legendary figure, which means it is of a very different ilk than ad hoc letters; and 4 Ezra is likewise a document attributed to an ancient figure. It is thus hard to see how these examples support the notion that Jews or Jewish Christians would not have had problems with a pseudonymous letter, especially if it claimed to be by a near contemporary or apostolic figure.[12] As Richard Bauckham himself says in evaluating the possibility of a document like James or Ephesians or 1 Peter (which are circular documents) being pseudepigrapha, "the more exegesis tends toward envisaging a specific situation as address in these letters, the less likely pseudepigrapha becomes."[13] We may add also that, the closer they were written to the time of their putative author, the less likely they could pass as genuine.

It is a helpful point of Bauckham's that only 2 Peter among New Testament letters contains indications that it is addressing its immediate *and* a later audience (see 2 Peter 1.12–15, especially the last verse).[14] This suggests it has a broader intended scope than ad hoc letters. In fact, it appears to be the only document that is not really situation specific in the entire New Testament. It could then be a pseudepigraph, but only if it did not contain a Petrine source, which it certainly appears to do, just as it contains source material from Jude and elsewhere.

It is also not cogent to argue, as Dunn does, that we may distinguish the attitude of Jewish Christians in the first century A.D. from Gentile Christians in the second. We have no historical basis for such a distinction that suggests that falsely attributed letters were fine by early Jewish Christians in the first century, but not for later Gentile Christians.

There are indeed clear objections by second- and third-century Christians to such a practice. For example, the Muratorian canon list, perhaps our earliest canon list (other than that of Marcion), makes note of the Epistle to the Laodiceans and the Epistle to the Alexandrians as "forged in Paul's name" by Marcion's supporters. Two other classic examples would be the supposed correspondence between Jesus and King Abgar or Paul and Seneca. There was a document named 3 Corinthians, composed by a bishop (!) in the second century, who said he did it out of admiration for Paul. But when he confessed that he was actually the originator of this document, Tertullian says that he lost his ecclesiastical position (Tertullian, *On baptism* 17).

One may also point to Tertullian's judgment in the very same document cited previously of the Asiatic presbyter who composed the "Acts of Paul and Thecla." The man was brought to trial and defrocked for the composition of this document, and Tertullian said this is exactly what should happen to a forger. One could also point to the famous story of Bishop Serapion of Antioch, who around A.D. 200 first approved the reading of the Gospel of Peter in Rhossus in Syria. When he read the book, he realized it was being used to support the docetic heresy, and he found some parts of the book to be unorthodox and therefore a forgery (see Eusebius, *Hist. Eccl.* 6.12, 3–6).

One then can understand the argument that Dunn made, that these sorts of judgments happened, because by the second century and later there were heretics running around in the church, and there was a heightened concern about what documents were and were not authentic. But this concern about forgeries and false teaching did not arise for the first time in the second-century church. In fact, we already see this concern in 2 Thessalonians 2.2 and elsewhere in the Pauline corpus where Paul takes the trouble to sign his documents to guarantee they are from him (see Gal. 6.11; 2 Thess. 3.17; 1 Cor. 16.21).

Forgery was certainly an issue in the first century A.D., and not just within the confines of the church.[15] In his classic study, B. M. Metzger, followed now by T. Wilder and B. Ehrman, showed that there was definitely a concept of intellectual property in the ancient Greco-Roman world, and it was seen as a scurrilous practice to put words into someone else's mouth to damage them, or even to secure greater credence and authority for one's own ideas (the latter being more to the point for our interests).[16] First, Metzger is able to show that authors, such as Galen, had serious concerns about the production of forgeries using their names. For this reason, Galen even wrote a book entitled *On His Own Books* to let people know which works were genuine and which were not.[17] In this book, he both listed and described his original works to avoid pseudepigrapha being pawned off as his own work.[18]

In addition, there were specific literary practices that ancient writers used within their documents to protect their intellectual property from being co-opted, added to, or subtracted from. Wilder puts it this way: "A writer could protect his work by (1) pronouncing a curse in the document to warn others against altering it [see Rev. 22.18–19]; (2) binding the authorial attribution with the text by means of a seal or an acrostic; (3) making known the document's size by citing the exact number of lines in it [e.g., see the very end of Josephus's *Antiquities*]; (4) informing others of what the work contained in chronological order; or (5) using trusted friends to circulate his writings before they could be altered or distorted."[19] All of these practices were known and used in the first century A.D., and we find some of them in use in the New Testament. Another practice used for such authentication was the use of a personal signature as Paul did, which was not in fact a regular practice in ancient letter writing in the Greco-Roman era.

Furthermore, we find evidence that, when falsification was discovered, there were moves to correct the problem. For example, Diogenes Laertius tells us *(Lives of Eminent Philosophers* 7.34) that the librarian of Pergamum, Athenodorus, was caught having falsified some existing Stoic works. Once discovered, the falsified material was eliminated, and the original writings restored to their original form. Another good example is the lament of Quintilian that only one of his famous rhetorical court speeches was properly published (*emiseram*). He goes on to complain that although many speeches circulated under his name, they had few words in them that were actually his (*Inst. Or.* 7.2.24).

Suetonius even says that Augustus himself condemned those who wrote under another person's name (*Lives of the Caesars* Vol. 2.LV). He adds a story involving Emperor Claudius about a man found guilty of forgery. He had his hands cut off once he was convicted of the crime (*Lives of the Caesars* V.XV.2). There are many such examples.[20] These examples are quite enough, however, to make the point.

F. Torm was right when he concluded, "The view that religious circles of Greco-Roman antiquity 'understood pseudonymity as a literary form and straightway recognized its rightness' is a modern invention."[21] In antiquity, it was not seen as an acceptable literary practice; rather, it was seen as a serious literary problem in the Greco-Roman world, and there could even be criminal repercussions for such acts. Christian reactions to forgery in the second and third centuries, as mentioned earlier, were not atypical of the entire early Christian period. Plagiarism was recognized as a real problem, not an approved literary device. In summary, even though ancients did not have copyright laws as moderns do, they had their own ways of identifying falsifications and protecting intellectual property.

> Thus, pseudepigrapha in the canon, whether attributed to Paul or someone else would be a problem because such documents do intend to deceive the audience. This would clearly not pass the ethics test of any genuine New Testament author. Fortunately, we probably don't have to worry about this. Not even the Pastoral Epistles or 2 Peter are likely genuine examples of pseudepigrapha.

AND SO?

Some New Testament scholars have frankly recognized the problem with pseudonymous letters and have drawn the logical consequence for how one should view documents such as the Pastoral Epistles if they are pseudepigrapha. L. R. Donelson puts it this way: "In the interest of deception [the author of the pastorals] fabricated all the personal notes, all the . . . commonplaces in the letters . . . and any device that . . . might seem necessary to accomplish his deception."[22] This is the honest and inevitable conclusion once one realizes there was no accepted ancient literary convention that involved epistolary pseudepigrapha *if*—and it is a big if—one concludes that the pastorals, or other New Testament documents for that matter, are pseudepigrapha.

E. E. Ellis goes on to show at length how one has to conclude that if documents like the pastorals or 1 and 2 Peter are pseudepigrapha, then they surely did intend to deceive the audience about this matter, for they excoriate all guile, hypocrisy, and deceit, while at the same time practicing it in literary form.[23] Ellis is particularly concerned about apostolic pseudepigrapha (i.e., using the names of Paul, Peter, James, and Jude). He concludes,

> The role of the apostle in the earliest church, the evidence for literary fraud in Greco-Roman antiquity, and the New Testament letters themselves combine to show that apostolic pseudepigrapha were a tainted enterprise from the start. At no point in the church's early history could they avoid the odor of forgery. Only when the deception was successful were they accepted for reading in the church, and when they were found out, they were excluded.[24]

One must then ask how in the world this might comport with one further factor. Early Christian writers such as Paul believed that both orally and in writing they were speaking the word of God, a truthful word, not merely the words of human beings. This is already evident in what is generally recognized as Paul's earliest letter. He says, "And we thank God continually because, when you received the word of God, which you heard from us, you accepted it not as a human word, but as it actually is, the word of God, which is at work in you who believe" (1 Thess. 2.13). The word of God was spoken and written by such figures as Paul, and this is how they viewed their communications. The documents attest to a concern about truthfulness in all things, especially because the word of God was being communicated.

Finally, it is worth reiterating why successfully devising a pseudepigraph would have been especially difficult. C. J. Classen puts his finger on it clearly:

> Most poems, works of fiction, novels are written for the world at large for future generations; and this applies to historical accounts as well. Letters, on the other hand, are more immediately relevant, addressed to an individual or a specific group at a specific time in a particular situation, though there are, of course letters composed to be preserved and published and appreciated also later for their literary form or for their content.[25]

Just so, and this remark sets up a series of questions one would need to ask about the letters we are dealing with in the New Testament, but most of all, it makes clear how difficult it would be to produce a successful pseudepigraph—it would likely have to be situation and content specific, but for a situation and with a content that did not actually address the putative audience but rather another and later one.

Here are the questions for our study: (1) Do the letters in the New Testament appear to be situation specific? The answer would seem to be yes, with the exception of 2 Peter.[26] (2) If they are not situation specific, do they show signs of addressing a broader audience over a longer period of time? Again, 2 Peter would seem to be such a document, but not these other letters. (3) Do these letters have literary pretensions? We must distinguish here between a facile use of literary and rhetorical devices and literary pretensions. We do find the former in some of our documents, but one would be hard-pressed to argue that any of these documents, including 2 Peter, were deliberately written for the purpose of publication or later literary appreciation. We may question whether any of these documents would then have been viewed as valuable or of lasting merit if they are pseudepigrapha.

In light of all these considerations, what must we conclude? At the very least, we must conclude that the older paradigm of F. C. Bauer and others who assumed the general acceptability of epistolary pseudepigrapha to early Jews and Christians because they were part of an acceptable literary genre or literary practice must be rejected. There were various inhibiting factors to such letters being accepted either within or outside of the Jewish and Christian sectors of society. There was indeed a concept of intellectual property and also of plagiarism in the Greco-Roman world.

Thus, although there *may* be pseudepigrapha within the New Testament, the burden of proof must fall squarely on the shoulders of those who claim such a thing. Although our modern notions of authorship require some emendation when we are asking about how the subject was viewed in antiquity, especially when it came to composite documents, nevertheless it is right to say that the ancients were certainly capable of critical thinking. Deception, especially about religious matters, was not deemed an acceptable literary practice, or even honest. In my view, a strong case for the Pastoral Epistles being Pauline in character can be made and is the most reasonable view. Indeed, it is likely that there are no epistolary pseudepigrapha in the whole New Testament.

FOR FURTHER READING

Bauckham, R. J. "Pseudo-Apostolic Letters." *Journal of Biblical Literature* 107, no. 3 (1988): 469–494.

Metzger, B. M. "Literary Forgeries and Canonical Pseudepigrapha." *Journal of Biblical Literature* 91 (1972): 3–24.

Richards, E. R. *Paul and First Century Letter Writing: Secretaries, Composition and Collections.* Downers Grove, IL: InterVarsity Press, 2004.

Witherington, B. *Letters and Homilies for Hellenized Christians.* Vol. 1, *A Socio-Rhetorical Commentary on Titus, 1-2 Timothy and 1-3 John.* Downers Grove, IL: InterVarsity Press, 2006.

STUDY QUESTIONS

What does the word *pseudonymous* mean?

How is the term applied to New Testament documents, and why is it especially applied to New Testament letters?

Do you think ancient peoples were as capable of critical thinking as moderns are? Why or why not?

If there are pseudepigrapha in the New Testament, how would that affect your view of these documents and their authority?

NOTES

1. R. J. Bauckham, "Pseudo-Apostolic Letters," *Journal of Biblical Literature* 107, no. 3 (1988): 469–494.
2. Ibid.
3. Ibid.
4. I. H. Marshall, "The Problem of Non-Apostolic Authorship of the Pastoral Epistles" (paper presented at Tyndale Fellowship Cambridge, England, 1985), 1–6, here 1.
5. D. G. Meade, *Pseudonymity and Canon: An Investigation into the Relationship of Authorship and Authority in Jewish and Early Christian Tradition* (Grand Rapids, IL: Eerdmans, 1986). This study can profitably be compared and contrasted with T. L. Wilder, *Pseudonymity, the New Testament, and Deception* (Lanham, MD: University Press of America, 2004).
6. B. D. Ehrman, *Forged: Writing in the Name of God—Why the Bible's Authors Are Not Who We Think They Are* (New York: HarperCollins, 2011).
7. B. Witherington with D. Hyatt, *Paul's Letter to the Romans: A Socio-Rhetorical Commentary* (Grand Rapids, MI: Eerdmans, 2004).
8. Wilder, *Pseudonymity*, 3.
9. For example, the discussion in L. R. Donelson, *Pseudepigraphy and Ethical Argument in the Pastoral Epistles* (Tubingen, Germany: Mohr Siebeck, 1986), 24–55; and D. deSilva, *An Introduction to the New Testament: Contexts, Methods & Ministry Formation* (Downers Grove, IL: InterVarsity Press, 2004), 686–687.
10. Here, we must reject the attempt to lump together anonymous and pseudonymous documents by K. Aland, "The Problem of Anonymity and Pseudonymity in Christian Literature of the First Two Centuries," *Journal of Theological Studies* ns 12 (1961): 39–49. The former sort of documents do not appear to be part of an attempt to deceive anyone about their provenance. For a pseudonymous document to be successful, be believed, and have its intended effect of being the word of its reputed author, it must successfully deceive its intended audience; otherwise, it was seen as disreputable or of lesser value, as the older study of F. Torm on Greco-Roman, Jewish, and Christian literature shows. Torm is helpful and correct about

the psychological dynamics involved. See F. Torm, *Die Psychologie der Pseudonymitat im Himblick auf die Literatur des Urchristentums* (Guterloh, Germany: Bertelsmann, 1932). He rightly points out that in antiquity, the defense of "rhetorical impersonation" is never used to justify creating such a document.

Equally unconvincing is the argument of Aland that, if a person was speaking in the Spirit, it did not matter who he claimed to be or who others later claimed he was, so long as the voice was from God. There were, no doubt, oracles of the risen Lord spoken, for example, in Revelation through John of Patmos. But they are presented as exactly that, oracles of the risen Lord spoken by John, not words of the historical Jesus during his ministry. In other words, one should not claim that the pneumatic nature of early Christianity led to a blurring of the concern about who said what and when, and then extend that reasoning to provide a justification or explanation for pseudepigrapha.

11. J. D. G. Dunn, *Unity and Diversity in the New Testament* (London: SCM Press, 1977), and his *The Living Word* (London: SCM Press, 1987), 83–84.
12. E. E. Ellis, "Pseudonymity and Canonicity of New Testament Documents," in *Worship, Theology, and Ministry. Essays in Honor of Ralph P. Martin*, eds. M. J. Wilkins and T. Page (Sheffield, England: Sheffield Academic Press, 1992), 212–224.
13. Bauckham, "Pseudo-Apostolic Letters," 488.
14. Ibid.
15. Again, the recent study by Bart Ehrman called *Forged,* should be consulted at this point.
16. cf. B. M. Metzger, "Literary Forgeries," 3–24; Wilder, *Pseudonymity,* 35–73.
17. Metzger, "Literary Forgeries," 6.
18. Wilder, *Pseudonymity,* 42–44.
19. Ibid.
20. Ibid. 45–46.
21. Torm, *Die Psychologie,* 19.
22. Donelson, *Pseudepigraphy,* 24, 55.
23. Ellis, "Pseudonymity," 220–223.
24. Ibid. 223–224.
25. C. J. Classen, *Rhetorical Criticism of the New Testament* (Tubingen, Germany: Mohr Siebeck, 2000), 46.
26. Ephesians is a circular letter, but to a specific Pauline group of churches, and thus is situation specific.

GLOSSARY

Abba An Aramaic term that means "father dearest." The term is not slang for "daddy." The term denotes intimate relationship with deep respect.

Abrahamic Covenant The covenant God made with Abram described in Genesis 15:18–21. God promises that Abram's descendants would inherit the land of many other nations. Genesis 12:1–3 also describes the promise that God made to Abram, namely, that he would be the father of many nations. In Genesis 17:9–14, God directs Abraham to circumcise all males as a sign of the covenant.

Ad Hoc Document A document written to address specific issues with specific audiences at a specific point in time.

Agonistic The Greek word *agon,* from which we get the word agony, refers to struggle and hence to a culture based on struggle and competitions of various sort to get ahead. In such a culture, "honor challenges" (or as we might call them today, "spitting contests") would be engaged in by rivals to see who was best at one thing or another—speaking, wrestling, throwing the javelin, business, you name it. Winning was the way to gain honor, and with losing came shame. Competition and rivalries were such a part of ancient culture that whole tribes and kin groups would go to war with others over a simple challenge of honor (recall what prompted the Trojan War and the story of Helen of Troy).

Alethinos A Greek word that means true. In certain cases, it may also mean authentic or genuine.

Alpha The first letter of the Greek alphabet. The letter is also used to refer to the beginning of something.

Amnos A Greek word for "lamb."

Anachronistic The description of a term, concept, idea or event that does not fit accurately into the time in which it is being discussed. In other words, the usage is chronologically incorrect. For example, it would be anachronistic (or an anachronism) to refer to the use of cell phones in the first century A.D.

Ancient of Days A phrase used to refer to God.

Anonymous An adjective that describes a work by an unknown author.

Anothen A Greek word that means either "again" or "from above."

Aphorism A short saying that reveals a general truth.

Apocalypsis A Greek word, from which the English word *apocalyptic* is derived, which refers to the revelation of divine secrets.

Apocalyptic Literature A genre of revelatory literature with a narrative framework, in which a revelation is mediated by an otherworldly being to a human recipient, disclosing a transcendent reality that is both temporal, insofar as it envisages eschatological salvation, and spatial insofar as it involves another, supernatural world.

Aramaic A Semitic language (not to be confused with Arabic) like Hebrew, which Jews acquired while they were in exile in Persia. The name itself comes from the region called Aram in central Syria. It is thus a northwest Semitic language like Hebrew and Phoenician. During its 3,000-year written history, Aramaic has served as a language of administration of empires and a language of worship. It was the day-to-day language of Israel in the Second Temple period (539 B.C.–A.D. 70), was the language spoken by Jesus, is the language of sections of the biblical books of Daniel and Ezra, and is the main language of the later collection of Jewish teachings called the Talmud.

Areopagus This word literally means Mars Hill, and refers to a locale in Athens. It is debated whether the reference is to a little knoll in the shadow of the acropolis and the Parthenon, or in fact Acts 17 is referring to the court in the stoa or marketplace below which Paul was tried for preaching new deities.

Arnion A Greek word for "lamb."

Asiatic Rhetoric Rhetoric that employs a preferred form of style and diction in the Province of Asia and neighboring areas. Common features include very long and ornate sentences and fanciful style.

Atonement Within Christianity this term refers to the suffering and death of Jesus Christ, which makes amends for sin and makes possible a relationship between humanity and God. In other words, the term draws a connection between the death of Jesus and the forgiveness of or release from sins.

Beza Theodore Beza, a Frenchman, was involved in the Reformation of the sixteenth century. Beza was mentored by John Calvin.

Biography A written account of a person's life history.

Canon A measuring device, like a rule. In reference to the Christian canon, the term refers to a limited collection of authoritative books. These books are considered to be sacred Scripture, inspired by God and authoritative for the faith and practice of Christians.

Chiasm A literary device in which one uses a sort of parallel construction to focus on key points, such that three topics are mentioned and then brought up again in reverse order in the passage in question, but the focus of the passage is on its center.

Chreia A short story or anecdote told about a person to reveal his or her character, usually concluding with a famous saying or deed of the person. Forming such tightly packed pithy narratives was part of elementary rhetorical training in antiquity, and Mark uses this form regularly.

Christianos A Greek term that means adherents of Christ or those belonging to Christ.

Christology The study of the person, nature, and actions or deeds of Jesus Christ. This study is founded mainly on the gospel accounts of the New Testament.

Christos A Greek term that correlates with the Hebrew term *Mashiach* and means "anointed one."

Cicero A Roman philosopher, politician, and orator. He gained prominence as one of Rome's best orators.

Clement of Alexandria A second century church father and theologian of the Christian faith who taught in the Catechetical School of Alexandria.

Codex The precursor to modern books, being pages of texts, sometimes on papyrus, sometimes on parchment, in book rather than roll form. The great codexes, such as *Vaticanus,* include all or almost all the New Testament in one codex, but they come from the fourth century and later.

Composite Document A document that collects materials from other sources and depends on them.

Constantine A Roman Emperor from A.D. 306–337 Constantine is known especially as the first Roman Emperor to become a convert to Christianity and to promote the Christian faith within the Empire.

Council of Nicea A meeting of Church Bishops in A.D. 325 that established a doctrine of the nature of the relationship between the Son and the Father. The Nicene Creed was also a product of this council.

Deliberative Rhetoric The rhetoric of the public assembly. Deliberative rhetoric is characterized by advice and consent and focuses on future events. For example, in Philippians, we find an example of deliberative rhetoric that tries to persuade the Philippians to follow good examples and avoid bad ones. This sort of rhetoric involves persuading the audience about their future behavior.

Diaspora A term used in reference to Jews who were dispersed outside of the Holy Land.

Diatribe A form of rhetorical writing that often involves an imaginary debate partner, speech in character, and the use of rhetorical questions. The goal is to confront or debate in an imaginative way for an instructive purpose.

Docetic A person who denies that Jesus, the Son of God, actually took on human flesh. Instead, the belief is that Jesus merely appeared to take on human flesh. Docetism is the formal name of this heresy.

Domitian A Roman emperor who ruled from A.D. 81–96. Christians experienced another persecution under Domitian.

Dyadic/Collectivistic Personality An identity chiefly formed by the group and the effect of the group on the individual. In other words, the identity of an individual was not defined by the ways one stood out from the crowd. Rather, individual identity was defined by what crowd one was associated with. As a result, individuals did not seek to form their own personal identity, as identity was derived from group association.

Dynamis A Greek word meaning "mighty works" when applied to deeds.

Ebionite A term literally meaning "the poor," used as a reference to a small but important sect of Jewish Christians, who seem to have had issues with Paul and his Gospel and also had a low Christology, believing that Jesus was not part of the Godhead. The Ebionites should not be confused with James or Jude, who do not reflect that sort of low Christology. It is possible they were a continuation of a group called the Judaizers in the New Testament—Pharisaic Jewish Christians believing in strict adherence to the Mosaic law for all followers of Jesus (see Acts. 15.1–3). They seem to have nonetheless claimed James the brother of Jesus as their first leader.

Ecclesiology A term used to refer to the study of the church.

Ekklesia A Greek word usually translated as "church" in modern translations.

Emperor Cult The Emperor cult was an organized form of religion that worshipped the emperor or dynasty of emperors. Emperors were divinized and worshipped as gods. The cult is also referred to as the Imperial cult.

Encomium A rhetorical style in which certain aspects of one's life are praised. Elements that are typically praised are noble birth, notable ancestors, titles, offices that are held, title, economic status, and morality among others.

Encyclical Document A document meant to circulate throughout various churches. Encyclical documents often have a general character, as they are intended for a larger audience.

Enthymemes A form of rhetoric that employs incomplete syllogisms in which the hearer is expected to understand the logic of the argument and supply the missing member of the argument.

Epideictic Rhetoric The rhetoric of the funeral oratory and public speeches lauding some person, place, or event. Epideictic rhetoric is characterized by praise and blame and focuses on the present.

Eschatology A study of end time events.

Essenes A Jewish sect that most likely produced and collected the Dead Sea scroll collection. The Essenes felt that they were the true Jewish people, and they separated themselves from the Jews in Jerusalem. The community consisted of mostly males (Philo and Josephus record their number at about 4,000). Discipline and study of the Scriptures characterized the activity of the community. Ceremonial baptisms were also performed. In addition, the group believed that they lived in the end times. As a result, they expected the coming of two messiahs: a priestly messiah and a kingly messiah.

Ethnos/ethne A Greek word that may be used to refer to either Gentile nations or to the Jewish nation. Context will help to determine the correct usage. For example, in Revelation, the term refers to the Gentile nations. In John, it refers to the Jewish nation.

Ethos The way a speaker comes across to an audience especially in relation to his/her authority, character, or disposition.

Euangelion A Greek word that literally means "good news" and is the origin of the English words *Gospel* and *evangelist*.

Eusebius A Roman historian who later became the Bishop of Caesarea Maritima. Eusebius is referred to as the "Father of Church History," as he chronicled much of the church's history in his work called *Ecclesiastical History*. His historical writings span three centuries.

Euthus A Greek word loosely translated as "immediately." In Mark, the term is not to be taken literally. Rather, it ought to be translated as "next," "after that," or "after awhile."

Exordium/Opening Remarks The beginning of a speech that was meant to establish rapport with the audience and make them well disposed to receive what follows.

External Evidence Evidence that is found externally such as in documents from the church fathers or other earlier, contemporaneous, or later documents.

Extra-Canonical Books Books that not only Protestants exclude from the Old Testament canon, but also Catholics and Orthodox in the case of books like 1 Enoch or the Testament of Abraham. In addition, Protestants exclude some books (e.g., Sirach, Wisdom of Solomon) that are counted as having secondary or deutero-canonical status by some non-Protestants.

Eyewitness A person who is present to witness an event personally and is able to present an account of the event from his/her own perspective.

1 Enoch An apocalyptic Jewish writing that describes the fall of the angels and the story of the joining of the angels with the daughters of men (referred to in Genesis 6.2). Further, it tells of Enoch's trip to heaven as well as his dreams and visions.

First-Order Moral Discourse The type of discourse one would use when addressing an audience for the first time. The goal is to begin the discussion and meet the audience where they are at before persuading them to move in a different direction.

Forensic Rhetoric The rhetoric of the law courts. Forensic rhetoric is characterized by attack and defense and focuses on past times. An example would include the arguments of attack and defense given by lawyers in a courtroom setting.

Gematria A system or code that assigns symbolic values to numbers. For example, the number seven is significant as it is often referred to as the number of perfection. A fascination with symbolic numbers is commonly present in apocalyptic literature.

Genre From the French *genre,* "kind" or "sort"; from Latin *genus* (stem *gener-*); from Greek *genos,* the term for any category of literature or other forms of art or culture; and in general, any type of discourse, whether written or spoken, auditory or visual, based on some set of stylistic criteria. Genres are formed by conventions that change over time as new genres are invented and old ones are discontinued.

Gnosticism The English term "Gnosticism" derives from the use of the Greek adjective *gnostikos* ("learned," "intellectual") by Irenaeus (ca. A.D. 185) to describe the school of Valentinus as "the heresy called Learned (gnostic)." This occurs in the context of Irenaeus's work *On the Detection and Overthrow of Knowledge Falsely So Called.* There is no clear historical evidence of a Gnostic movement before sometime in the second century A.D. The movement was mainly called Gnostic because of its claims to have special, even secret, knowledge about reality.

Gospel A term that originally meant the oral proclamation of the Good News about Jesus. Later it became common to use the term to refer to a document. In the New Testament, the term refers to Matthew, Mark, Luke, and John.

Gymnasium The term itself refers to a place where youths train their bodies in the nude (the very meaning of the Greek word *gymnos* is "naked"). Gymnasium complexes, however, were more than just places for physical training or places with adjoining baths near gyms, although these were included. There were also educational facilities involved in a gymnasium complex, as the Greek ideal was the complete training and discipline of both mind and body.

Hegesippus A second-century Christian who chronicled some events of the early church. He also wrote apologetically against the Gnostics and Marcion. What remains of his writings is quoted by Eusebius.

Hellenizing The practice of spreading Greek culture, language, architecture, and habits first begun by Alexander the Great as he conquered the then-known world east of Macedonia.

Hendiadys A figure of speech that expresses one idea with two words (typically joined by a conjunction). For example, the words "coming in power" express one major idea. A hendiadys is interchangeable with the use of an adjective and a noun such as "powerful coming."

Historical Monograph A written account of a certain period within history. For example, Luke's Gospel and the Acts of the Apostles are a two-volume ancient historical monograph that document the life and death of Jesus and the growth of the New Testament church.

Household Codes Ancient household codes included details about how the head of the household was to treat and engage with the other members of the home. It was also common to find discussions of how husbands related to wives, fathers related to children, and masters related to slaves.

Hyperbole A form of exaggeration that functions rhetorically to emphasize something or draw attention to it in order to inculcate a strong positive response from the audience. Hyperbole is not intended to be taken literally.

Incarnation A term used to refer to Jesus as a divine being who deliberately limited himself in order to also become fully and truly human. In other words, the term points toward Jesus' assumption of full humanity while also remaining fully divine.

Incorporative Personality A phrase that reflects the realities of a collectivist culture, a culture where the group identity is primary and individual identity is secondary.

What happens in such a culture is that some illustrious ancestor is seen not merely as the group's forefather but also as acting for them, as their representative, such that in some sense they were present with, say, Abraham or in the Greco-Roman world with brave Odysseus. Thus, people in these cultures can see themselves as being "in" their ancestor, part of his doings in the past. Thus, for Paul, Christ can be said to be "the seed" of Abraham, summing up and representing all Abraham's descendants and acting for them all. In addition, Paul sees Christ as incorporating all those who are his followers, and in this case, Christ is viewed as God the Father in that regard.

Insinuatio A rhetorical technique by which the author first says nice things in order to establish rapport with the audience before getting to the bone of contention. The technique attempts to soften up the audience before matters of contention are approached.

Internal Evidence Evidence that is found internally or within a text itself.

Irenaeus A church father who lived in the second century. Irenaeus was Bishop of Lugdunum in the Gaul region. One of Irenaeus' popular writings is titled *Against Heresies*. This work is an apologetic against Gnosticism.

Isolationist Sect A very inwardly oriented religious community that works hard to preserve its boundaries with the world, which of course makes real evangelism difficult.

Johannine Literature A phrase used to reference books in the New Testament that are traditionally attributed to John including John (the Fourth Gospel), 1–3 John, and Revelation.

Josephus A Jewish historian who lived during the first century A.D. and referred to Jesus in his writing. Key writings include *The Jewish War, Antiquities of the Jews,* and *Against Apion*.

Judaizers Pharisaic Jewish Christians who insisted that, to be true followers of Jesus and part of his community, even Gentiles must keep the whole Mosaic covenant, including circumcision, the Sabbath, and the food laws.

Judith A Jewish story written in the second century B.C. about a heroine named Judith who devised a plan to save the people of Israel from the persecution of the pagan king. Judith gained trust with the Assyrian king by using her beauty. When the king was found drunk, Judith decapitated him and took his head as a trophy back to her people.

Koinonia A Greek word literally meaning a sharing or participation of something in common by various persons, although sometimes translated as "fellowship." The word, however, speaks more to the process of sharing than the result of a close-knit community.

Kosmos A Greek term that is loosely translated as "world" in Johannine literature. The English cognate is cosmos.

Lector A literate person trained to read an important manuscript (a sacred text, a public proclamation) to an audience with appropriate feeling, pauses, and insight.

Logos The logical arguments of a rhetorical discourse. The arguments are based on the authority of the speaker (*ethos*).

Macro-Culture The dominant culture within a certain context.

Martus A Greek term often translated as "witness." It is the term from which we get the English word "martyr."

Melancthon Philip Melancthon (1497–1560) worked alongside Martin Luther as a German Reformer. Together, they started the Lutheran movement.

Messianic Secret A theory proposed by William Wrede. Wrede purported that Mark imposed a "messianic secret motif" on his source material (material used as sources in the writing process) to cover up the historical fact that Jesus did not really present himself as a messianic figure during his lifetime. The theory does not hold up well in light of other evidence in Mark itself, the other Gospels, Pauline material, and elsewhere in the New Testament.

Micro-Culture A subculture that exists under the umbrella of a macro-culture. Those who are part of a micro-culture may speak a different language or may define identity or rules differently than those who are predominantly a part of the macro-culture or culture at large.

Milieu A term used to refer to a social and cultural setting.

Mosaic Covenant The covenant that God made with Moses on Mt. Sinai concerning Israel. The covenant outlines the way of life for the Israelite people and the way in which they will be in relationship with God and other peoples.

Muratorian Canon This ancient fragment is one of the first documents to contain a list of the books that were accepted as part of the New Testament. The canon dates to the second century A.D.

Myth Greek myths, the stories about the gods, could be seen as stories that were not literally true or grounded in history. However, these myths expressed religious, moral, or philosophical truth in pictorial form.

Narratio/Narration A narration of pertinent facts, explaining the nature of the disputed matter, or facts that needed to be taken into account as a basis for argument and persuasion.

Nero A Roman Emperor (from A.D. 54–68) who is known for his severe persecution of Christians.

New Perspective A perspective or interpretation of Paul that typically interprets the key phrase "works of the law" in Pauline literature as boundary-defining rites of circumcision, food laws, and Sabbath keeping. These rites were used to distinguish Jews from other persons in the Greco-Roman world.

Omega The last letter of the Greek alphabet. The letter is also used to refer to the end or culmination of something.

Oral Culture A culture in which a large part of the communication takes place by the spoken word rather than by written text.

Oral Text A text that is read aloud for an audience. The text is meant to be heard out loud rather than studied privately in silence.

Oral Tradition A tradition that is passed down from generation to generation by word of mouth and not by written text.

Orthodoxy A term used to describe correct or approved theological and ethical beliefs. Heresy occurs when a belief does not agree with orthodox beliefs.

Orthopraxy A term used to describe correct practices based on proper theological and ethical beliefs.

p75 An abbreviation for Papyrus 75 that is called Papyrus Bodmer. This early papyrus codex contains the first volume of Luke-Acts. At the end is the ancient title *Euangelion kata Loukan*, Greek for "the Gospel according to Luke." p75 dates to sometime between A.D. 175 and 225 (or a bit earlier).

Pantaenus A Greek theologian and philosopher from the second century who converted to Christianity and was a key thinker and head of the Catechetical School of Alexandria. Pantaenus was a teacher of Clement of Alexandria.

Papias A church father who lived at the end of the first century A.D. and the beginning of the second century A.D. Papias was the Bishop of Hierapolis. His important writings include some fragments that discuss oral tradition and how the canonical gospels originated.

Papyrus A common material written on by the earliest Christians. Papyrus is a reed from which the stem is harvested and then cut into thin strips. The strips are rolled and hammered together using sap from the stem to glue them together. This process produces individual pages that are then hung to dry. Pages were on average 11 inches high by 8 inches wide and were glued side by side to produce papyrus rolls.

Parakletos A Greek word used in John in reference to the Holy Spirit. The term refers to the Holy Spirit as another advocate for Jesus' message and person, just as Jesus was the Father's advocate when he came to earth. The term also means a counselor, one who instructs, gives advice, ministers comfort, and more.

Parousia A Greek word that can mean "arrival" or "coming," or even sometimes "presence." It was a term like *epiphania* ("appearing") used by early Christians to talk about the second coming of Christ the King because this very same language was used for the "coming" or "appearing" of the so-called divine emperor to a city. Christ was seen as the divine reality, of which the emperor was just a pale parody.

Passion Narrative A term that is commonly used to refer to the narrative of Jesus' suffering and death.

Pathos The emotional response of the audience when the author appeals to their emotions in order to persuade.

Peasant A class of people who lived in an agrarian society. Peasants were part of the lower class, often illiterate, and were not landowners.

Peirasmos A Greek word that can be translated as either "test" or "temptation."

Peroratio/Final Emotional Appeal The recapitulating of the main thesis statement, including a final emotional appeal to the deeper feelings of the audience to cap off the total act of persuasion.

Pharisee This term seems to derive from the Hebrew root *prs,* which means either "separate" or "interpret"—probably the former. The Pharisees were the "Separate Ones" probably because of their attempt to distinguish themselves in the careful observance of the law from less-observant Jews and from Gentiles. It is possible to say that Pharisees were a holiness movement that believed that the way to purify the land was not by violence but through a more detailed attention to the Levitical laws. The Pharisees, unlike the Sadducees, believed that oral traditions were passed on by Moses since Mt. Sinai and were as binding on a Jew as the written traditions in the Old Testament. They used these oral traditions to meet new dilemmas and situations. The Sadducees by contrast were for strict adherence to the letter of the Old Testament, particularly the Pentateuch. This is in part why the Pharisees, but not the Sadducees, affirmed the concept of bodily resurrection, rewards and punishments after death, and the reality of demons (see Ant. 18.11–25; 13.171–73, 297–98; *Jewish Wars* 2.119–66).

Polycarp A church father who was the Bishop of Smyrna. According to Irenaeus, Polycarp was a disciple of John the Apostle. He lived in the second half of the first century and into the second century. Polycarp died as a martyr and was burned for his faith.

Polycrates A second-century A.D. church father who was the Bishop of Ephesus.

Praxis The application or practice of a concept or idea.

Presbyteros A Greek term that may mean either "the elder," "the old man," or even "the older man."

Prescript The initial greetings and address of the audience or audiences at the beginning of an ancient letter. In ancient letters, both the author and the audience are mentioned at the outset, whereas we put the author's name at the end of a letter.

Probatio/Arguments Pro The essential arguments *for* the proposition.

Prognōsin A Greek term from which the English term "prognosis" is derived and means foreknowledge.

Propositio/Proposition The essential proposition or thesis of a discourse that the following arguments are to support.

Pseudonymous A book falsely, and usually deliberately, attributed to a famous person as if he or she authored it.

Q An abbreviation for *Quelle,* which means "source." Q is a hypothetical document that contains the non-Markan collection of Jesus' sayings. The contents of Q are typically drawn from Matthew and Luke.

Qumran The home of a Jewish community, possibly the Essenes. The Essenes felt that they were the true Jewish people, and they separated themselves from the Jews in Jerusalem. The Dead Sea Scrolls were discovered in caves at Qumran starting in 1947.

Refutatio/Arguments Con Arguments intended to dismantle objections or the opposition's arguments against the thesis statement.

Rhetoric The verbal art of persuasion that had long been a staple of ancient education since the time of Alexander the Great, who was influenced by people like Aristotle and his successors who wrote treatises on rhetoric.

Rhetorical Discourse A discourse that employs rhetoric in order to persuade an audience.

Sadducees A sect of Jews who believed in strict adherence to the letter of the Old Testament, particularly the Pentateuch (the first five books of the Old Testament). The Sadducees did not affirm the concept of bodily resurrection, rewards and punishments after death, and the reality of angels or demons.

Sapiential Literature A form of literature that discusses wisdom.

Second-Order Moral Discourse Discourse that attempts to move the audience to a position that is further than what was presented at the first-order level.

Semeion A Greek word used in John to refer to "signs."

Semitic When used as an adjective and in reference to a language, the term denotes the characteristics or features of the Semitic languages such as Hebrew or Aramaic. So, if a Greek phrase or passage has a Semitic feel, this means that it bears the influence of a Semitic language such as Aramaic or Hebrew on it.

Sirach A Jewish writing from the 2nd century B.C. that discusses Jewish wisdom and promotes the study and observance of the Mosaic Law.

Solecism A grammatical mistake or error.

Son of Man The phrase regularly used by Jesus to identify himself and his mission in life. Although some scholars suggest that the use is a circumlocution (a roundabout way of saying something) for "I" or "a man in my position," this explanation does not do justice to the use of the phrase in Mark or by Jesus himself. Rather, the term refers both to a ruler who is human and yet so much more than human. The term also refers to Jesus' divinity as one who has God's authority to forgive sins, to change the way Sabbath is viewed and observed, to sit at the right hand of God, and to judge both the living and the dead.

Soteriology The discussion of salvation, whereas *eschatology* refers to the study of the end times.

Stoicheia A Greek term that refers to elementary religious traditions or sometimes to the basic elements believed to make up the world—earth, air, fire, water.

Superstitio A Greek term from which the English term "superstition" is derived. The term delineated a form of unsanctioned, unauthorized, or illegal religion.

Syllogism A form of argumentation that builds an argument using a major premise and a minor premise. The audience must employ deductive reasoning in order to extract the conclusion of the argument, which is based on the major and minor premise.

Symbolic Universe The sum total of fixed ideas and concepts in a person's mental world that are "givens," not debated, but taken for granted. To Paul, such concepts would be God and sin and redemption. These ideas are configured in relationship to one another through stories.

Synkrisis A rhetorical device used to compare and contrast two things. For example, Paul contrasts the earthly bodies we have now and the resurrection bodies we shall obtain at the resurrection.

Synoptic Gospels The Synoptic Gospels include Matthew, Mark, and Luke. They are called the Synoptic Gospels due to the amount of similarity between the three gospels. Whereas John does have similarities with the Synoptic Gospels, John also contains many differences that do not cohere at the same level as the material or order and events in Matthew, Mark, and Luke.

Tacitus A Roman historian who lived in the first century A.D. and referred in his writing to Jesus who was crucified on a cross by Pontius Pilate. Key writings include his *Annals* and his *Histories*, which report historical events contemporaneous with his lifetime.

Tertullian Tertullian, a church father of the second to third century, was the first Christian theologian and writer to compose documents in the Latin language. He wrote many apologetic works in order to defend the Christian faith against heresy.

Testament of Abraham A Jewish work written sometime during the 1st or 2nd century A.D. about events surrounding Abraham's death.

Testament of the Twelve Patriarchs A Jewish writing that reports stories about the final words and the nearing of death of each of the twelve patriarchs. The stories tell of the character of the patriarchs and their thoughts of what would occur among their descendants after their deaths.

Third-Order Moral Discourse A type of discourse that one has with a person or audience that he/she has an intimate relationship with. The discussion is more frank and to the point.

Tiberius A Roman Emperor (from 42 B.C.–A.D. 37). Tiberius ruled over the procurator Pontius Pilate under whom Jesus was sent for crucifixion.

Tobit A Jewish story written in the 3rd to 2nd century B.C. about a righteous Jew named Tobit. The story centralizes around Tobias, Tobit's son, who while traveling with Raphael (an angel disguised as a man), meets a Jew named Sarah during his travels to collect money from his father's friend. Sarah's previous engagements had ended, as just before the consummation of the marriages, her seven fiancés were murdered by a demon named Asmodeus who loved Sarah. Tobias learns a prophylaxis from Raphael and is able to marry Sarah.

Wisdom of Solomon A pseudonymous work (attributed to but not actually written by King Solomon) written by a Hellenized Jew. The sapiential work discusses matters of righteousness and wisdom in the Jewish context.

INDEX

Note: Page numbers followed by *f* indicate illustrations.

Abba, 94
Abraham, 16, 187, 198, 346*f*
  rhetoric about, 219–20
  in Romans, 219–21, 223
  Sermon of James and, 287
Abrahamic covenant, 175, 198
Acro-Corinth, 211*f*
Acropolis, 165*f*, 255*f*
Acts, 11, 13. *See also* Luke–Acts
  2.9-11, 315–16
  10-11, 272
  15, 37
  20, 160
  apostles in, 319–20
  Apostolic Decree in, 166, 289
  Good News in, 113–18
  Holy Spirit in, 115–18
  James in, 282
  logical structure of, 113–14
  missions in, 294, 296
  Paul in, 127–28, 160, 173
  Peter in, 127–28, 321
  "Son of Man" in, 119–20
Adam, 224–25, 377
adherents of Christ (*Christianos*), 176, 313
ad hoc documents, 210, 253
Adoptionist Christology, 122
Agabus, 171
again (*anothen*), 148
agape, 152, 156n7
agonistic culture, 179–80
alethinos (true), 389–91, 400–401, 425
Alexander the Great, 42, 178
Alexandria, 5, 332, 355, 440
Alpha, 416–17
alphabetical letters, 3–4, 3*f*
Ambrose, 7
"Amen," 148
amnos. See lamb
anachronistic, 26–27
analogies, 74–75, 277
anatolia, 311
ancient biographies, 57–59
ancient education, 176–78, 213
ancient of days, 69–70
Andrew, 440
angels, 77, 120–21, 151, 342

anonymous, 251
  Hebrews as, 331–32
  pseudonymous compared to,
    252–53, 353
anothen (again, from above), 148
Antioch, Syria, 88, 166, 321
Antiochus III, 311
Antipas, 402. *See also* Herod Antipas
Antiquities 20.9.1, 25–26
anti-Semitism, 226, 449
antitheses, 93
aphorisms, 67
apocalypsis, 66–68
apocalyptic documents, 15–16
apocalyptic literature, 16
  definition of, 419
  historical, 420
  numerology in, 422–23
  politics in, 422
  rectification in, 423
  Revelation as, 419–24
apocalyptic prophecy, 16, 420, 423,
    426–27
apocalyptic worldview, 44
Apollos, 334–35
Apollo Temple, *158*, 165*f*
apostles, 228, 320
  canon related to, 439–40, 448–49,
    451n11
  Johannine epistles related to, 357–58
  in Jude, 296
  in 1 Peter, 318–19
  in 2 Peter, 383
  Spirit and, 319
Apostolic Decree, 166, 289
apostolic tradition, 389–90
appearance, physical, 23–24, 24*f*
"appearing" (*epiphania*), 383
Apuleius (Met. 11.2), 14
Apuleius Florida 9, 8
aqueducts, *40*, 163*f*
Aquila, 167, 212, 228
Aramaic, 28, 42
Arch of Titus, 61*f*, 62*f*
Areopagus, 26–27, 27*f*, 118
Aretas IV (king), 162
arguments, 256–57, 407

  in Galatians, 197–98
arguments con, 180, 182–83
arguments pro, 180, 182–83, 196, 342
Aristotle, 177, 203
arnion. See lamb
arrival (*parousia*), 383–84, 391–94
Artemis, 48, 401*f*
artisans, 28, 39n2
Ascension, 120
Asia Minor
  emperor cult in, 412–14, 430n32
  Jews in, 311–12
  Johannine epistles and, 353
Asiatic Greek, 316, 381–82
Asiatic rhetoric, 231–33, 316
assembly (*ekklesia*), 84, 179–80, 184
Assumption of Moses, 302–3
Athanasius, 450
Athens, 165*f*
atonement, 122
  sacrifice and, 370–71
audience
  of Galatians, 196
  of Hebrews, 331–32,
    336–37
  of Johannine epistles, 355, 357–58,
    361–64
  of John, 146
  of Jude, 300–302
  of Mark, 74
  of Matthew, 88
  of 1 Peter, 311–14, 321–23
  of 2 Peter, 382
  of Revelation, 401–2
  of Romans, 221–22
Augustine, 7, 430n26
Augustus, 42*f*, 202
Aune, David, 118
authority
  in Colossians, 236–37
  in 2 Corinthians, 216
  of Enoch, 437
  in Galatians, 196
  of John the Elder, 355–56
  in Jude, 302–3
  of Paul, 173–74
  in Revelation, 406

authorship
   of canon, 434
   composite documents and, 252–53,
      309, 378
   definition of, 252
   God and, 378
   of Hebrews, 331–33
   history related to, 252–53
   of James, 273–74
   of Johannine epistles, 352–56, 373n2
   of John, 133–35, 138–40
   of John the Elder, 352–54
   of Luke, 36, 104
   of Mark, 60–61, 78–79
   of Matthew, 85–87, 253
   of New Testament, 16–17, 36, 447–48
   of Pastoral Epistles, 254–55, 266–67
   of Paul, 36, 252–55
   of 1 Peter, 309–10, 317–18, 327
   of 2 Peter, 379, 384–85, 395
   of Revelation, 135, 139, 400
   of Sermon of James, 280
autobiography, 197

Babylon, 310–11, 315, 410
   Rome as, 401, 430n26
Babylonian Talmud, 377–78, 436
banishment, 403–4
baptism, 64, 67, 68f. *See also* John
   the Baptist
Barabbas, 98
Barclay, John, 185
Barnabas, 37, 164, 335, 359
Barrett, C. K., 105, 176, 319, 438, 450n2
bartering, 50
Basilica di Santa Prassede, Rome, *292*
Bauckham, Richard, 135
   on Jude, 294, 296–97
   on 2 Peter, 380–81, 384
   on Revelation, 404, 410–11
Baumann, C., 91
beatitudes, 92–93
Bede, 353
behavior (*praxis*), 37, 203–4, 289
belief, 223–24
Beloved Disciple, 36, 134, 156n7,
      361–64
   at crucifixion, 137
   death of, 360
   identity of, 352–53, 358
   John the Elder and, 355–56, 358
   Lazarus as, 136–37, 139, 354
   Peter and, 137, 143
   Twelve and, 352, 357
Bengel, Johannes, 20
Bethsaida, 96, 145f
Beza, Theodore, 332–33

biographies, 12, 197
   Gospels as, 57–58
birth, 12, 26, *102*
birth narratives, 125
blasphemy, 71
Bock, Darrell, 446
Book of Glory, 141
Book of Revelation. *See* Revelation
Book of Signs, 141
Borgman, P., 104
brotherly love, 368
Brown, R. E., 356
Buechner, Frederick, 23

Caesara Phillipi, *306*
Caesarea Maritima, 162, 162f, *192*
Caiaphas, 71, 137, 137f
Callan, Therrance, 386
Calvin, John, 399
canon
   apostles related to, 439–40,
      448–49, 451n11
   authorship of, 434
   closure of, 443–44
   codexes in, 439–40, 444
   consciousness, 434–47
   dates of, 434
   definition of, 433–34
   extra-canonical books in, 436–37
   in First Century, 438–39, 444, 451n5
   history related to, 445–46
   Jewishness and, 443–44
   John as, 440–42
   Luke as, 438, 440–42, 444–46
   Muratorian, 107, 440–42
   New Testament and, 437–47
   of Old Testament, 434–36, 446
   orthodoxy and, 434
   Paul as, 439–42, 444–46
   in 2 Peter, 439
   regula canona, 444, 446–47
   in second century A. D., 439–41
   in third and fourth centuries A.D.,
      442–44
   Torah and, 445–46
   Wisdom of Solomon related
      to, 442–44
Capernaum, 88, 95f, 97, 250
captivity epistles, 128
   Asiatic rhetoric in, 231–33
   Colossians, 108, 231–37, 441
   date of, 231–32
   deliberative rhetoric in, 233
   Ephesians as, 231–33, 236–40
   household codes in, 231, 233
   marriage in, 233–34, 236–37, 249n1
   Philemon as, 108, 237, 239–40, 441

   Philippians as, 18, 179, 182,
      240–47, 441
   slavery in, 233, 236–37, 239–40
cartoon, 80, 80f
catholic epistles, 272–73. *See also* Hebrews;
      James; Johannine epistles; Jude; 1
      Peter
Catton, Bruce, 13
CEB. *See* Common English Bible
ceiling mosaics, 17f
Celsus Library, 167f, 168f, 259f
Cephas, 96
character, 23–24
Charles, J. Daryl, 298–99
chiasm, 368
chosen, 321–23
chreia, 60, 81n3
Christ, 17f
   Adam compared to, 244–45
   Domitian related to, 413–14
   of faith, 32–33
   as God, 243–44
   imitation of, 18, 245–46
   judgment related to, 415
   Lord as, 122–23
   in Luke, 119
   in Mark, 68–72
   in Matthew, 32–33
   name of, 247
   return of, 98, 200–202
   titles of, 415–16
Christian (*Christianos*), 176, 313
Christian graffiti, 278f
Christianity. *See also* early Christianity
   definition in, 118
   identity in, 118
   illegality of, 50
   Jewish, 271, 297, 300–303
   legitimation in, 118
   "Lost Christianities," 33–38, 448
   martyrs in, 337, 344, 402, 429n3, 448
   oral culture in, 7–8, 135, 177
   origins of, 33–34
   orthodoxy in, 33–34
   social context of, 283, 356–59, 412–15
Christianos (adherents of Christ,
      Christian), 176, 313
Christians
   circumcision of, 164–65, 194, 196
   Gentile, 226–28, 238–39, 271–72, 289
   Gnostic, 35–38, 442, 448–49
Christology, 308
   Adoptionist, 122
   in Hebrews, 340–44, 347
   of Jude, 299
   in Luke, 119–24
   in Matthew, 90

Christology (*continued*)
  in Philippians, 243–46
  of Revelation, 415–19
Christos, 123
chronology
  in biographies, 58
  of Gospels, 13
  of Mark, 60
  of Paul, 59, 161–72
Chrysostom, 331, 346
churches
  house, 357f, 361
  of Jewish Christianity, 307
  as witnesses, 425–26
Church History (Eusebius), 60
Cicero, 15, 179f, 294, 345
  on letters, 293
  rhetoric of, 178–79
  on style, 386
circumcision. *See also* Mosaic law
  of Christians, 164–65, 194, 196
  Hellenism and, 311
Circus Maximus, 337, 337f
Classen, C. J., 258
Claudius (emperor), 174, 336
cleansing, 97
1 Clement, 37–38
  Hebrews related to, 331–32
2 Clement, 84
Clement of Alexandria, 332, 440
Cleopatra, 255f
climate, 5
codexes, 439–40, 444
cognitive science, 185
Coliseum, 330, 407f
collectivist personality, 48–49
Colossians, 441
  4.14, 108
  angels in, 235–36
  Asian rhetoric in, 231–32
  authority in, 236–37
  Ephesians related to, 231–32, 236–37
  household codes of, 236–37
  rhetorical outline of, 234
  slavery in, 236–37
  stoicheia and, 235–36
  synopsis of, 234–36
columns, ionic, *376*
come o Lord (*Marana tha*), 155
Common English Bible (CEB), 8
comparisons. *See synkrisis*
compendium, 11
compilations, 252
composite documents, 252–53
  2 Peter as, 309, 378, 395
concessions, 227–28
confessions, 145–46

consciousness
  canon, 434–47
  Scripture, 435, 439
Constantine, 33, 434
continuity
  in Luke–Acts, 113–14
  in resurrection, 215
continuous flow, 3–7, 3f
contradictions, 204
conversion, 162, 176
Corinth, Greece, 165f, 167–68, 273f, 321
1 Corinthians, 174
  11, 18
  context in, 212–14
  marriage in, 211
  resurrection in, 214–15
  rhetorical outline of, 210
  Scripture consciousness in, 439
  trouble in, 167, 209–11
  wisdom in, 214
  women in, 211–14
2 Corinthians, 168, 174, 210, 215
  authority in, 216
  false teachers in, 216, 218
  irony in, 217–18
  Mosaic law in, 217
  pagans and, 217
  personal weaknesses in, 218
  rhetorical outline of, 216
  synopsis of, 216–18
Cornelius, 45, 116–18, 272
Council of Nicea, 33, 434, 450
covenant. *See also* Mosaic law
  Abrahamic, 175, 198
  in 1 Peter, 324
Craddock, F., 393
crucifixion, 14, 28–29, 77f, 153f
  Beloved Disciple at, 137
  cartoon about, 80, 80f
  in Mark, 66–67
  in Matthew, 98–99
  of Peter, 390
  shame of, 345–46
Cullmann, Oscar, 247
culture, 7–8, 135, 177
  agonistic, 179–80
  Greek, 27–28, 42, 43f
  history and, 51–52
  macro-, 310
  male-dominated, 258–59
  micro-, 310
  of shame, 47
  stories from, 186–87
customs, 146
  tradition, 24, 389–90, 420, 447
Cyprus Paphos Theseus, 163f

Damascus, 162, 162f
Daniel, 6, 42
  7, 69–71, 81n6
  ancient of days from, 69–70
  "Son of Man" in, 69, 81n6
  time in, 422–23
dates
  of canon, 434
  of captivity epistles, 231–32
  of Corinthians, 210
  of Galatians, 195–96
  of Hebrews, 331, 336, 338
  of Johannine epistles, 359
  of John, 135
  of Jude, 294, 298, 300
  of Matthew, 88
  of 1 Peter, 315
  of 2 Peter, 379–81
  of Philippians, 240
  of Revelation, 401
  of Romans, 219
  of Sermon of James, 280–81, 283
  of Thessalonians, 201
David, 70, 377
  Jesus and, 90–91, 97, 121–22
  Jewish Messiah and, 417–18
Davids, Peter, 282, 286
deacon, 228
Dead Sea scrolls, 44–46, 46f. *See also* Qumran
death. *See also* crucifixion; martyrs
  of Beloved Disciple, 360
  in biographies, 58
  of James, 180, 289f
  of Lazarus, 138, 139f
  of Paul, 172, 267
  of Peter, 389–90
  in Romans, 224
  tombs, 29, 30f, 56, 78f, 99, 114f, 139f, 376
Decapolis, 28
deliberative rhetoric, 180
  in captivity epistles, 233
  in Philippians, 179
  in 2 Timothy, 264–65
demands, 115
Demas, 108
Denny, J., 370–71
descendants, 298. *See also* genealogy
deSilva, David, 252
destiny, 225
Deut.19.15, 425
dialogue, 333–34
Diaspora, 310–12
Diaspora Jews
  Josephus on, 320–21
  1 Peter and, 310–13

diatribe, 275–76
Dibelius, Martin, 30, 275
Didache, 37–38, 39n6
Dio Chrysostom (Or. 12.5), 15
Diodorus Siculus, 391
Dionysius, 363*f*
Dionysius of Alexandria, 355
Dionysius the Short, 26
Diotrephes, 361, 366–67, 373n8
disciples, 116. *See also* apostles; Beloved
    Disciple
  women as, 99, 150
division of labor, 314, 356
docetics, 361–62
documents, 7–8
  ad hoc, 210, 253
  apocalyptic, 15–16
  composite, 252–53, 309, 378, 395
  encyclical, 314, 385–87
  on Jewish Christianity, 307
  of Johannine epistles, 351–52
Dodd, C. H., 75, 369
dominion, 76
Domitian (emperor), 315, 401, 403,
    407*f*, 412
  Christ related to, 413–14
Domus Augustana, Rome, 337*f*
Donaldson, Terry, 175
Donne, John, 19, 188
doxology, 417, 431n41
dualism, 421
Dunn, James, 379
dyadic personality, 48–49
dynamis (mighty works), 73, 145

early Christianity
  disputes within, 371–72
  evangelism in, 7–8
  formalization in, 388
  homes in, 357*f*
  from Judaism, 50
  Matthew related to, 84, 100
earthquakes, 99
Ecclesiastes, 397n11
Ecclesiastical History (Eusebius), 298
ecclesiology, 253
  in Galatians, 198–99, 198*f*
economy, 5–6, 50–51. *See also* wealth
education, ancient
  of Paul, 176–77
  rhetoric in, 177–78
  of women, 213
Egypt, 195*f*
ekklesia (assembly), 84,
    179–80, 184
elder (*presbyteros*), 353–56. *See also* John
    the Elder

Elijah
  John the Baptist and, 67
  Revelation and, 425
Elizabeth, 124–25
Elliott, John H., 274, 309–10, 314
emotional appeal, 180, 182–83, 196,
    342, 365
emotions, 240
emperor cult, 412–14, 430n32
empowerment, 115
encomium, 340–41, 343
encyclical document
  1 Peter as, 314
  2 Peter as, 385–87
Enoch, 44, 301, 437
1 Enoch, 44
enthymemes, 256–57
  in Sermon of James, 275–76
Epaphras, 234
Ephesians, 441
  Asian rhetoric in, 231–33
  Colossians related to, 231–32, 236–37
  epideictic rhetoric in, 238
  faith and, 238–39
  household codes of, 236–37
  Mosaic law in, 239
  2 Peter compared to, 385–86
  rhetorical outline of, 238
  synopsis of, 238–40
  unity in, 239
Ephesus, 169*f*, 236*f*, 354*f*, 414
  Celsus Library in, 167*f*, 168*f*, 259*f*
  homes in, 170*f*, 264*f*
epideictic rhetoric, 179–80, 200, 238, 365
epiphania ("appearing"), 383
equality, 49. *See also* slavery
Erastus, 166*f*
eschatology, 121, 200–201, 435
Essenes, 44–45
Esther, 436
ethical values
  in biographies, 58
  in First Century, 47
ethnos/ethne, 400–401
ethos, 181, 183
euangelion. *See* Good News
Eusebius, 60, 272–73, 298, 353, 443
euthus, 72
Eutychus incidents, 171
evangelism, 7–8, 59. *See also* missions
evidence, 134–35
exhortation, 232, 339–40
exodus, 390
exordium, 325, 365
exposition, 339–40
external evidence, 134–35
extra-canonical books, 436–37

eyewitnesses, 13, 36–37, 85
Ezekiel 40-48, 424–26
Ezra, 42, 377

faith, 9, 224, 341
  Christ of, 32–33
  Ephesians and, 238–39
  knowledge and, 32
  race of, 344–45
  regula fidei, 444, 446–48
  righteousness from, 221
  in Romans, 223
  Sermon of James on, 286–87
false prophets, 302
false teachers
  in 2 Corinthians, 216, 218
  docetics as, 361–62
  Jude and, 301–3
  in 2 Peter, 388–89, 391
  primary argument about, 256–57
famines, 51
favoritism, 285–86
Fee, Gordon, 229
Fekkes, J., 404, 406
Festus, 171
first and last, 416–17
First Apology (Justin Martyr), 35
First Century, 41
  bartering, 50
  canon in, 438–39, 444, 451n5
  collectivist personality, 48–49
  economy, 50–51
  ethical values in, 47
  fishing boat in, 34*f*, 295*f*
  Greece and Rome in, 42–43
  honor in, 47
  Jewish home in, 48, 48*f*
  limited goods in, 51
  patriarchy in, 47–48
  politics in, 50–51
  religion in, 50–51
  sexual double standard in, 48
  social history in, 47–51
  synagogue from, 88*f*
  wisdom literature in, 44–45
  women in, 47–48
first-order moral discourse, 233
fish, 31*f*
fishing boat, 34*f*, 295*f*
food, 51
food laws, 37, 164, 166, 174
Foote, Shelby, 13
foreknowledge (prognōsin), 322–23
  of God, 312, 318
forensic rhetoric, 179–80, 197–99
forgiveness, 97
Forum Basilica, Philippi, Greece, 164*f*

Francis of Assisi, 100
from above (*anothen*), 148
fulfillment
    in John, 141–42
    of Scripture, 118
    in Sermon on the Mount, 93
Fuller, R. H., 123
future, 19. *See also* prophecies

Gaius, 361, 366–67, 373n8
Galatians, 166, 193, 441
    1, 37
    1.13-14, 174
    Abrahamic covenant in, 198
    argument in, 197–98
    audience of, 196
    authority in, 196
    autobiography in, 197
    contradictions and, 204
    date of, 195–96
    ecclesiology in, 198–99, 198f
    against Judaizers, 194–99
    outline of, 196
    rhetorical structure of, 195–96
    Romans compared to, 219–20
    synopsis of, 196–99
    tone of, 194–95
Galilee, 34f, 144, 295f, 296f
    Jude and, 294–95, 298, 303
    Mark near, 64–65
    Matthew and, 88
    Sea of, 29
Garden of Gethsemane, 161f
gematria (symbolic numbers), 422–23
genealogy, 16, 97, 121–22
    in Matthew, 90–91
generosity, 242, 284–85
Genesis, 194f
    4.23-42, 97
genres, 12
    of Johannine epistles, 354–55
    of Revelation, 419–24
Gentile Christianity
    Jewish Christianity and, 226–28
    Johannine letters and, 358–59
    milieu and, 289
    Paul and, 238–39, 271–72, 356
    1 Peter and, 308–9
geographical orientation, 112–15
Giblin, C. H., 409–10
gladiator statue, 169f
Gnostic Christians, 34–36, 442, 448–49
    Judaizers and, 37–38
God
    authorship and, 378
    Christ as, 243–44
    foreknowledge of, 318, 321

image of, 19
Jesus and, 29–30, 140
kingdom of, 69
as love, 369–70
Moses and, 143
names for, 392
in Philippians, 246–47
"God-fearers," 310f, 311
God's Word, 285
Good News (euangelion)
    in Acts, 113–18
    euangelion as, 59
    in Mark, 63–64, 66, 68, 77
    oral preaching of, 59
goods, 51
Good Samaritan, 117f
Gospel Lectionary, 12f
Gospel of Judas, 34–35
Gospel of Mary, 34–35
Gospel of Philip, 34–35
Gospel of Thomas, 34–35
Gospels, 11
    beginnings of, 12
    as biographies, 57–58
    birth in, 12
    chronology, 13
    description of, 12–14
    as euangelion, 59
    focus of, 12–13
    history related to, 13–14
    literature of, 12–13
    mythological stories compared to, 14
    order of, 128–29
    Passion Narratives of, 13
    placement of, 159
    production of, 34
    term meaning of, 59
government
    in 1 Peter, 314–15, 327
    in Revelation, 314
    in Romans, 227
grace, 93–94
graffiti, Christian, 278f
grain, 28f, 51
Greco-Roman world, 364
    agonistic culture of, 179–80
    rhetoric in, 177–83
    stratification in, 178
Greece
    Athens, 165f
    Corinth, 165f, 167–68, 273f, 321
    in First Century, 42–43
    Philippi, 164f
Greek, 270
    Asiatic, 316, 381–82
    culture, 27–28, 42, 43f
    in Israel, 42–45

in Judea, 42–43
love in, 369
of Revelation, 400, 404, 429n7
Greek New Testament, 45
    continuous flow of, 3–7, 3f
    letters of, 3–4, 3f
    material of, 4–5
    understanding in, 8
Greek Old Testament, 45
Green, J. B., 112
Griffith, T., 362
guards, 99
Guthrie, G. H., 339
Gwyther, A., 413–14
gymnasium, 42

hand lamp, 217, 217f
Harrington, D. J., 333
Hartley, L. P., 41
healing
    in Mark, 64–65, 73–74
    in Matthew, 97
    wisdom for, 89, 101n5
hearers, 6–7
heaven on earth, 215
Hebrew Bible, 436. *See also* Old Testament
    Torah as, 24, 28, 142, 445–46
Hebrews, 15
    12.2, 9
    angels in, 342
    as anonymous, 331–32
    Apollos and, 334–35
    audience of, 331–32, 336–37
    authorship of, 331–33
    Christology in, 340–44, 347
    1 Clement related to, 331–32
    comparisons in, 340–41, 347
    core samples from, 343–46
    date of, 331, 336, 338
    dialogue and, 333–34
    encomium in, 340–41, 343
    exhortation in, 339–40
    images in, 341–42
    Jewishness of, 443
    Moses in, 336
    1 Peter and, 338
    provenance of, 332–33
    rhetoric of, 339–43
    rhetoric outline of, 342
    Scripture in, 332, 334, 345–46
    as sermon, 333–34
    social life in, 336
    witness in, 343–44
Hebrew Scriptures, 16–17
Hebrew writing, 26f
Hegesippus, 281, 298
Helholm, D., 431n43

Hellenism. *See also* Greco-Roman world
    circumcision and, 311
    of Herod Antipas, 42, 178
hendiadys ("powerful coming"), 391
Hengel, Martin, 439
Hermas, 442
Herod Antipas (Herod the Great), 43,
    126, 402
    Hellenism of, 42, 178
    palace of, 242*f*
Hierapolis, *208*, 443*f*
historical apocalyptic literature, 420
historical monographs, 13
history, 47–50
    authorship related to, 252–53
    canon related to, 445–46
    culture and, 51–52
    Gnostic Christians and, 34–35
    Gospels related to, 13–14
    intertestamental, 45–46
    Luke related to, 105, 119–22
    New Testament and, 41–42
    Old Testament and, 41–42
    theological history
        telling, 18–19
Holladay, Carl, 308–9
Holy Land, 5, 26, *144*
Holy of Holies, 171*f*
Holy Spirit
    in Acts, 115–18
    empowerment of, 115
    Mary and, 115
    moved by, 394
    Parakletos as, 154
    social elites and, 116
    universalization of, 115–16
Holy Writ, 395
Homer, 14
homosexuality, 222
honor, 29, 47, 205
hope, 29–30
hospitality, 366–67
house arrest
    of Paul, 171–72
    Philippians and, 240–42
house churches, 357*f*, 361
household codes, 231, 233
    of Colossians, 236–37
    of Ephesians, 236–37
House of Peter, 86*f*
House of the Fisherman, 96
Howard-Brook, W., 413–14
humanity, 19
    of Jesus, 121–22
human righteousness, 220–21
humility, 243–44
husband, 233–34, 236–37, 249n1

hymns, 243–46, 409
hyperbole, 362
hyperbolic generalization, 259

"I Am" sayings, 142, 153–54
identity, 49
    of Beloved Disciple, 352–53, 358
    in Christianity, 118
    of John of Patmos, 352, 354–55
    of Luke, 107–8
    in Mark, 67
    of Paul, 173–76
idols, 358–59
Ignatius of Antioch, 317, 387–88
illegality, 50
images, *270*
    of God, 19
    in Hebrews, 341–42
    of Jesus, 215, 225, 228
imagination, 189
imitation, 18, 245–46
Immanuel, 89, 99, 120
imperatives, 275–76
incarnation, *132*
    of Jesus, 143
    in Philippians, 246–47
incorporative personality, 187
Innocent (pope), 450
insinuatio, 219
internal evidence, 134–35
interpretation, 8, 259
intertestamental history, 45–46
invective, 302–3
invocation, 94
ionic columns, *376*
Irenaeus, 35, 440
    on John, 135–36
irony, 147, 217–18
Isaiah, 122
    5, 76
    61, 93, 118
    Philippians compared to, 244
    Suffering Servant in, 326
isolationist sect, 357
Israel, 187
"I" statements, 225

Jacob, 20
James. *See also* Sermon of James
    in Acts, 282
    authorship of, 273–74
    death of, 180, 289*f*
    in Jerusalem, 296
    Kümmel on, 280–81
    leadership of, 38, 127
    Mosaic law and, 290
    Paul and, 281

Zealots and, 282
Zebedees and, 280
Jerome, 379
Jerusalem, 114*f*
    Babylon compared to, 410
    Via Dolorosa in, 29*f*
    James in, 296
    in Mark, 65–66
    in Revelation, 401
    Symeon in, 296
Jerusalem Council, 37
Jerusalem Gold Gate, 113*f*
Jerusalem Temple, 42, 109*f*
    cleansing of, 97
    destruction of, 61–62, 62*f*, 126, 336
    Holy of Holies in, 171*f*
    measurement of, 424
    tax and, 96–97
    temple mount, *2*
    Temple Mount Pinnacle, 112*f*
Jesus
    birth of, 12, 26
    crucifixion of, 14, 28–29, 66–67, 77*f*,
        80, 80*f*, 98–99, 153*f*
    David and, 90–91, 97, 121–22
    existence of, 25–26
    God and, 29–30, 140
    Hebrews 12.2, 9
    humanity of, 121–22
    images of, 215, 225, 228
    Immanuel as, 89, 99
    incarnation of, 143
    as Jew, 26–28, 174
    as Jewish Messiah, 114, 122
    Josephus on, 25–26
    languages of, 42, 45
    literacy of, 28
    love related to, 243, 370–71
    Luke on, 12, 119–24
    Matthew on, 12, 90–91
    ministry of, 26, 28, 33
    Moses compared to, 89, 92–94, 123
    Nicodemus and, 147–49
    Passion Narratives of, 13, 66, 72,
        77–79, 126
    as peasant, 28
    perseverance of, 345–46
    Peter's breakfast with, 152
    Peter's name from, 96
    physical appearance of, 23–24
    Pontius Pilate and, 25–26, 45
    Sabbath and, 69–71
    sacred texts and, 435
    as sage, 89–90
    Samaritan woman and, 150–51
    Scripture related to, 445
    Spirit and, 154

Jesus (*continued*)
    stories of, 186–87
    Tacitus on, 25–26
    transfiguration of, 67, 347*f*,
        390–92, 425
    women and, 150–52
Jesus ben Sira, 283, 434
JESUSISNOWHERE, 4
Jewish Christianity, 34–36, 271, 297,
        300–303
    catholic epistles to, 272–73
    churches of, 307
    congregations of, 272
    documents on, 307
    Ebionites and, 308
    Gentile Christians and, 226–28
    in Rome, 336–37
Jewish home, 48, 48*f*
Jewish images, *270*
Jewish Messiah
    David and, 417–18
    Jesus as, 114, 122
Jewishness
    canon and, 443–44
    of Hebrews, 443
    of Jude, 443
    of Matthew, 87–88, 90
    of Revelation, 416, 443
Jewish numerology, 90–91
Jewish wisdom, 277–78
Jews
    in Asia Minor, 311–12
    Diaspora, 310–13, 320–21
    food laws and, 37, 164, 166, 174
    Jesus as, 26–28, 174
    King of the, 98–99
    leadership of, 271
    monotheistic, 34
    Paul as, 174–76
    Peter and, 272
    Sabbath of, 72
    Samaritans and, 149
Joel, 117
Johannine epistles
    apostles related to, 357–58
    Asia Minor and, 353
    audience of, 355, 357–58, 361–64
    authorship of, 352–56, 373n2
    core samples of, 367–71
    date of, 359
    documents of, 351–52
    genre of, 354–55
    Gentile Christianity and, 358–59
    Papias on, 353, 356
    Paul and, 356–57
    provenance of, 359–63
    rhetoric of, 363–64

    social context of, 356–59
    wisdom literature related to,
        357–59, 362
John
    1, 19
    3.16–17, 149
    7.53–8.11, 48
    audience of, 146
    authorship of, 133–35, 138–40
    beginning of, 12, 135
    Beloved Disciple and, 135
    as canon, 440–42
    climax of, 143, 145
    conclusion of, 154–55
    confessions in, 145–46
    date of, 135
    1 John compared to, 360
    fulfillment in, 141–42
    "I Am" sayings in, 142, 153–54
    Irenaeus on, 135–36
    Mary in, 140
    Mary Magdalene in, 151–52
    miracles in, 145
    Nicodemus in, 147–49
    oral culture of, 135
    outline of, 141
    passing explanations in, 146
    Peter in, 142, 152
    synopsis of, 153–54
    Synoptic Gospels compared to, 139–40,
        147, 153–54
    theological structure of, 140–43,
        145–46
    "we passages" in, 134–35, 138–39
    Zebedees and, 135–36
1 John, 135, 139, 353–54
    John compared to, 360
    placement of, 351–52
    rhetorical structure of, 365
1 John 4
    alliteration in, 368
    chiasm in, 367–68
    love in, 367–71
2 John, 351–54
    rhetorical structure of, 366–67
3 John, 351–54
    rhetorical structure of, 366–67
John Mark, 118
John of Patmos, 6, 139, 146
    banishment and, 403–4
    identity of, 352, 354–55
    Revelation and, 6, 400
Johnson, L. T., 275, 283, 291n12, 355
John the Apostle, 353
John the Baptist (John the Baptizer), 28
    apocalyptic worldview of, 44
    Elijah and, 67

    existence of, 25
    Qumran and, 45–46
John the Elder, 146, 360–61
    authority of, 355–56
    authorship of, 352–54
    Beloved Disciple and, 355–56, 358
John the prophet, *398*
John Zebedee, 156n3
Joseph, 90, 430n40
Josephus, 45
    on Diaspora Jews, 320–21
    on Jesus, 25–26
    on resurrection, 25
    on sacred texts, 435–36
journeying, 111
Judaism, 174
    early Christianity from, 50
Judaizers, 166, 308. *See also* Mosaic law
    Galatians against, 194–99
    Gnostic Christians and, 37–38
    Peter and, 37
Judas. *See* Jude
Judas Iscariot, 47, 298
Jude, 380, 383, 437, 442
    descendants of, 298
    Galilee and, 294–95, 298, 303
    Jewishness of, 443
    missions of, 294, 296–97
    name of, 294, 298
Jude (book)
    5-7, 302–3
    apostles in, 296
    audience of, 300–302
    authority in, 302–3
    Christology of, 299
    date of, 294, 298, 300
    false teachers and, 301–3
    invective in, 302–3
    Moses related to, 302–3
    2 Peter and, 380–81, 383
    purity language of, 300–301, 304
    rhetorical outline of, 300
    Sermon of James related to, 294, 296,
        298–300
    as speech, 293
    synopsis of, 302–3
Judea, *144*
    Greek in, 42–43
    ministry in, 140
Jude Thaddeus (saint), *292*
judgment, 402, 409, 415, 418
Judith, 45–46
Julius Africanus, 294
Justin Martyr, 35–36

Kasemann, E., 143
King, Martin Luther, Jr., 24

Kingdom, 76
    of God, 69
King James Translation, 8
King of the Jews, 98–99
Knidos, 449f
Knossos Palace, 382f
knowledge
    faith and, 32
    foreknowledge, 318, 321, 322–23
Koester, Craig, 336, 345
koinonia, 283
kosmos (world), 149, 358
Kraus, Thomas J., 385
Kümmel, W. G., 280–81

labor, division of, 314, 356
lamb (*arnion, amnos*), 400
    lion and, 418–19, 422, 423f
    in Revelation, 417–18, 430n40
Lamech, 97
lamp, hand, 217, 217f
languages. *See also* Greek
    Aramaic, 28, 42
    Asiatic Greek, 316, 381–82
    of 1 Peter, 310–12
    of Jesus, 42, 45
    Latin, 42–43
    of Matthew, 85–86
    purity, 300–301, 304
    of Sermon of James, 275, 277, 282
Laodicea, 403f, 414
Latin, 42–43
Law of Christ, 175, 206
laws. *See also* Mosaic law
    food, 37, 164, 166, 174
    of nature, 31–32
Lazarus
    as Beloved Disciple, 136–37, 139,
        352–54
    death of, 138, 139f
    resurrection of, 136, 138, 145
leadership
    of James, 38, 127
    of Jews, 271
    of Paul, 38, 128
    of Peter, 38
    in 1 Timothy, 261
    in Titus, 260
lector, 6
legacy, 59
legends, 14
legitimation, 118
letters. *See also* Paul's letters
    alphabetical, 3–4, 3f
    Cicero on, 293
    of New Testament, 14–15
    oral texts as, 14–15

in Revelation, 406–7
    rhetorical, 182–84
Leviticus, 313
Lewis, C. S., 11, 187–88
libraries, 5, 167f, 168f, 259f
limited goods, 51
Lincoln, Andrew T., 341
Linus, 384–85, 388
lion, 418–19, 422, 423f
literacy
    of Jesus, 28
    libraries, 5, 167f, 168f, 259f
    of Matthew, 84
    wealth and, 5–6
literature, 422. *See also* apocalyptic
        literature
    of Gospels, 12–13
    sapiential, 383–84, 397n11
    wisdom, 44–45, 75, 357–59, 362
Litfin, Duane, 181
Loader, W., 368
loaves and fishes, 31f
logical structure
    of Acts, 113–14
    of Luke–Acts, 109, 112–14
logos, 408, 415
logos protreptikos ("word of exhortation"),
        232
Loisy, Alfred, 100
Lord, 122–23. *See also* Christ; God; Jesus
Lord's prayer, 93f, 94–95
"Lost Christianities," 33–38, 448
love
    agape, 152, 156n7
    in 1 John 4, 367–71
    God as, 369–70
    in Greek, 369
    Jesus related to, 243, 370–71
    obedience related to, 371
    philo, 152
Lucretius, 391
Luke
    1.2, 13
    3.23, 26
    4, 93
    14.15–24, 106
    22.33, 105–6
    24, 29
    authorship of, 36, 104
    beginning of, 12
    as canon, 438, 440–42, 444–46
    Christ in, 119
    Christology in, 119–24
    Cornelius in, 116–18
    geographical orientation of, 112–15
    history related to, 105, 119–22
    identity of, 107–8

on Jesus, 12, 119–24
    Mark compared to, 105–6, 119–20,
        124–26
    Matthew compared to, 105–6, 119–20,
        124–26
    Nativity and, *102*
    papyrus in, 5, 105
    Passion Narrative in, 126
    Paul and, 107–8, 254–55
    Peter and, 126, 321
    Q relating to, 109, 117
    resurrection in, 121
    Scripture and, 437
    size of, 103–5, 130n6
    "Son of Man" in, 119–20
    sources of, 109
    Theophilus and, 104, 106–7, 111–12
    travel narrative in, 116–17
    "we passages" and, 108
    women in, 125
Luke–Acts
    continuity in, 113–14
    direction in, 113
    disciples in, 116
    journeying in, 111
    logical structure of, 109, 112–14
    ministry in, 110
    missionaries in, 111
    parallels in, 111, 117
    Pentecost in, 110
    prophet in, 123
    salvation in, 114–15
    separation of, 104, 128–29
    signification in, 112
    synopsis of, 124–28
    theological structure of, 113–15
    theology in, 123–24
    title of, 107
    unity of, 104, 128–29
Luther, Martin, 194, 274, 333
LXX, 107, 434
    Sermon of James compared to, 275, 278

Maccabean period, 42, 94–95
1-3 Maccabees, 45
macro-culture, 310
male-dominated culture, 258–59
manuscripts, 6
    ancient, 3–4, 3f
    placement of, 104
Marana tha (come o Lord), 155
Marc Antony, 255f
Marcion, 438, 441–42, 449, 450n2
Mark
    8.27–30, 63
    8.45, 63
    16.9–20, 78–79

Mark (*continued*)
  13.14, 6–7
  16.8, 77–79
  analogies in, 75
  apocalypsis in, 66–68
  arrangement of, 63–64
  audience of, 74
  authorship of, 60–61, 78–79
  baptism in, 64, 67
  beginning of, 12
  Christ in, 68–72
  chronology of, 60
  crucifixion in, 66–67
  dynamis in, 73
  ending of, 76–79
  exorcisms in, 73
  near Galilea, 64–65
  Good News in, 63–64, 66,
      68, 77
  healing in, 64–65, 73–74
  identity in, 67
  Jerusalem in, 65–66
  loss of, 79
  Luke compared to, 105–6, 119–20,
      124–26
  Matthew and, 79, 84–85, 105–6,
      119–22, 124, 126
  Messianic secret in, 66
  ministry in, 64–66
  miracles in, 73
  outline of, 63
  Papias on, 60–62
  parables and, 67, 73–76
  Passion Narrative in, 66, 72,
      77–79
  Peter and, 60–61, 63
  preparations in, 64
  questions in, 63
  resurrection in, 66, 77
  Satan in, 72
  Sermon on the Mount
      and, 73–74
  "Son of Man" in, 70–71
  synopsis of, 64–68
  teacher in, 73–76
  time in, 72
  transfiguration in, 67
  women in, 76–77
marriage
  in 1 Corinthians, 211
  in captivity epistles, 233–34, 236–37,
      249n1
  sex and, 214
Martial Satires 2.46, 104
Martin, Ralph, 380
martus. See witness
martyrs, 337, 344, 402, 429n3, 448

Mary
  genealogy and, 90–91
  Gospel of, 34–35
  Holy Spirit and, 115
  in John, 140
Mary Magdalene, 48, 99, 151–52
Matthew
  1, *82*
  1.1–17, 90
  4.28–34, 96
  5-7, 18, 91–95
  5.17–20, 93
  6.9–13, 94–95
  13.52, 87
  15.15, 96
  16.17–18, 96
  17.24–27, 96–97
  18.21, 97
  23, 87
  audience of, 88
  authorship of, 85–87, 253
  beatitudes in, 92–93
  beginning of, 12, 17
  Christ in, 32–33
  citations of, 84
  crucifixion in, 98–99
  date of, 88
  early Christianity related to, 84, 100
  Galilee and, 88
  genealogy in, 90–91
  healing in, 97
  Immanuel theme in, 89
  on Jesus, 12, 90–91
  Jewishness of, 87–88, 90
  language of, 85–86
  literacy of, 84
  Luke compared to, 105–6, 119–20,
      124–26
  Mark and, 79, 84–85, 105–6, 119–22,
      124, 126
  narratives in, 89
  Papias on, 85
  Peter principle, 95–97
  popularity of, 84
  Q related to, 86–87
  resurrection in, 99
  as scribe, 85–88
  Sermon of James compared to, 278–79
  Sermon on the Mount in, 91–95
  size of, 84
  status of, 84
  teachings in, 89, 97–98
  theological structure of, 89
Mayor, J. B., 275, 381
McIver, Robert K., 37
Melancthon, Philip, 332–33
Melito of Sardis, 436

menorah, *82*
mercy, 228
Messianic secret, 66
Metzger, Bruce M., 433, 448–49
Michaels, Ramsey, 385
micro-culture, 310
mighty works (*dynamis*), 73, 145
Miletus, 170*f*, 171
milieu, 289
  of 1 Peter, 309–10
ministry
  of Jesus, 26, 28, 33
  in Judea, 140
  in Luke–Acts, 110
  in Mark, 64–66
  of women, 212
miracles
  definition, 31
  in John, 145
  laws of nature and, 31–32
  loaves and fishes, 31*f*
  in Mark, 73
  open-mindedness and, 32
  of resurrection, 29, 31
The Missing Gospels (Bock), 447
missionaries
  hospitality to, 366–67
  in Luke–Acts, 111
missions
  in Acts, 294, 296
  of Jude, 294, 296–97
  of Paul, 166–68, 171–72
  in 1 Peter, 321
Mitchell, Margaret, 445
modesty, 213
monographs, historical, 13
monotheistic Jews, 34
moral discourses, 233–34
Mosaic law (Mosaic covenant), 26
  Abraham and, 219–20
  in 2 Corinthians, 217
  description of, 196
  in Ephesians, 239
  James and, 290
  obsolescence of, 198–99
  Paul and, 166, 174–75, 227
  in Romans, 224–25
mosaics, ceiling, 17*f*
Moses, 377
  Assumption of, 302–3
  God and, 143
  in Hebrews, 336
  Jesus compared to, 89, 92–94, 123
  Jude related to, 302–3
  Revelation and, 425
Mt. of Olives, 161*f*
Muratorian canon, 107, 440–42

Myers, Ched, 67
myth, 389–91
myth of origins, 34
mythological stories, 14

names, 49
    of Christ, 247
    for God, 392
    of Jude, 294, 298
    of Peter, 95–96
    of Roman citizen, 173
    titles, 107, 415–16
narration, 180, 182–83, 196
narratival ways, 185–86, 190n7
narratives, 58
    birth, 125
    in Matthew, 89
    Passion, 13, 66, 72, 77–79, 126
    travel, 116–18
narrative thought world, 185–87, 190n7
Nativity, 12, 26, *102*
nature, laws of, 31–32
Nazareth, 28, 39n2
Nehemiah, 436
Nero (emperor), 61, 128, 314–15
    persecution by, 337, 338*f*
    in Revelation, 421–22
New Living Translation (NLT), 8
new perspective, 174–75
New Revised Standard Version (NRSV), 8
New Testament
    authorship of, 16–17, 36, 447–48
    canon and, 437–47
    as compendium, 11
    Greek, 3–8, 3*f*, 45
    history and, 41–42
    letters of, 14–15
    Paul in, 160
    pseudonymous documents in, 447–48
    second century A.D. and, 307
    story of, 16–17
Neyrey, Jerome, 300–301, 394
Nicodemus, 147–49
Nike, Goddess of Victory, 169*f*
NLT. *See* New Living Translation
non-Biblical sources, 301–2
normality, 49
NRSV. *See* New Revised Standard Version
numerology
    in apocalyptic literature, 422–23
    Jewish, 90–91

obedience
    love related to, 371
    in 1 Peter, 323–24
    Sermon on the Mount and, 92, 94–95
old man (*presbyteros*), 353–56

Old Testament, 16–17
    canon of, 434–36, 446
    Christianity from, 34
    Greek, 45
    history and, 41–42
    prophecies and, 393–94
    at Qumran, 435
    in Revelation, 404–5
Olivet discourse, 98
Omega, 416–17
Onesimus, 239–40
Onesiphorus, 263–64
opening remarks, 180, 182–83
open-mindedness, 19–20, 32
oral culture, 7–8, 135, 177. *See also*
    rhetoric
oral preaching, 59
oral traditions, 24
Origen, 332
orthodoxy
    canon and, 434
    in Christianity, 33–34
    Didache on, 39n6
    Martyr on, 35–36
    organization of, 447
    Pliny on, 35–36
orthopraxy, 33–34, 447
Overbeck, Franz, 159

pagans
    1 Peter on, 311
    2 Corinthians and, 217
    temples of, 289
Painter, John, 351
palace, 242*f*
Pantaenus, 332
Papias, 443*f*, 445
    on Johannine epistles, 353, 356
    on John Zebedee, 156n3
    on Mark, 60–62
    on Matthew, 85
papyrus, *432*
    cost of, 4–5
    in Luke, 5, 105
    production of, 4
    pros and cons of, 5, *10*
    re-use of, 5
    size of, 5
Papyrus 46, 332, 335
Papyrus 75, 107
parables, 67, 73–76
Parakletos, 154
parallels, 111, 117, 409–10
parchment, 5
parousia (arrival), 383–84, 391–94
Parthenon, 179*f*
passing explanations, 146

Passion, 66, 72
Passion Narratives, 13, 126
    in Mark, 66, 72, 77–79
pastor, 212–14, 229, 247–48, 267
Pastoral Epistles, 128, 251–53, 259.
    See also Timothy; Titus
    authorship of, 254–55, 266–67
    false teachers in, 256–57
    rhetoric of, 255–58
pathos, 248, 263–64
Patmos, *398*, 403–4. *See also* John of
    Patmos
patriarchy, 47–48
patronage, 50–51, 106–7, 204–5
Paul, 160*f*
    in Acts, 127–28, 160, 173
    Areopagus and, 26–27, 27*f*
    authority of, 173–74
    authorship of, 36, 252–55
    Barnabas and, 37, 164
    as canon, 439–42, 444–46
    captivity epistles of, 231–49
    as Christian, 176
    chronology of, 59, 161–72
    contributions of, 188–89
    conversion of, 162, 176
    in Corinth, 167–68
    death of, 172, 267
    education of, 176–77
    ekklesia of, 179–80, 184
    Eutychus incidents and, 171
    food laws and, 164, 166, 174
    Gentile Christianity and, 238–39,
        271–72, 356
    hidden years of, 162, 164
    house arrest of, 171–72
    identity of, 173–76
    incorporative personality and, 187
    James and, 281
    as Jew, 174–76
    Johannine epistles and, 356–57
    Law of Christ and, 175
    leadership of, 38, 128
    Luke and, 107–8, 254–55
    missions of, 166–68, 171–72
    Mosaic law and, 166, 174–75, 227
    narrative thought world of,
        185–87, 190n7
    new perspective of, 174–75
    in New Testament, 160
    as pastor, 212–14, 229, 247–48, 267
    pathos from, 248
    of Paul's letters, 160, 184
    1 Peter related to, 320, 323, 389
    Pharisees and, 175–76
    pre-Christian, 161
    rhetorical letters of, 182–84

Paul (*continued*)
  rhetoric and, 176–82
  as Roman citizen, 173–74, 240–41, 312
  in Rome, 128, 171–72, 321
  on salvation, 206, 225–26
  Sermon of James and, 281, 284, 287–90
  severe letter from, 168
  shame and, 205
  status and, 173–74
  symbolic universe of, 176
  teachings of, 18
  visions and, 218, 235
Paul's letters, 154. *See also* captivity
    epistles; Corinthians
  Galatians, 37, 166, 174, 193–99, 204,
      219–20, 441
  opening of, 200
  against patronage, 204–5
  Paul of, 160, 184
  practicality of, 206
  rhetorical analysis of, 183–84
  Romans, 168, 174–75, 183–84,
      219–29, 441
  as Scripture, 383
  Thessalonians, 59, 193, 200–206, 439
peasant, 28
peirasmos, 94–95
Pentateuch, 24
Pentecost, 110, 116*f*
Perdue, L. G., 283
Perea, *144*
Pergamum, 413–14
persecution, 314–16
personality, 48–49, 187
personal remarks, 262
personal weaknesses, 218
Peter (Cephas, Simon bar Johan), 25,
      86*f*, *306*
  in Acts, 127–28, 321
  Beloved Disciple and, 137, 143
  Cornelius and, 45
  death of, 389–90
  Jesus' breakfast with, 152
  Jesus' name for, 96
  Jews and, 272
  in John, 142, 152
  Judaizers and, 37
  leadership of, 38
  in Luke, 126, 321
  Mark and, 60–61, 63
  name of, 95–96
  sermons of, 117–18
  threefold restoration of, 152
  walking on water by, 96
1 Peter
  apostle in, 318–19
  audience of, 311–14, 321–23

authorship of, 309–10, 317–18, 327
Babylon in, 310, 315
beginning of, 318–19
chosen in, 321–23
Christianos in, 313
covenant in, 324
date of, 315
Diaspora Jews and, 310–13
as encyclical document, 314
exordium in, 325
foreknowledge in, 322–23
Gentile Christianity and, 308–9
government in, 314–15, 327
Hebrews and, 338
language of, 310–12
milieu of, 311–12
missions in, 321
obedience in, 323–24
on pagans, 311
Paul related to, 320, 323, 389
persecution and, 314–16
2 Peter and, 381–83
prophets in, 325
resident aliens in, 309–10, 315, 323, 327
rhetorical outline of, 316–18
rhetoric of, 308–9
suffering in, 324–26
Sylvanus and, 317–18
synopsis of, 318–26
thesis statement in, 325
Twelve in, 319–20
2 Peter, 437, 443
  apostles in, 383
  Asiatic Greek in, 381–82
  audience of, 382
  authorship of, 379, 384–85, 395
  Babylonian Talmud and, 377–78
  canon in, 439
  as composite document, 309, 378, 395
  core samples in, 388–95
  date of, 379–81
  as encyclical document, 385–87
  Ephesians compared to, 385–86
  false teachers in, 388–89, 391
  1 Peter and, 381–83
  Jude and, 380–81, 383
  mystery of, 378–85
  myth related to, 389–91
  parousia in, 383–84, 391–94
  rhetorical outline of, 387
  rhetoric of, 385–88
  as sapiential literature, 383–84, 397n11
  Scripture in, 392–95
  sources of, 380, 384–85
  style of, 386–87
  transfiguration in, 391–92
  vocabulary of, 379

Peter principle, 95–97
Pharisees, 23–24, 24*f*
  Paul and, 175–76
Philadelphia, 414
Philemon, 108, 237, 239–40, 441
philia, 156n7
Philip, 171
Philippi, Greece, 164*f*
Philippians, 441
  2.5-11, 18
  Christology in, 243–46
  date of, 240
  deliberative rhetoric in, 179
  house arrest and, 240–42
  humility in, 243–44
  imitation in, 245–46
  incarnation in, 246–47
  Isaiah compared to, 244
  rhetorical outline of, 182, 241
  V-pattern in, 244–45
philo, 152
Philo, 391
Phoebe, 212, 228
physical appearance, 23–24, 24*f*
Plato, 204, 391
Pliny, 35–36, 49
Plutarch, 217
politics
  in apocalyptic literature, 422
  in First Century, 50–51
Polybius, 107
Polycarp, 359
Polycrates, 136
Pontius Pilate, 25–26, 43, 45
poor, 285–86
Porch of the Maidens, *22*
Powell, Mark Allan, 32–33
"powerful coming" (hendiadys), 391
praxis (behavior), 37, 203–4, 289
presbyteros (elder, old man), 353–56
prescript, 272
Price, Reynolds, 57
primary argument, 256–57
Priscilla, 117–18, 167, 212, 228
processive way, 185
prognōsin. *See* foreknowledge
prophecies, 405–7
  apocalyptic, 16, 420, 423, 426–27
  Old Testament and, 393–94
  of return, 98, 201–2
prophetic experience, 420–21
prophetic expression, 420
prophetic tradition, 420
prophets, 212–13, *398*, 435–36
  false, 302
  in Luke–Acts, 123
  in 1 Peter, 325

Protestants, 286
provenance
    of Hebrews, 332–33
    of Johannine epistles, 359–63
Proverbs, 252, 397n11
Psalm 22, 98–99
pseudonymous, 16
    anonymous compared to, 252–53, 353
    in New Testament, 447–48
Psidian Antioch Aqueduct, 163f
public communications, 6
purity language, 300–301, 304
pyramids, 195f

Q, 279
    Luke relating to, 109, 117
    Matthew related to, 86–87
Qoheleth, 397n11
Quintilian, 181
Qumran, 44, 73
    John the Baptist and, 45–46
    Old Testament at, 435

race, 265
    of faith, 344–45
Rahab, 90
Raphael, 45–46
reality, 185–86, 188–89
rebirth, 147–49
rectification, 423
redemptive judgment, 418
regula canona (rule of canon), 444, 446–47
regula fidei (rule of faith), 444, 446–48
Rehab, 287
Reicke, Bo, 381
relegation, 403–4
religion, 50–51
repentance, 116f
resident aliens, 309–10, 315, 323, 327
resurrection
    continuity in, 215
    in 1 Corinthians, 214–15
    Josephus on, 25
    of Lazarus, 136, 138, 145
    in Luke, 121
    in Mark, 66, 77
    Mary Magdalene and, 152
    in Matthew, 99
    miracle of, 29, 31
    in Thessalonians, 201
    of witnesses, 425–26
return, 98, 200–202
Revelation, 18, 353, 398, 428. See also
    Asia Minor
    as apocalyptic literature, 419–24
    arguments in, 407
    audience of, 401–2

authority in, 406
authorship of, 135, 139, 400
Christology of, 415–19
complexity of, 399–400
composition of, 406
core samples of, 424–27
date of, 401
dualism in, 421
Elijah and, 425
ending of, 418–19
first and last in, 416–17
first-person prophecies in, 405–7
genre of, 419–24
government in, 314
Greek of, 400, 404, 429n7
hymns in, 409
imminence in, 426–27
Jerusalem in, 401
Jewishness of, 416, 443
John of Patmos and, 6, 400
judgment in, 402, 409, 418
lamb in, 417–18, 430n40
letters in, 406–7
lion in, 418–19
logos in, 408, 415
Nero in, 421–22
Old Testament in, 404–6
parallels in, 409–10
place of, 401, 401f
prophetic experience in, 420–21
purpose of, 401–2, 407, 421
repetition in, 410–11
rhetorical outline of, 411
rhetoric of, 405–12
Scripture and, 358
seven in, 409–11, 422
social context of, 412–15
structure of, 408–10
style of, 406
symbols of, 414–15, 421–22
themes in, 406
visions in, 405–11, 414–16, 419–21,
    426, 429nn18–19
witnesses in, 402–3, 424–26
Revelation of John, 15–16
revenge, 97
rewards, 265
rhetoric
    about Abraham, 219–20
    Asiatic, 231–33, 316
    of Cicero, 178–79
    deliberative, 179–80, 233, 264–65
    enthymemes in, 256–57, 275–76
    epideictic, 179–80, 200, 238, 365
    ethos of, 181
    forensic, 179–80, 197–99
    in Greco-Roman world, 177–83

of Hebrews, 339–43
of Johannine epistles, 363–64
of Pastoral Epistles, 255–58
Paul and, 176–82
of 1 Peter, 308–9
of 2 Peter, 385–88
of Revelation, 405–12
of Sermon of James, 275–77
of 2 Timothy, 262–63
types of, 179–80
rhetorical analysis, 183–84
rhetorical discourses, 14–15
rhetorical letters, 182–84
Rhoda, 117–18
righteousness, 220–21, 223
rocks, 96
Roman bath, 208
Roman citizens, 173–74, 240–41, 312
Roman coins, 42f
Roman Empire, 43
Roman road, 232f
Romans, 168, 441
    10.4, 174–75
    Abraham in, 219–21, 223
    audience of, 221–22
    belief and, 223–24
    concessions in, 227–28
    critique in, 222
    date of, 219
    death in, 224
    destiny in, 225
    faith in, 223
    Galatians compared to, 219–20
    government in, 227
    homosexuality and, 222
    insinuatio in, 219
    "I" statements in, 225
    mercy in, 228
    Mosaic law in, 224–25
    rhetorical outline of, 183–84
    righteousness in, 220–21, 223
    Sermon on the Mount and, 227
    sin in, 223–24
    synopsis of, 221–28
    thesis statement of, 220–23
    trust in, 225–26
Rome, 292
    anti-Semitism in, 226
    as Babylon, 401, 430n26
    Circus Maximus in, 337, 337f
    coliseum in, 330
    Domus Augustana in, 337f
    in First Century, 42–43
    Jewish Christianity in, 336–37
    pagan catacombs in, 80, 80f
    Paul in, 128, 171–72, 321
    synagogue in, 335

Royalty, R., 408, 429n18, 430n32
rule of canon (*regula canona*), 444, 446–47
rule of faith (*regula fidei*), 444, 446–48
Ruth, 90

Sabbath
    Jesus and, 69–71
    of Jews, 72
sacred texts
    eschatology and, 435
    Jesus and, 435
    Josephus on, 435–36
sacrifice, 370–71
Sadducees, 24, 98
sage, 89–90
salvation
    in Luke–Acts, 114–15
    Paul on, 206, 225–26
    in 2 Timothy, 264
Samaritans, 149–51
Samaritan woman, 150–51
Sanders, E. P., 103
sapiential literature, 383–84, 397n11
Sarah, 45–46
Sardis, 311, 312f, 401f, 414, 436
Satan, 72
Saul of Tarsus. *See* Paul
sayings, 142, 153–54, 260–61
schism, 362–63
Schnabel, Eckhard, 296
scribes, 4, 85f, 378
    Matthew as, 85–88
    Paul and, 253–54
Scripture
    fulfillment of, 118
    Hebrew, 16–17
    in Hebrews, 332, 334, 345–46
    Jesus related to, 445
    Luke and, 437
    Paul's letters as, 383
    in 2 Peter, 392–95
    Revelation and, 358
Scripture consciousness, 435, 439
scrolls, 5
Sea of Galilee, 29
secondary argument, 257
second century A.D., 307
second-order moral
        discourse, 233
Samuel 7.12-17, 70
Second Temple period, 42
sectarian literature, 422
sects, 291n12, 357
Selwyn, E. G., 315
semeion (signs), 141, 145
Semitic, 275
Sepphoris, 245f, *270*, 297f

Sermon of James, 18, 25, 252–53
    2.14-26, 286–87
    Abraham and, 287
    authorship of, 280
    comparisons in, 277
    date of, 280–81, 283
    as diatribe, 275–76
    enthymemes in, 275–76
    on faith, 286–87
    favoritism in, 285–86
    generosity in, 284–85
    God's Word in, 285
    imperatives in, 275–76
    Jewish wisdom in, 277–78
    Jude related to, 294, 296, 298–300
    koinonia and, 283
    language of, 275, 277, 282
    LXX compared to, 275, 278
    Matthew compared to, 278–79
    outline of, 284
    Paul and, 281, 284, 287–90
    poor in, 285–86
    rhetoric of, 275–77
    social context of, 283
    suspicions about, 273–74
    synopsis of, 284–88
    teachers in, 287–88
    temptations in, 288
    wealth in, 284–86, 288
    wisdom in, 277–79
Sermon on the Mount
    fulfillment in, 93
    for insiders, 91–92
    intensity of, 92
    Lord's prayer and, 93f, 94–95
    Mark and, 73–74
    in Matthew, 91–95
    obedience and, 92, 94–95
    Romans and, 227
sermons
    Hebrews as, 333–34
    of Peter, 117–18
serpent, apple and, 197f
seven, 97, 423
    "I Am" Sayings and, 142, 153–54
    in Jewish numerology, 90–91
    in Revelation, 409–11, 422
sex, 214, 222
sexual double standard, 48
Shaliah, 319
shame
    of crucifixion, 345–46
    culture of, 47
    honor and, 29, 47, 205
    Paul and, 205
sheep, 318f
shunning, 205

signification, 112
signs (*semeion*), 141, 145
Silas, 166
Simon bar Johan, 95–96. *See also* Peter
sin, 223–24
Sirach, 44, 275, 278, 358
slavery, 233
    in Colossians, 236–37
    in Philemon, 237, 239–40
Smalley, S., 360
Smyrna, 414
social context, 283
    of Johannine epistles, 356–59
    of Revelation, 412–15
social elites, 116
social history, 47–51
social life, 336
social networks, 37
solecism, 8
Solomon, 89, 91, 101n5, 397n11
    Wisdom of, 44, 358, 436, 442–44
"Son of Man," 435
    in Acts, 119–20
    in Daniel, 69, 81n6
    in Luke, 119–20
    in Mark, 70–71
Sophia, 168f
soul, 150
speech, 293
Spirit, 319. *See also* Holy Spirit
    Jesus and, 154
Stamps, D. L., 364
Standard Sermons (Wesley), 100
Stanton, Graham, 439
Stark, Rodney, 311–12
statues, 169f, 386f
status
    of Matthew, 84
    Paul and, 173–74
    of women, 213–14
Stephen, 111, 119–20, 123
stoicheia, 235–36
stories
    imagination and, 189
    of Israel, 187
    of Jesus, 186–87
    of New Testament, 16–17
    reality in, 185–86
Stowers, S., 364
stratification, 178
submission
    mutual, 237
    women and, 234, 236–37, 249n1
suffering, 324–26
Suffering Servant, 326
summary statements, 142
Sunday, 35–36

sunergon, 108
superstitio (superstition), 337
syllogisms, 257–58, 275
Sylvanus, 317–18
symbolic numbers (*gematria*), 422–23
symbolic universe, 176
symbols, 414–15, 421–22
Symeon, 296
synagogues, 43*f*, 88*f*, *250, 270,* 273*f.*
    See also Jerusalem Temple
    in Rome, 335
    in Sardis, 311, 312*f*
    in Sepphoris, 245*f,* 297*f*
synkrisis (comparisons), 214–15, 258.
    See also specific books
synopsis
    of Colossians, 234–36
    of 2 Corinthians, 216–18
    of Ephesians, 238–40
    of Galatians, 196–99
    of John, 153–54
    of Jude, 302–3
    of Luke–Acts, 124–28
    of Mark, 64–68
    of 1 Peter, 318–26
    of Romans, 221–28
    of Sermon of James, 284–88
    of Thessalonians, 200–203
    of 1 Thessalonians, 200–202
Synoptic Gospels, 134
    John compared to, 139–40, 147,
        153–54

Tacitus, 25–26
Talmud, 42
Tannehill, R., 104
Tarsus road, 232*f*
Taurus Mountains, Turkey, 317*f*
tax, 96–97
Taylor, Vincent, 323–24
teachers. *See also* false teachers
    in Mark, 73–76
    in Sermon of James, 287–88
teachings
    in Matthew, 89, 97–98
    of Paul, 18
Tel Bethsaida, 145*f*
temple cleansing, 97
temple mount, *2*
Temple Mount Pinnacle, 112*f*
temples, *158,* 165*f,* 289, 413. *See also*
        Jerusalem Temple; synagogues
temptations, 94–95, 288
Ten Commandments, 312
tendentious, 58
Tertullian, 332–33
Testament of Abraham, 16

The Testament of Joseph, 430n40
Testament of Twelve Patriarchs, 45
testimonies
    of eyewitnesses, 36–37, 85
    Gnostic Christians and, 35–36
theater, 236*f*
theological history telling, 18–19
theological structure
    of John, 140–43, 145–46
    of Luke–Acts, 113–15
    of Matthew, 89
theology, 123–24
Theophilus, 104, 106–7, 111–12
thesis statement, 180, 220–23, 325
Thessalonians, 205–6, 441
    date of, 201
    resurrection in, 201
    return in, 201–2
    synopsis of, 200–203
1 Thessalonians, 59, 193, 439
    rhetorical outline of, 200
    synopsis of, 200–202
2 Thessalonians, 204
    prophecies in, 201
    rhetorical outline of, 203
    subjects in, 202–3
third-order moral discourse,
        233–34
Thomas, 145–46
Thuren, L., 386
Thyatira, 217*f,* 414
Thyen, H., 333
time, 265–66
    in Daniel, 422–23
    in Mark, 72
Timothy, 256, 338, 441
1 Timothy
    leadership in, 261
    outline of, 261
    personal remarks in, 262
    sayings in, 260–61
2 Timothy, 315
    3.16, 17, 435, 446
    deliberative rhetoric in, 264–65
    outline of, 263
    pathos of, 263–64
    race in, 265
    rhetoric of, 262–63
    salvation in, 264
    time in, 265–66
titles
    of Christ, 415–16
    of Luke–Acts, 107
Titus, 168, *330,* 441
    1.10-16, 256–57
    interpretation in, 259
    leadership in, 260

male-dominated culture
        and, 258–59
    outline of, 258
    women in, 259–60
TNIV. *See* Today's New International
        Version
Tobit, 45–46
Today's New International Version
        (TNIV), 8
tombs, 29, 30*f, 56,* 78*f*
    guards at, 99
    ionic columns on, *376*
    Jerusalem, 114*f*
    of Lazarus, 139*f*
tone, 194–95
Toorn, Karel van der, 83
Torah, 24, 28, 142
    canon and, 445–46
traditional prophecies, 420
traditions, 447
    apostolic, 389–90
    oral, 24
    prophetic, 420
transfiguration, 347*f,* 390
    in Mark, 67
    in 2 Peter, 391–92
    witnesses to, 425
translation, 8
    Hebrews 12.2, 9
    in John, 146
travel narrative, 116–18
Trebilco, Paul, 311
tree of life, 412, 412*f*
Trobisch, David, 451n5
true (*alethinos*), 389–91,
        400–401, 425
trust, 225–26
Turkey, 321
    inscriptions in, 386, 386*f*
    Taurus Mountains in, 317*f*
Twelve
    Beloved Disciple and, 352, 357
    in 1 Peter, 319–20

unity
    in Ephesians, 239
    of Luke–Acts, 104, 128–29
universalization, 115–16
universe, symbolic, 176

Vesapasian, *330*
Via Dolorosa, 29*f*
virginal conception, 90
visions, 29, 69, 218, 235
    in Revelation, 405–11, 414–16, 419–21,
        426, 429nn18–19
von Harnack, Adolph, 159